U.S. Laws, Acts, and Treaties

U.S. Laws, Acts, and Treaties

Volume 1

1776-1928

edited by

Timothy L. Hall

University of Mississippi School of Law

co-editor

Christina J. Moose

SALEM PRESS, INC.

Pasadena, California   Hackensack, New Jersey

Parts of this publication previously appeared in the following publications, copyrighted by Salem Press, Inc.: *Great Events from History: Human Rights* (© 1992), *Great Events from History: Business and Commerce*
(© 1994), *Great Events from History: Ecology and the Environment* (© 1995),
Ready Reference: American Justice (c 1996), *Great Events from History: Revised North American Series* (c 1997), *Ready Reference: Censorship* (© 1997),
Ready Reference: Women's Issues (© 1997), *Natural Resources* (© 1998),
Encyclopedia of Family Life (© 1999), *Racial and Ethnic Relations in America*
(© 1999), *The Sixties in America* (© 1999), *Aging* (© 2000), *Encyclopedia
of Environmental Issues* (© 2000), *Encyclopedia of the U.S. Supreme Court*
(© 2001), *Magill's Choice: American Indian History* (© 2002), and *Magill's
Choice: The Bill of Rights* (© 2002). New material has been added.

Library of Congress Cataloging-in-Publication Data
U.S. laws, acts, and treaties / edited by Timothy L. Hall.
    p. cm. — (Magill's choice)
Includes bibliographical references and index.
    ISBN 1-58765-098-3 (set : alk. paper) — ISBN 1-58765-099-1 (vol. 1 :
alk. paper) — ISBN 1-58765-100-9 (vol. 2 : alk. paper)— ISBN
1-58765-101-7 (vol. 3 : alk. paper)
    1. United States. Laws, etc. 2. Law—United States. 3. United
States—Foreign relations—Treaties. I. Title: US laws, acts, and
treaties. II. Hall, Timothy L. III. Series.
    KF385.A4U152 2003
    348.73'2—dc21
                                                      2002156063

Third Printing

CONTENTS

Publisher's Note ix
Contributors xiii
Introduction, *by Timothy L. Hall* xxiii
Contents by Popular Name xxix

Declaration of Independence (1776) 1
Articles of Confederation (1781) 4
Treaty of Paris (1783) 9
Fort Stanwix Treaty (1784) 13
Ordinance of 1785 17
Virginia Statute of Religious Liberty (1786). 21
Northwest Ordinance (1787). 24
U.S. Constitution: History (1787) 28
U.S. Constitution: Provisions (1787). 33
Three-fifths compromise (1787) 39
Judiciary Act of 1789 41
Bill of Rights (1789). 46
First Amendment (1789) 56
Second Amendment (1789) 61
Third Amendment (1789) 64
Fourth Amendment (1789). 66
Fifth Amendment (1789) 71
Takings clause (1789) 77
Sixth Amendment (1789). 85
Seventh Amendment (1789) 90
Eighth Amendment (1789). 91
Ninth Amendment (1789) 92
Tenth Amendment (1789) 98
Trade and Intercourse Acts (1790-1834) 102
Naturalization Act of 1790. 104
Federal Crimes Act (1790) 105
Fugitive Slave Act of 1793 106
Jay's Treaty (1794) 110
Eleventh Amendment (1798) 115
Fort Greenville Treaty (1795) 118
Pinckney's Treaty (1795) 123
Alien and Sedition Acts (1798) 127

Sedition Act of 1798 131
Judiciary Acts of 1801-1925 136
Treaty of Monfontaine (1801) 141
Black Codes of 1804-1807 143
Twelfth Amendment (1804). 147
Embargo Acts (1806-1807) 151
Anti-Slave Trade Bill (1807). 153
Fort Wayne Treaty (1809) 157
Horseshoe Bend Treaty (1814) 159
Treaty of Ghent (1814) 160
Rush-Bagot Agreement (1817) 165
Convention of 1818 167
Adams-Onís Treaty (1819). 169
Missouri Compromise (1820) 173
Land Act of 1820 178
Monroe Doctrine (1823) 181
Indian Removal Act (1830) 186
Treaty of Dancing Rabbit Creek (1830) 192
Force Act of 1833. 194
Preemption Act (1841) 199
Webster-Ashburton Treaty (1842). 202
Treaty of Wang Hiya (1844). 207
Independent Treasury Act (1846) 209
Treaty of Guadalupe Hidalgo (1848). 213
Oregon Act (1848). 217
Clayton-Bulwer Treaty (1850) 219
Fugitive Slave Act of 1850 221
Compromise of 1850. 225
Fort Laramie Treaty of 1851. 228
Pacific Railroad Survey Act (1853) 230
Fort Atkinson Treaty (1853). 235
Treaty of Kanagawa (1854) 236
Kansas-Nebraska Act (1854). 240
Confiscation Acts (1861-1862) 244
Homestead Act of 1862 245
Morrill Land Grant Act of 1862. 249
Militia Act (1862) 254
Emancipation Proclamation (1863) 259
National Bank Acts (1863-1864) 261
Freedmen's Bureau Act (1865) 265

Contents

Black Codes of 1865 269
Thirteenth Amendment (1865) 273
Civil Rights Act of 1866 278
Reconstruction Acts (1867) 280
Medicine Lodge Creek Treaty (1867) 287
Fourteenth Amendment (1868) 291
Burlingame Treaty (1868) 296
Fort Laramie Treaty of 1868 300
Fifteenth Amendment (1870) 302
Ku Klux Klan Acts (1870-1871) 305
Indian Appropriation Act (1871) 306
Treaty of Washington (1871) 310
General Mining Act (1872) 314
Coinage Act (1873) 316
Comstock Act (1873) 320
Page Law (1875) 322
Removal Act (1875) 326
Bland-Allison Act (1878) 327
Jim Crow laws (1880's-1954) 329
Chinese Exclusion Act (1882) 331
Indian Offenses Act (1883) 335
Pendleton Act (1883) 336
Major Crimes Act (1885) 340
Electoral Count Act (1887) 341
Interstate Commerce Act (1887) 343
General Allotment Act (1887) 347
Dependent Pension Act (1890) 351
Sherman Antitrust Act (1890) 353
Disfranchisement laws (1890) 358
Morrill Land Grant Act of 1890 362
Dingley Tariff (1897) 363
Treaty of Paris (1898) 367
Currency Act (1900) 369
Direct democracy laws (1913) 371
Reclamation Act (1902) 375
Platt Amendment (1903) 381
Burke Act (1906) 385
Pure Food and Drugs Act (1906) 387
Gentlemen's Agreement (1907) 391
Opium Exclusion Act (1909) 396

Copyright Act of 1909 397
Payne-Aldrich Tariff Act (1909) 403
Mann Act (1910) 409
Panama Canal Act (1912) 412
Sixteenth Amendment (1913) 414
Migratory Bird Act (1913) 415
Seventeenth Amendment (1913) 419
Alien land laws (1913) 421
Federal Reserve Act (1913) 425
Federal Trade Commission Act (1914) 430
Clayton Antitrust Act (1914) 432
Harrison Narcotic Drug Act (1914) 434
National Defense Act (1916) 435
National Park Service Organic Act (1916) 440
Immigration Act of 1917 446
Jones Act (1917) 448
Espionage Acts (1917-1918) 451
Migratory Bird Treaty Act (1918) 454
Eighteenth Amendment (1919) 460
Treaty of Versailles (1919) 464
Motor Vehicle Theft Act (1919) 469
Mineral Leasing Act (1920) 470
Federal Power Act of 1920 476
Nineteenth Amendment (1920) 478
Immigration Act of 1921 483
Sheppard-Towner Act (1921) 489
Cable Act (1922) 494
Equal Rights Amendment (1923-1983) 495
World War Adjusted Compensation Act (1924) 499
Immigration Act of 1924 501
Indian Citizenship Act (1924) 505
Oil Pollution Act of 1924 509
Halibut Treaty (1924) 514
Federal Corrupt Practices Act (1925) 518
Geneva Protocol (1925) 524
Air Commerce Act (1926) 530
Railway Labor Act (1926) 534
McFadden Act (1927) 541
Kellogg-Briand Pact (1928) 547

PUBLISHER'S NOTE

Magill's Choice: Laws, Acts, and Treaties offers librarians and students of U.S. history and law—as well as students of government, Native American studies, environmental law, political science, law sociology, women's issues, and American ethnic groups—a unique, one-stop resource for basic information and historical context on 433 major U.S. acts of Congress and U.S. treaties, from the Articles of Confederation and the Constitution through the Homeland Security Act of 2002.

These in-depth essays, averaging about 1,500 words in length (and ranging from 500 to 2,500 words), cover both the historical provenance and the main provisions of these core laws and treaties. In addition to describing the law's background and provisions, each essay lists known alternative popular names for the law, such as the "Dawes Act" for the General Allotment Act of 1887; title and section of the 2000 *U.S. Code* whenever the law is codified mainly within one title of the *Code*; categories of interest, such as civil rights, family life, health, the environment, or immigration; date of passage or presidential signing; and a list of "Sources for Further Study." A reference to the *United States Statutes at Large* by volume and page number is standard in all essays to which it applies (that is, all acts of Congress), employing the standard format of XX Stat. XXX, where XX is the volume and XXX the first page number on which the law appears. Public law numbers appear for all statutory laws after 1956, when the format for these was standardized to list the congressional session number followed by a hyphen and the number of the law.

Compiled from sixteen Salem reference works published within the past decade, essays have been updated, new ready-reference data have been added, and each has been subheaded to highlight key features of the law in question. In addition, 50 new essays, unique to this publication, have been added to fill historical gaps and ensure coverage through 2002. These new essays include, for example, the USA Patriot Act of 2001 and the U.S.-Russia Arms Agreement of 2002. Students and librarians alike will appreciate the resulting broad coverage of U.S. laws: both those that played key roles in the history of the Republic and those that remain important today. This scope is reflected in the wide variety of topical areas represented by these laws:

- African Americans
- Aging Issues
- Agriculture
- Animals
- Asia or Asian Americans
- Banking, Money, and Finance
- Business, Commerce, and Trade
- Children's Issues
- Civil Rights and Liberties
- Communications and Media
- Constitutional Law
- Copyrights, Patents, and Trademarks
- Crimes and Criminal Procedure
- Disability Issues
- Education
- Energy
- Environment and Conservation
- Food and Drugs
- Foreign Relations
- Government Procedure and Organization
- Health and Welfare
- Housing
- Immigration
- Judiciary and Judicial Procedure
- Labor and Employment
- Land Management
- Latinos
- Military and National Security
- Native Americans
- Natural Resources
- Privacy
- Property
- Religious Liberty
- Slavery
- Speech and Expression
- Tariffs and Taxation
- Transportation
- Treaties and Agreements
- Voting and Elections
- Women's Issues

The set's chronological arrangement allows the publication to function as an elaborate and detailed time line, offering students the opportunity to compare and contrast laws passed in the same era. At the same time, alphabetical access by the laws' popular names is ensured by the presence, at the beginning of each volume, of an alphabetical list of "Contents by Popular Name," including cross-references from "also known as" names.

Volume 3 offers several essential research tools, including a convenient reprint of the first "law" of the nation, the Declaration of Independence; the U.S. Constitution and its twenty-seven amendments; a list of legal research "Resources" including organizations and Web sites; a Categorized Index listing the laws by topic of interest; and a comprehensive Subject Index.

Very little one-stop reference on U.S. acts and laws exists—certainly not of this breadth and scope for the general reader. *U.S.*

Laws, Acts, and Treaties provides the much-needed service of selecting, from literally thousands of bills, those most likely to come up in classroom discussions, offering not only a summation of the laws' provisions and significance but also ample historical background and political context. Most other reference works in this area are either highly technical, requiring targeted searches (such as the U.S. government online databases), or limited in scope, geared to narrow thematic coverage by topics such as education, immigration, or civil rights. Salem's editors hope that this set will offer not only historical breadth but also a large number of laws in each of the main subject areas—accessible through the Categorized Index—that are likely to be of interest in high school and undergraduate history and government courses, allowing the student researcher quick access to (for example) the context and main provisions of historically significant environmental law, immigration law, laws affecting African Americans, or laws related to federal crime.

No work of this magnitude and diversity is possible, of course, without the major efforts of academicians and independent scholars in history, political science, government, and legal studies. All essays are signed by their original contributors, and a list of those individuals and their academic affiliations follows this note. In addition, we wish to acknowledge the contributions of Editor Timothy L. Hall of the University of Mississippi School of Law, without whose insight and oversight this publication would not have been possible. His Introduction, as well as his appendix "Resources on the Law," offers clarity and guidance through the tangled web of source materials fundamental to legal research.

CONTRIBUTORS

Timothy L. Hall, Editor
University of Mississippi School of Law

Craig W. Allin
Cornell College

William Allison
Weber State University

Leslie R. Alm
Boise State University

Thomas L. Altherr
*Metropolitan State College
of Denver*

Earl R. Andresen
University of Texas at Arlington

John Andrulis
Western New England College

Christina Ashton
National Writer's Club

Mary Welek Atwell
Radford University

Gayle Avant
Baylor University

James A. Baer
*Northern Virginia Community
College*

Nancy R. Bain
Ohio University

Siva Balasubramanian
Southern Illinois University

Ruth Bamberger
Drury College

Karen L. Barak
University of Wisconsin, Whitewater

Carole A. Barrett
University of Mary

Michael L. Barrett
Ashland University

Joseph E. Bauer
*State University of New York,
Buffalo State College*

Jonathan Bean
Southern Illinois University

Alvin K. Benson
Utah Valley State College

Milton Berman
University of Rochester

Cynthia A. Bily
Adrian College

Denis Binder
Western New England College

Nicholas Birns
New School University

Kent Blaser
Wayne State University

Amy Bloom
Harris Corporation

Daniel T. Boatright
*University of Oklahoma Health
Sciences Center*

Steve D. Boilard
California Legislative Analyst's Office

Margaret F. Boorstein
C. W. Post College of Long Island University

Michael R. Bradley
Motlow College

John Braeman
University of Nebraska

Elise M. Bright
University of Texas at Arlington

Daniel A. Brown
California State University, Fullerton

Laura R. Broyles
Independent Scholar

Susan J. Buck
University of North Carolina at Greensboro

Mary Louise Buley-Meissner
University of Wisconsin, Milwaukee

Kirk J. Bundy
Tulane University

Michael H. Burchett
Limestone College

Aubyn C. Burnside
Independent Scholar

Dale F. Burnside
Lenoir-Rhyne College

William H. Burnside
John Brown University

Joseph P. Byrne
Belmont University

Sherry Cable
University of Tennessee

Netiva Caftori
Northeastern Illinois University

Henry Campa III
Michigan State University

Richard K. Caputo
Yeshiva University

David Carleton
Middle Tennessee State University

Jon R. Carpenter
University of South Dakota

Nicholas A. Casner
Boise State University

Gilbert T. Cave
Lakeland Community College

Elisabeth A. Cawthon
University of Texas, Arlington

Richard N. Chapman
Francis Marion University

H. Lee Cheek, Jr.
Lee University

David L. Chesemore
California State University, Fresno

John G. Clark
University of Kansas

Lawrence Clark III
Independent Scholar

Michael D. Clark
Louisiana State University, New Orleans

Thomas Clarkin
San Antonio College

Douglas Clouatre
Independent Scholar

Contributors

William J. Cooper, Jr.
*Louisiana State University,
Baton Rouge*

Michael L. Coulter
Grove City College

David A. Crain
South Dakota State University

Stephen Cresswell
West Virginia Wesleyan College

Norma Crews
Independent Scholar

Edward R. Crowther
Adams State College

David H. Culbert
*Louisiana State University,
Baton Rouge*

Sudipta Das
*Southern University at
New Orleans*

Edward J. Davies II
University of Utah

Jennifer Davis
Independent Scholar

Merle O. Davis
*Louisiana State University, Baton
Rouge*

John H. DeBerry
Memphis State University

Juliet Dee
University of Delaware

Bruce J. DeHart
*University of North Carolina at
Pembroke*

Tyler Deierhoi
*University of Tennessee,
Chattanooga*

Bill Delaney
Independent Scholar

Judith Boyce DeMark
Northern Michigan University

Michael S. DeVivo
Bloomsburg University

Gerard Donnelly
University of Mississippi

Andrea Donovan
Western Michigan University

Paul E. Doutrich
York College of Pennsylvania

Colleen M. Driscoll
Villanova University

Joyce Duncan
East Tennessee State University

Eric Elder
Northwestern College

Robert P. Ellis
Independent Scholar

Daniel C. Falkowski
Canisius College

John L. Farbo
University of Idaho

Randall Fegley
Pennsylvania State University

David G. Fenton
Connecticut College

Anne-Marie E. Ferngren
Oregon State University

John W. Fiero
University of Louisiana at Lafayette

Linda E. Fisher
University of Michigan, Dearborn

Michael S. Fitzgerald
Pikeville College

George J. Fleming
Calumet College

Dale L. Flesher
University of Mississippi

John Fliter
Kansas State University

Donald W. Floyd
*State University of New York,
College of Environmental
Science and Forestry*

Richard H. Fluegeman, Jr.
Ball State University

George Q. Flynn
*State University of New York,
Plattsburgh*

Andrew M. Forman
Hofstra University

Donald R. Franceschetti
University of Memphis

C. George Fry
University of Findlay

Michael J. Garcia
Arapahoe Community College

John C. Gardner
Delaware State College

Louis Gesualdi
St. John's University

Jane M. Gilliland
Slippery Rock University

Richard Goedde
St. Olaf College

Robert Justin Goldstein
Oakland University

Nancy M. Gordon
Independent Scholar

Robert F. Gorman
Southwest Texas State University

Lewis L. Gould
University of Texas at Austin

Hans G. Graetzer
South Dakota State University

Phillip Greenberg
Independent Scholar

Manfred Grote
Purdue University, Calumet

Susan Grover
College of William and Mary

Michael Haas
Independent Scholar

Irwin Halfond
McKendree College

Timothy L. Hall
University of Mississippi

Susan E. Hamilton
Independent Scholar

Karen V. Harper
West Virginia University

Katy Jean Harriger
Wake Forest University

Jasper L. Harris
North Carolina Central University

Sandra Harrison
Drury College

Stanley Harrold
South Carolina State University

Fred Hartmeister
Texas Tech University

Contributors

Baban Hasnat
*State University of New York, College
at Brockport*

Robert M. Hawthorne, Jr.
Independent Scholar

James Hayes-Bohanan
Bridgewater State College

Peter B. Heller
Manhattan College

Arthur W. Helweg
Western Michigan University

Eric Henderson
University of Northern Iowa

Howard M. Hensel
*United States Air Force—
Air War College*

Maria A. Hernandez
Northern Arizona University

R. Don Higginbotham
*University of North Carolina at
Chapel Hill*

Kay Hively
Independent Scholar

Donald Holley
*University of Arkansas
at Monticello*

Eric Howard
Independent Scholar

Richard Hudson
Mercy College

William E. Huntzicker
University of Minnesota

Raymond Pierre Hylton
Virginia Union University

Andrew C. Isenberg
University of Puget Sound

Patricia Jackson
Davenport College

W. Turrentine Jackson
University of California at Davis

Robert Jacobs
Central Washington University

Julapa Jagtiani
Syracuse University

Duncan R. Jamieson
Ashland University

Albert C. Jensen
Central Florida Community College

Dwight Wm. Jensen
Marshall University

K. Sue Jewell
Ohio State University

Pamela R. Justice
Collin County Community College

Karen Kähler
Independent Scholar

Rajiv Kalra
Minnesota State University, Moorhead

Charles L. Kammer III
The College of Wooster

Manjit S. Kang
Louisiana State University

Burton Kaufman
Kansas State University

Richard Keenan
Wayne State College

Dan Kennedy
Independent Scholar

xvii

Vernon N. Kisling, Jr.
University of Florida

Benjamin J. Klebaner
City College, City University of New York

Howard M. Kleiman
Miami University

Mitchell Langbert
Clarkson University

David J. Langum
Samford University

Eleanor A. LaPointe
Ocean County College

Eugene Larson
Pierce College

Sharon L. Larson
University of Nebraska, Lincoln

Martin J. Lecker
Rockland Community College

Joseph Edward Lee
Winthrop University

Thomas T. Lewis
Mount Senario College

Paul Leyda
California Maritime Academy

Lester G. Lindley
Nova Southeastern University

R. M. Longyear
University of Kentucky

William C. Lowe
Mount St. Clare College

David C. Lukowitz
Hamline University

Richard B. McCaslin
High Point University

Jeanne M. McGlinn
University of North Carolina, Asheville

Priscilla H. Machado
U.S. Naval Academy

Edward J. Maguire
St. Louis University

Bill Manikas
Gaston College

Barry Mann
Independent Scholar

Nancy Farm Männikkö
Independent Scholar

Jo Manning
Independent Scholar

Nancy E. Marion
University of Akron

Chogallah Maroufi
California State University, Los Angeles

Lynn M. Mason
Lubbock Christian University

Patricia C. Matthews
Mount Union College

Michael E. Meagher
University of Missouri, Rolla

Elizabeth J. Miles
Independent Scholar

Laurence Miller
Western Washington University

Liesel Ashley Miller
Mississippi State University

Robert Mitchell
Independent Scholar

Wayne D. Moore
Virginia Tech

William V. Moore
College of Charleston

Christina J. Moose
Independent Scholar

Robert P. Morin
California State University, Chico

Jerry A. Murtagh
Fort Valley State University

Vidya Nadkarni
University of San Diego

William T. Neese
University of Arkansas at Little Rock

Cherilyn Nelson
Eastern Kentucky University

Joseph L. Nogee
University of Houston

Anthony Patrick O'Brien
Lehigh University

Charles H. O'Brien
Western Illinois University

Lisa Paddock
Independent Scholar

W. David Patton
Boise State University

Virginia Ann Paulins
Ohio University

Darryl Paulson
University of South Florida

Thomas R. Peake
King College

William D. Pederson
*International Lincoln Center,
   Louisiana State University*

William E. Pemberton
University of Wisconsin, La Crosse

Marilyn Elizabeth Perry
Independent Scholar

Doris F. Pierce
Purdue University Calumet

Erika E. Pilver
Westfield State College

George R. Plitnik
Frostburg State University

Mark A. Plummer
Illinois State University

Christina Polsenberg
Michigan State University

David L. Porter
William Penn University

Francis P. Prucha
Marquette University

Marc Georges Pufong
Valdosta State University

Srinivasan Ragothaman
University of South Dakota

Steven J. Ramold
Virginia State University

P. S. Ramsey
Independent Scholar

John David Rausch, Jr.
West Texas A&M University

Nim Razook
University of Oklahoma

E. A. Reed
Saint Mary's College of California

Merl E. Reed
Georgia State University

Jon Reyhner
Montana State University, Billings

Edward J. Rielly
Saint Joseph's College

Claire J. Robinson
Independent Scholar

Stephen F. Rohde
Rohde and Victoroff

Joseph R. Rudolph, Jr.
Towson University

Dorothy C. Salem
Cuyahoga Community College

Lisa M. Sardinia
Pacific University

Helmut J. Schmeller
Fort Hays State University

Kathleen Schongar
May School

John Richard Schrock
Emporia State University

Steven C. Schulte
Mesa State College

Stephen Schwartz
*State University of New York,
    Buffalo State College*

Larry Schweikart
University of Dayton

Rebecca Lovell Scott
College of Health Sciences

Elaine Sherman
Hofstra University

Paul A. Shoemaker
University in Shreveport

Thomas E. Shriver
University of Tennessee

R. Baird Shuman
*University of Illinois at Urbana-
Champaign*

Donald C. Simmons, Jr.
Mississippi Humanities Council

Jerold L. Simmons
University of Nebraska at Omaha

Sanford S. Singer
University of Dayton

Christopher E. Smith
Michigan State University

A. J. Sobczak
Independent Scholar

David R. Sobel
Independent Scholar

Robert Sobel
New College of Hofstra University

John A. Sondey
South Dakota State University

Glenn Ellen Starr
Appalachian State University

Barry M. Stentiford
Grambling State University

Robert J. Stewart
California Maritime Academy

Louise M. Stone
Bloomsburg University

Ruby L. Stoner
*Penn State University College of
Technology*

Leslie Stricker
Park University

Irene Struthers
Independent Scholar

Taylor Stults
Muskingum College

Glenn L. Swygart
Tennessee Temple University

Larry N. Sypolt
West Virginia University

Harold D. Tallant
Georgetown College

Susan M. Taylor
Indiana University

Carl A. Thames
Independent Scholar

John M. Theilmann
Converse College

Emory M. Thomas
University of Georgia

Susan L. Thomas
Hollins University

Donald J. Thompson
*California University of
Pennsylvania*

Vincent Michael Thur
Wenatchee Valley College

Leslie V. Tischauser
Prairie State College

Kenneth William Townsend
Coastal Carolina University

Paul B. Trescott
Southern Illinois University

Anne Trotter
Rosemont College

Robert D. Ubriaco, Jr.
Illinois Wesleyan University

Jiu-Hwa Lo Upshur
Eastern Michigan University

Theodore M. Vestal
Oklahoma State University

Sharon C. Wagner
Missouri Western State College

M. Mark Walker
University of Mississippi

Thomas J. Edward Walker
Pennsylvania College of Technology

Deborah D. Wallin
Skagit Valley College, Whidbey

Theodore O. Wallin
Syracuse University

Annita Marie Ward
Salem-Teikyo University

William C. Ward III
Kent State University

Donald A. Watt
Southern Arkansas University

William L. Waugh, Jr.
Georgia State University

Donald V. Weatherman
Lyon College

Marcia J. Weiss
Point Park College

Ashton Wesley Welch
Creighton University

D. Anthony White
Sonoma State University

Nancy A. White
Mississippi State University

Garrett L. Van Wicklen
University of Georgia

Thomas A. Wikle
Oklahoma State University

Theodore A. Wilson
University of Kansas

Thomas Winter
University of Cincinnati

Michael Witkoski
University of South Carolina

Frank Wu
University of Wisconsin, Madison

Cynthia Gwynne Yaudes
Indiana University

Clifton K. Yearley
State University of New York, Buffalo

Edward A. Zivich
Calumet College

Priscilla H. Zotti
United States Naval Academy

INTRODUCTION

Borrowing a phrase from John Adams, observers of American society frequently note that the United States is "a government of laws, and not of men." By this they mean that the destiny of American citizens does not—or at least, should not—depend on the whim of kings or priests or even talk show hosts, but on rights and obligations embodied in law. We tend to speak of "law" as though it were a seamless tapestry, a single magisterial whole. In fact, however, the rights and obligations that make the United States a "government of laws" do not reside in one book or even in one collection of volumes. What we know as the "laws of the land" are actually a vast assortment of legal rules that proliferate at every level and among every branch of American government. State, local, and federal governments all produce laws; and judges, legislators, and executives such as governors and presidents contribute to the creation of legal rules. Although state and local laws have a profound impact on the lives of American citizens, federal laws—while not necessarily more important than these—are by the terms of the U.S. Constitution the "supreme Law of the Land" and the focus of the present reference work. This series gathers together in three volumes more than 430 of the most important federal laws enacted in the course of U.S. history. Beginning with the Constitution itself, and including all the constitutional amendments, statutes, and treaties, readers will find collected here descriptions and historical backgrounds of the main laws that have shaped, and—in many cases—continue to shape the nation's life.

Each of the three main sources of law that are collected here—constitutional provisions, treaties, and statutes—have distinct methods of creation. The Constitution itself was drafted and approved by the Constitutional Convention that met in Philadelphia in 1787 and then ratified by the requisite number of states the following year. Amendments to the Constitution—of which there were twenty-seven by the beginning of the twenty-first century—may be proposed either by a vote of two-thirds of each House of Congress or in a constitutional convention called by two-thirds of the state legislatures. Although both possibilities exist under Article V of the Constitution, amendments in practice have always begun as proposals from Congress. However inaugurated, though, proposed amendments must be ratified by three-fourths of the states, acting either through their legislatures or through specially called constitutional conventions. The creation of treaties is more straightforward. These are negotiated by the president of the United States with foreign nations but require approval by the Senate to become effective.

Federal statutes make up the most common form of federal law, although their creation follows a more complicated path than either constitutional amendments or treaties. Congress derives its authority to make law from the Article I, section 1 of the Constitution, which provides that "[a]ll legislative Powers herein granted shall be vested in a Congress of the United States, which shall consist of a Senate and House of Representatives." Congress consists of two houses, or chambers (hence the term "bicameral legislature"), the House of Representatives and the Senate. The House has more than 430 members, drawn from the fifty states according to their populations. The Senate has 100 members, two from each of the fifty states. A new Congress begins in January of every second year and is numbered sequentially. The Congress meeting in the years 2003-2004, for example, is the 108th.

Federal laws enacted by Congress, referred to as "statutes," begin as a "bill"—or, less commonly, as a "joint resolution"—introduced in either the House of Representatives or the Senate. Congress passes both "public" and "private" laws: those which are "public" affecting Americans generally, and those which are "private" focusing on a specific individual or entity. Private laws, for example, may deal with issues such as whether a particular individual may remain in the country rather than be deported. (The laws covered in the present three volumes are exclusively "public laws.")

Although only members of the House or Senate may actually introduce a proposed law, ideas for laws come from a variety of sources. The president of the United States, for example, may propose that Congress pass particular legislation. Article II, section 3 of the Constitution specifies that the president shall "from time to time give to the Congress Information of the State of the Union, and recommend to their Consideration such Measures as he shall judge necessary and expedient." Groups and individuals interested in particular subjects may also seek the passage of legislation to give legal force to their views. Not only may such parties propose legislation to members of the House or Senate; they may also offer testimony in congressional hearings about a particular bill and may, as well, hire professional representatives—referred to as "lobbyists"—to speak to congressional members or their staffs in support of or in opposition to bills pending before Congress.

Bills or joint resolutions introduced first in the House are designated by a number that follows the abbreviations H.R. (for House of Representatives) or H.J.Res (for House Joint Resolution). Those originating in the Senate bear the labels S. or S.J.Res, followed by a number. A majority of bills introduced in each session of Congress actually originate in the House, and the Constitution specifically mandates that revenue bills must originate in the House. By tradition, moreover, appropriation bills are introduced in the House of Representatives rather than in the Senate.

Following the introduction of a bill in either the House or the Senate, it is sent to a committee or committees with oversight of the subjects addressed in the bill. Committees typically hold hearings on a bill, and these may include the opportunity for parties interested in the bill to testify before the committee. Following these hearings, committees meet to discuss the bill in detail, and these discussions often yield proposed amendments to the original bill. Eventually, members of the committee considering a bill vote on whether to report the bill—and any approved amendments—to the full House or Senate, or whether to table the bill—that is, to postpone, perhaps indefinitely, any further consideration of the bill. In cases in which a committee refuses to forward a bill to the full House or Senate, it is sometimes possible for supporters of the bill to retrieve it from the purgatory of a committee and to have it presented to the full chamber. In cases in which a committee reports the bill, it will prepare a report which discusses the background of the bill and the reasons the bill is being proposed.

Once a bill arrives before the full House or Senate from a committee, congressional members generally have the opportunity to debate the merits of the bill, as amended by the committee, and to offer proposed amendments of their own. Eventually, the bill and its amendments will be voted on. If the bill wins final passage in the House, then it will be forwarded for consideration by the Senate, and vice versa. To become law, a bill must be passed in both the House and the Senate in the same form. Sometimes a bill passed in one chamber of Congress will not be passed by the other. Often, however, the two chambers of Congress pass different versions of essentially the same bill. In this event, final passage of the bill requires that the two chambers negotiate their differences to produce an agreed-upon version of the bill. Commonly, such negotiations occur in a conference committee, with members from both the House and the Senate, whose purpose is to agree upon a version of the bill that can then be voted on again by the full House and Senate.

A bill approved by both the House and the Senate is said to be "enrolled" and is forwarded to the president. If the president signs the bill, or fails to return the bill to Congress with objections within ten days after receiving it, then it becomes law. However, the president may disapprove of the bill and may express this disapproval in the form of a veto. If the president vetoes a bill, then it does not become law unless Congress overrides the veto with a two-thirds majority vote in both the House and the Senate. Moreover, if a congressional term expires during the ten days in which the president has to object to a bill and the president has not signed the bill into law, then the bill is considered vetoed. The president's use of inaction to kill a bill at the end of a congressional term is referred to as a "pocket veto."

Once a bill becomes law, it generally remains effective indefinitely. Congress passes some laws, however, with built-in expiration dates, and these laws cease to be effective upon the arrival of their respective expiration dates. Congress may also pass a subsequent bill that repeals all or part of a previously enacted law. Finally, the U.S. Supreme Court may act to invalidate a law. Since the Court's decision in *Marbury v. Madison* (1803), which established the doctrine of "judicial review," the Court has been recognized as having authority to review laws passed at both the federal and state levels to determine whether their provisions are consistent with the U.S. Constitution. Occasionally, the Court determines that a law is unconstitutional, and when it does, the law ceases to be enforceable.

When a bill becomes a law, it receives a designation as a "public law," and a number indicating the Congress in which it was passed. For instance, the Aviation and Transportation Security Act, passed by Congress in 2001 in response to the terrorist attacks on September 11 that year on New York's World Trade Center towers and on the Pentagon, is designated Public Law (or "P.L.") 107-71. This designation means that the act was passed by the 107th Congress and that it was the 71st law passed by that Congress. The federal government publishes each public law separately in pamphlet form after it has been enacted, and this form of law is referred to as a "slip law." Eventually, though, the federal government binds public laws together and publishes them in an official series of volumes referred to as the *United States Statutes at Large*.

Were the *Statutes at Large* the only source for discovering the content of federal laws, then legal research—both by judges and lawyers and by the general public—would be extraordinarily difficult. This is so because any particular bill that is enacted may contain not only wholly new legal provisions but also revisions to one or more previously enacted laws. Thus, discovering the law on a particular subject might require investigating bills enacted by several different Congress over an extended period of years. Consequently, an important step in the life of an individual statute is its codification into the *U.S. Code*. The *U.S. Code* collects all the federal statutes currently in force and organizes them by subject matter in a series of nearly fifty "titles." The *Code* is itself revised every six years to incorporate laws enacted since the last revision. Once codified, a statute will be included with other federal laws having to do with the same subject. For laws that have been in force for several years or more, the *U.S. Code* (abbreviated as U.S.C.) is the authoritative reference source. The *Code* is available in many libraries, especially law libraries maintained by law schools or courts, as well as on the World Wide Web. The Library of Congress, for example, maintains a Web site containing the text of the U.S. Code at http://www.loc.gov/law/guide/uscode.html. For many of the laws appearing in this publication, we have listed the U.S. Code title and section numbers; these refer most often to the current version of the code as accessed via the Web. Many libraries also maintain an unofficial version of the U.S. Code called the *U.S. Code Annotated* (abbreviated as U.S.C.A.). The U.S.C.A. contains not only the text of the laws included in the *U.S. Code* but also annotations for each law addressing matters such as important Supreme Court cases that have interpreted the meaning of the law.

For recently enacted statutes, the various collections of public laws on the World Wide Web are the most accessible source. Again, the Library of Congress maintains an excellent web site, titled "Thomas: Legislative Information on the Internet." This site, located at http://thomas.loc.gov/, contains an index to and the text of public laws from the present back to the Ninety-third Congress, which met in 1973 and 1974. Perhaps of equal significance for legal researchers, the Thomas site contains a wealth of information about bills currently pending before Congress. This information allows citizens to track the progress of a bill from its introduction in the House or the Senate through its subsequent enactment or—as the case may be—failure to become enacted.

Surely "a government of laws" must be a government in which laws are not merely passed but in which they are *known*. That, at least, is the premise of the present reference set. "Ignorance of the law," courts are fond of saying, "is no excuse." Citizens are expected to inform themselves about the substance of the laws that govern their lives. Fortunately, there has never been a time when it is easier for them to do so. With the help of the following articles in this reference set, readers may understand better the laws that help to structure the lives of Americans at the beginning of the twenty-first century, as well as those which have guided the nation's course up to the present.

Timothy L. Hall
University of Mississippi

Contents by Popular Name

Adams-Onís Treaty (1819), 169

Age Discrimination Act (1975), 1285

Age Discrimination in Employment Act (1967), 1026

Agreed Framework of 1994. *See* North Korea Pact (1994)

Agricultural College Act. *See* Morrill Land Grant Act of 1890

Agricultural Marketing Act (1929), 551

Aid to Families with Dependent Children (1935), 647

Air Commerce Act (1926), 530

Air Pollution Control Act (1955), 839

Aircraft Noise Abatement Act (1968), 1060

Airline Deregulation Act (1978), 1343

Alaska Lands Act. *See* Alaska National Interest Lands Conservation Act (1980)

Alaska National Interest Lands Conservation Act (1980), 1380

Alaska Native Claims Settlement Act (1971), 1151

Alien Act (1798), 127

Alien land laws (1913), 421

Alternative Motor Fuels Act (1988), 1462

Amerasian Homecoming Act (1987), 1448

American Indian Citizenship Act. *See* Indian Citizenship Act (1924)

American Indian Religious Freedom Act (1978), 1333

Americans with Disabilities Act (1990), 1474

Animal Welfare Act (1966), 1009

Antarctic Treaty (1961), 898

Anti-Racketeering Act of 1934, 610

Anti-Racketeering Act of 1946. *See* Hobbs Act (1946)

Anti-Slave Trade Bill (1807), 153

Antitrust Procedures and Penalties Act (1974), 1248

Anzus Treaty. *See* Tripartite Security Treaty (1952)

Architectural Barriers Act (1968), 1066

Army Reorganization Act. *See* National Defense Act (1916)

Articles of Confederation (1781), 4

Atomic Energy Act of 1954, 828

Aviation and Transportation Security Act (2001), 1560

Banking Act of 1933, 590

Banking Act of 1935, 651

Bilingual Education Act (1968), 1029

Bill of Rights (1789), 46

Bipartisan Campaign Reform Act (2002), 1562

Black Codes of 1804-1807, 143

Black Codes of 1865, 269

Bland-Allison Act (1878), 327

Bonus Act. *See* World War Adjusted Compensation Act (1924)

Brady Handgun Violence Protection Act (1994), 1524

Bretton Woods Agreement (1944), 744

Buckley Amendment. *See* Privacy Act (1974)
Burke Act (1906), 385
Burlingame Treaty (1868), 296

Cable Act (1922), 494
Celler-Kefauver Act (1950), 800
Child Abuse Prevention and Treatment Act (1974), 1218
Child Care and Development Block Grant Act (1990), 1486
Child product safety laws (1970's), 1089
Child Protection and Toy Safety Act (1969), 1082
Child Support Enforcement Amendments (1984), 1415
Chinese Exclusion Act (1882), 331
Cigarette Warning Label Act (1966), 997
Civil Liberties Act (1988), 1456
Civil Rights Act of 1866, 278
Civil Rights Act of 1957, 863
Civil Rights Act of 1960, 875
Civil Rights Act of 1964, 933
Civil Rights Act of 1968, 1032
Civil Rights Act of 1991, 1500
Civil Rights Restoration Act (1988), 1452
Clayton Antitrust Act (1914), 432
Clayton-Bulwer Treaty (1850), 219
Clean Air Act (1963), 926
Clean Air Act Amendments of 1970, 1131
Clean Air Act Amendments of 1977, 1323
Clean Air Act Amendments of 1990, 1492
Clean Water Act and Amendments (1965ff.), 981

Coastal Zone Management Act (1972), 1192
Coinage Act (1873), 316
Communications Act (1934), 625
Communications Act Amendments (1960), 891
Communications Decency Act (1996), 1546
Communist Control Act (1954), 826
Comprehensive Crime Control Act (1984), 1418
Comprehensive Drug Abuse Prevention and Control Act (1970), 1117
Comprehensive Employment Training Act (1973), 1213
Comprehensive Environmental Response, Compensation, and Liability Act. *See* Superfund Act (1980)
Compromise of 1850, 225
Comstock Act (1873), 320
Confiscation Acts (1861-1862), 244
Constitution: History (1787), 28
Constitution: Provisions (1787), 33
Consumer Credit Protection Act (1968), 1044
Consumer Product Safety Act (1972), 1196
Convention of 1800. *See* Monfontaine, Treaty of (1801)
Convention of 1818, 167
Convention on the Prevention and Punishment of the Crime of Genocide. *See* Genocide Treaty (1948)
Copeland Act. *See* Anti-Racketeering Act of 1934
Copyright Act of 1909, 397
Copyright Act of 1976, 1295

Corrupt Practices Act. *See* Federal Corrupt Practices Act (1925)

Crime of 1873. *See* Coinage Act (1873)

Currency Act (1900), 369

Dancing Rabbit Creek, Treaty of (1830), 192

Dawes Act. *See* General Allotment Act (1887)

Declaration of Independence (1776), 1

Defense of Marriage Act (1996), 1551

Delaney Amendment. *See* Food Additives Amendment (1958)

Department of Energy Organization Act (1977), 1319

Dependent Pension Act (1890), 351

Digital Millennium Copyright Act (1998), 1555

Dingley Tariff (1897), 363

Direct democracy laws (1913), 371

Disfranchisement laws (1890), 358

Duck Stamp Act. *See* Migratory Bird Hunting and Conservation Stamp Act (1934)

Dyer Act. *See* Motor Vehicle Theft Act (1919)

Earned Income Tax Credit (1975), 1269

Eastern Wilderness Act (1975), 1254

Economic Opportunity Act (1964), 944

Economic Recovery Tax Act and Omnibus Budget Reconciliation Act (1981), 1397

Education for All Handicapped Children Act (1975), 1287

Eighteenth Amendment (1919), 460

Eighth Amendment (1789), 91

Eisenhower Doctrine (1957), 849

Electoral Count Act (1887), 341

Eleventh Amendment (1798), 115

Emancipation Proclamation (1863), 259

Embargo Acts (1806-1807), 151

Emergency Planning and Community Right-to-Know Act (1986), 1430

Emergency Price Control Act (1942), 728

Emergency Quota Act of 1921. *See* Immigration Act of 1921

Employee Retirement Income Security Act (1974), 1224

Employment Act (1946), 757

Endangered Species Act (1973), 1214

Endangered Species Preservation Act (1966), 1016

Endangered Species, Convention on International Trade in (1975), 1271

Energy Policy and Conservation Act (1975), 1288

Enforcement Acts. *See* Ku Klux Klan Acts (1870-1871)

Equal Access Act (1984), 1412

Equal Credit Opportunity Act (1974), 1233

Equal Employment Opportunity Act (1972), 1165

Equal Pay Act (1963), 909

Equal Rights Amendment (1923-1983), 495

Espionage Acts (1917-1918), 451

Ethics in Government Act (1978), 1349

Executive Order 8802 (1941), 723

Executive Order 11141 (1964),
929
Executive Orders 11246 and
11375 (1965, 1967), 980

Fair Credit Reporting Act (1970),
1108
Fair Housing Act (1968), 1035
Fair Labor Standards Act (1938),
704
Family and Medical Leave Act
(1993), 1513
Family Planning Services and
Population Research Act
(1970), 1118
Family Support Act (1988), 1458
Family Violence Prevention and
Services Act (1984), 1417
Farm Act of 1985. *See* Food
Security Act (1985)
Federal Aid in Wildlife Act. *See*
Pittman-Robertson Wildlife
Restoration Act (1937)
Federal Cigarette Labeling and
Advertising Act. *See* Cigarette
Warning Label Act (1966)
Federal Coal Mine Health and
Safety Act (1969), 1083
Federal Corrupt Practices Act
(1925), 518
Federal Credit Union Act (1934),
630
Federal Crimes Act (1790), 105
Federal Election Campaign Act
(1972), 1155
Federal Environmental Pesticide
Control Act (1972), 1182
Federal Firearms Act (1938), 619
Federal Food and Drugs Act. *See*
Pure Food and Drugs Act (1906)
Federal Food, Drug, and
Cosmetic Act. *See* Food, Drug,
and Cosmetic Act (1938)

Federal Land Policy and
Management Act (1976), 1300
Federal Power Act of 1920, 476
Federal Reserve Act (1913), 425
Federal Tort Claims Act (1946),
763
Federal Trade Commission Act
(1914), 430
Fifteenth Amendment (1870), 302
Fifth Amendment (1789), 71
First Amendment (1789), 56
Food Additives Amendment
(1958), 867
Food, Drug, and Cosmetic Act
(1938), 699
Food Security Act (1985), 1426
Force Act of 1833, 194
Force Acts. *See* Ku Klux Klan Acts
(1870-1871)
Foreign Agents Registration Act
(1938), 691
Forest and Rangeland Renewable
Resources Planning Act (1974),
1219
Formosa Resolution (1955), 834
Fort Atkinson Treaty (1853), 235
Fort Greenville Treaty (1795), 118
Fort Jackson Treaty. *See* Horseshoe
Bend Treaty (1814)
Fort Laramie Treaty of 1851, 228
Fort Laramie Treaty of 1868, 300
Fort Stanwix Treaty (1784), 13
Fort Wayne Treaty (1809), 157
Fourteenth Amendment (1868),
291
Fourth Amendment (1789), 66
Freedmen's Bureau Act (1865),
265
Freedom of Information Act
(1966), 1002
Fugitive Slave Act of 1793, 106
Fugitive Slave Act of 1850, 221

G.I. Bill (1944), 740
General Agreement on Tariffs and Trade of 1947, 780
General Agreement on Tariffs and Trade of 1994, 1537
General Allotment Act (1887), 347
General Mining Act (1872), 314
Geneva Protocol (1925), 524
Genocide Treaty (1948), 790
Gentlemen's Agreement (1907), 391
Ghent, Treaty of (1814), 160
Glass-Owen Act. *See* Federal Reserve Act (1913)
Gold Standard Act. *See* Currency Act (1900)
Good Neighbor Policy (1933-1945), 578
Guadalupe Hidalgo, Treaty of (1848), 213

Halibut Treaty (1924), 514
Harrison Act. *See* Harrison Narcotic Drug Act (1914)
Harrison Narcotic Drug Act (1914), 434
Hatch Act (1939), 709
Hate Crime Statistics Act (1990), 1471
Hawley-Smoot Tariff Act. *See* Smoot-Hawley Tariff Act(1930)
Hazardous Materials Transportation Act (1974), 1237
Hazardous Substances Labeling Act (1960), 886
Higher Education Act (1965), 995
Highway Beautification Act (1965), 966
Hobbs Act (1946), 761
Homeland Security Act (2002), 1566

Homestead Act of 1862, 245
Hoover-Stimson Doctrine (1932), 562
Horseshoe Bend Treaty (1814), 159
Housing Act of 1961, 901
Housing and Urban Development Act (1965), 976
Hundred Days legislation (1933), 573

Immigration Act of 1917, 446
Immigration Act of 1921, 483
Immigration Act of 1924, 501
Immigration Act of 1943, 736
Immigration Act of 1990, 1498
Immigration and Nationality Act Amendments of 1965, 985
Immigration and Nationality Act of 1952, 812
Immigration Reform and Control Act of 1986, 1435
Independent Treasury Act (1846), 209
Indian Appropriation Act (1871), 306
Indian Bill of Rights. *See* Indian Civil Rights Act (1968)
Indian Child Welfare Act (1978), 1355
Indian Citizenship Act (1924), 505
Indian Civil Rights Act (1968), 1040
Indian Education Acts (1972, 1978), 1176
Indian Gaming Regulatory Act (1988), 1465
Indian General Allotment Act. *See* General Allotment Act (1887)
Indian Offenses Act (1883), 335
Indian Removal Act (1830), 186

Indian Reorganization Act (1934), 620

Indian Self-Determination and Education Assistance Act (1975), 1262

INF Treaty (1987), 1444

Insanity Defense Reform Act (1984), 1420

Intelligence Identities Protection Act (1982), 1401

Inter-American Treaty of Reciprocal Assistance (1948), 778

Interest Equalization Tax Act (1964), 946

Internal Security Act (1950), 799

Internet Tax Freedom Act (1998), 1553

Interstate Commerce Act (1887), 343

Invalid Pension Act or Disability Pension Act. *See* Dependent Pension Act (1890)

Jacob Wetterling Crimes Against Children and Sexually Violent Offender Registration Act. *See* Megan's Law (1996)

Jay's Treaty (1794), 110

Jencks Act (1957), 861

Jim Crow laws (1880's-1954), 329

Johnson-Reid Act. *See* Immigration Act of 1924

Jones Act (1917), 448

Judiciary Act of 1789, 41

Judiciary Act of 1875. *See* Removal Act (1875)

Judiciary Acts of 1801-1925, 136

Juvenile Justice and Delinquency Prevention Act (1974), 1231

Kanagawa, Treaty of (1854), 236

Kansas-Nebraska Act (1854), 240

Kefauver-Harris Amendment (1962), 903

Kellogg-Briand Pact (1928), 547

Ku Klux Klan Acts (1870-1871), 305

Labor-Management Relations Act (1947), 769

Labor-Management Reporting and Disclosure Act. *See* Landrum-Griffin Act (1959)

Lame-Duck Amendment. *See* Twentieth Amendment (1933)

Land Act of 1820, 178

Land Grant Act of 1862. *See* Morrill Land Grant Act of 1862

Land Grant Act of 1890. *See* Morrill Land Grant Act of 1890

Landrum-Griffin Act (1959), 874

Law of the Sea Treaty (1982), 1403

Lead-Based Paint Poisoning Prevention Act (1971), 1141

Lend-Lease Act (1941), 719

Long-Range Transboundary Air Pollution, Convention on (1979), 1374

Low-Level Radioactive Waste Policy Act (1980), 1391

McCarran Act. *See* Internal Security Act (1950)

McCarran-Walter Act. *See* Immigration and Nationality Act of 1952

McFadden Act (1927), 541

McKinney Homeless Assistance Act (1987), 1440

Madison Amendment. *See* Twenty-seventh Amendment (1992)

Magnuson Act. *See* Immigration Act of 1943

Magnuson-Moss Warranty Act (1975), 1263

Maine Indian Claims Act (1980), 1377

Major Crimes Act (1885), 340

Mann Act (1910), 409

Marihuana Tax Act (1937), 674

Marine Mammal Protection Act (1972), 1189

Marine Plastic Pollution Research and Control Act (1987), 1449

Maternity Act. *See* Sheppard-Towner Act (1921)

Medicare and Medicaid Amendments (1965), 959

Medicine Lodge Creek Treaty (1867), 287

Megan's Law (1996), 1548

Menominee Restoration Act (1973), 1211

Mental Retardation Facilities and Community Mental Health Centers Construction Act (1963), 921

Migratory Bird Act (1913), 415

Migratory Bird Hunting and Conservation Stamp Act (1934), 603

Migratory Bird Treaty Act (1918), 454

Migratory Species of Wild Animals, Convention on the Conservation of (1979), 1372

Military Reconstruction Acts. *See* Reconstruction Acts (1867)

Militia Act (1862), 254

Miller-Tydings Fair Trade Act (1937), 675

Mineral Leasing Act (1920), 470

Mining Act. *See* General Mining Act (1872)

Mining and Minerals Policy Act (1970), 1137

Missing Children's Assistance Act (1984), 1421

Missouri Compromise (1820), 173

Monfontaine, Treaty of (1801), 141

Monroe Doctrine (1823), 181

Montreal Protocol (1990), 1472

Morrill Land Grant Act of 1862, 249

Morrill Land Grant Act of 1890, 362

Moscow Treaty. *See* U.S.-Russia Arms Agreement (2002)

Motor Vehicle Air Pollution Control Act (1965), 989

Motor Vehicle Theft Act (1919), 469

Motor Vehicle Theft Law Enforcement Act (1984), 1425

Multiple Use-Sustained Yield Act (1960), 879

Murray Act. *See* Employment Act (1946)

National and Community Service Trust Act (1993), 1517

National Arts and Cultural Development Act (1964), 952

National Bank Acts (1863-1864), 261

National Civil Service Act. *See* Pendleton Act (1883)

National Defense Act (1916), 435

National Defense Education Act (1958), 865

National Environmental Policy Act. *See* Clean Air Act (1963)

National Environmental Policy Act (1970), 1094

National Firearms Act (1934), 619

National Forest Management Act (1976), 1311

National Industrial Recovery Act (1933), 596

National Labor Relations Act (1935), 638
National Motor Vehicle Theft Act. *See* Motor Vehicle Theft Act (1919)
National Narcotics Act (1984), 1422
National Origins Act. *See* Immigration Act of 1924
National Park Service Organic Act (1916), 440
National Security Act (1947), 774
National Traffic and Motor Vehicle Safety Act (1966), 1014
National Trails System Act (1968), 1077
Native American Graves Protection and Repatriation Act (1990), 1496
Natural Gas Act (1938), 693
Naturalization Act of 1790, 104
Navajo-Hopi Land Settlement Act (1974), 1249
Navajo-Hopi Rehabilitation Act (1950), 797
Neutrality Acts (1935-1939), 657
Newlands Act. *See* Reclamation Act (1902)
News Room Search Act. *See* Privacy Protection Act (1980)
Niagara Power Act (1957), 859
Niagara Redevelopment Act. *See* Niagara Power Act (1957)
Nineteenth Amendment (1920), 478
Ninth Amendment (1789), 92
Noise Control Act (1972), 1203
Nonimportation Acts. *See* Embargo Acts (1806-1807)
Norris-La Guardia Act (1932), 565
North American Free Trade Agreement (1993), 1519
North Atlantic Treaty (1949), 792

North Korea Pact (1994), 1532
Northwest Ordinance (1787), 24
Nuclear Nonproliferation Treaty (1968), 1054
Nuclear Test Ban Treaty (1963), 913
Nuclear Waste Policy Act (1983), 1406

Occupational Safety and Health Act (1970), 1125
Ogdensburg Agreement (1940), 714
Oil Pollution Act of 1924, 509
Oil Pollution Act of 1990, 1480
Oklahoma Welfare Act (1936), 668
Older Americans Act (1965), 956
Older Workers Benefit Protection Act (1990), 1484
Omnibus Crime Control and Safe Streets Act (1968), 1052
Opium Exclusion Act (1909), 396
Ordinance of 1785, 17
Ordinance of 1787. *See* Northwest Ordinance (1787)
Oregon Act (1848), 217
Organized Crime Control Act (1970), 1103
Outer Space Treaty (1967), 1022

Pacific Railroad Survey Act (1853), 230
Pact of Paris. *See* Kellogg-Briand Pact (1928)
Page Law (1875), 322
Panama Canal Act (1912), 412
Panama Canal Treaties (1978), 1328
Panama Tolls Act. *See* Panama Canal Act (1912)
Parens Patriae Act (1974), 1232

Parental Kidnapping Prevention Act (1980), 1396
Paris, Treaty of (1783), 9
Paris, Treaty of (1898), 367
Part of the Civil Rights Act of 1968. *See* Fair Housing Act (1968)
Part of the Permanent Reciprocity Treaty of 1903. *See* Platt Amendment (1903)
Part of the Social Security Act. *See* Aid to Families with Dependent Children (1935)
Payne-Aldrich Tariff Act (1909), 403
Pendleton Act (1883), 336
Perkins Act (1990), 1483
Personal Responsibility and Work Opportunity Reconciliation Act (1996), 1549
Philippines Commonwealth Independence Act. *See* Tydings-McDuffie Act (1934)
Pinckney's Treaty (1795), 123
Pittman-Robertson Wildlife Restoration Act (1937), 681
Platt Amendment (1903), 381
Political Activities Act. *See* Hatch Act (1939)
Pollution Prevention Act (1990), 1487
Port and Tanker Safety Act (1978), 1337
Preemption Act (1841), 199
Pregnancy Discrimination Act (1978), 1352
Presidential Succession Act of 1947, 772
Price-Anderson Act (1957), 853
Privacy Act (1974), 1252
Privacy Protection Act (1980), 1378

Prohibition. *See* Eighteenth Amendment (1919)
Public Broadcasting Act (1967), 1024
Public Health Cigarette Smoking Act (1970), 1098
Public Law 280 (1953), 824
Public Protection of Maternity and Infancy Act. *See* Sheppard-Towner Act (1921)
Public Utility Regulatory Policies Act (1978), 1356
Puerto Rican Federal Relations Act. *See* Jones Act (1917)
Pure Food and Drugs Act (1906), 387

Racketeer Influenced and Corrupt Organizations Act (1970), 1105
Railway Labor Act (1926), 534
Reciprocal Trade Act of 1936, 670
Reclamation Act (1902), 375
Reconstruction Acts (1867), 280
Refugee Relief Act (1953), 820
Removal Act (1875), 326
Resource Conservation and Recovery Act (1976), 1306
Resource Recovery Act (1970), 1113
Rio Treaty. *See* Inter-American Treaty of Reciprocal Assistance (1948)
Robinson-Patman Antidiscrimination Act (1936), 662
Robinson-Patman Price Discrimination Act. *See* Robinson-Patman Antidiscrimination Act (1936)
Rush-Bagot Agreement (1817), 165

Safe Drinking Water Act (1974), 1242

SALT I Treaty (1972), 1171

SALT II Treaty (1979), 1367

Seabed Treaty (1972), 1157

Second Amendment (1789), 61

Second Morrill Act. *See* Morrill Land Grant Act of 1890

Securities Exchange Act (1934), 612

Sedition Act (1918 act). *See* Espionage Acts (1917-1918)

Sedition Act of 1798, 131

Servicemen's Readjustment Act. *See* G.I. Bill (1944)

Seventeenth Amendment (1913), 419

Seventh Amendment (1789), 90

Shays-Meehan Campaign Finance Reform Bill. *See* Bipartisan Campaign Reform Act (2002)

Sheppard-Towner Act (1921), 489

Sherman Act. *See* Sherman Antitrust Act (1890)

Sherman Antitrust Act (1890), 353

Sixteenth Amendment (1913), 414

Sixth Amendment (1789), 85

Sky Marshals Bill. *See* Aviation and Transportation Security Act (2001)

Smith Act (1940), 711

Smoot-Hawley Tariff Act(1930), 556

Social Security Act (1935), 642

Solid Waste Disposal Act of 1965, 992

Southeast Asia Resolution. *See* Tonkin Gulf Resolution (1964)

Speedy Trial Act (1975), 1260

START II Treaty (1993), 1509

Stimson Doctrine. *See* Hoover-Stimson Doctrine (1932)

Superfund Act (1980), 1386

Surface Mining Control and Reclamation Act (1977), 1317

Taft-Hartley Act. *See* Labor-Management Relations Act (1947)

Taiwan Relations Act (1979), 1363

Takings clause (1789), 77

Tariff Act of 1909. *See* Payne-Aldrich Tariff Act (1909)

Tariff Act of 1924. *See* Dingley Tariff (1897)

Tariff Act of 1930. *See* Smoot-Hawley Tariff Act(1930)

Tax Reform Act of 1986, 1434

Taylor Grazing Act (1934), 636

Tennessee Valley Authority Act (1933), 582

Tenth Amendment (1789), 98

Termination Resolution (1953), 815

Third Amendment (1789), 64

Thirteenth Amendment (1865), 273

Three-fifths compromise (1787), 39

Title I of the Consumer Credit Protection Act. *See* Truth in Lending Act (1968)

Title III of Superfund Amendments Reauthorization Act. *See* Emergency Planning and Community Right-to-Know Act (1986)

Title VII of the Civil Rights Act of 1964, 937

Title IX of the Education Amendments of 1972, 1178

Title IX of the Organized Crime Control Act. *See* Racketeer Influenced and Corrupt Organizations Act (1970)
Tonkin Gulf Resolution (1964), 942
Toxic Substances Control Act (1976), 1290
Trade and Intercourse Acts (1790-1834), 102
Trademark Act. *See* Trademark Law Revision Act (1988)
Trademark Law Revision Act (1988), 1469
Transcontinental Treaty. *See* Adams-Onís Treaty (1819)
Treaty of Monfontaine. *See* Monfontaine, Treaty of (1801)
Treaty of San Lorenzo. *See* Pinckney's Treaty (1795)
Tripartite Security Treaty (1952), 808
Truman Doctrine (1947), 764
Truth in Lending Act (1968), 1050
Tunney Act. *See* Antitrust Procedures and Penalties Act (1974)
Twelfth Amendment (1804), 147
Twentieth Amendment (1933), 571
Twenty-fifth Amendment (1967), 1020
Twenty-first Amendment (1933), 601
Twenty-fourth Amendment (1964), 928
Twenty-second Amendment (1951), 806
Twenty-seventh Amendment (1992), 1505

Twenty-sixth Amendment (1971), 1147
Twenty-third Amendment (1961), 896
Tydings-McDuffie Act (1934), 606

United States recognition of Vietnam (1995), 1541
Uniting and Strengthening America by Providing Appropriate Tools Required to Intercept and Obstruct Terrorism Act. *See* USA Patriot Act (2001)
U.S.-Japanese Treaty (1952), 810
U.S.-Russia Arms Agreement (2002), 1564
U.S.-Soviet Consular Treaty (1967), 931
USA Patriot Act (2001), 1558

Versailles, Treaty of (1919), 464
Victims of Crime Act (1984), 1424
Violence Against Women Act (1994), 1530
Violent Crime Control and Law Enforcement Act (1994), 1529
Virginia Statute of Religious Liberty (1786), 21
Vocational and Applied Technology Education Act. *See* Perkins Act (1990)
Voting Rights Act of 1965, 970
Voting Rights Act of 1975, 1274

Wagner-Connery Act. *See* National Labor Relations Act (1935)
Wang Hiya, Treaty of (1844), 207
War Brides Act (1945), 753
War Powers Resolution (1973), 1208
Washington, Treaty of (1871), 310

Water Pollution Control Act. *See*
  Clean Water Act and
  Amendments (1965ff.)
Water Pollution Control Act
  Amendments of 1956, 844
Water Pollution Control Act
  Amendments of 1972, 1159
Water Pollution Control Act of
  1948, 785
Water Power Act. *See* Federal
  Power Act of 1920
Water Resources Research Act
  (1964), 939
Webster-Ashburton Treaty (1842),
  202
Weeks-McLean Act. *See* Migratory
  Bird Act (1913)
Welfare Reform Act. *See* Personal
  Responsibility and Work
  Opportunity Reconciliation
  Act (1996)
Wheeler-Lea Act (1938), 685

Wheeler-Howard Act. *See* Indian
  Reorganization Act (1934)
White-Slave Traffic Act. *See* Mann
  Act (1910)
Wholesome Poultry Products Act
  (1968), 1071
Wild and Scenic Rivers Act
  (1968), 1077
Wilderness Act (1964), 954
Women in Apprenticeship and
  Nontraditional Occupations
  Act (1992), 1507
Women in Armed Services
  Academies Act (1975), 1280
Women's Educational Equity Act
  (1978), 1354
World War Adjusted
  Compensation Act (1924), 499

Yalta Conference agreements
  (1945), 750

U.S. Laws, Acts, and Treaties

DECLARATION OF INDEPENDENCE

DATE: Adopted July 4, 1776
U.S. STATUTES AT LARGE: 1 Stat. 1-4
CATEGORIES: Civil Rights and Liberties; Constitutional Law

The Declaration of Independence marks the beginning of the experiment in democracy that later became the United States of America, articulating the human rights and liberties on which the republic was founded.

In the opening months of 1776, the colonists faced a momentous decision. Should they content themselves with a return of British authority as it existed prior to 1763, or should they irrevocably sever all political ties with, and dependence upon, Great Britain? Since Great Britain was unwilling to give them that choice, offering instead only abject surrender to parliamentary sovereignty, Americans in increasing numbers concluded that complete independence, not merely autonomy within the British Empire, must be their goal. Many of the undecided were won over to defiance of the Crown as a result of Parliament's Prohibitory Act, which called for a naval blockade of the colonies, the seizure of American goods on the high seas, and the dragooning of captured provincial seamen into the royal navy. For many colonists, news of the British ministry's decision to employ German mercenaries for use in America was the last straw. The requirements of the struggle itself lent weight to the idea of complete separation. People would not do battle wholeheartedly for vaguely defined purposes, nor would French or Spanish aid, deemed essential to military success, be forthcoming if the colonies fought merely for a greater freedom within the empire.

In January, 1776, these colonial issues were the subject of Thomas Paine's *Common Sense*. Although it may be doubted that Paine's widely read pamphlet was the immediate impetus for the break, and although he advanced no new arguments, Paine expressed cogent and compelling arguments for a free America that would pursue its own destiny. Although Americans of almost every persuasion were already disputing the right of Parliament to rule over the colonies, there remained among the colonists a strong attachment to the British crown and to King George III. Monarchy in general, and the Hanoverian king in particular, received scathing denunciation from Paine, who asserted that kings were frauds imposed upon people capable of governing themselves. George III, Paine reasoned, was no exception and had engaged in oppressive acts that had destroyed every claim upon American loyalties. Paine held that the break should come immediately, while Americans were in arms and sensitive to their liberties. Independence, he argued, was inevitable for a wealthy, expanding continent that could not long be tied to a small and distant island controlled by "a Royal Brute."

One by one, the Southern and New England colonial assemblies authorized their delegates to the Continental Congress, meeting in Philadelphia, to vote for independence. On June 7, 1776, Richard Henry Lee, obeying instructions from Virginia, introduced at the congress a resolution declaring the colonies independent. Temporarily, the Middle Colonies hesitated to make such a drastic decision, causing a delay in acting on the matter; but on July 2, with only New York abstaining, the vote was 12-0 in favor of Lee's resolution declaring that "the United colonies are, and of right ought to be, free and independent States."

Anticipating the outcome, Congress had earlier formed a committee, composed of Thomas Jefferson, John Adams, Benjamin Franklin, Robert R. Livingston, and Roger Sherman, to prepare a statement concerning independence. The now-famous document was drafted by Jefferson with some assistance from Adams and Franklin. Congress, after first making some revisions, such as deleting Jefferson's passage denouncing the king for not ending the slave trade, adopted it on July 4.

PURPOSE AND PROVISIONS
The purpose of the Declaration of Independence was not to change the legal status of America; on July 2, Congress had voted to sever the colonies from the British Empire. The intent of Jefferson and his colleagues was rather to explain and justify the action of Congress in terms meaningful to Americans and Europeans alike. In doing so, Jefferson drew heavily upon the general cluster of ideas associated with the eighteenth century philosophies collectively known as the Enlightenment. Besides a preface and a conclusion, the Declaration of Independence consists of a statement of

the right of revolution based upon the philosophy of natural rights, a list of grievances against the king, and an account of the colonists' inability to obtain redress of grievances within the structure of the British Empire.

Some modern scholars consider the barrage of accusations heaped upon the king to be lacking in dignity and significance in relation to the rest of the document. They point out that George III was a strict constitutionalist whose conduct in the political arena was in accord with the practices and traditions of the earlier Hanoverian monarchs. Moreover, most of the programs and policies held to be reprehensible by the colonists hardly originated in the mind of the king. Still, George III favored a rigid policy of government, and he consistently turned a deaf ear to the remonstrances from the American assemblies and congresses. To counter the public mood of the times, it was essential for Jefferson to lay America's troubles at the feet of the king. Since the time of the First Continental Congress in 1774, patriot leaders had denied that there was any legitimate parliamentary authority to cast off; it was this lingering loyalty to the Crown that held many to the empire.

THE PRINCIPLE OF UNALIENABLE RIGHTS

The enduring significance of the Declaration of Independence transcends the Anglo-American conflict. The statement that "all men are created equal"—that they have certain unalienable rights under God that governments may not destroy—not only inspired people in that day but also has moved people in the United States and elsewhere ever since. The phrase, applied narrowly at first, came to be the focus of debate as women, people of color, the young, and the poor—excluded de facto from the document's guarantees—began to fight for full equality. Women were denied the right to vote in federal elections until ratification of the Nineteenth Amendment in 1920; African American men received this right in the Fifteenth Amendment, ratified in 1870; persons between eighteen and twenty-one years of age were given the right to vote by the Twenty-sixth Amendment in 1970. Rights and liberties other than voting—due process of law, fair housing and public accommodations, equal opportunity in employment and college admissions—have all been fought for and gradually won by groups previously discriminated against. The force that sparked the emergence of this powerful movement was the burning desire of the

3

supporters of the Declaration of Independence to be free to shape their own destiny. The message they conveyed has left a lasting imprint on the conscience of the world.

R. Don Higginbotham, updated by
Joseph Edward Lee

SOURCES FOR FURTHER STUDY

Bailyn, Bernard. *The Ideological Origins of the American Revolution.* Cambridge, Mass.: The Belknap Press of Harvard University Press, 1967.

Becker, Carl L. *The Declaration of Independence: A Study in the History of Political Ideas.* 2d ed. New York: Harcourt, Brace, & World, 1951.

Maier, Pauline. *From Resistance to Revolution.* New York: Alfred A. Knopf, 1972.

Middlekauf, Robert. *The Glorious Cause: The American Revolution, 1763-1789.* New York: Oxford University Press, 1982.

Norton, Mary Beth. *Liberty's Daughters: The Revolutionary Experience of American Women, 1750-1800.* Boston: Little, Brown, 1980.

Wills, Garry. *Inventing America: Jefferson's Declaration of Independence.* Garden City, N.Y.: Doubleday, 1978.

Wood, Gordon S. *The Radicalism of the American Revolution.* New York: Alfred A. Knopf, 1992.

SEE ALSO: Articles of Confederation (1781); U.S. Constitution: History (1787); U.S. Constitution: Provisions (1787); Bill of Rights (1789).

ARTICLES OF CONFEDERATION

DATE: Ratified March 1, 1781
U.S. STATUTES AT LARGE: 1 Stat. 4-9
CATEGORIES: Constitutional Law; Government Procedure and Organization

The Articles were the first constitution, the blueprint for an organized compact of the colonies, providing the first American system of government, although not a judicial system.

The American experience with nationalism ran counter to developments that had led to nationhood throughout much of the modern world. A sense of American nationalism scarcely existed during the colonial period. Nor did nationalism produce a revolution aimed at the creation of a single, unified American government. Slowly, almost imperceptibly, Americans' sense of oneness grew as the colonies stood together in opposition to Great Britain's post-1763 imperial program. As Americans traveled the long road to 1776 and became more aware of their shared principles and interests, they began to think simultaneously about independence and union. Because the independent states realized they must work cooperatively or perish, American patriots turned to the task of creating a confederacy of states.

BUILDING A LEAGUE OF FRIENDSHIP

In June, 1776, while Thomas Jefferson and his committee worked at a statement that justified independence, a second committee was appointed by the Continental Congress. Including one representative from each colony, the committee was instructed to draft a series of articles that would form a cooperative union of states, thus linking the thirteen self-governing states into a "league of friendship." With John Dickinson from Pennsylvania as chairman, the committee quickly proposed a plan for union, but in late July, opponents of such a union convinced the Continental Congress to reject Dickinson's document.

Nearly five years elapsed before all agreements and compromises could be reached within the Continental Congress and at state level. The exigencies of the war slowed the process as the Continental Congress grappled with enlistments, supplies, finances, and foreign aid. Lawmakers also twice fled, once to Baltimore and once to York, Pennsylvania, from approaching British armies. State governments were similarly distracted, which further slowed the process. Political clashes in and out of the Continental Congress about the contents of the proposed document added yet another obstacle to approval of the Articles. Historians have differed sharply over the nature of the struggles. Some contend that they were ideological in substance, between so-called radicals and conservatives; others contend that they were rivalries between the small and large states. However, few scholars deny that the conflicts over questions concerning local authority versus central authority were conditioned by the colonists' previous experience with remote, impersonal government control from London. Nor should it be forgotten that creating a central administrative authority for all thirteen states and participating in government beyond the colony level were experiences largely foreign to Americans.

Although the committee report, of which Dickinson was the primary architect, was placed before the Continental Congress as early as July 12, 1776, it languished as attention was focused on questions about administering the West and apportioning representation and financial burdens among the states. Most delegates favored a loose confederation, as opposed to a highly centralized and powerful national government. Sometimes explicitly, but more often implicitly, it seemed that the Dickinson draft left too much authority in the hands of Congress. Finally, in November, 1777, the Continental Congress agreed upon the Articles of Confederation and submitted the agreement to the states for ratification.

PROVISIONS

Under the Articles, the confederated Congress became the only branch of the central government. Each state would have one vote to cast, regardless of population, by delegates selected by the various state legislatures. A simple majority of states could decide issues, except for specified matters that required the consent of nine. Each state had the sole power to tax its population, although each state also was expected to contribute its share of money (based upon improved lands) to the upkeep of the Confederation. States also retained exclusive power to regulate their own commercial activities. Each state claiming territory in the trans-Appalachian region was allowed to keep its possessions instead of turning them over to the United States. Individually, the states were to retain their sovereignty, freedom, and independence, along with any rights not specifically granted to Congress. In turn, the Articles gave the confederated Congress the authority to make war and peace, make military appointments, requisition men and money from the states, send out and receive ambassadors, and negotiate treaties and alliances. Management of postal affairs and the authority to coin money, decide weights and measures, and settle disputes between states were also responsibilities that the Articles gave to the confederated administration.

Although the Articles of Confederation vested momentous responsibilities in confederated Congress, the agreement did not give the Congress the authority to discharge those responsibilities. Without the ability to tax or regulate trade and lacking powers of enforcement, Congress could only hope that the states would meet their assigned requisitions and cooperate with the confederated administration in other vital areas. Despite the limits on power built into the Articles of Confederation, some states were reluctant to give their consent to the proposed confederated Congress. Opponents continued to question jurisdictional responsibilities assigned to the central government.

By 1779, all states except Maryland had endorsed the Articles. Maryland's continuing opposition was driven largely by avaricious land speculators. Colonial charters had given Connecticut, Massachusetts, and all states south of the Potomac River land grants extending westward to the Pacific Ocean. Many people from the "landless" states felt that regions beyond the settled areas should be turned over to the Confederation, so that states with extensive western claims would not enter the union with distinct natural advantages over states without western claims. Likewise, "landless" representatives maintained that the West eventually would be won through the combined military efforts of all.

If Maryland land speculators (who hoped to fare better from Congress than from the Commonwealth of Virginia in having prewar claims recognized) had exercised a decisive role in their state's refusal to ratify, their stand did not invalidate the reasoning of others who demanded an equitable solution to the western land problem. To break the impasse, Congress reversed itself and recommended that the landed states relinquish generous portions of their transmontane territories. Virginia, with vast claims, held the key. Prompted by Thomas Jefferson, on January 2, 1781, Virginia offered the Confederation its rights to all lands north of the Ohio River. Equally important and far-reaching were Virginia's stipulations (ultimately accepted) that speculators' claims be canceled and that new states be created and admitted to the union on terms of equality with the original thirteen. New York also responded, abandoning its tenuous claims, as Connecticut abandoned its more solid ones. In time, the remaining landed states followed suit. Maryland, which had requested French naval protection, was prodded into ratification by the French envoy, the Chevalier de la Luzerne, and on March 1, 1781, Congress announced the formal creation of a "perpetual union."

Characterized as a league of friendship, the Confederation created a union of thirteen sovereign states. Time and circumstances during the 1780's, however, would demonstrate the inherent flaws in the Articles of Confederation. By the end of the decade, it had become apparent to many Americans that the Articles were not adequate for the needs of the thirteen member states. Instead, the states consented, for the first time, to create a national government.

R. Don Higginbotham, updated by
Paul E. Doutrich

SOURCES FOR FURTHER STUDY

Douglas, Elisha P. *Rebels and Democrats: The Struggle for Equal Political Rights and Majority Rule During the American Revolution.* Chapel Hill: University of North Carolina Press, 1955.

Henderson, H. James. *Party Politics in the Continental Congress.* New York: McGraw-Hill, 1974.

Hoffert, Robert W. *A Politics of Tension: The Articles of Confederation and American Political Ideas.* Boulder: University Press of Colorado, 1991.

Jameson, J. Franklin. *The American Revolution Considered as a Social Movement.* Princeton, N.J.: Princeton University Press, 1926.

Jensen, Merrill. *The Articles of Confederation.* 1940. Reprint. Madison: University of Wisconsin Press, 1970.

Main, Jackson T. *The Social Structure of Revolutionary America.* Princeton, N.J.: Princeton University Press, 1965.

Miller, John C. *Triumph and Freedom: 1775-1783.* Boston: Little, Brown, 1948.

Moore, Wayne D. *Constitutional Rights and Powers of the People.* Princeton, N.J.: Princeton University Press, 1996.

Morris, Richard B. *Forging of the Union, 1781-1789.* New York: Harper & Row, 1987.

Wood, Gordon. *The Creation of the American Republic, 1776-1787.* New York: W. W. Norton, 1969.

SEE ALSO: Declaration of Independence (1776); U.S. Constitution: History (1787); U.S. Constitution: Provisions (1787).

TREATY OF PARIS

DATE: Signed September 3, 1783
CATEGORIES: Foreign Relations; Treaties and Agreements

The treaty brought the American Revolution to a formal close and recognized the United States as a sovereign nation.

The United States' ultimate success in winning the Revolutionary War did not immediately translate into an easy peace. The new nation's primary objective was to gain formal recognition of its independence from Great Britain; it also needed agreements related to tangential issues, such as boundaries and fishing rights off Newfoundland and Nova Scotia. It quickly became evident that the United States could not expect altruistic generosity from either its friends or its former adversaries. France, an ally of Spain, hesitated to support U.S. interests against the wishes of its Bourbon neighbor. Madrid also objected to any new rising empire in the Western Hemisphere, fearing possible instability within its own Latin American colonies. If Great Britain appeared conciliatory toward the United States, its motives were dictated by a desire to weaken the Franco-American Alliance and maintain remaining North American interests. At the same time, as events later revealed, Great Britain and France were willing to cooperate surreptitiously to limit the territorial aspirations of the United States when it proved to be in the interest of either power.

THE NEGOTIATORS
The U.S. diplomats at the peace conference were a match for their French and English counterparts, despite problems in undertak-

ing their important task. Of those appointed by the Continental Congress to negotiate a peace, Thomas Jefferson did not serve because of the fatal illness of his wife, and Henry Laurens was a prisoner in England during the most crucial period of the peacemaking discussions. Two other appointees, John Jay at Madrid and John Adams at the Hague, were serving in previous diplomatic assignments and did not reach Paris until months after Benjamin Franklin began discussions with the British in April, 1782. (Jay reached Paris in late June, while Adams did not arrive until the end of October.)

In London, Lord North had been prime minister throughout the entire war, but King George III largely had dictated government policy. The revolt of the American colonies and their probable loss from the British Empire led to North's resignation in March, 1782. Lord Rockingham succeeded him but died several months later. William Petty, the earl of Shelburne, the home secretary in Rockingham's cabinet, had been assigned the responsibility of dealing with the Americans. Shelburne sent to Paris a Scottish merchant named Richard Oswald, an elderly acquaintance of Franklin, to start conversations aimed at luring the venerable commissioner away from France.

Oswald argued that the former British colonies in America could gain more by dealing separately with the mother country, but while Franklin revealed a willingness to speak with the British representatives, he remained firmly committed to the Franco-American military alliance created in 1778. He did, however, assure Oswald that a generous peace would go far toward rebuilding ties between the English-speaking nations. When Lord Rockingham died in July, Shelburne became prime minister but was reluctant to concede total independence to the former colonies.

When Jay finally arrived in Paris in June, he expressed his deep suspicion of French intentions, correctly believing that the comte de Vergennes, French minister of foreign affairs, favored Spanish ambitions in the disputed region between the Appalachian mountains and the Mississippi River. The conde de Aranda, Spanish ambassador to France, informed Jay of the unwillingness of Charles III, the Bourbon king of Spain, to recognize the United States' western claims to all lands to the east bank of the Mississippi River north of 31° north latitude and to free navigation of the entire river. Subsequently, Aranda and Gérard de Rayneval, Vergennes's secretary and diplomatic courier, proposed that the region between the Great Lakes and the Ohio River remain in British hands and that much of the Southwest should become a Spanish protectorate. When he learned that Rayneval had slipped away to London, Jay suspected that the Bourbons might negotiate with Great Britain at U.S. expense.

TREATY PROVISIONS
Led by Jay, who personally took the initiative in August, the U.S. commissioners assured Shelburne of their willingness to deal directly with the British if London would change Oswald's instructions to permit him to negotiate openly and with full authority with the representatives of the United States. This would be an implicit recognition of U.S. sovereignty, which Great Britain had hitherto refused to acknowledge. Shelburne now responded positively, believing that the Americans could be separated from France and would be more cooperative with Great Britain in the future. Oswald received his increased authority in September, and the negotiations rapidly clarified the details of an agreement.

Franklin was disappointed at not gaining Canada, one of his personal objectives in the negotiations, but the boundaries agreed upon in the preliminary treaty did meet the United States' aspirations in the northwest and southwest. The Mississippi River was designated as the primary western boundary of the United States. In addition, the new nation was given access to the Canadian fishing grounds, and British forces would be evacuated from U.S. soil. In return, the U.S. commissioners agreed to validate prewar debts owed to British subjects and to recommend to the states that they return confiscated Loyalist property. On balance, the United States gained more than the British in the concessions each side made to reach a satisfactory conclusion.

IMPACT
The preliminary articles, signed on November 30, 1782, although without the advice or consent of Vergennes, did not technically violate the letter of the Franco-American Alliance, for the treaty was not to go into effect until France and Great Britain also had come to terms. What the commissioners had violated, however, were the instructions given by Congress in June, 1781, that they do nothing without the knowledge and consent of France. At that time, Con-

gress had even withdrawn the requirement that the Mississippi River be the nation's western boundary, ordering its commissioners to insist only upon independence. The negotiators' coup enabled Vergennes, never really eager to keep fighting until Spain recovered Gibraltar from the British, to persuade Charles III's ministers to settle instead for the acquisition of the island of Minorca in the Mediterranean Sea, as well as the two Floridas.

The final treaties were signed at Paris on September 3, 1783, confirming the detailed Anglo-American understanding of the previous November. With the acceptance of the formal agreement and Congress's ratification of the treaty, the United States of America entered the community of nations.

R. Don Higginbotham,
updated by Taylor Stults

SOURCES FOR FURTHER STUDY

Bemis, Samuel Flagg. *The Diplomacy of the American Revolution.* Washington, D.C.: American Historical Association, 1935. Reprint. 1957.

Burt, Alfred L. *The United States, Great Britain, and British North America from the Revolution to the Establishment of Peace After the War of 1812.* 1940. Reprint. New Haven, Conn.: Yale University Press, 1968.

Cohen, Warren, ed. *Cambridge History of American Foreign Relations.* 4 vols. New York: Cambridge University Press, 1993.

Darling, Arthur B. *Our Rising Empire, 1763-1803.* 1940. Reprint. New Haven, Conn.: Yale University Press, 1972.

Dull, Jonathan R. *A Diplomatic History of the American Revolution.* New Haven, Conn.: Yale University Press, 1985.

Hoffman, Ronald, and Albert, Peter J., eds. *Peace and the Peacemakers: The Treaty of 1783.* Charlottesville: University Press of Virginia, 1986.

Morris, Richard. *The Peacemakers: The Great Powers and American Independence.* 1965. Reprint. New York: Harper & Row, 1983.

SEE ALSO: Jay's Treaty (1794); Treaty of Ghent (1814).

FORT STANWIX TREATY

DATE: Signed October 22, 1784
U.S. STATUTES AT LARGE: 7 Stat. 15
CATEGORIES: Native Americans; Treaties and Agreements

Through this treaty, Iroquois tribes ceded lands to the United States and were forced to move westward.

The Treaty of Fort Stanwix, signed in 1784, was a product of the American Revolution that involved colonists and the Iroquois nations. Because several Iroquois tribes had fought alongside the British during the war, victorious Americans maintained that they had won lands occupied by "defeated" Iroquois. The Treaty of Fort Stanwix marked the beginning of negotiations with Native Americans that dealt with them as a conquered people rather than as equals. The Revolutionary War and resulting treaty negotiations irreparably split the Iroquois Confederacy.

At the outbreak of the American Revolution, the Six Nations of the powerful Iroquois Confederacy were divided over whether to support the English, to side with the American rebels, or to remain neutral. The confederation had traded and fought alongside the English for many years and considered the English and colonists as the same. Both British and American Indian agents encouraged Native Americans throughout the colonies to remain neutral. Initially, the Iroquois remained nonpartisan. This allowed the Iroquois to deal with both the British in Canada and the Americans in the colonies, playing one against another as they had the French and British prior to the French and Indian War.

As the Revolutionary War progressed, however, both the British and the Americans saw the advantages of including American Indians in their ranks and urged Native Americans to ally themselves. The pressure to choose sides exerted by British and American agents split the six-nation Iroquois Confederacy into two groups. Unable to agree on which side to support, the confederation decided to allow each nation to choose which side, if either, to endorse. The Oneidas and Tuscaroras fought for the rebels. American attacks on Mohawk settlements encouraged the Mohawks to support the British; they were joined by the Onondagas, Cayugas, and

Senecas. These tribes were effective in British attacks on frontier locations, especially in the Mohawk Valley around Fort Stanwix.

COMPETING PROMISES

During the war, British officers had made promises of land to Native Americans who fought with them, but during the peace negotiations in Paris, the defeated British ignored the interests of their Native American allies. In 1783, the Treaty of Paris surrendered all the land east of the Mississippi River to the former colonists. Some of this land belonged to various Native American tribes and was not England's to grant.

New York State granted Iroquois lands to Revolutionary War soldiers as compensation for services during the war. New York tried to negotiate land sales with the Iroquois that would directly benefit the state. Congress, under the Articles of Confederation, admonished New York officials and appointed Indian commissioners Oliver Wolcott, Richard Butler, and Arthur Lee to negotiate peace and land cessions for the United States with the Mohawks, Onondagas, Cayugas, and Senecas. A peace conference was called and held in New York at Fort Stanwix near Oneida Lake. A number of Iroquois could not attend because of illness and other factors, and only a quickly formed irregular group of Iroquois representatives was present. The commissioners arrived at Fort Stanwix with an intimidating military escort. Rather than negotiating with the Iroquois as equals, as the English had done previously, American commissioners asserted political sovereignty over all tribal natives on American soil. Iroquois speeches were cut short and credentials challenged.

The commissioners insisted that the Iroquois tribes that fought on the side of the British were a conquered people. All lands held by those tribes, therefore, were forfeit to the United States as spoils of war. America would allow them to retain some of their lands but demanded land cessions in reparation for injuries inflicted on Americans during the war. The Iroquois contended (1) that England had had no right to cede tribal lands to America (2) that if the Iroquois were to surrender their lands to Americans, they expected something in return, and (3) that they had not, in any event, been defeated in battle and therefore were not party to peace negotiations.

MUTUAL CONCESSIONS

As part of the resulting Treaty of Fort Stanwix, the attending Iroquois ceded a strip of land that began at the mouth of Oyonwaye Creek on Lake Ontario four miles south of the Niagara portage path. The boundary line ran south to the mouth of the Tehosaroro, or Buffalo Creek, to the Pennsylvania line, and along its north-south boundary to the Ohio River. In effect, the treaty took all Iroquois lands west of New York and Pennsylvania and all of Ohio.

The United States released any claim it may have had by right of conquest to tribal lands west of that boundary. Iroquois property in the western region of New York state east of the Oyonwaye remained unaffected. The treaty assured the Oneida and Tuscarora who had fought on the side of the Americans continued peaceful possession of their lands. The United States agreed to protect the remaining Iroquois territories against encroachments, seizures, and other possible violations, and guaranteed the right of the Six Nations of the Iroquois Confederacy to independence.

Representatives for the Iroquois Confederacy agreed to peaceful relations with the United States. The tribes who had fought against the colonies promised to deliver up all prisoners, black and white, whom they had taken during the war. As guarantee of that promise, six Iroquois would be taken as hostages to Fort Harmar by General Arthur St. Clair, governor of the Northwest Territory.

Immediately after the congressional commissioners concluded their negotiations, commissioners from Pennsylvania negotiated for large land grants in their state. In return, the Iroquois received five thousand dollars in goods and supplies. Soon after, New York State, in defiance of Congress, negotiated land sales with the Oneida and Tuscarora. Additional land treaties quickly ensued. Congress's inability to prevent New York State from negotiating separate land sales and to uphold other aspects of the Treaty of Fort Stanwix highlighted the weaknesses in central government under the Articles of Confederation and served as a reminder that each state considered itself a sovereign nation.

In 1786, the Iroquois Confederacy held a council meeting at Buffalo Creek, New York. Disappointed and upset with their delegates, they refused to ratify the Treaty of Fort Stanwix and offered to return gifts presented to the delegates at the negotiations. Congress, however, considered the terms of treaty to be valid and acted on them accordingly.

BRITISH INTERFERENCE

After the American Revolution, British officials did little to discourage continued relations with northern Native American tribes. The English traded with and provided provisions to local tribes and allowed large councils to be held at British-held forts. After the council of Buffalo Creek, the Iroquois sought support from the British in their effort to denounce the treaty and continue their war against the United States. The Iroquois Confederacy soon discovered that the British had no intention of militarily supporting their former allies in defense of their land rights. Lacking the desire to go to war against the Americans alone, the Iroquois let the treaty stand.

On January 9, 1789, St. Clair negotiated the Treaty of Fort Harmar with a group of Senecas. The treaty reaffirmed the terms and boundaries set forth in the Treaty of Fort Stanwix. The Iroquois were given permission to hunt in their old lands "as long as they were peaceful about it."

The treaties of Fort Stanwix and Fort Harmar further fractionalized the confederation's six tribes, a process that had begun in 1777, when the Six Nations had split in choosing sides during the Revolutionary War. Joseph Brant led a group of Mohawk, Cayuga, and other tribe members out of the country and into Ontario, Canada, thereby splitting the confederacy in half. Those who remained in the United States were divided over other issues between the American Indians and the settlers. There was no single chief or council that could speak for the entire Iroquois Confederacy, and the Iroquois Confederacy was never again united.

Leslie Stricker

SOURCES FOR FURTHER STUDY

Downes, Randolph C. *Council Fires on the Upper Ohio: A Narrative of Indian Affairs in the Upper Ohio Valley Until 1795*. Pittsburgh: University of Pittsburgh Press, 1940.
Graymont, Barbara. *The Iroquois in the American Revolution*. Syracuse, N.Y.: Syracuse University Press, 1972.
Jennings, Francis, ed. *The History and Culture of Iroquois Diplomacy: An Interdisciplinary Guide to the Treaties of the Six Nations and Their League*. Syracuse, N.Y.: Syracuse University Press, 1985.

Trigger, Bruce G., ed. *Northeast.* Vol. 15 in *Handbook of North American Indians*, edited by William C. Sturtevant. Washington, D.C.: Smithsonian Institution, 1978.

Vaughan, Alden T. *Early American Indian Documents: Treaties and Laws, 1607-1789.* Washington, D.C.: University Publications of America, 1987.

Washburn, Wilcomb E., ed. *History of Indian-White Relations.* Vol. 4 in *Handbook of North American Indians*, edited by William C. Sturtevant. Washington, D.C.: Smithsonian Institution Press, 1988.

SEE ALSO: Treaty of Paris (1783); Ordinance of 1785 (1785); Trade and Intercourse Acts (1790-1834); Fort Greenville Treaty (1795).

ORDINANCE OF 1785

DATE: Adopted May 20, 1785
CATEGORIES: Constitutional Law; Land Management

The ordinance regulated the sale of the public domain through an orderly framework for land distribution.

By 1779, twelve of the thirteen American states, engaged at that time in the Revolutionary War, had ratified the Articles of Confederation. The recalcitrant state, Maryland, ostensibly refused to ratify the document until the states with land claims in the West ceded those lands to the new government. Pressure from the landless states and the exigencies of the war finally compelled the landed states, particularly New York and Virginia, to cede their western claims to the Revolutionary government. Maryland then ratified the Articles of Confederation early in 1781 and the confederation government came into existence as the owner of a vast public domain. Although little was done by that government to dispose of these lands during the war, in October, 1780, Congress passed an act declaring its intent to sell the public lands and create states out of the new territories.

SECURING THE "PUBLIC DOMAIN"

After the Treaty of Paris had been signed in 1783, the Confederation Congress turned to the formulation of a national land policy. To implement the intentions expressed in the Act of 1780, three problems had to be met. First, security against the natives was necessary before the new lands could be established, and some measure of success in this direction was achieved with General Anthony Wayne's victory at the Battle of Fallen Timbers. Second, some procedure had to be devised for the political organization of the new regions; this problem was resolved with the Northwest Ordinance in 1787. Third, a system for the survey and sale of the lands had to be established, and this was the purpose of the Ordinance of 1785.

The debate over disposal of the public domain brought into view two divergent approaches that persisted into the nineteenth century. There were those who desired rapid settlement of the land and who, therefore, favored a policy that would attract settlers by the cheapness of the land. Others, moved by a variety of motives, advocated less liberal terms to settlers. Some of this latter group were concerned about the grave financial situation of the government. The Articles of Confederation did not provide the government with an independent and reliable source of revenue. Proceeds from the sale of public lands might alleviate this situation. Some from eastern (tidewater) areas feared that the rapid growth of the West would quickly diminish the political power of the older states. Others, interested in the possibilities of land speculation, looked upon liberal policies as dangerous competition.

There was also disagreement as to the method of land disposal. Two basic forms were available. The more systematic approach was the New England practice of township settlement, which provided for concentrated patterns of ownership, security in communities, and such community institutions as schools and churches. The other approach, generally referred to as the southern method, resulted in dispersed settlement with each individual staking out a claim to hitherto unsettled lands. In the New England plan, survey preceded sale and the possibility of conflicting claims was considerably lessened.

PROVISIONS OF THE ORDINANCE

The matter was debated through 1784 and 1785, and when the Ordinance of 1785 was passed, it appeared to incorporate the basic features of the New England practice. The principle that survey should precede sale was adopted, as the act provided for rectangular surveys that divided the land into townships of six square miles. Townships were divided into tracts of 640 acres, or sections, which were to be sold at public auction for a minimum price of one dollar per acre. In each township, one lot was set aside for the support of public schools and four for the federal government. A provision giving similar support for religion was narrowly defeated.

This ordinance, with its minimal purchase requirement of 640 acres and its prohibition against indiscriminate settlement, seemed to favor the needs of speculators more than bona fide settlers. Few people of the type willing to carve a farm out of the wilderness in an area open to attack by American Indians had $640 in cash. Moreover, the disposition of the people who moved west was to settle where they lit, regardless of surveys, which were unable to keep up with settlement during the nineteenth century.

Congress itself, in its desperate need for ready money, compromised the intent of the act by disposing of vast tracts of land to private land companies for purposes of sale to settlers at a profit. The most famous of these companies was the Ohio Company of Associates. In 1787, Congress agreed to sell one and a half million acres of land to this group and another three and a half million to the Scioto Company. This latter speculative venture included many of the most important men in Congress, and their inclusion in the speculation made possible the passage of the Ohio Company grant. Also in 1787, the Symmes Purchase of two million acres was made at about sixty-six cents per acre.

IMPACT OF THE ORDINANCE
The confederation government did not realize much money from these sales, nor did these sales greatly stimulate settlement. Conditions were too precarious in the Ohio country. The Land Act of 1796, which raised the minimum price to two dollars per acre, did little to advance settlement. The change to a more liberal policy began with the Harrison Land Act of 1800.

Nevertheless, the ordinance established an orderly method of disposing of public lands into private hands—a method that solved several problems simultaneously. First, it brought settlers and farmers into the national effort to repay the Revolutionary War debts. Even if the sales did not achieve what Thomas Jefferson hoped, the concept showed that all the nation's citizens would be called upon to shoulder part of the price of independence. Second, the principle of organized and methodical settlement—although, again, far from perfect in reality—reflected a clear understanding about the importance of keeping populations reasonably dense for purposes of defense and development. Third, and perhaps most significant, the ordinance ratified the fundamental property rights that undergirded the entire economic system. Land, once only held by nobility, was available to anyone for a tiny sum. Along with Jefferson's Northwest Ordinance, the Ordinance of 1785 allowed people to settle new land, bring it into the Union, and participate as equals in the polity.

John G. Clark,
updated by Larry Schweikart

SOURCES FOR FURTHER STUDY

Atack, Jeremy, and Peter Passell. *A New Economic View of American History.* 2d ed. New York: W. W. Norton, 1994.

Harris, Marshall D. *Origin of the Land Tenure System in the United States.* Westport, Conn.: Greenwood Press, 1953.

Hibbard, Benjamin H. *A History of the Public Land Policies.* New York: Peter Smith, 1960.

Morris, Richard B. *The Forging of the Union, 1781-1789.* New York: Harper & Row, 1987.

Pattison, William D. *Beginnings of the American Rectangular Land Survey System, 1784-1800.* Chicago: University of Chicago Press, 1957.

Robbins, Roy M. *Our Landed Heritage: The Public Domain, 1776-1936.* New York: Peter Smith, 1962.

Treat, Payson Jackson. *The National Land System, 1785-1820.* New York: E. B. Treat, 1910.

SEE ALSO: Northwest Ordinance (1787); Land Act of 1820 (1820).

VIRGINIA STATUTE OF RELIGIOUS LIBERTY

DATE: Adopted January 16, 1786
CATEGORIES: Religious Liberty

The first state law to legislate religious liberty, Virginia's statute paved the way for the First Amendment's separation of church and state.

The adoption by the state of Virginia of the Statute of Religious Liberty was a pivotal episode in the long struggle for separation of church and state in the United States. The American colonies had inherited from England an organic concept of society that predominated in the Middle Ages and survived the Protestant Reformation. In England, the church and the state had been regarded ideally as parts of a greater and divinely sanctioned social order and so owed mutual support to each other. While the Puritans and other sects emigrated partly to practice their particular faiths without harassment, few were committed to genuine religious freedom. The legal toleration of all Christians in Maryland and Pennsylvania, and the complete toleration offered in Rhode Island, were exceptional in the seventeenth century, and even those colonies imposed penalties on Catholics by the time of the Revolutionary War. Whereas, in the later colonial period, toleration of dissenting sects was often a practical necessity, connections between the church and state persisted. The Church of England was established legally in the Southern colonies, and Protestant churches were supported by public funds in most of New England. Catholics and Jews remained under civil disabilities in some states until well into the nineteenth century.

SEPARATING CHURCH AND STATE

During the period of the American Revolution, there was an acceleration of the long-term evolution to a concept of society in which political and religious life existed in separate compartments and in which religion withdrew, theoretically, into the private sphere of activity. Part of the impetus behind the separation of church and state was religious. Some originally radical Protestant sects were committed to separation early, either because of their own experience with

21

persecution or out of more abstract considerations. Some agreed with the founder of Rhode Island, clergyman Roger Williams, that a church would be corrupted only by connection with the state. The Baptists were particularly energetic advocates of separation. Isaac Backus, Baptist leader of the fight for religious disestablishment in Massachusetts, has been characterized as the leading American advocate of religious liberty after Williams. In addition to these strains within American Protestantism, the philosophy of the Enlightenment, emphasizing the sanctity of the individual conscience, was influential, most notably among Thomas Jefferson and other leaders of the disestablishment struggle in Virginia. Perhaps the overriding factor in deciding the general issue in the United States, however, was a practical consideration: that because of the extreme multiplicity of sects in the country, in the long run it was not politically feasible to establish any one of them or even a combination.

IMPACT OF THE REVOLUTION
The American Revolution, bringing new state constitutions and the withdrawal of British support for the Anglican establishment, provided an occasion for the reform of relationships between church and state. Virginia's action in the period following the Declaration of Independence was particularly significant. Virginia— one of the largest and most important states in the new republic and the seat of the most deeply rooted of the Anglican establishments—took the lead in moving toward religious liberty and the complete separation of church and state. Only Rhode Island offered comparable liberty among the original states, although, despite its early toleration, Catholics and Jews had been barred from citizenship there in the late colonial period.

Revolutionary Virginia inherited a strongly antiestablishment sentiment, marked historically by disputes over clerical salaries and the long struggle by Baptists and Presbyterians against Anglican domination. The Declaration of Rights, adopted by the Virginia legislature three weeks before the Declaration of Independence, asserted that "all men are equally entitled to the free exercise of religion, according to the dictates of conscience. . . ." James Madison had suggested this liberal phrasing in preference to a more narrow statement of religious toleration. Later in 1776, penalties against those of dissenting religious persuasion were repealed, and dissenters were exempted from contributing to the support of the still-established Church of England. In 1779, the legislature moved in the direction of disestablishment by discontinuing the payment of salaries to clergy of the Church of England in Virginia.

PROVISIONS OF THE STATUTE

The conclusive debates in Virginia took place in 1784 and 1785. Patrick Henry led a move in Virginia's legislature to establish a general assessment for the support of Christian worship, which would have substituted a general Christian establishment for the Anglican establishment. Initially passed in November, 1784, this General Assessment Bill was sharply attacked by Madison and defeated on its final reading in October, 1785. Madison followed up this victory by securing a vote on the "Bill for Establishing Religious Freedom," proposed by Thomas Jefferson and originally introduced in the legislature in 1779. It was adopted and became law as the Statute of Religious Liberty in January, 1786. With a preamble asserting that God had "created the mind free" and that attempts to coerce it "tend only to beget habits of hypocrisy and meanness, and are a departure from the plan of the Holy Author of our religion," Jefferson's statute provided "that no man shall be compelled to frequent or support any religious worship, place or ministry whatsoever, nor shall be enforced, restrained, molested, or burthened in his body or goods, nor otherwise suffer on account of his religious opinions or belief. . . ." There remained some vestigial connections between the church and the state, but their separation had been completed by 1802.

STATES FOLLOW VIRGINIA'S LEAD

Few other states immediately followed Virginia's lead. Officeholders under many of the original state constitutions were required to be believers in God, Christians, or even Protestants. It was not until 1818 that Connecticut did away with compulsory public support of churches, and not until 1833 was a similar establishment completely eliminated in Massachusetts. The First Amendment to the federal Constitution, which prohibited religious establishment or infringement of religious liberty on the national level, helped to commend the example of Virginia to its sister states.

Michael D. Clark, updated by
Daniel A. Brown

SOURCES FOR FURTHER STUDY

Drakeman, Donald L. "Religion and the Republic: James Madison and the First Amendment." *Journal of Church and State* 25, no. 3 (1983): 427-445.

Howe, Mark De Wolfe. *The Garden and the Wilderness: Religion and Government in American Constitutional History.* Chicago: University of Chicago Press, 1965.

Noll, Mark A., ed. *Religion and American Politics: From the Colonial Period to the 1980's.* New York: Oxford University Press, 1990.

Peterson, Merrill D., and Robert C. Vaughan, eds. *The Virginia Statute for Religious Freedom: Its Evolution and Consequences in American History.* New York: Cambridge University Press, 1988.

Stokes, Anson P., and Leo Pfeffer. *Church and State in the United States.* Rev. ed. New York: Harper & Row, 1964.

Wald, Kenneth D. *Religion and Politics in the United States.* 2d ed. Washington, D.C.: CQ Press, 1992.

SEE ALSO: U.S. Constitution: Provisions (1787); Bill of Rights (1789) First Amendment (1789).

NORTHWEST ORDINANCE

ALSO KNOWN AS: Ordinance of 1787
DATE: Adopted July 13, 1787
U.S. STATUTES AT LARGE: 2 Stat. 514
CATEGORIES: Land Management; Slavery

The ordinance marked the rise of federal involvement in the organization of Western lands and the first sectional compromise over the extension of slavery.

In March, 1784, the Congress of the Confederation accepted the cession of lands Virginia had claimed west of the Appalachian Mountains. A congressional committee headed by Thomas Jefferson, delegate from Virginia, then took steps to provide for the political organization of the vast area south of the Great Lakes, west of the Appalachians, and east of the Mississippi River. The committee's task was to draft legislation for the disposal of the land and the government of its settlers. The proposal of Jefferson's committee met the approval of Congress as the Ordinance of 1784.

ORDINANCE OF 1784

The Ordinance of 1784 divided the West into eighteen districts. Each district would be admitted to the Union as a state when its population equaled that of the least populous of the original states. In the meantime, when the population of a district reached twenty thousand, it might write a constitution and send a delegate to Congress. As Jefferson envisaged it, as many as ten new states might be carved from the new lands, many of them provided with mellifluous classical names. In Jefferson's original version, slavery was to be excluded after 1800, but this was stricken from the ordinance when it was adopted in 1784. The Ordinance of 1784 was to become effective once all Western lands claimed by the states had been ceded to the government. Before the states ceded their lands, however, a new ordinance was adopted that superseded that of 1784.

ORDINANCE OF 1787

The Ordinance of 1787, known as the Northwest Ordinance, was passed, according to some historians, at the insistence of land speculators who opposed the liberality of the Ordinance of 1784. The new ordinance did indeed slow down the process by which a territory might become a state, but it also added certain important features and provided for the more orderly creation of new states. While the Northwest Ordinance may have been less liberal than its predecessor, it was not undemocratic.

PROVISIONS FOR TERRITORIES AND STATEHOOD

The Northwest Ordinance established government in the territory north of the Ohio River. The plan provided for the eventual establishment of a bicameral assembly, the creation of three to five states equal to the original thirteen states, freedom of religion, the right to a jury trial, public education, and a ban on the expansion of slavery. To accomplish these goals, legislation provided that the whole Northwest region should be governed temporarily as a single territory and administered by a governor, a secretary, and three judges appointed by Congress. When the population of the territory reached five thousand free adult male inhabitants, the citizens might elect representatives to a territorial assembly. Property qualifications for voting were established, but they were small. The general assembly was to choose ten men, all of whom owned at least five hundred acres, from whom Congress would choose five men to serve as the upper house of the legislature. The governor would continue to be selected by Congress and have an absolute veto over all legislation.

The territory was to be divided into not fewer than three nor more than five districts. Whenever the population of one of the districts reached sixty thousand free inhabitants, it would be allowed to draft a constitution and submit it to Congress. If the constitution guaranteed a republican form of government, Congress would pass an enabling act admitting the district into the Union as a state on an equal basis with those states already in the Union.

PROVISIONS FOR BASIC RIGHTS
The ordinance guaranteed certain basic rights to citizens who moved into the new lands. A bill of rights provided for freedom of religion and guaranteed the benefits of writs of habeas corpus, the right of trial by jury, bail, and the general process of law. The third article read: "Religion, morality and knowledge being necessary to good government and the happiness of mankind, Schools and the means of education shall forever be encouraged. The utmost good faith shall always be observed towards the Indians." The first of these moral injunctions was implemented as the inhabitants obtained the means to do so. The second, regarding the American Indians, has still to be achieved. The fourth article established the basis for relations between the general government and the territories and states that might be formed from them. The fifth article provided for equitable taxation and the free navigation of the waters leading into the Mississippi and St. Lawrence Rivers.

The sixth article was epoch-making. It read: "There shall be neither Slavery nor involuntary Servitude in the said territory otherwise than in the punishment of crimes, whereof the party shall have been duly convicted." This provision determined that the society that developed north of the Ohio River would eventually be free. Influenced by the French slaveholders inhabiting the region, the interpretation of Article VI forbade the further introduction of

26

slavery but did not abolish slavery or affect the rights of those holding slaves prior to 1787. No such provision was written into the act establishing the Southwest Territory, in 1790.

IMPACT

The pattern established by the Northwest Ordinance was more or less followed in the later admission of states into the Union. Some, such as Texas and California, came in without a territorial period. Others, such as Michigan, caused trouble because of boundary disputes with neighboring states. As for the Ohio country, Arthur St. Clair, president of the Confederation Congress in 1787, was appointed first governor of the territory. Indiana Territory was organized in 1803, the same year in which Ohio entered the Union. Indiana entered as a state in 1816, Illinois in 1818, Michigan in 1837, and Wisconsin in 1848. Statehood was delayed for Indiana and Illinois territories as a result of their repeated petitions seeking repeal of the restrictions in the ordinance against the expansion of further slavery in the territory. Congress refused to repeal or revise the section, making slaveholders reluctant to move into the area. The predominant settlement by nonslaveholders eventually led to strengthening of the antislavery movement in the region.

The Northwest Ordinance proved to be a crowning legislative achievement of the otherwise lackluster confederation government. However, while Congress was debating the Northwest Ordinance, the Constitutional Convention was occurring in Philadelphia. It has been argued that the antislavery provisions influenced the debates of the constitutional convention over congressional representation. Since each state won two seats in the Senate, Southern states acceded freedom to the Northwest Territory by limiting the number of free states formed from the region. In turn, the Southern states hoped for dominance in the House of Representatives through the three-fifths clause counting slaves for congressional representation. Under the new Constitution, Congress reenacted the Ordinance of 1787 as a model of territorial government.

John G. Clark,
updated by Dorothy C. Salem

SOURCES FOR FURTHER STUDY

Berwanger, Eugene H. "Western Prejudice and the Extension of Slavery." *Civil War History* 12 (September, 1966): 197-212.

Cayton, Andrew R. L. *The Midwest and the Nation: Rethinking the History of an American Region.* Bloomington: Indiana University Press, 1990.

Hyman, Harold M. *American Singularity: The 1787 Northwest Ordinance, the 1862 Homestead and Morrill Acts, and the 1944 G.I. Bill.* Athens: University of Georgia Press, 1986.

Johnson, Andrew J. *The Life and Constitutional Thought of Nathan Dane.* New York: Garland, 1987.

Konig, David Thomas. *Devising Liberty: Preserving and Creating Freedom in the New American Republic.* Stanford, Calif.: Stanford University Press, 1995.

Onuf, Peter S. *Sovereignty and Territory: Claims Conflict in the Old Northwest and the Origins of the American Federal Republic.* Baltimore: The Johns Hopkins University Press, 1973.

_____. *Statehood and Union: A History of the Northwest Ordinance.* Bloomington: Indiana University Press, 1987.

Swierenga, Robert P. "The Settlement of the Old Northwest: Ethnic Pluralism in a Featureless Plain." *Journal of the Early Republic* 9 (Spring, 1989): 73-105.

Vaughan, Alden T. *Early American Indian Documents: Treaties and Laws, 1607-1789.* Washington, D.C.: University Publications of America, 1987.

SEE ALSO: Ordinance of 1785 (1785); Three-fifths compromise (1787); Fugitive Slave Act of 1793 (1793); Missouri Compromise (1820); Land Act of 1820 (1820).

U.S. CONSTITUTION: HISTORY

DATE: Adopted September 17, 1787; ratified June, 1788
U.S. STATUTES AT LARGE: 1 Stat. 10-20
CATEGORIES: Constitutional Law; Government Procedure and Organization

The Constitution is the highest law of the United States of America, establishing the republic's government and the basic laws and principles that would guide all future lawmaking in the nation.

By the middle of the 1780's, much dissatisfaction with government under the Articles of Confederation had became evident throughout the United States. Many of those prominent in the political life of the United States—George Washington, Thomas Jefferson, John Jay, Alexander Hamilton, and Noah Webster, among others—in papers, letters, and conversations criticized the functioning of the Confederation Congress. Specific concerns included Congress's lack of power to tax, to regulate interstate commerce, and to force states to cooperate more effectively with the central government. All efforts to improve the Articles of Confederation seemed doomed to failure, because amendments required unanimous approval by the states. It became evident to many concerned persons that changes might best be accomplished by abandoning the Articles altogether.

THE 1785 CONVENTIONS

In March, 1785, a meeting of delegates from Virginia and Maryland initiated a series of meetings that culminated in the replacement of the Articles. At the March meeting, the two states worked out an agreement involving commercial regulations on the Potomac River. After the success of the meeting, Virginia called for another meeting to be held in Annapolis, Maryland, during the following year. It was hoped that the convention would provide an opportunity for those attending to discuss common problems and possible solutions. Nine states were invited, but only five sent delegates. The most important result of the Annapolis Convention was the publication of a report, probably drafted by Alexander Hamilton, that called for yet another convention. This one, scheduled for Philadelphia in May, 1787, was to include delegates from all states.

THE 1787 CONVENTION

The purpose of the convention was to address and correct the defects in the Confederation government. Copies of the report were sent to each state legislature with a request that delegates be appointed and sent to Philadelphia. Every state except Rhode Island honored the request and sent representatives. Seventy-four delegates were appointed to the convention, although only fifty-five attended. Thirty-nine signed the final document. The Virginia delegation was among the first to reach Philadelphia, arriving two weeks before the scheduled start of deliberations.

The Virginians brought with them the outline of a plan of government that they intended to offer to the convention. The plan, quite controversial at the time, proposed creating a new national government. The Virginians sought a strong government that would include three branches and a sophisticated system of checks and balances. During the days before the convention began, several of the Virginia delegates, particularly James Madison, conferred with other early arrivals to hone their plan.

The convention first met on May 25 and appointed George Washington as the presiding officer. The section was significant, because Washington was held in high regard by the American people. The presence of Benjamin Franklin, who at eighty-one years of age was the oldest delegate, also added prestige to the gathering. With two such notable figures participating, the American public anticipated notable results.

COMPETING PROPOSALS

On May 29, with the convention only four days old, the Virginia delegation proposed a series of resolutions that immediately were known as the Virginia Plan. Drafted largely by James Madison and introduced by Edmund Randolph, the plan argued that, rather than merely revise the Articles of Confederation, the convention should discard them altogether and create a constitution that embodied an entirely new frame of government. The proposed government would have far more authority than did the confederated administration, and it would not be subordinate to each state government. The proposals set off a fierce debate that dominated the convention throughout most of June. On one side were delegates who endorsed the Virginia Plan. On the other side were delegates who feared that a powerful national government might jeopardize many of the rights and liberties won during the Revolutionary War.

As the debate intensified, delegates from several of the smaller states devised a series of resolutions designed to counter the Virginia Plan. Introduced by William Patterson from New Jersey, the resolutions became know as the New Jersey Plan. These proposals rejected the need for a new national government and called instead for the convention to retain, but significantly revise, the existing confederated government.

Among the more active delegates in favor of establishing a strong federal government were James Madison and George Mason from Virginia, James Wilson and Gouverneur Morris from Pennsylvania, John Dickinson from Delaware, John Rutledge and Charles Pinckney from South Carolina, and Oliver Ellsworth from Connecticut. In addition to Patterson, the leading supporters of the New Jersey Plan included Roger Sherman from Connecticut, Elbridge Gerry from Massachusetts, and Luther Martin from Maryland.

DEBATES OVER REPRESENTATION

For almost a month, delegates intensely deliberated over the two plans. In late June, with the convention on the verge of dissolution, Benjamin Franklin implored the delegates to find a common ground. Spurred on by Franklin's pleas, the convention agreed to discard the Articles of Confederation and create a constitution that would embody a strong national government. With the initial differences resolved, other aspects of both the Virginia and New Jersey Plans were debated throughout the summer. Central to the discussions was the concern of less populated states, such as Connecticut and Maryland, that they would lose all power and authority to the national government if representation within the new government were determined exclusively according to population. Responding to these concerns, proponents of the national government agreed to create a dual system of representation within Congress: Membership in the House of Representatives would be determined according to population; in the Senate, each state, regardless of the size of its population, would be given two members. It also was agreed that before a bill could become a law, both houses of Congress would have to approve it.

THE GREAT COMPROMISE

The agreement concerning representation within the legislative branch, sometimes referred to as the Great Compromise, reflected the spirit of concession that marked convention proceedings during the late summer months. Many other issues, including the length of presidential terms, the electoral procedure, the responsibilities of the judicial branch, the amendment process, and slavery within the new nation, tested the delegates' ability to negotiate and cooperate. In the end, the document could not be considered the work of any one group or faction of delegates. It had become a synthesis of the plans of all the delegates.

In September, Gouverneur Morris, an outspoken Pennsylvania delegate, became chair of a committee that was instructed to write a final draft of the Constitution. After some preliminary discussions about style and content, the document was formally presented to the convention on September 17. Although few delegates agreed to all revisions, a large majority found the document as a whole acceptable. Signed by thirty-nine delegates, the Constitution was declared adopted "by unanimous consent." Upon endorsement by the convention, the Constitution was submitted to each state legislature for ratification. In late June, 1788, approval by nine states, the number required for ratification, was reached and implementation of the new national government began.

Edward J. Maguire, updated by
Paul E. Doutrich

SOURCES FOR FURTHER STUDY

Conley, Patrick, and John Kaminski, eds. *The Constitution and the States: The Role of the Original Thirteen in Framing and Adoption of the Federal Constitution.* Madison, Wis.: Madison House, 1988.

Farrand, Max. *The Records of the Federal Convention of 1787.* 4 vols. New Haven, Conn.: Yale University Press, 1966.

Jensen, Merrill. *The Making of the American Constitution.* Princeton, N.J.: Van Nostrand, 1964.

Kammen, Michael. *A Machine That Would Go of Itself.* New York: Alfred A. Knopf, 1986.

McDonald, Forrest. *"Novus Ordo Seclorum": The Intellectual Origins of the Constitution.* Lawrence: University Press of Kansas, 1985.

Peters, William. *A More Perfect Union: The Making of the United States Constitution.* New York: Crown, 1987.

Vile, John R. *A Companion to the United States Constitution and Its Amendments.* 3d ed. Westport, Conn.: Greenwood Press, 2001.

Wood, Gordon. *The Creation of the American Republic, 1776-1787.* New York: W. W. Norton, 1969.

SEE ALSO: Articles of Confederation (1781); U.S. Constitution: Provisions (1787); Bill of Rights (1789).

U.S. CONSTITUTION: PROVISIONS

DATE: Adopted September 17, 1787; ratified June, 1788
U.S. STATUTES AT LARGE: 1 Stat. 10-20
CATEGORIES: Constitutional Law; Government Procedure and Organization

The fundamental document establishing the national government of the United States of America, the Constitution describes the nature and limits of political power within the national government as well as the way the branches of government are structured.

The Constitution of the United States is an extraordinary document, both theoretically and historically. One of the most important aspects of the Constitution was that it was (and is) firmly based on a clear set of theoretical principles. To describe the Constitution as a document of the Enlightenment—an eighteenth century movement in European thought that celebrated the capacity of reason to solve human problems—would be to tell the truth but not necessarily the whole truth. Alexander Hamilton, a delegate to the 1787 Constitutional Convention from New York, claimed that the Constitution reflected what he described as a "new science of politics." According to Hamilton, this new science was based on principles either unknown to or not fully understood by previous generations. It is generally acknowledged that the most fundamental principles of the Constitution are separation of powers, federalism, and republicanism.

Each of these principles is critical to a clear understanding of the American system of government, but each was developed because of the Founders' commitment to a prior principle—the principle of limited governmental power. A government founded on the principle of limited powers must develop safeguards to ensure that the people who wield the powers of government do not go beyond the limits. Within the American constitutional system this is accomplished by the three principles cited above.

SEPARATION OF POWERS

Separation of powers was a political principle advocated by English philosopher John Locke and French philosopher Baron de Montesquieu. The Constitution of the United States was the first national political document to apply this concept of government. Distinct governmental powers had long been recognized, but the Constitution of the United States was the first to place these powers in separate branches of government. The first three articles of the Constitution describe the location and authority of the legislative, executive, and judicial powers of government.

LEGISLATIVE BRANCH

Article I, section 1 of the Constitution begins by stating: "All legislative Powers herein granted shall be vested in a Congress of the United States, which shall consist of a Senate and House of Representatives." In addition to establishing the location of the legislative powers, this statement declares that those powers will be shared by two separate legislative chambers. Bicameralism (the term used to describe a two-chambered legislature) permits the two legislative chambers to provide internal checks on each other.

The notes taken at the Constitutional Convention reveal that disagreements over how the representatives to Congress would be apportioned and selected were the most difficult for the delegates to settle. At one point, delegates threatened to withdraw from the convention over this issue. The solution to this dispute produced one legislative chamber that represents states equally (the Senate) and another that represents states according to their population (the House of Representatives).

The Senate consists of two senators from each state in the Union. Senators are elected for six-year terms; the long term was intended to give them relative freedom from the passing whims of the electorate. One of the rationales for such long terms was that the Senate would be freer to speak to the long-term needs of the nation. The Constitution requires staggered terms for the senators so that a third of the Senate seats are up for election every two years. This requirement provides a degree of stability and continuity in the national government.

In contrast, the members of the House of Representatives hold two-year terms. These shorter terms keep House members in much closer contact with the American voters. By requiring that House members seek reelection every two years, the Constitution provides the voting public with regular access to national lawmakers.

Legislators who desire new laws or want to alter old ones must be able to persuade a majority of the lawmakers in both legislative chambers of Congress. By design, this process was not intended to be quick or easy. The legislature was meant to be a deliberative group that carefully examines all proposed laws. In a bicameral legislature, proposals that might be rushed through one chamber may be examined carefully in the second chamber. The Framers of the Constitution believed that it was more important that laws be carefully and thoughtfully examined than that they be approved quickly.

EXECUTIVE BRANCH

Article II, section 1 of the Constitution places the executive powers of the United States government in the hands of "a President." The Constitutional Convention had considerable difficulties developing the executive branch of government. In part, this was attributable to their basic suspicion of executive power. They also realized, however, that one of the greatest shortcomings of the Articles of Confederation was the absence of a clearly defined executive branch. The first question was whether the executive authority should be placed in a single executive or multiple executives. The second question, and one of the last to be settled at the Convention, concerned the method for selecting the executive.

After much debate, the Convention settled on a single executive. In the words of Alexander Hamilton, only a single executive would provide the "unity and dispatch" modern governments required. This sentiment prevailed, and the Convention then had to determine how "the President of the United States" would be selected. The electoral college was the method upon which they eventually settled. This system utilizes the states as electoral units and follows the representative principle devised for Congress to distribute the votes among the states.

The president's basic responsibilities are to see that national laws are faithfully executed, to serve as the commander in chief of the national armed forces, to appoint the executive officers of the different federal agencies, and to recommend judges to serve on the Supreme Court and the lesser courts established by Congress. In addition to these responsibilities, the president has a limited veto over the acts of Congress.

JUDICIAL BRANCH

Article III of the Constitution describes the judicial branch of government. More specifically, it establishes the Supreme Court and any additional courts Congress may establish. One of the more unusual aspects of the Constitution is its establishment of an independent judiciary. Judges receive lifelong appointments, so they are as free from political influences as is humanly possible. The only qualification to this independence is that Congress has the power to impeach and remove judges if they behave in a manner that would warrant such removal. In this respect, judges are subjected to the same kind of scrutiny as are members of the executive branch of government.

One aspect of the separation of powers that is often given particular consideration is the concept of checks and balances. The Constitution provides that each of the three branches of government has certain "checks" on its power that are under the control of another branch. Congress, for example, controls the budget of the president and the judiciary. The president, on the other hand, can veto acts of Congress (Congress, in turn, can override a veto with a two-thirds vote in both houses). The president also appoints justices to the Supreme Court (with congressional approval). Finally, the Supreme Court can rule that the laws of Congress or the actions of the president are unconstitutional.

FEDERALISM

This aspect of the Constitution is one of the more ingenious creations to grow out of the Constitutional Convention. Historically, national governments had been either unitary governments or confederal governments. Unitary governments place all power in the hands of a centralized authority. The British government is an example of such a system. In a confederal system, the ultimate power is decentralized among member states. Some responsibility may be given over to a centralized authority, but the real power remains with the decentralized units of government. This was the case under the Articles of Confederation. The federal system established by the Constitution was unique in that it created a governmental system in which the real powers of the political system were truly divided between the centralized and decentralized units of government.

The distribution of powers between the states and the national government has created considerable political tensions during the course of American history. It is important to realize that these tensions were largely intended by the Founders. Federalism, like the separation of powers, was built into the constitutional system as a check on governmental powers. Article VI establishes the Constitution, acts of Congress, and treaties as the "supreme Law of the Land," but the Tenth Amendment to the Constitution declares the limits of that supremacy, stating that the states and the people possess all powers not delegated to the United States by the Constitution.

REPUBLICANISM

Article IV of the Constitution guarantees that every state in the union will have a republican form of government. The *Federalist Papers*, a collection of essays written by Alexander Hamilton, James Madison, and John Jay in 1787 and 1788, explain why a republican system of government was considered preferable to a democratic system. The tenth essay of this collection provides a detailed comparison of these two popular systems of government. The first advantage of republicanism is that governmental authority is delegated to a small group of citizens. The second is that republican governments can cover a much larger geographical area than a direct democracy can.

When a smaller group has the responsibility of representing a larger group, each of the representatives must speak for a variety of interests. By learning the interests and needs of a diverse number of groups, representatives approach governmental decision making with a broader perspective than they would if they were simply advocating their own interests and needs. Public opinion is thereby filtered through a select group of representatives who must keep the many needs of their district in mind.

The advantage of a large geographical area is that it produces a great diversity of interests. This diversity decreases the likelihood that a single interest will constitute a majority on any given issue. For example, while chicken processors may hold a majority interest in Arkansas or oil producers may be a major political force in Texas, neither of these groups can dominate a large geographical area such as the entire United States. Together, these factors increase the likelihood that governmental decisions will serve the general interests of the nation instead of one or a few dominant groups.

The existence of these basic principles within the Constitution creates a significant barrier to government guided by passion as opposed to government guided by reason. The many checks within the system provide numerous obstacles to laws that are not in the interest of a fairly wide and diverse group of citizens. The system also places a substantial burden of proof on those who want to change existing laws or develop new laws. The cumbersome nature of the political process exposes any legislative initiative to a series of examinations before a number of different bodies.

AMENDMENTS

The Constitution has been a remarkably stable political document. The method described in Article V for amending the Constitution has not been utilized very often. By 1995 there were only twenty-seven amendments to the Constitution. The first ten amendments, known as the Bill of Rights, were passed within three years of the Constitution's ratification.

Three amendments (thirteen through fifteen) were passed at the end of the Civil War to make the institution of slavery unconstitutional and to extend certain citizenship rights to African Americans liberated by the Civil War. One of these, the Fourteenth Amendment, through its requirements of "due process" and "equal protection of the laws," has been instrumental in expanding basic civil rights to a number of other groups as well. The Seventeenth Amendment instituted the direct election of senators, the Twenty-second Amendment limited presidents to two terms, and the Twenty-fifth Amendment provided for the transfer of power in cases of presidential disability. A number of amendments (the Fifteenth, Nineteenth, Twenty-third, Twenty-fourth, and Twenty-sixth) have expanded the electorate.

One of the reasons often cited for the Constitution not having gathered more amendments through the years is the role the federal courts have played in determining questions of constitutionality. This process, known as judicial review, has permitted the courts to clarify and fine tune aspects of the Constitution. At times the courts have been accused of taking undue advantage of this authority. President Woodrow Wilson, for example, once referred to the Supreme Court as an ongoing constitutional convention.

The Constitution has proved to be one of the most durable political documents of all time. One of the key reasons for this durability is the document's brevity. The Founders had a sense of what a constitution needed to specify and what it did not. Leaving many details unsettled, the Founders recognized that statutory laws, administrative law, and precedents could handle the more specific and transient details of government.

Donald V. Weatherman

SOURCES FOR FURTHER STUDY
Bloom, Amy. *Confronting the Constitution.* Washington, D.C.: AEI Press, 1990.
Hamilton, Alexander, James Madison, and John Jay. *The Federalist Papers.* Clinton Rossiter ed. New York: New American Library, 1961.
Kelly, Alfred H., Winfred A. Harbison, and Herman Belz. *The American Constitution: Its Origin and Development.* 6th ed. New York: W. W. Norton, 1983.
McDonald, Forrest. *Novus Ordo Seclorum: The Intellectual Origins of the Constitution.* Lawrence: University Press of Kansas, 1979.
Mansfield, Harvey C. *America's Constitutional Soul.* Baltimore: The Johns Hopkins University Press, 1991.
Vile, John R. *A Companion to the United States Constitution and Its Amendments.* 3d ed. Westport, Conn.: Greenwood Press, 2001.

SEE ALSO: Articles of Confederation (1781); U.S. Constitution: History (1787); Bill of Rights (1789).

THREE-FIFTHS COMPROMISE

DATE: Adopted September 17, 1787; ratified June, 1788
U.S. STATUTES AT LARGE: 1 Stat. 10
CATEGORIES: African Americans; Constitutional Law; Slavery

The Constitutional Convention in 1787 adopted the three-fifths compromise, whereby five slaves were counted as three people for purposes of taxation and representation.

Article I, section 2 of the U.S. Constitution states:

39

The House of Representatives shall be composed of Members chosen every second Year by the People of the several States, and the Electors in each State shall have the Qualifications requisite for Electors of the most numerous Branch of the State Legislature. . . . Representatives and direct Taxes shall be apportioned among the several States which may be included within this Union, according to their respective Numbers, which shall be determined by adding to the whole Number of free Persons, including those bound to Service for a Term of Years, and excluding Indians not taxed, three fifths of all other Persons.

The idea of the last part of this provision, which has become known as the "three-fifths compromise," originated as part of a 1783 congressional plan to base taxation on population. Congress rejected the three-fifths idea, but delegate James Wilson of Pennsylvania resurrected it as an amendment to the Virginia plan at the Constitutional Convention.

The Wilson amendment provoked heated debate over the counting of slaves. Most northern delegates regarded slaves as property and not deserving representation, while southern delegates insisted that blacks be counted equally with whites for purposes of representation. Northern delegates wanted slaves counted for taxation, while southern delegates disagreed.

Delegates also debated whether the Congress or a census every ten years should determine the apportionment of representatives in the national legislature. Several northern delegates wanted Congress to control apportionment because the West was developing rapidly. They considered the three-fifths idea pro-South and opposed its adoption. Southern delegates, meanwhile, threatened to reject the three-fifths idea if Congress controlled representation. Northern delegates eventually agreed to accept a census every ten years and count slaves as people rather than property, demonstrating the numerical strength of the proslavery interests. Until the Civil War, therefore, slaves were counted as three-fifths of nonslaves for purposes of taxation and representation.

David L. Porter

SOURCES FOR FURTHER STUDY
Vile, John R. *A Companion to the United States Constitution and Its Amendments.* 3d ed. Westport, Conn.: Greenwood Press, 2001.

SEE ALSO: Northwest Ordinance (1787); U.S. Constitution: History (1787); U.S. Constitution: Provisions (1787); Missouri Compromise (1820); Compromise of 1850 (1850); Thirteenth Amendment (1865).

JUDICIARY ACT OF 1789

DATE: September 24, 1789
U.S. STATUTES AT LARGE: 1 Stat. 73
CATEGORIES: Judiciary and Judicial Procedure

This act of the First Congress created the working structure of the federal judiciary, including the Supreme Court and a three-tier system of federal courts.

The Constitution, written during the summer of 1787 and ratified in 1788, established a new government that started working in April, 1789, when the newly formed Congress began meeting. President George Washington was sworn into office on April 30. At that point two of the three branches of the new government had been formed, but the judicial branch had yet to be created.

During the Constitutional Convention, most of the debate revolved around the executive and legislative branches. There was near complete agreement on the need for a federal judiciary, although there was considerable disagreement about what exactly the judiciary would do. That is, the supporters of both the Virginia and New Jersey plans during the Constitutional Convention favored the creation of a federal judiciary, something that did not exist under the previous governing document, the Articles of Confederation. The proposals for a federal judiciary were quite similar. Both supported the creation of a supreme court as well as the formation of inferior tribunals. The inferior courts would be trial courts, and the highest court would primarily be a court of appeals but would also hear some cases in the first instance. When the Committee on Detail, a small group formed by the men convened in Philadelphia, reported a draft to the full assembly on August 8, 1787, the section in the proposed Constitution regarding the judiciary was nearly identical to the final product of the Convention, which was signed on September 17, 1787.

CONSTITUTIONAL PROVISIONS

The new Constitution treated the judicial branch of government in Article III, which contains less detail than Articles I and II, which, respectively, lay out the structures and powers of Congress and the president. Article III, section 1, states that "the judicial Power of the United States, shall be vested in one supreme Court, and in such inferior Courts as the Congress may from time to time ordain and establish." The Framers of the Constitution did not believe it was prudent or even possible to determine the specifics of the structure of the federal judiciary. They left the exact structure to be determined by the legislative branch.

Moreover, Article III, section 2, states that "The judicial Power shall extend to all Cases . . . arising under this Constitution, [and] the laws of the United States" as well as matters specifically stated that were best suited for the federal judiciary.

A THREE-TIERED SYSTEM

Thus the Framers left it to Congress to determine the specifics, and Congress did so with the Judiciary Act of 1789. The Judiciary Act was the first bill introduced in the Senate and consumed much of the Senate's time during the summer of 1789. It had three principal authors: Oliver Ellsworth of Connecticut, a member of the Constitutional Convention and later a chief justice; William Paterson of New Jersey, previously the attorney general in New Jersey, a participant in the Constitutional Convention, and later an associate justice; and Caleb Strong of Massachusetts, who also attended the Constitutional Convention but was not an active participant.

The Judiciary Act, which was officially titled "An Act to Establish the Federal Courts of the United States," was signed by President Washington on September 24, 1789. The most significant aspects of the act were its establishment of a three-tier system of courts, establishing district courts along state boundaries and legislating the jurisdictions, both original and appellate, of the various courts.

The highest tier of the newly formed judicial system was the Supreme Court, which, according to the act, would "consist of a chief justice and five associate justices." The act also indicated that four justices needed to be present for the Court to operate and that the Court would have two sessions each year in the seat of the government.

The lowest tier of the federal judiciary would be the district courts. The act set the precedent that jurisdiction for district courts would follow state boundaries. It established thirteen district courts, one for each of the eleven states that had ratified the Constitution at that point and for the districts of Maine and Kentucky, which were not yet regarded as states. The arrangement of the district courts was a compromise between Federalists and Antifederalists. Some Antifederalists wanted state courts to adjudicate violations of federal law, and some Federalists wanted the boundary lines for district courts to be distinct from state boundaries. The judges appointed to each district court would hear criminal cases involving admiralty and maritime crimes as well as other cases involving federal law. All criminal cases would go before a jury. The district courts would also hear minor civil cases involving the federal government. These courts were to meet four times each year.

The other tier created by the act was the circuit courts of appeals. The act created three circuits: eastern, middle, and southern. The most remarkable characteristic of these courts to the modern observer is that there were no separate corps of judges for these courts. The judges for the circuit courts of appeals would consist of two Supreme Court justices along with a district court judge from within the territory of each circuit court of appeals. These courts were to be both trial and appellate courts. These courts would hold trials in cases of diversity of citizenship in civil cases as well in cases involving major federal crimes. These courts also heard appeals from the district courts. The act prevented district court judges from hearing appeals in cases in which they had already participated. Supreme Court justices were not prevented from hearing cases in their capacities both as circuit court of appeals judges and as justices of the Supreme Court. However, most justices removed themselves from any cases in which they had previously participated. Those justices appointed during the early years of the Court often served mostly as a circuit court judge because few cases made it to the high court.

ORIGINAL AND APPELLATE JURISDICTIONS

After the establishment of the courts, the most significant aspect of the Judiciary Act is the assignation of original and appellate jurisdiction for the various courts. In section 13, the act restated the original jurisdiction for the Supreme Court as outlined in Article III of the Constitution. The act also dictated what kind of appellate jurisdiction the Court would have. Section 13 further stated that the Court could issue writs of mandamus "in cases warranted by the principle and usages of law, to any courts appointed, or persons holding office under the authority of the United States." Such a writ would in effect force a higher-level official to act in a particular manner.

Regarding the jurisdiction of the Court, section 25 of the act indicated that the Court could hear appeals from the highest court in each state on matters of law alone. This section truly established the Court as the highest judicial authority in the new United States.

CASES INVOLVING THE ACT

The most famous of the Court cases involving the Judiciary Act of 1789 was *Marbury v. Madison* (1803). This decision set the precedent for judicial review because the Court ruled on the constitutionality of a statute. William Marbury, who had been appointed by President John Adams to be a justice of the peace in the District of Columbia, asked the Court to deliver a writ of mandamus forcing Madison, who was Jefferson's secretary of state to deliver his commission to him. Marbury asked for such an action by the Court because the Judiciary Act of 1789 gave the Court original jurisdiction regarding writs of mandamus. Chief Justice John Marshall declared in his decision that section 13 of the Judiciary Act of 1789 was unconstitutional because Article III of the Constitution indicated the specific kinds of cases in which the Court would have original jurisdiction, and issuing writs of mandamus was not one of those.

Another significant case involving the Judiciary Act of 1789 is *Martin v. Hunter's Lessee* (1816). In *Fairfax's Devisee v. Hunter's Lessee* (1813), the Court had overturned the decision of Virginia's highest court. The Virginia court of appeals refused to adhere to the Supreme Court's decision and declared that "the appellate power of the Supreme Court does not extend to this court." The Virginia court further stated that section 25 of the Judiciary Act of 1789 was not constitutional. The Supreme Court in *Martin* affirmed the constitutionality of this appellate jurisdiction. In the majority opinion, Justice Joseph Story affirmed the constitutionality of section 25, arguing that the Congress, except for specified cases, was given latitude in determining jurisdiction of the federal courts.

In *Cohens v. Virginia* (1821), the Court reaffirmed the constitutionality of section 25 of the Judiciary Act of 1789. This case is significant because Chief Justice John Marshall had not participated in *Fairfax's Devisee* or *Martin* because he and his brother had contracted to purchase some of the disputed land. In *Cohen*, Marshall was part of the majority in affirming the Court's jurisdiction in reviewing state supreme court decisions.

Michael L. Coulter

SOURCES FOR FURTHER STUDY
Brown, William G. *The Life of Oliver Ellsworth.* 1905. Reprint. New York: Da Capo Press, 1970.
Corwin, Edward S. *The Doctrine of Judicial Review.* Princeton, N.J.: Princeton University Press, 1914.
Goebel, Julius, Jr. *Antecedents and Beginnings to 1801.* Vol. 1 in *History of the Supreme Court of the United States.* New York: Macmillan, 1971.
Marcus, Maeva, ed. *Origins of the Federal Judiciary: Essays on the Judiciary Act of 1789.* New York: Oxford University Press, 1992.
Ritz, Wilfred. *Rewriting the History of the Judiciary Act of 1789.* Norman: University of Oklahoma Press, 1990.
Schwartz, Bernard. *A History of the Supreme Court.* New York: Oxford University Press, 1993.
Warren, Charles. *The Supreme Court in United States History.* Rev. ed. 2 vols. Boston: Little, Brown, 1932.

SEE ALSO: U.S. Constitution: Provisions (1787); Judiciary Acts of 1801-1925 (1801); Removal Act (1875).

BILL OF RIGHTS

DATE: Approved September 29, 1789; enacted December 15, 1791
U.S. STATUTES AT LARGE: 1 Stat. 97-98
CATEGORIES: Civil Rights and Liberties; Constitutional Law

The first ten amendments to the U.S. Constitution guaranteed individual rights, such as freedom of speech, freedom of the press, separation of church and state, the right to counsel, the right against self-incrimination, and due process. The Bill of Rights has posed an endless series of challenges for the Supreme Court to interpret the scope of personal liberties and the limits of government power.

When the Constitutional Convention adjourned in September, 1787, and submitted its new Constitution to a curious public, three of the remaining delegates refused to sign the new charter. One, George Mason of Virginia, declared that he would "sooner chop off this right hand than put it to a constitution without a Bill of Rights." Fearing that Mason and other Antifederalists might scuttle the ratification of the new Constitution, James Madison promised his fellow Virginians that if they supported the new charter (and elected him to the First Congress), he would sponsor a Bill of Rights. Each side kept its end of the bargain.

In December, 1791, the Bill of Rights was ratified, launching more than two hundred years of Supreme Court decisions interpreting, defining, and refining the nature of the relationship between the government and its citizens.

The Constitution was essentially a plan of government, establishing the legislative, executive, and federal branches and delineating their powers and responsibilities. Although the Constitution purported to grant only limited powers to Congress to pass laws in specified areas, it also provided that Congress had the authority to "make all Laws which shall be necessary and proper for carrying into Execution the foregoing Powers, and all other Powers vested by this Constitution in the Government of the United States, or in any Department or Officer thereof." This elastic catch-all clause worried those who feared that the Constitution would install an all-powerful national government, free to dominate the people and the states. It was the Bill of Rights that gave these critics some measure of solace that the new federal government would not become the same tyrannical seat of power that they had so recently fought to escape.

From the outset, the Supreme Court played a special role in giving meaning to the Bill of Rights. In March of 1789, Thomas Jefferson wrote to Madison that "the Bill of Rights is necessary because of the legal check which it puts into the hands of the judiciary." Jefferson was referring to a "legal check" on unwarranted government interference with the rights of the citizens.

The Bill of Rights touches on every realm of human affairs. It has fallen to the Supreme Court to interpret its elusive and elastic language. In every generation, the Court has been called on to grapple with the challenge of applying its 413 words, written in the late eighteenth century, to circumstances unknown to the authors, arising in the nineteenth, twentieth, and twenty-first centuries. The Bill of Rights protects both substantive and procedural rights. In contrast to the Constitution itself, which says what the government *can* do, the Bill of Rights says what the government *cannot* do.

FIRST AMENDMENT

The most powerful articulation of individual rights against government intrusion is found in the First Amendment, which is considered by many to be the most important of all the Amendments. The opening words speak volumes about the purpose and intent of the Bill of Rights: "Congress shall make no law . . ." These five words set the tone for all that follows. However, the simplicity is deceiving and the Supreme Court has the responsibility of deciding which laws pass constitutional muster and which do not.

Specifically, under the First Amendment, Congress is prohibited from making laws "respecting an establishment of religion or prohibiting the free exercise thereof." In one phrase, the First Amendment simultaneously guarantees the right of individuals to follow the beliefs and practices of their chosen religious faiths, while at the same time, it prohibits the government from singling out any particular religious denomination as a state-sponsored church. The First Amendment built what Jefferson called a "wall of separation" between church and state.

The free exercise and establishment clauses have generated great consternation for the Court on controversial issues. From prayer in school to religious symbols on public property, from religious invocations at high school graduations to vouchers using public funds to subsidize parochial schools, the Court has struggled to ensure that government remains neutral, but not hostile, in matters of religion.

The First Amendment next prohibits Congress from "abridging the freedom of speech, or of the press, or the right of the people peaceably to assemble, and to petition the Government for a redress of grievances." No portion of the Bill of Rights has engaged the Court's attention with more intensity, drama, and public interest than its protection of freedom of expression and freedom of assembly. Volumes have been written about how and why the Court decided whether particular speech or gatherings are constitutionally protected.

No majority of Supreme Court justices ever treated the protections guaranteed by the First Amendment as absolute. Instead, the Court has recognized exceptions for obscenity, libel, criminal solicitation, perjury, false advertising, and "fighting words." Within and beyond these categories, the Court has shifted, especially in times of war or during external threats, from the protection of wide-open, robust debate to the punishment of controversial ideas.

SECOND AMENDMENT

The Second Amendment has been controversial; however, it has been addressed by the Court only on rare occasions. It is popularly known for guaranteeing "the right of the people to keep and bear arms." However, in its most significant pronouncement, the Court unanimously held that this right is qualified by the opening phrase which reads: "A well regulated Militia, being necessary to the security of a free State . . ." In the light of that limitation, the Court has declined to hear an appeal from a lower court ruling upholding a municipal ban on hand guns.

THIRD AMENDMENT

The Third Amendment, prohibiting the quartering of soldiers in private houses in times of peace without the consent of the owner, or in times of war, except as prescribed by law, while vitally important when it was written, is no longer the subject of serious Court review.

FOURTH AMENDMENT

The Fourth Amendment is a catalogue of important personal rights that the Court has sought to interpret by balancing the right of privacy against the legitimate needs of law enforcement. It begins by declaring that the "right of the people to be secure in their persons, houses, papers, and effects, against unreasonable searches and seizures, shall not be violated." The very presence of the undefined term "unreasonable" has required the Court to delve into every manner of search and seizure, developing specific rules that police must follow in order to avoid the exclusion of evidence at trial. The Court has repeatedly articulated that the consequence for an illegal search or seizure is suppression of the evidence, thereby creating an incentive for police to scrupulously follow constitutional requirements.

The Fourth Amendment also guarantees that "no Warrants shall issue, but upon probable cause." Here again the Court developed rules to determine whether probable cause exists. In essence, the Court uses a standard of reasonableness based on all of the facts and circumstances surrounding a challenged search or arrest. The Court places itself in the position of the reasonable police officer, relying on particularized suspicion and past experience, but rejecting mere hunches or guesswork.

FIFTH AMENDMENT

The Fifth Amendment also protects the rights of persons charged with crimes. It prohibits double jeopardy ("subject for the same offence to be twice put in jeopardy of life or limb"), self-incrimination (being "compelled in any criminal case to be a witness against himself"), denial of due process (being "deprived of life, liberty, or property, without due process of law"), and a taking without compensation (having "private property . . . taken for public use without just compensation"). The Court takes these rights very seriously because they set critical boundaries on what government may do in prosecuting crime.

SIXTH AMENDMENT

The Sixth Amendment protects the rights of persons charged with criminal violations. Often mischaracterized as mere "technicalities" protecting the "guilty," Sixth Amendment rights were included in the Bill of Rights because the Founders had lived under a government that frequently arrested, jailed, convicted, and punished individuals without any semblance of fairness or justice.

Under the Sixth Amendment, the accused has a "right to a speedy and public trial." Both elements of this right are very important. The right to a trial is of little value if the accused is kept in jail for several months or years waiting to be tried. Generally speaking, unless the accused waives the time limit, he or she is entitled to go to trial within sixty days after arrest. Likewise, a "public" trial is vital to ensure that an overzealous prosecutor or corrupt judge does not trample on the rights of the accused. Exposing criminal trials to the bright light of public scrutiny allows the general public and the press to observe the proceedings and see for themselves whether the accused is getting a fair trial. The days of the notorious "Star Chamber," where Englishmen were tried in secret, are a thing of the past.

Anyone accused of a crime is also entitled to "an impartial jury" chosen from the geographical area where the crime was committed. The Sixth Amendment guarantees that no one may sit on a jury if he or she has a demonstrable bias or prejudice against the accused, either individually, or because of his or her gender, race, religion, ethnicity, or any other immutable characteristic. Generally, trial judges go to great lengths to question prospective jurors in order to ferret out those who cannot discharge their duties in an impartial manner.

Anyone accused of a crime has a right under the Sixth Amendment "to be informed of the nature and cause of the accusation." Obviously, in order to defend himself, the accused must know what he is being accused of so that he can establish an alibi or find witnesses who may assist in proving his innocence. Only by knowing the charges can the accused's attorney challenge the sufficiency of the indictment of the validity of the statute or regulation involved.

Closely allied to this right is the important right under the Sixth Amendment "to be confronted with the witnesses against him." An accused is entitled to know who will testify against him or her so that the accused and his or her lawyer can prepare adequate cross-examination. From experience, the Founders knew that it is more difficult to lie to another's face than to do so when the other person is not present.

Also, under the Sixth Amendment, an accused has the right "to have compulsory process for obtaining witnesses in his favor." In other words, the accused has the right to subpoena other persons and require them to come to court to testify and to bring papers and documents. Because the government already has this power, this right ensures a level playing field, where an accused can force reluctant witnesses to present evidence that may exonerate him or her or prove that a witness for the prosecution is lying. Without this right, an accused would be confined to presenting only testimony or documents from persons who voluntarily chose to take the time to come to court.

Finally, and perhaps most importantly, the Sixth Amendment guarantees the accused the right "to have Assistance of Counsel for his defense." No person should face a criminal trial without competent legal counsel at his or her side. Only attorneys trained in the rules of evidence and trial procedures can adequately navigate through the complexities of a criminal trial. Indeed, so vital is the right to legal counsel that the law requires the state to provide a lawyer free of charge for the most serious crimes where the accused cannot afford one.

It is worth noting, before leaving the Sixth Amendment, that it contains no reference to the fundamental principle considered the very foundation of Anglo-Saxon law that one is innocent until proven guilty. Indeed, the presumption of innocence appears nowhere in the Bill of Rights or the Constitution. Yet, this essential right has repeatedly been recognized by the courts and remains a vital guarantee of American justice.

SEVENTH AMENDMENT

The Seventh Amendment provides that in civil cases in federal courts at common law, where the value in controversy exceeds twenty dollars, "the right of trial by jury shall be preserved." Essentially, any civil case that entitled a litigant to a jury in 1791 still entitles the litigant to a jury today. Numerous rules (too extensive to be discussed here) have been developed by the courts to determine which civil claims must be tried before a jury and which may not.

The Seventh Amendment also guarantees that once a fact has been decided by a jury, it may not be otherwise reexamined in any federal court, except as provided by common law. Here again, because juries were viewed by the Founders as a protection against injustice and tyranny, it was important to ensure that once a jury had decided the facts in a case, a judge could not overturn that finding, except in limited circumstances provided in the common law.

EIGHTH AMENDMENT

Further protections for criminal defendants are found in the Eighth Amendment, beginning with the guarantee that "excessive bail shall not be required." Persons awaiting trial are entitled to be released from jail, provided they post reasonable bail, in cash or property, which will be returned as long as they appear in court where required. The prohibition against excessive bail ensures that an accused is not arbitrarily detained because a judge has set an unreasonably high bail.

Closely related is the Eighth Amendment's prohibition against "excessive fines." This provision ensures that once convicted, an individual will be fined in proportion to his or her crime or in keeping with guidelines for similar offenses under similar circumstances.

The most important provision of the Eighth Amendment states that "cruel and unusual punishment" shall not be inflicted. This prohibition limits the kinds of punishment that can be imposed on those convicted of crimes. It proscribes punishment grossly disproportionate to the severity of a crime, and it imposes substantive limits on what can be made criminal and punished as such. At its most basic level, the prohibition against cruel and unusual punishment was intended to eliminate torture and other barbaric methods of punishment, although as recently as 1963, twenty lashes as part of the sentence for robbery was found not to be in violation of the Eighth Amendment.

By far, the most serious and controversial application of the prohibition on cruel and unusual punishment came in 1972 when the Court used it to strike down the death penalty (which was then reinstated four years later). The Court found that to the extent the death penalty was administered in an arbitrary and capricious manner, amounting to little more than a lottery, it constituted cruel and unusual punishment in violation of the Eighth Amendment.

Generally, in determining whether a punishment is cruel and unusual, the courts consider a variety of factors, including the age of the defendant, the attitude of the defendant, the availability of less severe punishments, contemporary standards of decency, the frequency of imposition, the disparity in punishments for the same or lesser crimes, the proportionality to the offense, the inhuman shocking or barbarous nature of the punishment, and the totality of the circumstances.

NINTH AMENDMENT

One of the least known but most important provisions of the Bill of Rights is the Ninth Amendment, which in simple but meaningful terms states that the "enumeration in the Constitution, of certain rights, shall not be construed to deny or disparage others retained by the people." In many ways, these twenty-one words speak volumes about the very nature of the United States' constitutional democracy.

As set forth in the Declaration of Independence, people are born with certain inalienable rights. They are not granted their rights by a benevolent government; they are born with those rights and they establish governments in order to preserve and protect them. Thus, people speak of the Bill of Rights as "guaranteeing" constitutional rights, not "creating" them.

The Founders firmly believed in those principles. Indeed at first, the drafters of the Constitution did not include a Bill of Rights because they did not contemplate that the Constitution posed any threat to the inalienable rights of all citizens. However, as noted at the outset, many feared that a new and powerful national government would seize all the power it could, thereby jeopardizing personal rights and liberties.

However, when James Madison set about to draft the Bill of Rights during the First Congress in 1789, he faced a dilemma: How could he write a comprehensive list of *all* rights enjoyed by Americans without the risk of leaving some out? The solution was the Ninth Amendment. There, Madison, with utter simplicity, stated that the fact that "certain rights" were enumerated in the Constitution did not mean that "others retained by the people" were denied or disparaged. Consequently, any analysis of constitutional rights cannot stop by merely examining the specific rights; the "certain rights" spelled out in the first eight amendments. One must go further to determine whether there are "others retained by the people."

One of the most profound applications of the Ninth Amendment relates to the right of privacy. Few rights are more important to Americans than the right to be let alone, yet the right to privacy is nowhere mentioned in the Constitution or the Bill of Rights. To some extent, the entire Constitution and Bill of Rights express a right to privacy, that is, a set of limited and enumerated powers delegated to the government, with all other powers and rights held by the people. When the Supreme Court in the 1960's and 1970's began to address laws restricting contraception and abortion, it found that the right of privacy was rooted in several amendments, including the First, Fourth, Fifth, and Ninth, and what it called the "penumbras" emanating from all of the amendments.

Trivialized by certain judges and scholars as a mere "water blot" on the Constitution, the Ninth Amendment, on serious examination, may well reflect the true meaning of the Bill of Rights.

TENTH AMENDMENT

Parallel to the Ninth Amendment, the Tenth Amendment rounds out the Bill of Rights. It provides that the "powers not delegated to the United States by the Constitution, nor prohibited by it to the States, are reserved to the States respectively, or to the people." Thus, as all rights not expressed in the Constitution are retained by the people, all powers not delegated to the federal government are reserved to the individual States or to the people. The Tenth Amendment reemphasizes the limited nature of the national government, underscoring the fact that the government possesses only the powers expressly delineated in the Constitution and no others.

The Tenth Amendment is rather obscure on the question of whether the reserved powers belong to the states or to the people. This was surely intentional. Having made his point that the national government was a creature of limited powers, Madison and his colleagues left it to others, including state legislatures, state courts, and the people themselves to sort out their respective relationships when it came to these reserved powers.

The Bill of Rights continues to serve the majestic purposes for which it was written more than two hundred years ago. Sometimes with intentional ambiguity, often with passionate eloquence and always with elusive simplicity, the Bill of Rights represents one of the most masterful declarations of individual rights and civil liberties in human history. Yet, as a charter written by people to last the test of time, the Bill of Rights demands continuous study and interpretation to meet the challenges of the next century.

Stephen F. Rohde

SOURCES FOR FURTHER STUDY

Alderman, Ellen, and Caroline Kennedy. *In Our Defense: The Bill of Rights in Action.* New York: Bard, 1998.

Amar, Akhil Reed. *The Bill of Rights: Creation and Reconstruction.* New Haven, Conn.: Yale University Press, 1998.

Atherton, Herbert M., et al. *1791-1991: The Bill of Rights and Beyond.* Washington, D.C.: Commission on the Bicentennial of the U.S. Constitution, 1990.

Broadus, Mitchell, and Louise P. Mitchell. *A Biography of the Constitution of the United States: Its Origin, Formation, Adoption, Interpretation.* New York: Oxford University Press, 1965.

Butler, Lynda, et al. *The Bill of Rights, the Courts and the Law: The Landmark Cases that Have Shaped American Society.* 3d ed. Charlottesville, Va.: Virginia Foundation for the Humanities and Public Policy, 1999.

Hentoff, Nat. *Living the Bill of Rights: How to Be an Authentic American.* New York: HarperCollins, 1998.

Jensen, Merrill. *The Making of the American Constitution.* Princeton, N.J.: Van Nostrand, 1964.

Levy, Leonard W. *Origins of the Bill of Rights.* New Haven, Conn.: Yale University Press, 1999.

Levy, Leonard W., and Dennis J. Mahoney. *The Framing and Ratification of the Constitution.* New York: Macmillan, 1987.

Lloyd, Gordon, and Margie Lloyd, eds. *The Essential Bill of Rights: Original Arguments and Fundamental Documents.* Lanham, Md.: University Press of America, 1998.

Nardo, Don. *The Bill of Rights.* San Diego, Calif.: Greenhaven Press, 1998.

Renstrom, Peter G. *Constitutional Law for Young Adults: A Handbook on the Bill of Rights and the Fourteenth Amendment.* Santa Barbara, Calif.: ABC-CLIO, 1992.

Weinberger, Andrew D. *Freedom and Protection: The Bill of Rights.* San Francisco: Chandler, 1962.

SEE ALSO: U.S. Constitution: Provisions (1787); First Amendment (1789); Second Amendment (1789); Third Amendment (1789); Fourth Amendment (1789); Fifth Amendment (1789); Takings clause (1789); Sixth Amendment (1789); Seventh Amendment (1789); Eighth Amendment (1789); Ninth Amendment (1789); Tenth Amendment (1789).

FIRST AMENDMENT

DATE: Approved September 29, 1789; enacted December 15, 1791
U.S. STATUTES AT LARGE: 1 Stat. 97-98
CATEGORIES: Civil Rights and Liberties; Constitutional Law; Speech
and Expression; Religious Liberty

> *The First Amendment reads: "Congress shall make no law respecting an establishment of religion, or prohibiting the free exercise thereof; or abridging the freedom of speech, or of the press, or the right of the people peaceably to assemble, and to petition the Government for a redress of grievances."*

The wellspring of individual rights protected by the U.S. Constitution, the First Amendment presented the Supreme Court with endless challenges to decide the limits of governmental power and the scope of personal liberties. It guarantees freedom of speech, freedom of the press, religious liberty, separation of church and state, and the rights peaceably to assemble and to petition the government for redress of grievances.

Although the First Amendment, together with the other nine amendments known as the Bill of Rights, became part of the U.S. Constitution on December 15, 1791, the Supreme Court took little note of it until the beginning of the twentieth century. This was not for lack of federal laws impinging on free speech, from the Sedition Act of 1798 and the Comstock Act of 1873 to the Alien Immigration Act of 1930 and a wide variety of postal regulations. However, the Court never found that any of these laws violated the First Amendment. Indeed, in 1907 the Court upheld the conviction of an editor for contempt, rejecting a defense based on the First Amendment on the grounds that it only prohibited prior restraint.

It was inevitable that the Court and the First Amendment would travel together through U.S. constitutional law, frequently crossing paths, sometimes diverging, often forced by circumstances to retrace the same ground. Each clause of the First Amendment invites, indeed demands, judicial interpretation.

FREEDOM OF SPEECH

Beginning at the end of World War I, the Court tackled the task of devising a series of tests to determine whether particular speech was constitutionally protected. The Court could not merely cite the general language of the First Amendment; it had to apply those opaque terms to the real world of real cases.

The first test was articulated by Justice Oliver Wendell Holmes in 1919 in a series of cases challenging the convictions of antiwar activists under the Espionage Act of 1917. The "clear and present danger" test looked at whether the speech posed a real and immediate risk of a substantive evil that Congress had a right to prevent. Holmes captured the test in a powerful, albeit often misquoted, metaphor that persists to this day: "The most stringent protection of free speech would not protect a man in falsely shouting fire in a theatre and causing a panic."

Later in 1919, Holmes and his ally, Justice Louis D. Brandeis, dissented in *Abrams v. United States*, arguing for greater constitutional protection for controversial or even subversive speech. The majority of the Court continued to use the clear and present danger test to uphold the punishment of such speech.

Six years later, the majority of the Court tightened the noose on free speech by focusing on whether the expression had a bad tendency. Over bitter dissent from Holmes and Brandeis, the Court upheld a conviction under the New York State Criminal Anarchy Act, stating that a "single revolutionary spark may kindle a fire," and therefore the state may "suppress the threatened danger in its incipiency."

In 1951 the Court used a slightly reformulated test to uphold the convictions of eleven members of the Communist Party under the Smith Act (1940). Chief Justice Fred M. Vinson, writing for the Court, asked "whether the gravity of the 'evil' discounted by its improbability" would justify government limits on speech.

In 1964 Justice William J. Brennan, Jr., introduced a test that was far more protective of free speech. In the landmark case of *New York Times Co. v. Sullivan*, the Court held that false criticism of public officials was constitutionally protected unless it was made with knowledge that it was false or in reckless disregard of the truth. Instead of tilting the constitutional balance in favor of the government, the *Sullivan* test gave the advantage to the speaker.

The Holmes-Brandeis view in favor of more robust protection for free speech was finally vindicated in 1967 in *Brandenburg v. Ohio*, in which the Court declared that mere advocacy of the use of force or violation of the law could no longer be punished unless "such advocacy is directed to inciting or producing imminent law-less action and is likely to produce such action."

THE RELIGION CLAUSES

As in the field of free speech, the perplexing issues surrounding freedom of religion have required the Court to fashion several con-stitutional tests to ensure the free exercise of religion, without es-tablishing a state-sponsored religion. As the twentieth century ush-ered in an era of secularization, the dominance of religion in public life began to be seen as inconsistent with the First Amend-ment's promise of neutrality when it came to religious faith. Reli-gion was seen as a part of the private sphere of life, leaving the pub-lic sphere, including most visibly public schools, free of religious symbols, let alone indoctrination.

In several decisions spanning more than twenty years, from *Everson v. Board of Education of Ewing Township* in 1947 to *Lemon v. Kurtzman* in 1971, the Court developed the test that any govern-mental action touching on religion would survive invalidation un-der the establishment clause only if it had a secular purpose that neither endorsed nor disapproved of religion, had an effect that neither advanced nor inhibited religion, and avoided creating a re-lationship between religion and government that entangled either in the internal affairs of the other. The *Lemon* test has been criti-cized by all ends of the political and constitutional spectrum, but it has provided lower courts and legislators with some level of guid-ance in dealing with such thorny issues as prayer in schools and fi-nancial aid to religious institutions.

Meanwhile, the Court had to interpret the free exercise clause of the First Amendment in numerous cases in which believers claimed a right to ignore laws that required them to perform an act that violated their religious beliefs or that prohibited them from performing an act that was required by their religious beliefs.

Beginning in 1879 in *Reynolds v. United States* and for almost a hundred years, the Court dealt with most free exercise cases by up-holding laws that punished *actions* but struck down laws that pun-ished *beliefs*. However, the easy dichotomy began to break down when, in *Sherbert v. Verner* (1963), the Court ordered a state to pay unemployment benefits to a Seventh-day Adventist even though she would not make herself available for work on Saturday (her Sabbath). In 1972, in *Wisconsin v. Yoder*, the Court held that the

Amish were not required to send their children to public school past the eighth grade in violation of their religious beliefs.

By the 1980's, the pendulum had begun to swing against religious liberty as the Court issued a succession of decisions ruling against a Native American who sought to prevent the government from assigning his daughter a Social Security number, an Orthodox Jew who sought to wear a yarmulke in violation of Air Force uniform regulations, a Native American tribe that sought to prevent construction of a federal highway that would interfere with their worshiping, and two Native Americans who sought unemployment compensation after they were fired from their jobs for smoking peyote as part of tribal religious rituals.

The Court has found the religion clauses of the First Amendment fraught with interpretative dangers. Inevitably, the Court is criticized either for going too far in promoting religion or for exhibiting hostility toward religion. That alone may be evidence that the Court is doing its job as conceived by the Founders.

THE RIGHT TO PEACEABLY ASSEMBLE

Whereas freedom of speech and freedom to worship protect highly personal rights, the First Amendment's guarantee of the right "of the people peaceably to assemble" protects the right of association. These are the rights of the people as a community to join together to achieve certain political, social, economic, artistic, educational, or other goals.

For the Court, interpreting the right to assemble has been even more difficult than construing other aspects of the First Amendment, because by its very nature, assembly involves both speech *and* conduct. At first blush, the First Amendment has nothing to do with conduct. However, when the Court is confronted with cases involving public demonstrations, protests, parades, and picketing, it is apparent that these activities are intended to send a message— and communicating messages is clearly protected by the First Amendment.

However, blocking traffic, littering the streets, or physically obstructing others from going about their business is not protected by the First Amendment. Consequently, when it comes to freedom of assembly, the Court has used a balancing test, seeking first to determine whether the law regulating assembly is in fact a ruse to suppress a particular viewpoint, and if not, whether the law serves a compelling state interest unrelated to the suppression of free speech.

For example, in 1940 in *Thornhill v. Alabama*, the Court struck down a state law that prohibited all picketing. Although the First Amendment does not afford an absolute right to picket, the Court overturned the statute because instead of regulating specific aspects of labor demonstrations, it prohibited "every practicable method whereby the facts of a labor dispute may be publicized."

Closely aligned with freedom of assembly is freedom of association or the right of the people to form and join organizations in order to educate themselves and influence public policy on important issues of the day. Even during the hysteria of the Cold War in the 1950's, the Court held in *Yates v. United States* (1957) that when membership in the Communist Party involved nothing more than the advocacy or teaching of the abstract doctrine of the forcible overthrow of the government (as contrasted with the advocacy or teaching of direct action to achieve that end) convictions under the Smith were unconstitutional.

In 1958, in *National Association for the Advancement of Colored People v. Alabama*, the Court found that the forced disclosure of an organization's membership list violated the members' rights to pursue their lawful interests and to freely associate with like-minded persons. Although freedom of association is not expressly set forth anywhere in the Constitution, the Court nevertheless found freedom of association to be an integral part of the First Amendment.

THE RIGHT TO PETITION THE GOVERNMENT

The least controversial (and least litigated) right in the First Amendment is the right "to petition the government for redress of grievances." Aside from a doomed attempt in 1836 by the House of Representatives to impose a gag rule against the receipt of petitions from abolitionists who opposed slavery, Congress has not had the temerity to even attempt to restrict this quintessential right to write to your Congressperson, thereby sparing the Court the task of striking down such legislation.

Stephen F. Rohde

Sources for Further Study

Blanchard, Margaret A. *Revolutionary Sparks: Freedom of Expression in Modern America.* New York: Oxford University Press, 1992.

Eastland, Terry, ed. *Religious Liberty in the Supreme Court: The Cases That Define the Debate over Church and State.* Grand Rapids, Mich.: Wm. B. Eerdmans, 1995.

Flowers, Ronald B., and Robert T. Miller, eds. *Toward Benevolent Neutrality: Church, State, and the Supreme Court.* Waco, Tex.: Baylor University Press, 1998.

Gutman, Amy, ed. *Freedom of Association.* Princeton, N.J.: Princeton University Press, 1998.

Ingelhart, Louis E. *Press and Speech Freedoms in the World, from Antiquity Until 1998: A Chronology.* Westport, Conn.: Greenwood Press, 1998.

Murphy, Paul L. *Rights of Assembly, Petition, Arms, and Just Compensation.* New York: Garland, 1990.

Noonan, John Thomas, Jr. *The Believer and the Powers That Are: Cases, History, and Other Data Bearing on the Relation of Religion and Government.* New York: Macmillan, 1987.

Shiffrin, Steven H., and Jesse H. Choper. *The First Amendment: Cases, Comments, Questions.* St. Paul, Minn.: West Publishing, 1996.

Shumate, T. Daniel, ed. *The First Amendment: The Legacy of George Mason.* London: Associated University Presses, 1985.

See also: U.S. Constitution: Provisions (1787); Bill of Rights (1789); Sedition Act of 1798 (1798); Comstock Act (1873); Espionage Acts (1917-1918).

Second Amendment

Date: Approved September 29, 1789; enacted December 15, 1791
U.S. Statutes at Large: 1 Stat. 97-98
Categories: Civil Rights and Liberties; Constitutional Law; Military and National Security

The Second Amendment to the U.S. Constitution states: "A well regulated militia being necessary to the security of a free state, the right of the people to keep and bear arms shall not be infringed."

The Second Amendment provided the right of people to keep and bear arms. In comparison to other controversial constitutional guarantees, such as freedom of speech, the Supreme Court has had little to say about the Second Amendment. The Supreme Court's rare decisions on the Second Amendment have typically been narrowly drawn, leaving the broad issues of gun control and the intent of the Second Amendment unresolved. The Court has generally upheld criminal laws regarding firearms, but it has done so without attempting to establish a guiding interpretation of the amendment. Although the Court overturned two federal gun laws in two decisions during the 1990's, it did not rule on the laws as they pertained to the Second Amendment. Rather, in keeping with the Court's states' rights conservatism under Chief Justice William H. Rehnquist, the Court ruled on the laws as they pertained to the limits of the federal government's power to impose its laws on state and local authorities.

In *Printz v. United States* (1997), Jay Printz, the sheriff of Ravalli County, Montana, challenged a federal law that required him to perform background checks on people in his jurisdiction who sought to buy guns. The Court accepted his argument that the federal government may not compel the states to implement federal regulations, overturning the portion of the federal act that required local law enforcement agencies to conduct background checks. Before that, *United States v. Lopez* (1995) reached the Court after a student, Alfonso Lopez, was charged with violating the Gun-Free School Zones Act of 1990 when he carried a concealed handgun into a high school. The Court upheld an appellate ruling that the federal act exceeded the authority of Congress to legislate under the interstate commerce clause. To allow the act to stand, the Court wrote, would "require this Court to pile inference upon inference in a manner that would bid fair to convert congressional commerce clause authority to a general police power of the sort held only by the States." *Printz* and *Lopez* did not address the Second Amendment or rule on how it is to be interpreted. Nor is the controversy settled by a review of Court decisions touching on the Second Amendment.

EARLY DECISIONS
In *United States v. Cruikshank* (1876), William Cruikshank, a member of the Ku Klux Klan, was tried in federal court for violating the federal civil rights laws protecting the African American victims of a murderous riot he led. The trial court found Cruikshank guilty of

conspiring to deprive African Americans of their right to bear arms. The Supreme Court, however, ruled in favor of Cruikshank, arguing that the Second Amendment applied only to Congress and that people must look to local governments for protection against violations of their rights. The *Cruikshank* decision, like the *Slaughterhouse Cases* (1873), interpreted against use of the Fourteenth Amendment as a means to enforce the Bill of Rights at the state and local level. This interpretation of the Fourteenth Amendment, however, has since been abandoned in other decisions not relating to the Second Amendment.

The next major Second Amendment case was *Presser v. Illinois* (1886). Herman Presser led an armed group called the Lehr und Wehr Verein (Educational and Protective Association) on a march through the streets of Chicago. Presser argued that the Illinois law under which he was convicted was superseded by various provisions of federal law, including the Second Amendment. The Court upheld his conviction, arguing that to accept Presser's interpretations would amount to denying the rights of states to disperse mobs.

INDICATIONS OF AMBIVALENCE

The Court in *United States v. Miller* (1939) upheld the federal regulation against a shotgun's having a barrel less than eighteen inches long on the basis that the Court had no indication that such a weapon "was . . . ordinary military equipment or . . . could contribute to the common defense." It may be argued, therefore, that *Miller* indirectly defends the principle that a firearm that has some reasonable relationship to the efficiency of a well-regulated militia is protected by the Constitution. However, challenges to laws limiting civilian possession of machine guns and assault rifles, which are military weapons, have not met with success. A similar ambivalence can be inferred in *Cases v. United States* (1943), in which a lower court noted, "apparently . . . under the Second Amendment, the federal government can limit the keeping and bearing of arms by a single individual as well as by a group . . . but it cannot prohibit the possession or use of any weapon which has any reasonable relationship to the preservation or efficiency of a well-regulated militia." The Court made this observation, however, when declining to review a challenge to a provision of the Federal Firearms Act.

In *Quilici v. Village of Morton Grove* (1983), a circuit court refused to review a Second Amendment case and let stand a decision upholding an ordinance in Morton Grove, Illinois, banning possession of handguns. This decision has been cited to bolster the argument that the individual ownership of firearms is not a constitutional right, but the fact that the Court has done nothing to change the existing laws that allow individual possession of firearms undermines such an argument.

Eric Howard

SOURCES FOR FURTHER STUDY
Bijlefeld, Marjolijn, ed. *The Gun Control Debate: A Documentary History.* Westport, Conn.: Greenwood Press, 1997.
Bogus, Carl R., and Michael A. Bellesiles, eds. *The Second Amendment in Law and History: Historians and Constitutional Scholars on the Right to Bear Arms.* New York: New Press, 2001.
Cottrol, Robert J., ed. *Gun Control and the Constitution: Sources and Explorations on the Second Amendment.* New York: Garland, 1993.
Halbrook, Stephen P. *That Every Man Be Armed: The Evolution of a Constitutional Right.* Albuquerque: University of New Mexico Press, 1984.
Henigan, Dennis A. *Guns and the Constitution: The Myth of Second Amendment Protection for Firearms in America.* Northampton, Mass.: Aletheia Press, 1996.
Malcolm, Joyce Lee. *To Keep and Bear Arms: The Evolution of an Anglo-American Right.* Cambridge, Mass.: Harvard University Press, 1996.

SEE ALSO: Bill of Rights (1789); Brady Handgun Violence Protection Act (1994).

THIRD AMENDMENT

DATE: Approved September 29, 1789; enacted December 15, 1791
U.S. STATUTES AT LARGE: 1 Stat. 97-98
CATEGORIES: Civil Rights and Liberties; Constitutional Law; Privacy; Property

The Third Amendment reads: "No Soldier shall, in time of peace be quartered in any house, without the consent of the Owner, nor in time of war, but in a manner to be prescribed by law."

The last time the Third Amendment had serious literal application was during the Civil War (1861-1865), when property owners were made to house, feed, and generally support both Union and Confederate soldiers. Today, such literal application is rare. Contemporary use of the amendment by the Supreme Court has been simply as a reference exemplifying constitutional protections of property-based privacy rights against certain governmental intrusions. However, in *Engblom v. Carey* (1982), a federal appellate court held that striking corrections officers had a lawful interest in their living quarters, located at the prison and provided in the course of their employment, which entitled them to a legitimate expectation of privacy protected by the Third Amendment.

For development of privacy rights, the Supreme Court usually relied on provisions of other amendments, such as the Fourth Amendment protection against unreasonable searches and seizures and used the Third Amendment simply as a nominal reference to general constitutional protections. For example, in a footnote to *Katz v. United States* (1967), a landmark decision regarding Fourth Amendment privacy rights, Justice Potter Stewart merely listed the Third Amendment in his enumeration of constitutional protections.

This contemporary reliance is typified by *State v. Coburn* (1974), in which the Montana supreme court cited the First, Third, Fourth, and Fifth Amendments as the "umbrella of constitutional protections" afforded individual privacy.

Michael J. Garcia

SOURCE FOR FURTHER STUDY
Vile, John R. *Encyclopedia of Constitutional Amendments, Proposed Amendments, and Amending Issues, 1789-1995*. Santa Barbara, Calif: ABC-CLIO, 1996.

SEE ALSO: Bill of Rights (1789); Fourth Amendment (1789).

FOURTH AMENDMENT

DATE: Approved September 29, 1789; enacted December 15, 1791
U.S. STATUTES AT LARGE: 1 Stat. 97-98
CATEGORIES: Civil Rights and Liberties; Constitutional Law; Privacy

> *The Fourth Amendment reads: "The right of the people to be secure in their persons, houses, papers, and effects, against unreasonable searches and seizures, shall not be violated, and no Warrants shall issue, but upon probable cause, supported by Oath or affirmation, and particularly describing the place to be searched, and the persons or things to be seized."*

The Fourth Amendment protects people against unreasonable searches and seizures. The Framers of the Bill of Rights were concerned with the old English practice of issuing general warrants and writs of assistance. These two legal tools authorized searches with few stipulations on searching agents, allowing searches day or night on bare suspicion. Authorized by the monarch, they were valid for the duration of his or her lifetime. They were not required to name a specific person or place but could be stated in more general terms. No oath before a magistrate was necessary to secure a warrant, and probable cause was not required. Everything was left to the discretion of the holder of the warrant. The result was harassment. The colonists were victims of these general warrants and writs of assistance and purposely set out to outlaw them.

James Madison revised his initial draft of the Fourth Amendment, changing the word "secured" to "secure" and adding the clause "against unreasonable searches and seizures." Although Madison's goal was to eliminate general warrants and writs of assistance, scholars believe these alterations made the meaning of the amendment ambiguous. The Fourth Amendment outlaws only unreasonable searches and seizures, logically allowing those deemed reasonable. The Framers envisioned that searches conducted with a warrant, which required specifics such as who is to be searched, what is to be seized, and when, were constitutionally permissible. The warrant clause stipulated what was expected of police when conducting searches. However, left unanswered were the questions of whether there are times when it is reasonable to search without a warrant, what constitutes probable cause, and whether the amendment restricts only police or other governmental agents with searching authority.

In the early 1900's the Supreme Court began expanding the applications of the Fourth Amendment, balancing the rights of the accused against the safety of other people. The Court in *Wolf v. Colorado* (1949) made clear that search warrants had to be supported by probable cause and issued by a neutral and impartial magistrate. However, often searches are conducted without a search warrant.

EXCEPTIONS TO THE WARRANT REQUIREMENT

The Court created a number of exceptions to the search warrant requirement. Using the reasonableness clause of the amendment rather than the warrant provision, the Court rejected the idea of a bright-line rule in favor of a more fact-bound, case-by-case approach. The police do not need a warrant for searches incident to arrest; stop-and-frisk situations; when illegal or stolen items are in plain view during a legal search; administrative, consensual, and border searches; and searches involving exigent circumstances such as automobile searches.

When an individual is arrested on probable cause, a police officer is permitted to conduct a warrantless search of the person. This exception to the warrant requirement, search incident to arrest, rests on the understanding that the arresting officer must have the power to disarm the accused and preserve any evidence. Protecting the officer's safety and retaining probative evidence is reasonable. The officer may search not only the person but the areas of immediate control. In *Chimel v. California* (1969), the Court reasoned that the scope of a search incident to arrest included wherever the arrestee might reach to grab a weapon or piece of evidence.

If in the course of a valid search, an officer comes on stolen or illegal items in plain view, they may be seized and used as evidence. This inadvertent windfall is permissible and reasonable under the Fourth Amendment as long as the officer happens on the evidence in the course of conducting a legal search. Related is the plain feel exception. In *Minnesota v. Dickerson* (1993), the Court held that if an officer feels what seems to be contraband or evidence of a crime when patting down the outside of a suspect's clothing, the items can be seized.

In *Terry v. Ohio* (1968), the Court allowed for searches on the street that did not meet the standard of probable cause. In this case, it upheld the brief detention of a suspect for weapons on the grounds of reasonable suspicion rather than probable cause. Only a limited frisk was permitted with the lowered standard of cause. If the pat-down yielded a basis for an arrest, however, a full search incident to arrest could follow.

The Court has applied the Fourth Amendment to the increasing problems arising in a mobile society. Planes, buses, trains, and boats all raise exigency concerns because of the highly mobile nature of the place to be searched and the futility of the police in executing search warrants on moving objects. The most common exigent circumstance is created by the automobile. As early as 1925 in *Carroll v. United States*, the Court made clear that the automobile would not be afforded the same level of privacy rights protection as an individual's home or person. Stopping an automobile and searching it on the street without a warrant was reasonable. However, the particulars of the car have generated a volume of litigation aimed at answering questions such as whether the police can lawfully open the glove box, the trunk, or containers in the automobile or search the driver, passengers, and their personal items. Given the lower expectation of privacy in automobiles, the Court in *Michigan Department of State Police v. Sitz* (1990) allowed roadblocks to briefly stop all drivers to catch those driving under the influence of drugs and alcohol.

Employees of other governmental agencies, such as housing, fire, health, welfare, and safety inspectors, also have searching capabilities. These agents have a lesser standard than probable cause and often invoke an element of surprise, such as unannounced inspections of restaurants. Related to these types of searches are those to ensure safety in the workplace or school by drug-testing employees and students. In *National Treasury Employees Union v. Von Raab* (1989), the Court upheld suspicionless mandatory urinalysis testing for promotion on the grounds of safety (the employees would have access to firearms and secure information). By 1995 in *Vernonia School District v. Acton*, the Court upheld the right to drug-test all student athletes without requiring suspicion of individuals.

The courts have long recognized that individuals and items entering the United States may be searched at the international border without warrant or probable cause. The Court has placed some limits on these searches, such as the level of intrusion. Strip searches, for example, must be justified by real suspicion. In an attempt to stop the influx of illegal drugs, law enforcement developed the drug courier profile, a composite of variables that indicates the likelihood an individual is trafficking drugs. In *United States v. Sokolow* (1989), the Court upheld the use of the profile as a basis for detaining and searching individuals both at the border and within the continental United States.

In *Schneckloth v. Bustamonte* (1973), the Court acknowledged the use of consent searches, noting that individuals may waive their Fourth Amendment rights and allow a search without a warrant or probable cause. The key to the validity of such searches is that they must be voluntary; an individual must knowingly and freely consent to be searched. The waiver must be uncoerced, given without trickery or fear or promise of reward. Consent can be withdrawn at any time, and a refusal to give consent cannot then be used to establish probable cause.

The Fourth Amendment also applies to wiretapping and other forms of police surveillance. The Court in *Katz v. United States* (1967) reasoned that a person's expectation of privacy includes the seizure of intangible items such as words.

EXCLUSIONARY RULE

The Fourth Amendment describes the right to be secure against unreasonable searches and seizures without mentioning a remedy. The common-law remedy for search and seizure violations was a suit of trespass. This was used until *Weeks v. United States* (1914) when the Court adopted the exclusionary rule, which excludes illegally seized evidence from trials. The twofold purpose of the rule is to preserve the integrity of the judiciary and deter police misconduct. *Weeks* mandated the application of the exclusionary rule to searching agents of the federal government. In 1949 in *Wolf*, the Court incorporated the Fourth Amendment, thereby requiring states not to abridge the search and seizure rights of their citizens, yet allowing them to choose the remedy. This choice was eliminated in *Mapp v. Ohio* (1961) when the Court incorporated the remedy of exclusion from trials for all Fourth Amendment violations, by either state or federal officials.

Mapp's scope was limited by the Court. In *Linkletter v. Walker* (1965), the Court refused to apply the exclusionary rule retroactively. The exclusion remedy was limited in scope so that it did not include grand jury proceedings in *United States v. Calandra* (1974). The Court ruled in *United States v. Havens* (1980) that illegally seized evidence could be used to impeach the credibility of the defendant at trial and in *Nix v. Williams* (1984) that it could also be admitted into evidence if the police would have inevitably discovered the evidence by lawful means. In 1984 in *United States v. Leon* and *Massachusetts v. Sheppard,* the Court allowed the use of illegally obtained evidence if the police error was made in objective good faith. The Court was unwilling to exclude reliable probative evidence when the error made by the police was unintentional and made in the course of attempting to follow the law.

Priscilla H. Machado

SOURCES FOR FURTHER STUDY

Allen, Richard J., Richard B. Kuhns, and William J. Stunz. *Constitutional Criminal Procedure: An Examination of the Fourth, Fifth, and Sixth Amendments and Related Areas.* New York: Aspen Law and Business, 1995.

Amsterdam, Anthony. "The Supreme Court and the Rights of Suspects in Criminal Cases." *New York University Law Review* 45 (1970): 785.

Burger, Warren E. "Who Will Watch the Watchman?" *American University Law Review* 14 (1964): 1.

Griswold, Erwin N. *Search and Seizure: A Dilemma of the Supreme Court.* Lincoln: University of Nebraska Press, 1975.

Kamisar, Yale. "Is the Exclusionary Rule an 'Illogical' or 'Unnatural' Interpretation of the Fourth Amendment?" *Judicature* 62 (1978): 67

LaFave, Wayne. *Search and Seizure: A Treatise on the Fourth Amendment.* Mineola, N.Y.: Foundation Press, 1978.

Landynski, Jacob W. *Search and Seizure and the Supreme Court.* Baltimore: The Johns Hopkins University Press, 1966.

Lasson, Nelson B. *The History and Development of the Fourth Amendment to the United States Constitution.* Baltimore: The Johns Hopkins University Press, 1937.

O'Brien, David M. *Constitutional Law and Politics: Civil Rights and Liberties.* 3d ed. 2 vols. New York: W. W. Norton, 1997.

Taylor, Telford. *Two Studies in Constitutional Interpretation.* Columbus: Ohio State University Press, 1969.

Vile, John R. *Encyclopedia of Constitutional Amendments, Proposed Amendments, and Amending Issues, 1789-1995.* Santa Barbara, Calif: ABC-CLIO, 1996.

Wiley, Malcolm. "Constitutional Alternatives to the Exclusionary Rule." *South Texas Law Journal* 23 (1982): 531.

SEE ALSO: Bill of Rights (1789)

FIFTH AMENDMENT

DATE: Approved September 29, 1789; enacted December 15, 1791
U.S. STATUTES AT LARGE: 1 Stat. 97-98
CATEGORIES: Civil Rights and Liberties; Constitutional Law; Crimes and Criminal Procedure

The Fifth Amendment reads: "No person shall be held to answer for a capital, or otherwise infamous crime, unless on a presentment or indictment of a Grand Jury, except in cases arising in the land or naval forces, or in the Militia, when in actual service in time of War or public danger; nor shall any person be subject for the same offence to be twice put in jeopardy of life or limb, nor shall be compelled in any criminal case to be a witness against himself, nor be deprived of life, liberty, or property, without due process of law; nor shall private property be taken for public use without just compensation."

The Fifth Amendment provides a right to avoid self-incrimination, a right to a grand jury indictment in capital or infamous crime cases, a right to be free from double jeopardy, and a right to just compensation for property taken by the government. The Supreme Court has used the Fifth Amendment to protect citizens against government coercion.

THE RIGHT AGAINST SELF-INCRIMINATION
Although the Fifth Amendment includes more than just a right against self-incrimination, it has become virtually synonymous

with the right against self-incrimination. This right reflected the Framers' judgment that in a society based on respect for the individual, the government shouldered the entire burden of proving guilt and the accused need make no unwilling contribution to his or her conviction.

The Fifth Amendment is restricted on its face to "criminal cases." However, the Supreme Court ruled that the Fifth Amendment applies to criminal and civil cases and extends to nonjudicial proceedings, such as legislative investigations and administrative hearings. The protection of the clause extends only to people, not organizations such as corporations or unions, and is applicable to witnesses as well as to the accused.

The self-incrimination clause is violated if evidence compelled by the government incriminates the person who provides it. Given these standards, self-incrimination violations occur most commonly during police interrogations and government hearings. Although the purpose of the clause is to eliminate the inherently coercive and inquisitional atmosphere of the interrogation room, a person may voluntarily answer any incriminating question or confess to any crime, subject to the requirements for waiver of constitutional rights, even if his or her statements are intended as exculpatory but lend themselves to prosecutorial use as incriminatory.

The Court first addressed the meaning of the self-incrimination clause in *Twining v. New Jersey* (1908). The question was whether the right against self-incrimination was "a fundamental principle of liberty and justice which inheres in the very idea of free government" and therefore should be included within the concept of due process of law safeguarded from state abridgment. The Court decided against the right. It reaffirmed this position in *Palko v. Connecticut* (1937), in which the Court held that the right against compulsory self-incrimination was not a fundamental right; it might be lost, and justice might still be done if the accused "were subject to a 5duty to respond to orderly inquiry."

MIRANDA AND ITS IMPACT

The Court abandoned this position in its 1966 decision in *Miranda v. Arizona*, a tour de force on self-incrimination. The opinion announced a cluster of constitutional rights for defendants held in police custody and cut off from the outside world. The atmosphere and environment of incommunicado interrogation was held to be inherently intimidating and hostile to the privilege against self-incrimination. To prevent compulsion by law enforcement officials, before interrogation, people in custody must be clearly informed that they have the right to remain silent and anything they say may be used in court against them and that they have the rights to consult an attorney, to have a lawyer present during interrogation, and to have a lawyer appointed if they are indigent.

When Chief Justice Warren E. Burger replaced Chief Justice Earl Warren in 1964 and Justice Harry A. Blackmun replaced Justice Abe Fortas in 1970, they joined Justices Byron R. White, John Marshall Harlan II, and Potter Stewart in support of a narrow application of *Miranda*. These five justices constituted the majority in *Harris v. New York* (1971), indicating the beginning of a contracting trend for *Miranda*. Chief Justice Burger held that the prosecution is not precluded from the use of statements that admittedly do not meet the *Miranda* test as an impeachment tool in attacking the credibility of an accused's trial testimony.

The erosion of *Miranda* continued in several rulings in the 1970's. In *Michigan v. Tucker* (1974), the Court held that failure to inform a suspect of his or her right to appointed counsel before interrogation was only a harmless error in the total circumstances of the case. Then one year later in *Oregon v. Haas* (1975), the Court reaffirmed *Harris* and allowed the use of a suspect's statements for impeachment purposes though they had been made before arrival of counsel that he had requested before making any statements. And the next year in *Michigan v. Mosley* (1976), the Court did not construe *Miranda* as invoking a "proscription of indefinite duration on any further questionings . . . on any subject." This ruling approved an interrogation process in which a suspect had initially used the shield of Miranda rights to remain silent but several hours later in a different room was administered the Miranda rights again and proceeded to respond to questions about a different crime.

By the mid-1980's it was clear that the Court under Chief Justice William H. Rehnquist would continue to construe *Miranda* very narrowly. In *New York v. Quarles* (1984), for example, the Court held that when a danger to public safety exists, police may ask questions to remove that danger before reading Miranda warnings. Answers given to the police may be used as evidence. In *Illinois v. Perkins* (1990), the Court ruled that Miranda warnings are not required when a suspect is unaware he or she is speaking to the police and gives a voluntary statement. The case concerned a jailed defendant who implicated himself in a murder when talking to an undercover agent placed in his cell. Justice Anthony M. Kennedy wrote in the opinion, "*Miranda* forbids coercion, not mere strategic deception." Finally, in *Arizona v. Fulminante* (1991), the Court admitted that the defendant's confession was coerced by the threat of physical attack. However, the Court held that if such testimony is erroneously admitted as evidence, a conviction need not be overturned if sufficient independent evidence supporting a guilty verdict is also introduced.

At the turn of the century, the Court's decision to maintain the precedent with continued narrow application of *Miranda* appeared well entrenched. The majority of the justices appeared to be comfortable with that approach, and changes appeared unlikely.

DOUBLE JEOPARDY CLAUSE

Also under the Fifth Amendment, a person shall not be subject "for the same offense to be twice put in jeopardy of life or limb." The underlying premise of the double jeopardy clause is to prohibit the government from making repeated attempts to convict an individual. Acquittal acts as an absolute bar on a second trial. The meaning of acquittal, however, often divides the Court.

The Court ruled that there is no double jeopardy in trying someone twice for the same offense if the jury is unable to reach a verdict—in *United States v. Ball* (1896), the jury is discharged—in *Logan v. United States* (1892), or an appeals court returns the case to the trial court because of defects in the original indictment—in *Thompson v. United States* (1894). The Court also unanimously ruled in three cases—*Jerome v. United States* (1943), *Herbert v. Louisiana* (1926), and *United States v. Lanza* (1922)—that a person may be prosecuted for the same act under federal law and state law. The theory is that the person is being prosecuted for two distinct offenses rather than the same offense.

The double jeopardy clause also prohibits prosecutors from trying defendants a second time for the express purpose of obtaining a more severe sentence. However, in 1969 the Court decided that there is no constitutional bar to imposing a more severe sentence on reconviction (after the first conviction is thrown out), provided the sentencing judge is not motivated by vindictiveness. In *North Carolina v. Pearce; Chaffin v. Stynchcombe* (1973), it ruled that the guarantee against double jeopardy requires that punishment already exacted must be fully credited to the new sentence.

The double jeopardy clause also bars multiple punishments for the same offense. In *United States v. Ursery* (1996) and *Kansas v. Hendricks* (1997), the Court narrowly construed this right. The latter case involved a challenge to a statute that permitted the state to keep certain sexual offenders in custody in a mental institution after they had served their full sentence. The Court ruled that the civil confinement was not a second criminal punishment but a separate civil procedure, thus not a violation of the double jeopardy clause.

RIGHT TO A GRAND JURY

The Fifth Amendment also provides that "no person shall be held for a capital, or otherwise infamous crime, unless on a presentment or indictment of a grand jury, except in cases arising in the land or naval forces, or in the militia, when in actual service in time of war or public danger." The grand jury procedure is one of the few provision in the Bill of Rights that has not been incorporated into the due process clause of the Fourteenth Amendment and applied to the states. Instead the Court ruled that states may prosecute on a district attorney's "information," which consists of a prosecutor's accusation under oath in *Hurtado v. California* (1884) and *Lem Wood v. Oregon* (1913). The Court held in *Costello v. United States* (1956) that, unlike in a regular trial, grand juries may decide that "hearsay" evidence is sufficient grounds to indict. In 1992 the Court issued an opinion in *United States v. Williams* (1992) indicating that an otherwise valid indictment may not be dismissed on the ground that the government failed to disclose to the grand jury "substantial exculpatory evidence" in its possession. In 1974 the Court decided in *United States v. Calandra* that witnesses before a grand jury may invoke the Fifth Amendment privilege against self-incrimination. This privilege is overridden if the government grants immunity to the witness. Witnesses who then refuse to answer questions may be jailed for contempt of court. Witnesses may not refuse to answer because questions are based on illegally obtained evidence.

THE TAKINGS CLAUSE

Finally, the Fifth Amendment provides that private property shall not "be taken for public use, without just compensation." This is referred to as the takings clause, or the just compensation clause. The Court incorporated the takings clause under the due process clause of the Fourteenth Amendment in *Chicago, Burlington, and Quincy Railroad Co. v. Chicago* (1897); therefore, states are also forbidden from taking private property for public use without just compensation. Not every deprivation of property requires compensation, however. For example, the Court held in *United States v. Caltex* (1952) that under conditions of war, private property may be demolished to prevent use by the enemy without compensation to the owner. When compensation is to be paid, a plethora of 5-4 decisions by the Court—including *United States v. Fuller* (1973) and *Almota Farmers Elevator and Wholesale Co. v. United States* (1973)— demonstrate fundamental disagreements among the justices about the proper method of calculating what is "just."

Court decisions in the early and mid-1990's underscore the complexity and reach of the takings clause. Several cases broadened the powers of the states, and others expanded property rights. In *Yee v. Escondido* (1992), a unanimous Court held that a rent-control ordinance did not amount to a physical taking of the property of owners of a mobile home park. A more significant ruling, *Lucas v. South Carolina Coastal Commission* (1992), narrowed the rights of states to rely on regulatory takings that completely deprive individuals of the economic use of their property. To be exempt from compensating a property owner, a state must claim more than a general public interest or an interest in preventing serious public harm.

The Court broadened property rights by holding that land use requirements may be "takings." The decision in *Dolan v. City of Tigard* (1994) dealt with the practice of local governments giving property owners a permit for building a development only on the condition that they donate parts of their land for parks, bike paths, and other public purposes. These conditions are valid only if the local government makes "some sort of individualized determination that the required dedication is related both in nature and extent to the impact of the proposed development." This 5-4 decision underscores the Court's inability to reach agreement on constitutional principles under the Fifth Amendment.

Susan L. Thomas

Sources for Further Study

Allen, Richard J., Richard B. Kuhns, and William J. Stunz. *Constitutional Criminal Procedure: An Examination of the Fourth, Fifth, and Sixth Amendments and Related Areas.* New York: Aspen Law and Business, 1995.

Bodenhamer, Davd. *Fair Trial: Rights of the Accused in American History.* New York: Oxford University Press, 1992.

Ely, James. *The Guardian of Every Other Right: A Constitutional History of Property Rights.* New York: Oxford University Press, 1992.

Epstein, Richard. *Takings: Private Property and the Power of Eminent Domain.* Cambridge, Mass.: Harvard University Press, 1985.

Fireside, Harvey. *The Fifth Amendment: The Right to Remain Silent.* Springfield, N.J.: Enslow, 1998.

Holmes, Burnham. *The Fifth Amendment.* Englewood Cliffs, N.J.: Silver Burdett Press, 1991.

Lewis, Anthony. *Gideon's Trumpet.* New York: Vintage, 1964.

Vile, John R. *Encyclopedia of Constitutional Amendments, Proposed Amendments, and Amending Issues, 1789-1995.* Santa Barbara, Calif: ABC-CLIO, 1996.

See also: Bill of Rights (1789); Takings clause (1789).

Takings Clause

Date: Approved September 29, 1789; enacted December 15, 1791
U.S. Statutes at Large: 1 Stat. 97-98
Categories: Civil Rights and Liberties; Constitutional Law; Property

> *The takings clause is a provision in the Fifth Amendment that prohibits the taking of private property for public use unless the owner is appropriately compensated.*

The takings clause is one of the most important and vigorously contested constitutional provisions, at the center of numerous cases before the Supreme Court. The clause pits fundamental capitalist principles of private ownership against the doctrines of state sovereignty and the public good.

The U.S. Constitution contains a number of provisions that seek to protect private ownership of property and property rights more generally. Chief among these is the takings clause of the Fifth Amendment. The clause provides that "private property [shall not] be taken for public use without just compensation." In including this provision, the Framers paid respect to a long-standing, basic individual right with roots in seventeenth century English legal tradition.

The takings clause seeks simultaneously to protect the property rights of individuals—crucial to the American capitalist economic system and its cultural value of individualism—and to ensure that the state is able to acquire private property when necessary in order to promote the public good. In other words, it is not a person's *property* that is inviolable; rather, a person is entitled to the *value* of that property in the event that the state has a compelling need to acquire ("take") it. Such state takings of property (usually land) follow the principle of eminent domain—essentially, that the government retains the ultimate right to secure private property for the good of the state because the existence of the state is a precondition of property itself. However, while the principles of eminent domain and just compensation work together neatly under the concept of the takings clause, the business of defining what specific instances warrant the exercise of eminent domain and what level of compensation is just, is fraught with controversy. The Supreme Court has issued a number of landmark decisions on these questions over the years.

CONDEMNATION

Governments exercise eminent domain—that is, they take private property through a process of "condemnation"—in order to advance projects deemed to be in the interest of the public or the government. For example, state and local governments exercise eminent domain over private property that stands in the way of a planned road expansion, a proposed state building, a public works project such as a dam, or any of a number of other projects. Such condemnation of property typically is construed as a taking and thus requires payment of fair market value to the property owner. Eminent domain can be exercised by all levels of government, as well as some quasi-governmental entities such as public utilities.

Disputes may arise over what constitutes the fair market value for a property that is taken by the government through condemnation, but the principle of eminent domain is well established and seldom open to a constitutional challenge. As long as just compensation is provided, the threshold for a valid exercise of eminent domain is relatively low.

Sometimes a government may seize property without providing just compensation. For example, a number of laws at the state and federal level provide for the forfeiture of a person's assets under certain circumstances, including conviction for specified crimes. For example, federal laws permit the forfeiture of certain property, including boats and homes, that were purchased with illicit drug proceeds. Such laws have been challenged as unconstitutional, but generally it is the Eighth Amendment (which prohibits "excessive fines") that is invoked. Because seizures of this type are considered penalties, they do not require compensation.

There are several other circumstances under which the government can seize property without granting compensation. In certain cases, a government may destroy private property in order to preserve public health and safety. For example, the Court has long upheld the right of the state to demolish structures posing a fire hazard as in *Bowditch v. Boston* (1880), to destroy diseased trees that threaten the health of other trees as in *Miller v. Schoene* (1928), or otherwise to abate nuisances, all without compensation. In these cases, property is *not* seized for public use; rather, the state is performing a remediation action where a property owner has failed to meet requirements specified in laws and ordinances.

The takings issue becomes much more complicated when a government seeks not outright condemnation of property but rather to restrict its use. Regulating the use of property is a fundamental and indispensable facet of a government's police powers. Land use restrictions of various kinds have long been a recognized prerogative of government.

For example, federal, state, and local governments impose habitability standards for housing, hotels, mobile homes, and other structures. Local governments typically zone different sections of land under their jurisdiction for different uses, such as housing, retail businesses, or parks in order to impose order and promote compatible uses. Some such zoning ordinances restrict liquor stores or adult bookstores from areas near churches or schools. Zoning may also be used to restrict residential construction from flood-plains and other hazardous areas. Local ordinances may limit noise from a factory or amphitheater in order to preserve quiet for nearby neighborhoods. Land developers may be required to provide open space for habitat conservation or public recreation. Easements may be required to facilitate public access to natural resources such as shorelines or parks. In these and myriad other ways, government exercises a long-accepted right to restrict the use of property.

REGULATORY TAKINGS

Governmentally imposed restrictions on the use of property, such as zoning restrictions, can be construed as "regulatory takings" when new restrictions are imposed on a piece of property after a person has purchased it. Presumably restrictions that exist on a property at the time of its purchase are reflected in the purchase price, and thus no governmental compensation is necessary.

The idea that regulatory (nonphysical) takings require compensation has evolved slowly and remains controversial. Until the early 1900's most courts rejected the argument, made by some property owners, that postpurchase regulatory takings warranted compensation under the Fifth Amendment. For example, in *Euclid v. Ambler Realty Co.* (1926), the Court rejected a property owner's argument that he deserved compensation for a local zoning ordinance that banned industrial development on his land. The Court held that the restriction was a valid exercise of police powers exercised by the government for legitimate reasons. *Euclid* thus upheld the constitutionality of zoning ordinances. At about this time, the Court began to recognize the possibility that zoning and other land use regulations, if restrictive enough, could indeed amount to takings deserving of just compensation. For example, in *Nectow v. City of Cambridge* (1928), the Court considered another ordinance prohibiting industrial development. In this case, the ordinance would permit only residential development on land under contract to be sold for industrial use. The Court found that the ordinance amounted to a taking because it allowed for "no practical use" of the particular parcel.

Many naturally sought guidance on identifying the point at which an otherwise legitimate government exercise of police powers becomes a taking under the Fifth Amendment. The issue was addressed, albeit incompletely, in the Court's opinion in *Pennsylvania Coal Co. v. Mahon* (1922). In that case, the first to address nonphysical takings, the Court found that "Government hardly could go on" if every governmental regulation that diminished the value of property had to be accompanied by compensation. Rather, "some values are enjoyed under an implied limitation and must yield to the police power." At the same time, however, "the implied limitation must have its limits or the contract and due process clauses are gone." In this case, the Court held that restrictions that prevented coal mining on a particular piece of property made that property virtually worthless, and therefore the owner deserved compensation. Justice Louis D. Brandeis issued a dissenting opinion, however, highlighting some difficult and controversial aspects to the Court's attempt at balancing public and private interests. Brandeis's dissent presaged many of the debates that would come into full bloom a half-century later.

For many decades after the 1920's the Court largely avoided takings cases, leaving them to be resolved by state and federal courts. Allowing for some variation among states and regions, legal development during much of the century generally took a fairly conservative approach to the takings clause, emphasizing the need for compelling, often extraordinary state interests in order to effect a taking without compensation. In the 1980's and 1990's, however, the Court heard and decided a number of landmark cases that generally had the effect of strengthening the government's ability to pursue regulatory takings, particularly with the goal of advancing environmental protection.

BALANCING

In the 1980's the Court identified two major criteria for determining whether a taking had occurred. This approach, which the Court set forth in *Agins v. City of Tiburon* (1980), called for considering whether the restriction still permitted an economically viable use of the property and whether the regulation advanced a legitimate state interest. This approach is typically referred to as "balancing of public benefit against private loss." In the *Agins* decision, the Court determined that a local zoning ordinance that restricted but did not prohibit residential development did not constitute a taking.

It is important to note that denying a property owner the "highest and best" use of his or her property is not adequate grounds for a takings claim. Certainly a regulation eliminating all viable economic use would be considered a taking. This was illustrated in *Whitney Benefits v. United States* (1989), which held that federal legislation that deprived a mining company of all economic use of its property amounted to a taking without just compensation. Similarly, in *Lucas v. South Carolina Coastal Commission* (1992), the Court found that the denial of a beachfront building permit effectively prohibited all economic use of the land and thus amounted to a taking deserving of compensation. (Lucas allowed an exception for nuisance abatement.) Aside from such extreme cases as *Whitney* and *Lucas*, however, it is somewhat difficult to establish whether a regulatory action or zoning ordinance permits "economically viable use." One case that did so is *Goldblatt v. Hempstead* (1962), wherein the Court found that an ordinance that effectively prohibited the operation of a gravel pit did nevertheless allow for other, economically viable uses for the property. A similar conclusion was arrived at in *Agins*.

In another landmark case from the 1980's, the Court ruled in *First English Evangelical Lutheran Church of Glendale v. County of Los Angeles* (1987) that even a temporary taking requires just compensation. In this case, a church sought to rebuild some structures on its property that were destroyed in a flood. The county, however, had adopted an interim ordinance preventing construction (including reconstruction) of buildings on the floodplain where the church's buildings had been located. The Court found that a taking, such as that created by the county ordinance, requires just compensation even when the taking is temporary. This decision closed a potential loophole of long-lived, though putatively temporary, land use restrictions.

OPEN SPACE AND ENVIRONMENT
The increasing concern with environmental issues in the latter part of the twentieth century was accompanied by greater governmental regulation of private property to provide open space and public access to natural resources. Although the Court has generally supported such goals as legitimate public purposes, it has also had occasion to identify circumstances in which takings have resulted, thus requiring just compensation. For example, in *Kaiser*

Aetna v. United States (1980), the Court held that requiring a landowner to provide public access to a private pond amounted to a taking deserving of just compensation. The Court pushed this decision further in *Nollan v. California Coastal Commission* (1987), holding that a state agency's demand for a coastal easement on private property amounted to a regulatory taking that required just compensation. In the case of *Nollan*, it was a public resource (the coastline of the Pacific Ocean), rather than a private pond, for which public access was required.

It would seem that the Court accepted a broad range of resource-related goals as legitimate grounds for the exercise of eminent domain. At the same time, the Court seemed to be viewing open space requirements and demands for easements as bona fide takings requiring just compensation. A distinction was generally drawn for open space requirements imposed on land developers whose proposed development would itself generate a need for such open space. For example, a housing development on agricultural land would increase the population of the area, thus arguably creating a need to preserve and create access to some open space, such as parks or greenbelts. Requirements for such environmental impact-mitigating measures might therefore not warrant compensation. However, in *Dolan v. City of Tigard* (1994), the Court struck down a city's requirement that a hardware store owner dedicate a portion of property for a trail in order to be permitted to expand the store. The Court held that the city had not satisfactorily established that the requirement was needed to offset any anticipated increase in traffic from the expansion. Dolan thus underscored the need to link mitigating measures to the actual impacts of a proposed project.

LATER DECISIONS

In the late 1990's the Court seemed to continue its support for environmentally based regulatory takings, while maintaining or even expanding the requirement that such takings, when significant, require just compensation. The state has a right to insist on property restrictions that protect the environment, the Court seemed to say, but the state must be willing to pay when these restrictions significantly restrict use.

A major case from this period was *Suitum v. Tahoe Regional Planning Agency* (1997). In this case, a property owner sought to build a home on an undeveloped lot she had purchased fifteen years earlier. The lot, in Nevada near Lake Tahoe, fell under the jurisdiction of the Tahoe Regional Planning Agency (TRPA). The agency, charged with protecting environmental quality in the Lake Tahoe Basin, prohibited the development as likely to cause unacceptable environmental damage. TRPA essentially denied all economic use and offered as compensation "transferable development rights." Such rights could not be used to build on Suitum's lot but could be sold to a different landowner in the Tahoe basin where such development would not be prohibited. By purchasing those rights, the property owner could build a larger structure than otherwise allowed.

Suitum had been told by a lower court that her case was not "ripe"—that she had not accepted and tried to sell the transferrable development rights. However, the Supreme Court held that Suitum's case was indeed ripe and must be decided by the District Court of Nevada.

Transferable development rights are one of a number of the sometimes innovative, sometimes complicated, and frequently controversial approaches that were developed by various governmental bodies in order to regulate land use without running afoul of the Fifth Amendment. Other approaches involve development fees, open space dedications, habitat conservation plans, and statutory compensation programs.

Steve D. Boilard

SOURCES FOR FURTHER STUDY

Allen, Richard J., Richard B. Kuhns, and William J. Stunz. *Constitutional Criminal Procedure: An Examination of the Fourth, Fifth, and Sixth Amendments and Related Areas.* New York: Aspen Law and Business, 1995.

Bethell, Tom. *The Noblest Triumph: Property and Prosperity Through the Ages.* New York: St. Martin's Press, 1998.

Congressional Budget Office. *Regulatory Takings and Proposals for Change.* Washington, D.C.: Author, 1999.

Innes, Robert, et al. "Takings, Compensation, and Endangered Species Protection on Private Lands." *Journal of Economic Perspectives* (Summer, 1998): 35-52.

Kanner, Gideon. "Just Compensation Is by No Means Always Just." *The National Law Journal* (March 24, 1997): A23.

Laitos, Jan. *Law of Property Rights Protection: Limitations on Governmental Powers.* Gaithersburg, Md.: Aspen Law and Business, 1998.

Meltz, Robert, et al. *The Takings Issue: Constitutional Limits on Land Use Control and Environmental Regulation.* Washington, D.C.: Island Press, 1998.

Skouras, George. *Takings Law and the Supreme Court: Judicial Oversight of the Regulatory State's Acquisition, Use, and Control of Private Property.* New York: P. Lang, 1998.

SEE ALSO: Bill of Rights (1789); Fifth Amendment (1789).

SIXTH AMENDMENT

DATE: Approved September 29, 1789; enacted December 15, 1791
U.S. STATUTES AT LARGE: 1 Stat. 97-98
CATEGORIES: Civil Rights and Liberties; Constitutional Law; Crimes and Criminal Procedure

The Sixth Amendment reads: "In all criminal prosecutions, the accused shall enjoy the right to a speedy and public trial, by an impartial jury of the State and district wherein the crime shall have been committed; which district shall have been previously ascertained by law, and to be informed of the nature and cause of the accusation; to be confronted with the witnesses against him; to have compulsory process for obtaining witnesses in his favor, and to have the assistance of counsel for his defence."

The Sixth Amendment specifies the rights of defendants in the trial stage of the criminal law process, including the rights to a speedy and public trial, an impartial jury in the locale where the alleged crime was committed, information about the nature of charges being prosecuted, an opportunity to confront accusers and adverse witnesses, a compulsory process for obtaining favorable witnesses, and the assistance of counsel.

For most of U.S. history, the Sixth Amendment and other provisions of the Bill of Rights protected individuals against actions by the federal government only. However, during the twentieth century, the Supreme Court ruled that many provisions of the Bill of Rights, including the Sixth Amendment, also applied to state and local governments. Therefore, defendants in all criminal prosecutions came to benefit from the protections afforded by the Sixth Amendment.

RIGHT TO COUNSEL

Before the twentieth century, the right to counsel provided by the Sixth Amendment simply meant that the government could not prevent a criminal defendant from hiring an attorney when the defendant could afford to do so. Defendants who lacked the necessary funds were required to defend themselves in court without professional assistance.

The Court first expanded the right to counsel in *Powell v. Alabama* (1932). *Powell,* also known as the Scottsboro case, involved several African American defendants who were accused of raping two white women. The young men were convicted and sentenced to death in a quick trial without being represented by any attorneys. The case was heard at a time when African Americans were subjected to significant racial discrimination in the legal system, especially in southern states. There were troubling questions about the defendants' guilt, particularly after one of the alleged victims later admitted that she lied about what happened. Given the circumstances, the Court found the legal proceedings to be fundamentally unfair and declared that defendants facing the death penalty were entitled to representation by attorneys.

The Court expanded the right to counsel in *Johnson v. Zerbst* (1938) by declaring that all defendants facing serious charges in federal court are entitled to be provided with an attorney when they are too poor to afford to hire their own. The Court expanded this rule to cover all state and local courts in *Gideon v. Wainwright* (1963), a well-known case initiated by an uneducated prisoner who sent the Court a handwritten petition complaining about a judge denying his request for an attorney. In *Douglas v. California* (1963), the Court declared that the government must supply attorneys for poor defendants for their first appeal after a criminal conviction. Subsequently, the Court ruled in *Argersinger v. Hamlin* (1972) that regardless of the seriousness of the charges, criminal defendants are entitled to be represented by an attorney if they face the possibility of serving time in jail. Because people who possess the necessary funds are expected to hire their own attorneys, the Court's Sixth Amendment decisions primarily protected poor defendants who would not receive professional representation if it were not provided by the government. Although the Court expanded opportunities for poor defendants to receive representation during criminal trials, the right to counsel does not apply to civil trials or to cases pursued by prisoners after they have presented their first postconviction appeal.

TRIAL BY JURY

The Court did not interpret the Sixth Amendment to apply the right to trial by jury to all serious cases in both state and federal courts until 1968. In *Duncan v. Louisiana* (1968), the Court overturned the conviction of an African American defendant whose request for a jury trial had been denied when he was convicted and sentenced to sixty days in jail for allegedly slapping a white man on the arm. After the conviction was overturned, the federal courts prevented Louisiana from prosecuting the man again because he and his attorney had been subjected to discrimination and harassment by local law enforcement officials during the course of his arrest and trial.

The right to trial by jury does not, however, apply to all criminal cases. In *Lewis v. United States* (1996), the Court ruled that the Sixth Amendment right to a jury trial does not apply to defendants facing petty offense charges with six months or less of imprisonment as the possible punishment for each charge. Therefore, defendants may be denied the opportunity for a jury trial if they face multiple petty offenses that, upon conviction, could produce cumulative sentences in excess of six months through separate sentences for each charge. Such defendants are entitled to a trial, but the trial will be before a judge rather than a jury.

In its early decisions, the Court expected that juries would be made up of twelve members who reach unanimous verdicts. However, the Court's interpretation of the Sixth Amendment changed during the 1970's. In *Williams v. Florida* (1970), the Court determined that juries could have as few as six members in criminal cases. In *Apodaca v. Oregon* (1972), the Court declared that states could permit defendants to be convicted of crimes by less than unanimous jury verdicts. It ruled that Oregon could convict defendants with 10-2 jury votes and Louisiana with 9-3 votes. The right to trial by jury is not implemented in identical fashion in all courts throughout the country.

OTHER TRIAL RIGHTS

The Sixth Amendment's right to a speedy trial prevents the government from holding criminal charges over a defendant's head indefinitely without ever pursuing prosecution. People are entitled to have charges against them resolved in a timely manner. Because the Sixth Amendment provides no guidance on how long the government may take in pursuing prosecution, the Court had to establish guidelines through its Sixth Amendment rulings. The Court clarified the right to a speedy trial in *Barker v. Wingo* (1972), in which a defendant was forced to wait for more than five years for a trial after he was charged with murder. The delay occurred because the prosecution sought to convict a codefendant first but the codefendant's appeals led to orders for new trials. Therefore, it took several trials to obtain an error-free conviction of the codefendant. When the Court examined the claim that a five-year delay constituted a violation of the Sixth Amendment right to a speedy trial, the Court refused to set a firm time limit for speedy trials. Instead, the Court said the individual circumstances of each case must be examined. The Court ruled that judges must determine whether the right to a speedy trial was violated by considering four aspects of the delay: its length, the reason for it, whether the defendant complained about the delay, and whether it harmed the defendant's case, such as through the death or disappearance of a key witness. In this case, the Court found that because the defendant never complained about the delay and his case was not disadvantaged by the delay, the five-year wait for a trial did not violate the defendant's rights despite the fact that the prosecution caused the lengthy delay. Although the Court clarified the factors to be considered in evaluating a speedy trial claim, the exact nature of the right was not clearly defined.

The defendant's right to confront adverse witnesses is intended to prevent the government from holding trials without the defendant's knowledge or declaring the defendant guilty without permitting the defendant to challenge the prosecution's evidence. The adversary system underlying the U.S. criminal law process presumes that the best way to reveal the truth at a trial is to permit both sides to present their evidence and arguments to the judge and jury during the same proceeding.

The Court struggled with its attempts to provide a clear definition of the extent of the confrontation right. For example, in *Coy v. Iowa* (1988), the justices were deeply divided when they decided that it was not permissible for the state to place a screen in the courtroom to prevent a defendant from having eye contact with child victims who were presenting testimony about an alleged sexual assault. A few years later in *Maryland v. Craig* (1990), a narrow majority of justices approved the use of closed-circuit television to permit child victims to present testimony from a different room in the courthouse than the courtroom in which the trial was taking place. Thus the defendant could see the witnesses on television, but the children would not risk being traumatized by coming face to face with the person accused of committing crimes against them. The significant disagreements among the justices about the right to confrontation indicate that the Court may need to clarify the circumstances in which it is permissible to use devices to separate defendants from direct contact with witnesses testifying against them. Traditionally, defendants and witnesses were expected to be face to face in the same courtroom, but growing sensitivity to the psychological trauma experienced by crime victims who must testify in court has led to experiments with screens, closed-circuit television, and other techniques that collide with traditional conceptions of the right to confrontation.

Other Sixth Amendment issues to come before the Court include whether excessive pretrial publicity prevents the selection of an unbiased jury and in what circumstances judicial proceedings can be closed to the public. When addressing these issues, Court justices tend to focus on their assessment of factors and circumstances that may interfere with a criminal defendant's opportunity to receive a fair trial.

Christopher E. Smith

SOURCES FOR FURTHER STUDY

Decker, John. *Revolution to the Right.* New York: Garland, 1992.

Garcia, Alfredo. *The Sixth Amendment in Modern American Jurisprudence.* New York: Greenwood Press, 1992.

Goodman, James. *Stories of Scottsboro.* New York: Random House, 1994.

Heller, Francis Howard. *The Sixth Amendment to the Constitution of the United States: A Study in Constitutional Development.* Westport, Conn.: Greenwood Press, 1989.

Hensley, Thomas R., Christopher E. Smith, and Joyce A. Baugh. *The Changing Supreme Court: Constitutional Rights and Liberties.* St. Paul, Minn.: West Publishing, 1997.

Lewis, Anthony. *Gideon's Trumpet.* New York: Random House, 1964.

Vile, John R. *Encyclopedia of Constitutional Amendments, Proposed Amendments, and Amending Issues, 1789-1995.* Santa Barbara, Calif: ABC-CLIO, 1996.

Whitebread, Charles, and Christopher Slobogin. *Criminal Procedure.* 3d ed. Mineola, N.Y.: Foundation Press, 1993.

SEE ALSO: Bill of Rights (1789); Seventh Amendment (1789); Speedy Trial Act (1975).

SEVENTH AMENDMENT

DATE: Approved September 29, 1789; enacted December 15, 1791
U.S. STATUTES AT LARGE: 1 Stat. 97-98
CATEGORIES: Civil Rights and Liberties; Constitutional Law

> *The Seventh Amendment reads: "In Suits at common law, where the value in controversy shall exceed twenty dollars, the right of trial by jury shall be preserved, and no fact tried by a jury shall be otherwise re-examined in any Court of the United States, than according to the rules of the common law."*

The Seventh Amendment, part of the Bill of Rights, was ratified in 1791. It guaranteed the right to trial by jury in federal civil cases. The amendment was designed to preserve the common law distinction between issues of law and issues of fact. In *Baltimore and Carolina Line v. Redman* (1935), the Court held that the judge should remain the trier of law, deciding unresolved issues of law, and the jury should remain the trier of fact, resolving issues of fact under appropriate instructions by the court.

The amendment's guarantee applies to all courts under the authority of the United States, including territories and the District of Columbia. Generally, the amendment does not apply to state courts, except when the state court is enforcing a federally created right. When a federal court is enforcing a state-created right, it may follow its own rules based on the interests of the federal court system.

In *Colgrove v. Battin* (1973), the Court held that a federal district court's authorization of civil juries composed of six persons instead of the traditional twelve was permissible under the Seventh Amendment.

Patricia Jackson

SOURCES FOR FURTHER STUDY
Summer, Lila E. *The Seventh Amendment.* Vol. 7 in *American Heritage History of the Bill of Rights.* Morristown, N.J.: Silver Burdett Press, 1991.
Vile, John R. *Encyclopedia of Constitutional Amendments, Proposed Amendments, and Amending Issues, 1789-1995.* Santa Barbara, Calif: ABC-CLIO, 1996.

SEE ALSO: Bill of Rights (1789)

EIGHTH AMENDMENT

DATE: Approved September 29, 1789; enacted December 15, 1791
U.S. STATUTES AT LARGE: 1 Stat. 97-98
CATEGORIES: Civil Rights and Liberties; Constitutional Law; Crimes and Criminal Procedure

The Eighth Amendment reads: "Excessive bail shall not be required, nor excessive fines imposed, nor cruel and unusual punishments inflicted." The Eighth Amendment is the only part of the Constitution that places substantive limits on the severity of punishments in criminal cases.

The Eighth Amendment is derived almost verbatim from the English Bill of Rights (1689). Adopted in 1791 as part of the Bill of Rights, the amendment was intended to prohibit the abuse of federal government power, but the precise meaning of the amendment is unclear and requires interpretation by the Supreme Court.

The first two clauses of the Eighth Amendment (prohibiting excessive bail and fines) have not been applied to the states. Although the Court has never established an absolute right to bail, it has reviewed whether bail has been set higher than necessary to ensure that a defendant appears for trial.

The Court has taken a flexible interpretation of the cruel and unusual punishment clause, stating in *Trop v. Dulles* (1958) that punishments should be evaluated in light of the "evolving standards of decency" of a maturing society. The clause was formally applied to the states in *Robinson v. California* (1962). Barbaric punishments are prohibited, but the Court has refused to hold that the death penalty itself is cruel and unusual punishment. Punishments disproportionate to the crime, the treatment of prisoners, and conditions of confinement, may also violate the Eighth Amendment.

John Fliter

SOURCES FOR FURTHER STUDY

Buranelli, Vincent. *The Eighth Amendment*. Morristown, N.J.: Silver Burdett Press, 1991.

Vile, John R. *Encyclopedia of Constitutional Amendments, Proposed Amendments, and Amending Issues, 1789-1995*. Santa Barbara, Calif: ABC-CLIO, 1996.

SEE ALSO: Bill of Rights (1789)

NINTH AMENDMENT

DATE: Approved September 29, 1789; enacted December 15, 1791
U.S. STATUTES AT LARGE: 1 Stat. 97-98
CATEGORIES: Civil Rights and Liberties; Constitutional Law; Privacy

The Ninth Amendment reads: "The enumeration in the Constitu-tion, of certain rights, shall not be construed to deny or disparage oth-ers retained by the people." Relying on the Ninth Amendment, the Su-preme Court has not confined itself to rights directly stated in the Constitution but has also enforced unenumerated rights, such as the right to privacy.

The Ninth Amendment is among the most enigmatic parts of the Bill of Rights. At one level, the thrust of the amendment is rela-tively clear. The Bill of Rights and other parts of the constitutional text do not contain an exhaustive listing of the people's rights. However, the questions of what other rights the Constitution pro-tects and from whom, as well as who may enforce such rights and how they relate to delegated and reserved governmental powers, raise complex interpretive problems.

HISTORICAL ORIGINS AND EARLY INVOCATIONS
Federalist James Madison apparently drafted the amendment to address concerns that adding a bill of rights to the constitutional text might imply that the people held only the rights listed in that document. Claims that the people held other rights were often linked to a premise that the Constitution delegated limited powers to the federal government. Accordingly, the Ninth Amendment was viewed as a companion to the Tenth Amendment, which re-served for the states or the people all powers "not delegated to the United States by the Constitution, nor prohibited by it to the States."

Even before the Bill of Rights was ratified by three-fourths of the states, Madison relied on the terms of these two amendments to support arguments that Congress had no authority to establish a national bank. In debates within the House of Representatives on February 2, 1791, Madison claimed the Ninth Amendment "guard[ed] against a latitude of interpretation" and the Tenth Amendment "exclude[ed] every source of power not within the Constitution itself."

The Supreme Court's decision in *McCulloch v. Maryland* (1819) had implications for interpreting the Ninth and Tenth Amend-ments. In arguing that Congress had authority to establish a na-tional bank, Chief Justice John Marshall rejected a narrow rule of construction for interpreting the Constitution's delegations of power. He argued instead that the Constitution gave Congress "vast powers," on whose execution "the happiness and prosperity of the nation so vitally depends."

Variations of this reasoning would eventually support expansive conceptions of federal power and correspondingly narrow conceptions of residuals—including reserved powers and retained rights. In *Fletcher v. Peck* (1810), however, Chief Justice Marshall suggested that judges might enforce unenumerated rights as limits on the states. In subsequent cases, the justices linked the idea of unenumerated rights to principles of limited federal power.

THE NINTH AMENDMENT AND SLAVERY

In *Scott v. Sandford* (1857), Chief Justice Roger Brooke Taney argued in his majority opinion that the Missouri Compromise Act of 1850 was invalid because it exceeded constitutional delegations, encroached on reserved powers, and abridged retained rights. Referring to rights of slave ownership, Taney wrote, "The powers over person and property of which we speak are not only not granted to Congress, but are in express terms denied, and they are forbidden to exercise them." More specifically, he argued that Congress "has no power over the person or property of a citizen but what the citizens of the United States have granted."

Reinforcing Taney's arguments, Justice John A. Campbell quoted statements made by the authors of the Constitution intended to assure Antifederalists that the federal government would be limited to certain enumerated powers. Despite these assurances, the Constitution's critics demanded an "explicit declaration" that the federal government would not assume powers not specifically delegated to it. As a result, Campbell said, the Ninth and Tenth Amendments were "designed to include the reserved rights of the States, and the people . . . and to bind the authorities, State and Federal . . . to their recognition and observance." Claiming faithfulness to these interpretive premises, Campbell denied that Congress had power to prohibit slavery in the territories.

The Civil War Amendments (especially the Thirteenth and Fourteenth) overturned the central holdings of *Scott* and formalized the results of the Civil War by invalidating slavery and making all native-born people, including African Americans, citizens. However, these changes, along with others, did not end controversy over the scope of delegated powers or their relationship to reserved and retained prerogatives. Accordingly, the justices continued to deal with the problems of constitutional construction that were at the heart of the Ninth Amendment.

TWENTIETH CENTURY PRECEDENTS

These problems came to a head again during the New Deal era. The mid-1930's inaugurated an increasingly deferential approach to assertions of national power and had corresponding implications for interpreting limitations on those powers. In this context, the Ninth Amendment made its first substantial appearance in a majority opinion for the Court.

In *Ashwander v. Tennessee Valley Authority* (1936), the justices upheld the operation of the Wilson Dam by the Tennessee Valley Authority, an agency of the U.S. government. Among other things, the plaintiffs argued that the sale of electric energy generated by the dam exceeded constitutional delegations of power and abridged rights protected by the Ninth Amendment. Chief Justice Charles Evans Hughes, writing the majority opinion, dismissed both arguments. Referring to the Ninth Amendment, he claimed that "the maintenance of rights retained by the people does not withdraw the rights which are expressly granted to the Federal Government. The question is as to the scope of the grant and whether there are inherent limitations which render invalid the disposition of property with which we are now concerned."

In this passage, Chief Justice Hughes relied on normative premises similar to those implicit in debates by the creators of the Constitution on matters of structure. Following Madison's example, the chief justice treated delegated powers and retained rights as mutually exclusive and reciprocally limiting prerogatives. However, Hughes suggested that a finding of delegated power precluded opposing claims of retained rights. He characterized the latter, like reserved powers, as residuals beyond the legitimate reach of federal delegations.

Eleven years later, Justice Stanley F. Reed commented further on the Ninth Amendment in his opinion for the majority in *United Public Workers v. Mitchell* (1947). In that case, the justices upheld a section of the Hatch Act (1939) that prohibited employees of the federal government from active participation in political campaigns. Reed accepted the employees' stance that "the nature of political rights reserved to the people by the Ninth and Tenth

Amendments are involved. The rights claimed as inviolate may be stated as the right of a citizen to act as a party official or worker to further his own political views." The justice claimed, however, that "these fundamental human rights are not absolutes" and thus were subject to reasonable governmental restriction.

By this time, the Court had already enforced many of the guarantees of the Bill of Rights against the states through the Fourteenth Amendment's due process clause. In such cases, the Court repeatedly treated popular rights as "trumps" capable of preempting otherwise legitimate assertions of governmental power. The Court had also repeatedly interpreted enumerated rights as similar limitations on federal powers. In *Mitchell,* however, Justice Reed did not explore the possibility of judges' enforcing unenumerated rights as such limitations. Absent such a reconceptualization, the Ninth Amendment—along with the Tenth—would have diminished practical significance. Claims of unenumerated rights would be preempted by increasingly expansive conceptions of delegated powers.

THE RIGHT OF PRIVACY

In the 1960's, the Court first relied on the Ninth Amendment to enforce unenumerated rights as limits on state powers. The Court made this move in the landmark case of *Griswold v. Connecticut* (1965). The majority opinion, written by Justice William O. Douglas, invoked the Ninth along with the First, Third, Fourth, Fifth, and Fourteenth Amendments, to support the Court's invalidation of a state law prohibiting the use of contraceptives by married couples. According to Douglas, the state law abridged a right of privacy that was "older than the Bill of Rights." He presumed that the government's purpose was valid but suggested that the means chosen "swe[pt] unnecessarily broadly and thereby invade[d] the area of protected freedoms."

Justice Arthur J. Goldberg in his concurrence offered his view of the Ninth Amendment's relevance in this context. In the most extensive explicit analysis of the Ninth Amendment in a Court opinion to date, Goldberg reviewed commentary on the amendment by Madison and Joseph Story, along with judicial precedents enforcing fundamental liberties in addition to enumerated rights. His central claim was that the Ninth Amendment supported interpreting the Fourteenth Amendment as embracing unenumerated along with enumerated liberties.

Justice Hugo L. Black in his dissent criticized both the majority opinion and Justice Goldberg's concurrence. He denied that the Constitution protected a right of privacy and claimed that relying on the Ninth Amendment to enforce such a right against the states turned somersaults with history. He stated that the Ninth Amendment was added to constitutional text "to assure the people that the Constitution in all its provisions was intended to limit the Federal Government to the powers granted expressly or by necessary implication."

In *Roe v. Wade* (1973), the Court extended its holding in *Griswold*. Justice Harry A. Blackmun, in the majority opinion, wrote, "The right of privacy, whether it be founded in the Fourteenth Amendment's concept of personal liberty and restrictions upon state action, as we feel it is, or, as the District Court determined, in the Ninth Amendment's reservation of rights to the people, is broad enough to encompass a woman's decision whether or not to terminate her pregnancy." Blackmun hesitated to rely squarely on the Ninth Amendment to strike down the challenged state law. Following Douglas and Goldberg's opinions in *Griswold*, however, he suggested connections between the Ninth and Fourteenth Amendments.

A SAVING CLAUSE

In *Richmond Newspapers v. Virginia* (1980), Chief Justice Warren E. Burger announced the Court's ruling that the First and Fourteenth Amendments guaranteed a right of the public and press to attend criminal trials. Burger relied on the Ninth Amendment to rebut arguments that such a right was not protected simply because it was nowhere spelled out in the Constitution. In his view, the Ninth Amendment was significant as a saving clause designed to allay fears that the explicit listing of certain guarantees could be interpreted as excluding others. The amendment prevented people from claiming that "the affirmation of particular rights implies a negation of those not expressly defined." Burger pointed out, moreover, that the Court repeatedly enforced fundamental rights going beyond those explicitly defined in the Constitution, including the rights of association, of privacy, to be presumed innocent, to travel freely, and to be judged by a standard of proof beyond a reasonable doubt in criminal trial.

It is impossible to ascertain with confidence the extent to which justices have relied on the Ninth Amendment as an interpretive guide but not cited it in their opinions. However, Chief Justice Burger's opinion in *Richmond Newspapers* is a reminder that justices have not confined themselves to protecting enumerated rights. They have also protected unenumerated rights and taken positions on what rights the people hold in connection with interpreting the character and scope of federal and state governmental powers.

Wayne D. Moore

Sources for Further Study

Barnett, Randy E., ed. *The Rights Retained by the People: The History and Meaning of the Ninth Amendment.* 2 vols. Fairfax, Va.: George Mason University Press, 1989-1993.

Hyman, Harold, and William P. Hobby, eds. *The Ninth Amendment: Preservation of the Constitutional Mind.* New York: Garland, 1990.

Massey, Calvin R. *Silent Rights: The Ninth Amendment and the Constitution's Unenumerated Rights.* Philadelphia: Temple University Press, 1995.

Moore, Wayne D. *Constitutional Rights and Powers of the People.* Princeton, N.J.: Princeton University Press, 1996.

Vile, John R. *Encyclopedia of Constitutional Amendments, Proposed Amendments, and Amending Issues, 1789-1995.* Santa Barbara, Calif: ABC-CLIO, 1996.

See also: Bill of Rights (1789); Tenth Amendment (1789); Fourteenth Amendment (1868); Hatch Act (1939).

Tenth Amendment

Date: Approved September 29, 1789; enacted December 15, 1791
U.S. Statutes at Large: 1 Stat. 97-98
Categories: Civil Rights and Liberties; Constitutional Law

The Tenth Amendment reads: "The powers not delegated to the United States by the Constitution, nor prohibited by it to the States, are reserved to the States respectively, or to the people."

The Tenth Amendment protects the reserved powers of the state, those not delegated to the federal government by the U.S. Constitution. The First Congress received numerous requests to include a means of protecting the reserved powers of the states. These concerns arose in many quarters during the Constitutional Convention of 1787 and ratification process, especially among the Antifederalists, who feared that an overbearing national government would assume the authority of the states. Article II of the Articles of Confederation had contained explicit provisions for protecting states, initiating a system whereby "each state retains its sovereignty." Various early state constitutions included provisions outlining the primacy of states in the confederal arrangement.

FEDERALISTS AND ANTIFEDERALISTS
The most popular form of amendment requested during the state ratification conventions and proposed to the First Congress concerned a reserved powers clause. The defenders of the Constitution argued that such a provision was unnecessary. James Madison suggested in No. 39 of *The Federalist* (1788) that each state was "a sovereign body," bound only by its voluntary act of ratification. Other Federalists at the Virginia ratifying convention, including James Wilson, Alexander Hamilton, and John Marshall, held that such a provision was already present in the Constitution and that the new government would have only the powers delegated to it.

Opposition to and suspicion of the proposed Constitution on the grounds that it would infringe on the privileged status of the states was widespread. The defenders of state authority viewed the states as the repository of reserved power, and many believed that states were invested with an equal capacity to judge infractions against the federal government. In the Virginia ratifying convention, George Nicholas and Edmund Randolph, members of the committee reporting the instrument of ratification, noted that the Constitution would have only the powers "expressly" delegated to it. If Federalists disagreed with the stress on state authority, they generally viewed a reserved power clause as innocuous, and Madison included such a provision among the amendments he introduced in 1789.

In the First Congress, Elbridge Gerry, a Founder and Anti-federalist elected to the House of Representatives, introduced a proposal reminiscent of the Articles of Confederation, leaving to the states all powers "not expressly delegated" to the federal government. Gerry's proposal was defeated, in part because of concerns about the similarity between the language of his amendment and that of the articles.

Others who took a states' rights or strict constructionist view of the Constitution, including Thomas Jefferson, persisted in defending state power. Before ratification of the Tenth Amendment, Jefferson advised President George Washington that incorporating a national bank was unconstitutional, basing his opinion on the amendment. Jefferson would later compose the Kentucky Resolves, which defended the states as the sovereign building blocks of the American nation and noted that the states retained a means of protection when threatened. To describe the process of state action, Jefferson supplied a new term, nullification, to note the immediacy and severity of the "remedy" necessary to prohibit the federal government from absorbing state authority.

Defenders of the federal government, sometimes described as nationalists or loose constructionists, argued that Congress must assume more power if the needs of the country were to be met. Most prominent among the advocates of increased federal authority was Hamilton. For Hamilton, the Tenth Amendment was unnecessary as the political order already protected states. The Constitution, according to the nationalists, already contained provisions for the exercise of federal power, including the necessary and proper clause and supremacy clause.

THE COURT AND THE AMENDMENT
The Supreme Court addressed the controversy in *McCulloch v. Maryland* (1819). The Court upheld the constitutionality of a national bank, even though such an institution was not specified in the Constitution. In dismissing a strict delineation of state and federal authority, the Court, under the leadership of Marshall, extended the powers of Congress at the expense of the states. However, the Marshall Court also affirmed the notion that police powers belonged exclusively to the states. Under Chief Justice Roger Brooke Taney, the Court assumed more of a strict constructionist posture.

With the Civil War and Reconstruction, the authority and influence of the federal government were greatly increased. The role of the Tenth Amendment was essentially disregarded as federal troops occupied southern states and Congress provided governance. The authority of the states continued to suffer, resulting in part from a series of Court decisions in the twentieth century. In *Champion v. Ames* (1903), the Court affirmed a congressional act that prohibited the sale of lottery tickets across state lines as an effort to limit gambling. Before *Champion*, decisions regarding gambling were made by the states. The decisions of the Court were not consistent, and it soon adopted a view of the relationship between states and the federal government that allowed each to be authoritative in its own sphere, exempting "state instrumentalities" from federal taxation. In *Hammer v. Dagenhart* (1918), the Court ruled in favor of state power in terms of commerce. The Tenth Amendment would, however, suffer its most severe criticism in *United States v. Darby Lumber Co.* (1941). In this decision, Chief Justice Harlan Fiske Stone discredited the amendment as "redundant" and a "constitutional tranquilizer and empty declaration."

Although Stone dismissed the amendment, continued authentication of its importance can be seen in *Fry v. United States* (1975), in which the Court affirmed that the amendment "expressly declares the constitutional policy that Congress may not exercise power in a fashion that impairs the States' integrity or their ability to function effectively in a federal system." In *Printz v. United States* (1997), the Court again forcefully affirmed the amendment, noting that the amendment made express the residual state sovereignty that was implicit in the Constitution's conferring of specific governmental powers to Congress.

H. Lee Cheek, Jr.

SOURCES FOR FURTHER STUDY

Berger, Raoul. *Federalism: The Founders' Design.* Norman: University of Oklahoma Press, 1987.

Berns, Walter. "The Constitution as Bill of Rights." In *How Does the Constitution Secure Rights?*, edited by Robert A. Goldwin and William Schambra. Washington, D.C.: American Enterprise Institute, 1985.

_____. "The Meaning of the Tenth Amendment." In *A Nation of States*, edited by Robert A. Goldwin. Chicago: Rand McNally, 1963

Calhoun, John C. "A Discourse on the Constitution and Government of the United States." In *Union and Liberty: The Political Philosophy of John C. Calhoun*, edited by Ross M. Lence. Indianapolis, Ind.: Liberty Fund, 1992.

Hickok, Eugene W., Jr. "The Original Understanding of the Tenth Amendment." In *The Bill of Rights*, edited by Hickok. Charlottesville: University of Virginia Press, 1991.

Kaminski, John P., et al., eds. *The Documentary History of the Ratification of the Constitution, Volumes VIII-X: Ratification of the Constitution by the States, Virginia*. Madison: State Historical Society of Wisconsin, 1993.

Lofgren, Charles A. "The Origins of the Tenth Amendment, History, Sovereignty, and the Problems of Constitutional Intention." *Constitutional Government in America*, edited by Ronald K. L. Collins. Durham, N.C.: Carolina Academic Press, 1980.

Story, Joseph. *Commentaries on the Constitution of the United States.* Vol. 2. Boston: C. C. Little and J. Brown, 1833.

Vile, John R. *Encyclopedia of Constitutional Amendments, Proposed Amendments, and Amending Issues, 1789-1995*. Santa Barbara, Calif: ABC-CLIO, 1996.

SEE ALSO: Bill of Rights (1789); Ninth Amendment (1789).

TRADE AND INTERCOURSE ACTS

DATE: 1790-1834
U.S. STATUTES AT LARGE: 1 Stat. 137 (1790 act)
CATEGORIES: Business, Commerce, and Trade; Native Americans

These acts represent early efforts by the U.S. government to restrain private settlement and enterprise by European Americans in Indian territory; the restrictions eroded as a part of the market revolution of the nineteenth century.

In the late eighteenth and early nineteenth centuries, the United States government feared that rapacious private traders and land-grabbing settlers were creating resentment among Indians that could lead to war on the frontier of white settlement. Therefore, the government sought to prevent the wholesale migration of white settlers westward to lands controlled by Indians, regulate the trade in furs between Indians and European Americans, and acculturate Indians to Euro-American norms. The government hoped that these efforts would preserve peace between Indians and European Americans. The vehicles for these goals were the successive Indian Trade and Intercourse Acts. The first Trade and Intercourse Act was passed in 1790 and was scheduled to expire at the end of the congressional session of 1793. Before expiration, a new Trade and Intercourse Act was passed in 1793. Further laws were enacted in 1796, 1799, and 1802. The 1802 act was made permanent; it stood until 1834.

The Trade and Intercourse Acts built upon precedents established by the Continental Congress in an ordinance of August 7, 1786. The Ordinance of 1786 empowered the federal government to issue licenses to United States citizens allowing them to reside among or trade with Indians. Like the later Trade and Intercourse Acts, the ordinance was an assertion of federal over state power in the regulation of Indian affairs.

The Trade and Intercourse Act of 1790 provided for the licensing of private traders and outlined the penalties for trading without a license. The act of 1790 also detailed the punishments for crimes committed by whites against Indians. The act of 1793 reiterated the provisions of the 1790 act in stronger terms and further authorized the distribution of goods to Indians to promote acculturation to Euro-American mores. In response to the continuing influx of white settlers, the act of 1796 delineated the boundaries of territories belonging to Indians, the first such delineation by the federal government. The acts of 1799 and 1802 were substantially similar to the act of 1796.

In 1834, the federal government for the last time passed an Indian Trade and Intercourse Act. The 1834 act defined Indian territory as all lands west of the Mississippi River excluding the states of Missouri and Louisiana and the territory of Arkansas. The 1834 act banned liquor from the trade and outlawed white fur trappers from operating in Indian territory. Unlike any of the previous acts, however, the 1834 law empowered the federal government to use force to stop intertribal wars in order to protect the interests of fur trade companies. Ironically, a series of acts that began in 1790 by reining in white traders in order to preserve peace ended in 1834 by policing Indians in order to protect traders.

Andrew C. Isenberg

SOURCE FOR FURTHER STUDY
Prucha, Francis P. *American Indian Policy in the Formative Years: The Indian Trade and Intercourse Acts, 1790-1834.* Lincoln: University of Nebraska Press, 1970.

SEE ALSO: Maine Indian Claims Act (1980).

NATURALIZATION ACT

DATE: March 26, 1790
U.S. STATUTES AT LARGE: 1 Stat. 103
CATEGORIES: Immigration

Naturalization is the legal process by which a state or country confers citizenship on a person not born in that nation. This law established the means for non-U.S. citizens to become citizens.

After the American colonies gained their independence from Britain in 1787, each state adopted different rules for conferring U.S. citizenship upon its residents. President George Washington suggested that a uniform naturalization act at the federal level was needed.

Article I, section 8 of the U.S. Constitution empowers Congress to pass uniform laws for naturalization. Congress exercised this power for the first time when it passed "An act to establish an uniform Rule of Naturalization" on March 26, 1790. This act granted "all free white persons" with two years of residence the right of citizenship. In addition, the act stated that "the children of citizens of the U.S. that may be born beyond sea, or out of limits of the U.S., shall be considered as natural born citizens."

In effect, the act created two separate classes of people: free and white citizens, able to hold political office and entitled to the rights and privileges of citizenship, and nonwhite persons, ineligible for membership in the U.S. community. The act further reinforced the part of the Constitution that limits membership in Congress to citizens who meet stipulated residence requirements and the presidency to natural-born citizens. The Naturalization Act was repealed five years later.

Stephen Schwartz

SOURCES FOR FURTHER STUDY

Aleinikoff, Thomas Alexander. *Between Principles and Politics: The Direction of U.S. Citizenship Policy.* Washington, D.C.: Carnegie Endowment for International Peace, 1998.

Madison, James. *Writings.* Edited by Jack N. Rakove. New York: Library of America, 1999.

Neuman, Gerald L. *Strangers to the Constitution: Immigrants, Borders, and Fundamental Law.* Princeton, N.J.: Princeton University Press, 1996.

SEE ALSO: Alien and Sedition Acts (1798); Sedition Act of 1798 (1798).

FEDERAL CRIMES ACT

DATE: April 30, 1790
U.S. STATUTES AT LARGE: 1 Stat. 112-119
CATEGORIES: Crimes and Criminal Procedure

This law identified a number of federal crimes, established penalties for their commission, and established the foundation for the U.S. Criminal Code.

105

When the U.S. Constitution was adopted in 1789, it specifically charged the federal government with a narrow criminal jurisdiction, covering only counterfeiting and piracies and other felonies committed on the high seas. Yet the Constitution granted Congress the authority to make laws it deemed "necessary and proper for carrying into execution" the broad powers granted to it. It was by this authority that the first Congress passed the Federal Crimes Act in 1790.

The act specified penalties for a range of federal crimes, including counterfeiting and piracy, as well as treason, murder and manslaughter within a federal jurisdiction, receiving property stolen in a federal crime, bribery and perjury in connection with federal suits, and other crimes. Penalties ranged from fines of three hundred dollars to death by hanging.

Most of the penalties specified by the act have since been altered, and some of the crimes themselves have been redefined. More important, what began as a relatively modest catalog of federal crimes has since expanded to more than one thousand general criminal statutes.

Steve D. Boilard

SOURCES FOR FURTHER STUDY
Levasseur, Alain A., and John S. Baker, eds. *An Introduction to the Law of the United States*. Lanham, Md.: University Press of America, 1992.
Marion, Nancy E. *A History of Federal Crime Control Initiatives, 1960-1993*. Westport, Conn.: Greenwood Press, 1994.

SEE ALSO: U.S. Constitution: Provisions (1787); Judiciary Act of 1789 (1789); Judiciary Acts of 1801-1925 (1801).

FUGITIVE SLAVE ACT OF 1793

DATE: February 12, 1793
U.S. STATUTES AT LARGE: 1 Stat. 302
CATEGORIES: African Americans; Business, Commerce, and Trade; Civil Rights and Liberties; Slavery

This law established a federal procedure for slave owners to recover slaves who fled north, aggravating sectional conflict between free and slave states.

In colonial America, the return of fugitives within and between jurisdictions was a common practice. These fugitives were usually felons escaping from jails; persons charged with crimes; apprentices and indentured servants fleeing from their employers; or black, white, or Native American slaves running away from their masters. Their rendition between jurisdictions depended on comity among colonial authorities. The articles of the New England Confederation of 1643 included a provision for the return of fugitive slaves and servants. Like all subsequent American legislation on the topic, it did not provide for a trial by jury.

ANTISLAVE VS. SLAVE STATES

In the late eighteenth century, with the growth of antislavery sentiment in the North and the settlement of territory west of the Appalachian Mountains, a uniform method for the return of fugitive slaves became necessary. Article VI of the Northwest Ordinance of 1787 excluding chattel slavery provided that persons escaping into the territory from whom labor or service was lawfully claimed in any one of the original states might be returned to the person claiming their labor or service. The provision did not distinguish between slaves and indentured servants.

The United States Constitution of the same year incorporated the provision, without limiting the claimants to residents of the original states of the union. One of several concessions intended to win support from the slaveholding states, Article IV, section 2, states that "no person held to service or labor in one state, under the laws thereof, escaping into another, shall, in consequence of any law or regulation therein, be discharged from such service or labor, but shall be delivered up on claim of the party to whom such service or labor may be due."

In 1793, Congress decided to set federal rules for the rendition of alleged fugitives. This action was prompted by Pennsylvania's attempt to recover from Virginia several men accused of having kidnapped John Davis, a free black man. Unable to receive satisfaction, the governor of Pennsylvania brought the matter to the attention of President George Washington, who referred it to the Congress.

VARIOUS PROPOSALS

A committee of the House of Representatives, led by Theodore Sedgwick of Massachusetts, reported a rendition bill on November 15, 1791, but no action was taken. A special Senate committee, consisting of George Cabot of Massachusetts, Samuel Johnston of North Carolina, and George Read of Delaware, submitted a bill on December 20, 1792, establishing a ministerial procedure for the extradition of judicial fugitives. It also provided a system for the recovery of fugitives from labor or service. A claimant had to present a written deposition from one or more credible persons to a local magistrate who would order officers of the court to seize the fugitive and turn him or her over to the claimant. The bill set penalties for harboring a fugitive, neglecting a duty, or obstructing an arrest. After debate, the bill was recommitted with instructions to amend, and John Taylor of Virginia and Roger Sherman of Connecticut were added to the committee.

On January 3, 1793, a revised bill was reported to the Senate by Johnston, allowing the claimant or his agent to seize a fugitive and bring that person to a federal court or a local magistrate. Oral testimony or an affidavit certified by a magistrate of the master's state sufficed to establish a claim. To guard against the kidnapping of free African Americans, residents of the territory or state in which they were seized, the new bill included a proviso assuring them their rights under the laws of that territory or state. This meant they were entitled to a judicial inquiry or a jury trial to determine their status. They were also to be presumed free, until proven otherwise, and allowed to testify on their own behalf.

PROVISIONS OF THE 1793 LAW

After two debates, during which the proviso was dropped, the bill passed the Senate on January 18. It was entitled "An act respecting fugitives from justice and persons escaping from their masters." The House passed it with little discussion, February 5, by a vote of 48 to 7. Seven days later, President Washington signed the bill into law.

The first two sections of the act, known popularly as the Fugitive Slave Act of 1793, dealt with the interstate rendition of fugitives from justice. The third section provided that when a person held to labor escaped into any state or territory of the United States, the master or a designated agent could seize that individual and bring him or her before a judge of the federal courts in the state or before any magistrate of a county, city, or incorporated town. Title was proven by the testimony of the master or the affidavit of a magistrate in the state from which the escapee came, certifying that the person had escaped. The judge or magistrate then had to provide a certificate entitling the petitioner to remove the fugitives.

The act applied to fugitive apprentices or indentured servants as well as to slaves, a provision important at that time to representatives of the northern states. The act did not admit a trial by jury, and it contained no provisions for the alleged fugitives to offer evidence on their own behalf, although they were not prevented from doing so if the presiding judge or magistrate agreed.

Section 4 provided criminal penalties, a fine of five hundred dollars, in addition to any civil action the owner might have under state law, for obstructing the capture and for rescuing, harboring, aiding, or hiding fugitives.

AFTERMATH AND IMPACT

Although many attempts were made to amend the act, it remained the law of the land until the abolition of slavery, its constitutionality repeatedly upheld by the Supreme Court. It was amended and supplemented, not replaced, by the Second Fugitive Slave Law of 1850, part of the Compromise of 1850.

The statute contributed significantly to acerbating the growth of sectional conflict within the United States. Efforts to enforce its provisions encountered immediate resistance in Northern states, isolated and scattered at first but increasingly well organized and vigorous (for example, the Underground Railroad), as slavery prospered in the Old South and spread to western lands. Many Northern states passed personal liberty laws (Indiana in 1824, Connecticut in 1828, New York and Vermont in 1840). Designed to prevent the kidnapping of free African Americans, these laws provided for trial by jury to determine their true status. The effectiveness of the statute was further diminished by the Supreme Court's decision in *Prigg v. Commonwealth of Pennsylvania* (1842) that state authorities could not be forced by the national government to act in fugitive slave cases. Subsequently, Massachusetts (1843), Vermont (1843), Pennsylvania (1847), and Rhode Island (1848) forbade their officials to help enforce the law and refused the use of their jails for fugitive slaves. Because the Fugitive Slave Act of 1793 provided no federal means of apprehending fugitive slaves, owners had to rely on the often ineffectual and costly services of slave catchers. With the outbreak of the Civil War, the law ceased to apply to the Confederate States. It was considered valid in the loyal border states until it was repealed June 28, 1864.

Charles H. O'Brien

Sources for Further Study
Campbell, Stanley. *The Slave Catchers: Enforcement of the Fugitive Slave Law, 1850-1860.* Chapel Hill: University of North Carolina Press, 1970.
Finkelman, Paul. "The Kidnapping of John Davis and the Adoption of the Fugitive Slave Law of 1793." *The Journal of Southern History* 56, no. 3 (August, 1990): 397-422.
_____. *Slavery in the Courtroom: An Annotated Bibliography of American Cases.* Washington, D.C.: Library of Congress, 1985.
McDougall, Marion G. *Fugitive Slaves, 1619-1865.* 1891. Reprint. New York: Bergman, 1969.
Morris, Thomas D. *Free Men All: The Personal Liberty Laws of the North, 1780-1861.* Baltimore: The Johns Hopkins University Press, 1974.
Wiecek, William M. *Liberty Under Law: The Supreme Court in American Life.* Baltimore: The Johns Hopkins University Press, 1988.
_____. *The Sources of Antislavery Constitutionalism in America, 1760-1848.* Ithaca, N.Y.: Cornell University Press, 1977.

See also: Northwest Ordinance (1787); U.S. Constitution: Provisions (1787); Fugitive Slave Act of 1850 (1850).

Jay's Treaty

Date: Signed November 19, 1794; Senate ratified June 24, 1795
Categories: Foreign Relations; Treaties and Agreements

This resolution to outstanding conflicts between Britain and the United States led to large-scale settlement of the Northwest Territory but opened a rift with France.

After Great Britain's recognition of the United States as an independent nation in the 1783 Treaty of Paris, the United States had to make that independence meaningful and permanent. For the next three decades, the new nation struggled to maintain its integrity by achieving security against hostile forces facing it to the north and south. The southern and western boundaries were in dispute with Spain. There also existed many outstanding problems in Anglo-American relations after 1783, a number of which stemmed from the apparent unwillingness of either side to abide fully by the Treaty of Paris. The British in Canada, for example, refused to evacuate military posts in the Northwest Territory, which the Treaty of Paris recognized as belonging to the United States. Disputes over exact boundaries and fishing rights of Americans along the Grand Banks created further tensions.

EUROPEAN CONFLICTS
To compound this unstable situation, Britain and other European powers went to war in 1793 with France to put down the subversive doctrines evolving from the French Revolution and the later military ambitions of Napoleon Bonaparte. The war between France and the rest of Europe continued from 1793 to 1815, with only brief pause, and the United States was buffeted first by one belligerent and then by the other. The 1794 treaty negotiated by John Jay of New York is an episode in the struggle of the United States to cope with these difficulties.

The United States and Great Britain by 1793 found themselves competing in commercial affairs. In an effort to secure trade for British vessels, Great Britain prohibited American vessels from carrying goods to British colonial ports. At the same time, Great Britain enjoyed a virtual monopoly of American markets for manufactured goods. Even though it became evident that Great Britain could best supply credit and merchandise to the United States, many Americans resented their economic subservience to Great Britain. The administration of President George Washington only with difficulty prevented the passage of commercial legislation designed to retaliate against alleged British discriminatory practices. The United States therefore attempted to increase its trade with France.

When war between France and Great Britain broke out in 1793, new grievances added to the old, and relations between Great Britain and the United States took a rapid turn for the worse. The position of the United States as the major maritime neutral was critical. There was also residual hostility toward Great Britain in contrast to a generally favorable attitude toward France, the United States' important military ally during the Revolutionary War.

NEUTRAL SHIPS SEIZED

The British quickly gained mastery of the oceans, which substantially isolated the French West Indies. These islands could no longer trade with France in French ships. Into this vacuum flowed the merchant fleet of the United States, which gained great profits from this opportunity. The British realized that their naval and commercial supremacy was being weakened. In November, 1793, a British Order in Council ordered British naval commanders to seize all neutral vessels trading with the French islands. So suddenly was this order implemented that approximately 250 U.S. ships were seized and about half of them condemned to be sold as lawful prizes.

Such action led to widespread anti-British opinion in the United States. James Madison, then congressman from Virginia, led a vigorous campaign to pass retaliatory legislation. Secretary of the Treasury Alexander Hamilton successfully thwarted this effort, with Washington's blessing. To blunt Madison's attack further, the president sent John Jay to London as envoy extraordinary to negotiate with the British government. Washington apparently believed that war with Britain was inevitable unless Jay, at that time chief justice of the United States, returned with an acceptable settlement.

NEGOTIATIONS AND TREATY PROVISIONS

The treaty that Jay negotiated in London struck many contemporary observers as barely acceptable. Nevertheless, parts of the agreement do show Jay's success. It required the British to surrender the military posts which they held on American soil in the Northwest Territory, by June of 1796. It also provided for the creation of a joint commission to settle the claims of British citizens for unpaid prerevolutionary U.S. debts, to settle the claims of Americans for the illegal seizures of their ships, and to determine the disputed boundary between Maine and Canada. The rest of the treaty dealt with commercial matters and was to be in force for twelve years. It stated that the "most favored nation" principle was to operate between the United States and the United Kingdom.

American vessels were promised the same privileges as British in both Great Britain and the East Indies.

Jay failed, however, to gain British acceptance of several important U.S. objectives. American trading rights with the British West Indies were so restricted that the United States struck out that part of the treaty when it was submitted to the Senate. The agreement included a broad definition of contraband, but said nothing on the important matters of the rights of visit and search and impressment. Other issues were not resolved or included. A number of these issues later contributed to the underlying causes of the War of 1812.

CONTROVERSIAL PASSAGE

The agreement was signed on November 19, 1794, in London, and Jay returned to the United States satisfied with his efforts. When the terms of the treaty became known, however, advocates of U.S. commercial rights and anti-British opinion criticized Jay for his apparent failure to obtain complete success in the London negotiations. The Republicans charged the Washington administration with selling the nation out to the British. Effigies of Jay were burned throughout the country. Political pamphleteers and journalists entered the fray.

Congress debated the controversial treaty. The Senate ratified it June 24, 1795, by a vote of 20 to 10, barely meeting the two-thirds minimum required under the Constitution. After ratification by the Senate in a strictly partisan vote (Federalists for, Republicans against), the arguments continued both in Philadelphia and elsewhere. Secretary of State Edmund Randolph was forced to resign in a scandal related to the treaty's adoption. Washington, disappointed by the unevenness of the treaty, reluctantly signed it because he believed its acceptance the only alternative to war. Only an intense effort by his administration prevented the Republicans in the House of Representatives from undercutting the treaty by their threat to refuse to appropriate the funds necessary for its implementation. The essential legislation passed the House in 1796 by a narrow margin of only three votes (51 to 48).

IMPACT

The effects of Jay's Treaty were significant. Most important, it kept the peace between the United States and Great Britain. It also induced Spain to conclude a treaty the following year (Pinckney's Treaty) that was very favorable to the United States, and it prepared the way for the large-scale settlement of the Northwest Territory. The disagreements over the treaty completed the organization of the opposition Republican Party, intensified by Jefferson's and Madison's antagonism to Hamilton and his policies. The Federalists also were divided and weakened. Washington's invulnerability to political attack was breached.

The restraining influence of the British on the Indians along the northwestern frontier was withdrawn, creating further problems in that region. Most significant, the French First Republic was incensed at this apparent repudiation by the United States of the Franco-American Treaty of 1778. While relations with Great Britain improved temporarily, the United States and France drifted apart. This rift between the only republican governments in the world culminated in an undeclared war and proved to be the dominant issue during the administration of President John Adams (1797-1801). Positive relations with Great Britain eventually deteriorated, culminating in the War of 1812.

John G. Clark,
updated by Taylor Stults

Sources for Further Study

Bemis, Samuel F. *Jay's Treaty: A Study in Commerce and Diplomacy.* 2d ed. New Haven, Conn.: Yale University Press, 1962.

Cohen, Warren, ed. *Cambridge History of American Foreign Relations.* New York: Cambridge University Press, 1993.

Combs, Jerald A. *The Jay Treaty: Political Battleground of the Founding Fathers.* Berkeley: University of California Press, 1970.

McColley, Robert, ed. *Federalists, Republicans, and Foreign Entanglements, 1789-1815.* Englewood Cliffs, N.J.: Prentice-Hall, 1969.

Monaghan, Frank. *John Jay.* 1935. Reprint. Indianapolis: Bobbs-Merrill, 1972.

Reuter, Frank T. *Trials and Triumphs: George Washington's Foreign Policy.* Fort Worth: Texas Christian University Press, 1983.

See also: Treaty of Paris (1783); Pinckney's Treaty (1795); Treaty of Monfontaine (1801); Treaty of Ghent (1814).

ELEVENTH AMENDMENT

DATE: Ratified February 7, 1795; certified January 8, 1798
U.S. STATUTES AT LARGE: 1 Stat. 402
CATEGORIES: Constitutional Law; Judiciary and Judicial Procedure

The Eleventh Amendment has been cited as the justification for many Supreme Court decisions that extend far beyond what it states overtly.

The Eleventh Amendment was the first amendment to the U.S. Constitution following the adoption of the ten original amendments known as the Bill of Rights in 1791. It reads:

> The Judicial power of the United States shall not be construed to extend to any suit in law or equity, commenced or prosecuted against one of the United States by Citizens of another State, or by Citizens or Subjects of any Foreign State.

CHISHOLM V. GEORGIA

The Eleventh Amendment was adopted specifically to overrule a Supreme Court decision, *Chisholm v. Georgia* (1793). In this decision, the Court ruled that a default judgment in favor of the plaintiff, who served as executor for the estate of a South Carolina merchant, was valid because the defendant, the state of Georgia, had refused to appear in its own defense at the trial. Georgia claimed that, as an independent and sovereign state, it enjoyed immunity from such litigation.

Article III, section 2, of the U.S. Constitution grants jurisdiction to federal courts in the case of controversies between a state and citizens of another state. In a 4-1 decision, with only justice James Iredell dissenting, the Court set a precedent by ruling that the plaintiff in *Chisholm* had the right to sue the state of Georgia and that the state of Georgia was legally remiss in not responding to that suit. Opinions by Justices John Jay and James Wilson reiterated the nationalist view that sovereignty rests in the people of the United States for the purposes of union. In regard to these purposes, Georgia, in the eyes of these justices, did not meet the criterion of being a sovereign state.

PASSAGE AND RATIFICATION

Within a year of the *Chisholm* decision, Congress, on March 4, 1794, drafted the Eleventh Amendment and urged its passage. By February, 1795, the legislatures of the requisite three-quarters of the states had ratified this amendment, which officially made it a law and a part of the U.S. Constitution. By an odd circumstance, however, the amendment was not officially declared a part of the Constitution until January 8, 1798, when President John Quincy Adams declared it so in a presidential message. The date on which the Eleventh Amendment officially became a part of the Constitution is often given as January 8, 1798, although it is now conceded that presidents play no official role in the amendment process, so the Eleventh Amendment officially became a part of the Constitution after its ratification in 1795. The only states not voting for it were Pennsylvania and New Jersey.

PROVISIONS AND COURT CASES

Under the Eleventh Amendment, federal courts are prohibited from deciding lawsuits brought against states by two specific classes of people, citizens of other states and citizens or subjects of foreign states. As time passed, however, the Eleventh Amendment was interpreted more broadly than had perhaps been originally intended by its framers.

In *New Hampshire v. Louisiana* (1883), the Supreme Court ruled that one state could not sue another state if it did so in the interests of one or more of its citizens rather than in its own interest. Shortly thereafter, in *Hans v. Louisiana* (1890), the Court held that citizens of a state could not sue their own state in the federal courts. A further extension of the Eleventh Amendment occurred in *Ex parte New York* (1921), when the Court found that the amendment applied to admiralty jurisdiction so that sovereign states, as defined by the Court, could not be sued in federal courts for events that took place in the waters that adjoined those states.

In *Monaco v. Mississippi* (1934), the Court clearly found that foreign sovereigns could not sue sovereign states of the United States in federal courts. The decision in *Edelman v. Jordan* (1974) established, again under the jurisdiction of the Eleventh Amendment, that in situations where state officials are sued and compensation for past misdeeds would have to be paid from state treasuries, the complainants cannot pursue their actions in federal courts.

EXCEPTIONS

To ensure fairness, however, certain exceptions have been made to this amendment. Although a law exists stating that parties may not bestow jurisdiction on courts, individual states may, in some situations, waive their protection under the Eleventh Amendment and consent to being sued. Congress, under the enforcement powers accorded it in the Fourteenth and Fifteenth Amendments, may approve private causes of action against states, invoking the commerce clause of the Constitution.

Perhaps no amendment to the Constitution has been interpreted as variously as the Eleventh. Some noted legal scholars have called for its restatement and simplification. Others have proposed that the amendment be interpreted literally from the forty-three words that constitute it. At present, however, citizens who have cause to take action against states must resort to political action or work within the framework of exceptions resulting from the complexities that varying interpretations of the Eleventh Amendment have evoked.

R. Baird Shuman

SOURCES FOR FURTHER STUDY

Baum, Lawrence. *The Supreme Court.* 4th ed. Washington, D.C.: Congressional Quarterly, 1991.
Orth, John V. *The Judicial Power of the United States: The Eleventh Amendment in American History.* New York: Oxford University Press, 1987.
Spaeth, Harold J. *Studies in U.S. Supreme Court Behavior.* New York: Garland, 1990.
Vile, John R. *Encyclopedia of Constitutional Amendments, Proposed Amendments, and Amending Issues, 1789-1995.* Santa Barbara, Calif: ABC-CLIO, 1996.
Wagman, Robert J. *The Supreme Court: A Citizen's Guide.* New York: Pharos Books, 1993.

SEE ALSO: Indian Gaming Regulatory Act (1988).

FORT GREENVILLE TREATY

DATE: Signed August 3, 1795
U.S. STATUTES AT LARGE: 7 Stat. 49
CATEGORIES: Native Americans; Treaties and Agreements

The Fort Greenville Treaty, combined with Jay's Treaty, served as an important benchmark in the tripartite Anglo-American-Indian struggle for control of the region between the Great Lakes and the Ohio River.

During the twenty years following the end of the American Revolution in 1783, the question of which power—American Indians, the United States, or England—would control the region between the Ohio River and the Great Lakes constituted one of the greatest challenges confronting the new government of the United States.

HISTORICAL BACKGROUND

According to the terms of the Treaty of Paris (signed on September 3, 1783), Great Britain agreed to remove its commercial and military presence from the region between the Great Lakes and the Ohio River, a region then called the Old Northwest. Notwithstanding this commitment, however, the British delayed in implementing this treaty provision. Several factors accounted for this delay, but one of the most significant was the conviction of many influential Britons that the region north of the Ohio was too strategic to surrender to the Americans. Instead, they believed that Britain should attempt to maintain at least an indirect presence in the area, thereby placing Great Britain in an advantageous position should the loosely confederated United States politically disintegrate. It was in this context that the British considered the possibility of sponsoring the creation of a British satellite or buffer state spanning the territory between the Ohio River and the Great Lakes and consisting of a confederation of Indian tribes. Thus, in the hope of promoting such an entity (there were also other reasons), London opted to maintain its commercial and military presence south of the Great Lakes. Indeed, not only did the British continue their presence at Michilimackinac, Detroit, Fort Niagara, Oswego, and other locations on American soil, but also, in 1786, British authorities issued a directive to hold or, if necessary, recapture these sites should the United States attempt to seize them.

Simultaneously, beginning in 1785, British agents actively attempted to promote the establishment of a pro-British confederation among the tribes. For their part, the Indians were extremely dissatisfied with Congress's policy toward the tribes and the northwest region generally. The Indians thought that the treaties of Forts Stanwix, McIntosh, and Finney, which had been concluded between several of the tribes and the United States government, were unfair to Indian interests. Indeed, many of the original signatory tribes had subsequently repudiated these treaties. Those tribes that had not been parties to these treaties naturally refused to abide by their terms. The treaties, however, provided the context for an infusion of American frontiersmen into the lands north of the Ohio River. The small military force that Congress had raised from the states was clearly insufficient either to prevent the frontiersmen from intruding into Indian territory or to overawe the tribes into abiding by the treaties—to say nothing about convincing them to make additional territorial concessions. Consequently, the British agents sent to promote the establishment of the Indian confederation north of the Ohio under British protection met with a receptive audience.

Finally, in 1788, the Chippewa, Delaware (Lenni Lenape), Iroquois, Miami, Ottawa, Potawatomi, Shawnee, and Wyandot (Huron) tribes formed a confederation and repudiated the treaties of Forts Stanwix, McIntosh, and Finney, agreed not to cede any additional land to the United States without the consent of the entire confederation, and demanded U.S. recognition of an Indian state between the Ohio River and the Great Lakes. This development, combined with the continued British military and commercial presence on U.S. territory south of the Great Lakes, provided London with a strong bargaining position as the United States and Great Britain opened regular diplomatic relations. Great Britain's new ambassador to the United States arrived in Philadelphia in October, 1791, with instructions from his government to agree to the evacuation of the British presence south of the Great Lakes only if the United States agreed to abide by the British interpretation of the terms of the Treaty of Paris and accepted the establishment of the Indian state, de facto under British protection, between the Ohio River and the Great Lakes.

The Washington administration totally rejected the British stance as a violation of U.S. territorial integrity and sovereignty. With only a small military force, the administration attempted to negotiate a new treaty with the Indians. In the negotiations, held at Fort Harmar in January, 1789, the territorial governor, Arthur St. Clair, capitalized on dissension among the tribes and succeeded in concluding a treaty that, while providing some compensation to the Indians, reaffirmed the boundaries established under the terms of the treaties of Forts McIntosh and Finney. By the autumn of 1789, however, war had erupted along the frontier as a result of continued Indian resentment of U.S. policy generally and the Treaty of Fort Harmar specifically, as well as the continued provocations from the American frontiersmen in Indian country.

MILITARY OPERATIONS, 1790-1794

Yielding to pressure from the westerners, the Washington administration dispatched a series of military expeditions into the wilderness north of the Ohio River. The first two of these expeditions, in October, 1790, and August-November, 1791, under the successive leadership of Josiah Harmar and St. Clair, designed to overawe the Indians and assert U.S. control over the region, yielded disastrous results. Harmar's October, 1790, expedition resulted only in the destruction of a few Miami villages along the Maumee River and the death of a small number of Indians at the cost of 75 regulars and 108 militiamen killed and another 31 wounded. Similarly, St. Clair's late summer and autumn 1791 expedition resulted in a second disastrous defeat with 623 soldiers killed and 258 wounded. Indeed, St. Clair's defeat was considered an especially significant setback in asserting U.S. sovereignty over the region north of the Ohio. Conversely, the Indians were euphoric with success and, encouraged by British expression of support for the Indian Confederation, intensified warfare against the American frontiersmen while demanding U.S. recognition of their confederation.

In the autumn of 1793, the new U.S. military commander in the Ohio Valley, Major General Anthony Wayne, initiated a new offensive against the Indians. Throughout the winter and spring of 1794, Wayne carefully launched a limited operation into Indian country. He methodically constructed a series of forts to serve both as a line of defense and as a base for a new offensive against the tribes. Moreover, his emphasis on training and his focus on troop discipline, combined with his perseverance during the harsh winter, impressed the Indians.

Meanwhile, throughout the winter, as Wayne consolidated his position, the British reinforced their policy in the Northwest. In February, 1794, the British governor in Canada told the Indians that when war between the United States and the tribes came, Britain would support the Indian attempt to regain full control over their lands. Simultaneously, the British began construction of a new post, Fort Miami, on U.S. soil along the Maumee River. The new fort was intended to solidify the British position in Indian country further as well as to provide an advance defense for the British presence at Detroit. These developments convinced the Indians that London would support them against General Wayne's army. Hence, confident of future success, the tribes assembled approximately two thousand warriors outside Fort Miami.

On June 30 and July 1, 1794, the Indians attacked Wayne's forces but were repulsed and withdrew into the wilderness along the Maumee River. On July 28, Wayne, now reinforced (bringing his total force to about thirty-five hundred men), advanced into Indian country. Although he reached the Maumee River on August 8, he delayed in assaulting the Indians until he had secured his lines of communications and established a forward base (Fort Defiance). Finally, on August 20, after a series of deceptive initiatives, Wayne surprised and defeated the Indians at the Battle of Fallen Timbers. Following the battle, the defeated Indians retreated to Fort Miami, whereupon the British refused to provide any refuge or assistance. Realizing that they had been betrayed by the British, the disillusioned Indians retired to the forest.

THE TREATIES

The dramatic change in the British policy toward the Indians reflected a larger transformation in British policy toward the United States. During the spring of 1794, the British government moved toward a rapprochement with the Americans; during the summer of 1794, negotiations were opened in Britain between the U.S. representative, John Jay, and British officials. It was in the context of this change in the complexion of Anglo-American relations that the British decided to abandon the Indians rather then precipitate a crisis on the Maumee River that could, in turn, lead to the collapse of Anglo-American negotiations before they had begun and possibly provoke a war between the two powers. Eventually, on November 19, 1794, the negotiators concluded a new treaty, Jay's Treaty, which resolved the outstanding Anglo-American disputes stemming from the 1783 Treaty of Paris. Under the terms of Jay's Treaty, London, among other things, agreed finally to evacuate the British posts on U.S. soil.

Deprived of British support, the demoralized Indians entered into new negotiations with General Wayne from a position of weakness. On August 3, 1795, Wayne and chiefs representing the Delaware, Miami, Shawnee, and Wyandot Indians and the United States delineated a demarcation separating Indian lands from those open to settlement. The line ran along the Cuyahoga River, across the portage to the Tuscarawas River, westward to Fort Recovery, and finally southward to the Ohio River across from its confluence with the Kentucky River. Hence, the U.S. government opened for settlement all of the future state of Ohio, except the north-central and northwest portions of the state, as well as opening the extreme southeastern corner of the present-day state of Indiana. In addition, the U.S. government reserved a series of specific sites within Indian country primarily for commercial and/or military purposes. Thus, as a result of the Fort Greenville Treaty and Jay's Treaty, a new balance between the Americans and the Indians was struck along the northwestern frontier. Almost immediately, however, pressure began to mount which soon challenged the supposed permanence of the Fort Greenville Treaty line, and the stage was set for the next phase in American westward expansion at the expense of the Indians.

Howard M. Hensel

SOURCES FOR FURTHER STUDY

Bemis, Samuel Flagg. *Jay's Treaty.* Rev. ed. New Haven, Conn.: Yale University Press, 1962.
Billington, Ray Allen. *Westward Expansion.* New York: Macmillan, 1949.
Kohn, Richard H. *Eagle and Sword.* New York: Free Press, 1975.
Philbrick, Francis S. *The Rise of the West, 1754-1830.* New York: Harper & Row, 1965.
Prucha, Francis Paul. *The Sword of the Republic.* New York: Macmillan, 1969.

Williams, Robert A. *Linking Arms Together: American Indian Treaty Visions of Law and Peace, 1600-1800.* New York: Oxford University Press, 1997.

See also: Treaty of Paris (1783); Fort Stanwix Treaty (1784); Ordinance of 1785 (1785); Jay's Treaty (1794).

PINCKNEY'S TREATY

Also known as: Treaty of San Lorenzo
Date: Signed October 27, 1795
Categories: Foreign Relations; Treaties and Agreements

Wars in Europe prompt Spain to recognize the United States' western boundary claims, ensuring free navigation of the Mississippi River.

The negotiation of Pinckney's Treaty clearly demonstrates how European conflicts contributed to American diplomatic success and facilitated the nation's territorial growth and expansion during its formative years. With Spain, France, and Great Britain involved in yet another series of wars during the French Revolution, the European powers found it extremely difficult to maintain control over their empires in North America. This situation was complicated by the expanding westward moving population of the United States, and Spain quickly realized that it needed to settle its dispute with the United States in the West in order to sufficiently mobilize all of their resources for the European war. Once again, as the historian Samuel Flagg Bemis concluded, the United States benefited from European distress.

SPANISH AMERICA
One of the most pressing diplomatic problems facing the United States after 1783 was Spanish occupation of, and claims to, a large portion of the southern and southwestern continent of North America. The Spanish had enjoyed undisputed possession since 1763 of the territory that had been French Louisiana. They had

also regained Florida in 1783, after Great Britain had temporarily obtained control over this region between 1763 and 1783. Spanish power rested solidly along the entire Gulf Coast of North and Central America, both banks of the Mississippi River from its mouth to a point midway between present-day Baton Rouge, Louisiana, and Natchez, Mississippi, and the west bank of the river north to the Missouri River and west to the Pacific Ocean. In addition to these vast holdings, the Spanish claimed by right of conquest during the American Revolution a large portion of the present-day states of Alabama, Mississippi, and Tennessee. In other words, Spain held or claimed both banks of the Mississippi from its mouth to the mouth of the Ohio River and east to the western slopes of the Appalachian Mountains. Yet with American settlers and commerce expanding rapidly into this disputed territory, a potentially volatile diplomatic dispute erupted between the Washington administration and Spain.

RIGHTS TO THE MISSISSIPPI

The United States had received the right to navigate the Mississippi from Great Britain in the Treaty of Paris in 1783. Since Spain, however, had not been a party to this treaty, it refused to accept this settlement and closed the Mississippi to all but Spanish commerce. This action directly threatened both the commercial and political success of the American settlers crossing the Appalachians.

In an attempt to thwart American westward expansion, the Spanish, as did the English in the north, manipulated Native American antagonism toward the settlers and encouraged Indian raids in this region. At the same time, the Spanish, intermittently schemed with dissident western Americans who were dissatisfied with the lackluster western policies of the federal government. Looking to strengthen its position within the southeastern region of North America, Madrid tried to convince the settlers to abandon their ties with the United States and form a new republic aligned with Spain. Spain was desperately seeking a face-saving solution to its problem in America due to its inability to control and manage its affairs in the region. Aggressive and lawless in nature, the frontiersmen threatened the Spanish with an invasion because of the closure of the Mississippi River and Spanish-sponsored Indian raids on American settlements.

Military conflicts, separatist sentiments, and navigation rights posed grave problems for the United States. The Washington administration, fearful over the potential establishment of an independent republic on its southern border, recognized that the right to free navigation of the river was an absolute necessity to the west, since the river was the only economically feasible route to the market. The federal government was also under pressure by western speculative interests whose landholdings suffered in value as a result of Spanish-supported Indian attacks. Washington realized that if he failed to mollify western interests, it could significantly undermine American territorial growth.

Little progress was made in solving the disputes until 1794. Until that time western intrigues, Spanish fears of a Franco-American invasion, and Indian wars were recurrent themes along the southern border. The Spanish attempted, with the aid of the American Major-General James Wilkinson and others, to stimulate disunion in the West. The Spanish, in an attempt to generate momentum for the separatist movement, opened up trade on the Mississippi to Americans on payment of a 15 percent duty. This somewhat mollified the West but failed to produce any meaningful support for separation. Then, in 1794-1795, the French revolutionary wars brought relations to a crisis. In this instance, as has often been the case throughout American history, European wars provided the United States with the opportunity of achieving a striking diplomatic victory without surrendering any of its initial demands.

NEGOTIATING WITH SPAIN
Spain had joined with Great Britain in the war against the French First Republic. In 1794-1795, when the war turned against Spain, it began to look for a way out. In 1794, even before Spain made its decision relative to the war, it indicated willingness to negotiate with the United States. As a result of this offer, President Washington dispatched Thomas Pinckney, minister to Great Britain, as envoy extraordinary and minister plenipotentiary to Madrid. Pinckney arrived in 1795, and since Spain's military position had so deteriorated that it had decided to make a separate peace with France, the delay worked to America's advantage. Spain was also apprehensive concerning John Jay's diplomatic mission to Great Britain. These negotiations convinced the Spanish foreign minister, Don Manuel de Godoy, that a possible Anglo-American rapprochement was about to take place, and that a joint attack on Spain's overseas empire might coincide with the signing of Jay's Treaty. Furthermore,

Spain was about to abrogate its alliance with Great Britain and re-enter the war allied with France. Thus Godoy feared British retaliation. Pinckney was able to capitalize on Spain's anxieties in negotiating the Treaty of San Lorenzo, or Pinckney's Treaty, signed on October 27, 1795. The Spanish conceded point after point, while the United States gave up virtually nothing in return. Spain recognized American sovereignty to the east bank of the Mississippi north of the thirty-first parallel; granted permission to Americans to navigate the river; established a place to deposit American goods for transfer to oceangoing vessels; and recognized the American definition of neutral rights. Both powers promised to restrain the Native Americans. This was a tacit admission by Spain that it had incited them in the past. In addition, the treaty did not affect the drive of westward expansion.

AMERICA'S ADVANTAGE

The Spanish implementation of the treaty came slowly. Because of Spain's unfavorable situation in Europe, however, Godoy's government had little choice but to acquiesce to Washington's demands. Spain pulled out of the disastrous war with the French First Republic in the secret Treaty of Basel in 1795. The following year, in the secret Treaty of San Ildefonso, Spain plunged into an equally disastrous war as an ally of the French against Great Britain. With Spain preoccupied with the war in Europe, the United States emerged from Pinckney's negotiations completely victorious. Thus, as Samuel Flagg Bemis concluded, this treaty represents an excellent example of how "America's advantage" resulted from "Europe's distress."

For the second time the possibility of an Anglo-American alliance against Spain compelled Spain to placate the United States. The Treaty of San Lorenzo was executed in full by 1798. In negotiating the Treaty of Greenville (1795) with the Indians, Jay's Treaty, and Pinckney's Treaty, the Washington administration had achieved much in the field of diplomacy. The separatist movement was dead, and the West was secured to the Union.

John G. Clark, updated by
Robert D. Ubriaco, Jr.

SOURCES FOR FURTHER STUDY

Bemis, Samuel Flagg. *Pinckney's Treaty: A Study of America's Advantage from Europe's Distress.* Baltimore: The Johns Hopkins University Press, 1926.

Darling, Arthur B. *Our Rising Empire, 1763-1803.* New Haven, Conn.: Yale University Press, 1940.

Deconde, Alexander. *Entangling Alliances: Politics and Diplomacy Under George Washington.* Durham, N.C.: Duke University Press, 1958.

Tucker, Robert W., and David C. Hendrickson. *Empire of Liberty: The Statecraft of Thomas Jefferson.* New York: Oxford University Press, 1990.

Young, Raymond A. "Pinckney's Treaty: A New Perspective." *Hispanic American Historical Review* 43, no. 4 (1963): 526-535.

SEE ALSO: Treaty of Paris (1783); Jay's Treaty (1794); Treaty of Monfontaine (1801); Treaty of Ghent (1814); Adams-Onís Treaty (1819); Treaty of Guadalupe Hidalgo (1848).

ALIEN AND SEDITION ACTS

DATE: 1798: June 18 (Naturalization Act); June 25 (Alien Act); July 6 (Alien Enemies Act); July 14 (Sedition Act)

U.S. STATUTES AT LARGE: 1 Stat. 566 (Naturalization Act), 1 Stat. 570 (Alien Act), 1 Stat. 577 (Alien Enemies Act), 1 Stat. 596 (Sedition Act)

CATEGORIES: Immigration; Speech and Expression

The four laws collectively known as the Alien and Sedition Acts—the Alien Act, the Alien Enemies Act, the Naturalization Act, and the Sedition Act—were ostensibly passed to avoid war with France but led to a debate regarding the function of the Bill of Rights during wartime, the role of the federal government in legislating for the states, and the process of judicial review.

News of the XYZ affair—in which three French officials had demanded a bribe from Americans during during negotiations between the two countries to forestall war—descended upon the

American people and their representatives in Congress like a thunderbolt. It galvanized the government into action on the high seas; it helped unite Americans against the French, just as the initial news of British seizures had united them against Great Britain; it seriously weakened the infant Republican Party, which was associated with Francophilism; and it firmly entrenched the Federalists in power. Even President John Adams, for a time, seemed to relish the thought of leading the United States against its newest antagonist, but Adams regained his sense of moderation in time to prevent a catastrophe. The same cannot be said of certain elements of the Federalist Party, which exploited the explosive situation to strike out at their political opponents.

FEDERALISTS AND FOREIGN AFFAIRS

The Federalist Party, or at least its old guard, deeply resented gains made by the Republican opposition. Many of the Federalist leaders resented the very existence of the other political party. The High Federalists were by no means committed to a two-party system and rejected the idea of a loyal opposition. With the Republican tide at low ebb, these Federalists intended to strike a killing blow at two sources of Republican strength: the immigrant vote and the manipulation of public opinion through the use (and abuse) of the press. In selecting these targets, the Federalists demonstrated an acute awareness of the impact of the press on the growth of political parties, and they intended to use their political power to muzzle the Republican press, while leaving the Federalist press intact. Furthermore, Federalists expressed a deep xenophobia, as they viewed people of foreign birth as threats to the fabric of ordered liberty they believed the Federalists had built and must preserve.

Many Federalists had a long history of antiforeign sentiment. With the United States on the verge of war with France, the Federalists were apprehensive over the loyalty of thousands of French West Indian refugees who had flocked to the United States in an effort to escape the ferment of the French Revolution and its accompanying "Terror." The Federalists were further concerned by the fact that the refugees who became U.S. citizens generally aligned themselves with the Republican Party. Much the same was true of the Irish, who supported anyone who opposed the English. Such conditions threatened the continued hold of the Federalists on political power in the national government. To deal with such potential subversives, foreign and domestic, the Federalist-controlled Congress passed a series of four acts, known collectively as the Alien and Sedition Acts.

THE ACTS

Three of the acts dealt specifically with aliens or immigrants. The Sedition Act declared speech or writing with the intent to defame the president or Congress to be a misdemeanor. The Alien Act permitted the president to deport allegedly dangerous aliens during times of peace. Neither act was enforced, however. The Naturalization Act struck at the immigrant vote. Previously, aliens could become naturalized citizens after residing for five years in the United States. The new act raised the probationary period to fourteen years.

The Sedition Act was by far the most notorious. It imposed heavy fines and imprisonment as punishment on all those found guilty of writing, publishing, or speaking against the federal government. By allowing a defendant to prove the truth of statements as a defense, the Sedition Act was a definite improvement over the English laws of sedition libel. The fact remains, however, that its intent was the repression of political opposition and the annoying Republican press, and the Sedition Act seemed plainly to ignore the First Amendment. Under the law, suits were initiated against the editors of eight major opposition presses. The principal target was the Philadelphia *Aurora*, whose editor, William Duane, was prosecuted under the act. Congressman Matthew Lyon of Vermont received a jail sentence of four months and was fined one thousand dollars for disparaging remarks he made about President Adams. Some of these suits gave a comic air to the gross abuse of power. One gentleman was fined one hundred dollars for wishing out loud that the wadding of a salute cannon would strike President Adams in his backside.

IMPACT AND OPPOSITION

Republican opposition to these laws was immediate. Vice President Thomas Jefferson, himself a Republican, believed that the Alien and Sedition Acts were designed to be used against such leading Republicans as the Swiss-born congressman from Pennsylvania, Albert Gallatin. Republicans were convinced that the Sedition Act was designed to destroy them as an organized political party. The act had passed the House strictly along sectional-party lines. The vote was 44 to 41, with only two affirmative votes coming from south of the Potomac River, where the Republicans were strongest.

From the Federalist point of view, the acts were completely unsuccessful in suppressing the opposition. They were resented by many, and it soon became obvious even to those who first supported the new laws that they were as unnecessary as they were ineffective. The handful of "subversives" prosecuted under the Sedition Act hardly compensated for the fact that its existence gave the Republicans another campaign issue. Jefferson through the Kentucky legislature, and Madison through the Virginia legislature, penned immediate responses to the Alien and Sedition Acts. These remonstrances, known as the Virginia and Kentucky Resolves, aroused little enthusiasm at the time but did point out not only some of the basic principles of the Republican Party but also some striking differences between two streams of thought within the party.

Both resolutions maintained that the Constitution was a compact between sovereign states that granted to the federal government certain narrowly defined powers, while retaining all other enumerated powers. If the states created the Constitution, they had the power to decide when the federal government had overstepped its proper bounds. Jefferson, in the Kentucky Resolves, went much further than Madison in assigning to the states the power to nullify a federal law—to declare it inoperable and void within the boundaries of a state. South Carolina was to do so in 1832, when it nullified the Tariff of 1828. The Virginia and Kentucky Resolves had no immediate effect, but they had spelled out the theoretical position that those advocating states' rights could, and ultimately did, take.

The Alien and Sedition Acts took their place among a growing list of grievances against the Federalist Party. The Alien Act expired in 1800 and the Sedition Act in the following year. The Naturalization Act was repealed by the Republican-controlled Congress in 1802. The only tangible effect of these measures was to contribute to the defeat of Federalism in 1800. However, the mood that led to their passage was to return in later days.

John G. Clark, updated by
Edward R. Crowther

SOURCES FOR FURTHER STUDY

Elkins, Stanley, and Eric McKitrick. *The Age of Federalism: The Early American Republic, 1788-1800.* New York: Oxford University Press, 1993.

McCoy, Drew R. *The Elusive Republic: Political Economy in Jefferson's America.* Chapel Hill: University of North Carolina Press, 1980.

Miller, John C. *Crisis in Freedom: The Alien and Sedition Acts.* Boston: Little, Brown, 1951.

Sharp, James Roger. *American Politics in the Early Republic: The New Nation in Crisis.* New Haven, Conn.: Yale University Press, 1993.

Smith, James Morton. *Freedom's Fetters: The Alien and Sedition Laws and American Civil Liberties.* Ithaca, N.Y.: Cornell University Press, 1966.

SEE ALSO: Sedition Act of 1798 (1798); Force Act of 1833 (1833).

SEDITION ACT OF 1798

DATE: July 14, 1798
U.S. STATUTES AT LARGE: 1 Stat. 596
CATEGORIES: Speech and Expression

Federal statute enacted in 1798 that made interference or attempted interference with operations of the U.S. government a crime, criminalized oral and written utterances that tended to bring the government into disrepute, and liberalized the common law of seditious libel.

Among the 1978 laws that came to be known as the Alien and Sedition Acts, one, the Sedition Act, stands out for its historical significance and later impact. The Sedition Act had three substantive sections.

PROVISIONS

Section 1, the least controversial, provided that opposition to governmental operations or antigovernment conspiracies could be punished by fines up to five thousand dollars and confinement between six months to five years.

Section 2, the most controversial, codified the common law of seditious libel. It penalized certain kinds of political speech and permitted criminal prosecution for "knowingly and willingly" writing, publishing, or uttering statements that were "false, scandalous, and malicious" with the intent to defame the government, Congress, or president or to bring them into disrepute. Statements that turned people against the government or that promoted opposition to the nation's laws were likewise actionable. Conviction allowed imprisonment for up to two years and a maximum fine of two thousand dollars.

Section 3 liberalized seditious libel procedures. Under the common law, libel charges against the government were actionable if they tended to disturb the public peace or create animosities. Prosecutors had to prove publication and bad tendency to secure convictions. The common law allowed truth as a defense to private libel but not to libel aimed at the government or public officials. The reformed procedures provided that juries, not judges, decided issues of publication and bad tendency. Judges continued to charge juries and explain the law, but juries decided the facts and the law and judged a statement's truth or falsity. These procedural reforms shifted decision making from judges to juries.

EARLY VIEWS

The Supreme Court never ruled directly on the Sedition Act, but from its enactment to its expiration in March, 1801, justices riding on circuit upheld the measure, some heartily. Chief Justice Oliver Ellsworth believed it limited the dangers that the national government confronted. Associate Justice Samuel Chase was the Court's most ardent defender of the measure. In cases against James T. Callendar and Thomas Cooper, prominent Antifederalist writers, Chase was, in essence, more a prosecutor than a neutral justice. Chase's overzealous involvement in Sedition Act cases was reflected in several charges in the articles of impeachment brought against him in 1804 by the House of Representatives. Justices William Cushing, William Paterson, and Bushrod Washington all warmly endorsed the act. Like Chase, they informed juries that it was constitutional and encouraged convictions.

Jeffersonian Republicans (also referred to as Democratic-Republicans) opposed the act from the outset and fought vigorously for its repeal in 1799, but failed. They insisted that it violated the freedom of speech and press clauses of the First Amendment and secured resolutions to that effect from the legislatures of Virginia and Kentucky. After becoming president, Thomas Jefferson pardoned those who had been convicted under the act and remitted some fines, stating that the act was unconstitutional. In 1840 Congress agreed and repaid the remaining Federalist-imposed fines.

LATER VIEWS

In a well-known dissent to *Abrams v. United States* (1919), Associate Justice Oliver Wendell Holmes wrote, "I had conceived that the United States through many years had shown its repentance for the Sedition Act." Louis D. Brandeis joined his dissent. Some thirty years later, in a dissenting opinion in *Beauharnais v. Illinois* (1952), Associate Justice Robert H. Jackson, chief prosecutor in the Nuremberg War Crimes trial, observed that the enactment of the Sedition Act had come to be viewed as "a breach of the First Amendment." Continuing, he wrote that "even in the absence of judicial condemnation, the political disapproval of the Sedition Act was so emphatic and sustained that federal prosecution of the press ceased for a century."

The Sedition Act met considerable condemnation in the latter half of the twentieth century. In *New York Times Co. v. Sullivan* (1964), Justice William J. Brennan, Jr., noted that "although the Sedition Act was never tested in this Court, the attack upon its validity has carried the day in the court of history." Associate Justices Hugo L. Black and William O. Douglas concurred in Brennan's judgment that the court of history condemned the act. They noted that it had "an ignominious end and by common consent has generally been treated as having been a wholly unjustifiable and much to be regretted violation of the First Amendment." In a concurring opinion in *Garrison v. Louisiana* (1964), Douglas and Black quoted Holmes's 1919 observation that the nation had repented for having passed the act. A decade later, they reiterated their contempt for the 1798 measure in *Gertz v. Robert Welch* (1974), noting that it was a congressional attempt to "muzzle" the First Amendment, "a regrettable legislative exercise plainly in violation of the First Amendment."

FREEDOM VS. UNITY

In *Sullivan,* Brennan summarized not only the modern view of the act but also the classic reason for conflicting views about its constitutionality. Brennan wrote, "Thus we consider this case against the background of a profound national commitment to the principle that debate on public issues should be uninhibited, robust and wide-open, and that it may well include vehement, caustic, and sometimes unpleasantly sharp attacks on government and public officials." Although Brennan severely criticized the act and praised Jefferson for pardoning those sentenced under it, his method of interpretation comports well with that of both the Federalists and Democratic-Republicans in the early national era. National commitments were central to Brennan and those who supported or opposed the act during its short life. Expressive freedoms were not ends in themselves but served broad national commitments. When those commitments changed, interpretations of the freedom of speech and press clauses changed.

The Federalists and Democratic-Republicans had different commitments and dramatically different notions about speech and press functions. Both parties had a keen pride of accomplishment in winning the American Revolution and securing the Constitution. However, each viewed itself as the true revolutionary heir, and in the 1790's, they accused each other of deliberately squandering dearly won freedoms embodied in the Constitution. Each came perilously close to thinking of the other as an illegitimate faction, animated by a party spirit that threatened to undermine the benefits that the Revolution had secured. It seemed clear that if the other party threatened the nation, it should be suppressed. They agreed that limitations on expressive freedoms were instrumental to preserving the Revolution and protecting the Constitution but split decisively over which level of government was responsible for protecting the nation from illegitimate factions.

The Federalists passed the politically inspired Sedition Act in an attempt to suppress the Democratic-Republicans. Federalist prosecutors targeted only Democratic-Republican editors, newspapers, and party leaders, enforcing the act most vigorously just before the election of 1800 in order to dampen attacks by the opposition party and to maintain control of the national government. In all, twenty-four or twenty-five individuals were arrested for violating the act. At least fifteen were indicted, and of the eleven who went to trial, ten were convicted. Because Supreme Court justices accepted the Federalist position, they upheld the act's constitutionality.

In the early nineteenth century, after Jefferson became president, Democratic-Republicans—sometimes with Jefferson's approval, if not urging—prosecuted Federalist editors. Like their Federalist counterparts, Democratic-Republican prosecutors targeted political speech. Neither party tried to curb completely the other's speech. Prosecutions were intermittent, inconsistent, and unpredictable. Each party used law to create a legal environment that forced the other to be self-censoring; if self-censorship was glaringly ineffective, prosecutors might spring into action.

THE TWO-PARTY SYSTEM

Americans of the early national era believed they had good but fragile institutions, worthy of careful nurturing. Federalists and Democratic-Republicans felt obligated to shield the nation from unwarranted partisan attacks and to preserve revolutionary gains by limiting the other party's expressive freedom. In essence, the two parties bitterly contested the legitimacy of competing parties. They agreed that the other's licentious speech needed curbing but split over whether the national or state governments should impose the limits. In *Dennis v. United States* (1951), Associate Justice Felix Frankfurter noted that the central issue in the case was federalism rather than free speech or press. Jefferson, he wrote, had not condemned the Sedition Act because it limited political speech but because he thought states, not Congress, had "the right to enforce restrictions on speech."

By the end of the 1820's Americans believed that competing parties were a logical analog to the Constitution; parties gave an additional method of checking power. When one party put forth a program or set of policies, the competing party sponsored an alternative and thus acted as a check on the first party. As the party system gained legitimacy, the need for restraints on speech and press, such as those in the Sedition Act, disappeared. In the twentieth century, the Court consistently condemned the Sedition Act; however, it sustained restrictions on expressive freedoms when, as the Federalists believed in the 1790's, a good society with decent institutions was under unwarranted assault.

Lester G. Lindley

SOURCES FOR FURTHER STUDY

Berns, Walter. "Freedom of the Press and the Alien and Sedition Laws: A Reappraisal." *Supreme Court Review* (1970): 109-159.

Costa, Gregg. "John Marshall, the Sedition Act, and Free Speech in the Early Republic." *Texas Law Review* 77 (1999): 1011-1047.

Elkins, Stanley, and Eric McKitrick. *The Age of Federalism: The Early American Republic, 1788-1800.* New York: Oxford University Press, 1993.

Hofstadter, Richard. *The Idea of a Party System: The Rise of Legitimate Opposition in the United States, 1780-1840.* Berkeley: University of California Press, 1970.

Levy, Leonard W. *Emergence of a Free Press.* New York: Oxford University Press, 1985.

_____. *Freedom of Speech and Press in Early American History.* Cambridge, Mass.: Harvard University Press, 1960.

McCoy, Drew R. *The Elusive Republic: Political Economy in Jefferson's America.* Chapel Hill: University of North Carolina Press, 1980.

Miller, John C. *Crisis in Freedom: The Alien and Sedition Acts.* Boston: Little, Brown, 1951.

Sharp, James Roger. *American Politics in the Early Republic: The New Nation in Crisis.* New Haven, Conn.: Yale University Press, 1993.

Smith, James Morton. *Freedom's Fetters: The Alien and Sedition Laws and American Civil Liberties.* Ithaca, N.Y.: Cornell University Press, 1966.

Stevens, John D. "Congressional History of the 1798 Sedition Law." *Journalism Quarterly* 13 (Summer, 1966): 247-256.

SEE ALSO: First Amendment (1789); Alien and Sedition Acts (1798).

JUDICIARY ACTS OF 1801-1925

DATE: February 13, 1801; April 10, 1869; March 3, 1891; February 13, 1925

U.S. STATUTES AT LARGE: 2 Stat. 89 (1801); 16 Stat. 44 (1869); 26 Stat. 826 (1891); 42 Stat. 936 (1925)

CATEGORIES: Judiciary and Judicial Procedure

These laws established the number of justices who sit on the Supreme Court, created federal courts other than the Supreme Court, and defined jurisdictions of all federal courts, including, except for what is constitutionally mandated, the Supreme Court. The Judiciary Acts changed required review of cases by the Supreme Court to discretionary review, eliminating routine appeals affecting only individual litigants and allowing the Court to deal with those cases in which the decisions are of wide public significance.

The status of the federal judiciary in the beginning of the nineteenth century was determined by the first Judiciary Act, enacted on September 24, 1789, in the first session of Congress. According to the act, the Supreme Court was to consist of a chief justice and five associate justices. Each justice, in addition to Supreme Court duties, was required to serve as circuit judge in one of the three judicial circuits that ran the length of the Eastern seaboard. These circuit courts had original jurisdiction in some cases, which meant that they acted as the court of the first instance or the trial court. The circuit courts also had appellate jurisdiction in that they heard appeals on some cases from the federal district courts.

Riding the circuit immediately proved to be burdensome. Great distances needed to be covered as the court traveled from district to district within the several states that comprised the circuit. At the time, travel conditions were primitive and the health of some justices precluded it. The dual role as a circuit judge also created an anomaly in that an justice might decide a case as circuit judge and then have to decide it again if it was appealed to the Supreme Court.

JUDICIARY ACT OF 1801

In February, 1801, the outgoing Federalist Congress passed the Judiciary Act of 1801. Six new circuit courts were created to be staffed by newly appointed judges. The Supreme Court justices were relieved of their circuit court duties and the number of Supreme Court justices reduced to five. President John Adams, whose term of office was expiring in a few weeks, quickly made the judicial appointments, which were speedily confirmed by the Senate. This law was widely viewed by the incoming administration of President Thomas Jefferson as a ploy by his political opponents to name a new group of federal judges and protect the Supreme Court from any immediate change through an appointment made by Jefferson. Consequently, the repeal of the Judiciary Act of 1801 was one of the first items of legislative action of the incoming Congress and was passed on March 8, 1802. The Supreme Court justices therefore had to resume their roles as circuit judges, a job that was not eliminated until 1891.

Because of population growth, especially in Ohio, Kentucky, and Tennessee, an additional justice was added to the Supreme Court in 1807, bringing the total to seven. The next significant legislation was the Judiciary Act of 1837, which created three new judicial circuits and added two justices to the Supreme Court. This enabled President Andrew Jackson to make two appointments and ensured the domination of the Court by Southern Democrats. In 1863 President Abraham Lincoln secured passage of legislation to add a tenth seat to the court. Although the appointment of a tenth justice could on the surface be justified because of the creation of a circuit court for California and Oregon, Lincoln sought a majority on the Court in support of his war policies, a group that would uphold the constitutionality of his war powers. Such political maneuvering continued after Lincoln's assassination. His successor, President Andrew Johnson, was anathema to the Radical Republican leadership in Congress. To prevent Johnson from nominating any Supreme Court justices, in 1867 Congress reduced the number of justices on the Court from ten to seven.

JUDICIARY ACT OF 1869

The election of popular war hero Ulysses S. Grant to the presidency in 1868 eliminated the reason for the reduction of justices, and the membership of the Court was increased to nine justices in the Judiciary Act of 1869. The act also alleviated some of the circuit court duties of the Supreme Court justices. A separate circuit court judiciary was established consisting of one circuit court judge for each of the nine circuit court districts that now existed. The Supreme Court justices still had circuit court responsibilities, but they now had to attend circuit court proceedings only once every two years.

Until 1869, Supreme Court justices did not receive retirement benefits, which meant that a number of justices who found it difficult to carry out their duties because of age or disability hesitated to submit their resignations. This problem was partly remedied by the 1869 act, which provided that any federal judge or justice who attained the age of seventy with at least ten years of service could resign and continue to receive the same salary for life.

A problem not addressed by the 1869 act was the increasing caseload of the Court. From the end of the Civil War to the 1890's, it was not unusual for a case to be on the docket for two or three years before it could be argued before the Court. Litigants had the right to appeal a decision of a lower federal court to the Supreme Court, which was required to decide the appeal. It was not until the enactment of legislation in 1891 and later in 1925 that the hearing of most appeals would be made discretionary for the Court.

CIRCUIT COURT OF APPEALS ACT OF 1891

Chief Justice Melville W. Fuller, an energetic and able administrator, put the weight of his office behind court reform. He cultivated the important members of the Senate Judiciary Committee and convinced them of the need for reform. He was advised that the committee members would like recommendations from the justices. The justices, in a report prepared by Justice Horace Gray, recommended the establishment of circuit courts of appeals. Because the Supreme Court justices would not be expected to sit in the new courts, it would relieve them of circuit duty.

Senator George F. Edmunds, a key member of the Judiciary Committee, introduced a bill designed to relieve docket congestion in the Supreme Court and to eliminate the circuit court obligations of its justices. The Circuit Court of Appeals Act of 1891 created the U.S. circuit courts of appeals, intermediate appellate courts, to hear appeals from the federal district courts and the federal circuit courts. The circuit courts of appeals were to consist of three justices appointed to each of the nine judicial regions or districts. The act eliminated the circuit riding responsibilities of the Supreme Court justices. The old circuit courts that existed after 1789 were not abrogated by this legislation but were abolished in 1911.

The 1891 act also reduced direct appeals to the Supreme Court from the lower federal courts. The decisions of the circuit courts of appeals would be final except in certain cases such as those involving constitutional issues, capital crimes, jurisdictional issues, and those cases in which different circuit courts of appeals ruled differently on the same point of law.

JUDICIARY ACT OF 1925

A committee of justices set up by Chief Justice William H. Taft became actively engaged in promoting court reform to relieve the Court's congested docket. The Judiciary Act of 1925 was largely the result of the Court's efforts.

According to Justice Taft, the philosophy of the 1925 act was to ensure that the rights of each litigant were protected by the court of the first instance and the trial court, and if still aggrieved, be given one review by an intermediate court of appeal. The function of the Supreme Court was not to remedy the wrongs of particular litigants on appeal on a case-by-case basis but to consider those cases involving principles in which the application would be of wide public significance.

The act sharply curtailed appeals of right made to the Court. Decisions of the circuit courts of appeals could be appealed only if the appeals court found a state law invalid under the Constitution or because of a federal law or treaty. In such cases, review was limited to the federal question involved. From state courts, the only appeals of right were in cases where a state law was upheld despite a constitutional challenge or where a federal law or treaty was held invalid by the state court. Having eliminated most of the cases that it was heretofore required to review, the makeup of the Court's docket became largely a discretionary matter. This discretion was exercised by any four of the justices agreeing to issue a writ of certiorari so that a case could be heard and decided by the Court. This transformed the Court from a mere tribunal of the last resort to an institution with the ability to form social policy equal to or beyond that of the executive or legislative branch

Gilbert T. Cave

SOURCES FOR FURTHER STUDY

Baum, Lawrence. *The Supreme Court.* Washington, D.C.: Congressional Quarterly, 1981.

Biskupic, Joan, and Elder Witt. *Supreme Court at Work.* Washington, D.C.: Congressional Quarterly, 1997.

Foster, Roger. *The Federal Judiciary Acts of 1875 and 1887, with an Appendix Containing the Equity Rules.* New York:: L. K. Strouse, 1887.

Freund, Paul A., ed. *Supreme Court of the United States.* 11 vols. New York: Macmillan, 1971.

Marcus, Maeva, ed. *Origins of the Federal Judiciary.* New York, Oxford University Press, 1982.
Paddock, Lisa. *Facts About the Supreme Court.* New York: H. W. Wilson, 1996.
Schwartz, Bernard. *A History of the Supreme Court.* New York: Oxford University Press, 1993.
Witt, Elder, ed. *Guide to the U.S. Supreme Court.* Washington, D.C.: Congressional Quarterly, 1979.

SEE ALSO: Judiciary Act of 1789 (1789); Eleventh Amendment (1798); Removal Act (1875)

TREATY OF MONFONTAINE

ALSO KNOWN AS: Treaty of Mortefontaine; Convention of 1800
DATE: Ratified December 21, 1801
CATEGORIES: Foreign Relations; Treaties and Agreements

Among the earliest of American foreign treaties, the Treaty of Monfontaine preserved relations with the French as the United States maneuvered to ensure its independence from Great Britain.

In 1777, Americans, fighting the British for their independence, asked France for assistance, which France granted. Worried that support for America would lead to war with England, France insisted that America commit itself to mutual defense in return for military support, supplies, preferred trading status in French ports, and direct loans to the American treasury. The agreement came to be known as the Franco-American Treaty of 1778.

While vital to victory over the British, the treaty with France restricted America's efforts to create an independent foreign policy after the war. First, the war with England ended after the victory at Yorktown in 1781, but until England and France settled their differences America officially remained at war. Second, the French believed that their granting of preferred trading status to America gave the French a monopoly on American trade, and American at-

141

tempts to establish economic and diplomatic contacts with England after the Revolution suffered accordingly. Last, the treaty language implied that the treaty was in effect for perpetuity, a condition that became troublesome when the French Revolution and the subsequent European wars threatened to include the United States.

In 1793, France, under Napoleon Bonaparte, was entering a war with Great Britain and many of its European neighbors that would last until 1815. The effect of the older American-French alliance was placing pressures on the young American republic, and in 1794 the American negotiator John Jay arranged a treaty between the United States and Great Britain. The new treaty strained the relationship between France and the United States. The French, feeling betrayed by its American ally's signing treaties with its English enemy, responded by seizing U.S. vessels as economic retaliation.

While unhappy with the French action, President John Adams was unwilling to abrogate the French treaty that protected America from British dominance. Instead of a direct war with France, Adams initiated an undeclared conflict, since known as the Quasi War. French and American warships fired upon each other and seized any opposition merchant vessels they encountered. After three years in inconclusive conflict, both sides sought to end the struggle. France was again at war with its European neighbors, and President Adams's popularity had suffered in an election year. Therefore, the French proved receptive when Adams offered to end the Quasi War and redefine the Franco-American agreement of 1778, and Adams dispatched William Vans Murray to negotiate the American position.

Murray insisted on two points: financial compensation for the American ships captured during the Quasi War and an end to the mutual defense portion of the 1778 treaty. France countered that Americans could not have it both ways: America had to have a treaty (and hence diplomatic relations) with France to demand compensation, or America could demand compensation after reaffirming the 1778 treaty. Murray agreed to drop the issue of compensation in order to assure future American diplomatic freedom.

The terms of the subsequent Treaty of Monfontaine formally ended the Quasi War, guaranteed the return of all captured merchant vessels, voided any American claim to financial compensation, and formally ended the mutual defense agreement from

1778. Each side granted open trade to the other with no preferred status. While losing the economic benefits of preferred trade with France, the United States, through the Treaty of Monfontaine, was guaranteed economic and diplomatic freedom with England, which proved far more beneficial in the long term.

Steven J. Ramold

SOURCES FOR FURTHER STUDY
McCullough, David G. *John Adams.* New York: Simon and Schuster, 2001.
Stagg, John C. *Mr. Madison's War: Politics, Diplomacy, and Warfare in the Early American Republic.* Princeton, N.J.: Princeton University Press, 1983.

SEE ALSO: Treaty of Paris (1783); Jay's Treaty (1794); Pinckney's Treaty (1795); Embargo Acts (1806-1807); Treaty of Ghent (1814).

BLACK CODES OF 1804-1807

DATE: 1804, 1807
CATEGORIES: African Americans; Civil Rights and Liberties; Slavery

These Ohio laws denied civil rights to African Americans and discouraged black immigration to that state.

The Northwest Territory was established in 1787 and ultimately became the states of Ohio, Indiana, Michigan, Illinois, and Wisconsin. In 1800, what was to become the state of Ohio separated from the rest of the territory. Two years later, Ohio elected delegates to a constitutional convention in preparation for a statehood petition, which was approved in 1803.

SLAVERY IN OHIO?
Although the Northwest Ordinance of 1787 prohibited slavery in that territory, Ohio's constitutional convention debated the issue

during its sessions. With the slaveholding states of Virginia on Ohio's eastern boundary and Kentucky on its southern boundary, there was considerable pressure for Ohio to recognize slavery. Many of the immigrants to Ohio came from slave states and saw nothing evil in the system. While many southern Ohioans did not object to slavery, persons in the northern part of the state were more likely to oppose it. Immigrants from New England, New York, and Pennsylvania tended to accept the concepts of the Enlightenment, as expressed in Thomas Paine's *The Rights of Man* (1791-1792) and the Declaration of Independence, which proclaimed the concepts of liberty and equality for all people. Northern Ohioans, many of whom had little contact with African Americans, usually opposed slavery from an idealistic perspective. Thus, a geographic division with regard to slavery existed within the state from the first.

Delegates at Ohio's 1802 constitutional convention debated several questions that focused on African Americans. Should slavery be permitted in Ohio? If slavery were prohibited, what about indentured servitude? Regardless of the outcome of those two discussions, the place of African Americans in the new state needed to be defined: Should they be allowed to vote? Should they be granted civil rights? Should they be encouraged to emigrate to Ohio? Should their immigration to the state be discouraged?

Edward Tiffin, from Virginia, was president of the convention. Before leaving Virginia, he had freed his slaves. He did not necessarily support the concept of equal rights for African Americans, however. When there was a tie in the vote on granting African Americans the right to vote, Tiffin cast the deciding ballot against it. There was no strong feeling for instituting slavery in Ohio; there was, however, strong opinion in favor of limited rights for African Americans.

AFRICAN AMERICANS IN OHIO

When the constitutional convention, held in Chillicothe, began on November 1, there were approximately five hundred African Americans in the Ohio territory, representing approximately 10 percent of the population. None of them was represented in the constitutional convention, however, because none could meet the property qualifications required for voting. After a major debate over allowing African Americans to vote, it was decided not to delete the word "white" from the qualifications for the franchise. Nevertheless, the African American population grew from five hundred in 1800 to nearly two thousand by 1810; it is probable that most of the growth occurred before the passage of the first Black Laws.

THE 1804 LAW

Former Southerners living in Ohio were responsible for the Black Codes. In 1804, the legislature debated and passed the first of these laws, "An Act to Regulate Black and Mulatto Persons." The intent of this legislation was clearly to discourage African Americans from moving into Ohio and to encourage those already there to leave. Many delegates from areas near Virginia and Kentucky undoubtedly acted based on their geographic location. Ohio shared a 375-mile border with those two states, and many legislators did not want to see a mass migration of African Americans to Ohio. Early Ohioans generally rejected slavery, but not strongly enough to protest against it. At the same time, they opposed African Americans living in Ohio as free citizens.

The law, which went into force in January, 1804, had several provisions designed to control African Americans. First, no African American or mulatto could settle in Ohio without a certificate of freedom from a United States court. African Americans or mulattoes already residing in Ohio had until June 1 to produce such a certificate. Certificates cost twelve and one-half cents each, and were required of children as well as adults. It was a criminal offense for a white to employ, for more than one hour, an African American or mulatto who did not have the appropriate certificate. The fine was at least ten dollars but not more than fifty dollars for each offense, with half the money going to the informant. An additional fifty cents a day had to be paid to the African American's owner; the law assumed that a black or mulatto who did not have a certificate must be a slave. Penalties for aiding a fugitive from slavery remained the same, but the fine for assisting a fugitive slave attempting to escape from the state could be as much as one hundred dollars.

Again, the vote was split, with those in the northern half of the state opposed to the restrictions on African Americans and delegates from the south of Ohio supporting them. The bill passed in the House by a vote of 19 to 8 and in the Senate by a vote of 9 to 5, although the geographic lines in the Senate were not as clearly drawn as they were in the House.

THE 1807 LAW

A few years later, an even stronger bill to restrict African Americans was presented in the Senate. In its final version, it forbade African Americans from settling in Ohio unless they could present a five-hundred-dollar bond and an affidavit signed by two white men that attested to their good character. Fines for helping a fugitive slave were doubled. Finally, no African American could testify against a white in court. While there is no record of the vote in the Senate, the bill passed the House twenty to nine and became law in January, 1807.

However restrictive the original Black Codes were, the new law was far worse. African Americans were stripped of legal protection and placed at the mercy of whites. Whites did not need to fear being tried for offenses against African Americans unless there was a white witness who would testify. There is evidence of at least one African American being murdered by whites, with only African American witnesses to the crime. African American witnesses could not provide evidence against a white assailant. Even if a case went to court, it would be heard by an all-white jury before a white judge. African American victims could not testify on their own behalf, because of the restrictions against providing testimony against whites. Because they could not vote, African Americans could neither change nor protest these laws.

THE CODES' FATE

While the Black Codes of 1804 and 1807 were enforced only infrequently, they still were the law and were a constant reminder that African Americans in Ohio had only the barest minimum of human and civil rights, and that those rights existed only at the whim of white society. The laws fell into disuse and finally were repealed in 1849, long after the abolitionist movement, with its western center located in Oberlin, Ohio, was well under way, and long after the Underground Railroad had opened several stations in Ohio.

Duncan R. Jamieson

SOURCES FOR FURTHER STUDY

Bell, Howard H. "Some Reform Interests of the Negro During the 1850's As Reflected in State Conventions." *Phylon* 21, no. 2 (1960): 173-181.

Erickson, Leonard. "Politics and the Repeal of Ohio's Black Laws, 1837-1849." *Ohio History* 82, nos. 3/4 (1973): 154-175.
Franklin, John Hope. *From Slavery to Freedom.* New York: McGraw-Hill, 1994.
Knepper, George W. *Ohio and Its People.* Kent, Ohio: Kent State University Press, 1989.
Rodabaugh, James H. "The Negro in the Old Northwest." In *Trek of the Immigrants: Essays Presented to Carl Wittke.* Rock Island, Ill.: Augustana College Library, 1964.
Wilson, Charles Jay. "The Negro in Early Ohio." *Ohio Archeological and Historical Quarterly* 39, no. 4 (1930).

SEE ALSO: Northwest Ordinance (1787); Three-fifths compromise (1787); Fugitive Slave Act of 1793 (1793); Missouri Compromise (1820); Fugitive Slave Act of 1850 (1850); Black Codes of 1865 (1865); Jim Crow laws (1880's-1954); Disfranchisement laws (1890).

TWELFTH AMENDMENT

DATE: Ratified June 15 or July 27, 1804; certified September 25, 1804
U.S. STATUTES AT LARGE: 2 Stat. 306
CATEGORIES: Constitutional Law; Government Procedure and Organization; Voting and Elections

This amendment simplified procedures for electing the president and vice president of the United States.

The Twelfth Amendment to the United States Constitution was necessitated by a basic flaw in the original document. Article II, section 1, clause 3 of the Constitution had established a most complicated and confusing procedure for electing the president and vice president. According to this procedure, the election was to be determined by the vote of an electoral college composed of electors from each of the states. Each state was entitled to the same number of electors as it had representatives in Congress. These electors, appointed in whatever manner the individual state legislatures chose, were to vote for two persons, presumably one for president and the other for vice president, although the ballots were not so labeled. The person receiving the highest number of votes, provided he received a majority of the electoral votes possible, was elected president. The person having the next highest number of votes was elected vice president.

ELECTION PROBLEMS

If there were more than two major candidates for either the presidency or the vice presidency, it was possible that none would receive a clear majority of the electoral vote. In this situation, the House of Representatives would elect the president from the top five candidates. Two-thirds of the members constituted a quorum for this purpose, and each state had one vote—a measure designed to ensure that the smaller states had equal weight. A simple majority vote in the House was required for election. If the same situation occurred in the vice presidential election, the Senate would elect the vice president from the top two vote-getters by majority vote. Again, there was one vote for each Senator, and a quorum was two-thirds of the Senate. If the president should die or become disabled between the time of the popular election and determination of the electoral voter, the vice president would become president. This was similar to the case of the president's death during his term of office.

PROBLEM ELECTIONS

When the Constitution was written, it was presumed that many worthy candidates would receive votes from the various electors and that seldom, if ever, would anyone receive a majority of the electoral vote. The electoral college was intended to serve only as a nominating procedure to provide five good candidates for consideration by the House. The Framers did not anticipate the development of political parties, which began forming in the 1790's. The election of 1796 found Federalist John Adams, from Massachusetts, opposed by Republican Thomas Jefferson, from Virginia. Adams won the election, but his running mate, Thomas Pinckney, from South Carolina, finished in third place, nine votes behind Jefferson. This unusual election resulted in a situation in which presidential rivals, representing different political parties, were forced to serve four years together as president and vice president.

A different, but equally awkward, result came out of the electoral balloting in 1800. In this election, Jefferson and his vice presidential running mate, Aaron Burr, from New York, received the same number of votes. This election went into the House of Representatives, where Federalist opposition to Jefferson was strong. Although it was common knowledge that the electors who voted for Jefferson and Burr intended to place Jefferson in the top position, many die-hard Federalists were determined to thwart their intentions and to put Burr into the presidency. Moderate Federalists, influenced by Burr's home-state rival Alexander Hamilton, finally tipped the scales in favor of Jefferson. The Virginian was elected on the thirty-sixth ballot, dangerously close to Inauguration Day.

PROPOSALS FOR CHANGE

The somewhat bizarre results of the elections of 1796 and 1800 brought forth a demand for a change in the electoral system. John Taylor and other Jeffersonian Republicans prepared a series of resolutions suggesting an appropriate amendment to the Constitution. The resolutions were introduced into Congress, where support from several states was immediately evident. The major objection to changes in the electoral college came from smaller states and from the Federalists. The smaller states feared that their role in the presidential elections might be diminished if the electoral college was abandoned. The Federalists merely hoped to disrupt or confuse the election of 1804.

After much debate, agreement was finally reached in Congress in December of 1803. An amendment was written and sent to the states for ratification. Within a year, the necessary number of states, thirteen out of seventeen, had ratified the amendment. (New Hampshire's legislature approved on June 15 but the state's governor vetoed that ratification; Tennessee then approved on July 27. Some argue for the earlier date, seeing the gubernatorial veto as unconstitutional.) On September 25, 1804, Secretary of State James Madison announced the adoption of the Twelfth Amendment in time for the election of 1804.

THE AMENDMENT'S EFFECT

Although the Twelfth Amendment did not abolish the electoral college or radically change the method of electing the president and vice president, it did remedy some basic defects. Separate ballots were provided for the election of president and vice president, thus preventing the problem of 1796. Provision was also made for the vice president to take over as acting president if the House should delay too long in selecting a president, which almost occurred after the election of 1800. When no candidate received a majority vote in the electoral college, the House of Representatives was to choose a president from the three candidates who received the most votes, rather than from five. Equality among the states was maintained when presidential or vice presidential elections went into the House or the Senate.

Three times in the history of the United States, a president has been elected despite having received a smaller percentage of the popular vote than an opponent. The first time, in 1876, Rutherford B. Hayes assumed the presidency after an election so close that ballots from at least four states were in dispute. A special commission was set up to decide the outcome. The second time, in 1888, Grover Cleveland had a majority of the vote but lost the presidency to Benjamin Harrison. Finally, in 2000, Republican George W. Bush was elected over Democrat Al Gore when a hotly contested Florida electoral vote went to Bush despite a narrow majority of the national popular vote for Gore.

There has been, from time to time, discussion about amending the Twelfth Amendment to ensure that such an election cannot happen again. The usual proposal is that the electoral vote be counted in proportion to the popular vote. If there were two candidates for president and a state had ten electoral votes, a candidate who received 60 percent of the popular vote would receive six electoral votes, and the opponent would receive four electoral votes.

Edward J. Maguire, updated by
Susan M. Taylor

SOURCES FOR FURTHER STUDY

Hockett, Homer C. *The Constitutional History of the United States.* Vol. 1. New York: Macmillan, 1939.

Holder, Angela Roddey. *The Meaning of the Constitution.* New York: Barron's, 1987.

Kuroda, Tadahisa. *The Origins of the Twelfth Amendment: The Electoral College in the Early Republic, 1787-1804.* Westport, Conn.: Greenwood Press, 1994.

Luttbeg, Norman R. *American Electoral Behavior, 1952-1992.* 2d ed. Itasca, Ill.: F. E. Peacock, 1995.
Roseboom, Eugene H. *A Short History of Presidential Elections.* New York: Collier Books, 1967.
Rule, Wilma, and Joseph Zimmerman. *Electoral Systems in Comparative Perspective: Their Impact on Women and Minorities.* Westport, Conn.: Greenwood Press, 1994.
Vile, John R. *Encyclopedia of Constitutional Amendments, Proposed Amendments, and Amending Issues, 1789-1995.* Santa Barbara, Calif: ABC-CLIO, 1996.
Wright, Russell O. *Presidential Elections in the United States: A Statistical History, 1860-1992.* Jefferson, N.C.: McFarland Press, 1995.

SEE ALSO: U.S. Constitution: Provisions (1787); Electoral Count Act (1887); Presidential Succession Act (1947); Twenty-second Amendment (1951); Twenty-fifth Amendment (1967).

EMBARGO ACTS

ALSO KNOWN AS: Nonimportation Acts
DATE: April 18, 1806 (Nonimportation Act); December 22, 1807 (Embargo Act)
U.S. STATUTES AT LARGE: 2 Stat. 451 (Embargo Act)
CATEGORIES: Business, Commerce, and Trade; Foreign Relations

European wars that interfere with American trade led Thomas Jefferson to urge passage of these acts, which nevertheless failed to secure American trade neutrality.

The nineteenth century opened with England and France once again at war with one another. In addition to conducting battlefield operations, each nation attacked the other's economy by trying to restrict its foreign trade. The United States declared its neutrality in the conflict and continued to trade with both nations, but European conflicts would soon seriously affect America's economy.

SEIZURE OF U.S. SHIPS

Through a series of edicts, Napoleon banned neutral ships trading with England from landing in French-controlled ports. In retaliation, England's Orders in Council required all ships trading with France or her colonies first stop in British ports. The United States' neutral rights were violated when French and English officials boarded American merchant ships for inspection. British naval officers seized not only goods but also American citizens and impressed them into the British navy, claiming the sailors were deserters.

Thomas Jefferson was determined to use "peaceable coercion" rather than war to settle the issue. When diplomatic channels failed, he urged Congress to pass the Nonimportation Act (April 18, 1806). The measure established a boycott on all British goods. However, before the measure went into effect the British frigate *Leopard* tried to board and search the American *Chesapeake*. When the *Chesapeake*'s captain refused to be boarded, the *Leopard* fired upon her, killing three Americans. The British boarded the ship and impressed four of her sailors. Outraged Americans called for war.

At Jefferson's urging Congress passed the Embargo Act on December 22, 1807. The act forbade U.S. ships from leaving the United States to trade with any country anywhere in the world. Furthermore, commercial foreign ships were forbidden from entering American ports. In effect, the Embargo Act shut down all external American commerce. Jefferson hoped European nations would suffer without America's business and rescind their offending edicts and orders.

FAILURE OF THE ACTS

Unfortunately, Jefferson's economic sanctions did not produce the desired effect in Europe. French ports were already blockaded by the English and Britain simply increased its trade with Latin American countries to offset any losses suffered from the United States' embargo. Conversely, the Embargo Act had a devastating effect on the U.S. economy. American sailors, merchants, dockworkers, and tradesmen were immediately out of work. Manufacturers lost worldwide markets for their wares, and farmers suffered the loss of their largest customers for cotton and tobacco. As a result, Americans found numerous ways to circumvent the "dambargo" by smuggling and trading through inland waterways with Canada.

To stem the tide of illegal activity, Congress passed the Enforcement Act in 1809, closing trade along inland waterways and giving government officials more power against smugglers. The Enforcement Act, however, served only to anger Americans further. New England states that were heavily invested in a naval economy discussed seceding from the Union, and Jefferson's own political party split on the issue.

Congress repealed the Embargo Act, replacing it with another nonimportation act shortly before Jefferson left office. This act allowed Americans to trade with both nations. Should either England or France repeal its edicts, the United States would trade solely with that country. Neither country rescinded its restrictions, and the United States eventually found it necessary to fight for her rights in the War of 1812.

Leslie Stricker

SOURCE FOR FURTHER STUDY
Sear, L. M. *Jefferson and the Embargo*. London: Octagon Books, 1967.

SEE ALSO: Treaty of Paris (1783); Jay's Treaty (1794); Treaty of Monfontaine (1801).

ANTI-SLAVE TRADE BILL

DATE: March 2, 1807
U.S. STATUTES AT LARGE: 2 Stat. 426-430
CATEGORIES: African Americans; Business, Commerce, and Trade; Foreign Relations; Slavery

The outlawing of a two-century tradition failed to condemn slavery outright, reflecting the young nation's moral ambiguity.

By the seventeenth century, England had begun to gain ascendancy by developing the notorious "triangular slave trade," involving importation of African slaves to the North American colonies from coastal Africa and the Caribbean. This trade had reached its peak at the time Great Britain's American colonies revolted and established the United States of America. Thus, by 1790, there were three-quarters of a million African Americans, almost nine-tenths of whom labored as slaves in the Southern states, with Virginia alone claiming three hundred thousand of them. About 28 percent of African Americans in the North were free, but only one American city, Boston, had no black slaves at all. The American struggle for political independence did not effect freedom for the slaves and their offspring.

ROOTS OF ABOLITIONISM

Antislavery sentiment was growing at the time of the American Revolution but needed competent leadership to challenge the long-standing practice of people enslaving their fellow humans. The Society of Friends (Quakers), some of whose members had a long history of opposition to slavery, led the antislavery, or abolitionist, movement in Pennsylvania, beginning shortly before the outbreak of the American Revolution, and a few clergymen of other religious congregations in England and America took up the cause. Arguments against slavery at the Constitutional Convention of 1787 foundered on threats that delegates from South Carolina and Georgia would ratify no constitution that outlawed the slave trade.

Not all opposition to slavery was high-minded. The French Revolution of 1789 had led to African American efforts to end tyranny over blacks in the French colony of St. Dominque, or San Domingo, on Hispaniola (the island of the twentieth century Dominican Republic and Haiti). In the United States, fear of a similar uprising was probably a more powerful motive than democratic or humanitarian sentiments in the antislavery agitation of the 1790's.

THE RISE OF KING COTTON

Several states had outlawed slavery by that time, sometimes through legislation that instituted abolition gradually or at least banned traffic in slaves. Maryland, Massachusetts, Connecticut, New York, and New Jersey had all passed legislation in the 1780's, as did even South Carolina for a few years. Piecemeal legislation could not stop the trade in human beings, however, particularly after 1793, when Eli Whitney's invention of the cotton gin made cotton a more profitable crop by greatly increasing the speed at which seeds could be separated from the picked cotton, thus increasing plantation owners' desire for more cotton pickers. It has been said that slavery would have died out in the United States but for the New Englander's invention. Northern merchants, although not slave owners themselves, had few scruples against supplying new slaves for the cotton-growing states, and New England textile mill owners' delight over the burgeoning supply of cotton was not likely to make abolitionists of them. It has been estimated that no fewer than twenty thousand new slaves were imported in Georgia and South Carolina in 1803.

WEAK LEGISLATION, WEAK ENFORCEMENT
In December, 1805, Senator Stephen R. Bradley of Vermont introduced legislation that would prohibit the slave trade beginning in 1808, but the bill was stalled for some months. A similar bill was offered in the House of Representatives by Barnabas Bidwell of Massachusetts, again to no effect. Later that year, President Thomas Jefferson urged passage of the bill in his message to Congress. On March 2, 1807, Congress enacted a law specifying a twenty-thousand-dollar fine and forfeiture of ship and cargo for importing slaves, as well as other penalties for acts ranging from equipping a slave ship to knowingly buying an imported slave. The disposition of illegally imported slaves was left to the states, however. The law also prohibited coastal trade in slaves carried in vessels smaller than forty tons. Enforcement of the law was delegated first to the secretary of the treasury and later to the secretary of the navy.

Antislavery forces rejoiced in this new and symbolically important law, but enforcement proved weak. An exhaustive census of the slave trade published in 1969 estimated that 1.9 million slaves were imported illegally between 1811 and 1870; more recent research has called that estimate low. Probably one-fifth of the Africans who became Americans involuntarily arrived after 1808, when the law took effect. Although more than one hundred slave vessels were seized and their officers arrested in the years between 1837 and 1862, and nearly as many cases were prosecuted, convictions were difficult to attain, and when they were attained, judges often pronounced light sentences. Furthermore, because of meager press coverage, few Americans were aware of the extent of the violations. Just as white Americans for a century after the Civil War tended to regard African Americans as sharing in their own entitlement as citizens, most people in the decades following the 1807 law thought of slave importation as something of the past. Some people, particularly in the South, continued to sympathize with the slave trade.

Another weakness of the 1807 law was that it permitted the continuation of slave traffic between states. An owner could take his slaves into another slave state or, according to the Missouri Compromise of 1820, into a western territory south of 36°30', an area greatly increased by the annexation of Texas in 1845. Nor was a runaway slave out of danger in a "free" state. A half century after the 1807 law, according to the Fugitive Slave Act of 1850, anyone capturing a fugitive slave anywhere in the United States was legally obliged to return that slave to his or her owner.

Moral Compromise

It was morally important that Stephen Bradley and Barnabas Bidwell took initiatives to end the sanctioning of U.S. participation in the transatlantic slave trade and that Thomas Jefferson, who owned slaves and whose ambiguous attitude toward slavery has continued to cause debate among historians, used his presidential influence to secure passage of the law. It was one step in the direction of a free society, and if not a highly effective step, it was a necessary one in a new nation that could not agree to condemn slavery outright at that nation's birth or in its early decades. Yet, the underlying problem with the law forbidding importation of slaves was the institution of slavery itself. As long as a person could be someone else's property, that person would inevitably be subject to slave trade of some sort. It was illogical to try to restrict the buying and selling of men, women, and children as long as slavery itself continued to be legal. Nothing better illustrates the problems of compromise between holders of diametrically opposed convictions than the long series of compromises over slavery. Ultimately, the nation could find no better solution for its ambiguous struggle with slavery than the bloody Civil War of 1861-1865.

Robert P. Ellis

Sources for Further Study

Blackburn, Robin. *The Overthrow of Colonial Slavery, 1776-1848.* New York: Verso, 1988.

Davis, David Brion. *Slavery and Human Progress.* New York: Oxford University Press, 1984.

Eltis, David, and James Walvin, eds. *The Abolition of the Atlantic Slave Trade: Origins and Effects in Europe, Africa, and the Americas.* Madison: University of Wisconsin Press, 1981.

Franklin, John Hope. *From Slavery to Freedom: A History of Negro Americans.* 5th ed. New York: Alfred A. Knopf, 1980.

Howard, Warren S. *American Slavers and the Federal Law: 1837-1862.* Berkeley: University of California Press, 1963.

Rawley, James A. *The Transatlantic Slave Trade: A History.* New York: W. W. Norton, 1981.

Walvin, James. *The Slave Trade.* Sutton, 1999.

SEE ALSO: Three-fifths compromise (1787); Fugitive Slave Act of 1793 (1793); Fugitive Slave Act of 1850 (1850); Emancipation Proclamation (1863); Thirteenth Amendment (1865).

FORT WAYNE TREATY

DATE: Signed September 30, 1809
U.S. STATUTES AT LARGE: 7 Stat. 113
CATEGORIES: Native Americans; Treaties and Agreements

Negotiated by William Henry Harrison and repudiated by Tecumseh, the leader of a pan-Indian movement, this treaty precipitated a chain of events that culminated in the Battle of Tippecanoe.

On September 30, 1809, governor of the Indiana Territory William Henry Harrison met with leaders of the Delaware (Lenni Lenape), Miami, and Potawatomi in the fort built by General "Mad" Anthony Wayne. They signed the Treaty of Fort Wayne, which exchanged 2.5 million acres of Indian land southeast of the Wabash River for goods worth about $7,000 and an annuity of $1,750. Later that year, a separate treaty with the Kickapoo and Wea added half a million acres. While the exchange rate of two cents per acre was higher than usual for such treaties, it was still an unfair exchange.

The treaty culminated a process begun in 1795 with the Fort Greenville Treaty, which had ceded a meager 6 square miles of Miami land to the United States government. In the ensuing period, more than fifteen treaties had been signed, most of them negotiated by Harrison, relinquishing control of Indian lands. While Harrison was able to maintain friendly relations with the major tribal leaders, the loss of native lands had started a countermovement.

Led by the Shawnee prophet Tenskwatawa, a pan-Indian movement developed that was based on opposition to the cession of Indian lands and to the tribal leaders who had negotiated the treaties. Tenskwatawa, his brother Tecumseh, and their followers refused to recognize the validity of the treaties on the ground that the land belonged to all Indian peoples so the chiefs had no authority to sign the lands away. To show defiance of the treaties, Tenskwatawa established new Indian towns at Greenville from 1806 to 1808 in defiance of the Fort Greenville Treaty. From 1808 to 1811, he established Prophetstown at Tippecanoe to show that his movement did not honor the Treaty of Fort Wayne.

As Harrison continued his plans to open the recently acquired lands, Tecumseh assumed the role of war chief and took command of the nativist movement. He warned Harrison to keep surveyors and settlers out of the territory. So threatening was his presence that for two years, virtually no settlement occurred. In order to break the stalemate, Harrison led troops on Prophetstown in 1811 while Tecumseh was farther south trying to gain allies among the Creek, Choctaw, and Cherokee. The ensuing Battle of Tippecanoe efficiently removed Tecumseh's followers from the immediate area. It was also, however, the opening action of a war that would last until 1815 and would see Tecumseh ally his forces with the British in the War of 1812.

Charles L. Kammer III

SOURCES FOR FURTHER STUDY

Deloria, Vine, and Raymond J. Demallie. *Documents of American Indian Diplomacy: Treaties, Agreements, and Conventions, 1775-1979.* Norman: University of Oklahoma Press, 1999.

Falkowski, James E. *Indian Law/Race Law: A Five Hundred Year History.* New York: Praeger, 1992.

Prucha, Francis Paul. *American Indian Treaties: The History of a Political Anomaly.* Reprint. Berkeley: University of California Press, 1997.

SEE ALSO: Fort Stanwix Treaty (1784); Trade and Intercourse Acts (1790-1834); Fort Greenville Treaty (1795); Horseshoe Bend Treaty (1814).

HORSESHOE BEND TREATY

ALSO KNOWN AS: Fort Jackson Treaty
DATE: Signed August 9, 1814
CATEGORIES: Native Americans; Treaties and Agreements

This agreement eliminated any possibility of an effective Creek alliance against U.S. expansion and thus facilitated the removal of the Creek people to the trans-Mississippi region during Andrew Jackson's presidency.

After his defeat of the Red Stick faction of the Creeks at Horseshoe Bend, General Andrew Jackson took full advantage of his authorization to secure a peace agreement. His purpose was twofold: to secure large tracts of land as compensation for the cost of his campaign and to eliminate Creek political power by isolating them. In the Horseshoe Bend Treaty, also known as the Treaty of Fort Jackson, signed on August 9, 1814, Jackson received, on behalf of the United States, 22 million acres in south Georgia and central Alabama, or half of the Creek domain.

Cessions in the west isolated the Creeks from the Choctaws and Chickasaws, while those in the south created a buffer against the Seminoles and the Spanish. Ironically, only one Red Stick signed the treaty; the remaining signatories were Creek allies of Jackson, who lost much of their own land. Each Creek ally was allowed to keep a square mile of land as long as they or their family used it, but the United States reserved the right to build forts, trading posts, and roads on Creek lands.

Richard B. McCaslin

SOURCES FOR FURTHER STUDY

Deloria, Vine, and Raymond J. Demallie. *Documents of American Indian Diplomacy: Treaties, Agreements, and Conventions, 1775-1979.* Norman: University of Oklahoma Press, 1999.

Falkowski, James E. *Indian Law/Race Law: A Five Hundred Year History.* New York: Praeger, 1992.

Prucha, Francis Paul. *American Indian Treaties: The History of a Political Anomaly.* Reprint. Berkeley: University of California Press, 1997.

SEE ALSO: Fort Stanwix Treaty (1784); Trade and Intercourse Acts (1790-1834); Fort Greenville Treaty (1795); Fort Wayne Treaty (1809).

TREATY OF GHENT

DATE: Signed December 24, 1814; in force February 17, 1815
CATEGORIES: Foreign Relations; Treaties and Agreements

The Treaty of Ghent brought a formal end to the War of 1812, the United States' "second war for independence."

Chances of a negotiated, honorable peace ending the War of 1812 appeared remote in the summer of 1814. The United States ostensibly had gone to war to protect its rights on the high seas. President James Madison and Secretary of State James Monroe had repeatedly stated that the recognition of such rights, and particularly an end to the practice of impressing U.S. sailors into the British navy, was essential to any settlement.

WAR OF 1812: FINAL DAYS

The British had refused to abandon impressment, and the war continued. Militarily, the conflict had been inconclusive. In many ways, the British were in the stronger position at the outset of the talks. By the summer of 1814, they and their allies had defeated Napoleon; now Great Britain could turn its attention and energies to the war with its former colonies. With France subdued and veteran troops available for North American duty, Great Britain seemed in a position to end the war by military conquest. Moreover, the United States was divided over "Mr. Madison's War." The Federalist Party and New England generally had opposed the war from its beginning. The Republican administration faced the unpleasant prospects of political humiliation, military defeat, or both, should it continue to pursue its war aims.

NEGOTIATORS

Such were the circumstances when U.S. and British commissioners met in Ghent on August 9, 1814. The British had agreed to direct meetings as an alternative to mediation by Alexander I, czar of Russia, and evinced no haste to deal with the U.S. upstarts. Ghent was chosen as a convenient, easily accessible site—a pleasant, neutral city in what was then the Austrian Netherlands, soon to be part of the Kingdom of the United Netherlands and a major city in Belgium after that country's independence in 1830.

The United States government dispatched five commissioners, representing a broad spectrum of backgrounds. John Quincy Adams, a Massachusetts Republican and nominally the head of the delegation, was a staunch nationalist. Henry Clay and Jonathan Russell were "war hawks" from Kentucky and Rhode Island, respectively. James A. Bayard, a Delaware Federalist, and Albert Gallatin, a Pennsylvania Republican, were moderates; the latter, because of his role as peacemaker among his colleagues, emerged as the functional leader of the U.S. delegation at Ghent. The representatives from the United States often quarreled among themselves, but they stood firmly together in the face of their British counterparts.

Adams and Russell arrived in Ghent on June 23 and the others, by July 6. Clearly, the talks were going to be protracted, and so the U.S. delegates moved out of their hotel and into the Lovendeghem House in the heart of the city. Far from being the "five lonely Americans" as they have been often described, they became active in local intellectual and cultural life.

Negotiations began in an atmosphere of distrust as a result of a monthlong wait by the U.S. delegates for their British counterparts. The British delegation included Admiralty lawyer Dr. William Adams, Vice-Admiral Lord Gambier, and Henry Goulburn of the Colonial Office. Accompanied by a secretary, Anthony J.

Baker, they took up residence in a former Carthusian monastery at Meerhem. Their principal role was not so much to negotiate as to act as the messengers of Viscount Castlereagh (Robert Stewart), the British foreign secretary.

NEGOTIATIONS

Although the United States had always posed as the injured party in the conflict, the British dominated the early months of the conference. They proposed the establishment of an American Indian buffer state in the American Northwest and asked for a substantial cession of land along the border between Canada and the United States. The U.S. representatives refused. The British, anticipating the capture of New Orleans, then suggested that each party continue to occupy the territory it held at the conclusion of hostilities (*uti possidetis*). Again, the United States refused, holding to its principle of the restoration of territory as it was held prior to the outbreak of war (*status quo ante bellum*).

Finally, the constancy and apparent unanimity of the U.S. delegation bore fruit. Throughout the negotiations, the British cabinet had debated whether to conquer or conciliate the United States. Foreseeing greater good in Anglo-American friendship than in lasting enmity between the kindred nations, Castlereagh led the way toward compromise.

Several factors, some only vaguely relating to the war, confirmed Castlereagh's judgment. The British were having difficulties at the Congress of Vienna with their recent allies in the Napoleonic Wars. It seemed for a time that war with Russia was imminent. France was restive, portending Napoleon's return from Elba in 1815. At home, the British people were war-weary and growing resentful of taxation. To make matters worse, the United States won a timely victory at Plattsburg on September 11, 1814. The architect of the victory over Napoleon, the duke of Wellington, estimated that a conquest of the United States would come only at a heavy cost of men, money, and time. At this juncture, the British decided to compromise.

The commissioners at Ghent still bargained hard, but the stakes were no longer so great. On November 11, 1814, the United States presented a proposal that would maintain prewar boundaries. They agreed that the treaty would say nothing about impressment, which would be unnecessary in a post-Napoleonic Europe. The

British abandoned their designs on U.S. territory and their desire for a buffer state. They still demanded the islands in Passama-quoddy Bay, the right of navigation on the Mississippi River, and prohibitions on U.S. rights to dry fish in Newfoundland.

In the end, the participants at Ghent delegated these matters to commissions to resolve after peace had been concluded. The Peace of Ghent provided for a return to the *status quo ante bellum,* the state of affairs prior to the war. The two sides signed the treaty on Christmas Eve, 1814. Given the slow communications of the era, the treaty only took effect on February 17, 1815, after ratification by the governments of both sides. In the meantime, the British suffered a humiliating defeat in the Battle of New Orleans on January 8, 1815.

SOVEREIGNTY SECURED, FRIENDSHIP FOUND
Called America's second war for independence, the War of 1812 had several important results. Spawning a legacy of bad feeling between Great Britain and the United States, which persisted for many years, the war gave the U.S. people a greater feeling of national identity, simultaneously paving the way for the decimation of native populations. The war stimulated the growth of manufacturers and turned the U.S. people increasingly toward domestic matters and away from foreign affairs.

The treaty had a major impact on the United States' relationships with both Canada and the American Indian nations. Future war was averted by the Rush-Bagot Agreement of 1817, which limited armaments around the Great Lakes. Boundary commissions and subsequent treaties in 1818, 1842, and 1846 determined most of the border between the United States and British North America (Canada). The Red River Valley went to the United States; the borders of Alberta, Manitoba, and Saskatchewan were moved south to 49° north latitude. Oregon Territory (Oregon, Washington, and British Columbia) was to be jointly administered by Great Britain and the United States. The United States agreed to exact no retribution and to take no land from the American Indians who had fought for the British. However, the defeat of the British and their American Indian allies helped to open the Old Northwest and Southwest to the waves of settlement that would lead to white domination east of the Mississippi and eventually beyond.

At the time, the treaty was, in many ways, a victory for neither side. Yet for the United States, there was cause for rejoicing. The United States had stood firm against a great power. Castlereagh and the British had recognized U.S. military potential and decided to court instead of conquer. Most important, the peace that both sides wanted and needed was secure. The treaty provided a steady foundation for an Anglo-American relationship that, over a century, would transform the two nations' foreign policies from suspicious opposition to firm friendship.

Emory M. Thomas, updated by
Randall Fegley

SOURCES FOR FURTHER STUDY

Bemis, Samuel Flagg. *John Quincy Adams and the Foundations of American Foreign Policy.* New York: Alfred A. Knopf, 1949.

Burt, A. L. *The United States, Great Britain, and British North America from the Revolution to the Establishment of Peace After the War of 1812.* New Haven, Conn.: Yale University Press, 1940.

Coles, Harry. *The War of 1812.* Chicago: University of Chicago Press, 1965.

Dangerfield, George. *The Era of Good Feelings.* New York: Harcourt, Brace, 1952.

Engelman, Fred. *The Peace of Christmas Eve.* New York: Harcourt, Brace, 1962.

Gallatin, James. *The Diary of James Gallatin.* New ed. Westport, Conn.: Greenwood Press, 1979.

Horsman, Reginald. *The War of 1812.* New York: Alfred A. Knopf, 1969.

Perkins, Bradford. *Castlereagh and Adams: England and the United States, 1812-1823.* Berkeley: University of California Press, 1964.

Vannieuwenhuyse, Johan. *The Treaty of Ghent.* Ghent: Museum Arnold Vander Haeghen-Stadsarchief, 1989.

SEE ALSO: Treaty of Paris (1783); Jay's Treaty (1794); Treaty of Monfontaine (1801); Rush-Bagot Agreement (1817).

RUSH-BAGOT AGREEMENT

DATE: Accepted April 28, 1817; Senate ratified April 16, 1818
CATEGORIES: Foreign Relations; Treaties and Agreements

This agreement, the first example of reciprocal naval disarmament in the history of international relations, began the demilitarization of the U.S.-Canadian border and remained in force for more than a century.

The Treaty of Ghent (1814), ending the War of 1812, failed to deal with the problem of naval forces on the Great Lakes. Both nations maintained warships there, and both sides continued to build more vessels, raising the possibility of an expensive arms race. Americans had earlier wanted to demilitarize the lakes, which would clearly be advantageous to the United States. President John Adams had proposed limiting armaments on the Great Lakes when negotiating the 1783 Treaty of Paris, and John Jay unsuccessfully raised the issue again in 1794.

SECURING THE GREAT LAKES

American minister to Britain John Quincy Adams, acting upon instructions from Secretary of State James Monroe, proposed to Viscount Castlereagh, the British foreign secretary, that both nations limit warships on the lakes to those necessary for guarding against smuggling. Adams made the proposal informally in February of 1816, repeating the offer in writing on March 21. Because Adams lacked authority to conclude a definitive agreement, Lord Castlereagh transferred the negotiations to Washington, where British minister Charles Bagot could deal directly with Monroe. While negotiations continued, Adams and Castlereagh entered into a gentlemen's agreement not to introduce new armaments in the Great Lakes region.

On August 2, 1816, Monroe proposed specific terms, which Bagot transmitted to Castlereagh in London. By the time Castlereagh's response arrived, Monroe had been elected president and Richard Rush was acting secretary of state. Bagot sent Rush a note dated April 28, 1817, formally notifying the United States of British acceptance of Monroe's terms; on the following day Rush replied, expressing the president's satisfaction with the British response. Although Rush played no role in negotiating the accord, his signature on the second note attached his name to the Rush-Bagot Agreement. The following year, Monroe submitted the pact to the Senate, which unanimously approved it on April 16, 1818, giving it the status of a treaty.

TREATY PROVISIONS

The basic provisions of the treaty limited each country to one vessel on Lake Ontario, one ship on Lake Champlain, and two vessels on the upper lakes. Each ship could be of no more than one hundred tons' burden and carry only a single eighteen-pound cannon. All other armed vessels on the lakes were to be dismantled. Nothing in the text dealt with land fortifications or armies.

The agreement was the first example of reciprocal naval disarmament in the history of international relations. However, both countries continued to fortify the land frontier for the next fifty years, as it still seemed a likely place of future conflict. The treaty began the demilitarization of the U.S.-Canadian border and, as land fortifications became obsolete in the twentieth century, they were retained only as historical monuments. The naval treaty remained unmodified for 122 years. When the United States, Canada, and Britain allied against Adolf Hitler's Germany, agreements in 1940 and 1941 permitted construction of warships and naval training on the Great Lakes.

Milton Berman

SOURCES FOR FURTHER STUDY

Bemis, Samuel Flagg. *John Quincy Adams and the Foundations of American Foreign Policy.* New York: Alfred A. Knopf, 1949.

Perkins, Bradford. *Castlereagh and Adams: England and the United States, 1812-1823.* Berkeley: University of California Press, 1964.

Stacy, C. P. *The Undefended Border: Myth and Reality.* Ontario: Canadian Historical Association, 1953.

SEE ALSO: Treaty of Paris (1783); Jay's Treaty (1794); Treaty of Monfontaine (1801); Treaty of Ghent (1814); Convention of 1818 (1818).

CONVENTION OF 1818

DATE: Signed October 10, 1818; Senate ratified January 25, 1819
CATEGORIES: Foreign Relations; Treaties and Agreements

This agreement settled questions of the United States' northern border as well as issues of access to territory west of the Rockies.

The Treaty of Ghent (1814) ended the War of 1812 but left many issues unresolved. The major American grievance concerning impressment of American seamen by the British was not addressed in the treaty. Other disputes involved the northwest boundary with Canada, the status of the Oregon Country, compensation by the British for American slaves seized during the war, the right of Americans to fish off the coasts of Newfoundland, and access to trade with the British islands in the West Indies.

Lord Castlereagh, the British foreign secretary, suggested arbitration of the disputes, but President James Monroe preferred negotiation. When the Convention of 1815, dealing with transatlantic trade, needed renewal, Monroe suggested that a joint commission settle all outstanding questions. He appointed Richard Rush, American minister to Britain, and Albert Gallatin, minister to France, to negotiate for the United States.

Two issues proved intransigent. The negotiators came close to an agreement on impressment but failed to settle essential details. Even though American ships had freely traded with the West Indies before independence, the American delegates could not convince Britain to modify its long-standing policy excluding non-British ships from its colonies.

AGREEMENT PROVISIONS

The final agreement covered five points. The commission easily agreed at its first meeting to extend the Commercial Convention of 1815 for ten years. The issue of compensation for slaves taken by the British went to arbitration by Czar Alexander I of Russia, who awarded the United States $1,204,960. The British contended that American privileges to fish off the coast of Newfoundland, secured in the 1783 Treaty of Paris, had been abrogated when the United States declared war in 1812; Americans insisted on retaining all such rights. A compromise granted Americans substantial fishing rights, displeasing Canadians who hoped to displace them and upsetting New Englanders facing reduced access to Canadian shores and waters.

Two sections of the treaty dealt with boundary disputes. The 1783 peace treaty, working with poor maps, located the northern boundary of the United States on a line extending from the northwestern point of Lake of the Woods due west to the Mississippi River. Exploration later revealed the source of the river to be more than one hundred miles south of Lake of the Woods. The British wanted to move the boundary southward to approximately the latitude of Minneapolis, thus opening navigation of the Mississippi to them. The Americans refused. The British finally accepted a line from Lake of the Woods to the Rocky Mountains along the forty-ninth parallel.

The conferees compromised conflicting claims to the Northwest Coast by providing that, for ten years, all territory west of the Rocky Mountains claimed by Great Britain or the United States would be free and open to the vessels, citizens, and subjects of both powers. This joint occupation of Oregon continued until 1846, when the British agreed to divide the region along the 49-degree line, originally proposed by the Americans in 1818.

Milton Berman

SOURCES FOR FURTHER STUDY
Bemis, Samuel Flagg. *John Quincy Adams and the Foundations of American Foreign Policy.* New York: Alfred A. Knopf, 1949.
Powell, J. H. *Richard Rush, Republican Diplomat, 1780-1859.* Philadelphia: University of Pennsylvania Press, 1942.

SEE ALSO: Treaty of Paris (1783); Treaty of Ghent (1814); Rush-Bagot Agreement (1817); Oregon Act (1848).

ADAMS-ONÍS TREATY

ALSO KNOWN AS: Transcontinental Treaty
DATE: Signed February 22, 1819; in force February 22, 1821
U.S. STATUTES AT LARGE: 5 Stat. 252
CATEGORIES: Foreign Relations; Treaties and Agreements

After Spain ceded Florida to the United States in this treaty, a definitive western boundary for the Louisiana Purchase territory was established.

Following the end of the War of 1812, the United States intensified its efforts to resolve long-standing disputes with Spain. Spanish difficulties with the United States had entered a critical new phase during the undeclared naval war with France (1798-1800). As an ally of France at that time, Spain had permitted its ships to assist in ransacking U.S. commerce on the high seas and allowed the French to seize U.S. ships in Spanish ports. The United States later demanded compensation from Spain for the loss of these vessels and cargoes.

In 1802, the Spanish suspended the right of the United States to deposit and transfer goods at New Orleans, causing economic damage to the trans-Appalachian West. Although the Treaty of San Lorenzo of 1795 (known also as the Pinckney Treaty) between the United States and Spain had guaranteed U.S. deposit rights and prohibited privateering by either nation upon the other, the Spanish balked at paying compensation for its transgressions, leaving the issue deadlocked by 1805.

THE LOUISIANA PURCHASE

The United States' purchase of Louisiana from France in 1803 added serious complications to Spanish-American relations. The French had obtained the territory from Spain in the Treaty of San Ildefonso of 1800. By this agreement, France had pledged not to transfer Louisiana to another power without first offering to restore the territory to Spain. The Spanish thus considered the Louisiana Purchase to be illegal and continued to demand its return until 1818. The United States soon adopted an extensive definition of Louisiana's boundaries, which included two adjacent Spanish provinces: Texas and West Florida. U.S. claims to the latter territory were dubious at best, and Spanish rights to western and central Texas were solidly founded upon the chain of forts and missions established there by 1800. East Texas, however, was largely unsettled and would become the crux of the dispute after the War of 1812.

U.S. interest in Spanish territory also extended to areas to which the United States could make no plausible claim. East Florida was such an area, and the United States negotiated continuously for its purchase, beginning in the 1790's. U.S. leaders believed that possession of Florida would give their nation command of the Gulf of Mexico and would secure from foreign interference the trade that passed through the Mississippi River. After 1808, U.S. prospects for acquiring both West and East Florida improved greatly: Napoleon had invaded Spain, diverting that nation's resources to a life-or-death struggle against France.

WAR OF 1812

In the summer of 1810, the United States colluded in the successful rebellion of settlers in the Baton Rouge region of West Florida. Later in the same year, the area was legally annexed to the United States up to the Pearl River, eventually becoming part of the state of Louisiana. After the United States went to war with Great Britain in 1812, the U.S. government came under domestic pressure to use the opportunity to expand at Spain's expense. In the spring of 1813, Congress authorized the occupation of Mobile, the principal port in the section of West Florida between the Pearl and Perdido Rivers. The Spanish responded to U.S. aggression by allowing the British to use Pensacola as a base, and by assisting the Creek Indians in their 1813-1814 war against the United States. The War of 1812 thus dramatically illustrated U.S. vulnerability: In the hands of Spain, Florida had become a yawning gap in the United States' coastal defenses—a highway through which the interior of the country could be penetrated easily.

THE FIGHT FOR EAST FLORIDA

After peace with Great Britain was concluded in early 1815, the acquisition of East Florida became the prime goal of U.S. foreign policy. Spain recognized that it had only two choices to avoid a shameful abandonment of the region: to gain the support of a European ally, or to attain a semblance of honor in the affair by winning from the United States favorable territorial concessions west of the Mississippi. At first, the Spanish were successful in securing the support of the British, who warned the United States against further encroachments on their neighbors. Bolstered by Britain's encouragement, Spain's minister to the United States, Luis de Onís, successfully sparred with his counterpart, Secretary of State James Monroe, throughout 1815 and 1816. The Spaniard demanded the return of Louisiana and West Florida and protested against the United States' supplying of Spain's rebelling Latin American colonists and the privateers operating out of Baltimore against Spanish shipping. Soon, Spain had developed its own list of financial claims against the United States and was demanding compensation. President James Madison declined to intensify the diplomatic struggle, because delay only aided the United States, which would grow stronger in the future while Spain progressively weakened.

The inauguration of James Monroe as president in March, 1817, placed the negotiations in impatient, decisive hands. Monroe was determined to push the Spanish to an agreement and appointed a secretary of state, John Quincy Adams, who shared his views. In the fall of 1817, the U.S. cabinet decided to adopt a new attitude toward Spain, a decision that resulted in the dispatch of an army under the command of Major General Andrew Jackson into Florida— ostensibly to pursue Seminoles, who were raiding in retaliation for the destruction of one of their villages.

Jackson's orders from Washington were ambiguous: He was authorized to enter Florida to punish the Seminoles, but forbidden to attack them if they sheltered under a Spanish fort. At the same time, he was also enjoined to adopt the measures necessary to end the conflict. Once Jackson was actually in Florida, he discovered evidence of Spanish aid to the Seminoles. Relying on the discretion allotted to him, he judged that only the capture of Spanish forts would end the conflict. Jackson accordingly adopted these "necessary measures" by seizing St. Marks and Pensacola, effectively wresting Florida from Spain.

Although the U.S. administration would later deny having intended that Jackson should take such extreme action, Adams used the military pressure to cajole the Spanish into retreating from their extreme negotiating positions. International conditions also encouraged Spain to accommodate U.S. demands. By early 1818, Great Britain had made it clear that it would not risk another war with the United States by seeking to enforce mediation of Spanish-American disputes. European commitments and dangers had caused the British to reconsider their support for Spain and to seek détente with the United States. In the summer, Great Britain agreed to negotiate with the United States over all outstanding issues. These talks resulted in the Convention of 1818. Anglo-American rapprochement thus ended Spanish pretensions to power.

NEGOTIATIONS

Negotiations between the United States and Spain resumed in the fall of 1818, after the United States had agreed to restore the forts to the Spanish. Near the end of the year, the two nations agreed upon a western boundary that went up the Sabine River from its mouth and continued north to the Red River, zigzagged westward along the Red and Arkansas Rivers, followed the crest of the Rocky Mountains to the forty-second parallel, and then turned westward to the Pacific Ocean. On February 22, 1819, Adams and Onís signed the treaty that bears their names. It embodied the compromise western boundary and resolved nearly all disputes between their two nations. The Spanish retained Texas but gave up claims to the Oregon Country. Spain ceded all territory east of the Mississippi to the United States. Both nations renounced their claims for damages, although the United States agreed to assume the claims of its citizens against Spain up to a maximum of five million dollars. Adams successfully avoided guaranteeing that the United States would not recognize the Latin American nations.

King Ferdinand VII of Spain initially refused to ratify the treaty because the United States had failed to provide such guarantees. In January, 1820, a revolution in Spain brought to power a liberal regime whose leaders were inclined to accommodate the United States. France and Russia, who feared that the Spanish-American quarrel threatened world peace, pressured the new government to settle. Spain finally ratified the treaty in October, 1820, and the Adams-Onís Treaty (also known as the Transcontinental Treaty) became effective on February 22, 1821.

IMPACT

This agreement was crucial to determining the course of North American history. It signified the decay of Spanish power in the New World and provided conclusive evidence of British acquiescence in limited United States expansion. The acquisition of Florida strengthened the United States materially and enhanced its national security by closing a gap in its coastal defenses. Spain's recognition of U.S. rights in Oregon signaled the beginning of the United States' role as a global power. Resolving problems with Spain largely freed the United States from European entanglements for several decades. The treaty was also the decisive event in modern Seminole history. By replacing stagnant Spanish rule with that of a demographically and economically expanding United States, the treaty ensured that the Seminoles could not long remain in possession of their lands. Their removal westward inevitably followed during the 1830's.

Michael S. Fitzgerald

SOURCES FOR FURTHER STUDY
Bemis, Samuel F. *John Quincy Adams and the Foundations of American Foreign Policy*. New York: Alfred A. Knopf, 1949.
Brooks, Philip C. *Diplomacy and the Borderlands: The Adams-Onís Treaty of 1819*. Berkeley: University of California Press, 1939.
Cox, Isaac J. *The West Florida Controversy, 1798-1813: A Study in American Diplomacy*. 1918. Reprint. Gloucester, Mass.: P. Smith, 1967.
Griffin, Charles C. *The United States and the Disruption of the Spanish Empire, 1810-1822*. New York: Columbia University Press, 1937.
Weeks, William E. *John Quincy Adams and American Global Empire*. Lexington: University Press of Kentucky, 1992.

SEE ALSO: Treaty of Paris (1783); Jay's Treaty (1794); Pinckney's Treaty (1795); Treaty of Monfontaine (1801); Treaty of Ghent (1814); Treaty of Guadalupe Hidalgo (1848).

MISSOURI COMPROMISE

DATE: March 6, 1820
U.S. STATUTES AT LARGE: 3 Stat. 545
CATEGORIES: African Americans; Slavery

The Missouri Compromise was an attempt to pacify both Northern and Southern sectional interests by allowing slavery to exist in the southern part of the Louisiana Purchase territory.

Between 1818 and 1819 both the territories of Missouri and Maine petitioned the U.S. Congress to be admitted as new states. The Missouri Territory had been created from the Louisiana Purchase (1803) and was promised constitutional protection. However, Congress could not decide if the right of property applied to the institution of slavery. Should it be allowed in Missouri and the rest of the Louisiana Purchase, or did Congress have the moral responsibility to rectify the issue of slavery that had been avoided since the Constitutional Convention of 1787? It would take three sessions of Congress between 1818 and 1821 before Missouri was fully admitted as a state. The issue of slavery sparked by the ensuing debate spread throughout the country and threatened to cause disunion between the northern and southern regions.

THE SLAVERY QUESTION

At the time that Missouri and Maine applied for statehood, the United States consisted of eleven free states and eleven slave states. This political balance had been achieved since 1789 by admitting a slave state and then a free state determined by geographical location and each region's history with regard to slavery. This arrangement supplied each section with an equal number of senators (two per state) and attempted to equalize representation in the House of Representatives through the three-fifths clause.

The three-fifths compromise, added to the final draft of the Constitution, allowed slave states to count each slave as three-fifths of a person to balance their representative power against that of the more densely populated North. Nevertheless, the North had a majority of representatives in Congress (105 to 81). Missouri's admission as a free or slave state therefore became an important issue in the very body that would resolve it. Missouri threatened either to extend the influence of the industrial free North in the Senate or to provide the majority to the agrarian slaveholding South.

In 1818, Missouri's boundaries were approximately the same as those of today, and the territory was estimated to have between two thousand and three thousand slaves. Slavery was a historical byproduct of prior French and Spanish colonial policies. Missouri reasoned that slavery should be allowed to continue as it had in other territories that had been granted statehood since 1789.

In February, 1819, the House of Representatives responded to this debate by adopting the Tallmadge amendment. Representative James Tallmadge of New York proposed an amendment to the bill allowing Missouri to frame a state constitution. The two clauses in the amendment would restrict the further introduction of slavery into Missouri and provide that all children born to slaves would be free at age twenty-five. Both clauses passed the House. Southern senators were shocked by the bitterness of the debate in the House and the ability of the North to muster votes. They saw the Tallmadge amendment as the first step in eliminating the expansion of slavery. Voting along sectional lines, the Senate rejected both clauses.

Admission of Maine and Missouri

Congress adjourned session until December 6, 1819. During this interim, Maine formed a constitution and applied for admission as a free state. Maine had been incorporated into the Massachusetts Bay Colony in 1691 but had started to agitate for separate statehood during and after the War of 1812. Its application for statehood as a free state seemed to provide a possible solution to the Missouri debate that threatened the stability of the young nation. On February 18, 1820, the Senate Judiciary Committee joined the two measures and the Senate passed Maine's and Missouri's applications for statehood but without mentioning slavery. This infuriated Maine, which had, as part of Massachusetts, outlawed slavery in 1780. What should have been a routine confirmation of new states became part of the most explosive issue to face the country. Maine would be allowed to separate from Massachusetts and gain statehood as long as Congress approved it by March 4, 1820, or the nine counties would revert back to Massachusetts. Even so, many of Maine's constituency urged that Maine's application fail so that slavery would not spread into Missouri.

Sectional Polarization

Senator J. B. Thomas of Illinois offered a compromise amendment to the Senate bill that would admit Missouri as a slave state with the proviso that the remaining territories in the Louisiana Purchase above 36°30', Missouri's southern border, would be free of slavery. The Northern-controlled House responded by rejecting this Thomas amendment and passed a proviso prohibiting the further introduction of slavery anywhere. The result was polarization along sectional lines. In turn, the Senate struck out the antislavery provision and added the Thomas amendment. Thus began the final debate over whether slavery would be allowed to expand.

Senator Rufus King of New York continued the debate by stating that Congress, under Article IV, section 3 of the Constitution, was empowered to exclude slavery from the territory and to make slavery an issue for statehood: "New states *may be* admitted by the Congress into this Union." A precedent had been established under Article IV, section 3 of the Constitution which forbade slavery in lands above the Ohio River in the Northwest Ordinance of 1787. Therefore, in the minds of many of the northern congressmen, they should take this opportunity to eliminate slavery from any point west of the Mississippi. In response, Senator William Pickering of Maryland stated that the United States was composed of an equal number of slave states and free states; Missouri should be allowed to determine its own fate.

Missouri responded with anger and frustration, asserting that the issue was not about slavery but rather the issue of state sovereignty. Congress had delayed its admission for years. Missouri, like other states, had the right to choose its property laws. In Missouri as well as the rest of the South, the issue swung from one dealing with slavery to one dealing with property rights and the equality of states within the United States. These issues captured the attention of citizens throughout the country and led to heated debates on all levels. For the first time, slavery was being justified and defended as a good way of life by not only southern politicians but also the southern clergy. Would the country be influenced by restrictionists who sought to control this institution, or would states' rights be preserved?

THE COMPROMISE

A compromise between the two houses was eventually reached in a conference formed to break the deadlock. Speaker of the House Henry Clay of Kentucky stated that he would not support Maine's admission unless Missouri was admitted with no restrictions. The Senate took the House bill and inserted the Thomas amendment. The House under Henry Clay's leadership voted to admit Maine as a free state and Missouri as a slave state and restricted slavery north of 36°30′. It is interesting to note that seven of Maine's nine representatives in the Massachusetts delegation voted against Maine's admission so that their state would not be used to provide a solution to the slavery issue.

Missouri continued to be an issue when it presented a state constitution in November, 1820. As if to get the final word, the Missouri Constitutional Convention had incorporated into its constitution a provision excluding free blacks and mulattoes from the state. This provision incited the antislavery factions in the Senate and House and threatened to destroy the fragile compromise. A "Second Missouri Compromise" was needed which stated that Missouri would not gain admission as a state unless its legislature assured Congress that it would not seek to abridge the rights of citizens. The Missouri legislature agreed to this in June, 1821. On August 10, 1821, President James Monroe admitted Missouri as the twenty-fourth state. After waiting a short time, Missouri's state congress sought to have the last say when it approved statutes forbidding free blacks from entering the state.

The Missouri Compromise would stand for the next three decades. During that time it served to mark a clear delineation between the growing regional and sectional problems of the North and South and made states' rights the rallying cry for the South until the Civil War.

Vincent Michael Thur

SOURCES FOR FURTHER STUDY

Brown, Richard H. *The Missouri Compromise: Political Statesmanship or Unwise Evasion?* Boston: D. C. Heath, 1964.

Clark, Charles E. *Maine: A Bicentennial History.* New York: W. W. Norton, 1977.

Commager, Henry Steele, ed. *Documents of American History.* New York: Appleton-Century-Crofts, 1958.

Hurt, R. Douglas. *Agriculture and Slavery in Missouri's Little Dixie.* Columbia: University of Missouri Press, 1992.

McPherson, James M. *The Battle Cry of Freedom: The Civil War Era.* Oxford, England: Oxford University Press, 1988.

Moore, Glover. *The Missouri Controversy, 1819-1821.* Gloucester, Mass.: Peter Smith, 1967.

Nagel, Paul C. *Missouri: A Bicentennial History.* New York: W. W. Norton, 1977.

Nash, Gary B., ed. *The American People: Creating a Nation and a Society.* 2d ed. New York: Harper & Row, 1990.

SEE ALSO: Northwest Ordinance (1787); Three-fifths compromise (1787); Fugitive Slave Act of 1793 (1793); Anti-Slave Trade Bill (1807); Black Codes of 1804-1807 (1804-1807); Compromise of 1850 (1850); Fugitive Slave Act of 1850 (1850); Kansas-Nebraska Act (1854).

LAND ACT OF 1820

DATE: April 24, 1820
U.S. STATUTES AT LARGE: 3 Stat. 566
CATEGORIES: Land Management

The 1820 Land Act formed the basis for transferring the public domain to individual U.S. citizens for the next two decades.

The British colonies in North America had been, from the beginning, colonies of settlement. By the time of the Revolutionary War, most of the good agricultural land in the original thirteen colonies had been turned into farms by the settlers, and many were anxious to move west of the Alleghenies, to the area later known as the Old Northwest. The British, in order to ensure the friendship of the natives in that section, had forbidden settlement. With British defeat in the Revolutionary War, the area now belonged to the thirteen colonies, where the pressure to open it to settlement was overwhelming.

PRESSURES FOR SETTLEMENT

In 1785, the Confederation Congress first began deliberations about how to arrange the transfer of land in the Old Northwest, as well as those portions of the Old Southwest, acquired by the 1783 Treaty of Paris with Britain. Several principles were agreed on:

Before settlement and transfer of title, the land would have to be ceded by treaty with the Native Americans; the land would have to be surveyed, in square township units, and sale would be by portions of the surveyed townships; and the proceeds of the sale would be used to pay down the federal debt. These principles were embodied in the Ordinance of 1785, which continued to bind the federal government after the adoption of the Constitution in 1789.

In addition to pressure from would-be settlers, the federal government owed obligations to thousands of veterans of the Revolutionary War, who had been promised land grants in lieu of pay during the war. Many of the veterans had received scrip, redeemable in grants from the public domain. As a result, the federal government attempted to begin surveying the land; once at least a modest proportion had been mapped, it could be subdivided into townships and offered for sale. Treaties had been negotiated with some of the native tribes in 1784, 1785, and 1786, in which those tribes ceded much of western New York and western Pennsylvania and large portions of southern Ohio to the United States; the belief prevailed in the Congress that this laid the foundation for surveying and subsequent settlement by Euro-Americans. However, some of the Indians refused to accept the treaties, and battles were fought in the early 1790's between the natives and federal troops. The natives won the first battle, in 1791, but lost in 1794 to a force commanded by General Anthony Wayne at the Battle of Fallen Timbers. Wayne then ravaged the Indian settlements in northern Ohio and forced them to accept the Fort Greenville Treaty, in 1795, by which they accepted confinement to a reservation in northwestern Ohio and ceded the rest of Ohio, as well as parts of Indiana, Illinois, and a small part of Michigan, to the United States. In the Old Southwest—which would become the states of Mississippi and Alabama, as well as parts of western Georgia—numerous treaties were concluded with the tribes located there, defining their tribal lands and opening up significant lands for Euro-American settlement, mostly in the southern portions of the area.

SURVEYS AND SALES

Alexander Hamilton, at the Treasury, had begun organizing the system that would administer sales of the land, which, according to the Ordinance of 1785, was to be sold at auction for at least one dollar per acre after being surveyed. Sales were to be administered by the Treasury, and surveying would be supervised by the U.S. geographer (a post abolished in 1796 and replaced by the surveyor general). Surveys were to be of townships in six-mile-square units. In 1796, the price was raised to two dollars per acre, but plots of 640 acres were allowed. However, sales on this scale proved disappointing.

In 1800, William Henry Harrison induced Congress to change the terms of sale. Sales of smaller parcels were allowed, and purchasers were permitted to buy on the installment plan, with payments to be made over a four-year period. Simultaneously, Albert Gallatin, at the Treasury, put in place an organization of land offices located in the areas to be sold; in 1812, these were subordinated to a General Land Office that supervised the local offices, rapidly increasing in number as more land was surveyed and put up for sale. This rearrangement of the system, particularly the inclusion of purchases on credit, laid the basis for a large land boom in the period between 1812 and 1819.

WEAKENED ECONOMY
The land boom revealed the weakness of the system created in 1800. Purchases on credit were hard to keep track of, with the limited clerical help in the local land offices and in the General Land Office; and Congress had passed a number of relief acts since 1800, extending the time limits on credit purchases. By 1820, only about a third of the purchase price of the lands recorded as sold had been collected. Federal finances were in perilous shape as a result of the War of 1812, which had raised the federal debt to new heights. Since receipts from land sales, along with tariff receipts, were the only sources of federal income, and as the South opposed any increases in tariff, reform of the sales of public lands was needed.

PROVISIONS OF THE 1820 LAND ACT
The Land Act of 1820 abolished credit purchases, requiring full payment in cash. However, the price was reduced from $2 per acre to $1.25 per acre, and those who still owed money on previous credit purchases were given more time to complete payments. Purchasers who still owed money would be allowed to surrender part of the land they had bought to cover the remaining debt due. Al-

though this law dealt with some of the problems in the system of selling off the public domain, it failed to still criticism, for the public lands issue had become deeply enmeshed in sectional politics, which would determine subsequent modifications.

Nancy M. Gordon

SOURCES FOR FURTHER STUDY
Carstensen, Vernon, ed. *The Public Lands: Studies in the History of the Public Domain.* Madison: University of Wisconsin Press, 1963.
Clark, Thomas D., and John D. W. Guice. *Frontiers in Conflict: The Old Southwest, 1795-1830.* Albuquerque: University of New Mexico Press, 1989.
Gates, Paul W. *History of Public Land Law Development.* Washington, D.C.: Zenger, 1968.
North, Douglas C., and Andrew R. Rutten. "The Northwest Ordinance in Historical Perspective." In *Essays on the Economy of the Old Northwest,* edited by David C. Klingaman and Richard K. Vedder. Athens: Ohio University Press, 1987.
Rohrbough, Malcolm J. *The Land Office Business: The Settlement and Administration of American Public Lands, 1789-1837.* New York: Oxford University Press, 1968.
Sword, Wiley. *President Washington's Indian War: The Struggle for the Old Northwest, 1790-1795.* Norman: University of Oklahoma Press, 1985.

SEE ALSO: Ordinance of 1785 (1785); Northwest Ordinance (1787); Preemption Act (1841).

MONROE DOCTRINE

DATE: Delivered December 2, 1823
CATEGORIES: Foreign Relations

The Monroe Doctrine became the primary articulation of the United States' foreign policy in the Western Hemisphere.

On December 2, 1823, President James Monroe delivered his annual message to Congress. Although most of his remarks concerned domestic matters and largely have been forgotten, his foreign policy declaration became the cornerstone of U.S. policy in the Western Hemisphere. "The American Continents," Monroe declared, "by the free and independent condition which they have assumed and maintain, are henceforth not to be considered as subjects for future colonization by a European power." The president then turned to European colonial policy in the New World:

> With the existing Colonies or dependencies of any European power, we have not interfered, and shall not interfere. But with the Governments who have declared their independence, and maintained it, and whose Independence we have, on great consideration, and on just principles, acknowledged, we could not view any interposition for the purpose of oppressing them, or controlling in any other manner, their destiny, by any European power, in any other light than as the manifestation of an unfriendly disposition towards the United States.

THREE PRINCIPLES

Monroe's message contained three main points outlining the United States' new role as defender of the Western Hemisphere. First, the president announced to Europe that the United States would oppose any attempt to take over any independent country in the Western Hemisphere (the no-transfer principle). Second, he promised that the United States would abstain from European quarrels (non-intervention). Third, Monroe insisted that European states not meddle in the affairs of the New World countries. In other words, Monroe declared that the United States would not take sides in European disputes, but in return, Europe could not tamper with the status quo in the Western Hemisphere.

Monroe's bold message offered no threat to such nations as Great Britain and France. In 1823, the United States lacked the power to enforce its new role in the Western Hemisphere. Fortunately for the United States, Great Britain desired just such a policy as Monroe suggested. The British fleet, not Monroe's declaration, would maintain the independence of Latin America. It was not until 1852 that anyone referred to Monroe's declaration as the Monroe Doctrine, and it was not until the twentieth century that the United States had enough power to insist on international acceptance of the Monroe Doctrine.

QUINTUPLE ALLIANCE AND THE CONCERT OF EUROPE

Even so, Monroe's words reflected the change in unfriendly relations between the United States and Great Britain that had led to the War of 1812. The explanation lies in the decisions made at the Congress of Vienna in 1815. Napoleon had been defeated; Prussia, Russia, Austria, France, and Great Britain set out to turn the clock back, through establishing a Quintuple Alliance to undo the damage wrought by Napoleon's ambition. The establishment of the alliance led to the Concert of Europe, which sponsored four congresses between 1818 and 1822. The congresses created the modern system of conference diplomacy, although the various members failed to agree on Europe's future.

Autocratic reactionaries hampered the Quintuple Alliance's effectiveness from the beginning. Czar Alexander I of Russia led the way, convincing the monarchs of Austria and Prussia to join him in the Holy Alliance, which dedicated itself to upholding autocratic rule. Great Britain chose not to join, but continued to be a member of the Quintuple Alliance. As a member of the Quintuple Alliance, Great Britain seemed to support a policy of reestablishing monarchy and opposing revolution. By refusing to join the Holy Alliance, however, the British avoided appearing as the bastion of the conservative reactionaries. When put to the test, Great Britain's actions proved that it favored a system of monarchy and a European balance of power, but not systematic oppression of revolution in others parts of the world.

"Other parts of the world" referred to the newly independent states in the New World. Spain, for one, demanded the return of its New World colonies. In 1820, when Prince Clemens von Metternich, the architect of reaction, suggested that the Concert of Europe had a sacred duty to crush revolution, Great Britain protested. Metternich's proposal would have meant sending an army to Latin America to overthrow the new republics. Great Britain distinguished between a European balance-of-power system, in which revolution would not be permitted, and a colonial empire in the New World where revolution would be allowed to occur. In addition, Spain had monopolized trade with its colonies; only as independent republics could the former colonies maintain a profitable trade with the British.

Alexander I also tried to extend his interests in North America. Through an imperial decree on September 14, 1821, Russia claimed territory on the Pacific coast south to the fifty-first parallel (well into Oregon Country) by insisting that all foreign ships must remain a substantial distance from the coast that far south. Secretary of State John Quincy Adams vigorously opposed the decree, citing the U.S. principle of noncolonization. Russia never enforced the decree.

THE POLIGNAC MEMORANDUM

Viscount Castlereagh, the British foreign secretary, decided that Spanish claims to territory in the New World were less important to Great Britain than profitable trade with Spain's former colonies. Accordingly, the British began devising an arrangement with the United States that would prevent European powers from taking new, or regaining old, colonies in the Western Hemisphere.

In August, 1823, George Canning, Castlereagh's successor, suggested to Richard Rush, the U.S. minister to Great Britain, that the two countries jointly declare that they would oppose further colonization of the New World. Rush was reluctant to agree to such a bold move without consulting his own superior, Adams. Canning began a series of discussions with Prince Jules de Polignac, the French ambassador in London, seeking some guarantee that France would not help Spain regain lost colonies in the New World. On October 12, 1823, the ambassador gave Canning the specific assurances he wanted, in a document known as the Polignac Memorandum. France's promise to Great Britain, not the Monroe Doctrine, ended any chance of Spain regaining its colonies in the New World. Unaware of the Polignac Memorandum, Adams advised Monroe against a joint noncolonization declaration with the British. Instead, he suggested that the United States make a unilateral declaration opposing further European colonization in the Western Hemisphere. The resulting declaration came in the president's message to Congress in December, 1823.

IMPACT

Since 1823, Monroe's message has gained much greater significance. During the Civil War, France established a puppet government under Austria's Archduke Maximilian in Mexico. In 1867, by invoking the Monroe Doctrine and threatening invasion, the United States ensured the collapse of Emperor Maximilian's government. In December, 1904, President Theodore Roosevelt added a corollary to the Monroe Doctrine, in which he stated that the United States would not interfere with Latin American nations that conducted their affairs with decency. Should they fail to do so, the United States would then intervene and exercise international police power to ensure the stability of the Western Hemisphere. In 1930, President Herbert Hoover formally repudiated the Roosevelt Corollary by revealing the publication of the Clark Memorandum adjuring any right of the United States to intervene in Latin America. The Monroe Doctrine would thus be applied only as originally intended—to protect Latin America from European intervention.

The United States, however, has found reasons for intervening in the affairs of countries in the Western Hemisphere since 1930. In 1965, President Lyndon Johnson ordered U.S. troops into the Dominican Republic to prevent a takeover of that country by a communist government, although the official justification for that action was the protection of U.S. citizens and property. The same justification was used by President Ronald Reagan in 1983 to invade the small island nation of Grenada. President George Bush, in 1989, used hemispheric stability and his war on drugs to invade Panama and capture Panamanian dictator and alleged drug lord Manuel Noriega.

David H. Culbert, updated by
William Allison

SOURCES FOR FURTHER STUDY

Bemis, Samuel Flagg. *The Latin American Policy of the United States: An Historical Interpretation*. New York: Norton Library, 1967.

Donovan, Frank Robert. *Mr. Monroe's Message: The Story of the Monroe Doctrine*. New York: Dodd, Mead, 1963.

Hart, Albert Bushnell. *The Foundations of American Foreign Policy*. New York: Da Capo Press, 1970.

May, Ernest R. *The Making of the Monroe Doctrine*. Cambridge, Mass.: The Belknap Press of Harvard University Press, 1975.

Rappaport, Armin, ed. *The Monroe Doctrine.* New York: Holt, Rinehart and Winston, 1964.
Ronfedlt, David F. *Rethinking the Monroe Doctrine.* Santa Monica, Calif.: Rand, 1985.
Smith, Gaddis. *The Last Years of the Monroe Doctrine, 1945-1993.* New York: Hill & Wang, 1994.

SEE ALSO: Clayton-Bulwer Treaty (1850); Good Neighbor Policy (1933); Inter-American Treaty of Reciprocal Assistance (1948).

INDIAN REMOVAL ACT

DATE: May 28, 1830
U.S. STATUTES AT LARGE: 4 Stat. 411-413
CATEGORIES: Native Americans

The act marked the beginning of forced resettlement of sixty thousand eastern Native Americans to lands west of the Mississippi River.

Cherokees and other members of the so-called Five Civilized Tribes—Choctaw, Chickasaw, Cherokee, Seminole, and Creek—established independent republics with successful governments. Adapting to their white neighbors, they became farmers, miners, and cattle ranchers. Some had plantations, even owning slaves. They built schools and churches, wrote constitutions, and established independent governments. Eventually, they learned a bitter lesson: Whites wanted their land, not their assimilation into Euro-American society.

WHITE-NATIVE CONFLICTS
As a local militia leader and politician, Andrew Jackson negotiated the acquisition of fifty million acres of Georgia, Alabama, Tennessee, and Mississippi even before he became president of the United States in 1828. By then, the Cherokees had lost their land outside Georgia, and neighbors had grown increasingly jealous of Cherokee success. For generations, Cherokees had provided a textbook picture of Jefferson's ideal nation of farmers. Sequoyah, a young

man of Cherokee and white blood, invented a phonetic alphabet, or syllabary, that enabled almost every member of his nation to become literate within a few months. To hold their remaining land, Cherokees made the sale of any additional land to whites a capital offense.

Yet violent conflicts between whites and natives became so common that many friends and enemies alike advocated removal to protect Cherokees from white citizens who routinely attacked them. In 1817, some Cherokees exchanged land in North Carolina for space in Arkansas. Within two years, six thousand had moved voluntarily, but the move only worsened Cherokee problems. By 1821, the Cherokees were at war with the Osages who had been in Arkansas Territory already, and both groups fought whites who continued to move onto their land.

EARLY REMOVALS

These early voluntary removals proved so disastrous that the Cherokees and Choctaws remaining in Georgia vowed to stay on their native land. Although President James Monroe proposed removal again in 1825, neither Monroe nor his successor, John Quincy Adams, could get the measure through Congress. Only the enthusiasm of President Jackson got removal approved on a close vote in 1830. In 1829, President Jackson admitted that the five republics had made "progress in the arts of civilized life," but he said American Indians occupied land that whites could use. Beyond the Mississippi River lay enough land for Native Americans and their descendants to inhabit without interference "as long as grass grows or water runs in peace and plenty."

Meanwhile, the Georgia legislature extended its power over the Cherokee nation and stripped Native Americans of civil rights. These laws forbade anyone with American Indian blood to testify in court against a white man, annulled contracts between Native Americans and whites, and required an oath of allegiance to Georgia by white people living among American Indians. The laws also prevented Native Americans from holding meetings or digging for gold on their own land.

LEGAL CHALLENGES

Instead of going to war, the Cherokees hired two prominent Washington lawyers and went to the U.S. Supreme Court. They lost their first case, challenging Georgia for hanging a Cherokee man convicted under Cherokee law. The second case (*Worcester v. Georgia*) challenged the loyalty oath designed to remove teachers, missionaries, and other whites from the reservation. The Reverend Samuel Worcester and other missionaries among Cherokees refused to sign the loyalty oath, despite public humiliation, abuse, and imprisonment.

Chief Justice John Marshall declared repressive Georgia laws unconstitutional. American Indian nations, Marshall said, were "domestic dependent nations" that could have independent political communities without state restrictions. President Jackson, who had fought American Indians in the South, suggested that Georgia could ignore the Court's decision. The president, not the Court, controlled the army.

CREATION OF INDIAN TERRITORY

Congress also took up Georgia's cause. The Indian Removal Act of 1830 began a process of exchanging Indian lands in the twenty-four existing states for new lands west of the Mississippi River. In 1834, Congress established Indian Territory, now much of Oklahoma, as a permanent reservation. Major Ridge and his family had been among the strongest opponents of removal, and Cherokee lobbyists, including John Ridge, celebrated their Supreme Court victory in *Worcester*. However, they had thought Whigs in Congress would prevail against Jackson's removal policy.

The federal removal law did not say that Native Americans could be forced to move, but the Ridge family and Cherokee newspaper editor Elias Boudinot began to see the move as necessary to protect Cherokees from increasing violence. Principal Chief John Ross, however, still resisted removal. Believing it in their nation's best interests, the Ridge family signed a removal treaty without approval of the tribal council.

RESISTANCE TO REMOVAL

Many natives resisted removal from their ancient homelands. The Alabama Creeks were forcibly removed, some of them in chains. Choctaws were forced out of Mississippi in winter, with no chance to bring provisions against the cold. Some were tricked into getting drunk and signing away their possessions. Others signed away their lands, believing the promises of government officials. Forced marches of Creeks, Choctaws, and Cherokees brought sickness, starvation, and death to thousands of people throughout the 1830's.

The Cherokees faced a special horror. Georgia's repressive laws had created a climate of lawlessness. Whites could steal land, and Cherokees could not testify in court against them. In one notorious case, two white men enjoyed dinner in the home of a family whose father was part Cherokee. In the evening, the parents left temporarily and the guests forced the children and their nurse from the home and set it on fire, destroying the house and all of its contents. The men were arrested, but the judge dismissed the case because all the witnesses were part Cherokee. Only pure-blooded whites were allowed to testify in court.

Finally, Jackson's successor, President Martin Van Buren, ordered General Winfield Scott, with about seven thousand U.S. soldiers and state militia, to begin the forced removal on May 26, 1838. Soldiers quietly surrounded each house to surprise its occupants, according to James Mooney, a researcher who interviewed the participants years later. Under Scott's orders, the troops built stockades to hold people while being prepared for the removal. "From these," Mooney wrote,

> squads of troops were sent to search out with rifle and bayonet every small cabin hidden away in the coves or by the sides of mountain streams, to seize and bring in as prisoners all the occupants, however or wherever they might be found. Families at dinner were startled by the sudden gleam of bayonets in the doorway and rose up to be driven with blows and oaths along the weary miles of trail that led to the stockade.

Men were taken from their fields, children from their play. "In many cases, on turning for one last look as they crossed the ridge, they saw their homes in flames." Some scavengers stole livestock and other valuables, even before the owners were out of sight of their homes. "Systematic hunts were made by the same men for Indian graves, to rob them of the silver pendants and other valuables deposited with the dead." Some sympathetic soldiers allowed one family to feed their chickens one last time, and another to pray quietly in their own language before leaving their home.

Within a week, the troops had rounded up more than seventeen thousand Cherokees and herded them into concentration camps. In June, the first group of about a thousand began the eight-hundred-mile journey. Steamboats took them on the first leg down the Tennessee River. The oppressive heat and cramped conditions fostered disease and caused many deaths. Then the Cherokees walked the last leg of the trip to beyond the western border of Arkansas. Because of the oppressive heat, Cherokee leader John Ross persuaded General Scott to permit them to delay the largest removal until fall. Thus, the largest procession—about thirteen thousand people—started on the long overland march in October, 1838. Most walked or rode horses; they drove 645 wagons.

THE TRAIL OF TEARS

Dozens of people died of disease, starvation, or exposure on each day of the journey. More than four thousand Cherokees died on the journey that the survivors named the Trail of Tears. The procession reached the Mississippi River opposite Cape Girardeau, Missouri, in the middle of winter. Most had only a single blanket to protect themselves from the winter winds as they waited for the river ice to clear. In March, 1839, they reached their destination in Indian Territory. Many were buried along the road, including Chief John Ross's wife, Quatie Ross, who died after giving up her blanket to a sick child in a sleet- and snowstorm. Her death left Ross to grieve both his wife and his nation.

In his last message to Congress, President Jackson said he had settled the Native American problem to everyone's satisfaction and saved the race from extinction by placing them "beyond the reach of injury or oppression." Native Americans would now share in "the blessings of civilization" and "the General Government will hereafter watch over them and protect them." Between 1778 and 1871, 370 treaties stipulated land cessions to whites. Jackson ridiculed the idea of making treaties with Native Americans and called the idea of treating American Indians as separate nations an absurd farce.

By the end of June, 1838, Georgians could boast that no Cherokees remained on their soil, except in the stockade. Sixty thousand members of the five republics had been removed beyond the Mississippi River. As many as fifteen thousand men, women, and children died of starvation and disease. The Choctaw had moved in

1832; the Chickasaw in 1832-1834, the Seminole in 1836, and the Creek in 1836-1840. In June, 1839, members of the Ross faction, in revenge for the law that John Ridge signed into effect, murdered John Ridge, Major Ridge, and Elias Boudinot for their signing a removal treaty selling Cherokee land.

William E. Huntzicker

SOURCES FOR FURTHER STUDY
Foreman, Grant. *Indian Removal: The Emigration of the Five Civilized Tribes of Indians.* 2d ed. 1953. Reprint. Norman: University of Oklahoma Press, 1985.
Green, Michael D. *The Politics of Indian Removal: Creek Government in Crisis.* Lincoln: University of Nebraska Press, 1982.
Guttmann, Allen. *States' Rights and Indian Removal: "The Cherokee Nation v. the State of Georgia."* Boston: D. C. Heath, 1965.
Hoig, Stanley. *Night of the Cruel Moon: Cherokee Removal and the Trail of Tears.* New York: Facts On File, 1996.
McLoughlin, William G. *Cherokee Renascence in the New Republic.* Princeton, N.J.: Princeton University Press, 1983.
_____. *Cherokees and Missionaries, 1789-1839.* New Haven, Conn.: Yale University Press, 1984.
Mooney, James. *Historical Sketch of the Cherokee.* Chicago: Aldine, 1975.
Moulton, Gary E. *John Ross, Cherokee Chief.* Athens: University of Georgia Press, 1978.
Remini, Robert V. *The Legacy of Andrew Jackson: Essays on Democracy, Indian Removal, and Slavery.* Reprint. Baton Rouge: Louisiana State University Press, 1990.
Wallace, Anthony F. C. *The Long, Bitter Trail: Andrew Jackson and the Indians.* New York: Hill & Wang, 1993.
Wilkins, Thurman. *Cherokee Tragedy: The Ridge Family and the Decimation of a People.* Rev. ed. Norman: University of Oklahoma Press, 1986.

SEE ALSO: Treaty of Dancing Rabbit Creek (1830); Preemption Act (1841); Indian Appropriation Act (1871); General Allotment Act (1887).

TREATY OF DANCING RABBIT CREEK

DATE: Signed September 27, 1830
U.S. STATUTES AT LARGE: 7 Stat. 333
CATEGORIES: Native Americans; Treaties and Agreements

In the first treaty signed after passage of the Indian Removal Act of 1830, the experience of the Choctaws foreshadowed that of many tribes as they sold their lands in Mississippi and agreed to move west.

The Choctaws originally occupied much of present-day Mississippi. The tribe prided itself on good relations with the United States and the fact that it had never fought against the United States. Instead Choctaws had fought as American allies in the Creek War (1813-1814) and War of 1812.

FORCED CESSION OF LANDS
Nevertheless the Choctaws came under increasing pressure from American settlers as the area filled rapidly after the War of 1812. In treaties going back to 1801, the Choctaws had ceded land to facilitate settlement. Pressed by General Andrew Jackson, in 1820 the tribe agreed to the Treaty of Doak's Stand. Five million acres of land in western and west-central Mississippi were sold to the United States; in return, the Choctaws acquired thirteen million acres west of the Mississippi. The acquisition of western land clearly raised the prospect of removal, though few Choctaws chose to emigrate.

American pressure mounted, however, especially after Jackson's election to the presidency in 1828. Encouraged by his administration's stated goal of removing the tribes east of the Mississippi, in January, 1830, the Mississippi legislature voted to extend state jurisdiction over Choctaw lands, effectively ignoring tribal claims to the land. Feeling pressured and believing that American power was irresistible, Choctaw leaders agreed to negotiate. Terms proposed by Greenwood LeFlore, recently elected principal chief of the tribe, were rejected as too expensive. The Choctaws then agreed to a new round of negotiations at Dancing Rabbit Creek.

TERMS OF THE TREATY
There in September, 1813, chiefs LeFlore, Mushulatubbee, and Nitekechi and six thousand Choctaws met American commission-

ers John Eaton and John Coffee. The Americans had made elaborate preparations to feed and entertain the Choctaws and to create a festive air for the negotiations. Reluctantly, the chiefs agreed to the terms requested: In return for a $20,000, twenty-year annuity and other financial considerations, the Choctaws would give up the remaining ten million acres of their land in Mississippi and move to their lands in present-day southeastern Oklahoma. Choctaws who wished to stay in Mississippi would receive one-square-mile allotments and U.S. citizenship, provided they registered within six months of the treaty's ratification and lived on their lands for five years. Relatively few Choctaws remained under this provision.

REMOVAL

Though a few hundred Choctaws had departed for Indian Territory in 1830 in hopes of locating the best land, removal of the bulk of the tribe began in 1831 and extended over a three-year period. Much hardship accompanied the Choctaw Trail of Tears, especially in 1831, and about 15 percent of the tribe died during removal. The Choctaws were the first major tribe to be moved under the Indian Removal Act, and their experience established an important precedent that would be followed with other eastern tribes.

William C. Lowe

SOURCES FOR FURTHER STUDY

Deloria, Vine, and Raymond J. Demallie. *Documents of American Indian Diplomacy: Treaties, Agreements, and Conventions, 1775-1979.* Norman: University of Oklahoma Press, 1999.

Falkowski, James E. *Indian Law/Race Law: A Five Hundred Year History.* New York: Praeger, 1992.

Prucha, Francis Paul. *American Indian Treaties: The History of a Political Anomaly.* Reprint. Berkeley: University of California Press, 1997.

SEE ALSO: Indian Removal Act (1830).

FORCE ACT OF 1833

DATE: March 2, 1833
U.S. STATUTES AT LARGE: 4 Stat. 632
CATEGORIES: Business, Commerce, and Trade; Tariffs and Taxation

*When the South invoked states' rights and the doctrine of nullifica-
tion to counter tariffs, the Jackson administration passed the Force
Act of 1833 to make North Carolina and other states adhere to federal
law, in this early conflict between South and North, federal and state
governments.*

By the late 1820's, the southeastern section of the nation was economically depressed. Most of its fiscal ailments were blamed on the
Tariff of 1828, which protected the North against competition for
its textile goods but limited the South's disposing of its agricultural
commodities in the world market. While the South languished, the
industrial Northeast flourished. In truth, the soil in the older
Southern states was worn out, which meant that the region could
not compete on equal terms with the new Gulf states. Leadership
in the fight against the tariff fell to South Carolina, where the
planter aristocrats enjoyed political power and the relative decline
in prosperity was the greatest.

THE ANTITARIFF SOUTH

The key to South Carolina's defiance against the tariff was its racial
demography and a very conservative political structure, different
from that of its slaveholding neighbors. In 1830, South Carolina
was the only state with an absolute majority of blacks. Most of them
were concentrated on the sea islands and tidal flats south of
Charleston. The low-country planters controlled state politics.
Very high property qualifications for holding office kept power in
the hands of the planter elite. This elite controlled the state legislature, which appointed most officials and therefore had tremen-
dous leverage on public opinion in the state.

A cotton state, South Carolina had experienced a collapse of
cotton prices in the Panic of 1819, soil erosion, competition from
cotton produced on cheaper, more fertile western lands, and an
exodus of its white population. Up-country slaveholders incurred

heavy losses when upland cotton prices fell 72 percent by 1829, and they were receptive to the argument of the antitariff advocates, or Nullifiers, who blamed the tariff for their plight. Tariff rates had increased up to 50 percent by 1828, and the Nullifiers argued that these high tariffs caused prices on domestic manufactured goods to rise and potentially limited export markets for agricultural goods. The tariffs penalized one class for the profits of another. Along with the tariff issue, there was the issue of slavery. The leaders of Nullification were rice and sea-island cotton planters whose greater fear was not losing cotton profits but losing control over their African American majority.

THE NULLIFICATION DOCTRINE

South Carolina's most eloquent spokesman was John C. Calhoun, who by the late 1820's had completed his philosophical change from ardent nationalist to states' rights advocate. Calhoun then advocated the ultimate in states' rights thinking—a belief in, and support of, the doctrine of nullification, first stated by Thomas Jefferson and James Madison in the Kentucky and Virginia Resolves of 1798. In 1828, while running as a vice presidential candidate, Calhoun anonymously wrote the "South Carolina Exposition and Protest." This essay was a protest against the Tariff of 1828, known as the Tariff of Abominations by Southerners because of its high protective duties. Calhoun's authorship of this document remained secret, and for four years South Carolina did not act upon it, hoping that President Andrew Jackson would fight for a lower tariff. The "Exposition" and a later paper called "A Disquisition on Government" explained Calhoun's doctrine of nullification.

Contrary to popular belief, Calhoun's theory did not advocate secession; rather, he believed that nullification would prevent the disruption of the Union. Calhoun saw nullification as an antidote to secession. The basic tenets of his argument were that sovereignty was, by its very nature, absolute and indivisible. Each state was sovereign, and the Union was a compact between the states. Each individual state entered into an agreement with the others, and the terms of this covenant went into the Constitution. The Constitution provided for a separation of powers between the states and the federal government, but not a division of sovereignty. Sovereignty was not the sum of a number of governmental powers but the will of the political community, which could not be divided without being destroyed. The states had been sovereign under the Articles of Confederation, and they had not given up their supreme authority when they joined the new Union. Since the Union had been created by the states, and not vice versa, it logically followed that the creator was more powerful than the creature. As the federal government was not supreme, it could exercise only those powers given it by the states, as embodied in the Constitution. Should it exceed these powers, the measures enacted would be unconstitutional.

Who was to be the arbiter of constitutionality? Certainly not the Supreme Court, for it was an instrument of the federal government; and if the federal government were not sovereign, then a branch of that government could not be sovereign. The supreme authority rested solely in the people of the states. When a state believed that a federal law exceeded the delegated powers of Congress, that state could declare the law null and void and prevent its enforcement within its own boundaries. When passing on the constitutionality of a law of the federal government, the state acted through a convention called for the express purpose of considering this question, for this was the only way in which the people of a state could give expression to their sovereign will. This action, however, should be taken only as a last resort to protect its rights. Congress could then counter by offering an amendment authorizing the powers that the state contested. If the amendment were not ratified, the law was to be annulled not only for the state but also for the entire nation. Should it pass, the dissatisfied state would have to yield or secede—it could not remain in the Union without accepting the amendment. Thus, the final arbiter would be the same power that created the Constitution, the people of the states. Calhoun was sure that this would prevent secession, for after three-fourths of the states had spoken against her, rarely would a state secede.

TARIFF OF 1832 AND SOUTHERN NULLIFICATION
After simmering for four years, the issue of nullification erupted in 1832 over a new tariff. In December, 1831, President Andrew Jackson recommended to Congress a downward revision of the tariff and the elimination of the worst features of the Tariff of 1828. Such a bill finally was pushed through on July 14, 1832, but the new tariff was not low enough for the Southern planters. Although some of the "abominations" were removed, the general level of the duties

was only slightly lower. The greatest reductions were made on non-competitive manufactured items, and the protective make-up of the tariff hardly had been changed.

By mid-1832, the South Carolina extremists were ready to put the nullification theory into action. Many denounced the Tariff of 1832 as unconstitutional and oppressive to the Southern people. In the subsequent state election that fall, the States' Rights and Unionist parties made the tariff and nullification the chief issues, and when the States' Rights Party elected more than two-thirds of the legislature, it promptly called for a state convention. The convention met in November, 1832, and by a vote of 136 to 26 adopted an Ordinance of Nullification on November 24. Both the Tariffs of 1828 and 1832 were declared null and void. After February 1, 1833, the tariff duties were not to be collected, and should the federal government attempt to collect them forcibly, South Carolina would secede.

JACKSON'S FORCE BILL
Jackson met this challenge in typical fashion. He boldly proclaimed on December 10, 1832, that the Constitution formed a government, not a league, and that the power of a single state to annul a federal law was "incompatible with the existence of the Union, contradicted by the letter of the Constitution, unauthorized by its spirit, inconsistent with every principle on which it was founded, and destructive to the great object for which it was formed." He called nullification an "impractical absurdity" and concluded that "disunion by armed force is treason." This "Proclamation to the People of South Carolina" received the enthusiastic support of nationalists.

While Jackson was bold, he was also conciliatory. In his fourth annual message to Congress, in December, 1832, Jackson promised to press for further reduction of the hated tariffs. This was repeated later the same month when the president issued a proclamation to the people of South Carolina. On January 16, 1833, Jackson sent a message to Congress reviewing the circumstances in South Carolina and recommending measures that would enable him to cope successfully with the situation. Tension mounted as the Senate passed the Force Bill in February. This measure authorized Jackson to use the United States Army and Navy to enforce the federal laws, if necessary.

Fulfilling his promise to see that the tariffs were reduced, Jackson did his best to see that legislation giving him full power to force obedience to the laws was accompanied by bills to reduce the tariffs. While the Force Bill was being debated, Henry Clay brought forward a new compromise tariff bill calling for the gradual reduction of tariff duties over the next ten years. By 1842, the tariff was not to exceed 20 percent. South Carolinians waited anxiously to see what would happen, for it was already apparent that no Southern states were coming to her aid, and she would have to fight it out alone. Calhoun, who had resigned the vice presidency after the passage of the Tariff of 1832 and had been elected immediately to the Senate, objected to the Force Bill but feared that strong opposition might hurt the chances of reconciliation that were presented by the Compromise Tariff. He and Clay worked to push the new tariff bill through Congress, and on March 2, 1833, Jackson signed into law both the Force Bill and the Compromise Tariff of 1833.

EFFECTS

Once the Compromise Tariff was passed, South Carolina repealed its Ordinance of Nullification (January 21); however, in a last gesture of defiance, the convention declared the Force Bill null and void. Jackson ignored this final face-saving move on the part of South Carolina, for the Force Bill was irrelevant if the tariff duties were being collected.

Both sides claimed victory. Nationalists declared that the power of the federal government had been upheld by both the president and Congress, while South Carolina asserted that nullification had proved an effective method of sustaining states' rights. However, the failure of any other Southern state to rally to South Carolina's defense showed that the doctrine of nullification was unpopular, and from that time forward, militant Southerners looked to the doctrine of secession as their best redress of grievances.

John H. DeBerry,
updated by Bill Manikas

SOURCES FOR FURTHER STUDY

Bancroft, Frederic. *Calhoun and the South Carolina Nullification Movement.* Baltimore: The Johns Hopkins University Press, 1928.

Barney, William L. *The Passage of the Republic.* Lexington, Mass.: D. C. Heath, 1987.

Bedford, Henry F., and H. Trevor Colbourn. *The Americans: A Brief History.* New York: Harcourt Brace Jovanovich, 1976.

Boucher, Chauncey S. *The Nullification Controversy in South Carolina.* Chicago: University of Chicago Press, 1916.

Capers, Gerald M. *John C. Calhoun: Opportunist.* Gainesville: University of Florida Press, 1960.

Coit, Margaret L. *John C. Calhoun.* Boston, Houghton Mifflin, 1950.

Smith, Page. *The Nation Comes of Age: A People's History of the Antebellum Years.* New York: McGraw-Hill, 1981.

SEE ALSO: Tenth Amendment (1789); Alien and Sedition Acts (1798).

PREEMPTION ACT

DATE: September 4, 1841
U.S. STATUTES AT LARGE: 5 Stat. 456
CATEGORIES: Land Management

The Preemption Act gave the West a sectional victory in the drive for free land.

The passage of the Land Act of 1820 did not terminate the debate over public land policy in the United States. Indeed, the western portion of the United States became more insistent and demanding concerning the liberalization of land laws. With migration feeding the West with a never-ending stream of inhabitants and with numerous Western territories ready for admission to the Union as states, this section of the nation gained political power. As the West grew in influence, the Northeast and the Southeast vied with each other to gain the political support of the West.

GROWTH OF SECTIONALISM
Between 1815 and 1850, the political life of the nation became increasingly sectionalized. Each section had a position on the major

issues of the day, which included land policy, tariffs, internal improvements, and fiscal policies. These issues assumed more importance as the national debt was paid off, freeing up resources for other purposes.

On most issues, the Northeast and the Southeast were on opposite sides. This allowed the West to embark on protracted negotiations designed to win support for liberalization of land policies in return for support on issues of major significance in the Northeast or Southeast. It was in this context that the West was able to push for its pet objectives, preemption and graduation. This pressure also led to the decision of the Jackson administration to force the tribes of the Old Southwest—the Cherokees, Creeks, Chickasaws, Choctaws, and Seminoles—to move to new lands west of the Mississippi River. These lands, now the state of Oklahoma, were designated Indian Territory. The forced transfer of these, the Five Civilized Tribes, became the infamous Trail of Tears. Meanwhile, the West pressed for liberalization of the laws governing sale of the public lands.

GRADUATION

Graduation was a device whereby the price of land would be reduced proportionate to the time that the land had been on the market unsold. At the end of a specified period of time, unsold land would be turned over to the state in which it was located. Senator Thomas Hart Benton of Missouri introduced such legislation in 1824 and again in 1830, but it was not until 1854 that the Graduation Act was passed; it contributed to the land boom of the mid-1850's.

PREEMPTION

Preemption meant recognition of the legal right of squatters on the public domain to purchase the land they occupied when it was offered for sale. As early as 1807, with the Intrusion Act, effective preemption was provided retrospectively for squatters on public land; between 1799 and 1830, a number of preemption acts had been passed, but they were all retrospective, of limited duration, and restricted to specific localities. In 1830, Congress passed the first general preemption law, the Preemption Act of 1830, permitting squatters cultivating the land in 1829 to buy up to 160 acres at the minimum price. This kind of legislation proved very difficult to administer, and there were numerous instances of fraud. Nevertheless, several hundred thousand acres of land were sold to settlers under the terms of this law.

What the West wanted, however, was permanent and prospective preemption. Henry Clay and the Whigs preferred distribution, that is, turning over the receipts from sale of the public lands to the states to finance internal improvements. After extensive and complex political maneuverings, a Distribution-Preemption Act passed Congress in September of 1841, with the proviso tacked on that if the tariff rose above 20 percent, distribution would be halted. This occurred in 1842, and distribution was halted, but preemption remained a permanent part of the public land laws of the United States.

PROVISIONS AND IMPACT

The Preemption Act of 1841 recognized that settlement prior to purchase did not constitute trespassing, and that the use of the land for settlement was more important than for raising revenue, although the latter goal had been the original objective of selling off the public lands. Under the law, any adult citizen (or an alien who had declared his intention to become a citizen) who had occupied, cultivated, and erected a dwelling on the public lands could purchase a tract of up to 160 acres at the minimum price. Theoretically, the provision still applied only to surveyed lands; however, squatting on unsurveyed lands increased, and the original settlers, if interested, were normally allowed to benefit from the Preemption Act once the lands were surveyed.

The Preemption Act of 1841 proved to be only a waystation in the process of moving the distribution of public lands to free lands. This principle was incorporated in the Homestead Act of 1862, whose passage then became possible because the South had withdrawn from the Union and the West had the power to achieve its ultimate end, free land for settlers.

John G. Clark, updated by
Nancy M. Gordon

SOURCES FOR FURTHER STUDY

Carstensen, Vernon, ed. *The Public Lands: Studies in the History of the Public Domain.* Madison: University of Wisconsin Press, 1968.

Feller, Daniel. *The Public Lands in Jacksonian Politics.* Madison: University of Wisconsin Press, 1984.

Gates, Paul W. *History of Public Land Law Development.* Washington, D.C.: Zenger, 1968.

North, Douglas C., and Andrew B. Rutten. "The Northwest Ordinance in Historical Perspective." In *Essays on the Economy of the Old Northwest*, edited by David C. Klingaman and Richard K. Vedder. Athens: Ohio University Press, 1987.

Rohrbough, Malcolm J. *The Land Office Business: The Settlement and Administration of American Public Lands, 1789-1837.* New York: Oxford University Press, 1968.

SEE ALSO: Land Act of 1820 (1820); Homestead Act (1862); Morrill Land Grant Act of 1862 (1862).

WEBSTER-ASHBURTON TREATY

DATE: Signed August 9, 1842
CATEGORIES: Foreign Relations; Treaties and Agreements

The settlement of a U.S.-Canadian boundary dispute sets a precedent for amicable relations between North American neighbors.

The Webster-Ashburton Treaty settled a boundary controversy that had irritated Anglo-American relations since the Treaty of Paris had been signed in 1783. This dispute in the Northeast involved sovereignty over portions of northern Maine and the Canadian province of New Brunswick. The area involved was not large, the region was remote and lightly populated, but again and again from 1783 to 1842, conflict between America and Great Britain intruded to prevent some rational settlement of the dispute.

THE BOUNDARY PROBLEM
The boundary problem was the result of ignorance about the geography of the northeastern region and of the failure of the negotiators at Paris in 1783 to attach maps to the treaty with the boundary

line clearly marked upon them. The treaty language stated that the Maine-New Brunswick boundary was to be the St. Croix River from Passamaquoddy Bay to its source, and then "a line drawn due north, from the source of the St. Croix River, to the Highlands which divide those rivers which empty into the River St. Lawrence from those which fall into the Atlantic Ocean." Unfortunately, British-American surveyors could not agree on which of two streams emptying into Passamaquoddy Bay was the St. Croix River; nor were the highlands described in the treaty identified to the satisfaction of both sides. As a result, until the boundary was definitely fixed, the inhabitants of an area of approximately 7.7 million acres did not know whether they owed allegiance to Canada or to the United States.

Numerous efforts were made to settle the conflict. One provision of Jay's Treaty in 1794 was for a mixed commission to identify the "real" St. Croix River and chart its course. Its findings, which offered a compromise solution to the dispute, were made part of a general convention signed in 1803. Congress refused, however, to consent to this agreement, largely because of the article dealing with the Northwest boundary question involving Oregon. Nothing further was attempted until the negotiations at Ghent in 1814 called to end the War of 1812. There, the British tried hard to win a favorable Canadian boundary settlement because, during the war, they had become aware of the importance of the area for the construction of a projected military highway from Montreal and Quebec to the Maritime Provinces. The United States refused to accede to British demands, and the peace treaty merely created four commissions to mark the entire boundary from the Atlantic to the Lake of the Woods, west of Lake Superior. With regard to the Northeast, the treaty provided that, should the commission fail to agree, the question would be given over to arbitration by a third state.

When the joint commission failed to reach agreement, the king of the Netherlands was asked to arbitrate the matter in 1827. The royal arbitrator proposed to divide the disputed territory almost equally between the two parties. Great Britain was willing to accept this compromise, as was President Andrew Jackson, but the states of Maine and Massachusetts opposed a solution that gave away a large piece of Maine's territory. Jackson submitted the issue to the Senate, which rejected the solution that had been proposed by the king of the Netherlands. Political pressures and concern for national prestige prevented the issue from being resolved for another decade.

THE *CAROLINE* AFFAIR

The 1830's witnessed numerous incidents related to the boundary issue, which further heightened the tension between the United States and Great Britain. The Canadian insurrection of 1837 elicited great sympathy from Americans along the frontier, and the *Caroline* affair (in which a U.S. citizen, Amos Durfee, was killed on U.S. soil by Canadians assisting British authorities) inflamed opinion against Great Britain throughout the United States. The arrest and trial in 1840 of Alexander McLeod, a Canadian deputy sheriff, for the murder of Durfee, which most historians believe he did not commit, brought anti-British sentiment to a peak and stood in the way of any compromise on the boundary issue. Great Britain threatened war if McLeod was convicted. McLeod was acquitted and the threat passed, but the incident underscored the danger of letting the tension between Great Britain and the United States over Canadian border issues continue to simmer.

More directly related was the so-called Aroostook War—a threatened conflict between Maine and New Brunswick forces in 1839. The fertile Aroostook Valley was, in this period, the scene of incidents of claim-jumping and furious competition for timber and land, and there was increasing violence. The danger of an armed clash was averted through a truce arranged by General Winfield Scott, but the basic problems remained to imperil the peace.

NEGOTIATIONS

The conflict was finally resolved in 1841, soon after Daniel Webster became secretary of state and Baron Ashburton (Alexander Baring), who had married a Philadelphia heiress and had extensive financial interests in the United States, was appointed special envoy for Great Britain with powers to resolve the boundary controversy. Ashburton's appointment signified the new priority placed by the British on Canadian issues. In the aftermath of Lord George Durham's report, which had called attention to Great Britain's previous neglect of the Canadian situation, the British government now was determined to take Canadian matters in hand. Ashburton was instructed to negotiate amicably with the

United States and to settle the border issue once and for all. Even before Ashburton's arrival, Webster had announced that the United States would consider a compromise boundary in the Northeast. Webster, as pro-British as any U.S. politician of his era, was convinced that the dispute must be settled. To do so, however, the McLeod case would have to be resolved and the state of Maine would have to be persuaded to accept a surrender of territory claimed as its own. McLeod was acquitted by a New York jury, but direct intervention by Webster was required to accomplish the second aim.

The negotiation of the Canadian border treaty was a high personal priority for Webster. He saw it as the capstone of his tenure as secretary of state and prolonged his tenure in that office just to negotiate the treaty. William Henry Harrison, the Whig president who had appointed Webster to the State Department, had died in 1841 after only a month in office, leaving the presidency to his vice president, John Tyler, who was a Democrat by party. Most of Harrison's cabinet were Whigs, and most resigned when Tyler showed he had no intention of following Whig policies. Webster, although also a Whig, stayed on because he believed the negotiation of the treaty with Great Britain would be a crucial and fundamental diplomatic achievement.

TREATY PROVISIONS

Webster and Ashburton began informal conversations in the autumn of 1841 and made rapid progress. They agreed to "split the difference" over the territory in dispute between Maine and New Brunswick; the United States won the line north of latitude 45° north as the boundary of New York and Vermont; minor adjustments were made in the region of Lake of the Woods in Minnesota and articles dealing with extradition, suppression of the international slave trade, and the *Caroline* affair were drafted.

The objections of Maine and Massachusetts to a compromise settlement, which were overcome only after strenuous efforts, culminated in the payment of $150,000 to each of the two states by the federal government. Jared Sparks, a noted historian, lobbied for the treaty in the Maine legislature, for which he was paid $14,500 by Ashburton. The treaty was signed on August 9, 1842, and was approved by the Senate less than two weeks later.

IMPACT

The Webster-Ashburton Treaty was an important achievement. It removed a source of potential conflict and brought about immediate improvement in Anglo-American relations. Historians agree that settlement of the Oregon controversy would have been exceedingly difficult without use of the Webster-Ashburton Treaty as a precedent. Nevertheless, the negotiations, or more precisely Webster's role in them, are accounted by some as a failure in United States diplomacy. By the treaty's terms, the United States conceded approximately five thousand of the twelve thousand square miles of disputed territory to Great Britain. There now exists strong evidence (much of which was available to Secretary of State Webster, had he wished to uncover it) to support the validity of the original U.S. claims. On the other hand, concessions made by Ashburton in the Lake of the Woods region gave the United States clear title to sixty-five hundred square miles of territory that later revealed valuable deposits of iron ore.

The United States had fought two previous wars against British troops based in Canada. The Webster-Ashburton Treaty did much to ensure that such a circumstance would never happen again. Although Webster was accused of sacrificing more territory to the British than necessary, his flexibility no doubt contributed to British willingness to let the United States have the richest portions of the Oregon Territory only a few years later. Webster and Ashburton did much to guarantee the unprecedented amity and peace that prevailed on the United States-Canadian border in the centuries after their agreement.

Theodore A. Wilson, updated by
Nicholas Birns

SOURCES FOR FURTHER STUDY

Bourne, Kenneth. *Britain and the Balance of Power in North America, 1815-1908.* Berkeley: University of California Press, 1967.

Jones, Howard. *To the Webster-Ashburton Treaty: A Study in Anglo-American Relations, 1783-1843.* Chapel Hill: University of North Carolina Press, 1977.

Peterson, Merrill D. *The Great Triumvirate: Webster, Clay, and Calhoun.* New York: Oxford University Press, 1987.

Raddall, Thomas. *The Path of Destiny.* Garden City, N.Y.: Doubleday, 1957.

Stevens, Kenneth R. *Border Diplomacy: The Caroline and McLeod Affairs in Anglo-American-Canadian Relations, 1837-1842.* Tuscaloosa: University of Alabama Press, 1989.

SEE ALSO: Treaty of Paris (1783); Jay's Treaty (1794); Treaty of Ghent (1814); Rush-Bagot Agreement (1817); Convention of 1818 (1818); Treaty of Washington (1871).

TREATY OF WANG HIYA

DATE: Signed July 3, 1844
CATEGORIES: Asia or Asian Americans; Foreign Relations; Treaties and Agreements

This treaty opened China to American trade.

Although the quality of Chinese ceramics, silk, and tea was much valued, for centuries China was not interested in establishing normal commercial relations. Often, European merchants visiting China were held hostage or killed.

In 1786, one year after the first American ship traded with China, Major Samuel Shaw of Boston was appointed the first American consulate general to China. In 1787, England tried to send an ambassador. Both were unsuccessful in normalizing trade with China, which was largely handled by a guild of Chinese merchants in Canton who were known for capriciousness and corruption.

THE FIRST OPIUM WAR
Meanwhile, Britain and other countries began to make huge profits by selling opium grown in India and elsewhere on the black market in Canton; the supply increased sevenfold from 1821 to 1837. In 1839, China declared a war on drugs that ultimately led to blockading the foreign community in Canton, stopping all trade, arresting a leading foreign dealer, and demanding that merchants surrender all their opium, which was then burned. One day during the antiopium campaign, drunken British sailors killed a Chinese

man. Although British officials followed the common practice of bringing them to justice in a British tribunal, Chinese authorities insisted that they be tried in a Chinese court. British officials in Canton refused. The conflict escalated, London sent gunboats, and the First Opium War began in November, 1839. The Treaty of Nanking of August, 1842, concluded the war.

U.S. TRADE DELEGATION

After the Nanking treaty won trade advantages for Britain, other counties sought the same. Accordingly, U.S. president John Tyler, with congressional approval, dispatched a trade mission, including a small naval escort, headed by Congressman Caleb Cushing. His assignment was to present American diplomatic credentials to the emperor in Beijing and to negotiate a commercial treaty. After the mission arrived in Portuguese Macao in February of 1844, Cushing, through two American Cantonese-speaking members of his delegation, asked Chinese officials if he could proceed to Canton, Tientsin, and Beijing, but his requests were denied. Instead, he waited until the emperor sent Commissioner Ch'i-ying, the negotiator of the Nanking treaty, who arrived along with other officials at Macao on June 20. When Cushing finally dropped his persistent request to go to Beijing, the Chinese negotiator came to terms, and the Treaty of Wang Hiya was completed and signed on the same day.

TREATY PROVISIONS

Similar to the Nanking treaty, Wang Hiya opened five ports to American trade, consular representatives were allowed with extraterritoriality privileges, and China granted most-favored-nation status; that is, British and any future favorable concessions would be automatically granted to the United States. Unlike the Nanking agreement, The Wang Hiya treaty prohibited trade in opium, and the United States did not demand to appropriate Chinese territory.

Terms of the Treaty of Wang Hiya were not consistently observed. After the Second Opium War, China signed several treaties in Tientsin during 1858, granting much more favorable terms. The American treaty of Tientsin, also known as the Burlingame Treaty, was revised in 1868 to provide a temporary basis for importing Chinese laborers to build the transcontinental railroad.

Michael Haas

SOURCES FOR FURTHER STUDY
Hewes, Agnes Danforth. *Two Oceans to Canton: The Story of the Old China Trade.* New York: Knopf, 1944.
Swisher, Earl. *China's Management of the American Barbarians: A Study of Sino-American Relations, 1841-1861.* New York: Octagon Books, 1972.

SEE ALSO: Burlingame Treaty (1868).

INDEPENDENT TREASURY ACT

DATE: August 6, 1846
U.S. STATUTES AT LARGE: 9 Stat. 59
CATEGORIES: Banking, Money, and Finance; Government Procedure and Organization; Tariffs and Taxation

Management of Treasury funds was removed from state-chartered banks, resulting in a federal means of regulating the monetary system.

Creation of the Independent Treasury system, finally achieved in 1846, was the outgrowth of the controversy arising from President Andrew Jackson's refusal to accept recharter of the Second Bank of the United States. In 1833, Jackson and his secretary of the Treasury, Roger B. Taney, determined to withdraw government deposits from the Second Bank and transfer them to state-chartered banks. Since there was a hint of political patronage in this process, the newly selected deposit banks were soon termed the "pet banks." There were few checks on how these banks were to operate.

BOOM AND BUST
The years from 1833 to 1836 were a time of economic boom. Gold flowed into the country in payment for cotton exports and foreign investment. The gold entered bank reserves and banks responded by expanding loans, note issues, and deposits. There was a strong upsurge in sales of public lands by the government, bringing a

flood of revenues and enabling the government to pay off the national debt. Government deposits expanded rapidly, and in June of 1836, Congress voted to distribute the surplus to the states.

In 1837, however, a deflationary panic occurred, partly in response to the withdrawal of specie from banks to carry out the distribution of the surplus. The Panic of 1837, and the depression that followed, resulted in the failure of numerous banks, including some that held government deposits. More commonly, banks continued to operate but refused to redeem their liabilities in specie. As the economic depression reduced government revenue, the Treasury was hard-pressed by the unavailability of its bank deposits. Furthermore, there was widespread public resentment against the banking system, which was blamed for the panic and depression. The Treasury found itself obliged to make some of its payments using depreciated notes of its deposit banks. An element among the Jacksonian politicians had long held the view that banks' privilege to issue banknote currency should be curbed. This view was reflected in government directives restricting the acceptability of small-denomination banknotes in payments to the government, and in the Specie Circular of July, 1836, which ordered that payments to the government for public-land purchases be made in gold or silver.

However, the Panic of 1837 proved short-lived. Most banks resumed specie payments in the spring of 1838, a process facilitated by continued inflow of gold from overseas. Then, during 1839, deflationary conditions returned. This time, there were heavy gold exports and downward pressure on money and credit, leading to a 30 percent decline in prices between 1839 and 1843. Concern for the Treasury deposits and antibank sentiment combined to provide support for creating an Independent Treasury—independent of the banks, that is.

DEVELOPING THE INDEPENDENT TREASURY
Proposals for an Independent Treasury system began as early as 1834 in Congress, when William F. Gordon, an anti-Jackson Democrat, introduced such a measure to curb the potential political influence involved in relations with the "pet banks." President Martin Van Buren, in a message to a special session of Congress on September 5, 1837, called for a specie currency, criticized the operation of state-chartered banks, and suggested a plan to open Trea-

sury depositories independent of the banks. Congress debated the idea for the next nine years and finally passed the Independent Treasury Act on June 30, 1840, only to repeal it on August 13, 1841. On August 1, 1846, such a system was enacted again. It served as the basis for managing government funds until the inception of the Federal Reserve System in 1914.

The Independent Treasury Act adopted in 1840 reflected the antibank sentiments of Jacksonian Democrats. The election of 1840 shifted power to the Whigs, who repealed the 1840 law before it had much effect. The Independent Treasury was replaced as an issue by the efforts of Henry Clay and the Whigs to charter a new national bank. However, the untimely death of President William Henry Harrison brought John Tyler into the presidency. Tyler, a strong proponent of states' rights, vetoed two bills to create a new national bank. The victory of James K. Polk and the Democratic Party in 1846 allowed the reenactment of the Independent Treasury.

THE NEW SYSTEM

Under the new system, subtreasuries were established in six leading cities, with responsibility for receiving, safeguarding, and paying out government funds. The government's mints participated in these operations. All government transactions were to be conducted either in gold and silver coin or in Treasury notes. The latter were short-term, interest-bearing securities issued as part of the national debt. Some of them were issued with very low interest rates and were clearly designed to circulate as paper currency, even though they were not technically legal tender. The government now maintained no deposit accounts with banks, nor could it receive checks or banknotes for payments to the government.

Although technically independent of the banks, the Treasury's operations soon displayed substantial influence on banking conditions. At times, government revenues exceeded disbursements, and specie accumulated in the Treasury offices, draining off reserves from the banks and putting banks under pressure to contract loans, with deflationary consequences. At other times, government deficits led to a net flow of specie from Treasury to banks, with expansionary effects that were not always desirable. Ingenious methods were devised by secretaries of the Treasury to try to prevent these operations from causing financial damage. During the early 1850's, for example, boom conditions—arising in part from the California gold discoveries—led to a large increase in specie held in the Treasury. The national debt had increased substantially since 1836. This gave Secretary of the Treasury James Guthrie the opportunity to buy government securities in the open market. These purchases helped transfer funds from the Treasury to the banks and relieve them from deflationary pressure. Such operations became an important element in Treasury operations during the remainder of the period until to 1914.

The Civil War altered the character of the system. In 1863 and 1864, with the passage of the National Bank Acts, the government adopted a system of chartering local banks, to be called national banks. These were eligible to hold government deposits. Legal-tender government paper currency, the "greenback," was introduced in 1862. Both government and banks went off the specie standard until 1879, so government transactions were conducted with paper money. However, the subtreasuries continued to operate and to influence bank reserves and monetary conditions.

Paul B. Trescott

SOURCES FOR FURTHER STUDY

Hammond, Bray. *Banks and Politics in the United States from the Revolution to the Civil War.* Princeton, N.J.: Princeton University Press, 1957.

McPaul, John M. *The Politics of Jacksonian Finance.* Ithaca, N.Y.: Cornell University Press, 1972.

Schlesinger, Arthur M., Jr. *The Age of Jackson.* New York: Mentor Books, 1945.

Taus, Esther Rogoff. *Central Banking Functions of the United States Treasury, 1789-1941.* New York: Columbia University Press, 1943.

Timberlake, Richard H. *Monetary Policy in the United States: An Intellectual and Institutional History.* Chicago: University of Chicago Press.

SEE ALSO: National Bank Acts (1863-1864); Coinage Act (1873); Currency Act (1900); Federal Reserve Act (1913).

TREATY OF GUADALUPE HIDALGO

DATE: Signed February 2, 1848
U.S. STATUTES AT LARGE: 9 Stat. 922
CATEGORIES: Foreign Relations; Latinos; Native Americans; Treaties and Agreements

The treaty ended the Mexican-American War, forcing Mexico to cede about half its national territory to the United States and disrupting the lives of native peoples in the ceded territory.

The Treaty of Guadalupe Hidalgo, drafted and signed at the Mexican village of Guadalupe Hidalgo, near Mexico City, ended the Mexican War (1846-1848). The war had been prompted partly by hawkish adherents of "manifest destiny," a belief in the inevitable expansion of the United States through the whole of North America, although it had nominally erupted over disputed territories shortly after the United States annexed the Republic of Texas in 1845. The specific cause of the war was the dispute over which river—the Rio Bravo del Norte or the Nueces—marked a boundary line between the two countries. War had been declared formally in April of 1846, after Mexican and U.S. troops clashed in the disputed territory between the two rivers.

THE MEXICAN WAR

In Mexico, political turmoil and poor military strategy and preparedness at first led to fairly easy U.S. victories. Successful campaigns in northeastern Mexico by General Zachary Taylor caused the collapse of the Mexican government and the recall from exile of General Antonio López de Santa Anna, who fought a close but losing battle against Taylor at Buena Vista in February of 1847. The tide turned fully against Mexico when General Winfield Scott invaded Mexico at Veracruz and fought his way inland against tough resistance to capture Mexico City. The crucial battle in Scott's march from the sea was fought against Santa Anna at Cerro Gordo on April 18, 1847; even with Santa Anna's defeat, Scott's army had difficulty, and it was not until September 14, 1847, that his troops entered and took control of the Mexican capital.

NEGOTIATIONS BEGIN
Santa Anna, threatened with impeachment for his conduct of the war, went once more into exile. In order to take direct command of the Mexican forces, he earlier had named Manuel de la Peña y Peña interim president and eventually had to ask the Peña government for permission to leave Mexico. It was Peña who was forced to agree to the terms of the Treaty of Guadalupe Hidalgo, negotiated under the weakest possible conditions for Mexico. For a payment of $15 million and $3.25 million in claims of Mexican citizens, Mexico ceded to the United States the territories of New Mexico and Upper California. The agreement also established the Mexican-American boundary, which followed the course of the Rio Grande from the Gulf of Mexico to the southern border of New Mexico, west to the Gila and Colorado Rivers, and eventually to a point just south of San Diego on the Pacific Ocean.

The negotiations leading up to the treaty were complex. In April of 1847, President Polk had sent Nicholas P. Trist of the Department of State to Scott's camp with a secret treaty proposal drafted by James Buchanan, secretary of state. Trist was empowered to consider counterproposals and secure an armistice, which was actually arranged in late August of that same year. Scott had been in secret communication with Santa Anna, who, without the knowledge of the Mexican government, was trying to arrange treaty terms on his own. Santa Anna assured Scott that hostilities could be suspended and a treaty negotiated if and when Scott's army laid siege to Mexico City. Scott had even written a memorandum in which he avowed that he would fight a battle in view of the capital and then "give those in the City an opportunity to save the capital by making a peace."

A BREAK IN THE ARMISTICE
Scott, with victories at Contreras and Churubusco in August, 1847, had met Santa Anna's conditions. The road to Mexico City was open, and the remnants of Santa Anna's army had been put to disordered flight, taking refuge within the capital. Scott was certain that a peace with a compliant Santa Anna could be quickly negotiated. Santa Anna, however, was as deceitful and crafty as Scott was forthright and naïve. He knew that Scott's army was wracked by disease, declining morale, and logistics problems, and he believed that time was an invisible ally. As his blame-shifting maneuvers

made clear, he also wanted to avoid making any treaty concessions that would tarnish his national image. Thus, although a cease-fire was arranged and agreed to, the efforts to draft a mutually acceptable set of terms at the ensuing peace conference proved futile and were probably doomed from the outset. The armistice broke off on September 6, and on September 14 Scott took Mexico City. Santa Anna had already fled.

When it became clear to Buchanan and Polk that Santa Anna was stalling, Polk ordered the recall of Trist, in part to counteract the impression that the United States was anxious to achieve a peace, a view gaining currency among the Mexican people. Trist did not return, however; he stayed on after the futile negotiations broke off and fighting resumed. The war dragged on past the departure of Santa Anna, who met his final defeat at Puebla on October 11. It was abundantly clear that Mexico could not turn the war's tide, and within two months, it sued for peace. Trist, never having returned home, became the chief U.S. negotiator at Guadalupe Hidalgo, where the treaty was finally signed.

TREATY PROVISIONS
The drafted terms, readied by January 24, 1848, more fully realized the territorial ambitions of the United States than the terms that had been discussed during the earlier armistice conference, which had at least left the Texas border question open. However, even from the outset of the earlier negotiations, it had been clear that the United States was determined to annex both Upper California and New Mexico. In the end, Santa Anna's delaying tactics had proved a bit more costly to Mexico.

Because a flawed map was used during the treaty negotiations, the boundaries between Mexico and the United States remained open to interpretation. Surveyors could not agree on the identity of the first branch of the Gila River, one of the important demarcation lines, and the boundary line between Mexico and the United States in the area separating the Gila River and the Rio Grande was not settled. However, both the Rio Grande and the Gila River were established as principal boundaries. Mexico thereby ceded territories south of the Nueces River and all of Upper California from one nautical league south of San Diego to the Northwest Territories. The United States gained all of the Territory of New Mexico, the disputed lands in southern Texas, and Upper California. In consideration for ceding this vast acreage, the United States was to pay only the stipulated $15 million plus the $3.25 million in claims. It was a grand bargain for the expansionist believers in manifest destiny. The treaty terms were quickly accepted by Polk and, with some amendments, ratified by the U.S. Senate on March 10, 1848.

The Treaty of Guadalupe Hidalgo did not immediately end the boundary issue. In 1853, during the administration of Franklin Pierce, the current border between Mexico and the United States was finally set when the United States purchased the Arizona Territory from Mexico in the Gadsden Purchase and described the boundary line between the two countries in the disputed area.

An important provision of that treaty, Article VII, granted U.S. citizenship with full constitutional rights to the Mexicans living in the ceded territories and guaranteed them ownership of their land. However, through the invalidation of Spanish and Mexican land grants, federal courts and the U.S. Congress allowed government agencies, ranchers, land speculators, and business and railroad magnates to gobble up acreage that, by the terms of the treaty, rightly belonged to Mexican Americans. Over two generations, almost twenty million acres of their land was lost to private owners and state and federal agencies.

John W. Fiero

Sources for Further Study

Brack, Gene M. *Mexico Views Manifest Destiny, 1821-1846: An Essay on the Origins of the Mexican War.* Albuquerque: University of New Mexico Press, 1975.

Callahan, James M. *American Foreign Policy in Mexican Relations.* New York: Macmillan, 1932.

McAfee, Ward, and J. Cordell Robinson, comps. *Origins of the Mexican War: A Documentary Source Book.* 2 vols. Salisbury, N.C.: Documentary Publications, 1982.

Pletcher, David M. *The Diplomacy of Annexation: Texas, Oregon, and the Mexican War.* Columbia: University of Missouri Press, 1973.

Singletary, Otis A. *The Mexican War.* Chicago: University of Chicago Press, 1960.

See also: Adams-Onís Treaty (1819); Oregon Act (1848).

OREGON ACT

DATE: August 14, 1848
U.S. STATUTES AT LARGE: 9 Stat. 323
CATEGORIES: Land Management

This bill organized the Oregon territory and laid the groundwork for its later statehood.

The need to organize an Oregon government arose after the United States and Great Britain agreed to divide the Oregon region at the forty-ninth parallel in June of 1846. When Congress convened in December, President James K. Polk recommended that Oregon be recognized as a territory eligible for statehood. Polk did not expect difficulties. The residents of Oregon had already created a provisional government and in 1844 passed two laws: the first prohibiting slavery, the second forever forbidding residence by free black persons. No one doubted that Oregon would be free territory.

WILMOT PROVISO
When Polk asked for an Oregon bill, he also requested three million dollars to purchase land from Mexico, thus entangling Oregon in the Mexican territory dispute. Northern congressmen angered southern defenders of slavery when they tried attaching the Wilmot Proviso, banning slavery from any land acquired from Mexico, to Polk's Three-Million Bill. The House Committee on Territories reported an Oregon bill on January 14 using the language of Thomas Jefferson's Northwest Ordinance of 1787 to exclude slavery. A southern congressman proposed an amendment stating that Oregon was free territory because it lay north of the 36°30′ Missouri Compromise line. Northerners objected that this reversed the Wilmot Proviso's objective, implying that land south of the line could be slave territory. The amendment lost on a strictly sectional vote of 83 to 118. When a Senate committee took the slavery ban out of the Oregon Bill, northern senators tabled the bill rather than accept it in that form. Even though Northerners and Southerners agreed that Oregon would be free, they could not disentangle this agreement from their disagreement over territories in gen-

217

eral. Their opposing positions hardened into demands that slavery either be sanctioned in all territories or prohibited in all territories.

PROVISIONS FOR STATEHOOD
When an Indian war broke out in Oregon, underscoring the urgency of organizing the region, Polk, in June 1848, again requested Congress to accept the Missouri Compromise line. The Senate approved a bill specifying the 36°30′ line as the basis for excluding slavery, but the House defeated the measure. On August 12, three slave-state senators shifted their votes and accepted a bill specifying that Oregon would be free of slavery under the provisions of the 1787 ordinance and existing local laws. Polk signed the bill on August 14.

The bill provided that voters could elect a territorial legislature and send a nonvoting delegate to Congress. The president appointed the governor, secretary, judges, and governor's council. When the population reached sixty thousand, Oregon could hold a convention and submit a constitution to Congress for approval. The 1857 convention asked voters to separately consider the two articles banning slavery and prohibiting admission of free blacks. Both provisions passed by margins of eight to one. The exclusion clause was not repealed until 1926. Oregon became a state within its present boundaries in 1859 and voted for Abraham Lincoln in 1860.

Milton Berman

SOURCES FOR FURTHER STUDY
Nevins, Allan. *Fruits of Manifest Destiny, 1847-1852.* Vol. 1 in *Ordeal of the Union.* New York: Charles Scribner's Sons, 1947.
Potter, David M. *The Impending Crisis, 1848-1861.* New York: Harper & Row, 1976.

SEE ALSO: Northwest Ordinance (1787); Treaty of Ghent (1814); Convention of 1818 (1818); Missouri Compromise (1820); Treaty of Guadalupe Hidalgo (1848).

CLAYTON-BULWER TREATY

DATE: Signed April 19, 1850
CATEGORIES: Foreign Relations; Transportation; Treaties and Agreements

Although criticized for violating the Monroe Doctrine, this treaty between Great Britain and the United States was negotiated to ensure U.S. and British neutrality in building land routes and waterways across the Central American isthmus.

After the United States acquired Oregon in 1846 and California in 1848, the need for quicker communications between the Atlantic and Pacific coasts stimulated American interest in a canal across Central America. Great Britain, the major maritime power of the world, alarmed the United States by its activities in that region. Britain had established a protectorate over the Mosquito Indians on the east coast of Nicaragua and occupied Greytown at the mouth of the San Juan River. Many observers believed the most feasible canal route crossed Nicaragua, reaching the Atlantic via the San Juan River. Britain appeared intent on controlling that path.

NEGOTIATING NEUTRALITY

A worried American secretary of state, John M. Clayton, had the American minister in London ask the British foreign secretary if his country intended to establish new colonies in Central America and whether Britain would join the United States in guaranteeing the neutrality of any interoceanic canal. Britain denied any intention of establishing new colonies and sent Sir Henry Lytton Bulwer to Washington in December, 1849, to negotiate an agreement reconciling the views of the two countries regarding Central America.

After much diplomatic sparring, Clayton and Bulwer signed a treaty the following April providing that neither nation would try to control any canal or railroad built across Central America. Both agreed not to fortify a future canal, to cooperate in guaranteeing the neutrality of any that might be built, and to assure equal access for all nations to the prospective waterway. Article I pledged that neither country would colonize or exercise dominion over any part of Central America.

Article I proved a source of bitter dispute between the two countries. The phraseology on noncolonization was deliberately ambiguous; Clayton had wanted the British to pledge the return of the Mosquito Coast and Greytown to Nicaragua, but Bulwer would not admit that Britain's actions were improper. When the United States later requested that Britain withdraw from the Mosquito country, the British refused, insisting the treaty could not be applied retroactively to existing British positions.

AN UNPOPULAR TREATY

The treaty was persistently unpopular in the United States. Critics said it violated the Monroe Doctrine by treating Great Britain as an equal partner in the Western Hemisphere. In the latter half of the nineteenth century, American opinion began to demand exclusive American control of any Isthmian canal. Presidents, beginning with Ulysses S. Grant, tried without success to convince Great Britain to revoke the Clayton-Bulwer Treaty and permit sole United States construction and control of a canal.

Acquisition of the Philippines increased American desire for a canal. Diplomatic difficulties during the Boer War influenced Great Britain to be more flexible. The 1901 Hay-Pauncefote agreement granted the United States the right to construct, own, and operate an Isthmian canal and empowered the United States to fortify the waterway, as long as it was available to all nations on an equal basis. When the canal opened in 1914, it crossed Panama rather than Nicaragua.

Milton Berman

SOURCES FOR FURTHER STUDY

Van Alstyne, Richard W. "British Diplomacy and the Clayton-Bulwer Treaty, 1850-1860." *Journal of Modern History* 11 (1939): 149-183.

Williams, Mary Wilhemine. *Anglo American Isthmian Diplomacy, 1815-1915.* Washington, D.C.: American Historical Association, 1916.

SEE ALSO: Monroe Doctrine (1823); Panama Canal Act (1912); Panama Canal Treaties (1978).

FUGITIVE SLAVE ACT OF 1850

DATE: September 18, 1850
U.S. STATUTES AT LARGE: 9 Stat. 462
CATEGORIES: African Americans; Slavery

This law, aimed at making the rendition of fugitive slaves from Northern states easier for Southern slaveholders, exacerbated tensions between North and South.

Congress passed the Second Fugitive Slave Law in September, 1850, as part of the Compromise of 1850. This compromise, its supporters hoped, would provide a permanent settlement of the long-standing dispute between the North and the South over slavery. The dispute had reached crisis proportions in 1848, after the United States forcibly acquired from Mexico huge territories in the Southwest, which raised the issue of the status of slavery in those territories. Most of the provisions of the Compromise of 1850 dealt with that issue. Southern white spokespersons also insisted that the government do something to prevent slave escapes into the North and to make it easier for masters to reclaim fugitive slaves from there.

SLAVE ESCAPES
Slave escapes had been common long before the United States became an independent country. It was the decision of the Northern states following the Revolutionary War to abolish slavery within their bounds that created a sectional issue. As a result, in 1787, Southern influence brought about the insertion in the U.S. Constitution of a clause providing that slaves escaping from one state to another were not to be freed but returned to their masters.

This clause established the constitutional basis for fugitive slave laws. The first such law, passed by Congress in 1793, allowed masters, on their own, to apprehend escaped slaves in the free states. Although this law provided no legal protection for persons accused of being fugitive slaves, neither did it authorize state or federal assistance for masters attempting to reclaim slaves.

PERSONAL LIBERTY LAWS
Several events in the 1840's prompted Southern whites to intensify demands for a stronger fugitive slave law. First, the number of slave

221

escapes increased as the slave labor system in the border slave states weakened. Second, a few black and white abolitionists became active in helping slaves escape. Third, Northern states began passing "personal liberty laws" requiring jury trials to determine the status of African Americans accused of being fugitive slaves. Such trials provided protection to those falsely accused and also made it more difficult for masters to reclaim actual escapees.

The Supreme Court addressed this last issue in the case of *Prigg v. Commonwealth of Pennsylvania* (1842). In *Prigg*, the Court ruled that a state could not interfere with the right of a master to recapture slaves. The Court also ruled, however, that, because the power to legislate on the fugitive slave issue was purely national, states were not required to assist in the enforcement of the First Fugitive Slave Law. This ruling allowed for a new series of personal liberty laws that denied masters the support they needed to apprehend alleged slaves. For many Southern whites, who feared that slave escapes were a major threat to the existence of slavery in the border slave states, the fugitive slave law issue loomed as large as the issue of slavery in the territories in the late 1840's. In response to these concerns, Senator James Mason of Virginia proposed the passage of a new and stronger fugitive slave law, on January 3, 1850.

HARSH PROVISIONS

When Mason's much-amended bill became law nine months later, it appeared to be all that Southern whites demanded. It provided that United States marshals had to assist masters in arresting fugitive slaves and that the marshals could, in turn, summon Northern citizens to help. It provided that United States circuit courts appoint numerous commissioners who were empowered to evaluate the truth of a master's claim and authorize the return of fugitives to a master's state. Accused fugitives were not permitted to testify before the commissioners. The commissioners would receive a fee of ten dollars if they accepted a master's claim and only five dollars if they did not. Anyone who interfered with the apprehension of alleged fugitive slaves or who helped such persons escape was subject to a fine of up to one thousand dollars and imprisonment for up to six months.

To many Northerners, the new law seemed to be excessively harsh and corrupting. Even Northerners who expressed no opposition to slavery in the South had little enthusiasm for assisting in the rendition of fugitive slaves. The denial to the accused of the right to testify, of the writ of habeas corpus, and of a jury trial appeared to be invitations for the unscrupulous to use the new law to facilitate kidnapping of free African American Northerners. That commissioners were paid more to remand to the South persons accused of being fugitive slaves than to exonerate such persons seemed to be a bribe in behalf of the putative masters. The official explanation of the different fees—that to send the accused back to the South required more paperwork than to reject a master's claim—seemed a disingenuous excuse to many Northerners. Finally, because the law was retroactive, fugitive slaves who had lived safely in the North for many years were now subject to recapture.

To abolitionists, who opposed the very existence of slavery and encouraged slaves to escape, and to antislavery politicians, who contended that the South was seeking to expand its slave system into the North, the new law was anathema. The law's harshness and its apparent invasion of Northern states' rights led less committed Northerners to oppose it as well. Even as the bill that became the Second Fugitive Slave Law made its way through Congress, antislavery senators Salmon P. Chase of Ohio and William H. Seward of New York attempted, without success, to defeat it or to include in it provisions for jury trials. Antislavery Northerners denounced Senator Daniel Webster of Massachusetts for his March 7, 1850, endorsement of the bill. When it became law on September 18, there were protests throughout the North, although most Northerners acquiesced in its enforcement.

RESISTANCE

In many instances, however, enforcement was very difficult. As soon as the law went into effect, African Americans escaping from the South went to Canada, beyond the reach of the law. Others who had lived in the North for years took refuge across the Canadian border in times of danger. New personal liberty laws in a number of Northern states—several of which required jury trials—not only protected those falsely charged with being fugitive slaves but, by adding expenses, discouraged masters from pressing claims. Harriet Beecher Stowe's best-selling novel, *Uncle Tom's Cabin*, first published in serial form in 1851-1852, both reflected and encouraged Northern antipathy to the Second Fugitive Slave Law. By portraying slavery as a brutal system and depicting fugitive slaves sympathetically, Stowe aroused an emotional Northern reaction against the law.

Most striking, blacks and whites physically resisted enforcement of the law throughout the 1850's. Shortly after the law went into effect, former slave Harriet Tubman, with the help of black and white abolitionists, began her career of leading bands of slaves out of the South. Meanwhile, in Boston, Massachusetts; Christiana, Pennsylvania; Syracuse, New York; Wellington, Ohio; Milwaukee, Wisconsin; and elsewhere in the North, armed biracial mobs obstructed the enforcement of the act.

While the law was peacefully enforced in large regions of the North, its most important effect was to widen the gulf between the North and South. Many Northerners considered the law to be unconstitutional and an immoral Southern aggression, in behalf of an oppressive institution, upon not only African Americans but also the rights and values of Northern whites. White Southerners, many of whom had predicted that the new Fugitive Slave Law would be ineffective, regarded Northern resistance to it as another sign of antipathy toward the South and its institutions. What had been designed as part of a compromise to quiet sectional animosities, instead increased those animosities and helped lead the nation into civil war in 1861.

Stanley Harrold

SOURCES FOR FURTHER STUDY

Brandt, Nat. *The Town That Started the Civil War.* Syracuse, N.Y.: Syracuse University Press, 1990.

Campbell, Stanley W. *The Slave Catchers: Enforcement of the Fugitive Slave Law, 1850-1860.* New York: W. W. Norton, 1972.

Hamilton, Holman. *Prologue to Conflict: The Crisis and Compromise of 1850.* New York: W. W. Norton, 1964.

Potter, David M. *The Impending Crisis, 1848-1861.* Completed and edited by Don. E. Fehrenbacher. New York: Harper & Row, 1976.

Slaughter, Thomas P. *Bloody Dawn: The Christiana Riot and Racial Violence in the Antebellum North.* New York: Oxford University Press, 1991.

SEE ALSO: Fugitive Slave Act of 1793 (1793); Missouri Compromise (1820); Compromise of 1850 (1850); Kansas-Nebraska Act (1854).

COMPROMISE OF 1850

DATE: September 20, 1850
U.S. STATUTES AT LARGE: 9 Stat. 452 (statute on California)
CATEGORIES: African Americans; Slavery

Following the Missouri Compromise of 1820, the 1850 law was a last national attempt to resolve the question of slavery in the territories.

The U.S. Constitution, while creating a mechanism for the addition of states and acknowledging the right of each state to permit and even encourage slavery within its boundaries, made no mention of slavery's status in future states. Congress, when it admitted a state, could impose any condition it wished. The national government had first addressed the issue of slavery in territories and new states when the Confederation Congress passed the Northwest Ordinance of 1787. This ordinance excluded slavery from the unsettled area north of the Ohio River to the Mississippi River's eastern bank, the edge of the United States' holdings.

THE MISSOURI QUESTION

The issue reemerged in 1817, when Missouri, where between two thousand and three thousand slaves lived, applied to join the United States as a slave state. The question came before the Congress in 1819, and sectional tensions erupted. The U.S. Senate had eleven states each from the free North and the slave-owning South, but the North's growing population gave it a decisive advantage in the House of Representatives, so proslave forces committed themselves, at the minimum, to maintaining a balance between the regions in the Senate.

A temporary solution emerged in 1820, when Senator Henry Clay of Kentucky brokered a solution to the crisis. The Missouri Compromise stipulated that Missouri would be admitted to the Union as a slave state, while Maine, which had petitioned for statehood in late 1819, was admitted as a free state. The compromise also prohibited slavery from the remainder of the Louisiana Purchase in the area north of 36°30′ north latitude, while permitting it south of that line. Between 1820 and 1848, this solution maintained national peace, and the Senate remained balanced.

THE SOUTHWEST AND CALIFORNIA

The Mexican-American War disrupted the relative peace. The United States received millions of acres of land spanning the area from the Continental Divide west to the Pacific Ocean and south from the forty-ninth parallel to Mexico. Before the war ended, David Wilmot, a member of the House of Representatives from Pennsylvania, attached an amendment to an appropriations bill stipulating that any territory acquired from Mexico must exclude slavery in perpetuity. Although the bill failed to win passage, the Wilmot Proviso fueled the smoldering fires of sectionalism, as many assumed that any additional western lands would be governed by the Missouri Compromise.

In 1849, just a year after the discovery of gold in California, the young California Republic petitioned the Senate for admission to the Union. Besides disrupting the balance between slave and free states, California straddled the 1820 compromise's line and threw the prior agreements into chaos. In both houses of Congress, the question of slavery became paramount: Southerners rejected any attempt to exclude the practice from the West by nearly unanimous margins, while Free-Soilers from the North rejected the possibility of losing equal economic competition by similar percentages. Left in the middle were some elements of the national Whig Party, which struggled to preserve the Union while remaining a national party. The idea of disunion grew. Senator John C. Calhoun of South Carolina, long a firebrand for states' rights, proposed the formation of a sectional party to guarantee the practice of slavery. William Seward, an abolitionist representative from New York, also rejected the possibility of a compromise, citing the immorality of slavery. President Zachary Taylor, a hero of the Mexican-American War and a southerner, supported California's admission as a free state while rejecting the extreme position of persons such as Calhoun.

FIVE RESOLUTIONS

The first concrete proposal for compromise came from Senator Clay on January 29, 1850. Clay proposed a series of five resolutions: that the California Republic join the United States as a free state;

that the rest of the territory acquired in the Mexican Cession be organized without any decision on slavery; that Texas receive monetary compensation in exchange for giving up its claims to parts of contemporary New Mexico; that the slave trade within the District of Columbia be abolished (although the actual practice of slavery would not be affected); and that a more rigorous fugitive slave law be enacted.

On February 5 and 6, Clay presented his resolutions and spoke for the Union's preservation. One week later, Mississippi senator Jefferson Davis rejected Clay's proposals, using bitter language that also attacked northern intentions. On March 4, the ailing Calhoun, in a speech delivered by Virginia's James Mason, rejected compromise on the principle of slavery in the territories. On March 7, Daniel Webster acknowledged that both sides had just grievances and urged support for Clay's whole plan, calming some tensions with his eloquent plea that the Union be preserved. On March 11, Seward stated the abolitionist's opposition to the compromise because of the immorality of slavery.

In April, the Senate referred Clay's resolutions to a select committee. The committee reported back to the full Senate an omnibus bill that contained the substance of the five original resolutions and sparked another four months of debate. Two major stumbling blocks to the compromise disappeared in July, when President Taylor and Calhoun both died. Millard Fillmore, who supported the compromise's ideas, replaced Taylor, who had bitterly opposed the omnibus bill. While Clay was vacationing, Stephen A. Douglas broke the omnibus bill into five parts and steered them through the Senate, and the House of Representatives followed suit. By September 20, Congress had adopted the five bills that made up the Compromise of 1850.

KANSAS-NEBRASKA ACT

In 1854, the attempts at balancing the competing interests of the Free-Soil North with the proslave South ended when Senator Douglas proposed that the Kansas and Nebraska areas be organized using the concept of popular sovereignty. Congress adopted the Kansas-Nebraska Act that year, triggering the formation of a national political party dedicated to the idea of an exclusively free-soil policy in the West. The new Republican Party immediately became a force on the national political landscape, and its candidate,

John C. Frémont, came within four states of being elected president in 1856. Ultimately, the election of Abraham Lincoln in 1860, a man committed to both the preservation of the Union and the free-soil doctrine, drove the South to secession.

John G. Clark,
updated by E. A. Reed

Sources for Further Study

Collins, Bruce. *The Origins of America's Civil War.* New York: Holmes & Meier, 1981.

Foner, Eric, ed. *Politics and Ideology in the Age of the Civil War.* New York: Oxford University Press, 1980.

Holman, Hamilton. *Prologue to Conflict: The Crisis and Compromise of 1850.* New York: W. W. Norton, 1966.

Potter, David. *The Impending Crisis, 1848-1861.* New York: Harper & Row, 1976.

Stampp, Kenneth, ed. *The Causes of the Civil War.* Rev. ed. Englewood Cliffs, N.J.: Prentice-Hall, 1974.

See also: Fugitive Slave Act of 1793 (1793); Missouri Compromise (1820); Fugitive Slave Act of 1850 (1850); Kansas-Nebraska Act (1854).

Fort Laramie Treaty of 1851

Date: Signed September 17, 1851
U.S. Statutes at Large: 11 Stat. 749
Categories: Native Americans; Treaties and Agreements

In an unprecedented effort to promote peace during western expansion, a council was convened at Fort Laramie whereby ten thousand Indians of various nations gathered at one time to sign a peace treaty with representatives of the U.S. government.

During the mid-nineteenth century the continuing rush of covered wagon immigrants across the Plains of the United States began to have an unsettling effect on American Indian tribes living there. Wild game was driven out and grasslands were being cropped close by the immigrants' cattle and horses. U.S. government policy provided some reimbursement to Indians for losses of game, grass, and land caused by the continuing influx of white settlers. In 1847, Thomas Fitzpatrick was appointed the first U.S. government representative to the various nomad tribes of the High Plains. Aware of the mounting losses and the potential for Indian uprisings against the settlers, Fitzpatrick campaigned long and hard for congressional funding to help alleviate growing tensions.

PREPARING A TREATY COUNCIL

In February, 1851, Congress appropriated $100,000 for the purpose of holding a treaty council with the tribes of the High Plains. D. D. Mitchell, superintendent of Indian affairs at St. Louis, and Fitzpatrick were designated commissioners for the government. They selected Fort Laramie as the meeting location and September 1, 1851, as the meeting date. Word was sent throughout the Plains of the impending treaty council. By September 1, the first arrivals included the Sioux, Cheyennes, and Arapahos. Later arriving participants included the Snakes (Shoshones), and Crows. Because of the vast number of participants—more than ten thousand Indians and 270 soldiers—it became apparent that the forage available for Indian and soldier ponies and horses was insufficient. The council grounds were therefore moved about 36 miles south, to Horse Creek.

NEGOTIATIONS AND TREATY PROVISIONS

On September 8, the treaty council officially began. The assembly was unprecedented. Each Indian nation approached the council with its own unique song or demonstration, dress, equipment, and mannerisms. Superintendent Mitchell proclaimed that all nations would smoke the pipe of peace together. The proposed treaty asked for unmolested passage for settlers over the roads leading to the West. It included rights for the government to build military posts for immigrants' protection. The treaty also defined the limits of territory for each tribe and asked for a lasting peace between the various nations. Each nation was to select a representative, a chief who would have control over and be responsible for his nation. In return, the government would provide each Indian nation an annuity of $50,000 for fifty years, the sum to be expended for goods, merchandise and provisions.

After much discussion and conferencing, the treaty was signed on September 17 by the U.S. commissioners and all the attending chiefs. Adding to the festivities, on September 20, a delayed caravan of wagons arrived at the treaty council with $50,000 worth of goods and merchandise. These goods were summarily distributed to all the nations represented, and feelings of good will permeated the gathering. To further the sense of lasting peace, Fitzpatrick later took a delegation of eleven chiefs with him to Washington, D.C., where they visited with President Millard Fillmore in the White House.

John L. Farbo

SOURCES FOR FURTHER STUDY
Allen, Charles W., and Richard E. Jensen, eds. *From Fort Laramie to Wounded Knee: In the West That Was.* Lincoln: University of Nebraska Press, 1997.
Hafen, LeRoy, and Francis Young. *Fort Laramie and the Pageant of the West, 1834-1890.* Glendale, Calif.: Arthur H. Clark, 1938.
Hedren, Paul L. *Fort Laramie and the Great Sioux War.* Norman: University of Oklahoma Press, 1998.
_____. *Fort Laramie in 1876: Chronicle of a Frontier Post at War.* Lincoln: University of Nebraska Press, 1988.

SEE ALSO: Treaty of Guadalupe Hidalgo (1848); Fort Atkinson Treaty (1853); Medicine Lodge Creek Treaty (1867); Fort Laramie Treaty of 1868 (1868).

PACIFIC RAILROAD SURVEY ACT

DATE: March 2, 1853
U.S. STATUTES AT LARGE: 10 Stat. 201
CATEGORIES: Land Management; Transportation

This legislation was an attempt to break a political and economic deadlock over the location of the first transcontinental railroad.

On March 2, 1853, Congress passed the Pacific Railroad Survey Bill, which authorized the secretary of war, Jefferson Davis, to initiate exploration of possible routes across the trans-Mississippi West to the Pacific Ocean and to report findings to Congress within ten months. Davis decided to use officers of the Army Topographical Corps to make the surveys and placed them under Major William H. Emory.

A NORTHERN ROUTE
For years, there had been a proposal for a northern railroad route from Lake Michigan to the Columbia River, with a branch to San Francisco. Isaac Stevens, a young Army officer who had just accepted the governorship of Washington Territory, was placed in command of the northern survey, which covered the country between the forty-seventh and forty-eighth parallels. This party was divided into two sections: one group, led by Stevens, ascended the Missouri River to the mouth of the Yellowstone River at Fort Union and explored westward; a second party, led by Captain George B. McClellan, explored eastward from Puget Sound, seeking adequate passes through the Cascade Mountains. Numerous supposedly satisfactory passes across the Continental Divide were located, but no pass over the Cascades was found, because McClellan erroneously thought the snow of Snoqualmie Pass and elsewhere was too deep. Snowdrifts forty feet high could bury railroad workmen's cabins. Nevertheless, in 1853, Stevens enthusiastically reported that two practical routes through different passes over the Cascade Mountains were available. Citizens around Puget Sound were not convinced, and the legislature of Washington Territory commissioned Frederick West Lander, a civilian engineer, to survey another route from Puget Sound to South Pass.

CENTRAL ROUTES
South of Stevens's survey was a route near the thirty-eighth parallel along a line proposed by Thomas Hart Benton, senator from Missouri, with its starting point at St. Louis and its terminus in San Francisco. In 1848, Benton's son-in-law, John C. Frémont (called "Pathfinder" in a newspaper), had explored a portion of this route, named the Buffalo Trail. In seeking a satisfactory pass through the mountains in southern Utah, he had failed dramatically and disastrously by getting his group trapped twelve thousand feet up in the

Rocky Mountains in mid-December. Ten of his men starved or froze to death. When Lieutenant John W. Gunnison subsequently was placed in command of the official survey along the thirty-eighth parallel instead of Frémont, Benton, in disappointment, promoted two privately sponsored explorations along the same route. One, led by Frémont, was accompanied by newspaper reporters to publicize the route.

Gunnison's expedition, including topographer Richard H. Kern and a German botanist, Frederick Creuzefeldt, left Fort Leavenworth in June, 1853, and explored several new routes across the Great Plains. Gunnison was killed in October on the Sevier River in Utah by Paiute Indians. Before his death, he had reported that the railroad route along the thirty-eighth parallel was far inferior to the one along the forty-first parallel that had been used by emigrants in covered wagons. The death of his party closed the Buffalo Trail. Gunnison's was the only one of the four government survey expeditions to end in death.

Central route surveys were resumed the following spring, when Lieutenant E. G. Beckwith moved westward along the forty-first and forty-second parallels. His first responsibility was to reexamine the path traversed in 1850 by Captain Howard Stansbury, from Fort Bridge westward to Salt Lake. Beckwith found two satisfactory routes into the Great Basin through the Weber and Timpanagos Canyons. This route had elevations ranging from nine thousand to twelve thousand feet. Up to this point, contact with American Indian tribes had been peaceful, except with the Paiutes, who resisted the intrusion onto their lands. Authorized to continue the forty-first-parallel survey into California in February, 1854, Beckwith's party followed the customary emigrant route along the Humboldt River across Nevada, but upon reaching the sink of the stream, the party turned north to explore new passes across the Sierra Nevada and was successful in locating two: Madeline Pass and Nobles Pass.

SOUTHERN ROUTES

The third party, under Lieutenant Amiel Weeks Whipple, was ordered to explore the thirty-fifth-parallel route via Albuquerque and the Zuñi villages. This route was championed by California senator William H. Gwin, who hoped for a railroad from San Francisco to Albuquerque, from where several branches would go to Independence, Missouri; Fort Smith, Arkansas; Austin, Texas; and elsewhere. West of Albuquerque, the surveying group examined a route, later adopted by the Atchison, Topeka and Santa Fe Railroad. Whipple traversed the Mojave Desert to the Cajon Pass and crossed over into San Bernardino. He reported that this pass, so long used by traders and emigrants, was practical for railroad construction.

The southern, or thirty-second-parallel, route had already been explored by Emory, first when he was serving the Army of the West in the Mexican War and later as a member of the United States-Mexican Boundary Commission. Emory's survey of the boundary was accepted to bridge the gap from the Pima villages to the Colorado River, and Lieutenant R. S. Williamson was assigned the exploration in California. After extensive examination of the mountains of southern California, Williamson and his associates concluded that Walker Pass, long thought to be the southern gateway into California, was impractical for a railway because of its difficult westward approach. Nearby Tehachapi Pass was found to be superior. John G. Parke recommended a route from the mouth of the Gila River via the San Gorgonio Pass into Los Angeles, rather than a more southerly line to San Diego. From Los Angeles, a railway northward into the San Joaquin Valley could easily cross Tejon Pass.

These politically inspired routes were not properly engineered. The government surveys did not address the fact that railroads require grades no steeper than 116 feet to the mile and curves with a minimum three-hundred-foot radius to keep locomotives on track. It took the genius of Theodore Judah to engineer the first workable cut through the Sierras between California's American and Yuba Rivers, making possible the linking of east with west at Promontory Point, Utah, in 1869.

COASTAL ROUTES

The final phase for field operations of the Pacific Railroad surveys was that of Williamson and Lieutenant H. L. Abbott seeking the best routes from California into the Pacific Northwest. They located two practical coastal routes, one to the east and one to the west of the Cascades.

The officers of the Topographical Corps thus located most of the accessible routes through the mountain barrier to the Pacific Slope that were to be followed by modern railroads and highways. Their numerous reports, published in a series of quarto volumes at the direction of Congress in 1857, plainly showed that there was no unsurmountable difficulty in building a railroad to the Pacific. At least four routes were practicable, so instead of settling the sectional deadlock over the proposed route, as originally intended, the surveys stimulated new discussion. However, the surveys had reconnoitered the routes that later were used by the transcontinental railroads.

RELATIONS WITH NATIVE AMERICANS

Each of the survey groups met some of the many Native American tribes indigenous to the areas traversed. Using interpreters who had been captives of these tribes lessened the possibility of social error. Thus, the survey groups met with chiefs on equal terms. Gifts and goods were exchanged, and each could make only good reports of any encounter. Some survey groups made tribal lexicons, some having only twenty-eight words as an entire vocabulary. Whipple's group noted that nearly all the wealthy American Indians of central Oklahoma and western Arkansas had Mexican or African slaves. Lieutenant Whipple, in a letter dated June 30, 1855, to Jefferson Davis, said, "The quiet and peaceful manner in which we passed through the various tribes of Indians, usually hostile toward Americans is a proof of the sound discretion of those officers, and the good discipline of the men composing their command." Only after the intrusion of the wagon trains, the railroads, and white settlements did the Native Americans rise up in arms.

W. Turrentine Jackson, updated by
Norma Crews

SOURCES FOR FURTHER STUDY

Albright, George L. *Official Explorations for Pacific Railroads.* Berkeley: University of California Press, 1921.
Ogburn, Charlton. *Railroaders: The Great American Adventure.* Washington, D.C.: National Geographic Society, 1977.
Robertson, Donald B. *Encyclopedia of Western Railroad History.* Caldwell, Idaho: Caxton Books, 1986.
United States War Dept. *Reports of Explorations and Surveys to Ascertain the Most Practicable and Economical Route for a Railroad from the Mississippi River to the Pacific Ocean.* Washington, D.C.: Government Printing Office, 1855.

Wheeler, Keith, and the editors of Time-Life Books. *The Railroaders.* New York: Time-Life Books, 1973.

Williams, John H. *A Great and Shining Road: The Epic Story of the Transcontinental Railroad.* New York: Times Books, 1988.

SEE ALSO: Treaty of Guadalupe Hidalgo (1848); Oregon Act (1848).

FORT ATKINSON TREATY

DATE: Signed July 27, 1853
U.S. STATUTES AT LARGE: 10 Stat. 1013
CATEGORIES: Native Americans; Treaties and Agreements

This treaty was drawn to establish peace among southern Plains tribes in order to ease white passage westward and facilitate the building of a transcontinental railroad through Indian lands.

Personally negotiated by Thomas Fitzpatrick, a white trader and Indian agent of the Upper Platte Agency, the Treaty of Fort Atkinson was one of a series of U.S.-Indian treaties signed during the 1850's to open passage to America's Far West while promoting the Christianization and civilization of the Plains Indians. Fitzpatrick previously had helped to bring the Sioux and seven other Plains tribes together to sign the Treaty of Fort Laramie with the United States in 1851. The signatories to the Fort Atkinson Treaty agreed to establish peace among the affected Indian tribes, as well as between Indians and whites. It sanctioned the passage of whites through Indian lands, and acknowledged U.S. rights to establish military roads and posts thereon. It also provided for annuities to be paid by the United States (for a ten-year term) to the affected Indians.

Clifton K. Yearley

SOURCE FOR FURTHER STUDY

Ney, Virgil. *Fort on the Prairie: Fort Atkinson on the Council Bluff, 1819-1827.* Washington, D.C.: Command, 1978.

SEE ALSO: Fort Laramie Treaty of 1851 (1851).

TREATY OF KANAGAWA

DATE: Signed March 31, 1854
CATEGORIES: Asia or Asian Americans; Business, Commerce, and Trade; Foreign Relations; Treaties and Agreements

The treaty facilitated trade between the United States and the formerly isolationist nation of Japan.

The mission of Commodore Matthew Calbraith Perry to Japan from 1852 to 1854 was dramatic evidence of the United States' increasing interest in eastern Asia. It followed a series of overtures by other Western countries and coincided with a period of significant debate within Japan's ruling class over the prospect of opening the country to outside, particularly Western, influences.

JAPANESE ISOLATIONISM

From 1620 until Commodore Perry's squadron sailed into Edo Bay (later called Tokyo Bay), Japan had practiced a policy of rigid isolation and the exclusion of foreigners. In the sixteenth and early seventeenth centuries, Japan's experiences with Western missionaries and traders had been so negative that almost all contact with the outside world was broken off. Only the Dutch, Chinese, and Koreans were allowed to trade through one small port. In the nineteenth century, the desire to develop commercial relations, to exploit Japan's proximity to China, and to satisfy curiosity about Japan caused repeated attempts to open relations with Japan.

Prior to Perry's expedition, several European countries attempted to develop relations with Japan. Between 1771 and 1804, Russian individuals and government representatives made four separate, unsuccessful attempts to open Japan to trade. Japan redoubled its commitment to defend its northern islands against possible Russian advances, and no further interaction took place until Russia again exerted pressure in 1847. England was rebuffed in its 1818 effort to convince Japan to open trade. Following China's defeat in the Opium Wars, Japan was even further resolved to resist foreign influence.

PERRY'S MISSION

Perry's mission was at least the fourth U.S. effort to open relations with Japan. In 1832, President Andrew Jackson had sent an envoy, Edmund Roberts, to negotiate treaties in East Asia. He concluded treaties with Siam (later known as Thailand) and with the Sultan of Muscat (later part of Oman) but died en route to Japan in 1836. In 1837, the merchant ship USS *Morrison* attempted to land in Japan but was repelled by cannon fire. In 1846, Commodore James Biddle arrived in Japan with the same goal that Edmund Roberts had been unable to achieve, but the Japanese refused to negotiate.

By 1850, the U.S. government was being pressed to open Japan. There was a clamor for the negotiation of a convention to protect U.S. sailors shipwrecked in Japanese waters, and the growing use of steam-powered merchant ships led to the demand for coaling stations. There also was a great desire for new markets in the Far East. In 1852, Millard Fillmore, thirteenth president of the United States, sent another expedition in an attempt to break down Japan's seclusion. He chose Perry as its commander and minister plenipotentiary and gave him broad powers. Perry was assigned five steam warships and four sailing vessels; his instructions were to arrange for commercial relations and to negotiate a treaty.

Perry's expedition left Hampton Roads, Virginia, in November, 1852. Gifts were carried to demonstrate the United States' technological prowess, including a telegraph set and a miniature steam locomotive with cars and track. Eight months later, in 1853, Perry led four ships into Edo Bay. The Japanese, who had never seen steamships before, were greatly impressed. Perry was determined to avoid the mistakes of other Western envoys. Under strict orders to use force only if absolutely necessary, he assumed a confident bearing and insisted on dealing only with the highest officials. At first, representatives of the *bafuku*, or military government, demanded that the ships proceed to Nagasaki, the only port at which Westerners were permitted to have contacts with the Japanese government. Perry refused to be intimidated or to leave Edo Bay until he was assured that the dispatches he carried, including a letter from the president of the United States to the emperor of Japan, would be delivered in the appropriate quarters. When the Japanese finally promised that the emperor would receive the U.S. treaty proposals, Perry steamed away, but not before he informed the emperor's agents that he intended to return in the spring of 1854 with a larger force and with the expectation of a favorable response.

The *bafuku* solicited advice from members of the Japanese ruling class on how to respond to Perry's demands. Seven hundred proposals were submitted, with none offering an ideal solution. A group led by the lord of Mito, Tokugawa Nariaki, advocated resistance to invasion at all costs. The *Rangakusha,* or "masters of Dutch learning" school, which had learned something of the West through Japan's limited connections to the Netherlands, argued that Japan's substantial military capabilities would be no match for Western armies backed by modern industrial technologies. They also believed that Japan would benefit more than it would lose from more exposure to Western ideas and technologies.

While Emperor Komei and his advisers debated what response Japan should make to U.S. overtures, Perry returned to his exploration of the Far East. Believing that the glittering prospects for U.S. trade in the Far East required that the United States gain territorial footholds in the area, he took possession of certain of the Boning Islands, established a coaling station on Okinawa, and cast covetous eyes on Formosa; however, his superiors in Washington repudiated these actions.

In February, 1854, Perry returned to Japan with an impressive squadron of eight warships. The Japanese leaders had decided to deal with the North Americans as the least threatening of the Western powers. Japan was ready to accept, at least in part, the proposals of the United States. Perry exploited his advantage by demanding a treaty similar to the liberal agreement that the United States had negotiated with China in 1844, but the final terms, concluded in the Treaty of Kanagawa, signed on March 31, 1854, were less inclusive.

Treaty Terms

The United States was to be permitted to establish a consulate at Shimoda, a small port on Honshu near Edo Bay, but there was no provision allowing U.S. citizens to take up permanent residence, and U.S. citizens and merchant vessels were allowed to enter only two small ports, Shimoda and Hakodate. Japan bound itself to assist shipwrecked U.S. sailors and return them and their belongings to the proper authorities. The agreement did not provide for the establishment of coaling facilities or for extraterritorial rights for U.S. citizens, but it did contain an article ensuring that the United States would be offered any future concessions that might be offered to other powers. Japan soon reached similar agreements with England, France, Russia, and the Netherlands. The immediate and practical effects of the treaty negotiated by Perry were minimal, and even they were not supported fully by Emperor Komei and his advisers. The treaty prepared the way, however, for a broader commercial treaty that was signed by the emperor's senior councillor, Hotta Masayoshi, in 1858.

Theodore A. Wilson, updated by
James Hayes-Bohanan

Sources for Further Study

Fallows, James. "When East Met West: Perry's Mission Accomplished." *Smithsonian* 25, no. 4 (July, 1994): 20-33.

Hane, Mikiso. "The Fall of the Tokugawa Bakufu." In *Modern Japan: A Historical Survey.* 2d ed. Boulder, Colo.: Westview Press, 1992.

McDougall, Walter A. "Edo 1853." In *Let the Sea Make a Noise: A History of the North Pacific from Magellan to MacArthur.* New York: Basic Books, 1993.

Morison, Samuel Eliot. *"Old Bruin": Commodore Matthew C. Perry, 1794-1858.* Boston: Little, Brown, 1967.

Morton, W. Scott. "The Winds of Change: The Tokugawa Shogunate: Part II, 1716-1867." In *Japan: Its History and Culture.* New York: McGraw-Hill, 1984.

Preble, George Henry. *The Opening of Japan: A Diary of Discovery in the Far East, 1853-1856.* Edited by Boleslaw Szczesniak. Norman: University of Oklahoma Press, 1962. observations of the expeditions.

Wiley, Peter Booth, with Korogi Ichiro. *Yankees in the Land of the Gods: Commodore Perry and the Opening of Japan.* New York: Viking, 1990.

See also: Treaty of Wang Hiya (1844); Gentlemen's Agreement (1907).

KANSAS-NEBRASKA ACT

DATE: May 30, 1854
U.S. STATUTES AT LARGE: 10 Stat. 277
CATEGORIES: African Americans; Slavery

By subverting the Missouri Compromise and the Compromise of 1850, this act renewed the problem of slavery in the territories and escalated tensions between North and South.

The issue of the expansion of slavery was laid aside only temporarily with the passage of the Compromise of 1850, although the compromise had seemed to be fairly successful in the two or three years immediately following its enactment. Several events kept the compromise in the public eye, including the seizure in the North of African Americans under the provisions of the Second Fugitive Slave Law (1850), the publication of Harriet Beecher Stowe's *Uncle Tom's Cabin* in 1852, and the last of three filibustering expeditions launched from New Orleans in August, 1851, by Venezuelan Narcisco Lopez against Spanish Cuba.

THE SLAVERY QUESTION
Many people in the United States hoped that the slavery issue would disappear, and the economic pressures of life absorbed the attention of most average citizens. Moreover, no prominent politicians had captured the public's imagination. Lackluster, noncontroversial candidates were nominated in the presidential campaign of 1852—Franklin Pierce of New Hampshire for the Democrats and General Winfield Scott for the Whigs. The election, won by Pierce, was no more exciting than the candidates. Evidence of the desire of U.S. voters to maintain the status quo was demonstrated further in the poor showing of John P. Hale of New Hampshire, the standard-bearer of the Free-Soil Party. With the Democrats in control and apparently committed to the Compromise of 1850, the United States seemed destined to at least another four years of relative calm.

The issue of slavery in the federal territories was reopened in January, 1854, when Stephen A. Douglas of Illinois, chairman of the Committee on Territories, reported a bill to organize the Platte country west of Iowa and Missouri as the territory of Nebraska. Douglas's main interest was in opening the West to settlement and to the construction of a railroad to the Pacific coast. Douglas did not wish to deal with the slavery question and he (like his soon-to-be nemesis, Abraham Lincoln) doubted that the institution could survive on the Great Plains, but he realized that he needed Southern votes to get the territorial bill through Congress.

DRAFTING THE BILL

In the original form, the bill included a provision, similar to that found in the acts organizing the territories of Utah and New Mexico, that the territory would determine the question of its status as a slave or free state at the time of admission. The clause dealing with slavery was intentionally ambiguous, but it probably would have left in effect—at least during the territorial stage—the provisions of the Missouri Compromise that barred slavery in the Louisiana Purchase territory north of 36°30′ north latitude. The ambiguity of the bill bothered Southern political leaders, particularly the rabidly proslavery David R. Atchison of Missouri, president pro tempore of the Senate and acting vice president. Yielding to the pressure of Senator Atchison and other Southern leaders, Douglas and his committee added a section to the bill that permitted the people of the territory, acting through their representatives, to decide whether the territory should be slave or free. This "popular sovereignty" formula for dealing with the slavery question implied the repeal of the Missouri Compromise restriction on slavery.

The proslavery leaders were not satisfied with the implicit abrogation of the Missouri Compromise. As Whig senator Archibald Dixon of Kentucky pointed out, under popular sovereignty, the restriction of slavery would remain in effect until the territorial settlers acted to end it. In the interim, immigration of slaveholders into the territory would be prohibited. Proslavery leadership forced Douglas to amend the bill further so as to repeal explicitly that section of the Missouri Compromise prohibiting slavery north of 36°30′. In addition, the territory was divided at the fortieth parallel into the two territories of Kansas and Nebraska. Most Northerners considered the Missouri Compromise to be a sacred pledge, and its repeal was quite enough to destroy the relative political calm that had been prevalent in the nation since 1850.

Much more was at work, however. The Missouri Compromise had led to the creation of the political party system, utilized by the Democrats and finally adopted by the Whigs, under which party loyalty was ensured through the disposition of party and government jobs (known as patronage or the spoils system). Under that system, the tensions created by the Missouri Compromise were to be kept under control, for anyone could be controlled by the promise of employment, according to the assumptions of the new party system. The effect of the party system was to increase the size and scope of federal government operations in every election, because to get elected, a candidate had to promise more jobs than his opponent. The result for the slavery interests was that the South, slowly but surely, was being placed in a permanent minority status in the Senate and House. If an antislavery president were elected, the now-powerful federal government could act directly on slavery in the South.

The Kansas-Nebraska Act, especially Douglas's concept of popular sovereignty, offered hope to the South that the dynamic created by the spoils system could be short-circuited. If territories could decide whether or not to permit slavery, then slave interests could flood the new territories with proslavery settlers and vote in slavery, regardless of the attitudes of Congress or the president.

PASSAGE

Douglas still had to guide the bill through passage in the face of widespread and violent criticism from the North. The bill was certain of passage in the Senate, although it was the object of impassioned attack by Senators Salmon Chase of Ohio and Charles Sumner of Massachusetts. In the House, however, the issue was doubtful, and it was there that Douglas marshaled the power of the Pierce administration to force dissident Democrats into line behind the bill. By whip and spur, the Kansas-Nebraska Act was driven through the House by a large sectional vote of 113 to 100. Nearly all Southern Democrats supported the measure. All forty-five Northern Whigs opposed it, while thirteen of nineteen Southern Whigs, led by Alexander Stephens of Georgia, favored it. The divisiveness of the issue was represented best by the fact that of eighty-six Northern Democrats, forty-two voted against it in spite of patronage and other pressures brought to bear by administration leaders. In doing so, the Democrats showed the utter futility of basing a slavery strategy on the spoils system: Ideology proved stronger than economics, and the idea that the national debate over slavery could be contained with the promise of a few jobs was mortally wounded.

CONSEQUENCES

The passage of the Kansas-Nebraska Act had momentous consequences. The act touched off the forces that eventually brought war. It reopened sectional issues and embittered sectional relations by arousing the entire North. It destroyed the Whig Party in the deep South and increased Southern unity and influence in the Democratic Party. It contributed greatly to the demise of the Whig Party in the North and divided the Northern Democrats, inducing many of them to leave the party. Most important, it led to the formation, beginning in 1854, of the Republican Party. That party was founded in diametric opposition to the operating principles of the Democratic Party. Instead of holding that economic self-interest took precedence over ideology, the Republicans held that fundamental beliefs mattered more than temporal, material benefits in the long run. The Republicans thus made slavery—the issue that the Democrats and the Whigs refused to touch—the focal point of their campaigns.

On a personal level, Douglas gained little support in the South and lost an important part of his support in the North. Douglas, misinterpreting Northern sentiment toward this initially innocent piece of legislation, had opened a political Pandora's box. The legislation reflected Douglas's personal views accurately, though. He sincerely disliked slavery, but thought that it was an issue of choice of the slaveholder; therefore, the matter of human bondage was not a moral issue but simply a matter of votes. Douglas could say honestly that he opposed slavery personally, but supported a slaveholder's right to own slaves. Thus, the agony of Douglas and the struggle for Kansas had begun.

John C. Gardner, updated by
Larry Schweikart

SOURCES FOR FURTHER STUDY

Gienapp, William E. *The Origins of the Republican Party, 1852-1856.* New York: Oxford University Press, 1987.

Holt, Michael. *The Political Crisis of the 1850's.* New York: W. W. Norton, 1978.

Johannsen, Robert W. *Stephen A. Douglas.* New York: Oxford University Press, 1973.

McPherson, James W. *Battle Cry of Freedom: The Era of the Civil War.* New York: Oxford University Press, 1988.

Nevins, Allen. *A House Dividing, 1852-1857.* Vol. 2 in *Ordeal of the Union.* New York: Charles Scribner's Sons, 1947.

Nichols, Roy Franklin. "The Kansas-Nebraska Act: A Century of Historiography." *Mississippi Valley Historical Review* 43 (September, 1956): 187-212.

Wolff, Gerald. *The Kansas-Nebraska Bill: Party, Section, and the Coming of the Civil War.* New York: Revisionist Press, 1977.

SEE ALSO: Missouri Compromise (1820); Compromise of 1850 (1850).

CONFISCATION ACTS

DATE: August 6, 1861; July 17, 1862
U.S. STATUTES AT LARGE: 12 Stat. 319, 589
CATEGORIES: Military and National Security; Property

Congress permanently confiscated Confederate property and justified the action by declaring Confederates to be traitors.

Congress passed a law confiscating all property, including slaves, used in the Confederate war effort. The law required judicial proceedings before any property could be appropriated, and it left unclear whether any confiscated slaves would be freed.

The following July, Congress passed the Second Confiscation Act. The 1862 law, which also required a judicial hearing, declared that rebels were traitors whose property could be seized for the lifetime of the owner. The only property that would not be returned to the rebels' heirs was slaves, who were regarded as captives of war and set free after a period of sixty days. President Abraham Lincoln doubted that Congress possessed the constitutional authority to free slaves in the states. When he signed the bill into law, he included a statement of objections to its provisions. Although the power to confiscate rebel property was rarely used during or after the war, the difference between the first and second acts revealed the growing determination in the Union to end slavery and set the stage for the Emancipation Proclamation, which Lincoln issued in January, 1863.

Thomas Clarkin

SOURCES FOR FURTHER STUDY

Caton, Bruce. *Mister Lincoln's War.* Garden City, N.Y.: Doubleday, 1951.

McPherson, James M. *Abraham Lincoln and the Second American Revolution.* New York: Oxford University Press, 1990.

_____. *Battle Cry of Freedom: The Civil War Era.* New York: Oxford University Press, 1988.

SEE ALSO: Militia Act (1862); Emancipation Proclamation (1863).

HOMESTEAD ACT

DATE: May 20, 1862
U.S. STATUTES AT LARGE: 12 Stat. 392
PUBLIC LAW: 37-64
CATEGORIES: Agriculture; Land Management

Response to the demand for land in the West stimulated settlement of vast territories; this law was passed to encourage settlement and development of the land.

The United States grew enormously between 1840 and 1860. The continental limits of the nation were reached, with the exception of Alaska, by 1854, through the acquisition of Mexican territory ceded in the Treaty of Guadalupe Hidalgo (1848) and the Gadsden

Purchase (1853). The population continued its upward spiral, moving from slightly more than seventeen million in 1840 to more than thirty million in 1860. Canals, steamboats, turnpikes, and railroads knot the nation together into an integrated economic unit. Hundreds of thousands of people crossed the Atlantic to take up residence in the dynamic nation, while other hundreds of thousands moved into the western regions of the country.

The growth of the West was especially marked. While the population of all sections grew, the North and the South experienced less relative growth during these two decades than did the West. The West achieved a position of equality with the older sections during this period and became more insistent in its demands upon the government.

SECTIONALISM

The intensification of sectional antagonisms engendered by the controversy over slavery and its future in the nation fatally obstructed efforts at the national level to provide guidelines and incentives for growth. By the opening of the 1840's, sectional lines had hardened. Southern majorities in Congress consistently blocked legislation called for by the other sections of the country. This was true in debates over the tariff, internal improvements, central banking, and land policy. The West won a significant victory in the debate over the disposition of the public domain with the passage of the Preemption Act of 1841, which gave squatters the right to purchase up to 160 acres of land that they had settled and improved for $1.25 per acre. The next logical step for Westerners was for the government to provide completely free land as a reward for those who settled and developed the region.

THE FIGHT FOR FREE LAND

The campaign to achieve free land was waged on two fronts. Westerners such as Missouri senator Thomas Hart Benton consistently pushed for such legislation and were joined by increasing numbers of other Westerners committed to the free-soil idea. The slavery controversy erupted vigorously during the Mexican War, with efforts by free-soil Whigs to pass the Wilmot Proviso. It was obvious that the idea of free homesteads would work to the advantage of free-soil groups, by attracting into the newly won territories the more mobile population of the North. Therefore, the Free-Soil

Party made homestead legislation part of its platform for the 1848 campaign. By the 1850's, most Northerners accepted the idea that the land should be settled as rapidly as possible in order to bring it into production and to provide a stable population that would serve as a market for the industrial centers in the East. The Eastern-based Land Reform movement, led by George Henry Evans and supported by Horace Greeley and his *New York Tribune*, rounded out the alliance.

STRUGGLE FOR PASSAGE

The struggle for homestead legislation was waged in Congress during the 1850's. The congressional sessions of 1851, 1852, and 1854 devoted much time to such proposals. Southerners were opposed to the concept and argued that no benefits would accrue to their section. In spite of the leadership of Andrew Johnson of Tennessee, the Senate, dominated by the Southern wing of the Democratic Party, managed to block passage of several bills that passed the House of Representatives. When the Senate finally passed a homestead bill, in 1860, it was vetoed by President James Buchanan. The Republican Party committed itself to this policy and incorporated a homestead plank in its platform of 1860.

The election of Abraham Lincoln in 1860 did not guarantee the passage of homestead legislation, because the South still controlled the Senate. The secession of the Southern states made passage possible. During the special session of Congress in 1861, a bill was introduced into the House and passed in February, 1862. It passed the senate in May and was signed by President Lincoln on May 20.

PROVISIONS AND LATER LEGISLATION

Under the provisions of the bill, which was to go into effect January 1, 1863, a settler twenty-one years of age or older who was, or intended to become, a citizen and who acted as the head of a household could acquire a tract of acres of surveyed public land free of all but a $10 registration payment. Title to that land went to the settler after five years of continuous residence. Alternatively, after six months, the claimant could purchase the land for $1.25 per acre. Over the years, amendments and extensions of the act made it applicable to forest land and grazing land and enlarged the maximum acreage tract that the settler could acquire.

In 1873, the Timber Culture Act attempted to adjust the original act to more arid Western conditions by allowing the homesteading of an additional 160 acres on which the homesteader agreed to plant at least 40 acres (later reduced to 10 acres) of trees. The Desert Land Act of 1877 allowed Western ranchers to homestead up to a square mile, or 640 acres, of ranch land in certain areas. In the 1930's executive decisions by President Franklin Delano Roosevelt and the Taylor Grazing Act withdrew the remainder of the public domain from private entry. By then, 285 million acres had been homesteaded.

QUALIFIED SUCCESS

The Homestead Act was not the complete success its supporters hoped it would be. Homesteading was never attractive to the working class and urban poor in the East. There also were many competing forms of federal land distribution, including purchase by speculators, massive land grants to railroads, the sale of dispossessed Native American lands, and Morrill Act lands turned over to states for sale to support public education. Altogether, more than 80 percent of public lands were distributed through means other than homesteading. In addition, fewer than half of the nearly three million homesteaders who filed claims actually "proved up" and acquired title to the land after five years. A "Southern" Homestead Act of 1866, designed to provide land to former slaves, was especially disappointing. It was never effectively implemented and was strenuously opposed by Southern whites. Despite failures, the Homestead Acts helped several million families to obtain land and settle in the West, and it became an important symbol of the effort to create an egalitarian, middle-class, agrarian society in the United States in the nineteenth century.

John G. Clark,
updated by Kent Blaser

SOURCES FOR FURTHER STUDY

Fite, Gilbert C. *The Farmers' Frontier: 1865-1900.* New York: Holt, Rinehart and Winston, 1966.

Gates, Paul Wallace. *History of Public Land Law Development.* Washington, D.C.: Government Printing Office, 1968.

Hyman, Harold M. *American Singularity: The 1787 Northwest Ordi-*

nance, the 1862 Homestead and Morrill Acts, and the 1944 G.I. Bill. Athens: University of Georgia Press, 1986.

Lanza, Michael L. *Agrarianism and Reconstruction Politics: The Southern Homestead Act.* Baton Rouge: Louisiana State University Press, 1990.

Layton, Stanford J. *To No Privileged Class: The Rationalization of Homesteading and Rural Life in the Early Twentieth-Century American West.* Salt Lake City, Utah: Signature Books, 1988.

Shannon, Fred A. *The Farmer's Last Frontier: Agriculture, 1860-1897.* New York: Farrar and Rinehart, 1945.

Stratton, Joanna. *Pioneer Women: Voices from the Kansas Frontier.* New York: Simon & Schuster, 1981.

Tilghman, Wendy B. *The Great Plains Experience.* Lincoln, Nebr.: University of Mid-America, 1981.

SEE ALSO: Land Act of 1820 (1820); Preemption Act (1841); Morrill Land Grant Act of 1862 (1862); Morrill Land Grant Act of 1890 (1890); Taylor Grazing Act (1934).

MORRILL LAND GRANT ACT OF 1862

ALSO KNOWN AS: Land Grant Act of 1862
DATE: July 2, 1862
U.S. STATUTES AT LARGE: 12 Stat. 503
CATEGORIES: Agriculture; Education; Land Management

The federal government granted land to states for the establishment of agricultural and engineering colleges, paving the way toward higher education for the masses.

The author and successful promoter of the Morrill Land Grant Act of 1862 was Justin Smith Morrill, congressman from Vermont. Morrill was first elected to national office in 1854 as a Whig. With the demise of that party, Morrill helped to found the Republican Party in Vermont. In the House, Morrill served on both the Committee on Territories and the Committee on Agriculture, and he finally became chairman of the powerful Ways and Means Committee in 1861. Elected to the Senate in 1862, he served there until his death in 1898.

PRECEDENTS FOR PUBLIC EDUCATION
Several attempts to use land revenues to aid the promotion of public education had been made before Morrill's bill. The Ordinance of 1785 provided that the sixteenth section in each township was to be set aside for educational purposes. In 1848, when the Oregon Territory was organized, section 36 was added to section 16 in each township for common schools. The Preemption Act of 1841 (known also as the Distribution-Preemption Act) turned over to the states, for internal improvements, one-half million acres. Wisconsin, Alabama, Iowa, and Oregon used the proceeds from the sale of these lands for public schools. Revenues from the Swamp Lands Acts of 1849 and 1850 were applied in many states for the purpose of common education. Beginning as early as the 1840's, a movement made progress in the northeastern states for the establishment of agricultural colleges. In the 1850's, several states petitioned Congress for land to be used for educational purposes.

TRAINING IN AGRICULTURAL AND MECHANICAL ARTS
Morrill was interested in both education and agriculture. He regretted the fact that most existing institutions taught on the classical plan, so farmers, mechanics, and others employed at manual labor were not scientifically trained, and in most cases, they were doomed to the haphazard methods of self-education. In 1856, Morrill introduced a resolution that the Committee on Agriculture investigate the possibility of establishing one or more agricultural schools patterned after West Point and Annapolis. This resolution was not acted upon, but in 1857, Morrill introduced a bill that public lands be donated to the states for the purpose of providing colleges to train students in agricultural and mechanical arts. The land was to be apportioned to each state in a quantity of twenty thousand acres for each senator and representative the state had in Congress, and sixty thousand acres to each territory. Proceeds from the sale of this land were to be used in the state as a perpetual fund, the interest of which was to be appropriated to the support of a college. Within a period of five years after the passage of the bill, a college had to be established. If sufficient land for such a grant

were not available in a particular state, that state was to receive an equivalent amount of land scrip that could be used to purchase land elsewhere. This scrip had to be sold to private individuals, who could then choose holdings in the unoccupied areas of any public-land state according to the amount of scrip purchased.

DIFFICULT PASSAGE

Once the bill was presented to both houses of Congress, much opposition appeared. The South argued that it was inexpedient and unconstitutional, and many of the Western states believed that since the grants were to be made on the basis of population, it differed little from Henry Clay's distribution scheme. Many congressmen from states with large holdings attacked the bill on the grounds that large quantities of land scrip would be issued to the older Eastern states where there was no public domain, and the scrip soon would be acquired by land speculators who would claim large tracts of the best lands in the newer states. This land would then be held until the values had increased, and Western settlement and improvement thus would be retarded. In spite of this opposition, the bill passed both the House and the Senate by narrow margins.

President James Buchanan vetoed the land bill. It was, he said, unconstitutional and deprived the government of the needed revenue from land sales. It would make the state too dependent upon the federal government and would set up colleges in competition with existing institutions. Finally, the federal government could not compel the states to use the funds for the specified purpose if the states chose to do otherwise. A vote was quickly taken in the House to override the veto, but it failed to get the necessary two-thirds vote.

Unwilling to accept defeat, Morrill presented a second bill on December 16, 1861. It was almost identical to the first bill, except that the number of acres was increased to thirty thousand for each representative and senator. President Abraham Lincoln previously had informed Morrill that he would allow such a bill to become law. The issues were practically the same as before; however, in this instance, the representatives from the older Eastern states made a determined effort to force passage of the bill. With the passage of the Homestead Act virtually assured (it was signed into law in May and granted land acreage in 160-acre lots to anyone willing to re-

251

side upon it continuously for five years), the Easterners feared that their other chances to secure title to Western lands were materially reduced. President Lincoln signed the bill on July 2, 1862.

POPULIST PROVISIONS

The language of the Morrill Land Grant Act that Lincoln signed into law suggested a populist leaning. It provided for at least one college in each state at which studies of agriculture and the "mechanic arts" (engineering) would be available to support both a liberal and practical education of what were termed "the industrial classes," that is, the working class. Morrill no doubt was influenced by the rising democratic social climate in the United States; the growing power of workers and middle and lower managers; the importance of agriculture, industry, and commerce; and the growing body of scientific knowledge. The bill also struck a blow at the traditions of college education inherited from England and Germany that directed higher education to the preparation of well-to-do young men for careers as ministers, lawyers, scientists, college faculty, and high-level civil servants.

The concept of the land-grant college was a major contribution to the wider availability of higher education in the United States. The colleges were readily supported by the states. They made possible public college-level learning at low cost and established research as a legitimate activity of higher education. As a result, agricultural and engineering arts and sciences, as professions, were elevated to positions of academic respectability.

Most of the land-grant colleges received not land but scrip, which they used to purchase public land at $1.25 per acre. Under the terms of the act, eleven states received 1,769,440 acres of land. Public-land states later admitted to the Union received similar grants. Twenty-seven states eventually received scrip instead of land, and almost eight million scrip-acres were issued. The older states, which benefited because of their large populations, were authorized to select their acreage anywhere in the West. New York, for example, selected forest lands in Wisconsin and prairie lands scattered throughout the western Mississippi River Valley to use its 990,000-acre allotment. In all, the states received 140 million acres through the Morrill Land Grant Act and similar measures. None of this land was given to homesteads, and nearly all of it passed through the hands of speculators on its way to final users.

A second Morrill Land Grant Act was passed in 1890, stipulating that Congress was to make regular appropriations for the further support of land-grant colleges. The 1890 act resulted in the creation of seventeen agricultural and mechanical colleges in the South for African Americans. This act also established the practice of federal grants to institutions of higher education. Appropriations were increased in 1907, 1935, 1952, and 1960. By the 1960's, there was at least one land-grant institution in every state in the Union.

LONG-TERM IMPACT

Land-grant institutions have played a special role in developing several fields of study, particularly in agriculture and veterinary medicine. About 75 percent of the bachelor's degrees and 98 percent of the advanced degrees in these subjects are awarded by land-grant colleges. Engineering is another field that has been well developed in land-grant colleges, two-fifths of all such degrees coming from these institutions. Almost 51 percent of degrees in home economics are conferred by land-grant schools. A significant and little-known role is the one played by the land-grant college in military education. Thousands of officers have received their initial military training from these institutions.

Although the initial role of land-grant colleges was to teach the arts of agriculture and engineering. Over the years, as additional funds and needs arose, the institutions directed some of their efforts toward research and bringing the results of that research to the users through extension offices. In many instances, the colleges must not only satisfy the needs of their traditional clientele but also serve the interests of the general public. In addition, land-grant colleges increasingly face the challenges of international competition and environmental sensitivity and awareness.

John H. DeBerry, updated by
Albert C. Jensen

SOURCES FOR FURTHER STUDY

Cross, Coy F., II. *Justin Smith Morrill: Father of the Land-Grant Colleges.* East Lansing: Michigan State University, 1999.

Eddy, Edward D., Jr. *Colleges for Our Land and Time: The Land-Grant Ideas in American Education.* New York: Harper & Row, 1956.

Hyman, Harold M. *American Singularity: The 1787 Northwest Ordinance, the 1862 Homestead and Morrill Acts, and the 1944 G.I. Bill.* Athens: University of Georgia Press, 1986.

James, Edmund Janes. *The Origin of the Land Grant Act of 1862 (the So-Called Morrill Act) and Some Account of Its Author, Jonathan B. Turner.* Urbana-Champaign, Ill.: University Press, 1910.

Meyer, James H. *Rethinking the Outlooks of Colleges Whose Roots Have Been in Agriculture.* Berkeley: University of California Press, 1992.

_____. "The Stalemate in Food and Agriculture Research, Teaching, and Extension." *Science* 260 (May 14, 1993): 881, 1007.

Nevins, Allan. *The Origins of the Land-Grant Colleges and State Universities: A Brief Account of the Morrill Act of 1862 and Its Results.* Washington, D.C.: Civil War Centennial Commission, 1962.

Parker, William Belmont. *The Life and Public Services of Justin Smith Morrill.* Boston: Houghton Mifflin, 1924.

Rasmussen, Wayne D. *Taking the University to the People: Seventy-five Years of Cooperative Extension.* Ames: Iowa State University Press, 1989.

U.S. Department of the Interior. *Survey of the Land-Grant Colleges and Universities.* Directed by Arthur J. Klein, Chief of the Division of Collegiate and Professional Education. Washington, D.C.: Government Printing Office, 1930.

SEE ALSO: Ordinance of 1785 (1785); Land Act of 1820 (1820); Preemption Act (1841); Oregon Act (1848); Homestead Act (1862); Morrill Land Grant Act of 1890 (1890); G.I. Bill (1944).

MILITIA ACT

DATE: July 5, 1862
U.S. STATUTES AT LARGE: 12 Stat. 510
CATEGORIES: Military and National Security

The United States' first conscription act tapped Northern manpower to defeat the South.

The firing on Fort Sumter on April 12, 1861, came at a time when the regular army numbered only about sixteen thousand officers and troops. The traditional method of increasing the size of the army was to expand the state militias and to form a volunteer emergency national army recruited through the states. The immediate response of President Abraham Lincoln to the firing on Fort Sumter was to call for seventy-five thousand militia volunteers for three months' service. This call was exceeded, and some volunteers were turned away because the expectation was that a show of force would be sufficient to defeat the South.

THE NEED FOR A DRAFT

Congress and the president subsequently found it necessary, however, to call for more volunteers. Repeated defeats of the Union Army and the resultant loss of men caused President Lincoln to call for three hundred thousand volunteers in the summer of 1862. The difficulty of obtaining volunteers was soon apparent; bounties were increased and the threat of the draft was invoked. Congress passed the Militia Act of July, 1862, which allowed the states to draft men into the militia and encouraged enlistments. President Lincoln called for another three hundred thousand men to be enrolled into the militia. Although the Militia Act of 1862 gave the federal government power to enroll men in situations where state machinery was inadequate, the short-term (nine-month maximum) nature of the militia draft and the inequities of the system made it less than satisfactory.

Spurred by the loss of seventy-five thousand men, by news of a conscription law passed by the Confederacy, and by the failure of the states to provide men promptly for the various calls, Congress passed the Conscription Act of March 3, 1863. Henry Wilson, chairman of the Senate Committee on Military Affairs, was responsible for the introduction of a bill that eventually was passed and labeled "An Act for Enrolling and Calling Out the National Forces and for Other Purposes." This act was the first national draft law in the history of the nation. It called for the creation of the "national forces," which were to consist of all able-bodied male citizens and alien declarents between twenty and forty-five years of age, including African Americans. White opposition to blacks in federal army uniforms noticeably lessened as a result of the draft. In all, more than 168,000 African American recruits were drafted. Certain high officials, medically unfit persons, and hardship cases were exempted. Exemption could also be obtained by paying three hundred dollars or by securing a substitute.

THE CONSCRIPTION PROCESS

The system was operated by the War Department under the direction of Colonel James B. Fry, provost-marshal-general. Provost-marshals were appointed in districts similar to the congressional districts and enrollments began. Quotas were established and credit was given for enlistments. If the quotas were not met, drawings were held to determine who should be drafted. Small cards were placed in sealed envelopes in a large trunk, and the names were drawn in public by a trustworthy citizen wearing a blindfold. The system of paying three hundred dollars for exemption from service subsequently was abolished, but the privilege of hiring a substitute was continued. The names of more than three million men were gathered, but only about 170,000 were drafted, and 120,000 of those produced substitutes. The primary intent for passage of the law was to speed up voluntary enlistment, and more than one million men enlisted. The chief motivation for these enlistments was probably the threat of the draft.

RESISTANCE AND RIOTS

The draft brought President Lincoln and Secretary of War Edwin McMasters Stanton into conflict with state governors. Those governors who were unenthusiastic about the conduct of the war openly criticized the president and the draft, while governors who favored a more vigorous prosecution of the war often complained that their states had not been given full credit for previous enlistments. Lincoln and Stanton often temporized with the governors by granting postponements or additional credits as the end of the war drew near.

There was considerable resistance to the draft. Pennsylvania, Illinois, Indiana, and Kentucky had considerable problems with enrollment, and draft offices and officers were attacked in those states. The Irish in New York and New Jersey were particularly incensed by the draft, many viewing the conflicts as a rich man's war and a poor man's fight. With fifty-one categories of diseases qualifying men for medical exemption, the system was fraught with medical resistance problems. Surgeons administering medical qualifying exams were confronted by pretended hernias (the most widespread cause of exemption), eye problems caused by applying eye irritants, and feigned deafness. Giving incorrect birth dates, claiming false dependents, and even the enrollment of dead people were other methods of noncompliance. Finally, there were the runaways. Given time to settle their affairs before departing for camp, a considerable number of draftees either relocated or fled to Canada.

With the public generally hostile to the draft, the best way for a community to completely avoid it was to fill the quota with volunteers. Consequently, bounty taxes were implemented to raise revenues to attract foreigners, new immigrants, and the poverty-stricken to enlist. The paying of bounties corrupted the draft system. It produced bounty jumpers who, attracted by lump-sum payments, were willing to jump off trains or boats and escape.

Notorious resistance to the draft instigated the draft riots in New York City. Governor Horatio Seymour's speech of July 4, 1863, attacking the Lincoln administration for violations of individual liberty, did nothing to decrease the hostility of the New York Irish toward African Americans and the abolitionists. Antidraft rioting, which took place between July 13 and 15, destroyed property and physically harmed many African Americans. Some New York militia units that had been engaged at Gettysburg were hastily ordered back to New York to stop the rioting. Estimates of the casualties in the violence range up to more than one thousand. In spite of the violence, the federal government was determined to enforce the draft with even more fervor.

CONFEDERATE CONSCRIPTION

The Confederacy's calls for volunteers and its national conscription law antedated those of the Union. Jefferson Davis's call for one hundred thousand volunteers came before the firing on Fort Sumter, and the Conscription Act was passed on April 16, 1862, almost a year before similar legislation was passed by the United States. The Confederate act conscripted men from eighteen to thirty-five years of age; later the same year, it was extended to include those between seventeen and fifty years of age. The Confederate law included a substitute system and a controversial list of exempted persons held to be essential at home. The category that caused the most discussion was that which exempted one slave owner or overseer for each twenty slaves. The Confederate draft was also controversial because it was a national levy; it made no concession to the doctrine of states' rights for which most Southerners claimed to be fighting.

It appears that the Confederacy's early use of a conscription law enabled General Robert E. Lee's armies to continue their general success in the Civil War well into 1863. It was only after the North also began drafting men that President Lincoln could be confident of victory. The North, with a much larger population, was able to sustain its losses and to continue the war indefinitely; the Confederacy could not. Continuance of the draft underscored Northern determination to continue the war to its conclusion. The result was Lee's surrender at Appomattox and the restoration of the Union.

Mark A. Plummer, updated by
Irwin Halfond

Sources for Further Study

Bernstein, Iver Charles. *The New York City Draft Riots: Their Significance for American Society and Politics in the Age of the Civil War.* New York: Oxford University Press, 1990.

Geary, James W. *We Need Men: The Union Draft in the Civil War.* Dekalb: Illinois University Press, 1991.

Kohn, Stephen M. *Jailed for Peace: The History of American Draft Law Violation, 1658-1985.* New York: Praeger, 1987.

Murdock, Eugene C. *One Million Men: The Civil War Draft in the North.* Madison: State Historical Society of Wisconsin, 1971.

Shannon, Fred A. *The Organization and Administration of the Union Army, 1861-1865.* 1928. Reprint. 2 vols. Gloucester, Mass.: Peter Smith, 1965.

See also: Confiscation Acts (1861-1862).

EMANCIPATION PROCLAMATION

DATE: Issued September 22, 1862; effective January 1, 1863
U.S. STATUTES AT LARGE: 12 Stat. 1267
CATEGORIES: African Americans; Slavery

> *The Emancipation Proclamation was an order to the Union Army to free all slaves held in regions of the Confederacy still in rebellion against the Union. The proclamation provided the means by which the majority of American slaves became free.*

During the Civil War, 600,000 slaves freed themselves by escaping to Union Army lines, presenting military commanders with the question of what to do with the fugitives. In time, most commanders accepted the slaves into their lines because the Confederate war effort would be injured by denying it the use of slave labor. Although initially hesitant to turn the Civil War into a crusade against slavery, President Abraham Lincoln, too, embraced the idea that destroying slavery would weaken the Confederacy. Lincoln's Emancipation Proclamation of January 1, 1863, was a military order which freed all slaves in areas still in rebellion against the United States.

Lincoln's critics claimed that the Emancipation Proclamation had little real meaning because the Confederate slaves were beyond Lincoln's control. Critics also charged that Lincoln was not fully committed to emancipation, because the Emancipation Proclamation did not free the slaves in the loyal slave states or in parts of the Confederacy conquered before 1863. Such criticisms fail to note the real meaning of the Emancipation Proclamation. Lincoln's action turned the Union Army into an army of liberation which henceforward freed slaves in the parts of the South it occupied. Thus, the vast majority of American slaves obtained their freedom from the military actions of the Union Army operating under the orders of the Emancipation Proclamation. Lincoln's power to free the slaves came from his power, as commander in chief, to seize enemy property. Lincoln could not constitutionally use this power against loyal citizens of the Union or against defeated areas of the Confederacy which were no longer waging war against the United States. The sincerity of Lincoln's commitment to emancipation can be seen in the fact that both before and after he issued the Emancipation

259

Proclamation, Lincoln urged Congress to pass a constitutional amendment which would free all American slaves.

The Emancipation Proclamation ensured that slavery would be a casualty of the Civil War. Subsequently, most of the loyal slave states and conquered areas of the Confederacy bowed to the inevitable and abolished slavery by the actions of state legislatures during the Civil War: West Virginia (1863), Maryland (1864), Louisiana (1864), Tennessee (1865), and Missouri (1865). Only two loyal slave states, Kentucky and Delaware, refused to abolish slavery by state law. Slavery was abolished in these states and other scattered parts of the South by the Thirteenth Amendment to the U.S. Constitution (1865), which freed all remaining slaves owned by American citizens. The last black slaves on American soil to be emancipated were the property of American Indian nations. These slaves were freed by treaty between the Indians and the United States government in 1866.

Harold D. Tallant

SOURCES FOR FURTHER STUDY

Franklin, John Hope. *The Emancipation Proclamation*. Rev. ed. Wheeling, Ill.: Harlan Davidson, 1995.

Holford, David M. *Lincoln and the Emancipation Proclamation in American History*. Berkeley Heights, N.J.: Enslow, 2002.

Klingaman, Willam K. *Abraham Lincoln and the Road to Emancipation, 1861-1865*. New York: Viking, 2001.

Riehecky, Janet. *The Emancipation Proclamation: Abolition of Slavery in 1863*. Portsmouth, N.H.: Heinemann Library, 2002.

Tackach, James. *The Emancipation Proclamation: Abolishing Slavery in the South*. Farmington Hills, Mich.: Gale Group, 1999.

Vorenberg, Michael. *Final Freedom: The Civil War, the Abolition of Slavery, and the Thirteenth Amendment*. Cambridge Historical Studies in American Law and Society. Cambridge, Mass.: Cambridge University Press, 2001.

Young, Robert. *The Emancipation Proclamation: Why Lincoln Really Freed the Slaves*. New York: Dillon Press, 1994.

Zall, Paul M. *Lincoln's Legacy: The Emancipation Proclamation and the Gettysburg Address*. San Marino, Calif.: Huntington Library, 1994.

SEE ALSO: Thirteenth Amendment (1865).

NATIONAL BANK ACTS

DATE: February 25, 1863; June 3, 1864
U.S. STATUTES AT LARGE: 12 Stat. 665, 13 Stat. 99
CATEGORIES: Banking, Money, and Finance

This measure to finance the Civil War placed control of the United States' banking and monetary system under the auspices of the federal government.

Of the many crises faced by the federal government in conducting the war against the Confederacy, none was more difficult to resolve than financing the conflict. The government had to obtain revenue to pay for the war and at the same time expand support for the war among members of the financial community. Revenues declined while expenses mounted.

Salmon P. Chase, secretary of the Treasury in Lincoln's first administration, was reluctant to impose an income tax, aware that such taxes generated strong hostility. Chase, a Democrat, had no personal qualms about issuing paper money or about having government control the banks; he was much more interested in what he considered to be the larger issue—successfully prosecuting the war. An income tax was enacted in August, 1861, which commanded 3 percent of incomes exceeding eight hundred dollars per year, and that percentage rose in subsequent years. Nevertheless, taxation could raise only a small part of the income needed to fight the war. Foreign lenders, having recently lost money in the Panic of 1857, did not want to invest in a nation at war. Public confidence in the United States was low, especially after the early Union failures on the battlefield. The banks of the country had suspended specie payments by December, 1861. Lincoln's first administration met that crisis by issuing paper currency.

PAPER CURRENCY

The first Legal Tender Act of February 25, 1862, authorized the issue of $150 million in national notes, or "greenbacks." Subsequent acts raised the authorized total to $450 million. Since the federal government itself suspended specie payments, refusing to redeem the paper money in gold or silver, the greenbacks were an inconvertible paper money supported only by the credit of the government. More important to war financing, however, was the sale of bonds by the government through the efforts of financier Jay Cooke. He utilized mass-marketing strategies to reach new groups of middle-class investors with great success. Cooke and his associates sold more than $1 billion worth of federal securities. However, during the early days of the war, in 1862 and 1863, when the battlefield success of the Union was in doubt, even Cooke had difficulty selling the bonds.

The government ultimately sold its bond issues because of the relationship between bond purchases and the establishment of the national banking system. Prior to the Civil War, privately owned, state-chartered banks could issue their own money, backed by a specie reserve. The notes of those banks competed in the open market like other commodities, with weaker banks' notes trading at a substantial discount. Critics argued that the nation needed a uniform currency, and that the state banks were unstable. (Similar arguments had been made in the early nineteenth century by those wishing to establish the Bank of the United States.) The latter charge was not true; some systems, especially in the South, proved remarkably solvent and stable during the Panic of 1857, particularly where branch banking was permitted.

A NATIONAL SYSTEM

Some critics saw a national banking system as a way to link the uniform currency to a banking system that also would provide an outlet for the government's securities. In January, 1863, the Senate started work on such a system. State banks resisted, correctly fearing that a national banking system would have unfair competitive advantages. Thaddeus Stevens, a Republican congressman from Pennsylvania, opposed the new system. Secretary Chase, however, with support from Senator John Sherman of Ohio, pushed the bill through the Senate with a close vote. Stevens blocked the bill in the House for months, but it passed there in February, 1863. Many who voted for the bill opposed the concept in principle, but supported it at the request of Chase, who argued that it was necessary in order to continue the war. Cooke also threw his influence behind the bill.

The act provided for the creation of national banks, which were required to purchase government bonds as a condition of receiving their federal charters. They then were permitted to issue notes up to 90 percent of the market value of the bonds. In an amending act of June, 1864, Congress made provisions for converting state banks into members of the national banking system. Still, state banks resisted, and only the imposition of a federal tax of 10 percent upon state banknotes eliminated state bank competition. That act also ensured that the government would have a monopoly over the creation of money and could inflate at will. National banks were limited to note issues of $300 million, which, along with the greenbacks, became the national currency.

The system suffered from inadequate balance in its distribution of money across the nation—$170 million of the $300 million went to New England and New York—and the national banks proved to have inadequate redemption mechanisms. Demand for money in the West, especially, evolved into a considerable political issue after the Civil War. The laws also prohibited national banks from establishing branches (unless they entered the system with branches) and had other restrictions, including higher capital requirements, than banks with state charters had. On the positive side, only national banks could be chosen as depositories for the Treasury Department's tax revenues, and only national banks could issue notes. States retaliated by lowering their capital requirements, and state banks found that they could avoid the tax on banknotes by using demand deposits to finance their loans and investments, making state banknote issues irrelevant. Over time, the number of state-chartered banks overtook the number of national banks.

IMPACT

The national banking system did not eliminate financial crises or panics. Indeed, the poor redemption mechanisms and the lack of competitive currencies from state banks made panics more likely. Nationwide panics occurred in 1873, 1893, and 1907, eventually generating calls for reform that led to the creation of the Federal Reserve System in 1913. By 1900, deposits in national banks stood at $2.35 billion, while deposits in nonnational banks totaled $3 billion.

Creation of national banks and the corollary destruction of private note issue had another effect on the nation's banking system. After the Civil War, the South's banking system was devastated, and the prospects for either former Confederates or freedmen receiving federal charters were slim, if not nonexistent. Without national banks in the South, a dearth of capital occurred that retarded the postbellum growth of the region. Moreover, the destruction of competitive note issue by banks eliminated opportunities for the freedmen to create their own sources of capital. Thus, the National Bank Acts discriminated against the newly freed slaves. Whether the Radical Republicans in Congress intended to punish the South or the system accidentally discriminated against the South and West remains a matter of debate.

Another effect, almost surely unintended, was to destabilize the banking system by removing an important market constraint, namely the necessity for banks to maintain specie reserves for their notes. At the same time, the government had to reduce the number of greenbacks in circulation, and from 1865 to 1879, the amount of greenbacks fell. Nevertheless, international factors led to the long-term deflation that the nation experienced from 1865 to almost 1900. That deflation was viewed by farmers and miners as damaging, and helped create groups, such as the Populists, who sought inflation, either through "free silver" or through the renewed issue of greenbacks.

The Populists and others feared that the money power was concentrated in New York, particularly in the hands of New York Jewish bankers. Those fears were incorporated into the Federal Reserve Act, by which twelve Federal Reserve Banks were spread throughout the country. Most people unhappy with the national bank system, however, had failed to note the more serious threat: Note issue was centralized within the federal government in Washington, not with financiers in New York. Consequently, it proved relatively easy to move final authority over the nation's money and banking system to Washington, D.C., during the Great Depression.

John G. Clark, updated by
Larry Schweikart

SOURCES FOR FURTHER STUDY

Doti, Lynne Pierson, and Larry Schweikart. *Banking in the American West: From the Gold Rush to Deregulation.* Norman: University of Oklahoma Press, 1991.

Livingston, James. *Origins of the Federal Reserve System: Money, Class, and Corporate Capitalism, 1890-1913.* Ithaca, N.Y.: Cornell University Press, 1986.

Schweikart, Larry. *Banking in the American South from the Age of Jackson to Reconstruction.* Baton Rouge: Louisiana State University Press, 1987.

Sharkey, Robert P. *Money, Class, and Party: An Economic Study of Civil War and Reconstruction.* Baltimore: The Johns Hopkins University Press, 1959.

Timberlake, Richard H. *The Origins of Central Banking in the United States.* Cambridge, Mass.: Harvard University Press, 1978.

SEE ALSO: Independent Treasury Act (1846); Coinage Act (1873); Currency Act (1900); Federal Reserve Act (1913).

FREEDMEN'S BUREAU ACT

DATE: March 3, 1865
U.S. STATUTES AT LARGE: 13 Stat. 507
CATEGORIES: African Americans; Civil Rights and Liberties; Health and Welfare; Labor and Employment; Slavery

Congress created the Freedmen's Bureau to help newly freed African Americans to function as free men, women, and children.

On March 3, 1865, Congress created the Freedmen's Bureau, a temporary agency within the War Department. The Freedmen's Bureau, also known as the United States Bureau of Refugees, Freedmen, and Abandoned Lands, was administered by General Oliver Otis Howard from 1865 until it was dismantled by Congress in 1872. The primary objective of the Freedmen's Bureau was to help newly freed African Americans to function as free men, women, and children. In order to achieve this goal, the bureau was expected to assume responsibility for all matters related to the newly freed slaves in the Southern states.

The bureau's mission was an enormous undertaking because of limited resources, political conflicts over Reconstruction policies, and a hostile environment. The work of the bureau was performed by General Howard and a network of assistant commissioners in various states, largely in the South. The Freedmen's Bureau attempted to address many of the needs of the newly freed African Americans, including labor relations, education, landownership, medical care, food distribution, family reunification, legal protection, and legal services within the African American community.

LABOR RELATIONS

In the area of labor relations, the Freedmen's Bureau dealt with labor-related issues such as transporting and relocating refugees and the newly freed persons for employment, contract and wage disputes, and harsh legislation enacted by some states. Concerning the last issue, many Southern states had passed laws, called Black Codes, that required adult freed men and women to have lawful employment or a business. Otherwise, they would be fined and jailed for vagrancy, and sheriffs would hire them out to anyone who would pay their fine. Given the scarcity of jobs, this policy resulted in former slave owners maintaining rigid control over newly freed African Americans. Another discriminatory law gave the former owners of orphaned African Americans the right to hire them as apprentices rather than placing them with their relatives. Again, this law resulted in the continuation of free labor for many Southerners. The Freedmen's Bureau has been criticized for the failure of its agents to negotiate labor contracts in the interest of the newly freed. The bureau was frequently accused of protecting the rights of the Southern planters, instead.

EDUCATION

Obtaining an education was extremely important to the newly freed African Americans. They knew that learning to read and write would enable them to enter into contracts and establish businesses, and would aid them in legal matters. The Freedmen's Bureau provided some support, by providing teachers, schools, and books and by coordinating volunteers. The bureau also made a contribution to the founding of African American colleges and universities. Southern opposition to educating African Americans was a result of the Southerners' fear that education would make African Americans too independent and unwilling to work under the terms established by their former owners. Therefore, Southerners instituted control over the educational administration and classrooms and the entire system. Southern planters used a variety of methods to exert control: frequent changes in administrative personnel, the use of racial stereotypes regarding the intellectual inferiority of African Americans, and educational policy decision making based on paternalism and self-interest. Consequently, educational opportunities were significantly restricted for African American youth.

LAND DISTRIBUTION

The newly freed African Americans were eager to acquire property. They demonstrated their interest in owning their own land as individuals and formed associations to purchase large tracts of land. Their sense of family and community was the basis for their strong desire to own land. The Freedmen's Bureau was initially authorized to distribute land that had been confiscated from Southern plantation owners during the Civil War. Specifically, on the sea islands of South Carolina, the bureau was mandated to lease or sell lands that had been confiscated. This land was to be distributed in parcels of forty acres. The decision of Congress to authorize the distribution of land was based on a proposal made by Thaddeus Stevens, the Republican congressman from Pennsylvania. However, President Andrew Johnson acceded to pressure from the rebellious planters to return their lands. The plantation owners were pardoned, and their property rights were restored by President Johnson. Consequently, all land that had been distributed to African Americans was returned to its previous owners. African Americans then were encouraged to sign contracts to work on the land that they once owned. Many refused to comply with this arrangement. Others would not voluntarily leave the property they once owned. When the freed men and women refused to vacate this property, they were evicted.

HEALTH SERVICES

A medical department was created within the Freedmen's Bureau. It was to be a temporary service, to ensure that medical services were provided to African Americans until local governments assumed this responsibility. In spite of inadequate resources, the bureau founded forty-five hospitals in fourteen states. Some of the more common problems of the bureau's medical department were inadequately staffed hospitals, medical personnel with little control over health concerns, frequent personnel changes and relocation of hospitals, and lack of funds to purchase food for patients. In spite of these problems, the bureau experienced some success in providing for the medical needs of newly freed African Americans, rendering medical services to large numbers of former slaves, though unable to meet the medical needs of many.

Social Welfare

The Freedmen's Bureau also attempted to provide for the social welfare of the freed persons. The agency was noted for rationing food to refugees and former slaves; it assisted families in reuniting with members who had been sold or separated in other ways during slavery.

Protecting the rights of the former slaves was a major task of the Freedmen's Bureau. Republicans believed that African Americans should have the same rights as whites. However, many Southern states enacted Black Codes that severely restricted the civil rights of the freed men, women, and children. These laws, exerting social and economic control over African Americans, represented a new form of slavery. When state legislation prohibited African Americans' equal rights, the bureau attempted to invoke the 1866 Civil Rights Act, which offered African Americans the same legal protections and rights as whites to testify in courts, to own property, to enforce legal contracts, and to sue. The bureau found it extremely difficult to enforce the Civil Rights Act and to prosecute state officials who enforced laws that were discriminatory against African Americans. A shortage of agents and a reluctance among bureau commissioners to challenge local officials contributed to the agency's limited success in enforcing the Civil Rights Act. Finally, the Freedmen's Bureau also established tribunals to address minor legal disputes of African Americans within their own communities. In many instances, freed slaves were able to resolve their own problems. When they could not, they presented their legal concerns to bureau agents.

Assessment

The task assigned to the Freedmen's Bureau was monumental. The responsibilities of the bureau significantly exceeded the resources and authority granted to it by Congress. The bureau's ability to perform its varied tasks also was impeded by personnel shortages. President Johnson's Reconstruction policies represented another major challenge to the bureau, as they were not always supportive of the bureau's mandate and objectives. Myriad problems associated with the bureau meant that the newly freed men, women, and children were not able to receive the goods and services necessary to gain economic independence. Consequently, they developed extensive self-help networks to address their needs.

K. Sue Jewell

SOURCES FOR FURTHER STUDY

Crouch, Barry A. *The Freedmen's Bureau and Black Texans.* Austin: University of Texas Press, 1982.

Foster, Gaines M. "The Limitations of Federal Health Care for Freedmen, 1862-1868." In *The Freedmen's Bureau and Black Freedom,* edited by Donald G. Nieman. New York: Garland, 1994.

Franklin, John Hope. *From Slavery to Freedom: A History of Negro Americans.* New York: Alfred A. Knopf, 1988.

Magdol, Edward. *A Right to the Land: Essays on the Freedmen's Community.* Westport, Conn.: Greenwood Press, 1977.

Westwood, Howard C. "Getting Justice for the Freedmen." In *The Freedmen's Bureau and Black Freedom,* edited by Donald G. Nieman. New York: Garland, 1994.

SEE ALSO: Black Codes of 1865 (1865); Civil Rights Act of 1866 (1866); Reconstruction Acts (1867); Fourteenth Amendment (1868).

BLACK CODES OF 1865

DATE: Beginning November 24, 1865
CATEGORIES: African Americans; Civil Rights and Liberties; Labor and Employment; Slavery

Fearing the effects of the end of slavery, Southern states passed laws to control newly freed African Americans.

The months immediately following the end of the U.S. Civil War were a period of great uncertainty. Wartime president Abraham Lincoln had been killed, and his successor, Andrew Johnson, was wholly untested. No leadership could be expected from Capitol Hill, since Congress had gone into a long recess. In the Southern states, a host of questions required immediate answers; foremost among these were questions relating to the place of the recently freed slaves in postwar Southern society. Would the freed slaves continue to furnish an economical and reliable labor force for Southern cotton planters? Would the former slaves exact subtle or blatant revenge upon their former masters? Should lawmakers grant African Americans the vote in the Southern states? Should the U.S. government give them land? Should the states pay the cost of a basic education for them? What legal rights would these five million African Americans enjoy in the postbellum South?

JOHNSON'S RECONSTRUCTION PLAN

President Johnson developed a lenient plan for Reconstruction, one that called on the Southern states to quickly reorganize their state governments. His only major demands of these new governments were that they admit that no state had the right to leave the Union and that they ratify the Thirteenth Amendment, which ended slavery. As the new Southern state legislatures began to meet, their exclusively white members were most interested in passing laws that would answer some of the nagging questions about the future place of African Americans in Southern society. Many legislators believed the freed slaves would not work unless forced to do so, and they feared the double specter of an economy without a labor supply and a huge mass of people who would live on charity or plunder. In earlier years, laws known as the "slave codes" had controlled the African American population; some lawmakers now called for a renewal of the slave codes to control the freed black population.

MISSISSIPPI'S CODES

Mississippi's legislature was the first to take up the question of the rights of, or limitations on, African Americans. This body met in October, 1865, and quickly fell into arguments over what policies on racial matters should be enacted. Nearly half of the legislators favored laws that would, in almost every way, return African Americans to the position they had occupied in the time of slavery. Mississippi's governor, Benjamin G. Humphreys, intervened and urged lawmakers to ensure certain basic rights to the newly freed slaves. After Humphreys's intervention, the moderates in the Mississippi legislature had the upper hand and, on November 24, 1865, enacted a bill entitled "An Act to Confer Civil Rights on Freedmen."

As its title promised, Mississippi's new law did confer some basic rights on African Americans that they had not enjoyed as slaves. These rights included the right to sue and be sued, the right to swear out criminal complaints against others, the right to purchase or inherit land, the right to marry, and the right to draw up labor or other contracts. Although the law's title did speak of conferring civil rights, and a few new rights were indeed granted, this law—the first of the Black Codes of the Southern states—was remarkable primarily for the rights it denied to African Americans. It did give African Americans the right to own land, but it denied them the right to rent rural land—thus the legislators sought to perpetuate large gangs of landless agricultural workers. The act recognized the right to marry, but it also provided that interracial marriage would be punished by life imprisonment for both parties. The right to testify in court was eroded by certain provisions that said the right to testify did not apply to cases in which both parties in a lawsuit or criminal case were white, nor to criminal cases in which the defendant was African American.

Most ominous was the provision that every black citizen in the state must sign a one-year labor contract by January 1 of each year and must honor that contract. Should the employee leave the employer before the end of the year, law enforcement officers were empowered to return the worker forcibly to his or her place of employment. In a provision reminiscent of the old laws that forbade giving help to runaway slaves, this new law made it a crime to give food, clothing, or shelter to any African American worker who had left his or her employer while still under contract. The punishment for helping a runaway was up to two months in jail; for those who helped the fugitive find work in a state other than Mississippi, the punishment was up to six months in jail. Once again, securing a stable labor supply for the state was at the forefront of lawmakers' goals.

CODES IN OTHER SOUTHERN STATES

After Mississippi passed this first Black Code, a flood of other laws soon followed in Mississippi and the other Southern states. South Carolina's Black Codes forbade African Americans from pursuing any occupation other than agricultural work, unless the worker paid a prohibitively expensive fee. Black farm workers there were required by law to work from sunup to sundown and forbidden from leaving the plantation without the permission of their employer. South Carolina and Mississippi both enacted severe vagrancy laws that called for the arrest of idle persons, drunkards, gamblers, wanderers, fighters, people who wasted their pay, circus hands, actors, and even jugglers. If these persons were African American, they were to be considered vagrants and fined up to one hundred dollars and imprisoned. If unable to pay their fine, their labor would be auctioned off to a white employer, and their wages used to satisfy the fine.

The Black Codes varied from state to state, but their Northern opponents said they all had the common goal of returning the freed slaves to a system equivalent to bondage. In some Southern states, blacks were prohibited from owning guns. In other states, their assembly in groups was forbidden, or an evening curfew was imposed. President Johnson, himself a Southerner, saw little objectionable in the Black Codes, but many Northerners did. Occupying generals Daniel E. Sickles in South Carolina and Alfred H. Terry in Virginia overturned all or parts of the Black Codes in their areas, pending action in Congress. In Washington, Senator Lyman Trumbull wrote the Civil Rights Act of 1866, which declared that all persons born in the United States were U.S. citizens, and that all U.S. citizens enjoyed equality before the law. Congress passed this measure over the veto of President Johnson. By 1868, the Fourteenth Amendment brought this same promise of equality before the law into the Constitution itself.

WEAK ENFORCEMENT

The Black Codes were barely enforced. Overturned by the actions of occupying generals, and later by the U.S. courts, which found them in conflict with the Fourteenth Amendment, they were important chiefly for fueling a conflict in Washington between Johnson's lenient Reconstruction plan and Congress's insistence that the basic rights of African Americans be protected. These codes are also important for their role in bringing about passage of the Fourteenth Amendment. Although African Americans' rights generally were protected between 1866 and 1876, the Southern states found many ways to draft laws that were color-blind on their face but that could be enforced in a racially biased way. After Reconstruction, few Southern elected officials, and few officeholders nationwide, were very interested in championing African American civil rights.

Stephen Cresswell

SOURCES FOR FURTHER STUDY

Cohen, William. "Negro Involuntary Servitude in the South, 1865-1940: A Preliminary Analysis." *Journal of Southern History* 42 (February, 1976): 35-50.

Foner, Eric. *Reconstruction: America's Unfinished Revolution.* New York: Harper & Row, 1988.

Harris, William C. *Presidential Reconstruction in Mississippi.* Baton Rouge: Louisiana State University Press, 1967.

Litwack, Leon F. *Been in the Storm So Long: The Aftermath of Slavery.* New York: Alfred A. Knopf, 1979.

Wilson, Theodore B. *The Black Codes of the South.* Tuscaloosa: University of Alabama Press, 1965.

SEE ALSO: Black Codes of 1804-1807 (1804-1807); Fugitive Slave Act of 1850 (1850); Thirteenth Amendment (1865); Civil Rights Act of 1866 (1866); Reconstruction Acts (1867); Fourteenth Amendment (1868); Jim Crow laws (1880's-1954); Disfranchisement laws (1890).

THIRTEENTH AMENDMENT

DATE: Ratified December 6, 1865; certified December 18, 1865
U.S. STATUTES AT LARGE: 13 Stat. 567
CATEGORIES: African Americans; Civil Rights and Liberties; Constitutional Law; Slavery

The first of the Civil War amendments states that "neither slavery nor involuntary servitude . . . shall exist within the United States. . . ."

The antislavery and abolition movements did not begin with the Civil War. As early as 1652, the state of Rhode Island passed antislavery legislation. In 1773, Benjamin Franklin and Dr. Benjamin Rush formed the first abolition society in America. In 1832, the New England Anti-Slavery Society was formed by newspaper editor William Lloyd Garrison, who also helped found the American Anti-Slavery Society in 1833. The Society of Friends, or Quakers, a religious group who settled early in the history of the United States, were very active in the antislavery movement. Their religion forbade the holding of slaves. Quakers primarily settled in the northern part of the country.

EARLY ANTISLAVERY LAWS

In 1807, federal legislation was passed outlawing the importation of slaves after January 1, 1808. However, this did not end the use of slaves in the United States. The writers of the Constitution could not resolve the issue of slavery in America, and so had declared that the slave trade could end by 1808 or anytime later. Eventually, the inability of national leaders to resolve this issue would divide the nation. The Missouri Compromise of 1820 banned slavery in most of the western states and territories. This was overturned by the Supreme Court in 1857, in the famous *Dred Scott* decision (*Scott v. Sandford*).

The split between the states was well in place at this point. Congress, in an attempt to appease pro- and antislavery proponents, adopted five provisions in the Compromise of 1850. The most notable was the Second Fugitive Slave Law, passed as part of the Compromise of 1850, which provided for slaves who escaped from the South and were found in Northern antislavery states to be returned to slave owners. A great deal of violence erupted over this legislation, which led to the act's repeal on June 28, 1864. This split between the North and the South eventually resulted in the Civil War.

ABOLITIONISTS

The abolitionist movement had fought throughout the history of the United States for an end to the institution of slavery. Robert

Dale Owen, an abolitionist and legislator, struggled for the emancipation of slaves and is thought to have influenced President Abraham Lincoln with his *Policy of Emancipation* (1863), or Emancipation Proclamation. Another radical opponent of slavery was Wendell Phillips, a noted speaker and a graduate of Harvard Law School. He believed that the U.S. Constitution supported slavery and therefore was owed no allegiance by abolitionists. Harriet Tubman was active in the Underground Railroad, which was successful in bringing many slaves into Northern states that would not return them to their owners. John Brown adopted more violent means of expressing his abolitionist sentiment. He raided the federal arsenal at Harpers Ferry, Virginia, and encouraged a slave revolt. He was eventually hanged for his violent actions. Frederick Douglass was an important abolitionist who played a significant role in the passage toward freedom for the slaves. A runaway slave, he spoke eloquently about the need to redress the wrongs created by slavery.

EMANCIPATION PROCLAMATION

As Civil War broke out, the movement placed greater pressure on President Lincoln to issue the Emancipation Proclamation. Lincoln had focused a great deal of attention on the issue of slavery during the famous Lincoln-Douglas debates. The Emancipation Proclamation was issued on September 22, 1862, well after the beginning of the Civil War. It announced that in states that had seceded from the union, all slaves would be freed effective January 1, 1863. This proclamation did not free many slaves. It did not apply to states that were part of the Union and was unenforceable in those states involved in the Confederacy. The major function of the Emancipation Proclamation was to announce to all that the Civil War was about slavery.

At the time that the Civil War began, the African American population of the United States consisted of approximately four and a half million people, four million of whom were slaves. White supremacy was the general ideology of both Southerners and Northerners. Slaves were denied such rights as the right to legal marriage, choice of residence, and education, and existed in perpetual servitude. Without significant changes in institutional structures, there was no hope of freedom.

CIVIL WAR AMENDMENTS

The Thirteenth Amendment was one of three amendments (the others being the Fourteenth and Fifteenth) known as the Civil War amendments. The combined purpose of these three amendments was to free the slaves and promote their participation in their country. The Thirteenth Amendment states "neither slavery nor involuntary servitude, except as a punishment for crime whereof the party shall have been duly convicted, shall exist within the United States, or any place subject to their jurisdiction." One of the battles surrounding the Thirteenth Amendment in particular, and all the Civil War amendments in general, concerned the interpretation of the Tenth Amendment. The Tenth Amendment stated that no federal legislation could detract from the power of state government. Those who opposed the Thirteenth Amendment claimed that the right to allow slavery was not specifically denied in the Constitution and therefore fell within the authority of the state.

With the passage of this amendment, the long fight to abolish slavery was over. The amendment was ratified on December 6, 1865, and officially announced on December 18, 1865. For some abolitionists, such as William Lloyd Garrison, the battle had been won: Slavery was ended. Others saw the Thirteenth Amendment as only a beginning.

EXPECTATIONS AND IMPACT

Frederick Douglass did not have the same high hopes held by Garrison. Douglass believed that slavery would not be abolished until the former slaves acquired the right to vote. The passage of the Civil Rights Act of 1866 did not provide this right. It was not until the passage of the Fourteenth Amendment, in 1868, that citizenship and the rights thereof were guaranteed to "all persons born or naturalized in the United States." Finally, in 1870, former slaves were expressly given the right to vote. Within weeks, the first African American in the U.S. Senate, Hiram R. Revels, took his seat.

On April 15, 1865, President Lincoln died from wounds inflicted by an assassin the night before. Vice President Andrew Johnson took over the reins of the presidency and reconstruction of the nation. Johnson, however, was not highly supportive or sympathetic to the needs of the slaves. Johnson blocked every attempt to extend rights to former slaves. In fact, Johnson vetoed most of the bills that were passed by Congress, only to have his veto overridden

by a two-thirds majority of Congress. Impeachment charges eventually ensued, and Johnson was spared by only a one-vote margin.
At that point, Johnson withdrew from reconstruction activities and
allowed Congress to control the process.

Sharon L. Larson

SOURCES FOR FURTHER STUDY

Anastaplo, George. *The Amendments to the Constitution: A Commentary.* Baltimore: The Johns Hopkins University Press, 1995.

Commission on the Bicentennial of the U.S. Constitution. *1791 to
1991: The Bill of Rights and Beyond.* Washington, D.C.: Author,
1991.

Farber, Daniel A., William N. Eskridge, Jr., and Philip P. Frickey.
Constitutional Law: Themes for the Constitution's Third Century. St.
Paul, Minn.: West Publishing, 1993.

Foner, Eric. *Reconstruction: America's Unfinished Revolution, 1863-
1877.* New York: Harper & Row, 1988.

Franklin, John Hope. *From Slavery to Freedom: A History of Negro
Americans.* 3d ed. New York: Alfred A. Knopf, 1967.

Furnas, J. C. *The Road to Harpers Ferry.* London: Faber & Faber,
1961.

Klingaman, Willam K. *Abraham Lincoln and the Road to Emancipation, 1861-1865.* New York: Viking, 2001.

McKissack, Pat, and Fredrick McKissack. *The Civil Rights Movement
in America from 1865 to the Present.* 2d ed. Chicago: Children's
Press, 1991.

Owen, Robert Dale. *The Wrong of Slavery, the Right of Emancipation,
and the Future of the African Race in the United States.* Philadelphia:
J. B. Lippincott, 1864.

Richards, David A. J. *Conscience and the Constitution: History, Theory,
and Law of the Reconstruction Amendments.* Princeton, N.J.: Princeton University Press, 1993.

Riehecky, Janet. *The Emancipation Proclamation: Abolition of Slavery
in 1863.* Portsmouth, N.H.: Heinemann Library, 2002.

Vorenberg, Michael. *Final Freedom: The Civil War, the Abolition of
Slavery, and the Thirteenth Amendment.* Cambridge Historical
Studies in American Law and Society. Cambridge, Mass.: Cam-
bridge University Press, 2001.

See also: Anti-Slave Trade Bill (1807); Emancipation Proclamation (1863); Freedmen's Bureau Act (1865); Civil Rights Act of 1866 (1866); Fourteenth Amendment (1868); Fifteenth Amendment (1870).

Civil Rights Act of 1866

Date: April 9, 1866
U.S. Statutes at Large: 14 Stat. 27
Categories: African Americans; Civil Rights and Liberties

These statutes were designed to give legal protection for the fundamental rights of African Americans in the South but generally failed to provide long-term, effective protection because of Supreme Court decisions and public disenchantment.

After the Thirteenth Amendment abolished slavery throughout the United States in 1865, almost all freed blacks were without property or education, and most white southerners bitterly opposed any fundamental improvement in their political and social status. In 1865-1866, southern legislatures enacted the highly discriminatory Black Codes, and proponents of racial equality responded by calling for new federal laws.

Provisions of the Act

Congress, using its new authority under the Thirteenth Amendment, overrode President Andrew Johnson's veto to pass the first Civil Rights Act on April 9, 1866. This law conferred citizenship on African Americans, a measure necessitated by the Supreme Court's *Dred Scott* decision (*Scott v. Sandford*, 1857). The law included a list of enumerated rights, including the right to make and enforce contracts, to sue and give evidence in court, and to purchase and inherit all forms of property. It also punished public officials if they used their legal powers to deny equality to blacks. Since the law's constitutionality was questionable, many of its major provisions were incorporated into the Fourteenth Amendment. On July 16, 1866, Congress again overrode President Johnson's veto, this time to enlarge the scope of the Freedmen's Bureau. Among other items, this law authorized the bureau to use military commissions to try persons accused of violating the civil rights of freedmen.

SUBSEQUENT CIVIL RIGHTS LEGISLATION

Again voting to override a presidential veto on March 2, 1867, Congress passed the First Reconstruction Act. Dividing the South into five military districts, the act required southern states to call new constitutional conventions elected by universal male suffrage and to ratify the Fourteenth Amendment. Under the act, 703,000 blacks and 627,000 whites were registered as voters, with black majorities in five states.

As the Ku Klux Klan conducted a wave of terrorism against African Americans and Republicans in the South, Congress responded with the Ku Klux Klan Acts of 1870 and 1871, which provided police protection to enforce the rights guaranteed in the Fourteenth and Fifteenth Amendments. In several decisions, such as *United States v. Cruikshank* (1876), the Supreme Court ruled that key parts of the statutes exceeded the constitutional powers of Congress.

Finally, on March 1, 1875, President Ulysses S. Grant signed into law the Civil Rights Act of 1875. This far-reaching act, largely the work of Senator Charles Sumner, outlawed discrimination based on race in public accommodations (inns, businesses, theaters, and the like) and made it illegal to exclude blacks from jury trials. In the *Civil Rights* cases (1883), however, the Supreme Court struck down most of the 1875 law, holding that the Fourteenth Amendment did not authorize Congress to prohibit discrimination by private individuals. This decision ended almost all federal attempts to protect African Americans from private discrimination until the passage of the Civil Rights Act of 1964.

LONG-TERM IMPACT

Although the Civil Rights Acts of the Reconstruction era failed to guarantee any long-lasting equality for blacks, they did provide points of reference for the Civil Rights movement of the 1950's and 1960's. The Civil Rights Act of 1866 was resurrected in *Jones v. Alfred H. Mayer Company* (1968), when the Supreme Court upheld its use to outlaw private racial discrimination in economic transactions as a "badge of slavery."

Thomas T. Lewis

U.S. Laws, Acts, and Treaties

SOURCES FOR FURTHER STUDY

Abernathy, M. Glenn. *Civil Liberties Under the Constitution.* 5th ed. Columbia: University of South Carolina Press, 1989.

Asch, Sidney H. *Civil Rights and Responsibilities Under the Constitution.* New York: Arco, 1968.

Bardolph, Richard, ed. *The Civil Rights Record: Black Americans and the Law, 1849-1870.* New York: Thomas Crowell, 1970.

Blaustein, Albert P., and Robert L. Zangrando, eds. *Civil Rights and the American Negro: A Documentary History.* New York: Trident Press, 1968.

Chalmers, David M. *Hooded Americanism: The First Century of the Ku Klux Klan.* 3d ed. Durham, N.C.: Duke University Press, 1987.

Franklin, John Hope. *From Slavery to Freedom: A History of Negro Americans.* 3d ed. New York: Alfred A. Knopf, 1967.

Henry, Christopher E., and Wilbert Jenkinds. *Forever Free: From the Emancipation Proclamation to the Civil Rights Bill of 1875.* Broomall, Pa.: Chelsea House, 1995.

McKissack, Patricia, and Frederick McKissack. *The Civil Rights Movement in America, from 1865-Present.* 2d ed. Chicago: Children's Press, 1991.

Weinstein, Allen, and Frank Otto Gatell. *Freedom and Crisis: An American History.* 2 vols. New York: Random House, 1978.

SEE ALSO: Black Codes of 1804-1807 (1804-1807); Fugitive Slave Act of 1850 (1850); Thirteenth Amendment (1865); Reconstruction Acts (1867); Fourteenth Amendment (1868); Fifteenth Amendment (1870).

RECONSTRUCTION ACTS

ALSO KNOWN AS: Military Reconstruction Acts
DATE: Beginning March 2, 1867
U.S. STATUTES AT LARGE: 14 Stat. 428
CATEGORIES: African Americans; Civil Rights and Liberties; Government Procedure and Organization

280

These acts were passed to enlist military and other governmental aid in reconstruction of the Southern states following the Civil War.

The end of the Civil War brought on the enormously complex task of reconstructing the nation. The situation in the South was desperate: Its commercial heart had been destroyed and economic paralysis had set in; banks, money, and credit were nonexistent; people in many areas faced actual starvation; institutions such as churches, schools, and city and county governments had ceased to function. Were these seceded and now destitute Southern states to be treated as erring rebels and quickly returned to the Union?

TEN PERCENT PLAN

Abraham Lincoln, sixteenth president of the United States, consistently maintained that the "seceding" Southern states had, in fact, never left the Union; those Southern states, according to Lincoln, were to be brought back into their "proper relationship" with the federal government; then "safely at home, it would be utterly immaterial whether they had been abroad."

While the war was still in progress, Lincoln had turned his thoughts to the problem of reconciliation and had devised a plan to restore the South with maximum speed and minimum humiliation. The basis of this restoration would be a loyal minority in each state. To create such a body, Lincoln expected to use the presidential pardoning power. He granted amnesty to all ex-Confederates, except high civilian and military officials, who would take an oath of loyalty to the United States. When 10 percent of the 1860 electorate in the state took the oath, that state could then set up a new state government, which would then be recognized by the president. Lincoln proclaimed this "ten percent plan" in effect on December 8, 1863.

RADICAL RECONSTRUCTION

The more radical members of Congress—led in the House by Thaddeus Stevens of Pennsylvania and in the Senate by Charles Sumner of Massachusetts—were annoyed by the mildness of Lincoln's approach, and they repudiated the state governments of Tennessee, Arkansas, and Louisiana, which had been established under this plan. The electoral votes from these states were not counted in 1864, and their representatives were not seated in Congress. Forced by political necessity to provide an alternative, the Radical Republicans countered Lincoln by passing the Wade-Davis Bill in June, 1864. That measure stipulated that Congress was to put the Reconstruction program into effect. A majority of the number of persons who had voted in 1860, rather than ten percent, was required to swear allegiance before state governments could be established. Other rigid provisions were enumerated. The new state constitutions had to abolish slavery, repudiate the Confederate debt, and disfranchise Confederate military leaders. Prospective voters had to swear an "ironclad oath" of past as well as future loyalty in order to qualify for the franchise. Since the bill was passed an hour before the session of Congress ended, Lincoln, who objected to the harshness of the radical position, permitted the bill to die by pocket veto. The radicals then approved the Wade-Davis Manifesto, which bitterly attacked Lincoln for ostensibly usurping congressional power.

The sentiment behind a program of Radical Reconstruction had been present from the earliest days of the Civil War, but it coalesced around the Wade-Davis Bill, a measure that would have eliminated the Southern ruling class from participation in the political process. This measure came about as a response by Republicans in Congress who resented or eschewed the reconstruction proposals outlined by Lincoln in December, 1863.

JOHNSONIAN RECONSTRUCTION

Before any action could be taken by either side, Lincoln was assassinated in April, 1865. His death removed from politics a far-sighted statesman of tact and influence and a man well versed in handling recalcitrant congressmen. It elevated Andrew Johnson, a Southern Democrat from Tennessee, to the presidency. Not elected to this highest office, Johnson lacked the respect and gratitude of the nation that Lincoln had gained as the wartime president. Also, Johnson was stubborn and adamant, particularly when he believed his cause to be right. In such a time of crisis, the Tennessean was, perhaps, ill-suited for the presidency.

Although a Southerner and a former slave owner, Johnson was a devoted Unionist. Without calling Congress into session, he put into operation a plan of reconstruction that closely resembled Lincoln's. This, referred to by historians as "Presidential Reconstruction," was not revealed until May 29, 1865. The basic difference between Johnson's and Lincoln's plan was the number of people excluded from the amnesty; Johnson listed a total of fourteen categories of Southerners who were ineligible for pardon. Still, his pardon policy was extremely lenient, and by September of 1865, pardons were being issued "wholesale." In addition, he asked for explicit guarantees: The new state constitutions had to abolish slavery, declare the secession ordinances null and void, and repudiate the Confederate war debt. Majority consent, rather than 10 percent, was implied, but not specified, and the new legislatures were to ratify the Thirteenth Amendment, which abolished slavery. By the time Congress reconvened in December, 1865, all the ex-Confederate states except Texas had fulfilled Johnson's terms, and the president announced to the assembled legislators that Reconstruction was over.

Johnson's plan staggered many Republicans who determined to contest it. Seeking guarantees that the South accepted the results of the war, the Republicans instead saw that the Southern governments reestablished under the Johnson plan had enacted Black Codes, regulations that had the effect of placing African Americans in a kind of peonage system in Southern society. The Black Codes, in various forms in the Southern states, effectively kept newly freed slaves from voting, getting an education, finding homes, taking advantage of economic opportunities, and gaining equal access to the judicial system. Furthermore, Southern governments had failed to prevent race riots, had elected to office important ex-Confederates such as Alexander H. Stephens, the former vice president of the Confederacy, and generally had given little evidence of a suppliant mood. Politically, the Republicans did not want to jeopardize their position by the rapid return of the Democratic South. Economically, Northern business interests feared Southern opposition to high tariffs and government subsidies, and humanitarians from all sections of the country wanted to see African Americans given political and social equality. Perhaps the most important motivating force was psychological; many Northerners wanted to gloat over their victory and see some direct evidence of Southern repentance.

FOURTEENTH AMENDMENT

After many proposals and counterproposals, the Republicans in Congress proposed the Fourteenth Amendment to the Constitution, which they considered to be a peace treaty. If the South would accept it, the Southern states would be readmitted. The Four- teenth Amendment guaranteed African Americans citizenship, im- posed political disabilities upon ex-Confederates, and attempted to compel the former slave states to allow African American suf- frage by decreasing their representation in the House of Represen- tatives and the electoral college in the event of disenfranchise- ment. Given the temper of the North and of Republicans in the spring of 1866, it was an eminently moderate measure. Johnson op- posed it, however, and urged the Southern states to reject it. They did, and the measure failed.

Military Reconstructon
On March 2, 1867, Congress passed the first of the Military Recon- struction Acts. This act replaced civil administration with military rule, dividing the South into five military districts whose adminis- trating officers were to take orders from General Ulysses S. Grant rather than from the president. The first duties of these military re- gimes were to protect persons and property, to create a new elec- torate based on male suffrage, and to supervise the election of con- ventions that were to draft new state constitutions. The military governments were also given the right to replace civil officials who had been "fraudulently" elected and to remove "disloyal" members from the state legislatures.

The South was now ruled with a firm hand by its military gover- nors. Confederate veterans' organizations and historical societies were suppressed, state and local officials were removed from of- fice, and military tribunals assumed the duties of civil courts when it was found that those courts could not be depended upon to pun- ish violence against African Americans. The army of occupation, consisting of nearly twenty thousand men and aided by an African American militia, enforced military rule; but these forces, deeply resented by the local populace, were kept largely in the back- ground. In general, they were not called out except to supervise elections or to control civil disorders. In each Southern state, the new African American electorate that had been registered by the military helped to choose the conventions that drafted new state constitutions. The new constitutions gave African Americans the right to vote while denying this right to former Confederate lead- ers. Civil and political equality was also granted to freedmen.

By the summer of 1868, reconstructed governments had been established in seven of the Southern states. After their state legislatures had ratified the Fourteenth and Fifteenth Amendments, the states were formally readmitted to the Union and were allowed to send senators and representatives to Congress. The states of Mississippi, Georgia, Virginia, and Texas were not "reconstructed" until 1870.

This era of "Black Reconstruction" has been greatly misrepresented, for varied and often deceitful reasons, as a time when the South fell prey to uneducated African Americans, opportunistic Northern "carpetbaggers," and a minority of disloyal Southern "scalawags." In reality, however, African Americans never dominated any Southern state government, nor did they ever hold offices in proportion to their numbers within the population. The African Americans elected to office were most often equal in ability to their white predecessors; some, such as Hiram R. Revels, senator from Mississippi, were men of extraordinary talent and ability. Due to a lack of political experience, however, some African American officeholders were manipulated and exploited by avaricious whites. In general, the corruption that characterized several of the state governments in this period was a result of the triumph of white political sophistication and wiles over the political naïveté of the newly elected officeholders.

It is interesting to note that the new African American legislators never did attempt to pass vindictive laws aimed at their former masters. However, no matter what form the new reconstructed governments took, they were bound to be hated by the majority of Southern whites. A program of rebuilding the physical structure of the area—cities, roads, railroads—necessary for economic growth and recovery, resulted in deficit spending characterized by the crushing burden of taxation that was placed on the Southern gentry, plus the graft and bribery that took place on a large scale; such corruption was also common in the North at that time. To answer the threat of this alleged oppression, many Southern whites turned to the formation of secret white supremacist societies such as the Ku Klux Klan and the Knights of the White Camelia. A series of pillages, whippings, and even murders resulted. These actions resulted in the enactment of the Force Acts, or Ku Klux Klan Acts, authorizing the president to suspend *habeas corpus* and to send federal troops to areas that were considered to be the most unruly. By means of this congressional legislation, portions of which were later declared unconstitutional, the first incarnation of the Klan was largely stamped out by 1872 (it would resurface again in the twentieth century).

END OF RECONSTRUCTION

By 1874 the Democrats had captured control of the House of Representatives, marking the end of Northern Radicalism. The Amnesty Act of 1872 had restored full political rights to the disfranchised ex-Confederates. Factional splits in the Republican Party had been caused by struggles between carpetbaggers and scalawags. African Americans who had been promised "forty acres and a mule" by the Republicans began to desert the party when their hopes failed to materialize. Instead, they would turn to the old master class, in which they had more confidence. These white "redeemer" governments recaptured control of state political machinery between 1869 and 1871 in Tennessee, Virginia, North Carolina, and Georgia, and in 1874 to 1875 in Alabama, Arkansas, Texas, and Mississippi. With the Civil War a more distant memory by this time, the North no longer cared about the freedmen in the South, and shortly after the inauguration of Rutherford B. Hayes in 1877, Reconstruction came to an official end when President Hayes withdrew the last federal troops from Louisiana on April 24 of that year.

John H. DeBerry, updated by
Liesel Ashley Miller

SOURCES FOR FURTHER STUDY

Anderson, Eric, and Alfred A. Moss, Jr., eds. *The Facts of Reconstruction: Essays in Honor of John Hope Franklin.* Baton Rouge: Louisiana State University Press, 1991.

Burr, Virginia Ingraham, ed. *The Secret Eye: The Journal of Ella Gertrude Clanton Thomas, 1848-1889.* Chapel Hill: University of North Carolina Press, 1990.

Carter, Dan T. *When the War Was Over: The Failure of Self-Reconstruction in the South, 1865-1867.* Baton Rouge: Louisiana State University Press, 1985.

Foner, Eric. *Reconstruction: America's Unfinished Revolution, 1863-1877.* New York: Harper & Row, 1988.

Mcpherson, James M. *Ordeal by Fire: The Civil War and Reconstruction.* New York: Alfred A. Knopf, 1982.

Smith, Page. *Trial by Fire: A People's History of the Civil War and Reconstruction.* Vol. 5. New York: McGraw-Hill, 1982.

Sutherland, Daniel E. *The Confederate Carpetbaggers.* Baton Rouge: Louisiana State University Press, 1988.

SEE ALSO: Black Codes of 1804-1807 (1804-1807); Fugitive Slave Act of 1850 (1850); Freedmen's Bureau Act (1865); Thirteenth Amendment (1865); Civil Rights Act of 1866 (1866); Fourteenth Amendment (1868); Fifteenth Amendment (1870).

MEDICINE LODGE CREEK TREATY

DATE: Concluded October 21, 1867

U.S. STATUTES AT LARGE: 15 Stat. 589

CATEGORIES: Native Americans; Treaties and Agreements

Tribes of the Great Plains entered an agreement that ultimately resulted in total submission to the U.S. government.

For many years, five Native American tribes—the Comanche, the Kiowa, the Kiowa-Apache, the Southern Cheyenne, and the Arapaho—roamed the vast area of the southern Great Plains, following huge buffalo herds. This area became parts of Texas, Oklahoma, New Mexico, Colorado, and Kansas. Northern Cheyenne, Sioux, and other tribes lived a similar life on the northern Great Plains. Warfare was a part of the daily life of these tribes, generally as a result of intertribal rivalries and disputes concerning control of certain sections of the plains. This traditional life began to change when the first Europeans began to arrive on the Great Plains in the sixteenth century. Until the early nineteenth century, however, the changes were limited to the acquisition of steel knives, guns, and other products from European traders. The tribes soon became dependent on these items, but their day-by-day life changed very little.

The dominant leaders of the region were the Comanches, called the Lords of the Southern Plains. Joined by the Kiowas, with whom they established friendly relations about 1790, they controlled the smaller Kiowa-Apache tribe and all land south of the Arkansas River. Their chief rivals north of the Arkansas River were the southern Cheyenne. In 1840, the Comanches and Cheyennes established a fragile peace that also included the Arapaho, the less numerous allies of the Cheyenne.

PLAINS INDIANS AND THE UNITED STATES
This peace came at the beginning of a decade that would change forever the face of the southern Great Plains. In 1846, the United States annexed Texas. The end of the Mexican War in 1848 added New Mexico, Arizona, and other areas of the Southwest to the United States. For the next half century, the fragile Native American peace of 1840 became a strong bond of brotherhood for the southern plains tribes as they fought to defend themselves and their land against European American settlers, railroads, buffalo hunters, soldiers, and other newcomers.

With the acquisition of Texas, the United States inherited a long and bloody conflict between Texans and Comanches, who were described by some as the best light cavalry in the world. The Comanches had long hunted from the Arkansas River to the Rio Grande. In 1821, the government of Mexico began giving land grants in west Texas to settlers from the United States. These settlers immediately challenged the Comanches for control of the area.

COMANCHE RESERVATIONS
The first attempt to confine the Comanches to reservations was a May, 1846, treaty that created two small reservations on the Brazos River. The few Comanches who settled on them soon yearned for the nomadic life on the vast plains. By 1850, discoveries of precious metals from the southern Rocky Mountains to California were drawing numerous wagon and pack trains through the southern plains. These were soon followed by stagecoach lines and, later, railroads. The increase in traffic was paralleled by increased confrontation with the tribes, who were accustomed to unhindered pursuit of the buffalo.

Between 1846 and 1865, several treaties were signed between the Native Americans of the southern plains and the government of the United States. Lack of confidence and open contempt on both sides doomed these treaties to failure. The frustration felt by the Native Americans increased when cholera and other diseases carried by Europeans began rapidly decreasing the native populations.

In March of 1863, a party of Native American chiefs from the southern plains went to Washington, D.C., and met with President Abraham Lincoln. Returning home loaded with gifts, these leaders were convinced that coexistence with European Americans was possible. This confidence was hard to maintain after the bloody and unprovoked massacre of Cheyennes at Sand Creek, in Colorado, the following year. Nevertheless, Ten Bears of the Comanche, who had met President Lincoln, Black Kettle of the Cheyenne, who had escaped from Sand Creek, and other chiefs still felt that peace was their best protection and was possible to achieve.

TREATIES AND PEACE COMMISSIONS

The next effort toward peace was the Little Arkansas Treaty in October, 1865. Representatives of the five southern plains tribes met with U.S. commissioners at the mouth of the Little Arkansas River near Wichita, Kansas. The government wanted to end native American hindrances to movements in and through the plains. The treaty, little more than a stopgap measure, committed the tribes to reservations—the Cheyenne and Arapaho in northern Indian Territory (Oklahoma) and the Comanche, Kiowa, and Kiowa-Apache in western Texas and southwestern Indian Territory. These boundaries were impossible to enforce and did not end the violence, but the treaty set the stage for a more important meeting two years later.

In July, 1867, Congress created a peace commission to establish permanent settlements of grievances between Native Americans and European Americans on the Great Plains. The commission was led by Commissioner of Indian Affairs Nathaniel Taylor and included a senator and three generals. The group chose to meet representatives of the southern plains tribes on the banks of Medicine Lodge Creek in southwestern Kansas. Joining them there were more than four thousand Native Americans representing all five tribes, but not all bands of the tribes. Noticeably absent was the Quahadi, a Comanche band that wanted no peace with the United States government.

The council opened on October 19, 1867, with Senator John B. Henderson giving the opening remarks. Under a large brush arbor, he referred to reservation homes, rich farmland, livestock, churches, and schools for all Native Americans. Although most tribal leaders accepted the promises as positive, the idea of being restricted to reservations covering only a fraction of their beloved Great Plains was sickening. The Kiowa chief Satanta, or White Bear, lamented, "I love to roam over the prairies. There I feel free and happy, but when we settle down we grow pale and die." The Yamparika Comanche chief Ten Bears gave one of the most eloquent statements, declaring,

> I was born where there were no inclosures and where everything drew a free breath. I want to die there and not within walls. . . . when I see [soldiers cutting trees and killing buffalo] my heart feels like bursting with sorrow.

THE TREATY AND ITS CONSEQUENCES

In spite of such emotional appeals, Ten Bears and other Comanche chiefs signed the Treaty of Medicine Lodge Creek on October 21, 1867, thereby committing their people to life on the reservation. Black Kettle, with the horrors of the 1864 Sand Creek Massacre fresh in his mind, represented the Cheyenne at the council. He would not sign the treaty until other Cheyenne chiefs arrived on October 26. Although less happy with the treaty than the Comanche and Kiowa leaders, the Cheyenne chiefs signed, primarily to get ammunition for their fall buffalo hunt. The Arapaho chiefs soon did likewise. At the end of the council meeting, Satank rode alone to bid farewell to the Peace Commission. He expressed his desire for peace and declared that the Comanche and the Kiowa no longer wanted to shed the blood of the white man.

The Treaty of Medicine Lodge Creek restricted the five southern Plains tribes to reservations in the western half of Indian Territory. However, vague terminology and unwritten promises made the treaty impossible to understand or to enforce. Violence soon erupted on the southern plains. One year after Medicine Lodge Creek, Black Kettle was killed in a confrontation similar to the Sand Creek Massacre, this time on the Washita River in Indian Territory. The violence escalated for several years, then dwindled to isolated incidents before ending at Wounded Knee in 1890.

A poignant illustration of the ultimate effect of the treaty occurred on June 8, 1871, when the seventy-year-old Satank—who along with Satanta and a young war chief named Big Tree had been arrested for attacking a mule train carrying food that the ration-deprived Indians sorely needed—was being transported to Texas to stand trial for murder. Chewing his own wrists in order to slip out of his manacles, Satank then attacked a guard and was shot dead, fulfilling a prophecy that he had uttered only minutes before to fellow prisoners: "Tell them I am dead. . . . I shall never go beyond that tree."

Glenn L. Swygart

SOURCES FOR FURTHER STUDY
Brown, Dee. *Bury My Heart at Wounded Knee.* New York: Holt, Rinehart and Winston, 1970.
Grinnell, George Bird. *The Fighting Cheyennes.* 1915. Reprint. Norman: University of Oklahoma Press, 1956.
Hagan, William T. *United States-Comanche Relations.* New Haven, Conn.: Yale University Press, 1976.
Josephy, Alvin M., Jr. *500 Nations: An Illustrated History of North American Indians.* New York: Alfred A. Knopf, 1994.
Mooney, James. *Calendar History of the Kiowa Indians.* 1898. Reprint. Washington, D.C.: Smithsonian Institution Press, 1979.
Rollings, Willard H. *The Comanche.* New York: Chelsea House, 1989.

SEE ALSO: Indian Removal Act (1830); Treaty of Dancing Rabbit Creek (1830); Treaty of Guadalupe Hidalgo (1848); Fort Laramie Treaty of 1851 (1851); Fort Atkinson Treaty (1853); Fort Laramie Treaty of 1868 (1868); Indian Appropriation Act (1871); General Allotment Act (1887).

FOURTEENTH AMENDMENT

DATE: Probably ratified July 9, 1868; certified July 28, 1868
U.S. STATUTES AT LARGE: 15 Stat. 706-707
CATEGORIES: African Americans; Civil Rights and Liberties; Constitutional Law; Slavery

The first article of this amendment, perhaps the most important after the Bill of Rights, states, "All persons born or naturalized in the United States and subject to the jurisdiction thereof, are citizens of the United States and of the State wherein they reside. No State shall make or enforce any law which shall abridge the privileges or immunities of citizens of the United States; nor shall any State deprive any person of life, liberty, or property, without due process of law; nor deny to any person within its jurisdiction the equal protection of the laws. "

The Fourteenth Amendment was part of the plan for Reconstruction formulated by the Republican majority in the Thirty-ninth Congress. Before Congress met in December, 1865, President Andrew Johnson had authorized the restoration of self-government in the former Confederate states, and the congressmen and senators from those states waited in Washington to be seated in Congress. The state legislatures elected under Johnson's program had met to develop a series of laws called Black Codes, which restricted the rights of the former slaves.

REPUBLICANS FIGHT STATUS-QUO RECONSTRUCTION

While the Republican majority in Congress had no intention of permitting the Johnson approach to Reconstruction to prevail or of seating the unrepentant white Southern representatives, they had no comprehensive counterproposal. To gain time and to work out a positive approach, Republicans in the House and the Senate created the Joint Committee of Fifteen on Reconstruction. This committee was composed of six senators and nine representatives.

The Republican majority rejected Johnson's plan because, as the Black Codes demonstrated, the old Confederates could not be trusted to respect the rights of the freedmen. Moreover, the Republicans had no intention of permitting white Southerners, whom they regarded as rebels and traitors, to increase the representation in the House of Representatives of the Southern Democrats. The abolition of slavery had destroyed the old compromise under which five slaves counted as three free persons in apportioning representation in the House and the electoral college, and the Republicans wanted to make sure that the South did not add to its numbers in the House and thus profit from rebellion.

Between December, 1865, and May, 1866, the Republicans attempted to hammer out a program that would accomplish their purposes in the South, unite members of their party in Congress, and appeal to Northern voters. Given the diversity of opinion within the party, this undertaking proved to be difficult. The radicals wanted African American suffrage, permanent political proscription, and confiscation of the property of ex-Confederates. Some maintained they were authorized in these actions by the Thirteenth Amendment, which, they believed, gave Congress the power to abolish the "vestiges of slavery." Moderate Republicans, on the other hand, feared political repercussions from African American suffrage, as such a requirement would result in beginning the Reconstruction process over again. Many moderates also believed that an additional amendment to the Constitution was needed to provide precise authority for Congress to enact civil rights legislation.

From deliberations of the joint committee and debate on the floor of the House came the Fourteenth Amendment. Many Republicans believed that the proposal was in the nature of a peace treaty, although this view was not explicitly stated. If the South accepted the amendment, the Southern states were to be readmitted and their senators and representatives seated in Congress; in other words, Reconstruction would end. Republicans presented a united front during the final vote as a matter of party policy. Because the amendment was an obvious compromise between radicals and moderates, it was too strong for some and too weak for others.

PROVISIONS

The Fourteenth Amendment became the most important addition to the constitution since the Bill of Rights had been adopted in 1791. It contains five sections:

Section 1, the first constitutional definition of citizenship, states that all persons born or naturalized in the United States are citizens of the United States and of the state in which they reside. It includes limits on the power of states by providing that no state may abridge the privileges and immunities of citizens, deprive any person of life, liberty, or property without due process of law, or deny to any person within its jurisdiction the equal protection of law. This section was intended to guarantee African Americans the rights of citizenship, although the amendment's framers did not define exactly which rights were included. Nor did they define "state action" to specify whether the term meant only official acts of state government or the actions of individuals functioning privately with state approval. The courts later interpreted the due process clause to extend the rights of the accused listed in the Bill of Rights, which had applied only to the federal government, to the states. They expanded the notion of equal protection to include other categories, such as sex and disability, as well as race. They also interpreted the word "person" to include corporations as legal persons; under this interpretation, corporations found protection from much state regulation.

Section 2 gives a new formula of representation in place of the old three-fifths compromise of the Constitution, under which five slaves were counted as equal to three free persons in determining a state's representation in the House of Representatives and the electoral college. All persons in a state were to be counted for representation, but if a state should disfranchise any of its adult male citizens, except for participation in rebellion or any other crime, the basis of its representation would be reduced proportionately. While not guaranteeing suffrage to African Americans, this provision threatened the South with a loss of representation should black males be denied the vote.

Section 3 declares that no person who has ever taken an oath to support the Constitution (which included all who had been in the military service or held state or national office before 1860) and has then participated in the rebellion can be a senator or representative or hold any civil or military office, national or state. This disability could be removed only by a two-thirds vote of both houses of Congress. This section took away the pardoning power of the president, which congressional Republicans believed Andrew Johnson used too generously.

Section 4 validates the debt of the United States, voids all debts incurred to support rebellion, and invalidates all claims for compensation for emancipated slaves.

Section 5 gives Congress authority to pass legislation to enforce the provisions of the Fourteenth Amendment.

The correspondence and speeches of those who framed the Fourteenth Amendment do not support any theories of economic conspiracy or ulterior motives. The amendment's framers desired to protect the former slaves and boost Republicanism in the South by barring old Confederates from returning to Congress and the electoral college with increased voting strength. They hoped to do this without threatening the federal system or unduly upsetting the relationship between the central government and the states. At the same time, Republicans wanted to unify their party and project a popular issue for the approaching electoral contest against Andrew Johnson.

William J. Cooper, Jr., updated by
Mary Welek Atwell

SOURCES FOR FURTHER STUDY

Benedict, Michael Les. *A Compromise of Principle: Congressional Republicans and Reconstruction, 1863-1869.* New York: W. W. Norton, 1974.

Cox, LaWanda, and John H. Cox. *Politics, Principle, and Prejudice: Dilemma of Reconstruction America, 1865-1866.* New York: Free Press, 1963.

Hyman, Harold M., and William Wiecek. *Equal Justice Under Law: Constitutional Development, 1835-1875.* New York: Harper & Row, 1982.

Lively, Donald E. *The Constitution and Race.* New York: Praeger, 1992.

Nieman, Donald G. *Promises to Keep: African-Americans and the Constitutional Order, 1776 to the Present.* New York: Oxford University Press, 1991.

Perry, Michael J. *We the People: The Fourteenth Amendment and the Supreme Court.* New York: Oxford University Press, 2002.

Renstrom, Peter G. *Constitutional Law for Young Adults: A Handbook on the Bill of Rights and the Fourteenth Amendment.* Santa Barbara, Calif.: ABC-CLIO, 1992.

Richards, David A. J. *Conscience and the Constitution: History, Theory, and Law of the Reconstruction Amendments.* Princeton, N.J.: Princeton University Press, 1993.

Stampp, Kenneth M. *The Era of Reconstruction, 1865-1877.* New York: Alfred A. Knopf, 1965.

Vile, John R. *Encyclopedia of Constitutional Amendments, Proposed Amendments, and Amending Issues, 1789-1995.* Santa Barbara, Calif: ABC-CLIO, 1996.

SEE ALSO: Three-fifths compromise (1787); Black Codes of 1804-1807 (1804-1807); Emancipation Proclamation (1863); Black Codes of 1865 (1865); Thirteenth Amendment (1865); Civil Rights Act of 1866 (1866); Reconstruction Acts (1867); Fifteenth Amendment (1870); Jim Crow laws (1880's-1954); Disfranchisement laws (1890).

BURLINGAME TREATY

DATE: Signed July 28, 1868
CATEGORIES: Asia or Asian Americans; Foreign Relations; Treaties and Agreements

This treaty established reciprocal rights between China and the United States, including respect for territorial sovereignty and bilateral immigration.

Formal United States interest in China dates from the thirteen-thousand-mile voyage of the U.S. ship *Empress of China*, under the command of Captain John Green, which departed from New York City on February 22, 1784. The vessel returned from Canton in May, 1785, with tea, silks, and other trade goods of the Orient. Merchants in Philadelphia, Boston, Providence, and New York quickly sought profits in the China trade. By the late 1830's, "Yankee clippers" had shortened the transit time from America's Atlantic ports to Canton from a matter of many months to a mere ninety days.

Political problems, however, hindered commercial relations. The Manchu, or Ch'ing, Dynasty (1644-1912), fearful of Western intentions, restricted trade to one city, Canton, and sharply curtailed the rights of foreigners in China. Chafing at these limits, especially China's refusal to deal with Europeans on terms of equality, caused Great Britain to begin hostilities with the Manchu Dynasty, occasioned by the "unsavory issue" of England's trade in opium with China. The Opium War (1839-1842) resulted in the Treaty of Nanking (August 24, 1842), a triumph for the political and commercial interests of Great Britain in eastern Asia. England obtained the cession of the island of Hong Kong and the opening of four additional cities—Amoy, Ningpo, Foochow, and Shanghai—to British trade.

SEEKING TRADE WITH CHINA

The U.S. government desired similar rights and obtained them in the Treaty of Wang Hiya (named for a village near Macao) on July 3, 1844; Commissioner Caleb Cushing, although not formally received by China as a minister, was permitted to negotiate this landmark agreement. The United States secured access to the newly opened ports and was extended the right of extraterritoriality; that is, U.S. citizens were to be tried for offenses committed in China under U.S. law by the U.S. consul.

Within the next twenty years, trade with China grew. The United States acquired Washington, Oregon, and California, and, with Pacific ports, had greater access to Chinese markets. The California gold rush (1849) and the construction of the Central Pacific Railroad (completed in 1869), with its need for labor, encouraged Chinese emigration to the United States. Meanwhile, U.S. missionaries, merchants, travelers, and adventurers were arriving in China. Conditions in "the Middle Kingdom," however, were not good. The authority of the central government had been challenged by the anti-Western Taiping Rebellion (1850-1864) and was suppressed only with outside help. Further European incursions into China, epitomized by the Anglo-French War with the Manchus (1854-1858), threatened to curtail U.S. cultural and commercial opportunities in China. If the United States did not act, it would face the prospect of being excluded from China by European imperialism.

BURLINGAME GOES TO CHINA

Secretary of State William Henry Seward believed that it was time for the United States to have formal representation at the Manchu court. His fortunate choice was Anson Burlingame. Born on November 14, 1820, in rural New York, the son of a "Methodist exhorter," Burlingame had grown up in the Midwest, graduating from the University of Michigan. After attending Harvard Law School, Burlingame went into practice in Boston. With a gift of oratory and exceptional personal charm, Burlingame served in the U.S. House of Representatives (1855-1861) and was a pioneer of the new Republican Party. As a reward for his labor and in recognition of his talents, Burlingame was offered the post of U.S. minister to Austria, but the Habsburgs refused him because of his known sympathies with Louis Kossuth, the Hungarian revolutionary. As a second choice and a compensatory honor, Burlingame was given the assignment to China.

Because the United States was distracted with the Civil War, Burlingame was left on his own and could count on little U.S. military might to support his actions. Acquiring a great admiration for and confidence in the Chinese, Burlingame won the trust and respect of I-Hsin, known as Prince Kung, the co-regent of China with the dowager empress Tz'u-hsi. When Burlingame resigned as the U.S. minister to China, in November, 1867, the Imperial Manchu court asked him to head China's first official delegation to the West. The Burlingame mission toured the United States, being warmly received, and arrived in the United Kingdom as William Gladstone was assuming the prime ministership of that nation. Burlingame's brilliant career was cut short during a subsequent visit to Russia, where he contracted pneumonia, dying in St. Petersburg on February 23, 1870. Few had served their own country so well, and it was said that none had given China a more sincere friendship.

FAIR TREATY, NATIVIST FEARS

The most outstanding accomplishment of the Burlingame mission, the Burlingame Treaty, was signed on July 28, 1868, in Washington, D.C. This document dealt with a variety of issues between China and the United States. The United States pledged itself to respect Chinese sovereignty and territorial integrity, a position in sharp contrast to that of the European powers and one that anticipated the United States' subsequent "open door policy" (1899). The Burlingame Treaty accepted bilateral immigration between China and the United States, and by 1880 there were 105,000 Chinese living in the United States.

By the standards of the 1860's, the Burlingame Treaty was a landmark of fairness and justice. Unfortunately, the United States did not honor its spirit or letter. Anti-immigrant feeling focused on a fear of Chinese "coolie" labor. The infamous Sandlot Riots in San Francisco, in June, 1877, were symptomatic of both the mistreatment of Asian immigrants and the rising sentiment for Asian exclusion. On March 1, 1879, President Rutherford B. Hayes vetoed a congressional bill limiting the number of Chinese passengers on board ships bound for the United States as a violation of the Burlingame Treaty. Hayes did, however, send a mission to China to work for the revision of the Burlingame Treaty. In 1880, China recognized the United States' right to regulate, limit, and suspend, but not absolutely forbid, Chinese immigration.

Two years later, President Chester A. Arthur vetoed a twenty-year suspension of Chinese immigration as being a de facto prohibition, but on May 6, 1882, the Chinese Exclusion Act passed, suspending the importation of Chinese labor for a ten-year period. In 1894, another ten-year exclusion period was enacted; in 1904, exclusion was extended indefinitely. When, on December 17, 1943, Chinese immigration was permitted by an act of Congress, it was within the strict limits of the 1920's quota system, allowing the entrance of only 105 Chinese annually. Not until the mid-twentieth century did the United States depart from an immigration policy centered on ethnic origin, thus allowing the original intent of the Burlingame Treaty to be realized.

C. George Fry

SOURCES FOR FURTHER STUDY
Dulles, Foster Rhea. *China and America: The Story of Their Relations Since 1784*. Princeton, N.J.: Princeton University Press, 1946.
Fairbank, John K. *China Perceived: Images and Policies in Chinese-American Relations*. New York: Alfred A. Knopf, 1974.
Fairbank, John K., Edwin O. Reischauer, and Albert M. Craig. *East Asia: Tradition and Transformation*. Rev. ed. Boston: Houghton Mifflin, 1989.
Miller, Stuart Creighton. *The Unwelcome Immigrant: The American Image of the Chinese, 1785-1882*. Berkeley: University of California Press, 1969.
Mosher, Steven W. *China Misperceived: American Illusions and Chinese Reality*. New York: Basic Books, 1990.
Tsai, Shih-shan Henry. *China and the Overseas Chinese in the United States, 1868-1911*. Fayetteville: University of Arkansas Press, 1983.

SEE ALSO: Treaty of Wang Hiya (1844); Page Law (1875); Chinese Exclusion Act (1882); Opium Exclusion Act (1909); Alien land laws (1913).

FORT LARAMIE TREATY OF 1868

DATE: Signed November 5, 1868
U.S. STATUTES AT LARGE: 15 Stat. 635
CATEGORIES: Native Americans; Treaties and Agreements

This treaty was meant to provide a lasting peace through mutual concessions involving territorial rights and peaceful behavior, but it ultimately failed.

By mid-1800's, the vast area of land claimed by the Sioux Nation was subjected to inexorable pressures from America's westward expansion, which accelerated after the end of the Civil War in 1865. Pioneers, settlers, farmers, gold prospectors, railroads, and the army all encroached on Sioux territory. Inevitably, armed conflict between whites and Indians occurred. Attempts to arrive at a peaceful solution and compromise, such as the treaties of 1851, 1865, and 1866, provided only short-lived respites.

On July 20, 1867, after vigorous debate over whether to subdue the Indians militarily and punish them or reach a peaceful accord with them, both houses of Congress approved a bill which authorized a government commission to make peace with the Plains tribes. The commission was directed by Congress to establish peace, remove if possible the causes of war, safeguard frontier settlements and the rights-of-way for the transcontinental railroads, and establish reservations for the Plains Indians with adequate arable land so they could become self-sufficient farmers.

TERMS OF THE TREATY

The peace commission, headed by Commissioner of Indian Affairs Nathaniel Taylor, worked its way west, meeting various tribes of Sioux and listening to their demands. In April, 1868, the commission convened at Fort Laramie with a draft treaty that met many of these demands. Article 2 established the Great Sioux Reservation, which gave to the Sioux all of present-day South Dakota west of the Missouri River, including the sacred Black Hills, "for the absolute and undisturbed use and occupancy of the Sioux." Article 16 established the Powder River Country to the north and west of the Great Sioux Reservation as "unceded Indian territory," where whites were not permitted to go unless given permission by the Sioux. Article 11 gave the Sioux hunting rights along the Republican River and above the Platte River in Nebraska and Wyoming for "so long as the buffalo may range thereon in such numbers as to justify the chase." Other articles promised that all Sioux who resided within the Great Sioux Reservation would be provided with food for the next four years (until they learned to become farmers). The reservation was promised schools, mills, blacksmiths, doctors, and teachers and an agent to administer the various programs and maintain order. Additionally, no chief could unilaterally sign away treaty rights, as any sale of land had to be approved by three-fourths of all adult Sioux males.

In return, the United States asked for peace and asked that the Sioux make their permanent residence within the boundaries of the reservation. The Sioux relinquished the right to occupy any lands outside the reservation permanently, including the unceded territory. The Sioux were not to oppose the building of railroads on the plains and were not to attack settlers and their wagon trains or take white prisoners. Additionally, provisions would be distributed by the government not at the western end of the reservation, near traditional hunting grounds and where the Sioux customarily traded with whites, but at agencies established along the Missouri River in the eastern part of the reservation, in order to reorient Sioux life to these agencies.

FAILURE OF THE TREATY

Red Cloud was the final Sioux chief to sign the treaty, on November 5, 1868, only after the government abandoned its forts along the Bozeman Trail in Sioux territory. The treaty was rejected, however, by the influential and powerful Sioux chiefs Crazy Horse and Sitting Bull, who remained in the unceded territory and refused to live on the reservation.

In the end, this treaty proved no more effective in maintaining the peace and Sioux way of life than previous ones had been. Violations of Sioux territory by white emigrants and the army, the discovery of gold in the Black Hills (and the taking of the Black Hills by the government in 1877 without compensation), problems administering the reservation, and the refusal of Crazy Horse and Sitting Bull to live on the reservation despite government threats of war undermined any hope that the treaty's terms would be honored and observed. By 1880 the Sioux had been either killed or defeated and were confined to the reservation.

Laurence Miller

SOURCES FOR FURTHER STUDY
Allen, Charles W., and Richard E. Jensen, eds. *From Fort Laramie to Wounded Knee: In the West That Was.* Lincoln: University of Nebraska Press, 1997.
Hedren, Paul L. *Fort Laramie and the Great Sioux War.* Norman: University of Oklahoma Press, 1998.
_____. *Fort Laramie in 1876: Chronicle of a Frontier Post at War.* Lincoln: University of Nebraska Press, 1988.

SEE ALSO: Fort Laramie Treaty of 1851 (1851); Fort Atkinson Treaty (1853); Medicine Lodge Creek Treaty (1867); Indian Appropriation Act (1871).

FIFTEENTH AMENDMENT

DATE: Probably ratified February 3, 1870; certified March 30, 1870
U.S. STATUTES AT LARGE: 15 Stat. 346
CATEGORIES: African Americans; Civil Rights and Liberties; Constitutional Law; Voting and Elections

The Fifteenth Amendment to the U.S. Constitution, adopted in 1869 and ratified in 1870, stated that the right to vote could not be denied to any citizen "on account of race, color, or previous condition of servitude."

The purpose of the Fifteenth Amendment was to extend the franchise to the African American men who had been freed from slavery as a result of the Civil War. At the time, women were not regarded as citizens and were therefore not covered by the measure. The amendment marked a continuation of the program of the Republican Party to provide political rights for black men after the defeat of the Confederacy. The Thirteenth Amendment had ended slavery, and the Fourteenth Amendment had provided civil rights to all citizens born or naturalized in the United States. These amendments, however, had not ensured that black men could vote throughout the United States. To accomplish that end, the Republicans in Congress, in a lame-duck Congress that met in early 1869, decided that ensuring the right to vote would both carry on the moral impetus of Reconstruction (1863-1877) and act to offset any political comeback of the antiblack Democratic Party.

NEED FOR AN AMENDMENT

A constitutional amendment would have the additional benefit, as the Republicans saw it, of providing a clear legal basis for enforcement of voting rights in the South. In its language, the amendment did not ensure that blacks could hold public positions nor did it rule out such barriers to voting as literacy tests or property requirements. Nonetheless, it represented a clear forward step for African Americans and offered the promise of greater participation in elections and the operations of government.

The ratification process broke down along the existing party alignments of the Reconstruction era. Republicans favored the measure and Democrats resisted it in the state legislatures that addressed ratification. It required vigorous campaigning, especially in such key states as Ohio, to achieve approval from the requisite number of states by March, 1870.

WEAK ENFORCEMENT

The Fifteenth Amendment did not prevent southerners from excluding African Americans from the political process at the end of the nineteenth century. With a political stalemate between Republicans and Democrats in Washington, enforcement of the amendment proved difficult. Federal courts did not encourage a broad interpretation of the amendment. In 1889-1890, the Republicans endeavored to strengthen federal legislation to ensure fair elections in the South, but Democrats defeated their efforts. When the Democrats regained control of the White House and both branches of Congress in 1893-1895, they repealed the existing legislation that gave the government authority over elections. As a result, discriminatory practices kept African Americans from voting in many parts of the South for three-quarters of a century.

In the middle of the twentieth century with the rise of the Civil Rights movement, efforts resumed to revive the Fifteenth Amendment. The Voting Rights Act of 1965 enabled blacks to enter the political process in large numbers and, in so doing, to redeem the unfulfilled promise that the framers of the Fifteenth Amendment had originally envisioned.

Lewis L. Gould

SOURCES FOR FURTHER STUDY

Ball, Howard, Dale Krane, and Thomas P. Lauth. *Compromised Compliance: Implementation of the 1965 Voting Rights Act.* Westport, Conn.: Greenwood Press, 1982.

Braeman, John. *Before the Civil Rights Revolution: The Old Court and Individual Rights.* New York: Greenwood Press, 1988.

Dawson, Michael. *Behind the Mule: Race and Class in American Politics.* Princeton, N.J.: Princeton University Press, 1994.

Greenberg, Jack. *Race Relations and American Law.* New York: Columbia University Press, 1959.

Kousser, J. Morgan. *The Shaping of Southern Politics: Suffrage Restriction and the Establishment of the One-Party South, 1880-1910.* New Haven, Conn.: Yale University Press, 1974.

_____. *Colorblind Injustice: Minority Voting Rights and the Undoing of the Second Reconstruction.* Chapel Hill: University of North Carolina Press, 1998.

Lowenstein, Daniel Hays. *Election Law.* Durham, N.C.: Carolina Academic Press, 1995.

Richards, David A. J. *Conscience and the Constitution: History, Theory, and Law of the Reconstruction Amendments.* Princeton, N.J.: Princeton University Press, 1993.

Schwartz, Bernard, and Stephen Lesher. *Inside the Warren Court.* Garden City, N.Y.: Doubleday, 1983.

Thernstrom, Abigail M. *Whose Votes Count? Affirmative Action and Minority Voting Rights.* Cambridge, Mass.: Harvard University Press, 1987.

Vile, John R. *Encyclopedia of Constitutional Amendments, Proposed Amendments, and Amending Issues, 1789-1995.* Santa Barbara, Calif: ABC-CLIO, 1996.

SEE ALSO: Freedmen's Bureau Act (1865); Thirteenth Amendment (1865); Civil Rights Act of 1866 (1866); Reconstruction Acts (1867); Fourteenth Amendment (1868); Ku Klux Klan Acts (1870-1871); Disfranchisement laws (1890); Civil Rights Act of 1960 (1960); Twenty-fourth Amendment (1964); Voting Rights Act of 1965 (1965); Voting Rights Act of 1975 (1975).

KU KLUX KLAN ACTS

ALSO KNOWN AS: Enforcement Acts; Force Acts
DATE: May 31, 1870; February 28, 1871; April 20, 1871
U.S. STATUTES AT LARGE: 16 Stat. 140; 16 Stat. 433; 17 Stat. 13
CATEGORIES: African Americans; Crimes and Criminal Procedure; Voting and Elections

These laws were an attempt to enforce the Fourteenth and Fifteenth Amendments and to end Ku Klux Klan violence.

Also known as the Enforcement Acts, or Force Acts, these three laws were enacted by the U.S. Congress in response to the terrorist activities of the Ku Klux Klan and other groups committed to white supremacy in the South during the era of Reconstruction, immediately following the Confederate defeat at the end of the Civil War.

The first act, passed in May, 1870, made night riding (the practice of riding on horseback at night and committing various acts of intimidation and harassment) a federal felony and reaffirmed the rights of African Americans provided for in the Fourteenth and Fifteenth Amendments. Congress passed a second act in February, 1871, which provided for election supervisors to ensure against fraud and racial discrimination. Two months later, Congress approved a third statute aimed specifically at the activities of the Ku Klux Klan. This law made it a federal offense to violate anyone's voting rights. In addition, it allowed the president to proclaim areas in which state governments failed to curb domestic violence to be in "rebellion" and authorized the use of military force and the suspension of the writ of habeas corpus to end rebellions. In October, 1871, President Ulysses S. Grant used the law to declare nine counties in South Carolina to be in rebellion. These laws proved effective in suppressing white supremacy organizations.

Thomas Clarkin

SOURCES FOR FURTHER STUDY

Trelease, Allen W. *White Terror: The Ku Klux Klan Conspiracy and Southern Reconstruction.* Westport, Conn.: Greenwood Press, 1979.

West, Jerry Lee. *The Reconstruction Ku Klux Klan in York County, South Carolina, 1865-1877.* New York: McFarland, 2002.

Williams, Lou Falkner. *The Great South Carolina Ku Klux Klan Trials, 1871-1872.* Athens: University of Georgia Press, 1996.

SEE ALSO: Freedmen's Bureau Act (1865); Thirteenth Amendment (1865); Civil Rights Act of 1866 (1866); Reconstruction Acts (1867); Fourteenth Amendment (1868); Fifteenth Amendment (1870); Disfranchisement laws (1890); Civil Rights Act of 1960 (1960); Twenty-fourth Amendment (1964); Voting Rights Act of 1965 (1965); Voting Rights Act of 1975 (1975).

INDIAN APPROPRIATION ACT

DATE: March 3, 1871
U.S. STATUTES AT LARGE: 16 Stat. 544
CATEGORIES: Native Americans; Treaties and Agreements

Congress unilaterally determined that Native Americans no longer belonged to their own sovereign nations, thereby ending treaty-making between U.S. and tribal governments.

In 1871, Congress voted to end treaty making with Native American peoples. Since the origins of the republic, the U.S. government had dealt with tribes by recognizing each one as an independent nation living within the United States. Hence, ambassadors were sent out from Washington, D.C., to negotiate treaties, and each agreement had to be ratified by two-thirds of the Senate, as provided in the Constitution. Chief Justice John Marshall, in *Worcester v. Georgia* (1832), had determined that this process had to be followed because each tribe was self-governing and sovereign in its own territory.

The change took place because many people in the United States came to believe that the Native American nations no longer acted like sovereign states. They were too weak, post-Civil War whites believed, and many had become dependent on the federal government for their existence. Members of Congress expressed that view in a series of discussions on American Indian policy in 1870-1871. In the House of Representatives, the feeling also grew that the House was being ignored in the development of Indian policy. The only way the House could influence Native American relations would be by renouncing the treaty concept. The attack on treaty making gained strength during the debate over the money to be appropriated for the United States Board of Indian Commissioners. This agency had been created in 1869 to oversee money authorized to be spent on Indian programs.

POLICY CHANGES

The commissioners' first report suggested major changes in Indian policy. It called for ending the treaty system and dealing with "uncivilized" native peoples as "wards of the government." Board chair Felix R. Brunot echoed the views of many U.S. citizens when he declared that it was absurd to treat "a few thousand savages" as if they were equal with the people and government of the United States. President Ulysses S. Grant supported that view, as did his commissioner of Indian affairs, Ely S. Parker, a member of the Seneca nation. Parker believed that it was a cruel farce to deal with the tribes as equals; in his view, most were "helpless and ignorant wards" of the federal government.

The resentment of members of the House of Representatives at their exclusion from Indian policy making became apparent during debates over treaties negotiated in 1868 and 1869. A May, 1868, agreement with the Osage Nation in Kansas had ceded eight million acres of land to the government. The land then would be sold to a railroad company for twenty cents per acre. The House voted unanimously to recommend that the Senate not ratify the treaty because the land transfer had taken place outside the traditional methods of selling public property. The Senate responded to the House plea by rejecting the treaty. Later, however, the land was sold to the railroad company with the approval of the House.

The House took up the issue of treaty making again in 1869 during a debate over the Indian appropriation for 1870. It provided money for food, clothes, and education for tribe members living on reservations. The House refused to accept an increase in funds voted by the Senate. Representatives also began to question whether native peoples were capable of signing official treaties with the United States. Most members attacked the traditional system, although three congressmen spoke in favor of the treaty process. Representative William Windom of Minnesota argued that changing the process would be a breach of faith with the tribes. Revoking the process would create great confusion among Native Americans and add to their distrust of the U.S. government.

Representative John J. Logan, Republican of Illinois, responded for the majority, however, by declaring that "the idea of this Government making treaties with bands of wild and roving Indians is simply preposterous and ridiculous." Amid loud cheers and laughter, Logan attacked the character of native peoples and suggested that they were an inferior race that should not be treated as equal in status to the people of the United States. The House refused to approve the appropriation, and the Senate refused to compromise; therefore, no Indian appropriation bill passed Congress in 1869.

In the debate over the 1871 appropriation, both sides raised the same arguments. In the Senate, supporters of the treaty system argued that any change would severely injure any goodwill native peoples still held toward the U.S. government system. Senator Richard Yates reiterated the antitreaty sentiment, declaring that the tribes were not civilized and that making treaties with them had been a mistake. The Senate, however, passed an appropriation bill and sent it to the House. While the debate took place, many tribes were waiting for the money due to them under treaties negotiated in 1868 and 1869. Unless Congress agreed to an appropriation bill, they would receive nothing. In a compromise arranged between the two legislative branches, a sum of two million dollars was appropriated to pay off prior obligations. Debate over the appropriation for the next year bogged down in the House, however.

AGITATION AGAINST TREATIES

The Board of Indian Commissioners helped the House position by calling for an end to treaty making and for abrogating all existing agreements. Only Representative Eugene M. Wilson of Minnesota spoke in favor of continuing the historic policy. If Native Americans were not protected by treaties, they would be cheated out of their lands by white speculators and end up with nothing, he argued. Debate in the Senate and the House seemed far more concerned with constitutional technicalities than with the welfare of native peoples. Once more, no bill seemed possible. On the last day of the session, President Grant urged a compromise, or, he warned, a war with the tribes was sure to break out. Under this threat, Congress agreed to put aside its differences temporarily and passed a bill.

When the new Congress opened on January 4, 1871, Representative Henry Dawes of Massachusetts led the call for change. Dawes, who in 1887 would author a major bill in the Senate drastically changing policy toward native peoples, called for a quick program of assimilation in this earlier debate. If natives were to become Americanized—a policy he supported—they should be treated as individuals rather than as members of foreign nations. Native peoples were not and never had been equal to the United States. The House passed a bill denouncing "so-called treaties."

In the Senate, an amendment to delete the words "so-called" before "treaties" led to a vigorous debate. Senator William Stewart of Nevada objected to the amendment: "The whole Indian policy of feeding drunken, worthless, vagabond Indians, giving them money to squander . . . has been a growing disgrace to our country for years." Treaties with "irresponsible tribes" were no treaties at all. Only a few senators agreed with this amendment, however, and "so-called" was eliminated. This angered the House, which refused to accept the Senate version.

Many congressmen and senators were tired of the endless debate and seemed willing to compromise. A conference committee of senators and representatives agreed that past treaties would be accepted or the integrity of the United States would be compromised. It agreed that no more treaties should be negotiated with Native Americans, however. Most conferees agreed that the tribes remaining hardly seemed like legitimate nations, as they were too small, weak, and miserable. The final compromise asserted the validity of prior agreements but provided that in the future, "no Indian nation or tribe within the territory of the United States shall be acknowledged or recognized as an independent nation, tribe, or power with whom the United States may contract by treaty." Both the Senate and the House accepted the compromise, and President Grant signed it into law on March 3, 1871. Treaties would no longer be negotiated with Native American peoples. Native Americans would, instead, become "wards of the state."

Leslie V. Tischauser

SOURCES FOR FURTHER STUDY
Cohen, Fay G. *Treaties on Trial: The Continuing Controversy Over Northwest Indian Fishing Rights.* Seattle: University of Washington Press, 1986.
Heizer, Robert F. "Treaties." In *California.* Vol. 8 in *Handbook of North American Indians.* Washington, D.C.: Smithsonian Institution Press, 1978.
Jones, Dorothy V. *License for Empire: Colonialism by Treaty in Early America.* Chicago: University of Chicago Press, 1982.
Kvasnicka, Robert M. "United States Indian Treaties and Agreements." In *History of Indian-White Relations,* edited by Wilcomb E. Washburn. Vol. 4 in *Handbook of North American Indians.* Washington, D.C.: Smithsonian Institution Press, 1988.
Prucha, Francis Paul. *American Indian Treaties: The History of a Political Anomaly.* Berkeley: University of California Press, 1994.

SEE ALSO: Fort Laramie Treaty of 1868 (1868); General Allotment Act (1887); Burke Act (1906); Indian Citizenship Act (1924); Indian Reorganization Act (1934); Termination Resolution (1953).

TREATY OF WASHINGTON

DATE: Signed May 8, 1871
CATEGORIES: Foreign Relations; Treaties and Agreements

This U.S.-British settlement of differences became a milestone in international conciliation.

On February 27, 1871, official Washington shrugged off late-winter dreariness to celebrate the beginning of a momentous gathering of American and British dignitaries. The social festivities that took place did much to dissipate the feelings of bitterness and suspicion that had dominated Anglo-American relations since the Civil War years. The Washington Conference had been called to deal with the *Alabama* claims, the major legacy of Union-British conflict over neutral rights and duties during the Civil War. Proceedings began on a surprisingly cordial note, and within three months the two delegations had reached solutions or provided for later agreement on almost all matters at issue.

ALABAMA CLAIMS

Neither side would have believed when the negotiations were first arranged that such an explosive issue as the *Alabama* claims could be resolved with so little difficulty. In the years immediately following the Civil War, Anglo-American relations were dangerously tense. The principal cause was the lasting bitterness of Americans toward what they regarded as Great Britain's shamefully unneutral support of the Confederacy. The British government had on several occasions come perilously close to recognizing Confederate independence, an act tantamount to intervention on the South's behalf. Though that step was not taken, British sympathy for the Confederacy was manifested by toleration of repeated evasions of the Foreign Enlistment Act of 1819, especially that section which prohibited construction in British yards of warships for belligerent powers. The Confederacy hoped to break the blockade and drive Union commerce from the seas by building a navy in Great Britain. The gamble almost succeeded. Confederate warships produced by British shipbuilders sank or seized about 250 Union merchant ships. Three fast commerce destroyers, the *Florida*, the *Shenandoah*, and the notorious *Alabama*, accounted for almost one-fourth of the sinkings. The case of the *Alabama* was so blatant a violation of Great Britain's neutrality that just before her scheduled launching in July, 1862, proceedings were begun to detain the ship. However, the *Alabama* escaped to begin an amazing (and, to the British government, a most embarrassing) career. Although the British soon closed the loopholes in their neutrality laws, the United States government considered that the damage had been done and that Great Britain must be made to pay for its callous disregard of neutral obligations.

311

During the remainder of the war, Union claims for indemnity arising from depredations committed by the *Alabama* and her sister ships mounted steadily, but the ministry of Lord Palmerston refused to accept responsibility for the Confederate cruisers' activities. American determination to gain satisfaction culminated in the suggestion in 1869 by Senator Charles Sumner, chairman of the Senate Foreign Relations Committee, that Great Britain be made to pay for the damages caused by the Confederate cruisers (estimated at $15 million), the cost of catching them, destruction to the United States merchant marine ($110 million), and (since action by the cruisers had prolonged the war by two full years) an additional $2 billion to cover the cost of war for that period. Sumner's aim was not to bankrupt the British treasury but to force Great Britain to satisfy American demands by the cession of Canada to the United States. London dismissed Sumner's arguments as utter insanity but was forced to note that both President Ulysses S. Grant and his new secretary of state, Hamilton Fish, supported the proposal.

NEGOTIATIONS AND TREATY PROVISIONS

Great Britain decided to negotiate. Fish then adopted a more moderate position, asking for payment of existing claims by Great Britain and an expression of regret. Informal conversations were begun between Fish and Sir John Rose, a British-Canadian statesman and businessman residing in England, whom the British Foreign Office had chosen to convey its interest in pacific settlements of the various disputes. It was soon agreed that a joint commission should be convened to deal with all unresolved issues: the *Alabama* claims, a long-standing conflict over American fishing rights off the Canadian coast, the matter of ownership of the San Juan Islands in Puget Sound, and other minor problems.

Arbitration of the *Alabama* claims took place in Geneva, Switzerland, in December, 1871. The discussions nearly collapsed at the outset, for Charles Francis Adams, the United States commissioner, carrying out express instructions from Secretary of State Fish, revived the question (which the British had thought dead and buried) of indirect damages. Fish's motivation was not money, not Canada, but domestic politics. He desired that the tribunal deal with and reject the matter of indirect damages; otherwise, Congress might throw out the treaty. Although the British representative, Sir Alexander Cockburn, lord chief justice of England, was enraged by this tactic, the tribunal exceeded its jurisdiction and ruled out the indirect claims. This act allowed for adjudication of the direct claims. The court found in favor of the United States and awarded damages of $15.5 million.

The commission, comprising five American and five British representatives, met in Washington from February 27 to May 8, 1871. Buoyed by foxhunting weekends, liberal ministrations of fine liquor, and superb food, the commissioners agreed without serious difficulty on a fair settlement. Most important was the treaty provision regarding the *Alabama* claims. Great Britain offered regrets for the escape of the *Alabama* and other warships and agreed to submit the claims to binding arbitration. Furthermore, it accepted a definition of rules to govern neutral obligations toward belligerents. Although these regulations were not retroactive, the British were conceding victory to the American position in the forthcoming arbitration proceedings. This Anglo-American agreement was a historic one for the future of neutrality. The treaty also provided for a temporary resolution of the quarrel over fishing privileges, an agreement to submit the question of the San Juan Islands to arbitration, and numerous other economic and territorial agreements. The Washington Treaty was a remarkable accomplishment and had been termed by some as the greatest example of international conciliation ever known. It certainly represented a significant diplomatic victory for the United States.

Theodore A. Wilson

SOURCES FOR FURTHER STUDY

Allen, Harry C. *Great Britain and the United States: A History of Anglo-American Relations, 1783-1952.* New York: St. Martin's Press, 1955.

Boykin, Edward C. *Ghost Ship of the Confederacy: The Story of the Alabama.* New York: Funk and Wagnalls, 1957.

Cushing, Caleb. *The Treaty of Washington: Its Negotiation, Execution, and the Discussions Relating Thereto.* New York: Harper & Brothers, 1873.

Duberman, Martin B. *Charles Francis Adams, 1807-1886.* Boston: Houghton Mifflin, 1961.

Nevins, Allan. *Hamilton Fish: The Inner History of the Grant Administration.* 2 vols. New York: Dodd, Mead, 1936.

Smith, Goldwin A. *The Treaty of Washington, 1871: A Study in Imperial History.* Ithaca, N.Y.: Cornell University Press, 1941.

Winks, Robin W. *Canada and the United States: The Civil War Years.* Baltimore: The Johns Hopkins University Press, 1960.

SEE ALSO: Treaty of Paris (1783); Jay's Treaty (1794); Treaty of Ghent (1814); Rush-Bagot Agreement (1817); Convention of 1818 (1818); Webster-Ashburton Treaty (1842); Oregon Act (1848).

GENERAL MINING ACT

ALSO KNOWN AS: Mining Act
DATE: May 10, 1872
U.S. STATUTES AT LARGE: 17 Stat. 91
U.S. CODE: 30 § 22
CATEGORIES: Land Management; Natural Resources

The General Mining Law of 1872 fought post-Civil War economic depression and unemployment by opening the vast federal lands in the West for development. Amended many times over the years, this law still governs the exploitation of "hard-rock" minerals in the United States.

In its original form, the General Mining Law covered all mineral resources on more than one billion acres of federal land. It now covers only "hard-rock" minerals, those associated with igneous and metamorphic rocks. By the Mineral Leasing Act of 1920, the fossil fuels and some minerals were "withdrawn" from coverage under the law. The Common Varieties Mineral Act of 1955 withdrew sand, gravel, stone, and other common rocks and minerals. In 1976 the last of the national parks and monuments were withdrawn from coverage, thus protecting them from mining. As a result of these withdrawals, the total acreage now covered under the law is approximately four hundred million.

PROVISIONS OF THE 1872 LAW
The General Mining Law permits U.S. citizens to lay claim to federal land. In exchange, the claimant has only to pay a $100 fee and make minimal annual improvements ("assessments") to the land or pay a $100 annual assessment fee. Actual mining need not be done. Claimants possess the right to any mineral deposits below ground; they also possess the right to the exclusive use of the land surface. Claims can be of two types: placer or lode. Placer claims are for 20-acre sites, whereas lode claims, those designed to exploit localized veins of ore, are for tracts measuring 1500 by 600 feet. For a fee of $2.50 per acre (placer claim) or $5.00 per acre (lode claim), a claim can be "patented," or converted to private ownership.

PROS AND CONS
Opponents of the law find fault with it in three areas. First, the federal treasury receives no income from minerals taken from lands that belong to the public. Second, the law makes no provision for environmental concerns—concerns which did not exist in 1872. Third, abuses of the law abound, including the resale of claims for thousands of times the original purchase price.

Proponents of the law, primarily the major mining companies, argue that while royalties are not paid, mining provides thousands of jobs and significant tax revenue. The mining industry must compete in a global market against nations that exploit cheap labor and are government-subsidized. Whereas the original mining law took no cognizance of environmental concerns, any mining on federal lands is now covered by the same environmental legislation that governs all mining.

Proposed modifications to the law revolve around three key issues: royalty payments, patenting, and environmental concerns. Suggested levels of royalty payment range from 2 percent on the net value (after taxes and cost) to 8 percent on the gross value of the minerals produced. Either patenting would be eliminated or claimants would be allowed to purchase the mining patents for the fair market value of the land surface. Environmental concerns would be addressed by requiring restoration of the land and by using royalty payments to establish a fund for the cleanup of abandoned mine properties.

Donald J. Thompson

SOURCES FOR FURTHER STUDY
Barringer, Daniel Moreau. *The Law of Mines and Mining in the United States.* Reprint. Holmes Beach, Fla.: Gaunt, 2000.
Dobra, John L. *Congressional Testimony on the U.S. Mining Act of 1872.* Reno: Nevada Policy Research Institute, 1993.
Gelb, Bernard A. *Hardrock Mining, the 1872 Law, and the U.S. Economy.* Washington, D.C.: Congressional Research Service, 1994.
Gordon, Richard L. *Two Cheers for the 1872 Mining Law.* Policy Analysis 300. Washington, D.C.: Cato Institute, 1998.
Humphries, Marc. *The 1872 Mining Law: Time for Reform?* Washington, D.C.: Congressional Research Service, Library of Congress, 1998.
Maley, Terry S. *Mining Law.* 5th ed. Boise, Idaho: Mineral Land Publications, 1992.

SEE ALSO: Mineral Leasing Act (1920); Mining and Minerals Policy Act (1970); Surface Mining Control and Reclamation Act (1977).

COINAGE ACT

ALSO KNOWN AS: Crime of 1873
DATE: February 12, 1873
U.S. STATUTES AT LARGE: 17 Stat. 424
CATEGORIES: Banking, Money, and Finance

Proponents of free silver charged that this law, which made gold the sole monetary standard, represented a "gold conspiracy."

The Coinage Act of 1873 was known by its opponents as the Crime of 1873. The emotion-laden nickname was first used in 1876 by proponents of the free coinage of silver to express hostility toward the Coinage Act, passed on February 12, 1873, which made gold the sole monetary standard, with no provision for the coining of silver dollars. The money controversy, which the shibboleth "Crime of 1873" dramatized, raged between 1865 and 1896 and can best be understood in the context of the nation's antebellum and Civil War monetary policies.

BIMETALLISM

Until the Civil War, the United States functioned under bimetallism—a monetary system based on silver and gold, supplemented by the notes of its banks. The use of the two kinds of specie as money was deemed desirable because there were insufficient quantities of precious metals for the requirements of trade, commerce, and exchange. Under bimetallism, both silver and gold were acceptable for the payment of debts at a rate fixed by the government. The Currency Act of 1834 established a legal ratio between the two metals of sixteen ounces of silver to one ounce of gold (16:1). Under this "mint ratio," the Treasury was obligated to purchase either metal at the established price.

Bimetallism presented a problem in that the value of silver and gold fluctuated on the world market in response to changes in supply. New supplies of gold from Russia, Australia, and California during the 1840's, for example, caused gold gradually to decline in value. Therefore, silver was undervalued if priced at the mint ratio of 16:1. As predicted by Gresham's law—that higher-valued money is driven out of circulation by cheaper money—silver coins disappeared from circulation, because silver producers preferred to sell their bullion on the world market, where the price was higher than at the mint. By 1853, the market ratio of silver to gold was 15.4:1. In other words, silver producers needed sixteen ounces of silver to exchange for an ounce of gold at the mint, but only 15.4 ounces on the bullion market. Having been out of circulation for years, silver was reduced by Congress in 1853 to a subsidiary metal. Silver remained scarce and undervalued as coin until the 1870's.

PAPER CURRENCY

Under great pressure to raise money during the Civil War, the government abandoned the specie standard and passed the Legal Tender Acts of 1862, which authorized the printing of fiat money (greenbacks), unsupported by specie but legally acceptable (legal tender) for all debts except interest on government bonds and excise taxes. During the war, the Treasury circulated more than $450 million in greenbacks, which inflated precipitously by 1864. The use of gold became limited primarily to international trade.

When the war ended, the Treasury began urging a program of deflation leading to the eventual retirement of the greenbacks and a return to a specie standard. Resistance in Congress to this hard-money scheme came from a group of soft-money advocates, who opposed a return to specie but differed among themselves over the issue of inflation. Consequently, the Treasury received authority to retire only small quantities of greenbacks. Some soft-money advocates who favored inflation demanded the printing of more greenbacks to be used for payment of the national debt, a proposal that was written into the Democratic Party platform of 1868. By this time, the money controversy had caused factions to grow in the business community (among farmers, bankers, and manufacturers), in geographical regions, and to some extent in political parties, with soft-money supporters generally showing greater strength in the states west of the Appalachians. However, the Greenbackers suffered serious reverses with the passage of the Public Credit Act of 1869, which pledged payment of the national debt in gold, and the Resumption Act of 1875, which ordered the redemption of greenbacks with gold by 1879.

PASSAGE OF THE ACT
In the midst of the greenback controversy, John Jay Knox, comptroller of the currency, aided by special assistant Henry Richard Linderman, former director of the mint at Philadelphia, began preparing a revision of the laws dealing with the mints and coinage. One aspect of their work appeared in the Coinage Act of 1873, which discontinued the coinage of silver dollars. The following year, the *Revised Statutes of the United States* demonetized silver by limiting its legal tender function to debts not more than five dollars. Both laws gave belated recognition to the fact that silver had not circulated since the 1840's. At the time, the legislation disturbed no one, not even the silver miners who preferred to sell on the open market. Indeed, Senator William M. Stewart of the silver state of Nevada, who later used the slogan "Crime of '73," failed to oppose either law.

"CRIME OF '73"?
Even as the legislation was passed, however, new mines were opening in the Western states, augmenting the world supply of silver. The market ratio, 15.9:1 in 1873, climbed to 16.1:1 in 1874, and to

16.6:1 by 1875, or about ninety-six cents in gold. As silver prices dropped, mining interests discovered to their dismay that the Currency Act of 1873 blocked the profitable sale of silver to the mint at 16:1. On March 2, 1876, George M. Weston, secretary of the United States Monetary Commission, charged in a letter to the Boston *Globe* that the demonetization of silver was a conspiracy by the creditor class against the people. Weston's letter, which used the word "crime" for the first time, began the controversy over silver. Other advocates of silver took up the charge, demanding the free coinage of silver. Later, Greenbackers and other inflationists, fighting losing battles against resumption, also began supporting silver.

Agitation for the free coinage of silver continued until 1896, when new gold supplies began inducing the price increases that post-Civil War inflationists had desired. Congress, however, previously had passed legislation permitting limited silver coinage. The Bland-Allison Act of 1878 required the Treasury to buy between two and four million ounces of silver per month at the prevailing market price. According to the Sherman Silver Purchase Act of 1890, four million ounces had to be purchased each month. This legislation demonstrated that those who favored silver had far greater strength than the Greenbackers had a decade earlier.

The conspiracy charge against the Currency Act of 1873, which alleged that British financiers plotted to influence Congress, was rejected by most nineteenth century economists and writers. The issue was raised again in 1960 with the discovery of new evidence that seemed to indicate that Linderman foresaw an increase in silver output and, as a monometallist, allegedly plotted to omit silver coinage from the 1873 legislation. Nevertheless, most modern scholarship continues to reject the conspiracy thesis.

Merl E. Reed, updated by
Charles H. O'Brien

SOURCES FOR FURTHER STUDY

Barrett, Don Carlos. *The Greenbacks and Resumption of Specie Payments, 1862-1879.* Cambridge, Mass.: Harvard University Press, 1931.

Friedman, Milton, and Anna J. Schwartz. *A Monetary History of the United States, 1867-1960.* Princeton, N.J.: Princeton University Press, 1963.

Hixson, William F. *Triumph of the Bankers: Money and Banking in the Eighteenth and Nineteenth Centuries.* Westport, Conn.: Praeger, 1993.

Laughlin, J. Laurence. *The History of Bimetallism in the United States.* 4th ed. New York: Greenwood Press, 1968.

Studenski, Paul. *Financial History of the United States.* New York: McGraw-Hill, 1952.

Timberlake, Richard H. *Monetary Policy in the United States: An Intellectual and Institutional History.* Chicago: University of Chicago Press, 1993.

Unger, Irwin. *The Greenback Era: A Social and Political History of American Finance, 1865-1879.* Princeton, N.J.: Princeton University Press, 1964.

Weinstein, Allen. *Prelude to Populism: Origins of the Silver Issue, 1867-1878.* New Haven, Conn.: Yale University Press, 1970.

SEE ALSO: Independent Treasury Act (1846); National Bank Acts (1863-1864); Bland-Allison Act (1878); Currency Act (1900); Federal Reserve Act (1913).

COMSTOCK ACT

DATE: March 3, 1873
U.S. STATUTES AT LARGE: 17 Stat. 598
CATEGORIES: Communications and Media; Food and Drugs; Health and Welfare; Speech and Expression

The most restrictive antiobscenity statute ever passed by the U.S. Congress, this law expanded existing federal obscenity statues and effectively outlawed the advertisement and transportation of birth control and drugs that induced abortion.

In 1865, Congress passed the Postal Act, making it a crime to use the mails for sending any "publication of a vulgar or indecent character." Anthony Comstock, a tireless crusader against pornography, successfully lobbied Congress to make the postal regulations more restrictive. The resulting 1873 legislation created special agents with wide discretion to seize obscene matter and provided for criminal penalties of up to five years' imprisonment for the first offense. Books and magazines, including serious novels such as Theodore Dreiser's *Sister Carrie* (1900), were proscribed if they contained any references considered "lewd" or "lascivious" by Victorian standards.

By the 1930's, the Comstock Act had been amended to become less restrictive, but much of its language, while reinterpreted, continued into the 1990's. The Supreme Court affirmed the constitutionality of the law's principles in numerous cases after 1877, but beginning with the landmark case *Roth v. United States* (1957), the Court liberalized the law by insisting on a narrow definition of obscenity.

Thomas T. Lewis

Sources for Further Study

Bates, Anna Louise. *Weeder in the Garden of the Lord: Anthony Comstock's Life and Career.* Lanham, Md.: University Press of America, 1995.

Beisel, Nicola Kay. *Imperiled Innocents: Anthony Comstock and Family Reproduction in Victorian America.* Princeton, N.J.: Princeton University Press, 1997.

Bennett, Belinda. *Legal Narratives: From Comstockery to the Food and Drug Administration.* Madison: University of Wisconsin Institute for Legal Studies, 1989.

Boyer, Paul S. *Purity in Print: The Vice-Society Movement and Book Censorship in America.* New York: Scribner, 1968.

Broun, Heywood. *Anthony Comstock, Roundman of the Lord.* New York: A & C Boni, 1927.

SEE ALSO: First Amendment (1789); Racketeer Influenced and Corrupt Organizations Act (1970).

PAGE LAW

DATE: March 3, 1875
U.S. STATUTES AT LARGE: 18 Stat. 477
CATEGORIES: Asia or Asian Americans; Immigration; Women's Issues

The Page Law, designed to prohibit Chinese contract workers and prostitutes from entering the United States, eventually excluded Asian women in general.

On February 10, 1875, California congressman Horace F. Page introduced federal legislation designed to prohibit the immigration of Asian female prostitutes into the United States. Officially titled "An Act Supplementary to the Acts in Relation to Immigration," the Page Law evolved into a restriction against vast numbers of Chinese immigrants into the country regardless of whether they were prostitutes. Any person convicted of importing Chinese prostitutes was subject to a maximum prison term of five years and a fine of not more than five thousand dollars. An amendment to the law prohibited individuals from engaging in the "coolie trade," or the importation of Chinese contract laborers. Punishment for this type of violation, however, was much less severe and was much more difficult to effect, given the large numbers of Asian male immigrants at the time. As a consequence of this division of penalties, the law was applied in a most gender-specific manner, effectively deterring the immigration of Asian women into the United States. Within seven years following the implementation of the law, the average number of Chinese female immigrants dropped to one-third of its previous level.

ENFORCEMENT AND IMPLEMENTATION

An elaborate bureaucratic network established to carry out the Page Law's gender-specific exclusions was a catalyst for the decline in Chinese immigration rates. American consulate officials supported by American, Chinese, and British commercial, political, and medical services made up the law's implementation structure. Through intelligence gathering, interrogation, and physical examinations of applicants, the consulate hierarchy ferreted out undesirable applicants for emigration and those suspected of engaging in illegal human trafficking.

This investigative activity evolved well beyond the original intent of the law's authors. Any characteristic or activity that could be linked, even in the most remote sense, to prostitution became grounds for denial to emigrate. Most applications to emigrate came from women from the lower economic strata of society; low economic status therefore became a reason for immigration exclusion. The procedure was a complicated one. Many roadblocks were placed in the way of prospective immigrants. Acquiring permission to emigrate took much time and effort. Passing stringent physical examinations performed by biased health care officials was often impossible. Navigating language barriers through official interviews aimed at evaluating personal character often produced an atmosphere of rigid interrogation, bringing subsequent denial of the right to emigrate. Such a complex system aimed at uncovering fraudulent immigrants placed a hardship upon those wishing to leave China.

Because Hong Kong was the main point of departure for Chinese emigrating to the United States, all required examinations were performed there with a hierarchy of American consulate officials determining immigrant eligibility. In a sense, the Page Law actually expanded consulate authority beyond any previous level.

CORRUPTION CHARGES

Such increased power of the consular general in implementing the law provided an opportunity for possible abuses of power. In 1878, the U.S. consul general in Hong Kong, John Mosby, accused his predecessors of corruption and bribery. According to Mosby, David Bailey and H. Sheldon Loring were guilty of embezzlement. Both men were accused of setting up such an intricate system to process immigration applications that bribery soon became the natural way to obtain the necessary permission to do so. Mosby went on to charge that Bailey had amassed thousands of dollars of extra income by regularly charging additional examination fees regardless of whether an exam was performed. Mosby also accused Bailey of falsifying test results and encouraging medical personnel to interrogate applicants in order to deny immigration permission to otherwise legal immigrants.

Most of the allegations of corruption surrounded the fact that monies allotted by the federal government for implementation of the Page Law were far below the amount Bailey required to run his administration of it. Given this scenario, the U.S. government scrutinized Bailey's conduct. No indictments resulted from the official investigation, however, and Bailey, who had previously been promoted to vice consul general in Shanghai, remained in that position. Further examination of Bailey's tenure in Hong Kong has suggested that, if anything, he was an overly aggressive official who made emigration of Chinese women to the United States a priority issue of his tenure there rather than an opportunity for profit.

Bailey was replaced in Hong Kong by Loring. Unlike his predecessor, Loring did not enforce the Page Law with as much vigor, allowing a slight yet insignificant increase in the annual numbers of Chinese immigrants. Nevertheless, Loring did enforce the law in an efficient manner, publicly suggesting that any ship owner who engaged in the illegal transport of women would be dealt with to the fullest extent of the law. Even so, Loring was accused of sharing Bailey's enthusiasm for the unofficial expensive design of the immigration procedure. During Loring's tenure, questions about his character began to surface mostly on account of his past relationships with individuals who engaged in questionable business practices in Asia. By the time that Mosby replaced him, such questions had become more than a nuisance. The new U.S. consul to Hong Kong began to describe his predecessor as a dishonest taker of bribes. Once again, the official dynamics of such charges brought forth an official inquiry from Washington. Like the previous investigation of Bailey, however, this investigation produced no official indictment against Loring. The only blemish concerned an additional fee that Loring had instituted for the procuring of an official landing certificate. As there was precedent for such a fee, Loring, like his predecessor, was exonerated of all charges.

Having decided that his predecessors were indeed corrupt, yet unable to prove it, Mosby pursued enforcement of the Page Law with relentless occupation. Keeping a posture that was above accusations of corruption, Mosby personally interviewed each applicant for emigration, oversaw the activities between the consulate and the health examiners, and eliminated the additional charges for the landing permits. In the end, the numbers of Chinese immigrants remained similar to those of Loring and below those of Bailey, with the numbers of Chinese female immigrants continuing to decline. Aside from being free from charges of corruption, Mosby's tenure in office was as authoritative as those of his predecessors.

Regardless of the personalities of the consulate officials in charge of implementing the Page Law, the results were the same: The number of Chinese who emigrated to the United States decreased dramatically between the 1875 enactment of the law and the enactment of its successor, the Chinese Exclusion Act of 1882. Furthermore, the law's specific application to Chinese women ensured a large imbalance between numbers of male and female immigrants during the period under consideration. In the long run that imbalance negatively affected Asian American families who had settled in the United States. The barriers that the Page Law helped to erect against female Chinese immigrants made a strong nuclear family structure within the Asian American community an immigrant dream rather than a reality.

Thomas J. Edward Walker and
Cynthia Gwynne Yaudes

SOURCES FOR FURTHER STUDY
Cheng, Lucy, and Edna Bonacich. *Labor Immigration Under Capitalism.* Berkeley: University of California Press, 1984.
Foner, Philip, and Daniel Rosenberg. *Racism, Dissent, and Asian Americans from 1850 to the Present.* Westport, Conn.: Greenwood Press, 1993.
Peffer, George Anthony. "Forbidden Families: Emigration Experience of Chinese Women Under the Page Law, 1875-1882." *Journal of American Ethnic History* 6, Fall, 1986.

SEE ALSO: Treaty of Wang Hiya (1844); Burlingame Treaty (1868); Page Law (1875); Chinese Exclusion Act (1882); Opium Exclusion Act (1909); Alien land laws (1913); Immigration Act of 1921 (1921); Cable Act (1922); Immigration Act of 1924 (1924); Hoover-Stimson Doctrine (1932); Immigration Act of 1943 (1943); War Brides Act (1945).

REMOVAL ACT

ALSO KNOWN AS: Judiciary Act of 1875
DATE: March 3, 1875
U.S. STATUTES AT LARGE: 18 Stat. 470
CATEGORIES: Judiciary and Judicial Procedure

This act granted lower federal courts original and removal jurisdiction over federal question cases. After 1875 all cases arising under the Constitution, federal laws, or treaties could be prosecuted in federal district courts, expanding the power, influence, and decision-making scope of the federal judiciary, including the Supreme Court.

The Removal Act of 1875, also known as the Judiciary Act of 1875, provided federal courts with original and removal jurisdiction. The Judiciary Act of 1789 was Congress's initial exercise of the powers in Article III of the U.S. Constitution. It allowed state courts to retain jurisdiction over federal question cases, those cases arising under the Constitution, federal laws, or treaties. The end of the Civil War brought expansion and growth of federal government power. Three constitutional amendments and various congressional statutes were passed during the Reconstruction period. The primary purpose of these enactments was to secure equal rights for the newly emancipated slaves. Congress viewed the federal courts as necessary to the implementation of Reconstruction legislation and to the expansion of federal court jurisdiction and powers.

The Removal Act awarded federal courts jurisdiction over cases alleging that a state law or an action of a state official violated the Constitution. The Removal Act allowed a federal question suit to be filed in federal district court. Such actions filed in state court could be removed to federal district court for disposition. No subsequent jurisdictional statute enacted by Congress has so significantly enlarged the caseloads and jurisdiction of the federal courts. The Removal Act resulted in federal courts, including the Supreme Court, becoming the primary forum for litigating constitutional rights.

Robert P. Morin

SOURCE FOR FURTHER STUDY
Foster, Roger. *The Federal Judiciary Acts of 1875 and 1887, with an Appendix Containing the Equity Rules.* New York: L. K. Strouse, 1887.

SEE ALSO: Judiciary Act of 1789 (1789); Eleventh Amendment (1798); Judiciary Acts of 1801-1925 (1801).

BLAND-ALLISON ACT

DATE: February 28, 1878
U.S. STATUTES AT LARGE: 20 Stat. 25
CATEGORIES: Banking, Money, and Finance

This act represented an early victory for silver advocates in the gold-silver debate that dominated the 1880's, but it failed to establish silver as a basis for the U.S. currency.

During the latter half of the nineteenth century one of the great political debates focused on whether gold or silver should be the currency of the United States. In 1873 Congress made gold the single currency for the country. The Depression that followed led to turmoil and protests in favor of using silver as a form of currency. The Bland-Allison Act was one battle in that debate.

The act, passed by Congress in 1878, was sponsored by Missouri congressman Richard Bland and Iowa senator William Allison. Under the U.S. Constitution, Congress has the power to determine the proper currency for the country. During the presidential administration of Rutherford B. Hayes, several bills trying to make silver a currency equal with gold were passed by the House but rejected by the Senate.

Bland sought broad power for the Treasury to make silver a currency equal to gold. His bill passed the House in 1878. The Senate, led by Allison, watered down the original bill. The new piece of legislation required the Treasury Department to buy between two and four million dollars of silver every month. That silver would be coined and used as currency. The idea behind the act was that because silver was more plentiful than gold, the money supply would be inflated, which would help farmers repay their debts. The act would also aid silver mining interests in the West, which sought to sell more of their commodity on the open market. Finally, the act was seen as the first step in a bimetal approach to currency.

The act did not work as expected. President Hayes and his successors did not generally approve of silver being a form of currency. They purchased the minimum amount of silver and coined it, limiting how much silver would be circulated through the country and allowing gold to remain the dominant currency. Because of this limitation on the amount of silver used as currency, the political battles over the use of gold as a single currency continued past the Hayes administration. It divided the eastern half of the United States against the more rural western half of the country.

Yet the Bland-Allison Act did act as a guide for future congresses, which continued to debate using silver as currency. In 1890, the Sherman Silver Purchase Act was passed, vastly increasing the silver-purchasing power of the Treasury Department.

Douglas Clouatre

Sources for Further Study

Friedman, Milton, and Anna Schwartz. *A Monetary History of the United States.* Princeton, N.J.: Princeton University Press, 1963.

Hoogenboom, Ari. *The Presidency of Rutherford B. Hayes.* Lawrence: University of Kansas Press, 1988.

See also: Independent Treasury Act (1846); National Bank Acts (1863-1864); Coinage Act (1873); Currency Act (1900); Federal Reserve Act (1913).

JIM CROW LAWS

DATE: 1880's-1954
CATEGORIES: African Americans; Civil Rights and Liberties

Jim Crow laws were part of an organized attempt throughout the American South to subvert the Fourteenth Amendment and keep African Americans permanently in a socially subordinate status in all walks of life and to limit possibilities for any form of contact between people of different racial backgrounds.

The precise origins of the term "Jim Crow" are unknown. It may have first appeared in 1832, in a minstrel play by Thomas D. "Big Daddy" Rice. The play contained a song about a slave titled "Jim Crow." The expression was used commonly beginning in the 1890's. In 1904, the *Dictionary of American English* listed the term "Jim Crow law" for the first time.

Jim Crow laws had predecessors in the so-called Black Codes, passed in many southern states after the Civil War (1861-1865) to limit the freedom of African Americans and assure a continuous labor supply for the southern plantation economy. Radical Reconstruction, which placed most parts of the South under military government, put an end to this. Even after the official end of Reconstruction in 1877, race relations in the South remained in a state of flux.

THE JIM CROW ERA

Jim Crow laws emerged during the 1880's and 1890's as conflict over political control in the South between different parties and between factions within parties intensified. Disfranchisement of African Americans and the segregation of whites and blacks were intended to assure the permanent subjugation of the latter and the prevention of future biracial political movements which could challenge white rule in the South. Domestic politics do not bear the sole responsibility, however: Jim Crow laws emerged at a time when the United States acquired colonies in the Pacific and the Caribbean and in the process subjugated the indigenous populations of those areas. Race theories used to justify American imperialism did not substantially differ from the white supremacy rhetoric of southern politicians.

The first Jim Crow law was passed by the state of Florida in 1887, followed by Mississippi in 1888, Texas in 1889, Louisiana in 1890, Alabama, Arkansas, Georgia, and Tennessee in 1891, and Kentucky in 1892. North Carolina passed a Jim Crow law in 1898, South Carolina in 1899, and Virginia in 1900. Statutes requiring racial segregation had been quite common in northern states before the Civil War, but only in the post-Reconstruction South did racial segregation develop into a pervasive system regulating the separation of white and black in all walks of life. Jim Crow laws segregated public carriers, restaurants, telephone booths, residential areas, workplaces, public parks, and other recreational spaces. Mobile, Alabama, passed a special curfew law for African Americans in 1909. In Florida, the law required separate textbooks, which had to be separately stored. The city of New Orleans segregated white and black prostitutes in separate districts. Many states outlawed interracial marriages. Jim Crow laws were not even limited to life: Cemeteries, undertakers, and medical school cadavers were all subjects of segregation under the laws.

These laws, however, represented only symptoms of larger and even more pervasive patterns of discrimination and racial oppression. White vigilante groups, such as the Ku Klux Klan, often enforced their own brand of racial justice through violent means, frequently with the quiet consent and even cooperation of law enforcement officers. In addition, contract labor laws and corrupt law enforcement and prison officials created a system of peonage, which kept large numbers of African Americans in the turpentine and cotton belts in debt slavery.

U.S. SUPREME COURT
In the process of legally entrenching racial segregation through so-called Jim Crow laws, the U.S. Supreme Court served as a willing handmaiden. In the 1883 *Civil Rights* cases, the Supreme Court ruled that segregation in privately owned railroads, theaters, hotels, restaurants, and similar places comprised private acts of discrimination and as such did not fall under the Fourteenth Amendment. In the 1896 case of *Plessy v. Ferguson*, concerning the constitutionality of a Louisiana Jim Crow law, the Supreme Court redefined segregation from a matter of private prejudice into a mandate of state law. In *Plessy v. Ferguson*, the Supreme Court approved of segregation as long as facilities were "separate but equal." In the 1930's

and 1940's, the Supreme Court began to strike down segregation. Eventually, on May 17, 1954, the Supreme Court, in the landmark decision in *Brown v. Board of Education*, declared that separate facilities by their very nature were unequal, thereby reversing previous decisions.

Thomas Winter

Sources for Further Study

Daniel, Pete. *The Shadow of Slavery: Peonage in the South, 1901-1969.* Urbana: University of Illinois Press, 1972.

Finkelman, Paul, ed. *The Age of Jim Crow: Segregation from the End of Reconstruction to the Great Depression.* Vol. 4 in *Race, Law, and American History, 1700-1900.* 11 vols. New York: Garland, 1992.

Miller, Loren. *The Petitioners: The Story of the Supreme Court of the United States and the Negro.* New York: Pantheon Books, 1966.

Woodward, C. Vann. *The Strange Career of Jim Crow.* 3d rev. ed. New York: Oxford University Press, 1974.

See also: Black Codes of 1804-1807 (1804-1807); Black Codes of 1865 (1865); Ku Klux Klan Acts (1870-1871); Executive Order 8802 (1941); Civil Rights Act of 1957 (1957); Civil Rights Act of 1960 (1960); Civil Rights Act of 1964 (1964); Voting Rights Act of 1965 (1965); Civil Rights Act of 1968 (1968); Fair Housing Act (1968); Voting Rights Act of 1975 (1975).

CHINESE EXCLUSION ACT

Date: May 6, 1882
U.S. Statutes at Large: 22 Stat. 58
Categories: Asia or Asian Americans; Immigration

This act represents the first time the United States sought to exclude immigrants by race and nationality; it marked a turning point in what had been, until then, an open door to immigrants from around the world.

The Chinese Exclusion Act of 1882 suspended immigration by Chinese laborers to the United States for a period of ten years and prohibited Chinese residents in the United States from becoming naturalized citizens. Merchants, students, and tourists, however, were still permitted to enter the United States for visits. Although the Chinese Exclusion Act of 1882 was established as a temporary suspension of immigration by Chinese laborers, it was only the first of many laws designed to exclude Asians from entry into the United States.

This law was both a political and social reaction to increasing non-European immigration in the second half of the nineteenth century. As the country became more industrialized and its frontier began to disappear, Americans became increasingly apprehensive about employment and the role of immigrants. American labor organizations objected to what they perceived as unfair competition by Chinese laborers.

BACKGROUND

Chinese immigration to the mainland United States began in earnest after the Taiping Rebellion in 1848. Most Chinese immigrants headed for California, where the gold rush of 1849 led to an increased need for labor. In 1854, 13,100 Chinese came to the United States. This immigration, regulated by the Burlingame Treaty in 1868, was unrestricted; by 1880, the number of immigrants had risen to 105,465. The majority remained in California, where they were hired as laborers by the railroads, worked as domestics, and opened small businesses. San Francisco was the port of entry for many Chinese; the population of its Chinatown grew from two thousand to twelve thousand between 1860 and 1870.

The size and nature of this early Chinese immigration brought a long-lasting prejudice. Californians thought of Chinese laborers as "coolies"—that is, as cheap labor brought to the United States to undercut wages for American workers. Chinese workers were also accused of being dirty. Authorities in San Francisco suspected that crowded areas of Chinatown were the focus for disease and passed the Cubic Air Ordinance, prohibiting rental of a room with fewer than five hundred cubic feet of space per person. This municipal ordinance was later declared unconstitutional.

Discrimination and violence increased during the 1870's. In 1871, a mob attacked and killed nineteen Chinese people in Los Angeles. Denis Kearney, a naturalized citizen from Ireland, organized the Workingmen's Party in 1877 to oppose Chinese immigrants. Shouting, "The Chinese must go!" Kearney threatened violence to all Chinese immigrants. In July, 1877, men from an "anti-coolie club" led workers into San Francisco's Chinatown on a rampage that lasted several days.

Because most local ordinances against the Chinese had been declared unconstitutional, people who opposed Chinese immigration turned to Congress for new legislation. Congress responded in 1879 with a bill to limit Chinese immigration by prohibiting ships from bringing more than fifteen Chinese immigrants at a time. The bill was vetoed by President Rutherford B. Hayes on the grounds that it violated the Burlingame Treaty. With popular sentiment against continuing Chinese immigration, however, the treaty was amended in 1880, allowing the United States to limit the number of Chinese immigrants.

EXCLUSIONARY LEGISLATION
The Chinese Exclusion Act of 1882 was a response to the intensity of anti-Chinese feelings in the West and to close political elections that made western electoral votes critical. As signed into law by President Chester A. Arthur, the act suspended immigration by Chinese laborers for ten years. The vote in the House of Representatives reflected the popularity of the measure. There were 201 votes in favor, 37 against, and 51 absent. Representatives from every section of the country supported the bill, with southern and western House members voting unanimously for the legislation.

Later laws were even more draconian. An amendment in 1884 excluded all Chinese and Chinese residents living in other countries from entering the United States except as students, merchants, or tourists. The Scott Act of 1888 prohibited outright the entry of Chinese laborers and denied reentry to those who traveled abroad, even if they held reentry visas. The law also placed additional restrictions on those who were still permitted to come to the United States. In 1892 the Geary Act extended for an additional ten years the exclusion of Chinese immigrants, prohibited the use of *habeas corpus* by Chinese residents in the United States if arrested, and required all Chinese people to register and provide proof of their eligibility to remain in the United States. The act was renewed in 1902, and Congress made permanent the exclusion of Chinese immigrant laborers in 1904.

These exclusionary laws reflected a bias in American attitudes toward immigration by non-Europeans and increasing racial discrimination. Restrictions on intermarriage and land ownership by Chinese in many western states in the early 1900's led to a reduction in the number of Chinese residing in the United States from more than 100,000 in 1890 to 61,639 by 1920.

On December 17, 1943, the Chinese Exclusion Act was repealed. By then the threat of competition by Chinese labor was no longer an issue, and China was an ally of the United States in the war with Japan.

James A. Baer

SOURCES FOR FURTHER STUDY

Allen Jones, Maldwyn. *American Immigration.* 2d ed. Chicago: University of Chicago Press, 1992.

Barth, Gunther. *Bitter Strength: A History of the Chinese in the United States, 1850-1870.* Cambridge, Mass.: Harvard University Press, 1964.

Chan, Sucheng, ed. *Entry Denied: Exclusion and the Chinese Community in America, 1882-1943.* Philadelphia: Temple University Press, 1991.

Coolidge, Mary Roberts. *Chinese Immigration.* New York: Henry Holt, 1909.

Hoexter, Corinne K. *From Canton to California: The Epic of Chinese Immigration.* New York: Four Winds Press, 1976.

Knoll, Tricia. *Becoming Americans: Asian Sojourners, Immigrants, and Refugees in the Western United States.* Portland, Oreg.: Coast to Coast Books, 1982.

LeMay, Michael C. *From Open Door to Dutch Door: An Analysis of U.S. Immigration Policy Since 1820.* New York: Praeger, 1987.

Miller, Stuart Creighton. *The Unwelcome Immigrant: The American Image of the Chinese, 1785-1882.* Berkeley: University of California Press, 1969.

Takaki, Ronald. *Strangers from a Different Shore: A History of Asian Americans.* Boston: Little, Brown, 1989.

U.S. Commission on Civil Rights. *The Tarnished Golden Door: Civil Rights Issues in Immigration.* Washington, D.C.: Government Printing Office, 1980.

SEE ALSO: Treaty of Wang Hiya (1844); Burlingame Treaty (1868); Page Law (1875); Opium Exclusion Act (1909); Alien land laws (1913); Immigration Act of 1921 (1921); Cable Act (1922); Immigration Act of 1924 (1924); Hoover-Stimson Doctrine (1932); Immigration Act of 1943 (1943); War Brides Act (1945).

INDIAN OFFENSES ACT

DATE: 1883
U.S. STATUTES AT LARGE: 22 Stat. 400
CATEGORIES: Judiciary and Judicial Procedure; Native Americans

The federal government created courts, located on reservations, run by Native Americans, who were responsible for policing native cultural practices deemed offensive by European American society.

Courts of Indian Offenses were created by the Bureau of Indian Affairs in 1883. The judges of these courts were Indian men appointed by the federal agent on each reservation, and they heard only cases involving certain cultural practices, termed "Indian offenses," which were banned on the reservations. All decisions of the court were subject to the approval of the Indian agent.

Essentially, the Indian offenses were a list of common traditional practices that the government determined were "demoralizing and barbarous" and therefore should be discontinued so that Indians could become more assimilated into mainstream American culture and values. The list of Indian offenses included dancing, plural marriages, feasts, giveaways, and destroying the property of the dead (a funerary custom among some tribes). Additionally, and most devastating to many Indian people, traditional religious practices including sun dances, sweat-lodge ceremonies, vision questing, and shamanism were strictly prohibited in the hope that Indian people would be more likely to convert to Christianity. In short, Indian offenses were an extensive body of religious and cultural practices that the federal government banned because they were deemed disruptive to the smooth functioning of reservations. When living within the reservation context, Indian people were not granted constitutional protections.

Carole A. Barrett

SOURCES FOR FURTHER STUDY

Falkowski, James E. *Indian Law/Race Law: A Five Hundred Year History.* New York: Praeger, 1992.

Hoxie, Frederick E. *A Final Promise: The Campaign to Assimilate the Indians, 1880-1920.* Lincoln: University of Nebraska Press, 1984.

Prucha, Francis Paul, ed. *Documents in United States Indian Policy.* 2d ed. Lincoln: University of Nebraska Press, 1990.

Washburn, Wilcomb E., ed. *History of Indian-White Relations.* Vol. 4 in *Handbook of North American Indians,* edited by William C. Sturtevant. Washington, D.C.: Smithsonian Institution Press, 1988.

SEE ALSO: Major Crimes Act (1885); Indian Citizenship Act (1924); Indian Reorganization Act (1934); Termination Resolution (1953).

PENDLETON ACT

ALSO KNOWN AS: National Civil Service Act
DATE: January 16, 1883
U.S. STATUTES AT LARGE: 22 Stat. 403
CATEGORIES: Government Procedure and Organization

The act created the civil service system for federal employees to replace a corrupt political spoils system.

On July 2, 1881, President James A. Garfield prepared to leave Washington for a vacation in New York State. As the presidential party neared the waiting train, Garfield was shot in the back by Charles J. Guiteau, an unsuccessful aspirant to the office of consul to Paris. He shouted, "I am a Stalwart and Arthur is president now!"

GOVERNMENT CORRUPTION

Even in an age of widespread graft, Chester A. Arthur, the vice president, had been well known as the head of the New York Customs House, a classically corrupt government agency, and as a spoilsman in Roscoe Conkling's New York Republican political machine. Few expected him to change when he became president at Garfield's death on September 19, but he exhibited an unanticipated coolness toward the Stalwarts (professional machine Republicans) in selecting cabinet replacements and insisted on continuing the prosecution of the "Star Route" mail fraud case. These actions are credited with costing Arthur the presidential nomination in 1884, as well as providing the Democrats with numerous victories in the elections of fall, 1882. As a result, the outgoing Republican Congress was impelled to adopt civil service reform legislation in 1883.

CALLS FOR REFORM

However, a confluence of reasons were responsible, finally, for civil service reform. George Washington, when he was president, initiated the idea that persons of high competence and integrity should be sought to fill public service jobs. This approach resulted in a stable and fairly skilled workforce but contributed to its elite quality. When Andrew Jackson became president in 1829, he operated under the belief that the "common man" had as much right to a government job as the wealthy and that most government jobs could be done by people without special training. He democratized the civil service but also helped justify the spoils system.

By the 1880's, the number of public jobs had greatly increased, and the quality of those serving in them had declined. Several reform attempts failed. The first serious attempt to reform the system was led by Thomas Allen Jenckes, a Republican congressman from Rhode Island. Jenckes was a patent lawyer by profession and also had financial interests in several companies. In both activities he had to rely on the federal mail service, which was inefficient and corrupt. In 1865 he introduced his first civil service reform bill covering all federal agencies, including the post office. His proposal was patterned after the British system and would have covered all federal officials except those appointed by the president with the consent of the Senate. A decade later a number of organized reform groups around the country, concerned first with local and then with national corruption, were formed. A national reform movement was spearheaded by the National Civil Service Reform League, presided over by George William Curtis.

PASSAGE AND PROVISIONS

The assassination of Garfield was the spark that lit the smoldering coals not only of the reformers' attempts but also of elected officials' weariness with long lines of people seeking jobs, patronage appointees' weariness with blatant assessments of percentages of their salaries for political party support, and the Republican Congress's assessment that its power might be about to end. Therefore in 1883 the Republican Congress passed an act drafted by Dorman B. Eaton, secretary of the National Civil Service Reform League, and sponsored by Democratic senator George Pendleton of Ohio: the National Civil Service Act, commonly known as the Pendleton Act.

The act had two purposes: to eliminate political influence from administrative agencies and to assure more competent government employees. It established a three-member bipartisan Civil Service Commission appointed by the president with the consent of the Senate for indefinite terms. Eaton became the first chairman of the Civil Service Commission. About ten percent of the government positions were included initially, but other positions, to be designed by the president, could be "covered in"; that is, current patronage appointees could remain in their positions when those positions were included under the act. This provision gave outgoing presidents an incentive to "cover in" increasing numbers of positions over time, which is in fact what happened. The act provided that civil service positions were to be filled through open and competitive examinations; lateral entry was encouraged, and employees were assured tenure regardless of political changes at the tops of the organizations. Employees were also protected against political pressures such as assessments and required participation in campaign activities.

SUBSEQUENT LEGISLATION

The adoption of a merit system at the federal level was followed immediately by similar adoptions in some of the states. Widespread coverage at the state and local levels was subsequently brought about through requirements attached to most federal grant monies.

Over the years, legislation was added to improve the civil service system. The Classification Act of 1923 established a system for classifying jobs according to qualifications needed to carry them out and tying them to various pay grades, thus providing uniformity throughout the federal system. The Hatch Political Activities Act of 1939 prohibited national civil service workers from taking an active part in politics, and later amendments extended the ban to state and local employees whose programs were financed fully or in part by federal funds. In 1978 the Civil Service Reform Act reassigned the Civil Service Commission's often contradictory functions to two agencies: a new Office of Personnel Management, responsible for policy leadership, and a Merit Systems Protection Board, to handle investigations and appeals. A Senior Executive Service was also established, creating a separate personnel system for the highest-ranking civil service officials in an attempt to provide greater flexibility in assignments and incentives for top senior personnel.

Anne Trotter, updated by
Erika E. Pilver

Sources for Further Study

Cayer, N. Joseph. *Public Personnel Administration in the United States.* New York: St. Martin's Press, 1986.

Emmerich, Herbert. *Federal Organization and Administrative Management.* University: University of Alabama Press, 1971.

Hoogenboom, Ari. *Outlawing the Spoils: A History of the Civil Service Reform Movement, 1865-1883.* Urbana: University of Illinois Press, 1961.

Ingraham, Patricia, and Carolyn Ban, eds. *Legislating Bureaucratic Change: The Civil Service Reform Act of 1978.* Albany: State University of New York Press, 1984.

See also: Hatch Act (1939); Securities Exchange Act (1934); Ethics in Government Act (1978); Twenty-seventh Amendment (1992); Bipartisan Campaign Reform Act (2002).

MAJOR CRIMES ACT

DATE: March 3, 1885
U.S. STATUTES AT LARGE: 23 Stat. 385
U.S. CODE: 18 § 1153
CATEGORIES: Crimes and Criminal Procedure; Native Americans

The Major Crimes Act gave the U.S. government, rather than tribal courts, criminal jurisdiction to prosecute fourteen major crimes committed by one reservation Indian against another.

The Major Crimes Act gave the U.S. government jurisdiction over serious crimes committed by Indians on tribal lands. Congress reacted strongly to the *Ex parte Crow Dog* (1883) decision, in which an Indian who killed another Indian was released by the federal government because it lacked federal jurisdiction in Indian country. Two years after the Crow Dog incident, Congress passed the Major Crimes Act, which gave the United States the right to prosecute Indians for seven crimes: murder, manslaughter, rape, assault with intent to kill, arson, burglary, and larceny. This law applied to any Indian who committed a crime against another Indian on a reservation. Over the years, the list of criminal offenses expanded to include kidnaping, maiming, assault with a dangerous weapon, assault resulting in bodily injury, incest, theft, and sexual abuse. Indians accused of lesser crimes are tried in tribal court. However, federal court decisions narrowed the act so it covers only enrolled Indians who commit crimes on their own reservations. This act transformed the relationship between tribes and the federal government by limiting tribal sovereignty and the power of tribal courts and making it nearly impossible for tribes to deal with serious crimes committed on their reservations.

Carole A. Barrett

SOURCES FOR FURTHER STUDY
Falkowski, James E. *Indian Law/Race Law: A Five Hundred Year History.* New York: Praeger, 1992.
Hoxie, Frederick E. *A Final Promise: The Campaign to Assimilate the Indians, 1880-1920.* Lincoln: University of Nebraska Press, 1984.

Prucha, Francis Paul, ed. *Documents in United States Indian Policy.*
2d ed. Lincoln: University of Nebraska Press, 1990.
Washburn, Wilcomb E., ed. *History of Indian-White Relations.* Vol. 4
in *Handbook of North American Indians,* edited by William C. Sturtevant. Washington, D.C.: Smithsonian Institution Press, 1988.

SEE ALSO: Indian Offenses Act (1883); Indian Citizenship Act
(1924); Indian Reorganization Act (1934); Termination Resolution (1953).

ELECTORAL COUNT ACT

DATE: February 3, 1887
U.S. STATUTES AT LARGE: 24 Stat. 373
CATEGORIES: Voting and Elections

*This act, originally passed to correct the mistakes of the 1876 election,
played an important role in the outcome of the 2000 presidential election.*

In 1887, Congress passed the Electoral Count Act. The law was enacted to prevent a repeat of the 1876 election, in which Republican Rutherford B. Hayes narrowly defeated Democrat Samuel Tilden after a dispute over the slates of electors appointed by several states. The legislation established the criteria for deciding whether a state's choice of electors is the final list to be submitted to Congress when the body assembles to count the electoral votes. In states where the selection of an elector or electors is challenged, the act provided that the conflict would be settled according to state law in effect prior to election day. The law also specified that the dispute had to be settled at least six days before the electors were supposed to meet to vote for president and vice president.

Passage of the Electoral Count Act of 1887 marked the end of more than ten years of debate in Congress over legislation to correct the mistakes of the 1876 election. The Senate passed bills similar to the Electoral Count Act in 1878, 1882, 1884, and 1886. Each time the House of Representatives either rejected the legislation or passed bills that differed significantly from the Senate's bill.

THE 2000 PRESIDENTIAL ELECTION

The Electoral Count Act existed largely unnoticed in federal law for more than a century. It became an issue for the first time in the disputed presidential election of 2000. Vice President Al Gore, the Democratic nominee, held a slim lead over Texas Governor George W. Bush, a Republican, in the popular vote and the electoral vote. Because of some voting irregularities, the electors from the state of Florida were in dispute. A series of lawsuits resulted in the case *Bush v. Gore* (531 U.S. 98 [2000]) being taken to the United States Supreme Court. The court was asked to apply the provisions of the Electoral Count Act to the dispute.

Lawyers representing Vice President Gore argued that the law regulated each state's process only to resolve disputes over which electors could cast votes. According to Gore's lawyers, the court should accept a Florida Supreme Court decision issued after election day allowing manual recounts of ballots in that state. Lawyers for Governor Bush argued that the Florida Supreme Court decision was a law enacted after election day, a violation of the Electoral Count Act's provision that disputes be resolved using laws enacted before election day.

The Supreme Court ruled in Bush's favor. The 5-4 majority decided that the Electoral Count Act required that "any controversy or contest that is designed to lead to a conclusive selection of electors be completed by December 12," six days before electors were scheduled to meet in their respective state capitols. Vice President Gore conceded the presidency to Governor Bush.

John David Rausch, Jr.

SOURCES FOR FURTHER STUDY

Schickler, Eric, Terri Bimes, and Robert W. Mickey. "Safe at Any Speed: Legislative Intent, the Electoral Count Act of 1887, and *Bush v. Gore.*" *Journal of Law and Politics*, Fall, 2000, 717-764.

Sunstein, Cass R., and Richard A. Epstein, eds. *The Vote: Bush, Gore, and the Supreme Court.* Chicago: University of Chicago Press, 2001.

SEE ALSO: Seventeenth Amendment (1913); Twenty-third Amendment (1961); Federal Election Campaign Act (1972); Bipartisan Campaign Reform Act (2002).

INTERSTATE COMMERCE ACT

DATE: February 4, 1887
U.S. STATUTES AT LARGE: 24 Stat. 379
U.S. CODE: 49 § 10721, 10761
CATEGORIES: Business, Commerce, and Trade; Transportation

This law, which created the Interstate Commerce Commission, was passed to regulate the operation of the railroads.

By the 1880's, the United States had experienced more than fifty years of railroad expansion. Transcontinental railroad lines tied the nation together, while spurring the growth of industry and agriculture through the rapid transportation of both raw materials and finished goods. During much of this time, government had served as a willing partner to the rapid growth of the railroads. Both national and state governments had provided land for the railroad right-of-way, as well as other subsidies to underwrite the cost of this vital form of transportation.

MONOPOLIES AND PRICE-FIXING

By the end of the Civil War, however, many people in the United States had begun to have second thoughts about the railroads. Although almost no one doubted the need for railroads, many criticized the business practices of the railroad companies. Consumers suffered when railroad companies experienced either too much or too little competition. In regions where one company dominated, that company often took advantage of its monopoly of the market and charged its customers exorbitant fees for necessary services. Where competition was intense, the railroads too often resorted to unfair practices in order to attract and retain the business of large-volume shippers. They reduced rates in some areas to meet competition and raised rates in noncompetitive areas to compensate. They also engaged in such practices as offering rebates or kickbacks to large-volume shippers at the expense of the average consumer. The railroads entered into agreements, often referred to as "pools," among themselves to fix rates at a level higher than the free market permitted. They charged more for a short haul in order to offer special long-haul rates to large shippers. The railroads also were guilty of watering their stock, or overcapitalizing issues, to bilk the investor. These and other practices worked to the advantage of the railroads and a few favored customers. As a result of railroad manipulation of freight charges, it often cost small farmers more to ship their grain than they would receive in payment for it, while large mill owners would receive a discount on the shipment of the finished flour. The unethical business practices thus worked to the detriment of the ordinary shippers, farmers, and the public.

STATE REFORMS

The states responded first to the demands for railroad reform. Many states passed laws that compelled railroads to offer standard rates for all, and many states set up regulatory boards to supervise the practices of the railroad companies. The states, however, could not supervise interstate operations. Farmers shipping grain from the Dakotas to Minnesota mills or cattle from Texas to Chicago slaughterhouses were not protected by individual state regulations. In addition, the state regulatory laws and boards often created more problems than they solved. Finally, the railroads resisted attempts at state regulation and fought enforcement in the courts. In October, 1886, the Supreme Court (in *Wabash, St. Louis, and Pacific Railway v. Illinois*) held that a state could not regulate commerce that went beyond its boundaries. This meant that any regulation of interstate commerce would have to come from the federal government.

THE NEED FOR A FEDERAL LAW

Numerous groups and individuals had long pressed for national legislation to reform the railroads. Organizations of producers, shippers, and merchants demanded an end to practices by which railroad companies took advantage of the need for rail transportation. F. B. Thurber, a New York wholesale grocer, and Simon Sterne, chairman of New York's Board of Trade and Transportation, became active lobbyists. Some of the loudest demands for some system of national regulation began to come from the railroad companies themselves, particularly in the East, where competition was ruthless. Financiers such as Jay Gould recognized that without some reforms, public outrage could lead to harsh regulations in the future.

John H. Reagan, a congressman from Texas and the chairman of the House Committee on Commerce, during the 1870's and early 1880's introduced many bills in Congress that would outlaw specific practices, such as pools, rebates, and price discrimination between long and short hauls. Reagan's approach to the problem was an attempt to clean up the competition among the railroads on the assumption that fair competition was economically healthy for the entire nation. The proposed bills described what would constitute illegal practices but contained no provisions for investigation or regulation. Reagan's attempts to regulate the railroads met with little success until the first administration of President Grover Cleveland.

PASSAGE AND PROVISIONS

Cleveland, a Democrat, strongly opposed the growth of government but opposed the idea of government favors to business even more. Following the Supreme Court decision in *Wabash Railroad v. Illinois,* Cleveland urged Congress to take action to regulate the railroads. This time, Congress seemed ready to pass regulatory legislation. Reagan once again introduced a bill in the House of Representatives, while in the Senate, Shelby M. Cullom of Illinois proposed a more far-reaching solution. Cullom's approach, which emerged from extensive committee hearings, embodied a regulatory commission with broad powers to investigate and to bring into court railroad companies whose rates or practices were unfair. Cullom proposed that the federal government take positive action in laying down precisely what constituted unfair tactics and rates. The Reagan and Cullom bills went to a joint committee of the House and the Senate. President Cleveland exerted some influence in favor of Cullom's proposals. From the joint committee emerged the Interstate Commerce Act.

The act followed Reagan's suggestions and prohibited specific abuses, such as long- and short-haul discrimination. It also created the Interstate Commerce Commission (ICC). Under the provisions of the act, the commission would comprise five members whose duty it was to investigate and expose unfair rates and practices among interstate carriers. Congress empowered the commission to take unrepentant railroads into court. After decades of encouraging and subsidizing the railroads, the government had begun to regulate them.

WEAK ENFORCEMENT

The jubilation of the railroad reformers was short-lived. The courts and the ICC itself seemed determined to frustrate substantive reform. The commission, whose first chairman was Thomas M. Cooley, a professor of law at the University of Michigan, often dealt with the railroads in an extremely conservative manner, and the Supreme Court weakened the commission's powers. Cooley believed in a strict interpretation of the Constitution and was reluctant to expand the power of the federal government. When the railroads chose to dispute the rulings of the ICC, they generally won in court. Of the sixteen cases involving railroads and the ICC that were heard by the Supreme Court between 1887 and 1911, the railroads won fifteen. In the process, the Supreme Court destroyed the commission's power to act against fixing rates, pooling, and long- and short-haul discrimination. Government regulation had been established in theory, but not yet in practice. The Interstate Commerce Act was significant chiefly as a precedent for the genuine economic reform that followed in later years.

Emory M. Thomas, updated by
Nancy Farm Männikkö

SOURCES FOR FURTHER STUDY

Cullom, Shelby Moore. *Fifty Years of Public Service: Personal Recollections of Shelby M. Cullom.* New York: Da Capo Press, 1969.

Jones, Alan R. *The Constitutional Conservatism of Thomas McIntyre Cooley: A Study in the History of Ideas.* New York: Garland, 1987.

Neilson, James W. *Shelby M. Cullom: Prairie State Republican.* Urbana: University of Illinois Press, 1962.

Reagan, John H. *Memoirs, with Special Reference to Secession and the Civil War.* 1906. Reprint, edited by Walter Flavius McCaleb. New York: AMS Press, 1978.

Stone, Richard D. *The Interstate Commerce Commission and the Railroad Industry: A History of Regulatory Policy.* New York: Praeger, 1991.

Welch, Richard E. *The Presidencies of Grover Cleveland.* Lawrence: University Press of Kansas, 1988.

SEE ALSO: Sherman Antitrust Act (1890); Federal Trade Commission Act (1914); Clayton Antitrust Act (1914); Consumer Credit Protection Act (1968); Hazardous Materials Transportation Act (1974); Antitrust Procedures and Penalties Act (1974).

GENERAL ALLOTMENT ACT

ALSO KNOWN AS: Dawes Act; Indian General Allotment Act
DATE: February 8, 1887
U.S. STATUTES AT LARGE: 24 Stat. 388-391
U.S. CODE: 25 § 331
CATEGORIES: Land Management; Native Americans

This law established a policy of allotting land to individual Native Americans in severalty, a practice that effectively dissolved the tribal nations.

When the General Allotment, or Dawes, Act became law on February 8, 1887, proponents hailed it as the Indian Emancipation Act and Secretary of the Interior L. Q. C. Lamar called it "the most important measure of legislation ever enacted in this country affecting our Indian affairs."

LAND OWNERSHIP AND CITIZENSHIP

The law dealt primarily with Native American ownership of land. It authorized the president of the United States, through the Office of Indian Affairs in the Department of the Interior, to allot the lands on reservations to individual Native Americans, so that they would hold the land in severalty instead of the tribe's owning the land communally. Each head of a household would receive a quarter-section of land (160 acres); single persons over eighteen years of age and orphans would receive eighty acres; and other persons, forty acres. (In 1891, an amendment to the law equalized the allotments to provide eighty acres for each individual, regardless of age or family status.) The United States government would hold the allotments in trust for twenty-five years, during which time the Native American could not sell or otherwise dispose of his or her land. At the end of that period, he or she would receive full title to it. After the process of dividing up the reservation land for allotments, the federal government could sell the surplus land (often a considerable portion of the reservation) to willing purchasers (most of whom would be European Americans). The money from such sales would go to a fund to benefit Native American education.

The Dawes Act also provided for Native American citizenship. Native Americans who received allotments in severalty or who took up residence apart from their tribe and adopted what European Americans considered civilized ways became citizens of the United States and subject to the laws of the state or territory in which they lived. In 1924, Congress passed the Indian Citizenship Act, granting full citizenship to nearly all Native Americans who were not already citizens, and measures in the late 1940's extended such status to Arizona and New Mexico Native Americans that the 1924 law had missed.

PROPONENTS OF THE ACT

Two groups of European Americans especially welcomed the Dawes Act. Land-hungry settlers who had long cast covetous eyes on the reservation lands—which, to European American thinking, were going to waste because of the lack of productive agricultural practices by Native Americans—were now able to acquire the lands left over from the allotment process. No doubt, the less scrupulous among the settlers also looked forward to the day when individual Native Americans would receive full title to their land and be able to sell, lease, or otherwise dispose of it. Then pressure, legitimate or not, would likely induce the new owner to part with the acreage.

A second group, however, was more influential in securing passage of the Dawes Act. These were the humanitarian reformers of the day, who considered private ownership of land in severalty, U.S. citizenship, education, and consistent codification of laws to be indispensable means for the acculturation of the Native Americans and their eventual assimilation into the mainstream of U.S. society. As ministers from several Christian denominations, educators, civil servants, politicians, and even a few military personnel, these philanthropists exerted a clout beyond their numbers. Calling themselves the Friends of the Indian, these reformers had been meeting annually at the Catskills resort of Lake Mohonk to discuss ways to bring the tribal peoples to what the conveners deemed to be civilization.

Federal politicians had long considered private ownership of land essential to the civilizing process. Thomas Jefferson and the like-minded policymakers of his time had strongly advocated it, and in 1838 the Commissioner of Indian Affairs gave voice to a widespread view when he said, "Unless some system is marked out by which there shall be a separate allotment of land to each individual . . . you will look in vain for any general casting off of savagism. Common property and civilization cannot co-exist."

It was not until the post-Civil War years, when increasing European American pressures on the Native Americans created crisis after crisis, that humanitarians and philanthropists began a concerted drive for "Indian reform." Land in severalty would be the most important factor in breaking up tribalism. The reform groups that were organized—the Board of Indian Commissioners (1869), the Women's National Indian Association (1879), the Indian Rights Association (1882), the Lake Mohonk Conference of Friends of the Indian (1883), and the National Indian Defense Association (1885), to name the most important—all strongly espoused allotment in severalty. Nor were they satisfied with the piecemeal legislation that affected one tribe at a time; the panacea they sought was a general allotment law. Although supporters argued over the speed of implementing allotment, such proponents as Carl Schurz, Herbert Welsh, and the Reverend Lyman Abbott fought energetically for such legislation. They finally won to their cause Senator Henry L. Dawes, chairman of the Senate Committee on Indian Affairs, who successfully shepherded through Congress the measure that bears his name.

Voices Against Allotment

Only a few European American voices cried out against the proposal. Congressman Russell Errett of Pennsylvania and a few others protested that the bill was a thinly disguised means of getting at the valuable tribal lands. Senator Henry M. Teller of Colorado argued that the Native Americans did not want to own land in severalty and were not prepared to assume the responsibilities that went with private property and citizenship. He denied the contention of the reformers that private ownership of land would lead to civilization. Albert Meacham, editor of *The Council Fire*, maintained that there was little enthusiasm for severalty among traditionalist Native Americans, and anthropologist Lewis Henry Morgan believed that allotment would result in massive poverty. Presbyterian missionaries apparently were disunited on the subject of allotment, and their views fell by the wayside as the juggernaut of reform plunged ahead.

Native American response to allotment has largely gone unrecorded. The Cherokee, Creek, Chickasaw, Choctaw, Seminole, Sac, Fox, and a few other tribes in Indian Territory, as well as the Seneca in New York, contended that they already mostly owned land individually and won exclusion from the act's operation. By 1906, however, Congress extended allotment to them as well. Most of the complaints came after the act's passage, when Native Americans lost land and found farming difficult under its provisions.

ASSESSMENT

"February 8, 1887," one optimistic spokesman of the Board of Indian Commissioners commented, "may be called the Indian emancipation day." Although much sincere Christian goodwill motivated passage of the Dawes Act, it turned out to be a disaster for Native Americans. The sponsors of the Dawes Act had assumed an unrealistically romantic view of the Native American. People who had had firsthand experience with tribal peoples attempted to convince the reformers that the "noble savage" had never existed. In 1891, Congress allowed Native Americans to lease their allotments if they were not able to farm for themselves.

The allotments and the leasing moved faster and with less careful discrimination than Dawes and other promoters had intended. Instead of being a measure that turned Native Americans into self-supporting farmers, the act, through the rapid alienation of the Native Americans' lands, meant the loss of the land base on which the tribal peoples' hope for future prosperity depended. Tribal peoples held claim to about 150 million acres of land in 1887. The Dawes Act eventually diverted two-thirds of that acreage out of Native American ownership, down to about forty-eight million acres by 1934. Not until that year, with the passage of the Indian Reorganization Act (the Wheeler-Howard Act, also known as the "Indian New Deal"), did the federal government repeal the Dawes Act and encourage communal forms of ownership again, but by that time much of the former reservation land was gone as surplus sales, leases, or sales by the individual allottees.

Francis P. Prucha, updated by
Thomas L. Altherr

SOURCES FOR FURTHER STUDY
Gibson, Arrell Morgan. "The Centennial Legacy of the General Allotment Act." *Chronicles of Oklahoma* 65, no. 3 (1987): 228-251.
Greenwald, Emily. *Reconfiguring the Reservation: The Nez Perces, the Jicarilla Apache, and the Dawes Act.* Albuquerque: University of New Mexico Press, 2002.
Hoxie, Frederick E. *A Final Promise: The Campaign to Assimilate the Indians, 1880-1920.* Lincoln: University of Nebraska Press, 1984.
Mintz, Steven, ed. *Native American Voices.* St. James, N.Y.: Brandywine Press, 1995.
Prucha, Francis Paul, ed. *Americanizing the American Indians: Writings of the "Friends of the Indian" 1880-1900.* Lincoln: University of Nebraska Press, 1973.
Washburn, Wilcomb E. *The Assault on Indian Tribalism: The General Allotment Law (Dawes Act) of 1887.* Philadelphia: J. B. Lippincott, 1975.

SEE ALSO: Indian Removal Act (1830); Indian Appropriation Act (1871); Burke Act (1906); Indian Citizenship Act (1924); Indian Reorganization Act (1934); Termination Resolution (1953).

DEPENDENT PENSION ACT

ALSO KNOWN AS: Invalid Pension Act or Disability Pension Act
DATE: June 27, 1890
U.S. STATUTES AT LARGE: 26 Stat. 182
CATEGORIES: Health and Welfare

This law created the first large, government-supported pension program to assist Civil War veterans.

Civil War legislation relating to the benefits of Union veterans and their dependents began in February, 1862, a few months after the outbreak of the 1861-1865 conflict. Feelings of indebtedness to those who had served and sacrificed for the nation, the destitution of many veterans and their dependents, and the reluctance by men to volunteer because of family concerns motivated these laws. There followed the discovery that pension benefits could be used for patronage, partisanship, and political advantage. Indeed, the 1888 reelection defeat of Democratic president Grover Cleveland, who had vetoed the Dependent Pension Bill of 1887 (a forerunner of the 1890 act) as overly generous, had been a political object lesson. Frequent budget surpluses, driven by high tariffs, also helped, as did "soldier-president" General Benjamin Harrison, who signed the 1890 law following its passage by both Republican-dominated Houses of Congress.

Thus, in the quarter century that had elapsed since the end of the Civil War, much legislative tinkering and increasingly liberal administrative interpretations—spurred by such interest groups as Union veterans' organizations and pension lawyers filing benefit applications and collecting supporting evidence—expanded the number of those covered and the substance of the benefits, as witness the retroactive Arrears of Pension Act of January 25, 1879.

The 1890 law provided that the dependent parents of Civil War veterans who had served at least ninety days in the Union forces and had been honorably discharged would be entitled to a pension. Also, veterans suffering from a physical or mental disability from nearly any cause not of their own "vicious" habits would be entitled to a pension for as long as the disability lasted or even for life. A dependent widow and minor children under sixteen years of age would each qualify for a pension. Finally, the law set a maximum fee for intermediaries acting as agents for applicants. Amendments in 1900, 1907, 1908, and 1912 liberalized benefits for veterans and their widows even further.

Thus, an extensive social welfare system grew dramatically after passage of the 1890 act. In 1891 there were some 115,000 Civil War pensioners on the federal rolls. By 1893 there were nearly 460,000 costing taxpayers more than sixty-eight million dollars that year and aggregating to some five billion dollars by World War I. This benefits program was viewed by many as a system of national public care but only for the deserving members of a special generation.

Peter B. Heller

SOURCES FOR FURTHER STUDY

Glasson, William H. "Civil War Pensions: The Act of June 27, 1890." Chapter 3 in *Federal Military Pensions in the United States*. New York: Oxford University Press, 1918.

McClintock, Megan J. "Civil War Pensions and the Reconstruction of Union Families." *Journal of American History* 83, no. 2 (September, 1996): 456-480.

Skocpol, Theda. "Public Aid for the Worthy Many: The Expansion of Benefits for Veterans of the Civil War." Chapter 2 in *Protecting Soldiers and Mothers: The Political Origins of Social Policy in the United States*. Cambridge, Mass.: Harvard University Press, 1992.

SEE ALSO: World War Adjusted Compensation Act (1924); Social Security Act (1935); G.I. Bill (1944); Employee Retirement Income Security Act (1974).

SHERMAN ANTITRUST ACT

ALSO KNOWN AS: Sherman Act
DATE: July 2, 1890
U.S. STATUTES AT LARGE: 26 Stat. 209
U.S. CODE: 15 § 1 et seq.
CATEGORIES: Business, Commerce, and Trade; Crimes and Criminal Procedure

> *Among most important antitrust laws, this act outlawed certain trusts, or "loose combinations," and monopolies, empowering the U.S. attorney general to bring criminal or civil court actions against violators.*

The period following the Civil War was one of rapid economic growth and change in the United States. Creation of a nationwide network of railroads gave individual firms a way to serve a nationwide market, enabling them to grow to a large size to improve their efficiency or simply to gain strategic advantages. A conspicuous firm was Standard Oil, led by John D. Rockefeller. The firm was efficient and progressive in developing petroleum refining, but was heavily criticized for such actions as pressuring railroads for preferential rebates and discriminatory price-cutting to intimidate competitors.

STANDARD OIL

Standard Oil effectively controlled the petroleum-refining industry by 1879. In addition to lubricants, its principal product was kerosene, aggressively marketed worldwide as the first cheap and convenient source of artificial light. In 1882, the firm was reorganized in the form of a trust, facilitating the acquisition of competing firms. Although the trust form went out of use soon after, the term "trust" became a common name for aggressive big-business monopolies. Other large combinations were soon formed, so that by 1890, large companies controlled the production of such items as whiskey, sugar, and lead, and dominated the nation's railroads.

Opposition to big-business abuses spread among farmers and in small-business sectors such as the grocery business. Popular concern was fueled by writings such as Edward Bellamy's utopian novel *Looking Backward*, which had sold a million copies within fifteen years after its publication in 1881. Individual states adopted anti-monopoly legislation or brought court actions against alleged monopolists. By 1891, eighteen states had adopted some sort of antitrust legislation. Both major political parties adopted vague antimonopoly statements in their platforms for the 1888 election, but neither rushed to submit appropriate legislation at the next congressional session. President Benjamin Harrison was moved to ask for such a statute in his annual message of December, 1889. A bill introduced by Senator John Sherman of Ohio was extensively revised by the Senate Judiciary Committee, under the able guidance of George Hoar and George F. Edmunds. The resulting bill was passed by Congress with virtually no debate and only one opposing vote. President Harrison signed it into law July 20, 1890.

THREE MAIN PROVISIONS

The Sherman Antitrust Act contained three important types of provisions. First, the law outlawed "every contract, combination in the form of trust or otherwise, or conspiracy, in restraint of trade or commerce among the several states or with foreign nations. . . ."

This came to be viewed as dealing with "loose combinations" of several firms undertaking joint action. Second, the law made it illegal for any person to monopolize or attempt to monopolize any part of that trade or commerce. This was viewed as dealing with activities of individual large firms. The key terms were not defined, and it remained for lawyers and judges to try to find satisfactory and consistent meanings for them. Third, the law provided for a variety of means of enforcement. The attorney general was empowered to bring criminal or civil court actions against violators. Civil remedies often proved attractive, because the burden of proof was not so difficult to achieve, and the remedies could involve changing industry structure and behavior, not merely applying punishments. In addition, private individuals could sue offending firms for triple the value of their losses.

EFFECTS

Between 1890 and 1904, only eighteen suits were filed under the act. Several of these aimed at collusive rate-fixing by railroads, despite their regulated status under the Interstate Commerce Commission. At the time of the Pullman Strike (1894), the courts held that the Sherman Act could be applied to the activities of labor unions. Unions were repeatedly subjected to injunctions and triple-damage suits for strikes, picketing, and boycotts, even after Congress attempted, in the Clayton Act of 1914, to exempt most union activities from antitrust laws.

The Sherman Act's effectiveness was limited severely by the Supreme Court in an 1895 case against the sugar trust, *United States v. E. C. Knight Company.* The ruling defined commerce so narrowly that it excluded almost all forms of interstate enterprise except transportation. The Court was led to make a ruling of this type by the way in which the Justice Department, under Attorney General Richard Olney, framed the case. Collusive behavior among a number of separate firms, however, was not granted such a loophole. In 1899, activities by six producers of cast-iron pipe to agree on contract bids were held illegal in *Addyston Pipe and Steel Co. v. U.S.* These two cases indicated that activities involving several firms were much more likely to be found illegal than the operations of a single-firm monopolist. Perhaps in response, the decade of the 1890's witnessed an unprecedented boom in the formation of giant corporations through mergers and consolidations.

The process culminated in the creation of United States Steel Corporation in 1901, capitalized at more than one billion dollars. Again, public outcry arose. Congress appointed an Industrial Commission in 1899 to consider the trust problem. A preliminary report in 1900 observed that "industrial combinations have become fixtures in our business life. Their power for evil should be destroyed and their means for good preserved." The commission's 1902 report recommended stronger actions against price discrimination. Some large firms were prosecuted successfully. A giant railroad merger was blocked in the *Northern Securities* case of 1904, helping to gain for President Theodore Roosevelt a reputation as a vigorous trust-buster. In 1911, two notorious trusts, Standard Oil and American Tobacco, were convicted of Sherman Act violations. In each case, the convicted firm was ordered to be broken into several separate firms. The Standard Oil settlement made it much easier for new firms to enter petroleum refining, making possible the emergence of such new competitors as Texaco and Gulf Oil. However, prosecution of the ultimate corporate giant, U.S. Steel, was dismissed in 1920.

THE CLAYTON ACT
In 1914, Congress adopted the Clayton Act, which amended the Sherman Act to specify business actions to be prohibited. This outlawed price discrimination, tying and exclusive-dealing contracts, mergers and acquisitions, and interlocking directorships, where these tended to decrease competition or to create a monopoly. The Federal Trade Commission was also established in 1914, charged with preventing unfair methods of competition and helping to enforce the Clayton Act.

LATER IMPACT OF THE SHERMAN ACT
Until 1950, Sherman Act prosecutions tended to be relatively effective against collusive actions by separate firms in interstate commerce—situations involving, for example, price-fixing, and agreements to share markets, to boycott suppliers, or to assign market territories. On the other hand, individual firms were left relatively free, even if large and dominant. Treatment of individual large firms shifted somewhat after the government successfully prosecuted the Aluminum Company of America (ALCOA) in 1945. The court agreed with the prosecution that the firm's market share was

large enough to constitute a monopoly, and that ALCOA had delib-erately undertaken to achieve this monopoly. This case provided a basis for successful antitrust actions against United Shoe Machin-ery Company in 1954 and against American Telephone and Tele-graph (AT&T) in 1982. In the AT&T case, the telephone industry was drastically reorganized. The various regional operating compa-nies became independent, and entry into long-distance phone ser-vices was opened up for new competitors. The government's ability to block the formation of giant-firm monopoly was strengthened in 1950, when Congress passed the Celler-Kefauver Antimerger Act, which gave the government stronger authority to block merg-ers that seemed to threaten to produce monopoly.

Paul B. Trescott

SOURCES FOR FURTHER STUDY

Blair, Roger D., and David L. Kaserman. *Antitrust Economics*. Home-wood, Ill.: Irwin, 1985.

Kintner, Earl W., ed. *Federal Antitrust Laws and Related Statutes: A Legislative History*. Buffalo, N.Y.: William S. Hein, 1978.

Kovaleff, Theodore P., ed. *The Antitrust Impulse: An Economic, Histor-ical, and Legal Analysis*. 2 vols. Armonk, N.Y.: M. E. Sharpe, 1994.

Letwin, William L. *Law and Economic Policy in America: The Evolution of the Sherman Act*. New York: Random House, 1956.

Shenefield, John H. *The Antitrust Laws: A Primer*. 3d ed. Washing-ton, D.C.: American Enterprise Institute, 1998.

Sherman, Roger. *Antitrust Policies and Issues*. Reading, Mass.: Addi-son-Wesley, 1978.

Thorelli, Hans. *The Federal Antitrust Policy: Origination of an Ameri-can Tradition*. Baltimore: The Johns Hopkins University Press, 1955.

Walker, Albert H. *History of the Sherman Law of the United States of America*. Westport, Conn.: Greenwood, 1980.

Whitney, Simon N. *Antitrust Policies: American Experience in Twenty Industries*. 2 vols. New York: Twentieth Century Fund, 1958.

SEE ALSO: Interstate Commerce Act (1887); Federal Trade Com-mission Act (1914); Clayton Antitrust Act (1914); Celler-Kefauver Act (1950); Parens Patriae Act (1974); Antitrust Procedures and Penalties Act (1974).

DISFRANCHISEMENT LAWS

DATE: August, 1890
CATEGORIES: African Americans; Civil Rights and Liberties; Voting
and Elections

*In August, 1890, the Mississippi legislature passed laws that effec-
tively eliminated the black vote in the state.*

At the end of the nineteenth century, Mississippi and South Carolina had the largest black populations in the United States. In
1890, fifty-seven of every hundred Mississippians were black. The
Fifteenth Amendment to the U.S. Constitution (ratified in 1870)
provided that no state could deny the right to vote on account of
race; thus, Mississippi had a large black electorate. During the
early 1870's, Mississippi voters elected hundreds of black officeholders, including members of Congress, state legislators, sheriffs,
county clerks, and justices of the peace. In the mid-1870's, white
Democrats launched a counteroffensive, using threats, violence,
and fraud to neutralize the African American vote. After 1875, very
few blacks held office in Mississippi.

CIRCUMVENTING THE FIFTEENTH AMENDMENT

By 1890, many politicians in Mississippi were calling for a convention to write a new constitution for the state. They complained that
although only a small number of African Americans were voting,
this small number could prove decisive in close elections. Many
white leaders worked toward a new constitution with provisions
that effectively would disfranchise black voters. It would be difficult to draft such provisions, however, without running afoul of the
Fifteenth Amendment.

The state's two senators illustrated the divisions of opinion that
were so widespread among white Mississippians. Senator Edward
C. Walthall argued against a constitutional convention, warning
that it would only excite political passions for no good purpose.
He felt certain there was no way to eliminate black political participation without violating the Fifteenth Amendment, and that
if Mississippi made such an attempt, the U.S. government would

show new interest in enforcing African American voting rights. On the other hand, Senator James George attacked the old constitution, claiming that it had been drafted by carpetbaggers and ignorant former slaves. George urged that the "best citizens" should now take the opportunity to draft a new state constitution. He warned that black voting could revive unless the state took measures to reduce the black electorate by provisions of the state's highest law.

A bill calling a constitutional convention passed both houses of the state legislature in 1888, but Governor Robert Lowry vetoed it, warning that it was better to accept the state's existing problems than to run the risk of creating new ones by tampering with the state's constitution. Two years later, a similar bill passed both houses of the legislature, and the new governor, John M. Stone, signed the law. Election for delegates was set for July 29, 1890. The voters would elect 134 delegates, 14 of them from the state at large and the rest apportioned among the counties.

The state's weak Republican Party (to which many African Americans adhered as the party that had freed them from slavery) decided not to field a slate of candidates for at-large delegates. In heavily black Bolivar County, Republicans did offer a local delegate slate with one black and one white candidate. In Jasper County, the white Republican candidate for delegate, F. M. B. "Marsh" Cook, was assassinated while riding alone on a country road. In two black-majority counties, the Democrats allowed white conservative Republicans onto their candidate slates. In several counties, Democrats split into two factions and offered the voters a choice of two Democratic tickets. As it turned out, the constitutional convention was made up almost exclusively of white Democrats. The membership included only three Republicans, three delegates elected as independents, and one member of an agrarian third party. Only one of the 134 delegates was black: Isaiah T. Montgomery of Bolivar County.

THE MISSISSIPPI PLAN

Delegates elected the conservative lawyer Solomon S. Calhoon as president of the convention and immediately set about their work. Convention members had no shortage of ideas on how to limit the suffrage almost exclusively to whites without violating the Fifteenth Amendment. Some suggested that voters must own land, which few African Americans in Mississippi did. Others favored literacy tests, since African Americans, only a generation removed from slavery, had had fewer educational opportunities than whites and therefore were often illiterate.

As finally devised, the Mississippi plan for disfranchisement had a number of parts, the most important of which were a literacy test and a poll tax. Under the literacy test, the would-be voter must either be able to read or to explain a part of the state constitution when it was read to him. This latter provision, the so-called "understanding clause," was included as a loophole for illiterate whites. Delegates knew that voting registrars could give easy questions to white applicants and exceedingly difficult ones to African Americans. The poll tax provision stated that a person must pay a poll tax of at least two dollars per year, for at least two years in succession, in order to qualify to vote. The voter would have to pay these taxes well in advance of the election and keep the receipt. The tax was quite burdensome in a state where tenant farmers often earned less than fifty dollars in cash per year. Because Mississippi's African Americans were often tenant farmers, poorer than their white counterparts, it was thought they would give up the right to vote rather than pay this new tax.

DISCRIMINATORY IMPACT

In a notable speech, the black Republican delegate, Isaiah T. Montgomery, announced that he would vote for these new suffrage provisions. He noted that race relations in the state had grown tense and that black political participation in the state had often led whites to react violently. His hope now, Montgomery explained, was that black disfranchisement would improve race relations and as the years passed, perhaps more African Americans would be permitted to vote. The new constitution passed the convention with only eight dissenting votes; it was not submitted to the voters for their ratification.

The new suffrage provisions went into effect just before the 1892 elections. The new voter registration requirements disfranchised the great majority of African Americans in the state; they also resulted in the disfranchisement of about fifty-two thousand whites. The new registration resulted in a list of seventy thousand white voters and only nine thousand African American voters. The predominantly black state Republican Party had won 26 percent of the vote for its presidential candidate in 1888; after the new registration, in 1892, the Republican standard-bearer won less than 3 percent.

Under the Constitution of 1890, Mississippi had an almost exclusively white electorate for three-quarters of a century. This constitution served as a model for other Southern states, which eagerly copied the literacy test, the understanding clause, and the poll tax into their state constitutions. Only after passage of new laws by the U.S. Congress in 1964 and 1965 would African American voters again make their strength felt in southern elections.

Stephen Cresswell

SOURCES FOR FURTHER STUDY

Cresswell, Stephen. *Multiparty Politics in Mississippi, 1877-1902.* Jackson: University Press of Mississippi, 1995.

Kirwan, Albert D. *Revolt of the Rednecks: Mississippi Politics, 1876-1925.* Lexington: University Press of Kentucky, 1951.

Kousser, J. Morgan. *The Shaping of Southern Politics: Suffrage Restriction and the Establishment of the One-Party South, 1880-1910.* New Haven, Conn.: Yale University Press, 1974.

McLemore, Richard Aubrey, ed. *A History of Mississippi.* Hattiesburg: University and College Press of Mississippi, 1973.

Stone, James H. "A Note on Voter Registration Under the Mississippi Understanding Clause, 1892." *Journal of Southern History* 38 (1972): 293-296.

SEE ALSO: Black Codes of 1804-1807 (1804-1807); Black Codes of 1865 (1865); Thirteenth Amendment (1865); Civil Rights Act of 1866 (1866); Reconstruction Acts (1867); Fourteenth Amendment (1868); Ku Klux Klan Acts (1870-1871); Jim Crow laws (1880's-1954); Disfranchisement laws (1890); Civil Rights Act of 1960 (1960); Twenty-fourth Amendment (1964); Voting Rights Act of 1965 (1965); Voting Rights Act of 1975 (1975).

MORRILL LAND GRANT ACT OF 1890

ALSO KNOWN AS: Agricultural College Act; Land Grant Act of 1890; Second Morrill Act
DATE: August 30, 1890
U.S. STATUTES AT LARGE: 26 Stat. 419
U.S. CODE: 7 § 321
CATEGORIES: African Americans; Agriculture; Education; Land Management

The second Morrill Act expanded the land-grant colleges established by the first Morrill Act, supporting the establishment of higher education for African Americans.

In 1862, Congress passed the first Morrill Land Grant Act to authorize the establishment of a land-grant institution in each state to educate citizens in agriculture, mechanic arts, home economics, and other practical professions. Because of the emphasis on agriculture and mechanic arts, these institutions were referred to as A&M colleges. Because of the legal separation of the races in the South, African Americans were not permitted to attend these original land-grant institutions. This situation was rectified in 1890, when Congress passed the second Morrill Land Grant Act, expanding the 1862 system of land-grant colleges to provide support for the establishment of African American institutions of higher learning in states that lacked such facilities.

Each of the southern states that did not have an African American college by 1890 established one or more under the second Morrill Land Grant Act. The 1890 institutions evolved into a major educational resource for the United States. For more than a century, these institutions have provided the principal means of access to higher education for African Americans. They continue to be a major source of African American leaders who render valuable service to their communities, the nation, and the world.

Alvin K. Benson

SOURCES FOR FURTHER STUDY
Cross, Coy F., II. *Justin Smith Morrill: Father of the Land-Grant Colleges.* East Lansing: Michigan State University, 1999.

Hyman, Harold M. *American Singularity: The 1787 Northwest Ordinance, the 1862 Homestead and Morrill Acts, and the 1944 G.I. Bill.* Athens: University of Georgia Press, 1986.

James, Edmund Janes. *The Origin of the Land Grant Act of 1862 (the So-Called Morrill Act) and Some Account of Its Author, Jonathan B. Turner.* Urbana-Champaign, Ill.: University Press, 1910.

Nevins, Allan. *The Origins of the Land-Grant Colleges and State Universities: A Brief Account of the Morrill Act of 1862 and Its Results.* Washington, D.C.: Civil War Centennial Commission, 1962.

SEE ALSO: Ordinance of 1785 (1785); Land Act of 1820 (1820); Preemption Act (1841); Homestead Act (1862); Morrill Land Grant Act of 1890 (1890); G.I. Bill (1944).

DINGLEY TARIFF

ALSO KNOWN AS: Tariff Act of 1924
DATE: July 24, 1897
U.S. STATUTES AT LARGE: 30 Stat. 207
CATEGORIES: Business, Commerce, and Trade; Tariffs and Taxation

Successful protective tariff policies of the late 1890's become the focus of criticism after 1900.

One of the most controversial political issues of the late nineteenth century was the protective tariff. Republicans argued that high customs duties on imports to the United States protected U.S. businesses from foreign competition and provided jobs to farmers and workers. Democrats countered that the policy raised prices to consumers and favored some businesses at the expense of others. The tariff became a key issue dividing the two major parties, with the Republicans united behind protection and most Democrats advocating lower tariffs. In the presidential elections of 1888 and 1892, the two parties offered very different approaches to trade policy. The Republicans received support for protectionism in 1888; the Democrats elected Grover Cleveland in part on the promise of lower tariffs in 1892.

PROTECTIONISM VS. LOWER TARIFFS

Republicans enacted the protective McKinley Tariff in 1890 and saw their control of the House of Representatives vanish as voters rejected the higher prices associated with the law. When the Democrats regained the White House in 1893 under President Cleveland, they endeavored to pass a law to lower the tariff. Divisions within the party over other issues and the onset of the economic depression of the 1890's made it difficult for the Democrats to agree on a reform law. The result was the Wilson-Gorman Tariff of 1894, which lowered rates somewhat but also made concessions to protectionist sentiment within the Democratic Party in order to get a bill through Congress. Cleveland let the bill become law without his signature, and the Republicans hammered away at the measure in the congressional elections of 1894. When the Republicans regained the House of Representatives in that year, they promised that if a Republican president were elected in 1896, the tariff would be revised upward.

HAMMERING OUT THE TARIFF

The Republican nominee in 1896 was William McKinley, who had long been associated with the protective tariff in the House of Representatives. By this time, however, McKinley had decided that it would be wise to include a policy of reciprocal trade whereby the United States would moderate its tariff rates in return for concessions from other trading partners. The new president was not a free-trader. Reciprocity would occur within the protective system, but he envisioned an expansion of trade with this approach.

After he defeated William Jennings Bryan in 1896, McKinley urged Congress to move ahead quickly on a tariff law. He summoned the lawmakers into session in March, 1897. Advance planning meant that the House could act quickly on the tariff. The chairman of the House Ways and Means Committee, Nelson Dingley, reported out a new tariff bill, called the Dingley Tariff, on March 18, three days after the session opened. The Speaker of the House, Thomas B. Reed, used the power of the Republican majority to push the bsill through within three weeks of the opening of the session.

The situation was more complex in the Senate, where Republican control was less secure. There the Dingley Tariff became entangled with another issue. To achieve a greater use of silver in international trade, the United States had opened negotiations with

France about an agreement on a policy known as international bimetallism. The French indicated interest in helping the United States if they could receive some concessions for their products in the new tariff bill. These elements led Nelson Aldrich, chair of the Senate Finance Committee, to produce an initial tariff measure in the Senate that recognized French desires, including lower rates on French luxury products.

As time passed, however, the various interest groups within the Republican coalition increased the pressure for higher tariff rates. The result was a bill that raised duties on such products as wool and woolen clothing, while hiking rates on French items such as silks, gloves, and olive oil. When the bill became more protectionist, Senate supporters of international bimetallism pushed the idea of tariff reciprocity treaties as a way of promising future concessions to France and other nations. The Senate bill, as passed on July 7, included language that allowed the president to negotiate treaties for a reduction of up to 20 percent on the duties in the Dingley bill.

FINAL PROVISIONS
The conference committee of the House and Senate leaned more toward the protectionist side. The final bill retained the raised duties on wool, silk, and other products of concern to France. There was wording that allowed the president to offer countries reductions on specific items and to negotiate reciprocal trade treaties as well. The bill came out of conference on July 19, and both houses approved it by July 24, 1897. Despite not having a dependable majority in the Senate, the Republicans had passed a tariff bill quickly and with little intraparty friction. The French initiative on international bimetallism collapsed later in the summer, for reasons unrelated to the passage of the Dingley Tariff.

ARGUMENTS FOR RECIPROCITY
Public reaction to the bill was quiet. The returning prosperity of the summer of 1897 made the action of the Republican Congress seem appropriate. Although President McKinley tried to use the reciprocity sections of the law during the remainder of his term, and negotiated agreements with France, Jamaica, Argentina, and other nations, the strength of protectionist sentiment on Capitol Hill limited his accomplishments. In his last public speech, on September 5, 1901, in Buffalo, New York, McKinley argued for reci-

procity as a policy of the future and sought to guide public opinion to tolerance of freer trade. The next day he was shot and, with his death on September 14, 1901, reciprocity waned. The new president, Theodore Roosevelt, proved willing to let Congress have its way on the tariff.

Until 1900, the Dingley Tariff enjoyed general political acceptance. As the return of prosperity following the Spanish-American War became more apparent, consumer prices rose and inflation became an issue. The rise of large corporations and public fears about the trusts also were associated with the protective policy. Democrats charged that the tariff law had stimulated the growth of giant corporations and raised prices that average citizens had to pay. Within the ranks of the Republicans, sentiment to reform the tariff law grew, especially in the plains states of the Midwest. Party regulars remained steadfast in support of the law, and an internal dispute about the tariff marked the history of the Republicans during the first decade of the twentieth century.

LATER TARIFFS

In the presidential election of 1908, public pressure and the attacks of the Democrats led the Republicans to promise a revision of the tariff following the outcome of the race for the White House. The winner, William Howard Taft, followed through on this commitment and set in motion events that led to the enactment of the Payne-Aldrich Tariff of 1909. The controversy that stemmed from that event led, in turn, to a split in the Republican Party and the election of Democrat Woodrow Wilson in 1912. After Wilson took office, the Democratic Congress passed the Underwood Tariff in 1913, which lowered rates and finally replaced the Dingley Tariff completely.

The Republicans achieved substantial political benefits from the Dingley Tariff during the McKinley administration. After 1901, it became a source of persistent friction and opposition internally and from the Democrats. In that period, the law gained its enduring historical reputation as the embodiment of the high protective tariff policies associated with the Republican Party during the last twenty-five years of the nineteenth century.

*Lewis L. Gould, based on the
original entry by Anne Trotter*

SOURCES FOR FURTHER STUDY
Becker, William H. *The Dynamics of Business-Government Relations: Industry and Exports, 1893-1921.* Chicago: University of Chicago Press, 1982.
Gould, Lewis L. "Diplomats in the Lobby: Franco-American Relations and the Dingley Tariff of 1897." *Historian* 39 (August, 1977): 659-680.
_____. *The Presidency of William McKinley.* Lawrence: University Press of Kansas, 1980.
Taussig, Frank W. *The Tariff History of the United States.* New York: Augustus M. Kelley, 1967.
Terrill, Tom E. *The Tariff, Politics, and American Foreign Policy.* Westport, Conn.: Greenwood Press, 1973.
Wolman, Paul. *Most Favored Nation: The Republican Revisionists and U.S. Tariff Policy, 1897-1912.* Chapel Hill: University of North Carolina Press, 1992.

SEE ALSO: Payne-Aldrich Tariff Act (1909); Smoot-Hawley Tariff Act (1930).

TREATY OF PARIS

DATE: Signed December 10, 1898; Senate ratified February 6, 1899
CATEGORIES: Foreign Relations; Treaties and Agreements

The 1898 Treaty of Paris closed the Spanish-American War and ceded overseas territory to the United States.

Although traditionally anti-imperialist, America became increasingly interested in obtaining overseas colonies by the late nineteenth century. The remnants of Spain's once massive empire in the Western Hemisphere, now reduced to Cuba and Puerto Rico, seemed an attractive target. A Cuban rebellion against Spanish rule attracted American sympathy and prompted the trip of the battleship USS *Maine* to Cuba in February, 1898, to demonstrate American interest in the situation. When the *Maine* mysteriously exploded (killing 260 Americans), Americans believed Spain was responsible and demanded vengeance. Congress declared war a month later, and America moved to expel Spain from Cuba. Despite some military shortcomings, the United States defeated the Spanish garrison at Santiago, Cuba, and destroyed a small squadron of Spanish ships based there. American troops occupied Puerto Rico with little opposition, and American ships under the command of Commodore George Dewey destroyed Spanish naval power in the Philippine Islands and established American control there as well. Defeated on every front, Spain agreed to an armistice on August 12, 1898, and peace talks began in Paris.

OBSTACLES TO PEACE
While America's military had clearly defeated Spain on the battlefield and Cuban independence was also clearly presumed, two large hurdles to a formal peace agreement remained. First was the issue of the Philippines, which Spain was reluctant to give up. Spain agreed to grant independence to Cuba and cede Puerto Rico to the United States, as the cost of maintaining these islands exceeded the profits the islands generated. The Philippines, however, was another matter. Although facing a local rebellion, Spain had maintained strong control over the islands and the land remained profitable. Also, while Spain was willing to cede the two Caribbean islands, giving up the massive Philippine Archipelago (containing hundreds of islands) was too much for Spanish pride to bear. Only when the United States threatened to void the armistice and renew the war did Spain agree to American demands, signing the Treaty of Paris on December 10, 1898.

The other hurdle was the American Congress, where strong anti-imperialist elements in the Senate threatened to defeat the treaty's ratification. The anti-imperialists feared that empire would corrupt American values and possibly drag the United States into future wars around the world. American jingoism, however, overcame anti-imperialist efforts, and the Senate ratified the Treaty of Paris by a single vote on February 6, 1899.

TERMS OF THE TREATY
Under the terms of the treaty, Cuba became an independent country, although the Platt Amendment (1903) gave the United States rights to intervene in Cuban affairs at any time, essentially reduc-

ing Cuba to the status of an American protectorate until the United States abrogated the Platt Amendment in 1934. Spain ceded to the United States control of Puerto Rico, the Philippines, and the island of Guam. As compensation for the loss of the Philippines, the United States paid Spain $20 million. The United States inherited the Philippine rebellion along with the islands, and subsequent efforts to suppress the rebel Filipinos took another three years, costing 4,300 American and approximately 600,000 Filipino lives.

Steven J. Ramold

SOURCES FOR FURTHER STUDY
Blow, Michael. *A Ship to Remember: The Maine and the Spanish-American War.* New York: Morrow, 1992.
Millis, Walter. *The Martial Spirit: A Study of Our War with Spain.* New York: Houghton Mifflin, 1931.

SEE ALSO: Platt Amendment (1903); Jones Act (1917).

CURRENCY ACT

ALSO KNOWN AS: Gold Standard Act
DATE: March 14, 1900
U.S. STATUTES AT LARGE: 31 Stat. 45
CATEGORIES: Banking, Money, and Finance

The Currency Act reestablished the "gold standard" and stabilized the dollar after a period of economic upheaval.

In 1879, following the monetary disorder of the Civil War, the United States returned to a formal gold standard. Gold coins circulated, and bank deposits and paper currency could be freely exchanged for gold. A declining price level created many economic hardships, especially for farmers.

FREE SILVER DEBATE

Agitation arose for a more expansionary monetary policy and focused on coinage of silver as the means. Silver producers were a powerful lobby, pressuring the government to permit unlimited coinage of silver (at the initiative of private silver producers) at favorable values. The policy would increase the money supply and raise prices. Opponents feared a return to the inflationary monetary conditions of the Civil War. The issue was central to the presidential election of 1896. Democrat William Jennings Bryan advocated the "free silver" program but lost the election to Republican William McKinley, who opposed it.

One purpose of the Currency Act of 1900 was to solidify the position of gold in the monetary system. The law created a monometallic system with the dollar equivalent to 25.8 grains of gold, nine-tenths fine, equivalent to a price of $20.67 an ounce. The government would continue to issue silver coins, but in limited supply, so that their monetary value could exceed the market value of their silver content without inflationary results. To maintain government-issued paper currency and silver coins at parity with gold, the law provided for the Treasury to maintain a reserve fund of $150 million in gold.

Paper currency was also issued by national banks under federal supervision, and the law contained several provisions to increase the supply of this type of currency. Minimum capital required to start a national bank was reduced. National banks were allowed to issue more notes for a given amount of government securities which they held as security. Tax rates on national banks were reduced.

FOREIGN INVESTORS

The silver agitation of the 1890's had been very damaging to the international financial position of the United States. Foreign investors feared that the value of the dollar would fall. The Currency Act of 1900 eliminated this threat. As a result, funds flooded into the United States for investment in railroads, steel mills, petroleum refineries. The new law also helped produce a large increase in national banknotes, from $265 million in 1900 to $614 million in 1908. More than three thousand new national banks opened over that period.

However, the monetary and banking system still possessed serious defects, which were dramatized by financial panic in 1907. In response, the government adopted the Federal Reserve Act in 1913. The gold standard did not prevent severe inflation during World War I, and its shortcomings became painfully evident during the disastrous economic downswing of 1929-1933 known as the Great Depression. The United States and other nations adopted severely deflationary policies to maintain gold parities. The gold standard was essentially abolished by President Franklin D. Roosevelt in 1933. Issue of national-bank-note currency was discontinued in 1935.

Paul B. Trescott

SOURCES FOR FURTHER STUDY
Studenski, Paul, and Herman E. Krooss. *Financial History of the United States.* 2d ed. New York: McGraw-Hill, 1963.
Timberlake, Richard H. *Monetary Policy in the United States.* Chicago: University of Chicago Press, 1993.
Trescott, Paul B. *Money, Banking, and Economic Welfare.* New York: McGraw-Hill, 1960.

SEE ALSO: Independent Treasury Act (1846); National Bank Acts (1863-1864); Bland-Allison Act (1878); Currency Act (1900); Federal Reserve Act (1913).

DIRECT DEMOCRACY LAWS

DATE: June 2, 1902-May 31, 1913
CATEGORIES: Civil Rights and Liberties; Voting and Elections

During the first decade of the twentieth century, a slate of both state and federal measures were passed to increase the political tools of direct citizen involvement in government.

Although the Declaration of Independence asserted that all "men" are created equal and, in later years, Abraham Lincoln movingly spoke of government as being "of, by, and for" the people, there was a gap between such sentiments and political realities. Admittedly, by 1890 the franchise included all male citizens. Women, however, were excluded except in a few Western states, and even the enfranchised found their prerogatives circumscribed. They were unable to vote directly for their United States senators and lacked legal methods to force recalcitrant legislatures to take specific action or to rid themselves of unsuitable elected public officials before their terms ended. Clearly something had to be done to make government at all levels more responsive to the will of the people.

The Progressive movement provided the vehicle for change as it initially sought to bring about reforms on the municipal and state levels. Among those responsible for reform were Wisconsin's Robert La Follette and the virtually forgotten William U'Ren of Oregon. They were joined in their attempts to alter state government by hoards of urban reformers who realized that the city was so tied to the state that in order to correct fully the basic problems of the former, the latter had to be changed as well.

SECRET BALLOT

In one respect the burden was eased by an earlier reform—the Australian, or secret, ballot—whose ramifications were just beginning to be recognized fully. This new form of voting replaced the older system, under which different colored ballots, printed by the political parties or independent candidates, were distributed to the voters, who then deposited them in the proper box under the watchful eyes of their employers' representatives or the local political boss. Obviously the old system protected those in power. Fraud, bribery, and corruption were rampant. In an attempt to end these evils, Massachusetts adopted the secret ballot in 1888. Through the efforts of such individuals as Grover Cleveland, the system was used nationwide by the election of 1910. Additionally, many Progressive states enacted corrupt-practices laws and limited the amount of money a candidate could spend. Similar federal laws followed.

PRIMARY ELECTIONS

The early twentieth century also saw the election of the first great reform governor when La Follette bested the ruling Republican machine in Wisconsin. During his years in office, 1901-1906, he transformed that state into a Progressive commonwealth, a "laboratory of democracy." A major accomplishment was to give the voter increased control over the nomination of candidates for public office. On May 23, 1903, Wisconsin held the first statewide primary to select those who would run in the general election. The primary abolished the old boss-dominated party caucus which had previously chosen the candidates.

INITIATIVE, REFERENDUM, AND RECALL

La Follette's actions seemed to trigger a chain reaction across the West. In 1904 a young reformer, Joseph W. Folk, smashed the unusually corrupt machine running Missouri to become governor. Slowly but surely traditional frontier democracy, lost in the Gilded Age, reasserted itself as some states enfranchised women and almost all enacted fundamental political reforms. Nowhere was this trend more apparent than in Oregon, home of the little-known William U'Ren, who indirectly affected national political life as did few of his more famous contemporaries.

U'Ren, a blacksmith turned newspaper editor and lawyer, never held a major political office, yet because of his ability to marshal public opinion was the unofficial fourth branch of Oregon's government. He first became interested in direct democracy in the 1890's, after reading of its use in Switzerland, and spent a large part of his time working to introduce it into Oregon and the rest of the nation. Oregon adopted the initiative and referendum on June 2, 1902, the direct primary in 1904, and the recall in 1910, thereby putting direct democracy into practice.

Initiative and referendum made it possible for a majority vote of the electorate to pass laws when the legislature was unable or unwilling to do so, and to veto unpopular legislation. Recall allowed an elected official to be promptly removed if a majority of citizens were displeased with the person's conduct. This device was most often adopted in states west of the Mississippi, where its threat was generally sufficient to bring an official into line. Initiative and referendum, being less tinged with "radicalism" than recall, were usually adopted by the more conservative Eastern states.

DIRECT ELECTION OF SENATORS

Another drive occurring simultaneously was aimed at amending the U.S. Constitution to allow a direct vote for U.S. senators. The Constitution provided for their election by state legislatures as a means of removing the Senate from direct control by the "rabble." By the late nineteenth century, however, the office had become an item to be purchased like a loaf of bread. In 1907 Simon Guggenheim shocked the nation by publicly declaring what he had spent for the office in Colorado. As the stronghold of special privilege, the Senate had opposed and often thwarted Progressive measures such as tariff revision, the abolition of child labor, and revision of the method for selecting U.S. senators. Realizing that an amendment was out of the question, several Western states began holding primary elections to select Senate nominees. In some states the legislature was bound to abide by the decision of the voters. In 1912, with twenty-nine states using this device to circumvent the Constitution and public pressure for change mounting, the Senate reluctantly yielded and submitted an amendment to the states. The Seventeenth Amendment, providing for direct election of senators, was ratified on May 31, 1913.

With this ratification the major political reforms proposed by the Progressives had been accomplished. The responsibilities of the electorate had been dramatically enlarged. Control over the quality of government was now in the hands of the voter. The only question remaining was how the new powers would be exercised.

Anne Trotter

SOURCES FOR FURTHER STUDY

Cronin, Thomas E. *Direct Democracy: The Politics of Initiative, Referendum, and Recall.* Cambridge, Mass.: Harvard University Press, 1989.

Goldman, Eric F. *Rendezvous with Destiny.* New York: Alfred A. Knopf, 1952.

Hofstadter, Richard. *The Age of Reform: From Bryan to F. D. R.* New York: Alfred A. Knopf, 1955.

La Follette, Robert M. *Autobiography.* Madison: University of Wisconsin Press, 1911.

Mowry, George E. *The California Progressives.* Berkeley: University of California Press, 1951.

_____. *The Era of Theodore Roosevelt, 1900-1912.* New York: Harper & Row, 1958.

Nye, Russel B. *Midwestern Progressive Politics, 1870-1958.* Ann Arbor: University of Michigan Press, 1959.

Schmidt, David D. *Citizen Lawmakers: The Ballot Initiative Revolution.* Philadelphia: Temple University Press, 1989.

SEE ALSO: Seventeenth Amendment (1913); Nineteenth Amendment (1920); Twenty-third Amendment (1961); Twenty-sixth Amendment (1971).

RECLAMATION ACT

ALSO KNOWN AS: Newlands Act
DATE: June 17, 1902
U.S. STATUTES AT LARGE: 32 Stat. 388
CATEGORIES: Agriculture; Land Management; Natural Resources

The 1902 Reclamation Act provided for federal development of irrigated agriculture and eventually transformed the Western United States.

On June 17, 1902, the Reclamation Act (sometimes called the Newlands Act) became law after more than twenty years of discussion and failed federal land policy. Before 1902, irrigation and reclamation policies in the arid West were mostly aimed at promoting private and state initiatives to develop irrigated agriculture. The act represented the first of several conservation initiatives by the Theodore Roosevelt administration and set a precedent for active federal investment and direction of natural resources management.

ARID LANDS OF THE WEST

In 1878, John Wesley Powell's *Report on the Lands of the Arid Region of the United States* laid the groundwork for land classification according to land's capability to produce different kinds of goods and services. Early federal land policy initiatives such as the Homestead Act of 1862 and the Desert Land Act of 1877 failed to grasp both the scope of the problem of aridity and the cooperative approaches that would be required to overcome it. Powell proposed that federal lands be classified according to their best use and disposed of based on that classification. He suggested organizing lands and local governments on a watershed basis, providing homesteads of 2,560 acres that included a mix of irrigable land and rangeland, and creating cooperative irrigation districts.

Powell's ideas proved unpopular with Congress because they were at odds with the traditional image of the hearty, independent settler. Yet the Reclamation Act of 1902, which was passed a few months before Powell's death, incorporated many of his ideas. Public land scholars have come to recognize his report as one of the most significant documents in American conservation history.

WATER-RESOURCES INVENTORY

In 1888, Congress authorized the first water-resources inventory of the arid West. Frederick H. Newell, an assistant hydraulic engineer (and later chief hydrographer) of the U.S. Geological Survey, took charge of the project and set out to measure water supplies, survey potential dam and canal sites, and calculate the area of potentially irrigable land. Congress had authorized Powell, the director of the U.S. Geological Survey, to reserve all such sites from entry under the public land laws. Powell's reservation of 127 reservoir sites and 30 million acres of potentially irrigable public land angered Western congressmen. In 1890, Congress restored the right of entry to all the withdrawn land except that required for dam and reservoir sites.

Private funding of irrigation efforts had largely come to a halt by the mid-1890's. The most profitable sites had already been developed, and many private projects failed in the financial panic of 1893. State efforts to develop irrigation districts in California and Colorado met with little success. In 1894, Congress passed the Carey Act, which granted one million acres to each Western state to promote irrigation. The grants resulted in few projects, however, because there was limited available financing. A coalition that supported federal financing of reclamation projects eventually emerged among scientists such as Newell and Powell and Western economic development interests.

NEWLANDS AND THE ROOSEVELT ADMINISTRATION

Francis G. Newlands came to Nevada in the late 1880's to manage the estate of his wealthy father-in-law, Senator William Sharon. Nevada was rapidly losing population as a result of the end of the silver boom. Newlands recognized irrigated agriculture as one method to promote economic stability, and he became a principal in a privately financed project in the Truckee basin. The project failed, and Newlands suffered a financial loss; in the process, however, he had investigated and acquired many of the potential reservoir sites in the state, which he offered to sell to water-users' associations. Upon his election to the House of Representatives, he became one of the principal promoters of federal financing of irrigation and a prominent member of the National Irrigation Congress, an influential interest group that promoted reclamation.

Upon the assassination of William McKinley in 1901, Theodore Roosevelt became president. Roosevelt had already become familiar with Western land and water issues through his experience as a gentleman rancher in North Dakota. A progressive Republican, Roosevelt also recognized the political advantages that he might reap from running against large corporate interests and supporting public efforts to conserve natural resources. As governor of New York, he had advocated scientific management of natural resources and had already established a relationship with Newell and Gifford Pinchot, a leader of the forest-conservation movement.

At the prompting of Newell and Pinchot, Roosevelt made reclamation and forest conservation a major theme in his first address to Congress. Given new support from the president, Newlands's proposals gained momentum. His bill authorized federal funding of irrigation projects through a reclamation fund composed of proceeds from the sale of Western public lands. The bill gave the secretary of the interior discretion in selecting and constructing projects and withdrew the reclaimed areas from all but homestead entries. To promote development of family farms, Newlands included a provision that limited each individual to water rights for eighty acres. Newlands's intent was to deny speculation in the federal projects and to reinforce the ideal of the yeoman farmer.

Newlands's bill was opposed by Western representatives who wanted a larger water-rights acreage limitation and who wanted the lands to be open to other than merely homestead entries. Newlands compromised and raised the limitation to 160 acres, but the bill was defeated in the House. A rival measure with few of Newlands's provisions passed the Senate in early 1902, and Newlands introduced a new version of his bill. Roosevelt convinced the Senate to incorporate much of Newlands's language into an amended Senate version, and the Reclamation Act became law on June 17, 1902.

IMPACT OF THE ACT

Perhaps no single law has had a greater effect on the Western United States than the Reclamation Act of 1902. The projects that eventually evolved under the Bureau of Reclamation transformed the face and economy of half a continent. El Paso, Denver, Tucson, Phoenix, Los Angeles, and Salt Lake City could not have grown into great metropolises without the massive water developments and associated hydroelectricity made possible by the act. The agricultural and manufacturing economies of the Western states would also be wholly different without the act and the work it engendered.

Yet this transformation came at a substantial environmental price. The increased salinization of irrigated lands, the degradation of the Colorado River delta, the demise of salmon stocks in the Pacific Northwest, and the loss of biological diversity caused by conversion of unregulated rivers to reservoirs are some of the broader costs of irrigated agriculture and hydroelectric power production.

These costs must be balanced against the benefits that the Western states and the nation as a whole have derived from economic development. In fiscal year 1992, the Bureau of Reclamation delivered 30 million acre-feet of water to 28 million people and irrigated close to 10 million acres, producing annual crops valued at almost $9 billion. The bureau also operated fifty-two hydroelectric plants, generating 40 billion kilowatt hours, making it the eleventh-largest producer of electricity in the United States.

In addition to such obvious environmental impacts, the Reclamation Act of 1902 had a number of subtler but nevertheless important implications. Political scientists have observed that the concentration of political power among a "water aristocracy" in the Western United States is one result of the failure to implement the original policy of providing for a system of family farms. The act also set a precedent for a growing, activist federal presence in the West that directly controls or influences most forest, rangeland, and water resources in the region.

During the late 1940's, federal subsidies to reclamation programs became increasingly contentious. In the early and mid-1950's, the subsidy issue combined with an awakening environmental movement to block the construction of the Echo Park Dam, which had been proposed for Dinosaur National Monument in western Colorado.

Like other conservation programs designed during the Progressive Era, the Reclamation Act of 1902 envisioned an independent, self-financing funding mechanism to pay for efficient projects. The act had established a reclamation fund through the sale of Western federal lands. Homesteaders would repay the fund for project construction costs (without interest) within ten years of the time that water became available to them, and the repayments would then allow new projects. By 1914, all projects that could be developed within the ten-year framework had been exhausted. In subsequent acts, Congress extended the period for repayment to twenty years in 1914, to forty years in 1926, and to fifty years in 1934.

The last revision allowed for nonreimbursable allocation of project costs to flood control and navigation. This revision was subsequently interpreted to allow use of electricity-generation revenues to pay for irrigation costs that were beyond the financial ability of irrigators. Even with these provisions, however, the development and approval of projects by the secretary of the interior were limited by poor economic returns. When conservation groups, economists, and Southern California water interests combined to block construction of the Echo Park Dam and the larger Upper Colorado River Basin Project in the 1950's, it marked the end of an era and the once-potent dream of "making the desert bloom."

By the 1970's, growing environmental awareness and poor economic feasibility left the Bureau of Reclamation vulnerable to political change. One of the bureau's projects, the Teton Dam, failed on June 5, 1976, claiming eleven lives and causing damage estimated as high as $2 billion. In November, 1976, President Jimmy Carter was elected on a platform stressing environmental protection and governmental reform. In April, 1977, the Carter "hit list" successfully proposed eliminating five of the largest reclamation projects and reducing several others. In addition, the Carter administration proposed reduced budgets and several other reforms that substantially reduced the bureau's powers. Despite a political ideology that favored Western development, Carter's successor, President Ronald Reagan, implemented budget reforms that further constrained the growth of federal reclamation projects.

In the early 1980's, controversy arose over the original act's limitation on the size of farms that were eligible to receive federally subsidized water. The government failed to enforce the limitation of 160 acres per farm (320 acres per couple) and associated restrictions on leasing and residency. Attempts by the Carter administration to enforce the law led to the act's revision during the Reagan administration. The 160-acre limitation was raised to 960 acres, and growers were required to pay full cost for water used in excess of the 960-acre limit. By 1988, however, the General Accounting Office found that some farms that exceeded the limit had been divided into holdings of less than 960 acres but had continued to operate as a single unit. For example, the agency identified a 12,000-acre farm that had been divided into fifteen holdings so that it could continue to receive federally subsidized water at a savings of $500,000 per year.

One environmental problem facing many reclamation projects is that of increasing salinity. As fresh water evaporates, it may concentrate and deposit salt in the irrigated soil; the elevated salinity levels that result can retard or eliminate crop yields. By treaty, the United States must deliver water containing less than nine hundred parts per million of salt to Mexico from the Colorado River. Salinity levels have exceeded the legal limit, and the United States has built an expensive desalinization plant near Yuma, Arizona, to improve water quality.

In the San Joaquin Valley of California, a related problem has caused environmental concern. Increasing salinity prompted construction of a drainage system that concentrated used irrigation water in the Kesterson Reservoir. The reservoir acted as an artificial wetland, attracting many migratory waterfowl. In the early 1980's, biologists observed that many birds were being sickened or killed; by the mid-1980's, researchers confirmed that the cause was selenium poisoning. Selenium, a naturally occurring element in the region's soils, was being carried from irrigated soils and concentrated in the reservoir.

Overall, the Reclamation Act of 1902 proved successful in reaching its original goal of developing agriculture, commerce, and settlement in the West. The environmental consequences of that development were largely unforeseen at the time of the act's passage, but they have become increasingly problematic in the latter part of the twentieth century.

Donald W. Floyd

SOURCES FOR FURTHER STUDY
Clarke, Jeanne N., and Daniel McCool. *Staking Out the Terrain.* Albany: State University of New York Press, 1985.
Dana, Samuel T., and Sally K. Fairfax. *Forest and Range Policy.* New York: McGraw-Hill, 1980.
Hays, Samuel P. *Conservation and the Gospel of Efficiency.* Cambridge, Mass.: Harvard University Press, 1959.
Pinchot, Gifford. *Breaking New Ground.* Washington, D.C.: Island Press, 1947.
Reisner, Marc. *Cadillac Desert.* New York: Viking Penguin, 1986.
Stegner, Wallace. *Beyond the Hundredth Meridian.* Lincoln: University of Nebraska Press, 1982.
Stratton, Owen, and Phillip Sirotkin. *The Echo Park Controversy.* University: University of Alabama Press, 1959.
Wyant, William K. *Westward in Eden.* Berkeley: University of California Press, 1982.

SEE ALSO: National Park Service Organic Act (1916); Water Pollution Control Act (1948); Water Pollution Control Act Amendments of 1956 (1956); Multiple Use-Sustained Yield Act (1960); Water Resources Research Act (1964); Wilderness Act (1964); Clean Water Act and Amendments (1965); Wild and Scenic Rivers Act and National Trails System Act (1968); Water Pollution Control Act Amendments of 1972 (1972); Forest and Rangeland Renewable Resources Planning Act (1974); Federal Land Policy and Management Act (1976).

PLATT AMENDMENT

ALSO KNOWN AS: Part of the Permanent Reciprocity Treaty of 1903
DATE: Signed May 22, 1903
PUBLIC LAW: 56-803
CATEGORIES: Foreign Relations; Latinos; Treaties and Agreements

The Platt Amendment underscored Cuba's independence from Spain but at the same time secured U.S. influence in Cuba for the next three decades.

In 1895, Cuban revolutionaries initiated what was ultimately to become a successful revolt against Spanish colonial domination. The break from Spain was brought about by a variety of factors, the two most critical being the repressive nature of the colonial rule of Spain and a change in U.S. tariff policy as a result of the recessions and depressions in the United States during the 1890's. The Wilson-Gorman Tariff of 1894 imposed a duty on Cuban sugar arriving in the United States, which previously had entered duty-free. With the economy of Cuba reeling from dwindling Cuban-United States trade because of the new tariff, Cuban dissidents, who had been waiting for an opportunity to act, launched a revolution.

Led by José Martí, who had strong ties to the United States, the rebels who called for Cuban independence began a guerrilla war against the Spanish. Even after the death of Martí during the first year of fighting, the ranks of the Cuban rebel forces continued to increase. Spanish authorities responded to the groundswell of domestic support for the rebels by attempting to separate the rebels from their supporters in rural areas. Under a new policy known as reconcentration, more than a quarter-million Cubans were interred in concentration camps guarded by Spanish soldiers. Thousands of Cubans died in the camps, which served as breeding grounds for disease. U.S. sympathy for the Cuban rebels was stimulated by reports of atrocities occurring as a result of the new Spanish policy, and people in the United States began to call for an end to the conflict through reconciliation. The mysterious sinking of the battleship *Maine* in Havana harbor on February 15, 1898, ended all hope of a peaceful resolution to the conflict.

THE SPANISH-AMERICAN WAR

The sinking of the U.S. battleship, which had been ordered to Cuba in an effort to display U.S. concern for events unfolding on the island and to protect U.S. citizens, drew the United States further into the conflict. Naval investigators concluded that a Spanish mine had caused the explosion. U.S. president William McKinley responded to events by demanding that Spain grant Cuban independence. Finding the Spanish response unsatisfactory, McKinley requested on April 11, 1898, that Congress grant him authorization to stop the war in Cuba by force, if necessary. Following some debate, on April 19 Congress declared that Cuba was and should be independent, demanded an immediate withdrawal of Spain from

Cuba, authorized the use of force to accomplish that withdrawal, and vowed not to annex the island. Known as the Teller Amendment, the vow not to annex Cuba was perhaps the most controversial of the issues debated.

Despite the Teller Amendment, the entrance of the United States into the conflict initiated the beginning of an exploitive relationship between the United States and Cuba, which was dictated by the former. As the war drew to an end and Spanish withdrawal began to be realized, the United States downplayed the role of the Cuban rebels in the success of the military campaign. The Treaty of Paris, which halted the conflict, required Spain to surrender all claims to Cuba, but the McKinley administration refused to recognize the former Cuban rebels as a legitimate government or the Cuban people as being capable of self-rule. For two years, the U.S. military performed the functions of government. Although the U.S. military made substantial improvements in the infrastructure of Cuba and generally improved the quality of life on the island, Cubans resented the U.S. occupation. Many Cubans felt that they had traded one colonial master for another.

In 1900, Cubans were allowed to draft a constitution and hold elections. The United States refused to withdraw its troops, however, until provisions were made for the continuation of U.S. relations. Elihu Root, the U.S. secretary of war, proposed such provisions, which ultimately were included in a bill sponsored by Senator Orville H. Platt. Platt, a Republican from Connecticut, attached a rider to the Army Appropriations Bill of 1901 that essentially made Cuba a U.S. protectorate.

PROVISIONS OF THE PLATT AMENDMENT

The Platt Amendment, as the provisions would come to be known, severely restricted Cuba's ability to make treaties and its right to contract public debt. The United States also declared its right to intervene in Cuban affairs in order to preserve Cuban independence and maintain order. Cuba also was expected to give the United States the right to maintain naval bases and coaling stations on the island. The Cuban government reluctantly appended the provisions of the Platt Amendment to the Cuban constitution. The last U.S. forces finally withdrew from Havana in 1902. The Platt Amendment became a formal part of a U.S.-Cuba treaty on May 22, 1903.

The Platt Amendment formed the basis for United States-Cuban relations for the next sixty years, until Fidel Castro emerged as the leader of Cuba. Forced to submit to the will of the United States, Cuba was soon inundated with U.S. investment. Foreign investors controlled and manipulated Cuban politics and the economy. U.S. troops reoccupied Cuba from 1906 to 1909, under the authority of the Platt Amendment, following an uprising that protested, among other things, U.S. involvement in Cuban affairs.

THE 1930'S

The election of Franklin D. Roosevelt as U.S. president in 1933 initially brought little change in U.S.-Cuban relations, despite his "good neighbor policy," which was based on the belief that no state had the right to intervene in Latin America. Roosevelt was forced to deal with a Cuba in turmoil. President Gerardo "the Butcher" Machado y Morales, who had dominated Cuban politics for a decade, was forced to resign in 1933 because of popular opposition and U.S. pressure. His successor, Ramón Grau San Martín, was no more acceptable to the Roosevelt administration. Viewed as too radical by Roosevelt, the government of Grau was never recognized as legitimate by the U.S. administration.

It was not until Fulgencio Batista y Zaldívar led a coup and installed a government acceptable to the United States that the Roosevelt administration agreed to discuss revoking the Platt Amendment. The second Treaty of Relations, as it came to be known, eliminated the limitations on Cuban sovereignty imposed by the Platt Amendment. The new treaty did allow the United States to retain its naval base at Guantanamo Bay, which could be revoked only by mutual consent of both states.

Despite the formal end of U.S. involvement in Cuba, the new Cuba, which was controlled by Batista, was no less tied to the United States financially or politically. Batista was viewed by many international observers as a puppet for the U.S. government. Cuba attracted more U.S. investment under Batista than ever before. Many Cubans argued that despite the end of the Platt Amendment, Cuba was still a U.S. dependency. It was this sense of frustration over their inability to achieve a true sense of sovereignty that served as a catalyst for Fidel Castro's successful coup in 1959.

Donald C. Simmons, Jr.

Sources for Further Study

Abel, Christopher, and Nissa Torrents, eds. *José Martí: Revolutionary Democrat.* London: Athlone Press, 1986.

Langley, Lester D. *The Cuban Policy of the United States.* New York: Wiley, 1968.

Perez, Louis A., Jr. *Cuba: Between Reform and Revolution.* New York: Oxford University Press, 1988.

_____. *Cuba Under the Platt Amendment: 1902-1934.* Pittsburgh: University of Pittsburgh Press, 1986.

_____. *Intervention, Revolution, and Politics in Cuba, 1913-1921.* Pittsburgh: University of Pittsburgh Press, 1978.

Suchlicki, Jaime. *Cuba: From Columbus to Castro.* 3d rev. ed. Washington, D.C.: Brassey's (U.S.), 1990.

Thomas, Hugh. *Cuba: Or, The Pursuit of Freedom.* New York: Harper & Row, 1971. Perhaps the most extensive work written about the country.

See also: Treaty of Paris (1898); Good Neighbor Policy (1933).

BURKE ACT

Date: May 8, 1906
U.S. Statutes at Large: 34 Stat. 182
U.S. Code: 25 § 349
Categories: Land Management; Native Americans

Passed to improve the process of allotting tribal lands to individual American Indians, the Burke Act contributed to the large-scale loss of Indian land between 1887 and 1934.

In 1887, Congress passed the General Allotment Act (or Dawes Act). This act sought to make small farmers out of American Indians by dividing tribal lands into individual allotments. Indians taking allotments received United States citizenship; the government held the title for the lands in trust for twenty-five years, during which time they could not be sold. At the end of the period, the Indian would receive a fee patent assigning full ownership of the land.

CRITICISM OF ALLOTMENT

The administration of the General Allotment Act prompted considerable criticism. Many of those sympathetic to the Indians were concerned at the distinction between citizenship, which was taken up at the outset, and ownership, which came at the end of the trust period. The discrepancy became a source of worry in 1905 when the Supreme Court ruled that citizenship exempted an Indian from direct federal supervision, thus invalidating federal restrictions on liquor on allotments. Other people simply thought that the trust period postponed too long the time when an Indian might sell his allotment.

PROVISIONS AND IMPACT

In 1906, Congress passed the Burke Act, named for South Dakota Congressman Charles Henry Burke. The act provided that the trust period could be extended indefinitely on presidential authority, though it also permitted the secretary of the interior to cut the period short if requested by Indians who could prove competence to manage their own affairs. In either case, there would be no citizenship until the end of the trust period, during which individuals would remain subject to federal control.

The Burke Act had a major effect on the awarding of allotments, though not the one that some of its supporters had hoped. Though certificates of competency (and fee patents) were awarded cautiously at first, there were clear signs that many allotments quickly passed out of Indian possession once they could be sold or mortgaged. During the act's first decade of operation, roughly ten thousand fee patents were issued, the vast majority of allotments passing out of Indian ownership. When the ardent assimilationist Fred K. Lane became secretary of the interior in 1917, the process speeded up. Competency certificates and fee patents were often given without the requisite individual investigation, sometimes to Indians who had not asked for them. In four years twenty thousand fee patents were issued, again with much of the land quickly alienated.

During the 1920's, when Burke himself was commissioner of Indian affairs, the process slowed, but the overall trend of allotment lands passing into the hands of non-Indians continued. By 1934, when the Indian Reorganization Act finally stopped the allotment process, Indians had lost 86 million of the 138 million acres they had controlled in 1887. In the meantime the citizenship available under the Burke Act had been made redundant by Congress's grant of citizenship to all Indians in 1924.

William C. Lowe

SOURCES FOR FURTHER STUDY

Hoxie, Frederick E. *A Final Promise: The Campaign to Assimilate the Indians, 1880-1920.* Lincoln: University of Nebraska Press, 1984.

Prucha, Francis Paul, ed. *Americanizing the American Indians: Writings of the "Friends of the Indian" 1880-1900.* Lincoln: University of Nebraska Press, 1973.

Washburn, Wilcomb E. *The Assault on Indian Tribalism: The General Allotment Law (Dawes Act) of 1887.* Philadelphia: J. B. Lippincott, 1975.

SEE ALSO: General Allotment Act (1887); Indian Citizenship Act (1924); Indian Reorganization Act (1934).

PURE FOOD AND DRUGS ACT

ALSO KNOWN AS: Federal Food and Drugs Act
DATE: June 30, 1906
U.S. STATUTES AT LARGE: 34 Stat. 768
PUBLIC LAW: 59-384
U.S. CODE: 21 § 1ff.
CATEGORIES: Agriculture; Business, Commerce, and Trade; Food and Drugs; Health and Welfare

One of the earliest laws passed to protect consumer safety, this act prohibited the adulteration or mislabeling of specified food and drug products shipped in interstate or international commerce.

With the rise of the food processing and packaging industry at the end of the 1800's, consumers became increasingly concerned about the purity of their food. Ingredients that had once come from trusted local sources were now produced by machines and marketed by faceless corporations unaccountable to the public.

ADULTERATED FOOD

In 1883, Harvey Wiley became head of the U.S. Department of Agriculture's (USDA) Bureau of Chemistry. Wiley began to investigate and discover incidents of food adulteration, ranging from the use of nontoxic extenders and fillers to the presence of poisonous preservatives. Following the example of Great Britain, which had passed its first national food and drug act in 1875, Wiley began to campaign for a pure food law in the United States, but the powerful food industry lobby branded him a socialist and blocked his efforts, including an unsuccessful bill in 1889.

Despite Wiley's initial failures, public distrust of the food supply continued to mount, fomented by the deaths from botulism of U.S. soldiers who had eaten spoiled canned meat in the Spanish-American War (1898), early exposés of the meatpacking industry by William Randolph Hearst, and various other muckraking articles and pamphlets. With only scattered state regulation and none at the federal level, a "buyer beware" caveat governed food and drug consumption. Some housewives even performed their own chemical tests on their food at home to determine its makeup and quality.

Food manufacturers countered consumer concerns with advertising designed to emphasize the purity of their products, promoting them as hygienic and staging pure food fairs around the country with samples and cooking demonstrations. While such fairs were very popular and served to introduce processed food products into U.S. domestic life, consumer anxiety about manufactured food persisted.

SINCLAIR'S EXPOSÉ

In 1904, socialist journalist Upton Sinclair received a challenge from one of his editors: to investigate and write about the lives of the industrial working class. Already working on an article detailing an unsuccessful strike by meat packers in Chicago, Sinclair chose Packingtown there as his investigative site and undertook seven weeks of research, disguising himself as a stockyard worker to observe the meatpacking process at first hand. The result was *The Jungle* (1906), a novel about a family of Lithuanian immigrants destroyed by the brutality of stockyard work. The novel's story was tragic, but its true impact lay in passages graphically depicting unsanitary slaughtering and processing procedures, exposing the widespread practice of selling to the public products made from diseased and chemically tainted meats.

The horrors recounted in *The Jungle* included the sale of spoiled meat whose rot was concealed with chemicals; inclusion of rats' poisoned carcasses and feces in sausages; the prevalence of tuberculosis among workers handling meat; instances of workers falling into cooking vats, their flesh cooking off into the contents that were subsequently packaged and sold; the use of tripe, pork fat, and beef suet in potted chicken; the rechurning of rancid butter; and the treatment of milk with formaldehyde. In support of his allegations, Sinclair included footnotes quoting from the USDA's meat-inspection regulations.

Macmillan, the publisher initially contracted to publish *The Jungle*, declined to do so for fear of libel suits from the food industry. Sinclair finally found a potential buyer in Doubleday, Page, and Company, which sent investigators to Packingtown to confirm Sinclair's allegations. Convinced that the novel's descriptions could withstand legal challenge and despite pressure from the meat industry, Doubleday agreed to publish *The Jungle* with one of the first mass publicity campaigns for a book in U.S. history, ushering in the age of modern mass media.

Doubleday's campaign highlighted the novel's muckraking exposé and targeted everyone from newspaper editors to President Theodore Roosevelt himself, to whom the publisher sent an advance proof of the book. *The Jungle* was released in February, 1906, to an outraged public primed by advance publicity and became an immediate best-seller.

INVESTIGATIONS OF THE MEATPACKING INDUSTRY

The economic impact of *The Jungle*'s disturbing descriptions was dramatic and long-lasting: Domestic meat sales dropped by more than half and remained depressed for more than two decades, leading to an industrywide "eat more meat" campaign in 1928; publication of the book in Great Britain and in seventeen translations created an international scandal and caused Germany to raise its import duties on U.S. meat. The political result soon followed: President Roosevelt, after a personal consultation with Sinclair at the White House, wrote to Secretary of Agriculture James Wilson on March 12, 1906, requesting that he undertake a secret investigation of the meatpacking industry with Sinclair's collaboration. The resulting Neill-Reynolds report gave the president the ammunition he needed to support pure food legislation. Harvey Wiley drafted the law, and Indiana senator Albert Beveridge, the president's ally and an architect of Progressive reform, brought it to Congress.

PASSAGE, PROVISIONS, AND ENFORCEMENT

Beveridge's bill passed the Senate on May 26 as an amendment to the Agricultural Appropriations bill, but stalled in the House at the behest of the chair of the Committee on Agriculture, James W. Wadsworth, who was apparently under pressure from the meat lobby. Roosevelt responded by releasing the first part of the Neill-Reynolds report, which confirmed Sinclair's version of meat-processing practices and raised public outrage to fever pitch. The meat lobby conceded and, after minor compromises, Congress passed both the Pure Food and Drugs Act and the Meat Inspection Act on June 30, 1906.

The Pure Food and Drugs Act prohibited the interstate transportation and sale of adulterated food, including any product that is combined or packed with another substance that adversely affects its quality or strength; is substituted in whole or in part by another substance; has had any essential component removed; has been blended, coated, colored, or stained to conceal damage or inferiority; contains poisonous or harmful additions; is composed of filthy or decomposed animal or vegetable matter; or is the product of a diseased animal or one that died other than by slaughtering.

Enforcement of the act was consigned to the USDA's Bureau of Chemistry until 1928, when the Food, Drug, and Insecticide Administration (renamed the Food and Drug Administration in 1931) was formed to assume the responsibility. The act was amended in 1911, 1913, and 1919; then, amid charges that the law was inadequately enforced and served to benefit the largest food-processing companies, it was superseded by the Food, Drug, and Cosmetic Act of 1938. That act, supplemented by numerous amendments and acts addressing food processing and inspection procedures, fair packaging and labeling, and drug testing and safety, became the basis of food and drug law. The Food and Drug Administration has remained one of the nation's oldest consumer protection agencies, and its roots clearly extend back to the events of 1906.

Elizabeth J. Miles

SOURCES FOR FURTHER STUDY
Bloodworth, William A., Jr. *Upton Sinclair.* Boston: Twayne, 1977.
Harris, Leon. *Upton Sinclair: American Rebel.* New York: Thomas Y. Crowell, 1975.
Root, Waverly, and Richard de Rochemont. *Eating in America: A History.* New York: Ecco Press, 1995.
Shapiro, Laura. *Perfection Salad: Women and Cooking at the Turn of the Century.* New York: Farrar, Straus & Giroux, 1986.
Sinclair, Upton. *The Jungle.* 1906. Reprint. New York: New American Library, 1980.
U.S. Food and Drug Administration. *Milestones in U.S. Food and Drug Law History.* Washington, D.C.: Government Printing Office, 1985.

SEE ALSO: Food, Drug, and Cosmetic Act (1938); Food Additives Amendment (1958); Hazardous Substances Labeling Act (1960); Wholesome Poultry Products Act (1968); Food Security Act (1985).

GENTLEMEN'S AGREEMENT

DATE: March 14, 1907
CATEGORIES: Asia or Asian Americans; Foreign Relations; Immigration

Immigration from Japan to the mainland United States was limited to nonlaborers, laborers already settled in the United States, and their families.

From 1638 to 1854, Japan maintained a policy of isolation toward the world, both to preserve peace, which it had not enjoyed for several hundred years, and to protect its cultural values and feudal institutions from foreign influence. This long period of seclusion changed in 1852, when Commodore Matthew Calbraith Perry arrived in Edo, Japan, to deliver a letter from President Millard Fillmore to the emperor. Diplomatic relations between Japan and the United States began on March 31, 1854, when a treaty was signed opening two Japanese ports to U.S. ships and permitting the United States to receive any future concessions that might be granted to other powers. For the next thirty years, trade flourished between the two countries. A treaty of commerce and navigation in 1884 retained the most-favored-nation clause in all commercial matters.

JAPANESE IMMIGRATION
Until 1868, Japan prohibited all emigration. Without obtaining their government's permission to leave, a group of Japanese laborers, the *gannenmono* ("first-year" people), arrived in Hawaii on May 17, 1868. Japan was in transition during the 1870's and 1880's. During the Meiji Restoration period, following the overthrow of the Tokugawa shogunate (1603-1867), Japan's economy and government had been modernized extensively. However, industrialization in urban areas was not accompanied by similar developments in agricultural areas. By 1884, overpopulation, compounded with high unemployment, conditions of drought, crop failure, and famine, had engendered political upheaval and rioting. These changed circumstances led to the legalization of emigration in 1885.

The first Japanese immigrants who arrived in California in 1871 were mostly middle-class young men seeking opportunities to study or improve their economic status. By 1880, there were 148 resident Japanese. Their numbers increased to 1,360 in 1891, including 281 laborers and 172 farmers. A treaty between the United States and Japan in 1894 ensured mutual free entry although allowing limitations on immigration based on domestic interests. By 1900, the number of Japanese recorded in the U.S. Census had increased to 24,326. They arrived at ports on the Pacific coast and settled primarily in the Pacific states and British Columbia.

An increase in the demand for Hawaiian sugar in turn increased the demand for plantation labor, especially Japanese labor. An era of government-contract labor began in 1884, only ending with the U.S. annexation of Hawaii in 1898. Sixty thousand Japanese in the islands then became eligible to enter the United States without passports. Between 1899 and 1906, it is estimated that between forty thousand and fifty-seven thousand Japanese moved to the United States via Hawaii, Canada, and Mexico.

NATIVIST ANTAGONISM
On the Pacific coast, tensions developed between Asians and other Californians. Although the Japanese immigrant workforce was initially welcomed, antagonism increased as it began to compete with U.S. labor. The emerging trade-union movement advocated a restriction of immigration. An earlier campaign against the Chinese had culminated in the 1882 Chinese Exclusion Act, which suspended immigration of Chinese laborers to the United States for ten years. This act constituted the first U.S. law barring immigration based on race or nationality. A similar campaign was instigated against the Japanese. On March 1, 1905, both houses of the California State legislature voted to urge California's congressional delegation in Washington, D.C., to pursue the limitation of Japanese immigrants. At a meeting in San Francisco on May 7, delegates from sixty-seven organizations launched the Japanese and Korean Exclusion League, known also as the Asiatic Exclusion League.

President Theodore Roosevelt, who was involved in the peace negotiations between Japan and Russia, observed the developing situation in California. George Kennan, who was covering the Russo-Japanese War, wrote to the president:

> It isn't the exclusion of a few emigrants that hurts here . . . it's the putting of Japanese below Hungarians, Italians, Syrians, Polish Jews, and degraded nondescripts from all parts of Europe and Western Asia. No proud, high spirited and victorious people will submit to such a classification as that, especially when it is made with insulting reference to personal character and habits.

Roosevelt agreed, saying he was mortified that people in the United States should insult the Japanese. He continued to play a pivotal role in resolving the Japanese-Russian differences at the Portsmouth Peace Conference.

Anti-Japanese feeling waned until April, 1906. Following the San Francisco earthquake, an outbreak of crime occurred, including many cases of assault against Japanese. There was also an organized boycott of Japanese restaurants. The Japanese viewed these acts as especially reprehensible. Their government and Red Cross had contributed more relief for San Francisco than all other foreign nations combined.

STRAINED RELATIONS WITH JAPAN

Tension escalated. The Asian Exclusion League, whose membership was estimated to be 78,500 in California, together with San Francisco's mayor, pressured the San Francisco school board to segregate Japanese schoolchildren. On October 11, 1906, the board passed its resolution. A protest filed by the Japanese consul was denied. Japan protested that the act violated most-favored-nation treatment. Ambassador Luke E. Wright, in Tokyo, reported Japan's extremely negative feelings about the matter to Secretary of State Elihu Root. This crisis in Japanese-American relations brought the countries to the brink of war. On October 25, Japan's ambassador, Shuzo Aoki, met with Root to seek a solution. President Roosevelt, who recognized the justification of the Japanese protest based on the 1894 treaty, on October 26 sent his secretary of commerce and labor to San Francisco to investigate the matter.

In his message to Congress on December 4, President Roosevelt paid tribute to Japan and strongly repudiated San Francisco for its anti-Japanese acts. He encouraged Congress to pass an act that would allow naturalization of the Japanese in the United States. Roosevelt's statements and request pleased Japan but aroused further resentment on the Pacific coast. During the previous twelve months, more than seventeen thousand Japanese had entered the mainland United States, two-thirds coming by way of Hawaii. Roosevelt recognized that the basic cause of the unrest in California—the increasing inflow of Japanese laborers—could be resolved only by checking immigration.

NEGOTIATING AN AGREEMENT

Negotiations with Japan to limit the entry of Japanese laborers began in late December, 1906. Three issues were involved: the rescinding of the segregation order by the San Francisco school board, the withholding of passports to the mainland United States by the Japanese government, and the closing of immigration channels through Hawaii, Canada, and Mexico by federal legislation. The Hawaiian issue, which related to an earlier Gentlemen's Agreement of 1900, was the first resolved through the diplomacy of Japan's foreign minister, Tadasu Hayashi, ambassadors Wright and Aoki, and Secretary of State Root.

Before Japan would agree to discuss immigration to the mainland, it was necessary for the segregation order to be withdrawn. In February, 1907, the president invited San Francisco's entire board of education, the mayor, and a city superintendent of schools to Washington, D.C., to confer on the segregation issue and other problems related to Japan. On February 18, a pending immigration bill was amended to prevent Japanese laborers from entering the United States via Hawaii, Mexico, or Canada. Assured that immigration of Japanese laborers would be stopped, the school board rescinded their segregation order on March 13. An executive order issued by the president on March 14 put into effect the restrictions on passports. Subsequently, the Japanese government agreed to conclude the Gentlemen's Agreement. In January, 1908, Foreign Minister Hayashi agreed to the terms of immigration discussed in December, 1907. On March 9, Secretary of State Root instructed Ambassador Wright to thank Japan, thus concluding the negotiations begun in December, 1906.

As reported by the commissioner general of immigration in 1908, the Japanese government would issue passports for travel to the continental United States only to nonlaborers, laborers who were former residents of the United States, parents, wives, or children of residents, and "settled agriculturalists." A final provision prevented secondary immigration into the United States by way of Hawaii, Mexico, or Canada.

When the Gentlemen's Agreement of 1907 cut off new supplies of Japanese labor, Filipinos were recruited to take their place, both in Hawaii and in California, as well as in the Alaskan fishing industry. As U.S. nationals, Filipinos could not be prevented from migrating to the United States.

Susan E. Hamilton

SOURCES FOR FURTHER STUDY

Boddy, E. Manchester. *Japanese in America*. 1921. Reprint. San Francisco: R&E Research Associates, 1970.

Esthus, Raymond A. *Theodore Roosevelt and Japan.* Seattle: University of Washington Press, 1967.

Herman, Masako, ed. *The Japanese in America, 1843-1973.* Dobbs Ferry, N.Y.: Oceana, 1974.

Kikumura, Akemi. *Issei Pioneers: Hawaii and the Mainland, 1885 to 1924.* Los Angeles: Japanese American National Museum, 1992.

U.S. Department of State. *Report of the Hon. Roland S. Morris on Japanese Immigration and Alleged Discriminatory Legislation Against Japanese Residents in the United States.* 1921. Reprint. New York: Arno Press, 1978.

SEE ALSO: Treaty of Kanagawa (1854); Alien land laws (1913); Hoover-Stimson Doctrine (1932); War Brides Act (1945); U.S.-Japanese Treaty (1951).

OPIUM EXCLUSION ACT

DATE: February 9, 1909
U.S. STATUTES AT LARGE: 35 Stat. 614
CATEGORIES: Asia or Asian Americans; Business, Commerce, and Trade; Food and Drugs; Health and Welfare

The Opium Exclusion Act prohibited the use and importation of the drug for other than medicinal purposes. The sponsors of the act intended to suppress illicit uses of the drug and to send a signal to countries involved in the production and trade of opium to do the same.

Senator Henry Cabot Lodge of Massachusetts introduced the opium exclusion bill on January 4, 1909. Drafted by Elihu Root, chairman of the American Opium Commission, the bill was part of the commission's attempt to root out the Chinese opium trade through international cooperation. A bill regulating the importation of opium into the United States was needed as a signal to other countries.

Enemies of the bill opposed it on the grounds that the act, by placing the Department of Agriculture in charge of executing it, would give the federal government police powers constitutionally reserved for the states. To accommodate the critics, the authors of the bill changed it to transfer responsibility for implementing the law from the Agriculture Department to the Treasury Department, thereby declaring it a revenue bill.

Thomas Winter

SOURCES FOR FURTHER STUDY

Bewley-Taylor, David R. *The United States and International Drug Control, 1909-1997.* New York: Pinter, 1999.

Courtwright, David T. *Dark Paradise: A History of Opiate Addiction in America.* Enlarged ed. Cambridge, Mass.: Harvard University Press, 2001.

Musto, David F., ed. *Drugs in America: A Documentary History.* New York: New York University Press, 2002.

SEE ALSO: Treaty of Wang Hiya (1844); Burlingame Treaty (1868); Pure Food and Drugs Act (1906); Harrison Narcotic Drug Act (1914); National Narcotics Act (1984).

COPYRIGHT ACT OF 1909

DATE: March 4, 1909
U.S. STATUTES AT LARGE: 35 Stat. 1075
CATEGORIES: Business, Commerce, and Trade; Copyrights, Patents, and Trademarks

The Copyright Act of 1909 was the end product of hundreds of years of common and statutory copyright law.

Under copyright law in general, authors or creators of original works have the exclusive right to reproduce (or authorize others to reproduce) these works and are protected against unlawful copying, known as plagiarism or piracy. "Original" does not mean "unique." Original works are those created by the author's own intellectual or creative effort, as opposed to having been copied. Copying all or part of a work without permission of the author (or any agency the author has authorized for copying) constitutes copyright infringement. Willful unauthorized copying for the purpose of making a profit is a criminal offense punishable by fine or imprisonment. When authors suspect infringement but have no grounds for charging criminal intent, they can bring civil action against the alleged offender. Under certain circumstances, parts of authors' works can be copied without permission according to what is known as the fair use doctrine.

THE BASICS OF COPYRIGHT
Works are protected by copyright for a specific length of time. At the end of that time, a work is said to be in the public domain and can be copied without permission. Ever since the concept of the right to copy was established and codified, copyright has existed under both common and statutory law. Common law is unwritten law, based on tradition and precedent. Statutory law is written law passed by a legislative body, such as the British Parliament or the U.S. Congress.

In general, common law protects a work before it is published and statutory law protects it after it is published. In both common and statutory law, it is assumed that what is written or created is property. The creator of a work has sole ownership of the work and the right to dispose of it as one would any other type of property; that is, to sell it, lease it, transfer it, or leave it in a will. Upon publication of the work, the author gives up some of the ownership rights granted by common law but is given monetary rewards for doing so. The law is based on two sometimes conflicting principles: authors should be rewarded for their labors and knowledge should be made readily available to the pubic for the good of society as a whole. Much of the history of copyright law is concerned with attempts to reconcile these two principles.

HISTORICAL PRECEDENTS
The concept and fundamental issues of copyright date back at least as far as the fifteenth century. With the invention of printing, copies of both ancient and contemporary works began to proliferate and become readily available to the public. Early English copyright law began to address the questions of what should be printed, who

ultimately owned the works and for how long, how the owners should be compensated for them, and who should be authorized to copy them.

Throughout Europe, by the sixteenth century printing had developed from an unregulated cottage industry of craftsmen to a full-fledged profession and a thriving large-scale industry. Usually, the printers of books were also the vendors of them. In England, the printing and selling of books was done by a monopoly called the Stationers' Company. Copyright at this time was a license given to the Stationers' Company by royal decree. The decree gave the company exclusive rights to print all works the government deemed proper to print. The law was for the benefit of publishers and booksellers more than for authors. Furthermore, since the license to publish was granted on the basis of what the government decided could or could not be published, it was actually a form of censorship. It bore little resemblance to the laws that followed but did recognize that what was written in a book was as much property as was the book itself. Authors, who had hitherto been supported by wealthy, interested patrons rather than by sale of their work, could now earn money (although hardly a living wage) apart from patronage by selling their manuscripts to printers, who paid them a lump sum. It was generally accepted that once the manuscript was sold, the work was no longer the property of the author. Copyright infringement, which frequently consisted of printing unauthorized works outside the Stationers' monopoly, was more an offense against the publisher, or those who licensed the publisher, than against the author.

By the late seventeenth century, the English press was generally liberated from the dictates of the authorities. There was much less censorship, and licenses to the Stationers' Company were no longer renewed. Freedom of the press destroyed the Stationers' monopoly, for now anyone could print virtually anything. An unfettered press also meant a lack of protection for authors from piracy and plagiarism. Literary piracy long had been considered an outrage, if not actually a criminal offense, and was supposed to be prevented by common law, but there were few means of enforcing common law. Both authors and booksellers pressured Parliament for legislation that would protect authors from piracy and provide booksellers with enough security to allow them to stay in business. In 1710, Parliament responded with the Statute of Anne, named for the reigning queen. The Statute of Anne established time limits, with renewals, on how long a published work would be protected before it went into the public domain and outlined penalties for copyright infringement. The law was not clear, however, on how long an unpublished work was protected by common law or whether common law was superseded by statutory law after a work was published. It did not answer whether an author gave up all rights to a work after it was published. There were many cases in which publishers freely copied works for which the statutory term of protection had expired. When the authors of the works complained that this free copying was a violation of their common law rights, the English courts decided that once a work had been published and the term of protection had expired, common law rights no longer applied. This conflict sparked long and heated debates over ownership and the balance between authors' rights and the public good. These debates continued through the twentieth century.

Limited and controversial as it was, the Statute of Anne became the pattern for all subsequent copyright legislation in both England and the United States. Twelve of the thirteen original states adopted copyright statutes before the federal Constitution was drawn up. These statutes were summarized in Article I, section 8 of the federal Constitution, which says: "Congress shall have power . . . to promote the progress of science and useful arts by securing for limited times to authors and inventors the exclusive right to their respective writings and discoveries." The first federal copyright law, enacted in 1790, was revised in 1831 and 1879. On March 4, 1909, Congress passed a copyright law that remained in effect until revisions were made in 1976.

PROVISIONS OF THE 1909 ACT
The 1909 law states that the purpose of copyright is "not primarily for the benefit of the author, but primarily for the benefit of the public." Although unpublished works were still held to be covered by common law, publication was necessary in order for a work to be covered by statutory law, and an author's rights under statutory law were substantially different from what they were under common law. Under the 1909 law, there was no general protection of unpublished works. Omission of or serious error in a copyright notice or failure to deposit a copy in the Copyright Office resulted in loss or forfeit of copyright.

The Copyright Office, located in the Library of Congress in Washington, D.C., was established by the 1909 law to keep records and register works. The law outlined procedures for registration of copyright, detailed circumstances of and penalties for infringement, and listed fourteen categories of works that could be copyrighted. It codified the standard of copyrightability of a work as being original by the author and not copied from other work. It also lengthened the duration of copyright to twenty-eight years, renewable for twenty-eight more.

Just as the Statute of Anne had responded to the implications of the new technology of the printing press, so the law of 1909 tried to respond to the new technology of the early twentieth century. The 1909 law grew out of centuries of political upheaval, factional controversy, technological development, and legislative compromise. As English government swung from monarchy to republic and back to monarchy again, up to the early eighteenth century, written work was first strictly censored and then liberated to the point of anarchy. Printing had made works of all kinds widely available, and once the press was liberated in England, the rights of publishers, authors, and the public came into sharp conflict. Some of the conflicts were resolved by the Statute of Anne, which served as a pattern for American copyright law.

In the spirit of the original state laws and the federal copyright law of 1790, the 1909 law stated its purpose as being "primarily for the public," thus favoring the rights of the public over the rights of authors but allowing for reward to authors in order to encourage them to continue producing. In this way, the conflicting principles of rewards to creators and the "promotion of progress in science and useful arts" for the common good seemed to be reconciled. By extending the term of copyright coverage, it gave more protection to authors than previous legislation had. It provided no protection, however, for unpublished work, and it tended to supersede common law, since publication was a necessary condition for copyright. Nor did it address the special issues of copyright involved for writers as employees or contractors, such as newspaper reporters and freelance writers, who do what is known as "work for hire."

The fair use doctrine had been applied even in early copyright law and was based on the constitutional principle of public benefit from authors' works. In 1961, while the 1909 law was still in effect, the Copyright Office listed what could be copied without permission and for what purpose. Research, instruction, and literary review, for example, were given fairly broad rights to copy. Fair use was not codified until the copyright law revision of 1976.

NEW TECHNOLOGY, NEED FOR REVISION

As technology improved and became more varied, the 1909 law lagged in its provisions. In describing the classes of works that were copyrightable, the language of the 1909 law indicated that it was still largely based on the technology of the printing press. It protected the "writings" of an author, whereas later law protects "original works of authorship," thus broadening the definition of "author" and lengthening the list of what can be considered to be authors' works. Although the 1909 law listed motion pictures and sound recordings among the classes of copyrightable works, it made inadequate provision for the protection of what was disseminated via these new technologies and no provision at all for infringement issues arising from the use of photocopy machines, television, videotapes, computers, or cable and satellite communications.

Beginning in 1955, there were several attempts to revise the law, but it was not extensively revised until 1976 (effective in 1978). The most significant impact of the 1909 copyright law on the writing and publishing world and on society in general, as beneficiary of authors' work, is that it was specific, whereas prior legislation had been general. By establishing a Copyright Office, listing the kinds of works that could be copyrighted, and outlining how they could be protected, it sought to resolve the ongoing conflict between rewarding creators and benefiting their audiences.

Christina Ashton

SOURCES FOR FURTHER STUDY

Brylawski, E. Fulton, and Abe Goldman, eds. and comps. *Legislative History of the 1909 Copyright Act.* South Hackensack, N.J.: F. B. Rothman, 1976.
Bunnin, Brad, and Peter Beren. "What Is Copyright?" In *The Writer's Legal Companion.* Reading, Mass.: Addison-Wesley, 1988.
Dible, Donald M., ed. *What Everybody Should Know About Patents, Trademarks, and Copyrights.* Fairfield, Calif.: Entreprenuer Press, 1978.

Goldfarb, Ronald L., and Gail E. Ross. "What Every Writer Should Know About Copyright." In *The Writer's Lawyer.* New York: Times Books, 1989.
Johnston, Donald F. *Copyright Handbook.* 2d ed. New York: R. R. Bowker, 1982.
Kaplan, Benjamin. *An Unhurried View of Copyright.* New York: Columbia University Press, 1967.
Moore, Waldo, and Kirk Polking. "Ten Questions About the New Copyright Law." In *Law and the Writer,* edited by Leonard S. Meranus. Cincinnati, Ohio: Writer's Digest Books, 1978.
Wincor, Richard, and Irving Mandell. "Historical Background— Copyright Law." In *Copyright, Patents, and Trademarks.* Dobbs Ferry, N.Y.: Oceana Publications, 1980.

SEE ALSO: Copyright Act of 1976 (1976); Trademark Law Revision Act (1988); North American Free Trade Agreement (1993); General Agreement on Tariffs and Trade of 1994 (1994); Digital Millennium Copyright Act (1998).

PAYNE-ALDRICH TARIFF ACT

ALSO KNOWN AS: Tariff Act of 1909
DATE: August 5, 1909
U.S. STATUTES AT LARGE: 36 Stat. 95
U.S. CODE: 48 § 739
CATEGORIES: Banking, Money, and Finance; Business, Commerce, and Trade; Tariffs and Taxation

The Tariff Act of 1909 forced corporations, for the first time, to open their books to the United States government for inspection and audit.

The Tariff Act of 1909, also known as the Payne-Aldrich Tariff Act, can be characterized as one part of a growing progressive movement against rapid concentrations of wealth during the late nineteenth and early twentieth centuries. Social forces were driven by sentiment against those business tycoons perceived as reaping exorbitant profits at the expense of the masses of laborers. In the meantime, political figures, determined to address the concerns of their constituents, were also challenged by growing federal deficits. The need to finance and eradicate the national debt while circumventing the appearance of imposing an income tax, declared unconstitutional by the Supreme Court, was imperative.

PROVISIONS AND PENALTIES

The direct result was an excise tax on corporate forms of businesses. An indirect result was the authorization for the Internal Revenue Service to audit corporate records with respect to enforcing compliance with the excise tax. The invasion into corporate records and accounting practices, which were until that time considered highly guarded secrets, was as traumatic to business as was the tax itself.

Section 38 of the Tariff Act of 1909 authorized a special excise tax on net incomes of domestic corporations, joint stock companies, associations organized for profit and having capital stock represented by shares, insurance companies, and foreign corporations operating in the United States or United States territories. The tax was 1 percent of net incomes in excess of $5,000 after allowing deductions for ordinary and necessary operating expenses, losses, depreciation charges, interest and taxes paid, and dividends received from organizations subject to this new tax. All taxable incomes were assessed on a calendar-year basis, with tax returns due on March 1 of the following year.

Penalties were determined for fraud, failure to file, and late returns. Fraud carried a corporate penalty of 100 percent of the tax due and a fine with a minimum of $1,000 and a maximum of $10,000. Individuals responsible for fraud were subject to fines of up to $1,000, imprisonment of up to one year, or both. Failure to file a return carried a corporate penalty of 150 percent of the tax due and a fine with a minimum of $1,000 and a maximum of $10,000. Responsible individuals were subject to the same fines and imprisonment terms as set forth for fraud. Corporations were assessed a penalty of 5 percent of the tax due plus 1 percent interest, per month, of the tax due for late returns.

SOCIOECONOMIC CONDITIONS

The period from the late 1800's to the early 1900's was one in which the United States experienced an economic transition from an agricultural society to an industrial society. This transition caused a population shift from the country to cities. Wealth became concentrated among the few fortunate enough to own businesses. The business climate was ripe for increases in wealth for going concerns, as business was favored by cheap immigrant labor and raw materials, an expanding market, and high protective tariffs against imports, such as those imposed by the Dingley Tariff Act of 1897. Andrew Carnegie, J. P. Morgan, and John D. Rockefeller reached their financial zeniths during this time period in the steel, banking, and railroad industries, among others.

The recessions of 1893 and 1907 also contributed to wealth concentration, as they allowed or encouraged large corporations to buy out smaller firms unable to weather the financial storms. For example, the Morgan family bought the Morse shipping interests, a competitor to the Morgan New Haven Railroad. Morgan's United States Steel Corporation bought the troubled Tennessee Coal, Iron and Railroad Company.

Monopolies or highly concentrated markets were formed as a result of this financial concentration. For example, 95 percent of the railroad track in the United States was owned by six investment groups by 1900. The Sherman Antitrust Act of 1890 was designed to defuse monopoly power by breaking large monopolies into smaller, diversely owned entities. The Sherman Act was loosely enforced by the government, however, and corporations often appeared to have more wealth and political power than did the government. Industrialists circumvented antitrust law by breaking up their consolidated corporations and creating holding companies, which evaded antitrust legislation but in substance were essentially the same form of entities.

ORGANIZED LABOR

On the labor side, the experiences of the 1880's and 1890's brought a maturity to organized labor, which became strong enough to begin challenging corporate sovereignty. The oppression of labor through low wages, poor working conditions, and long hours encouraged the formation of labor unions. The American Federation of Labor (AFL) grew to a membership of approximately half a million by 1898 and more than 1.6 million by 1906, accounting for more than three-fifths of all trade-union workers.

The unity of labor, demonstrated by strikes, caused industrialists to become conciliatory toward labor, and corporate concessions were made. For example, the United Mine Workers of America (UMW) won an unprecedented victory in 1897 when the conditions of 100,000 striking mine workers were met, including a 20 percent pay increase, the eight-hour day, abolition of company stores, recognition of the union, and a provision for annual joint conferences with the mine operators. This newfound success encouraged labor to move toward a socialist philosophy, not to abolish capitalism but to share in corporate profits.

States also began exercising power over corporations by passing prolabor legislation in the early 1900's. Child protection laws were passed in all states, and many states passed laws to protect laborers, particularly women, from unsafe working conditions. Workers' compensation laws were passed in Maryland (1902), Montana (1909), Massachusetts (1909), and New York (1910). These laws were declared unconstitutional shortly thereafter but were constitutionally reinstated before 1920. Finally, the federal government saw the mood as right to challenge the power of corporate America.

IMMEDIATE IMPACT OF THE TARIFF
The convergence of social, political, and legal sentiment against large corporations led to the Tariff Act of 1909. The act was sponsored by senators Sereno Elisha Payne and Nelson W. Aldrich. Aldrich was a particularly powerful senator who wished to mitigate or repeal certain tariffs contained in the Dingley Tariff Act of 1897 pertaining to favored special interest groups. To offset the revenue reductions, however, new taxes had to be imposed to meet the $100 million federal deficit. Opposed to an income tax, Aldrich included an inheritance tax in his act. A coalition of Republican Party dissidents demanded that an income tax be included. To prevent a split within the Republican Party, President William Howard Taft stepped in and worked out a compromise. The result was the Tariff Act of 1909, authorizing an excise tax on the privilege of operating corporate forms of business with the excise based on corporate net incomes.

The immediate, and most significant, impact of the Tariff Act of 1909 was the intrusion of government into corporate financial affairs. Government had established an implicit control of corporations, at least in principle. The Internal Revenue Service was authorized to audit corporate records if it had reason to believe returns were incorrect or not filed as required. Authorization was also given to use the courts to force compliance.

CHALLENGING THE TARIFF'S CONSTITUTIONALITY

Looking more like an income tax than an excise tax, the special tax was challenged in *Flint v. Stone Tracy Company* in 1911. It was affirmed by the Supreme Court as constitutional. The Court ruled that this tax was an indirect tax, not a direct tax, on individuals through stock ownership and therefore was not subject to apportionment according to the population. The Court expounded that there were distinct advantages to operating in the corporate form of entity and that Congress had the right to tax that privilege with an excise tax. The tax could be based on any component of the corporation that Congress saw fit, including its income.

The 1911 decision made it apparent that corporations had no further recourse. For the first time in history, records of U.S. corporations were open to outside inspection. Laissez-faire no longer applied. Furthermore, the requirement to report corporate incomes on standardized government forms set in motion a standardization of accounting principles and an accountability to shareholders virtually nonexistent before.

Prior to 1909, corporate records were guarded closely by the few principal corporate owners. Most investment bankers and stockholders were uninformed regarding the financial position and operations of corporations. They relied on the reports of the principals, sometimes to their detriment. Moreover, investors were generally unsophisticated in financial matters and were therefore willing to accept the reports in blind faith. When investment bankers asked for audited financial statements, some corporations would refuse to sell securities through those individuals.

LONG-RANGE EFFECTS

Reporting behavior changed as a result of the excise tax. It was not uncommon for corporations to keep two sets of records, one for tax reporting and one for reporting to stockholders and other users of financial statements. Lower, and probably more accurate, earnings were reported to the government. Despite this new accountability to the government, shareholders had no protection from securities fraud until the Securities Acts of 1933 and 1934.

Depreciation policy received greater attention as a result of the act because this was the only expense deductible against income that could be based on estimates rather than determined on a cash basis. Before the Tariff Act of 1909, no method of depreciation allocation was prescribed, and accordingly, a multitude of methods was used. For example, Standard Oil Company applied depreciation rates of 6 to 35 percent around 1905, depending on the equipment, but the rates were not necessarily applied in proportion to the normal lives of the assets. John D. Rockefeller, the company's principal owner, thought that the company assets were undervalued around the time of the Tariff Act. Consequently, the public records of Standard Oil show "depreciation restored." It is uncertain whether this short-lived practice was used to recapitalize asset values for later tax deductions. Although the Tariff Act of 1909 required no standard method of depreciation, later tariff acts narrowed the methods acceptable for reporting purposes.

The corporate excise tax became a corporate income tax in 1913 with the passage of the Sixteenth Amendment, which allowed for direct taxation not apportioned according to population. The difference between the income tax of 1913 and the excise tax before 1913 was in name only. The reporting requirements remained the same. As later tariff acts refined income and expense reporting requirements, tax planning became an important corporate management function. When the Securities Acts of 1933 and 1934 created the Securities and Exchange Commission to regulate the accounting of corporations that publicly traded securities, many of the accounting methods established by the tariff acts, such as depreciation methods and inventory costing methods, were adopted by the commission. The Tariff Act of 1909 thus formed a basis for generally accepted accounting principles to be used by publicly owned corporations.

Paul A. Shoemaker

SOURCES FOR FURTHER STUDY

Anderson, Donald F. *William Howard Taft: A Conservative's Conception of the Presidency.* Ithaca, N.Y.: Cornell University Press, 1973.

Beth, Loren P. *The Development of the American Constitution 1877-1917.* New York: Harper & Row, 1971.

Carson, Gerald. *The Golden Egg.* Boston: Houghton Miffin, 1977.
Degler, Carl N. *Out of Our Past: The Forces That Shaped Modern America.* New York: Harper & Row, 1970.
Faulkner, Harold U. *The Decline of Laissez Faire, 1897-1917.* New York: Rinehart, 1951.
_____. *The Quest for Social Justice 1898-1914.* New York: Macmillan, 1931.
Kintner, Earl W., ed. *Federal Antitrust Laws and Related Statutes: A Legislative History.* 11 vols. Buffalo, N.Y.: William S. Hein, 1978, 1982-1985.
Ratner, Sidney. *Taxation and Democracy in America.* New York: John Wiley, 1967.
Seligman, Edwin. *The Income Tax: A Study of the History, Theory, and Practice of Income Taxation at Home and Abroad.* 2d ed. New York: Macmillan, 1914.

SEE ALSO: Sherman Antitrust Act (1890); Dingley Tariff (1897); Payne-Aldrich Tariff Act (1909); Sixteenth Amendment (1913); Smoot-Hawley Tariff Act (1930); Securities Exchange Act (1934).

MANN ACT

ALSO KNOWN AS: White-Slave Traffic Act
DATE: June 25, 1910
U.S. STATUTES AT LARGE: 36 Stat. 825
U.S. CODE: 18 § 2421 (for 1948)
CATEGORIES: Crimes and Criminal Procedure

This act prohibited the interstate transportation of women for immoral purposes and was the first national legislation specifically outlawing sexually oriented activities considered detrimental to the public welfare.

Prostitution in the United States is as old as the country. Until the Mann Act, it was regulated by state statutes that generally prohibited the practice. Enforcement, however, was universally lax. The powerful men who controlled the syndicates that owned many of the brothels and controlled the women who worked in them had the political influence it took to protect their operations even though laws existed in virtually every state that specifically prohibited prostitution.

Vigorous enforcement of antiprostitution laws generally occurred only after vice commissions or outraged citizens' groups, often religiously oriented, raised a loud outcry against prostitution in their communities. Enforcement stepped up when such outcries arose, then died down quickly and continued to be sporadic. Many law enforcement officials across the nation grew wealthy from the bribes they accepted from those who controlled prostitution.

"WHITE SLAVERY"

Beginning in the reform era of the 1890's and continuing into the early 1900's, however, sensational reports began to surface about the widespread existence of "white slavery," the name given to the transportation of women from depressed rural areas to large cities, where they were forced into prostitution. Such reports alarmed a public that had already been shocked by Stephen Crane's *Maggie: A Girl of the Streets* (1896) and Theodore Dreiser's *Sister Carrie* (1900), two influential novels that drew widespread attention to prostitution and aroused strong public sentiment against it. Lincoln Steffens's *The Shame of the Cities* (1904), which focused attention on the corruption that pervaded most major American cities of that period, also aroused the public.

At this time, it must be remembered, the many women's suffrage groups actively crusading to gain the franchise for women were focusing considerable attention upon women's rights. Also active in the 1890's and early 1900's were temperance groups, most of them dominated by women, who were calling for a constitutional amendment that would prohibit the sale of alcoholic beverages in the United States. Members of these groups, most notably members of the Anti-Saloon League, founded in 1893, were active in calling for strict enforcement of antiprostitution statutes.

PROVISIONS

The Mann Act was also enacted to comply with an international treaty prohibiting the movement of prostitutes between nations and to respond to domestic hysteria that a conspiracy of coerced prostitution, so-called "white slavery," was flourishing in U.S. cities. It prohibited the interstate transportation of women for "prostitution or debauchery, or for any other immoral purpose." The act initially imposed a fine of up to five thousand dollars and a prison term of up to five years, or both, upon those who violated this law. These penalties were doubled if the victims were minors. The legislative history is clear beyond serious argument that Congress did not intend the law to address premarital sex or extramarital affairs, not commercial in nature, that involved a woman crossing a state line.

SUPREME COURT DECISIONS

In *Hoke v. United States* (1913), the Supreme Court upheld the constitutionality of the statute against a charge that it exceeded the power of the federal government under the interstate commerce clause. Viewed with the hindsight of history, this was a modest expansion of federal power; far greater was yet to come.

Caminetti v. United States (1917) is the best known of the Mann Act cases to come before the Court. Two couples, in extramarital but totally noncommercial relationships, traveled from California to Nevada and were charged with violating the act. The defendants pointed to the legislative history of the statute and argued that the law was intended to criminalize the transportation of prostitutes only. The Court rejected this means of interpretation and declared that it would look only to the plain meaning of the statute. "Immoral purpose" had to mean something beyond prostitution; an extramarital relationship was "immoral," and therefore, the male defendants were guilty.

Although the Court occasionally revisited the Mann Act and further refined its meaning, *Hoke* and *Caminetti* are the most significant cases. During the 1910's and 1920's the act was vigorously enforced, especially in noncommercial interstate travel involving unmarried couples. As American mores changed, it was increasingly used to combat prostitution, its original purpose. Ultimately in 1986 Congress amended the law, changing the prohibition to apply to interstate transportation of women for prostitution or any other sexual activity that is punishable by law. Interstate travel involving legal, noncommercial sexual activity was no longer a federal felony.

R. Baird Shuman (through "White Slavery") and
David J. Langum ("Provisions" and
"Supreme Court Decisions")

SOURCE FOR FURTHER STUDY

Langum, David J. *Crossing Over the Line: Legislating Morality and the Mann Act.* Chicago: University of Chicago Press, 1994.

SEE ALSO: Violence Against Women Act (1994); Megan's Law (1996).

PANAMA CANAL ACT

ALSO KNOWN AS: Panama Tolls Act
DATE: August 24, 1912
U.S. STATUTES AT LARGE: 37 Stat. 560
U.S. CODE: 48 § 1305
CATEGORIES: Business, Commerce, and Trade; Foreign Relations; Transportation

> *The Panama Canal Act provided for the establishment, administration, and functions of government in the ten-mile-wide Panama Canal Zone.*

The Spanish-American War (1898) emphasized the need for a canal to be built across the isthmus of Central America to connect the Atlantic and Pacific Oceans. On June 28, 1902, Congress passed the Spooner Act, designating that the canal be constructed across Panama. Colombia controlled Panama and rejected offers made by the United States. In 1903, Panama revolted against Colombia and declared its independence on November 3. On November 18, 1903, Phillippe Jean Bunau-Varilla, the appointed Panamanian ambassador to the United States, and U.S. Secretary of State John Hay completed the Hay-Bunau-Varilla Treaty giving the United States the authority to construct and operate a canal across Panama. Construction on the canal began in 1906.

On August 24, 1912, the Panama Canal Act provided for the establishment, administration, and functions of government in the ten-mile-wide Panama Canal Zone. Under the direction of the president of the United States, a governor selected by the U.S. Senate would oversee the operation of the canal, as well as the duties associated with governing the Canal Zone. A U.S. district court would hold legal jurisdiction over the Canal Zone, with a judge appointed by the president of the United States. Appeals would go through the Fifth U.S. Court of Appeals headquartered in New Orleans. Provisions were made for the president of the United States to establish regulations for health matters, sanitation, tolls, and military control of the Canal Zone during times of war or other emergencies. The act exempted all U.S. vessels from the payment of canal tolls. The British protested, claiming that the exemption violated the Hay-Pauncefote Treaty of 1901. They demanded that the United States either repeal the toll exemption or arbitrate the dispute.

The act of 1912 provided the governance necessary to complete the colossal canal in August, 1914, at a cost of about four hundred million dollars. On June 15, 1914, at the request of President Woodrow Wilson, the U.S. Congress repealed the U.S. toll exemption clause from the act of 1912. Canal traffic increased dramatically after World War I. Almost all commercial and private interoceanic travel use the Panama Canal. Oil supertankers are an exception because they are too wide to pass through the locks of the canal.

On September 7, 1977, President Jimmy Carter signed the Panama Canal Treaty guaranteeing that the Panama Canal would be transferred to Panama by the year 2000. After a long and bitter debate, the U.S. Senate approved the treaty. On December 31, 1999, control of the canal was officially transferred to Panama, some eighty-seven years after the Panama Canal Act of 1912 was approved.

Alvin K. Benson

SOURCE FOR FURTHER STUDY

Chidsey, Donald Barr. *The Panama Canal: An Informal History.* New York: Crown Publishers, 1970.

LaFeber, Walter. *The Panama Canal: The Crisis in Historical Perspective.* New York: Oxford University Press, 1989.

McCullough, David G. *The Path Between the Seas: The Creation of the Panama Canal, 1870-1914.* New York: Simon and Schuster, 1977.

SEE ALSO: Clayton-Bulwer Treaty (1850); Panama Canal Treaties (1978).

SIXTEENTH AMENDMENT

DATE: Ratified February 3, 1913; certified February 25, 1913
U.S. STATUTES AT LARGE: 36 Stat. 184
CATEGORIES: Constitutional Law; Tariffs and Taxation

Adopted to overturn an 1895 Supreme Court ruling that found an income tax to be unconstitutional, this amendment permitted the imposition of an income tax without the need to apportion the tax among the states on the basis of population.

The Supreme Court, in *Pollock v. Farmers' Loan and Trust Co.* (1895), ruled that the income tax law of 1894 was unconstitutional and void. Because part of the tax applied to money received from the leasing of land, it was a direct tax and therefore needed to be apportioned among the states on the basis of population This decision raised a public outcry because the tax law, which affected only the wealthiest 1 percent of Americans, was very popular.

After his inauguration in 1909, President William H. Taft proposed a constitutional amendment to overturn the Court's ruling. The result was the Sixteenth Amendment, ratified in 1913, which gave Congress the power to impose an income tax without apportioning it. Although the explicit purpose of the amendment was to overturn the Court's ruling, the Court, in *Stanton v. Baltic Mining Co.* (1916), averred that the amendment conferred no new power of taxation but simply prohibited taking the income tax out of the category of indirect taxes, "to which it inherently belonged."

John Andrulis

SOURCE FOR FURTHER STUDY
Vile, John R. *Encyclopedia of Constitutional Amendments, Proposed Amendments, and Amending Issues, 1789-1995*. Santa Barbara, Calif: ABC-CLIO, 1996.

SEE ALSO: Payne-Aldrich Tariff Act (1909).

MIGRATORY BIRD ACT

ALSO KNOWN AS: Weeks-McLean Act
DATE: March 4, 1913
U.S. STATUTES AT LARGE: 37 Stat. 828, 847
CATEGORIES: Agriculture; Animals; Environment and Conservation

The Migratory Bird Act gave the U.S. Department of Agriculture authority to regulate the hunting seasons of migratory game and insectivorous birds.

On March 4, 1913, the U.S. Congress passed and President William Howard Taft signed the Weeks-McLean Act. Also known as the Migratory Bird Act, the law gave the Department of Agriculture authority to regulate the hunting season of a wide range of bird species. The act placed under U.S. protection all migratory game and insectivorous birds with northern or southern migration paths that passed through any U.S. state or territory.

The passage of the act was an important step in bird protection. While individual states had laws protecting resident bird species from excessive hunting, the laws did not protect birds that migrated from the Canadian Arctic to the American Gulf Coast. The Weeks-McLean Act extended federal protection to these species. Events in the late 1800's led to a changing public view of the need for bird protection. The slaughter of birds in their nesting grounds had severely depleted the populations of several species. The birds' plight, brought to the public's attention by the cooperation of many organizations, resulted in widespread support for the Weeks-McLean Act.

DECLINE OF SPECIES

At the beginning of the twentieth century, responsibility for bird protection rested mainly with a scientific group, the American Ornithologists' Union (AOU). The main purpose of the AOU, which was founded in 1883, was to help identify and classify bird species. Although the union supported state laws that prohibited the killing of certain endangered birds, it had no enforcement power.

The mass destruction of the passenger pigeon by commercial hunting did much to help change public attitudes. These birds were killed by the millions. Commercial hunters descended on breeding grounds covering up to forty-five square miles and slaughtered so many birds that the birds' bodies filled freight cars. Once numbering in the hundreds of millions, the pigeon was scarce by the 1880's. The species became extinct in 1914, when the last bird died in the Cincinnati Zoo. Less publicized was the destruction of nongame birds such as warblers, terns, and egrets. The feathered-hat craze of the late 1800's resulted in the mass slaughter of these nongame birds for their feathers. Commercial hunters invaded nesting areas, wiping out colony after colony.

LACEY ACT

Sportsmen's groups and state Audubon societies helped to pass the first federal legislation for bird protection, the Lacey Act of 1900. Sponsored by Representative John F. Lacey of Iowa, the law forbade the interstate shipment of any birds killed in violation of state laws. Although the Lacey Act's application was limited to species already protected by individual states, it placed the authority and enforcement powers of the federal government behind the bird-protection movement. Many protected songbirds were being killed and sold across state lines as game birds; other species were hunted as sources of hat feathers. The Lacey Act, wherever enforced, stopped these practices. The act made the Bureau of Biological Survey in the Agriculture Department responsible for enforcing the law.

The Biological Survey was charged with enforcing the Lacey Act, but Congress did not provide funding for a federal police force. The survey had to rely on the cooperation of states, conservation groups, and commercial interests to protect bird species. Sportsmen and nature lovers thus continued to fight for federal protection of migratory birds.

PASSAGE OF WEEKS-MCLEAN

In 1912, Representative John W. Weeks of New Hampshire and Senator George P. McLean of Connecticut proposed a bill to regulate migratory birds on the grounds that migration of waterfowl across state boundaries constituted interstate commerce. Because the bill extended federal powers, it was strongly opposed by states'-rights congressmen from the South and West. Widespread public support for bird protection urged the passage of the bill, but Congress would not act on it. Toward the end of the congressional session in March, 1913, the migratory bird legislation was attached as a rider to an agricultural appropriation bill. Concealed in this manner, it passed both houses of Congress and was signed by Taft during the last hours of his administration.

With the passage of the Weeks-McLean Act, the secretary of agriculture authorized the Biological Survey to draft suitable regulations prescribing and fixing hunting seasons. The regulations clearly defined the species considered to be migratory game and insectivorous birds. The regulations also provided a detailed schedule of closed hunting seasons on these birds for various zones throughout the United States. George Grinnell and John Lacey were among those appointed to an advisory board to assist the secretary of agriculture in making the law effective. The regulations went into effect on October 1, 1913.

IMPACT AND SUBSEQUENT LEGISLATION

The Weeks-McLean Act was the most sweeping action of its time taken by the country for the protection of wildlife, but its usefulness was hampered by Congress's failure to provide sufficient enforcement funding. The greatest blow to the Migratory Bird Act, however, came from a federal court case in Arkansas in 1914. An individual had killed birds in violation of the Weeks-McLean law and was indicted for the offense. The federal judge for the case rendered an opinion adverse to the law. He stated that no provision of the Constitution allowed Congress to claim that migratory birds were the property of the U.S. government. In his opinion, attempts to regulate the shooting of these birds were unconstitutional. The judge's decision effectively negated the Migratory Bird Act.

In the meantime, a bird-protection treaty was being negotiated between the United States and Canada. Supporters of the Weeks-McLean Act actively urged passage of the treaty. The Migratory Bird Treaty Act was passed by Congress in 1918. Its regulations had a firmer legal foundation; treaties take precedence over state laws. The treaty also gave the Biological Survey international responsibilities in protecting and regulating hunting of migratory birds.

Even though the Weeks-McLean Act itself was unsuccessful in protecting bird species, the massive public support for the law aided in the passage of the treaty. The regulations of the bird law formed the basis for the protection of migratory and insectivorous birds under the international treaty. This treaty was a major step in satisfying America's growing desire to protect its wildlife.

The Weeks-McLean Act formed the basis for future wildlife protection policy in the United States. The law's regulations recognized the importance of species other than game birds. Insectivorous birds are song and other perching birds that feed either entirely or chiefly on insects. The protection of these migratory birds would indirectly protect farmers, as many of the insects eaten by these birds are destructive to crops and fruit trees. The act also established the Biological Survey as a federal agency empowered to enforce its regulations. With the passage of the Migratory Bird Treaty Act, the survey became part of early international efforts to protect bird and other wildlife species. The survey would eventually become the U.S. Fish and Wildlife Service, with a wider range of responsibilities.

The regulations written for the Weeks-McLean Act recognized the importance of protecting birds in their nesting grounds from any hunting. Species could not reproduce adequately if breeding colonies were destroyed. This concept would later be expanded to include the protection of wildlife habitats by the Endangered Species Act of 1973.

Pamela R. Justice

SOURCES FOR FURTHER STUDY
Bird Lore. "The Federal Migratory-Bird Law in the Courts." July, 1914, 322-323.
_____. "Proposed Regulations for the Protection of Migratory Birds." July, 1913, 230-235.
Cooke, Wells W. "Saving the Ducks and Geese." *National Geographic,* March, 1913, 360-380.
Dunlap, Thomas R. *Saving America's Wildlife.* Princeton, N.J.: Princeton University Press, 1988.
Fox, Stephen. *John Muir and His Legacy: The American Conservation Movement.* Boston: Little, Brown, 1981.
Pearson, T. G. "Weeks-McLean Law." *Bird Lore,* March, 1913, 137-138.
Reiger, John F. *American Sportsmen and the Origins of Conservation.* Norman: University of Oklahoma Press, 1986.
Scientific American. "Federal Regulations for Protection of Migratory Birds." July 22, 1913, 66.

SEE ALSO: Migratory Bird Treaty Act (1918); Migratory Bird Hunting and Conservation Stamp Act (1934); Endangered Species Preservation Act (1966); Endangered Species Act (1973); Convention on the Conservation of Migratory Species of Wild Animals (1979).

SEVENTEENTH AMENDMENT

DATE: Ratified April 8, 1913; certified May 31, 1913
U.S. STATUTES AT LARGE: 37 Stat. 646
CATEGORIES: Constitutional Law; Voting and Elections

The Seventeenth Amendment provided for direct election of U.S. senators and represents one of the first advances in the movement toward direct democracy during the early twentieth century.

The Constitutional Convention of 1787 provided for a bicameral national legislature. The House of Representatives, voted on directly by the electorate, reflects a measure of direct, or pure, democracy. The other chamber, the Senate, was created to represent the states, thereby providing a check on the lower chamber. In contrast to the members of the House, who are voted on every two years, the Senate's members (according to the first clause of Article I, section 3 of the U.S. Constitution) were initially chosen by state legislatures. In cases of vacancy, section 2 allowed the state executive to make temporary appointments of senators pending state legislative action. Only one-third of the Senate seats are up for election every two years.

James Wilson of Pennsylvania proposed direct election of senators at the Philadelphia Convention in 1787, and in the mid-nineteenth century Andrew Johnson, a Democrat from Tennessee, advocated direct elections both as senator and as president, but there was virtually no support for that approach. After the Civil War, however, popular sentiment changed rapidly. Industrialization, large-scale immigration, and urbanization spawned big-city bosses, the rise of special interests, and public corruption. The

Senate heard increasing numbers of bribery cases, and states experienced legislative deadlock.

A groundswell of popular support for the direct election of senators emerged as a result of combined criticism voiced by the Populists—especially William Jennings Bryan, the Democratic Party, the mostly western Bull Moose progressive faction of the Republican Party, "muckraker" journalists in the vein of Lincoln Steffens, and influential newspaper publisher William Randolph Hearst. Southerners and the mostly industrial northeastern states, bastion of the conservative wing of the Republican Party, resisted the change. The House of Representatives, the people's voice in Congress, overwhelmingly passed direct election amendments, but the Senate consistently killed them in its Committee on Privileges and Elections.

Western states circumvented the status-quo Senate. In 1901, the "Oregon system" was launched. It provided for state primary elections that allowed the state legislature to ratify voters' preferences. After twenty-nine states adopted similar legislation and thirty-three state legislatures called for a direct election amendment, the Senate Judiciary Committee reported such legislation out on January 1, 1911. By then, membership of the Senate had changed and on May 13, 1912, Congress approved the bill. On April 8, 1913, the Seventeenth Amendment was ratified by three-fourths of the state legislatures. Representative democracy was enhanced significantly.

William D. Pederson

SOURCES FOR FURTHER STUDY

Bernstein, Richard B. *Amending America: If We Love the Constitution So Much, Why Do We Keep Trying to Change It?* New York: Random House, 1993.

Grimes, Alan P. *Democracy and the Amendments to the Constitution.* Lexington, Mass.: Lexington Books, 1978.

Rossum, Ralph A. *Federalism, the Supreme Court, and the Seventeenth Amendment: The Irony of Constitutional Democracy.* Lanham, Md.: Lexington Books, 2001.

Vile, John R. *A Companion to the United States Constitution and Its Amendments.* 3d ed. Westport, Conn.: Greenwood Press, 2001.

_____. *Encyclopedia of Constitutional Amendments, Proposed Amendments, and Amending Issues, 1789-1995.* Santa Barbara, Calif: ABC-CLIO, 1996.

SEE ALSO: Electoral Count Act (1878); Direct democracy laws (1913).

ALIEN LAND LAWS

DATE: Beginning May 20, 1913
CATEGORIES: Asia or Asian Americans; Immigration; Property

These measures deprived Japanese Americans of their property rights.

Immigration from Japan to the United States increased significantly during the final decade of the nineteenth century, with most of the Asian immigrants settling in the Pacific states. As the number of Japanese laborers arriving in California increased substantially, however, a strong anti-Japanese sentiment developed: Their success threatened and antagonized the emerging labor unions. The Asian Exclusion League was formed in 1905, and a campaign to bar Japanese immigration was launched. Negotiations begun in 1906 between the United States and Japan resulted in the Gentlemen's Agreement of 1907, which limited immigration from Japan to nonlaborers and to families who were joining previously settled laborers. In 1907, an immigration bill was amended to prevent Japanese laborers from entering the United States via Hawaii, Mexico, and Canada.

THE FIRST PROPOSALS
The California legislature's attempts to pass alien land bills began in 1907 when it appropriated funds to investigate Japanese agricultural involvement. The California State Labor Commission's report, which was favorable to the Japanese, resulted in a reprimand for the commissioner. In 1910, twenty-seven anti-Japanese proposals were introduced in the legislature. Enactment of the proposed anti-Japanese legislation was prevented that year by influence from

the White House and, in 1911, by President William Howard Taft's direct intervention.

On April 4, 1913, a California bill that would prohibit Japanese and other foreigners ineligible for citizenship from holding or leasing land in California prompted the Japanese ambassador, Viscount Chinda, to make an informal protest to the Department of State. The proposed bill in California was modeled on an 1897 federal law barring ownership of land by aliens ineligible for citizenship. The federal law, however, contained a proviso that it would not be applicable where treaty obligations conferred the right to own and hold land. The California bill included a clause prohibiting the leasing of land to Japanese, but the Japanese contended that this right had been conferred previously by the Treaty of 1894 and reenacted in the Treaty of 1911.

In Washington, D.C., the introduction of the 1913 California Alien Land bill was viewed seriously. The prevailing opinion was that its effect could be more sweeping than the problems of 1908 and could lead once again to talk of war. When Secretary William Jennings Bryan and Ambassador Chinda exchanged mutual assurances of continuing friendship between the United States and Japan on April 4, the Department of State expressed confidence that the matter would be resolved amicably. The following day, Bryan met with the California congressional delegation, which emphasized the necessity of the proposed legislation. Members of the delegation described how, in many parts of California, more than half the farms were operated by Japanese, and neither U.S. nor Chinese workers could compete with Japanese labor. They asserted that despite the Gentlemen's Agreement of 1907, "coolie laborers" were arriving continuously. The feeling in California was so strong, they reported, that people who leased land to the Japanese were ostracized by their neighbors. Members of the delegation intimated that violent protests against the increase in Japanese competition were imminent.

In Japan, the Tokyo press vehemently opposed the legislation. The Japanese government filed a formal protest on April 7. President Woodrow Wilson's position was to remain outside the conflict because he believed that the proposed legislation lay within the rights of a sovereign state.

The final draft of the new law was adopted by the California Senate on April 12. Ambassador Chinda presented his government's formal protest against the bill to the Department of State. Because of agitation in Tokyo, where the bill was denounced by the press and where demonstrators were calling for war, the California legislature, despite overwhelming margins in both houses, delayed further action until May 20, when the Alien Land Law, known also as the Webb-Henley bill, was signed into law by Governor Hiram Warren Johnson. The statute barred all aliens ineligible for citizenship, or corporations with more than 50 percent ineligible alien ownership, from the legal right to own agricultural land in California, and it limited land-leasing contracts in the state to three years' duration.

FURTHER RESTRICTIONS

To prevent the Japanese from circumventing the law, a more restrictive alien land bill was introduced in the California legislature in 1920 to forbid the Issei (first generation Japanese Americans) from buying land in the name of their U.S.-born children, the Nisei. It also prohibited the transfer of land to noncitizens by sale or lease and established criminal penalties for aliens caught attempting to bypass the 1913 law. In a statewide ballot, California voters passed the 1920 Alien Land Law by a three-to-one margin. A number of cases to test the constitutionality of the new law were instigated by the Japanese. In 1923, the U.S. Supreme Court ruled against the Issei in four of these cases. Further restrictions also were passed in a 1923 amendment, which, together with the 1924 Immigration Act, effectively denied further immigration and determined the status of Japanese immigrants in the United States. The alien land laws in California were not repealed until 1956.

During 1917, an alien land law was enacted in Arizona. In 1921, Washington, Texas, and Louisiana followed suit, as did New Mexico in 1922, and Oregon, Idaho, and Montana in 1923. Other states followed: Kansas in 1925; Missouri in 1939; Utah, Arkansas, and Nebraska in 1943; and Minnesota in 1945.

Susan E. Hamilton

SUPREME COURT DECISIONS

In 1923 the Supreme Court upheld alien land laws in four separate cases. In *Terrace v. Thompson*, the Court upheld a Washington state statute prohibiting citizens from leasing land to Japanese immigrants. *Porterfield v. Webb* involved a similar statute in California. In *Webb v. O'Brien*, the Court found sharecropping agreements between citizens and aliens to be illegal, and in *Frick v. Webb*, it upheld a statue prohibiting aliens from owning stock in certain types of agricultural corporations. Furthermore, two Court cases in 1922, *Yamashita v. Hinkle* and *Ozawa v. United States* upheld the constitutionality of denying naturalized citizenship to Japanese immigrants.

However, in *Oyama v. California* (1948), the Court declared California's 1920 alien land law to be "outright racial discrimination" and in violation of the equal protection clause of the Fourteenth Amendment. In 1952 the McCarran-Walter Act granted Japanese immigrants the right to naturalized citizenship. State referendums officially repealed the remaining alien land laws, with the last law reversed in Washington state in 1966.

Mary Louise Buley-Meissner

SOURCES FOR FURTHER STUDY

Chuman, Frank F. *The Bamboo People: The Law and Japanese-Americans.* Del Mar, Calif.: Publisher's Inc., 1976.

Curry, Charles F. *Alien Land Laws and Alien Rights.* Washington, D.C.: Government Printing Office, 1921.

Ichioka, Yuji. *The Issei: The World of the First Generation Japanese Immigrants, 1885-1924.* New York: Free Press, 1988.

McGovney, Dudley. "The Anti-Japanese Land Laws of California and Ten Other States." *California Law Review* 35 (1947): 7-54.

Nomura, Gail M. "Washington's Asian/Pacific American Communities." In *Peoples of Washington: Perspectives on Cultural Diversity*, edited by Sid White and S. E. Solberg. Pullman: Washington State University Press, 1989.

Takaki, Ronald, ed. *Iron Cages: Race and Culture in Nineteenth Century America.* New York: Oxford University Press, 1990.

SEE ALSO: Gentlemen's Agreement (1907); Immigration Act of 1917 (1917); Immigration Act of 1921 (1921); Cable Act (1922); Immigration Act of 1924 (1924); Immigration Act of 1943 (1943); War Brides Act (1945); Immigration and Nationality Act of 1952 (1952).

FEDERAL RESERVE ACT

ALSO KNOWN AS: Glass-Owen Act
DATE: December 23, 1913
U.S. STATUTES AT LARGE: 38 Stat. 251
U.S. CODE: 28 § 2671
CATEGORIES: Banking, Money, and Finance; Government Procedure and Organization

Money and the banking system are placed under control of a central bank, giving the federal government significant economic powers.

By the beginning of the twentieth century, the U.S. economy was the most powerful in the world, yet its banking system was less than efficient. The United States had two major types of commercial banks: those chartered by the states, and those chartered by the federal government.

NATIONAL BANKS, STATE BANKS

National banks received their charters through the authority of the National Bank Acts of 1863 and 1864, which required a bank seeking a national charter to purchase government securities and submit to federal regulation. The bank then could issue national banknotes, which became the national currency after greenbacks were withdrawn, beginning in 1865. Most important, the National Bank Acts either prohibited (in the case of national banks) or did not expressly permit branch banking, particularly interstate branch banking. That had the dual effect of subjecting the individual state systems to the vicissitudes of local or regional economic dislocations, and of producing state-line barriers to rapid transfers of money and capital in the event of such dislocations.

As a result, the nation's banking system operated under two regulatory systems, one for state banks and one for national banks. States had far lower capital requirements for banks, and some states permitted intrastate branch banking, making their systems far more attractive to prospective bankers when they determined to obtain a charter. Thus, after a brief period during which national charters expanded, state-chartered banks soon eclipsed those receiving federal charters. A more significant problem involved the inelasticity of the currency, which meant that the money supply could not expand and contract with the seasonal needs of the economy, particularly in agricultural areas. The system also suffered from flawed redemption mechanisms, making it even more difficult to contract the money supply in bad times than to expand it in prosperous periods.

Interstate branching would have solved many, if not all, of those problems, as would maintenance of the pre-Civil War system of competitive banknote issue, wherein any chartered bank could print its own money. The National Bank and Currency Acts, however, had placed a 10 percent tax on all non-national banknotes, giving the government a monopoly over currency creation. Thus, the government had the authority, but not the capability, to control the money supply, while private banks had the capability, but not the authority, to do so.

PROPOSALS FOR REFORM

Numerous reform measures were advanced to meet those problems in the latter half of the nineteenth century. The greenback movement of the 1870's and the Populists' agitation in the 1890's for "free silver"—unlimited coinage of silver at fixed (inflated) prices—both sought to address the long-term deflation caused by international economic forces. Both those plans would have required the federal government to inflate the money supply artificially. Other reformers wanted to place more control in the federal government, through creation of a central bank akin to the Bank of England. The United States had not had a central bank since President Andrew Jackson effectively destroyed the Second Bank of the United States by vetoing its recharter in 1832.

Two other factors accelerated the reform agenda. First, the Panic of 1907 persuaded many Americans, including the nation's premier banker J. P. Morgan, that no single private bank or group of banks could rescue the nation from depressions (as Morgan had in the Panic of 1893, when he loaned the government 3.5 million ounces of gold). Many bankers concluded that they needed a lender of last resort to keep banks afloat during periods of financial panic, and that such emergency loans themselves would quell the hysteria and impose financial stability. Second, with the Populists leading the way, Americans grew increasingly alarmed over the concentration of financial power in New York City. Many openly spoke of conspiracies—and especially linked "money power" to

Jews, even though the largest New York bankers, like Morgan, were Protestant Christians. As a result, the reform movement focused on creating a lender of last resort, adding elasticity to the system, and reducing the power of New York City.

Following the Panic of 1907, a National Monetary Commission, composed of members of Congress, was created in 1908 to devise a plan for a revision of the banking system. Headed by Senator Nelson W. Aldrich, the commission prepared the so-called Aldrich Plan. That plan called for a voluntary system headed by a central bank, the National Reserve Association, having branch banks that would issue currency and hold the deposits of the federal government, while furnishing reserve credit to member banks. Some large banks supported the Aldrich Plan, but by the time it was submitted to Congress in 1912, it faced strong opposition.

Many Progressives feared that, under the plan, Wall Street would retain control over the nation's financial markets. Unit bankers convinced Congress that interstate banking would permit large New York City banks to extend into middle America, driving the smaller country banks out of business. Woodrow Wilson, elected president in 1912, shared Progressive sentiments. The Democrats controlled the Congress but were divided on the banking issue. Southern and Western radicals followed William Jennings Bryan of Nebraska. Conservatives were headed by Congressman Carter Glass of Virginia, chairman of the House Banking Committee. Bryan, who was joined by William G. McAdoo, soon to be secretary of the Treasury, and Senator Robert L. Owen of Oklahoma, chairman of the Senate Banking Committee, insisted that the government control any banking system enacted and that it also control the money supply. Glass and his faction opposed any plan for a central bank and favored a loose, disconnected system of regional reserve banks.

CRAFTING A NEW BANKING LAW

In the weeks before Wilson's inaugural, Glass worked with Wilson and H. Parker Willis, a banking expert, on a new banking law to provide a privately controlled system of regional reserve banks, with a general supervisory and coordinating board. The plan developed by Wilson, Glass, and Willis resembled a decentralized version of the Aldrich Plan. After incorporating into it changes demanded by the radical faction, such as a federal guarantee of notes issued by the new system, the plan was submitted to Congress as the

Federal Reserve, or Glass-Owen, bill. After further changes, the measure was finally passed in December, 1913, almost a year after its inception.

The Federal Reserve Act had the stated purposes of providing for the establishment of no more than twelve regional Federal Reserve Banks, furnishing an elastic currency, affording means for rediscounting commercial paper, and establishing a more effective supervision of banking in the United States. The twelve "bankers' banks" neither accepted deposits from individuals nor loaned them money, and were controlled by a five-member Board of Governors (later increased to seven members) appointed by the president for ten-year terms. They worked along with the secretary of the Treasury and the comptroller (originally ex officio members) to oversee operation of the system. Member banks elected six of the nine directors of the district Federal Reserve Banks, whose capital was subscribed by the commercial banks that joined the system. Technically, the system was a corporation owned by the member banks, but the "Fed" (as it is called) came to act completely independently of the banks. Although it is directly responsible to Congress, neither Congress nor the president ever successfully exercised control over it. Thus, Fed policies had far-reaching effects on the U.S. economy, yet Fed leadership was virtually unaccountable.

IMPACT OF THE "FED"

The intent of the Federal Reserve Act was to decentralize power and move it out of New York City; therefore, most of the reserve banks were located in the West and South, with the state of Missouri alone containing two. Yet the New York Fed immediately emerged as the most powerful and quickly dominated the others, thanks to its brilliant governor, Benjamin Strong. Under Strong's leadership, the New York Fed merely took over the role that J. P. Morgan once had held. Strong died in 1928; his absence left a leadership void in New York as the worldwide economic crises of the 1920's reached their apex.

At that point, another set of factors grounded in the Federal Reserve Act exacerbated economic problems. First, the act essentially had undercut the role of the successful clearinghouse associations that had developed in the absence of interstate branching by the turn of the century. The associations had provided rapid information transmission among members—a task that the Fed assumed for itself. Second, the act had made little mention of the gold standard, assuming that it would continue to function. However, as European nations' economies collapsed in the 1920's, those nations left the gold standard. By the end of the decade, the United States was one of the few countries remaining on the gold standard, which led to a sharp outflow of gold from the United States. Federal Reserve notes were guaranteed by gold, and financial panics started.

The Fed then turned a recession into a disaster by raising interest rates, choking off the money supply at the very time business needed an expanding money supply to sustain growth. In addition, some economists have pointed to the misjudgment of the New York Fed in failing to rescue the Bank of the United States, triggering further runs. The result was the Great Depression, a cyclical downturn exacerbated by, if not caused by, Fed policies.

Congress reformed the banking system yet again during the Great Depression, instituting deposit insurance and separating banking and securities operations. An indirect result of those reforms was the savings and loan crisis of the 1980's, in which the Federal Savings and Loan Insurance Corporation (FSLIC) virtually went bankrupt attempting to support savings and loans that had collapsed due to federal restrictions on their lending. Through the mid-1990's, the Fed has maintained somewhat steady interest rates but has had little success supporting the value of the dollar internationally.

Merle O. Davis, updated by
Larry Schweikart

SOURCES FOR FURTHER STUDY
Friedman, Milton, and Anna J. Schwartz. *A Monetary History of the United States, 1867-1960.* Princeton, N.J.: Princeton University Press, 1963.
Greider, William. *Secrets of the Temple: How the Federal Reserve Runs the Country.* New York: Simon & Schuster, 1987.
Timberlake, Richard H. "Federal Reserve Act." In *Encyclopedia of American Business History and Biography: Banking and Finance to 1913,* edited by Larry Schweikart. New York: Facts On File, 1990.
Wheelock, David. *The Strategy and Consistency of Federal Reserve Monetary Policy, 1924-1933.* New York: Cambridge University Press, 1991.

White, Eugene Nelson. *The Regulation and Reform of the American Banking System, 1900-1929.* Princeton, N.J.: Princeton University Press, 1983.

SEE ALSO: Independent Treasury Act (1846); National Bank Acts (1863-1864); Coinage Act (1873); Currency Act (1900); Mcfadden Act (1927); Banking Act of 1933 (1933); Banking Act of 1935 (1935).

FEDERAL TRADE COMMISSION ACT

DATE: September 26, 1914
U.S. STATUTES AT LARGE: 38 Stat. 717
U.S. CODE: 15 § 41 et seq.
CATEGORIES: Business, Commerce, and Trade; Government Procedure and Organization

This act created the Federal Trade Commmission, which is mandated to protect the public against unfair and deceptive business practices.

Congress passed the Federal Trade Commission Act (FTCA) for the purpose of protecting consumers from unfair methods of competition and unfair or deceptive acts in commerce. The act created the Federal Trade Commission (FTC) to enforce the provisions of the act and to determine what is unfair competition and what constitutes deceptive acts. The passage of the act was the result of a program by President Woodrow Wilson to curtail the growth of business trusts and monopolistic businesses and to preserve competition as an effectual regulator of business.

PURPOSE AND PROVISIONS
The underlying philosophy of the act is that markets should generally be left to competitive market forces and that noncompetitive market structures should be prevented. The intent was to prevent unfair practices rather than punish perpetrators.

The fundamental objectives of the FTC are to initiate antitrust actions and to protect the consumer public. The FTCA was amended by the Wheeler-Lea Act in 1938, which prohibits a variety of deceptive practices in commerce. The FTCA gave the FTC power to promote free and fair competition through the prevention of price-fixing agreements, boycotts, combinations in restraint of trade, interlocking directorates, unfair acts of competition, false advertising, and other deceptive business practices. Businesses need not have committed a deceptive act to be in violation of the provisions of the FTCA. The law does not require an actual deception; a company may be held liable for unfair and deceptive acts when there is a possible likelihood that a consumer might be deceived. A company can be held liable for the unfair and deceptive acts of its employees, agents, or other representatives. The act applies to interstate and foreign commerce but does not apply to banking institutions, savings and loan institutions, federal credit unions, or common carriers—all of which are regulated by other federal agencies.

FEDERAL TRADE COMMISSION

The FTC consists of five commissioners who are appointed by the president with the advice and consent of the Senate. Not more than three of the commissioners can be from the same political party. Commissioners serve seven-year terms. Among the FTC's activities are the enforcement of the provisions of the Sherman Act of 1890, the Clayton Act of 1914, and amendments to these acts. The FTC also enforces the Truth in Lending Act of 1968 and some aspects of the Foreign Corrupt Practices Act of 1977. To enforce legislation, the FTC can investigate corporate conduct, hold hearings, and issue cease-and-desist orders. If a person or company fails to comply with the cease-and-desist order, the FTC turns to the Federal Circuit Court of Appeals for enforcement.

Over its history, several Supreme Court decisions have frustrated the work of the FTC, but the commission has done much toward ridding the economy of anticompetitive business practices.

Dale L. Flesher

SOURCES FOR FURTHER STUDY

Holt, William Stull. *The Federal Trade Commission: Its History, Activities, and Organization.* New York: D. Appleton and Company, 1922.

O'Dell, George T. "The Federal Trade Commission Yields to Pressure." *The Nation,* January, 1921, 36-37.
Rublee, George. "The Original Plan and Early History of the Federal Trade Commission." *Annals of the American Academy of Political and Social Science,* January, 1926, 115-117.

SEE ALSO: Interstate Commerce Act (1887); Sherman Antitrust Act (1890); Clayton Antitrust Act (1914); Wheeler-Lea Act (1938); Celler-Kefauver Act (1950); Truth in Lending Act (1968); Parens Patriae Act (1974); Antitrust Procedures and Penalties Act (1974).

CLAYTON ANTITRUST ACT

DATE: October 15, 1914
U.S. STATUTES AT LARGE: 38 Stat. 730
U.S. CODE: 15 § 12
CATEGORIES: Business, Commerce, and Trade; Labor and Employment

The Clayton Act outlawed a number of business practices limiting competition and strengthened the legal position of labor unions. While providing a symbolic victory for those seeking to halt the dominance of American industry by large corporations, the act proved disappointing in its impact.

The growing power of great corporations, or "trusts," was a major concern in the late nineteenth and early twentieth centuries. How best to deal with the problem was a major issue in the 1912 presidential campaign. Woodrow Wilson, the Democratic candidate, advocated a "New Freedom" platform that promised to cut trusts down to size and encourage a more competitive business environment.

STRENGTHENING SHERMAN
After Wilson's election, one approach of his administration was to remedy what was thought to be too general language of the

Sherman Antitrust Act (1890), the nation's primary antitrust law. In 1914, under the leadership of Congressman Henry D. Clayton, chairman of the House Judiciary Committee, Congress proceeded to pass a new antitrust measure whose main thrust was to foil would-be monopolists by outlawing tactics that in the past had fostered the growth of large corporations.

The Clayton Act attacked a range of business practices: acquisition of stock of a competitor, interlocking directorates (the same directors sitting on the boards of supposedly competing companies), price discrimination (giving some customers an advantage by charging them lower prices than their competitors), and exclusive or tying contracts. All these practices were outlawed "where the effect may be to substantially lessen competition or tend to create monopoly." The act also made corporate officials personally liable for the actions of their companies. Individuals or heads of firms who believed that they had been harmed by such tactics could seek an injunction to stop the objectionable practice, and they could sue for triple damages.

The act also sought to improve the legal position of organized labor. It declared that labor was not a commodity and that antitrust laws could not be used against legitimate union activities, such as peaceful strikes or boycotts. It also prohibited the use of injunctions in labor disputes unless danger threatened persons or property.

CIRCUMVENTING CLAYTON

The Clayton Act proved disappointing to many of those who had supported it. President Wilson switched his emphasis, trying to encourage greater competition in the economy through regulation provided by the Federal Trade Commission, also created in 1914. Corporate lawyers soon found ways to get around the act's provisions, especially since the courts found latitude in the act's wording that made violations difficult to prove. Though strengthened in 1936 and 1950, the act has been less important in antitrust law than the Sherman Act. Although labor leader Samuel Gompers had hailed the act as "labor's Magna Carta," it did not meet the hopes of its supporters in this arena either, for it failed to end the use of injunctions in labor disputes.

William C. Lowe

SOURCE FOR FURTHER STUDY
Kintner, Earl W., ed. *Federal Antitrust Laws and Related Statutes: A Legislative History.* 11 vols. Buffalo, N.Y.: William S. Hein, 1978, 1982-1985.

SEE ALSO: Interstate Commerce Act (1887); Sherman Antitrust Act (1890); Federal Trade Commission Act (1914); Wheeler-Lea Act (1938); Celler-Kefauver Act (1950); Truth in Lending Act (1968); Antitrust Procedures and Penalties Act (1974).

HARRISON NARCOTIC DRUG ACT

ALSO KNOWN AS: Harrison Act
DATE: December 17, 1914
U.S. STATUTES AT LARGE: 38 Stat. 785
CATEGORIES: Food and Drugs; Health and Welfare

The most comprehensive federal drug legislation at the time, the Harrison Narcotic Drug Act was designed to control the production and dispensation of narcotics; however, it raised issues of federal versus state authority and the protected physician-patient relationship.

Prompted by international treaty obligations under the 1912 Hague Convention and concerns over drug abuse, Representative Francis Burton Harrison, a Democrat, introduced H.R. 6282 on June 10, 1913. The bill passed Congress on December 14, 1914, and President Woodrow Wilson signed it on December 17, 1914. The Harrison Act required the registration of all producers and dispensers of narcotics with the district internal revenue collector and the payment of an annual fee of one dollar. Violations carried a penalty of up to two thousand dollars and five years' imprisonment.

Section 8 of the Harrison Act declared as unlawful the possession of specified drugs by unregistered persons unless the drugs were prescribed by a physician, and it placed the burden of proof on the defendant. Federal district courts ruled, however, that addicts could not be arrested for possession as long as they had obtained the drug by prescription. In June, 1916, the Supreme Court ruled in *Jin Fuey Moy v. United States* (1916) that the Hague Convention (which had banned narcotics trafficking) did not require the police powers specified in section 8, which overturned central portions of the act.

Thomas Winter

SOURCES FOR FURTHER STUDY

Temin, Peter. *Taking Your Medicine: Drug Regulation in the United States.* Cambridge, Mass.: Harvard University Press, 1980.

U.S. Food and Drug Administration. *Milestones in U.S. Food and Drug Law History.* Washington, D.C.: Government Printing Office, 1985.

SEE ALSO: Opium Exclusion Act (1909); Marihuana Tax Act (1937); Food, Drug, and Cosmetic Act (1938); Comprehensive Drug Abuse Prevention and Control Act (1970); National Narcotics Act (1984).

NATIONAL DEFENSE ACT AND MILITARY APPROPRIATIONS ACT

ALSO KNOWN AS: Army Reorganization Act
DATE: June 3, 1916; August, 1916
U.S. STATUTES AT LARGE: 39 Stat. 203
CATEGORIES: Military and National Security

On the eve of U.S. entry into World War I, these acts authorized the president to commandeer plants for production of war matériel and coordinated government, civilian, and military organizations through the Council of National Defense.

The War Industries Board (WIB) was organized on July 8, 1917, to coordinate and control the industrial resources of the United States in its World War I effort against Germany. Establishment of the WIB was the climax of several frustrating months of efforts to mobilize agencies of production and distribution following the nation's entry into the war in April.

MOBILIZING FOR WAR

Federal coordination of industry had begun in 1915, when Congress authorized the creation of a Committee on Industrial Preparedness to study the supply requirements of the Army and Navy. The committee's work was narrow in scope—its primary accomplishment was the preparation of an inventory of plants able to manufacture munitions. As the war emergency in the United States became more acute, the government extended its power over the nation's industrial life. By the National Defense Act of June, 1916, Congress authorized the president to place orders for war matériel with any source of supply and to commandeer plants when it was in the national interest to do so. Two months later, Congress approved a Military Appropriations Act, providing for a Council of National Defense consisting of the secretaries of war, navy, interior, agriculture, commerce, and labor, and an advisory commission comprising civilian representatives from all the major sectors of the nation's economy. The purpose of both committees was to plan for the most efficient use of the country's resources in case of war.

The advisory commission, which served as the executive committee of the Council of National Defense, did most of the work and mapped out extensive preparations to meet wartime needs. Each of the seven members of the commission took charge of a special segment of the economy, such as transportation, engineering and education, munitions and manufacturing, medicine and surgery, raw materials, supplies, and labor. The commission soon became the nucleus of numerous committees and boards that were the forerunners of several wartime agencies, including the WIB. Finally, Bernard Baruch, a Wall Street investor and the commissioner in charge of raw materials, formulated an elaborate plan whereby representatives of various businesses were organized into "committees of the industries" to work with the council in coordinating the country's resources. For their efforts, they received one dollar a year, and thus were known as the "dollar-a-year men."

COUNCIL OF NATIONAL DEFENSE

Because the Council of National Defense had been formed to plan for, rather than direct, industrial mobilization, its powers were only advisory. Moreover, its organization was extremely loose; many of its ablest men served only in a part-time capacity. It was ill-prepared, therefore, to assume the responsibility of directing mobilization, which was forced upon it after the United States' entry into war in 1917. That unpreparedness was readily apparent in the council's attempt to coordinate the purchases of the U.S. Departments of the Navy and War. For that purpose, the advisory commission first established a Munitions Standard Board and then a General Munitions Board, on which members of the commission and representatives from the military purchasing bureaus served. The power and authority of the board were poorly defined, and its machinery nearly broke down under the pressure of the war orders. Within a month after its establishment, it was found that the board merely overlapped in jurisdiction and authority with many of the other committees formed by the Advisory Commission. As a result, it was unable to coordinate the purchases of the military bureaus, which, jealous of their own prerogatives, continued to go their own ways. Realizing that a central coordinating agency was needed, the Council of National Defense, on July 18, 1917, replaced the General Munitions Board with the WIB, comprising five civilians and one representative each from the Army and the Navy.

WAR INDUSTRIES BOARD

Before the Civil War, the United States had adopted a policy of procuring many, if not most, wartime goods and weapons from civilian businesses. With the exception of a few shipyards or munitions plants, the government therefore relied primarily on private industry to provide a steady stream of war goods and combat weapons. Coordinating that production and flow was a major problem for a nation that allowed the market to determine the type and number of goods to be supplied. In wartime, the urgency of delivery dictated that coordination of production and delivery systems fall to the government.

While the War Industries Board was given broad responsibilities for the direction of war industry needs, its ability to do effective work suffered from the lack of any executive power. As a result, the government's effort to coordinate the nation's military and industrial efforts continued to flounder for the next eight months. The board's first chairman, F. A. Scott, broke down under the strain of the war; its second, Daniel Willard, resigned because he believed that the board lacked authority.

In the spring of 1918, President Woodrow Wilson reorganized the board and named Bernard Baruch as its chairman. In effect, the president transferred to Baruch the power to coordinate industry that Congress had granted to the president in the National Defense and Military Appropriations Acts of 1916, as well as giving Baruch certain controls over the military that Wilson had in his capacity as commander in chief. Endowed with this authority, Baruch was able to determine priorities, requisition supplies, conserve resources, commandeer plants, and make purchases for the United States and the Allies. The only important control he did not exercise directly was that of fixing prices, which was left to a separate committee within the board.

Despite some sharp criticism later by congressional critics regarding the extent of power that the War Industries Board assumed, the board was highly effective in coordinating the nation's industrial and military effort. The pattern of organization created by the board became the model for the war regulation of industry by the Allies in World War II. Moreover, the introduction of businessmen into government procurement placed professional business managers in close proximity with bureaucrats. This led to an appreciation by business for the role of control and planning, and convinced many in government that business management practices would be effective in improving the government during peacetime. Business already had undergone a managerial revolution that emphasized planning; therefore, the new, centralized control reinforced the notion that stability could be achieved by proper accounting and forecasting. The quintessential proponent of that approach was Herbert Hoover, elected president in 1928, who attempted to apply such nostrums to the Great Depression.

On December 31, 1918, President Wilson directed that the board be dissolved, and it was liquidated on July 22, 1919. Other wartime agencies that were involved in economic mobilization— such as the War Trade Board, which licensed exports and imports and rationed supplies to neutrals, and the United States Railroad Administration, which controlled the nation's railroads—also were dissolved gradually after the war ended.

IMPACT OF WAR MOBILIZATION
Aided by the National Defense and Military Appropriations Acts, the friendly relationship between big business and government that emerged from the war cemented an alliance that lasted until the Great Depression. In the short term, business thought that it was the beneficiary of that relationship, receiving government contracts and favorable treatment. Although the boom provided by the Roaring Twenties proved nourishing to many small businesses, as witnessed by the extensive growth of all business during that decade, the special treatment afforded to such new enterprises as airplane and some shipping companies, based on future wartime needs, served to align government with some industries at the expense of others.

More important, however, were the lessons learned by the government during wartime that were inapplicable during peacetime. The government assumed that wartime planning—based on the coercive powers yielded to bureaucrats by citizens facing a national emergency—would provide the same degree of effectiveness in the absence of the emergency. Since the national tendency of government was to increase during emergencies, but never to recede to its original levels, the war intruded federal authority into the lives of millions of people who had never before experienced it. Thus, although the WIB was disbanded after World War I, the notion that government planning and direct management of businesses could keep the economy stable was revived on a larger scale during the Great Depression.

Burton Kaufman, updated by
Larry Schweikart

SOURCES FOR FURTHER STUDY
Baruch, Bernard. *American Industry in the War.* New York: Prentice-Hall, 1941.
Clarkson, Grosvenor B. *Industrial America in the World War.* Boston: Houghton Mifflin, 1923.
Crowell, Benedict, and Robert F. Wilson. *How America Went to War.* New Haven, Conn.: Yale University Press, 1921.
Cuff, Robert D. "Bernard Baruch: Symbol and Myth in Industrial Mobilization." *Business History Review* 43 (Summer, 1969): 115-133.

Higgs, Robert. *Crisis and Leviathan: Critical Episodes in the Growth of American Government.* New York: Oxford University Press, 1987.
Schaffer, Ronald. *America in the Great War: The Rise of the War Welfare State.* New York: Oxford University Press, 1991.

SEE ALSO: Federal Trade Commission Act (1914); Espionage Acts (1917-1918); Treaty of Versailles (1919); World War Adjusted Compensation Act (1924).

NATIONAL PARK SERVICE ORGANIC ACT

DATE: August 25, 1916
U.S. STATUTES AT LARGE: 39 Stat. 535
U.S. CODE: 16 § 1
CATEGORIES: Environment and Conservation; Land Management

The act established the National Park Service to promote and regulate the use of national parks and monuments.

On August 25, 1916, President Woodrow Wilson signed the National Park Service Organic Act, establishing the National Park Service (NPS). Forty-four years had passed since President Ulysses S. Grant had signed the act on March 1, 1872, establishing Yellowstone National Park, the first area ever designated a national park. Many people and events would play important roles in the development of the national park system.

PREVIOUS CONSERVATION LEGISLATION
John Muir, a naturalist and conservationist, arrived in California's Yosemite State Park in 1868. A conservation prophet, explorer, advocate, and writer, he stayed there until his death in 1914. Muir led the fight to set aside a larger state-controlled area on the Sierra range, which caused Congress to establish a national park nearly the size of Yellowstone and focused attention on the giant sequoia trees that were being destroyed by logging.

Congress made an important distinction between national parks and national forests in the 1890's. In 1891, the Forestry Reserve

Act gave the president the authority to establish national forests from the public domain without congressional approval. National parks still required a separate act of Congress. Four presidents had set aside more than 175 million acres of national forest lands before the Forestry Reserve Act was abolished in 1907.

The year 1906 proved to be significant in the history of national parks. Legislation indicated that there could be other than scenic values in the parks. As early as 1880, people were outraged at the looting of cliff dwellings and Pueblo ruins in the Southwest. Many sites were plundered and vandalized to supply the demands of collectors. Mesa Verde National Park, Colorado, established on June 29, 1906, put historic preservation on the national level. Creation of the park gave permanent protection to the tableland two thousand feet above the surrounding country.

The Antiquities Act, passed that same year, proved one of the best pieces of park legislation ever devised. The act forbade the removal, destruction, or excavation of any historic or prehistoric object or ruin on public land. The act also allowed the president to declare any site on federal lands containing outstanding historic, scientific, or scenic value to be a national monument until Congress could be persuaded to make the area a national park. Caves, forts, canyons, battlefields, pueblos, and birthplaces of famous persons could be considered national monuments.

Also that year, President Theodore Roosevelt created four national monuments: Devils Tower in Wyoming, El Moro in New Mexico, Montezuma Castle in Arizona, and the Petrified Forest in Arizona. He was the first president to make conservation a national goal. Roosevelt also convened a conference on conservation at the White House in 1908, bringing together many national leaders and telling them that it was time for the country to take account of its natural resources.

In 1912, several national park supporters convinced President William Howard Taft that the disorganized way of handling national parks should be streamlined and given professional direction. At the time, each national park had one superintendent and little or no other staff. All were under the supervision of the secretary of the interior. There was no specific national park division. There was little or no funding for staff at the parks, and development was left up to private concessionaires or to those willing to erect a building in which guests could stay while visiting a park.

The U.S. Cavalry was in charge of Yellowstone National Park for many years, and other Army units were in charge of Yosemite and Sequoia during the summers. The U.S. Army Corps of Engineers was in charge of building roads in all the parks.

THE CAMPAIGN FOR A NATIONAL PARK SERVICE

Horace M. Albright went to work for Secretary of the Interior Franklin K. Lane in 1913. Albright had planned to work in Washington for one year and then go back to his native California. Working closely with Lane and Stephen Mather, whom Lane brought in to coordinate the national parks, Albright was instrumental in getting legislative support for the National Park Service Organic Act. He also developed policy issues and served as Mather's assistant. He devoted the next twenty years to the National Park Service. Mather was sworn in as an assistant to the secretary of the interior in charge of national parks in January, 1915.

Mather immediately began promoting the issue of a separate national park service. He brought prominent people together and courted those who had influence in business and politics. He generated great public interest in the national parks and enlisted *The Saturday Evening Post* and *National Geographic* to join his campaign. The railroads, which would benefit from an increase in the number of travelers, paid for a National Parks Portfolio publication, which was distributed free to more than 250,000 people. It was well worth the effort. President Woodrow Wilson signed the bill establishing the National Park Service on August 25, 1916.

PROVISIONS OF THE ACT

The act addressed in general terms the way the new organization should provide for public use while protecting park resources. The park service was established to promote and regulate the use of national parks and monuments, with the purpose of conserving the scenery and the natural and historic objects and the wildlife therein, and to provide for the enjoyment of the parks in such a manner as would leave them unimpaired for the enjoyment of future generations.

The National Park Service thus became a reality. The new federal agency initially oversaw fourteen national parks, twenty-one national monuments, Hot Springs Reservation, and Casa Grande Ruin. Mather and Albright were ready to put their plans for the new system in motion, but the necessary funding had not been approved.

The appropriation to organize the new agency came from Congress only a few days after war was declared on Germany in April, 1917, but it was not sufficient to provide proper personnel and equipment for the park system. Mather was appointed director on May 16, 1917, giving formal structure to the National Park Service.

GETTING STARTED

A special appropriation in the summer of 1918 enabled the new National Park Service to hire a qualified force of rangers for parks under its control. Many service policies and programs were established during these early years: uniformed ranger service, interpretive and information programs, concessionaires, and professional natural and cultural resources management functions.

In 1917, Mount McKinley National Park became the first national park to be created under the new agency. Despite the war and the ensuing Depression, the park system increased in size. For the first time in history, national parks were established in the most populated regions of the country. Land was donated east of the Mississippi River to establish national parks across the United States, making the system a truly national one.

The act creating the National Park Service resulted in many changes in the national parks. The Army was withdrawn from its governance of certain national parks, freeing troops for war service. Mather replaced the soldiers with a professional ranger corps. He publicized the beauty and other attractions of the parks with railroad lines and automobile clubs. Parks were promoted for both their beauty and historic culture.

The National Park Service became an official agency of the federal government, with its own staff, equipment, and budget. The way was paved for other lands and sites to become future national parks. Land in the eastern part of the United States was given national park status; the system thus covered the whole country.

MID-CENTURY

Stephen Mather, the first director of the National Park Service, suffered a stroke in 1928; he was succeeded by Horace Albright, who had been the field director of the service and superintendent of

Yellowstone National Park, in 1929. Albright's administrative talent set a pattern for all the parks. Growth of the park system and professionalization of personnel were Albright's two main goals. His most valuable contribution, however, was in the field of historic preservation.

The conservation movement in the late 1920's had almost no interest in historic preservation. Albright argued that the American heritage was made up of the unique grandeur of the geography of the nation's parks and the heroic deeds of its people, and that both should share in the conservation movement.

Three months after President Franklin D. Roosevelt was inaugurated in 1933, he signed two executive orders reorganizing the national park system. The reorganization orders consolidated all national parks and monuments, all military parks, eleven national cemeteries, all national memorials, and the parks of the nation's capitol under National Park Service authority. For the first time, almost all natural and historic parks in the country were under one agency. In many respects, the reorganization was a personal achievement of Horace Albright.

REORGANIZATION

The 1933 reorganization had three major consequences: It made the National Park Service the agency responsible for almost all federally owned parks, monuments, and memorials, greatly strengthening the system's institutional position and importance; it changed the idea of what the National Park Service should comprise by adding new kinds of areas not before considered as national parks or monuments; and it increased the number and geographic diversity of the Park Service's holdings by adding a dozen natural areas in ten Western states and fifty historical sites in seven Eastern states and the District of Columbia to the system.

The Civilian Conservation Corps (CCC) was established in 1933 as a conservation and reforestation measure. Many of the CCC camps were set up in national park-controlled properties for the purposes of planting trees, cutting fire and hiking trails, and constructing recreation and camping areas, roads, and shelters. The formal structure provided a natural work environment for the greatest reforestation program in U.S. history. It also brought new kinds of parks into the system, such as the Blue Ridge Parkway, the Skyline Drive, and Lake Mead, behind Hoover Dam.

The end of World War II brought instant growth in tourist travel. The park service budget had been reduced by war, and it was not until after the Korean War that the budget was raised to meet needs. Roads and trails had deteriorated because of the lack of repair money.

In 1956, President Dwight D. Eisenhower was presented a ten-year restoration program called "Mission 66." The program was to be completed by the fiftieth anniversary of the National Park Service. It would rehabilitate the parks and add interpretation centers and museums. These centers would explain the history, geology, and wildlife of the area being visited. New facilities would be constructed in all parks, and two new training centers were proposed that would provide Park Service employees with one of the most extensive training programs in the federal government.

More than 300 million visits are made to the national parks each year. Such visits were made possible by the foresight of men such as Lane, Mather, Albright, and Muir. Through their efforts, the natural beauty and historic areas of America have been preserved for the enjoyment of succeeding generations.

Larry N. Sypolt

SOURCES FOR FURTHER STUDY
Albright, Horace M. *The Birth of the National Park Service: The Founding Years, 1913-33.* Salt Lake City: Howe Brothers, 1986.
Everhart, William C. *The National Park Service.* Boulder, Colo.: Westview Press, 1983.
Mackintosh, Barry. *The National Park Service Administrative History: A Guide.* Washington, D.C.: National Park Service, 1991.
_____. *The National Parks: Shaping the System.* Washington, D.C.: Government Printing Office, 1985.
Olsen, Russell K. *Administrative History: Organizational Structures of the National Park Service, 1917 to 1985.* Washington, D.C.: Government Printing Office, 1985.

SEE ALSO: Pittman-Robertson Wildlife Restoration Act (1937); Wilderness Act (1964); Wild and Scenic Rivers Act and National Trails System Act (1968); National Environmental Policy Act (1970); Eastern Wilderness Act (1975); National Forest Management Act (1976).

IMMIGRATION ACT OF 1917

DATE: February 5, 1917
U.S. STATUTES AT LARGE: 39 Stat. 874
PUBLIC LAW: 64-301
CATEGORIES: Asia or Asian Americans; Immigration

The Immigration Act of 1917 significantly restricted immigration into the United States by use of a literacy test, among other measures.

Public concern over immigration prompted the U.S. Congress to establish a Joint Commission on Immigration in 1907. The commission consisted of three members of the Senate, three members of the House of Representatives, and three other appointees. In 1910 and 1911, the Dillingham Commission, named after the legislation's author and the commission's chairman, Senator William P. Dillingham of Vermont, issued a forty-two-volume report that advocated the restriction of immigration. It stated that recent immigrants from southern and eastern Europe were more likely to be unskilled, unsettled, and generally less desirable than the northern and western European immigrants who had arrived previously. Experts later disputed these conclusions, but the report was used to justify the new restrictions that Congress continued to write into law in the comprehensive Immigration Act of 1917.

LITERACY TESTS

A number of different ways to restrict immigration were suggested by the commission. They included instituting a literacy test, excluding unskilled laborers, increasing the amount of money that immigrants were required to have in their possession, and increasing the head tax. The commission also advocated the principle of racial quotas.

Major attention was directed toward the literacy test. Congress had introduced prior bills requiring literacy tests for immigrants. In 1897, such a bill was vetoed by President Grover Cleveland, who said that immigration restrictions were unnecessary. The House voted to override the president's veto on March 3, 195 to 37. The Senate referred the veto message and bill to the Committee on Immigration. When the bill resurfaced at the Sixty-second Congress, it was the Senate that voted to override President William Howard

Taft's veto on February 18, 1913, while the House voted to sustain it on February 19. During the Sixty-third Congress (1914-1917), the House voted to sustain the veto of President Woodrow Wilson.

At the second session of the Sixty-fourth Congress, a bill was introduced "to regulate the immigrating of aliens to, and the residence of aliens in, the United States." Again, Wilson vetoed the bill. On February 1, 1917, the House voted to override the president's veto, 287 to 106, and the Senate voted similarly on February 5, 1917, 62 to 19. The veto was overridden, and the bill became Public Law 301. The act excluded from entry "all aliens over sixteen years of age, physically capable of reading, who can not read the English language, or some other language or dialect, including Hebrew or Yiddish."

OTHER PROVISIONS

Other major recommendations made by the Dillingham Commission six years earlier were passed. The head tax was increased, and vagrants, alcoholics, advocates of violent revolutions, and "psychopathic inferiors" all were barred. A further provision created an Asiatic Barred Zone in the southwest Pacific, which succeeded in excluding most Asian immigrants who were not already excluded by the Chinese Exclusion Act and the Gentlemen's Agreement.

Susan E. Hamilton

SOURCES FOR FURTHER STUDY

Bernard, William S., ed. *American Immigration Policy.* Port Washington, N.Y.: Kennikat Press, 1969.
Cose, Ellis. *A Nation of Strangers.* New York: William Morrow, 1992.
Daniels, Roger. *Coming to America: A History of Immigration and Ethnicity in American Life.* New York: HarperCollins, 1990.
Harper, Elizabeth J. *Immigration Laws of the United States.* 3d ed. Indianapolis: Bobbs-Merrill, 1975.
Nugent, Walter. *Crossings: The Great Transatlantic Migrations, 1870-1914.* Bloomington: Indiana University Press, 1992.

SEE ALSO: Chinese Exclusion Act (1882); Gentlemen's Agreement (1907); Alien land laws (1913); Immigration Act of 1921 (1921); Cable Act (1922); Immigration Act of 1924 (1924); Immigration Act of 1943 (1943); War Brides Act (1945); Immigration and Nationality Act of 1952 (1952);.

JONES ACT

ALSO KNOWN AS: Puerto Rican Federal Relations Act
DATE: March 2, 1917
U.S. STATUTES AT LARGE: 39 Stat. 951
CATEGORIES: Foreign Relations; Immigration; Land Management;
Latinos

*The Jones Act of 1917 formed a unique relationship between the
United States and Puerto Rico.*

On December 10, 1898, the Treaty of Paris between Spain and
the United States ended the Spanish-American War and set forth
terms that became effective April 11, 1900. The agreement transferred the control of Puerto Rico to the United States, thereby
legitimizing the occupation of the island and its satellites by U.S.
forces. One of the provisions of the Treaty of Paris was as follows: "The civil rights and the political status of the native inhabitants of the territories hereby ceded to the United States shall be determined by the Congress." The natives of Puerto Rico, no longer
subjects of the Spanish crown, now found themselves without any
citizenship recognized under international law or U.S. domestic law.

The Organic Act of 1900 (known as the Foraker Act, after its
sponsor) established a political entity called the People of Porto
Rico (Puerto Rico), but there was no mention of U.S. citizenship
for those born on the island, only that they would be "held to be citizens of Porto Rico, and as such entitled to the protection of the
United States." Puerto Ricans were now stateless, essentially confined to their island because of the difficulty of traveling without a
passport. The U.S. Supreme Court, in cases such as *Downes v.
Bidwell* (1901), confirmed that Puerto Rico was merely a possession
of the United States, not an incorporated territory, to be disposed
of by the U.S. Congress.

THE CITIZENSHIP DEBATE
The reelection of William McKinley to the U.S. presidency in 1900
favored U.S. imperial expansion. Nevertheless, the debate as to
whether racially, culturally, and linguistically distinct peoples

brought under U.S. control should be granted U.S. citizenship and, if so, with what rights, continued intermittently between 1900 and 1916. In that year, the Philippines, also seized by the United States from Spain in the war, was promised independence by the Organic Act of the Philippine Islands (also known as the Jones Act of 1916). The Organic Act of 1917 (the Jones Act of 1917) did not similarly grant independence to Puerto Rico, but it did confer U.S. citizenship collectively on the natives of the island. Although the Jones Act of 1917 changed the status of Puerto Ricans from that of U.S. nationals—noncitizens, but owing allegiance to and subject to the protection of the United States—the granting of citizenship did not give the islanders the right to vote in U.S. federal elections because the territory fell short of statehood. In *Balzac v. Porto Rico* (1922), the Supreme Court ruled that as citizens of an unincorporated territory, the islanders enjoyed only fundamental provisions in the Bill of Rights of the U.S. Constitution, not procedural or remedial rights such as the guarantee of trial by jury.

The extent to which Puerto Ricans participated in the debate relating to their prospective status between 1900 and 1917 remains a matter of conjecture. For one thing, the spokesmen of the Puerto Rican community—such as Resident Commissioner Luís Muñoz Rivera and the Puerto Rican House of Delegates (the local legislature)—were ambivalent and contradictory on the subject. For another, much of the evidence placed before the Congress about the Puerto Ricans' preferences during the drawn-out debate was impressionistic and anecdotal rather than objective.

Accordingly, while some U.S. legislators talked of the yearnings, longings, and aspirations of Puerto Ricans to citizenship, critics claim that citizenship was pressed on the islanders. It is also charged that the expediency of acquiring additional recruits for military service only weeks before President Woodrow Wilson sought a declaration of war on Germany on April 4, 1917, was not absent from congressional thinking. Whatever the truth, making Puerto Ricans native U.S. citizens and the establishment of a seemingly permanent political link between the United States and Puerto Rico by the Jones Act of 1917 contrasted with the creation of an articulately temporary relationship between Washington, D.C., and the Philippines. In fact, the defining of the latter's status under the 1916 Jones Act catalyzed the following year's Jones Act relating to

Puerto Rico. The racist comments peppering the congressional debates were infinitely harsher as they related to Filipinos, partly because of their spirited resistance to U.S. occupation, than in regard to Puerto Ricans, who were much more receptive to occupation. Some legislators even produced statistics to "prove" that a high percentage of the islanders were white in order to justify their being granted U.S. citizenship.

PROVISIONS OF THE ACT

The final version of the 1917 Jones bill, introduced in the House on January 20, 1916, was only slightly different from Congressman Jones's earlier versions. The only noteworthy change was that Puerto Ricans residing on the island were allowed one year, instead of six months, to reject U.S. citizenship if they desired. The House passed the bill by voice vote on May 23, 1916; the Senate approved it on February 20, 1917; and the House-Senate Conference Committee followed suit on February 24, 1917. President Wilson, a Democrat, signed it into law on March 2, 1917. Only 288 Puerto Ricans legally declined to accept U.S. citizenship within the statutory period, thereby losing their right to hold or run for any public office on the island. Because the Jones Act had established five different categories in determining the status of different individuals, there was great confusion as to who qualified for citizenship. The U.S. Congress subsequently passed several additional laws in the interest of administrative simplification.

In 1952, the U.S. Territory of Puerto Rico became the Commonwealth of Puerto Rico, known in Spanish as a "free associated state." As such, Puerto Rico elected a nonvoting representative to the U.S. Congress but cast no vote in presidential, congressional, or senatorial elections. While islanders paid no federal taxes, the aid Puerto Rico received from Washington was less than it would have received had it been a state.

On November 14, 1993, a nonbinding referendum, which President Bill Clinton nevertheless pledged to respect, was held regarding the island's future status. Puerto Ricans who opted for continued commonwealth status cast 48.4 percent of the votes; statehood received 46.2 percent; and 4.4 percent of the 2.1 million ballots cast favored independence. The spread between the first two options had narrowed drastically since an earlier referendum in 1967. The issue of Puerto Rico's status—and thus the nature of the citizenship of the islanders—was far from over. It now was up to Puerto Ricans themselves, increasingly aware of their Latino roots, to decide their own political future.

Peter B. Heller

SOURCES FOR FURTHER STUDY

Cabranes, Jose A. *Citizenship and the American Empire: Notes on the Legislative History of the United States Citizenship of Puerto Ricans.* New Haven, Conn.: Yale University Press, 1979.
De Passalacqua, John L. A. "The Involuntary Loss of United States Citizenship upon Accession to Independence by Puerto Rico." *Denver Journal of International Law and Policy* 19, no. 1 (Fall, 1990): 139-161.
Gatell, Frank O. "The Art of the Possible: Luís Muñoz Rivera and the Puerto Rico Jones Bill." *The Americas* 17, no. 1 (July, 1960): 1-20.
Karst, Kenneth L. *Belonging to America: Equal Citizenship and the Constitution.* New Haven, Conn.: Yale University Press, 1989.

SEE ALSO: Platt Amendment (1903); Treaty of Paris (1898).

ESPIONAGE ACTS

ALSO KNOWN AS: Sedition Act (1918 act)
DATE: June 15, 1917; May 16, 1918
U.S. STATUTES AT LARGE: 40 Stat. 217, 40 Stat. 553
CATEGORIES: Crimes and Criminal Procedure; Speech and Expression

Espionage Act prosecutions led to the first significant attempts by the Supreme Court to interpret the free speech provisions of the First Amendment, including the original espousal of the "clear and present danger" test.

On June 15, 1917, two months after the United States entered World War I, Congress passed the Espionage Act. In addition to outlawing a wide variety of acts that fit the commonsense definition of "espionage," including the gathering, transmission, or negligent handling of information that might harm U.S. defense efforts, the law forbade, during wartime, the willful making or conveying of false information with intent to interfere with the nation's armed forces or to promote the success of its enemies, as well as willful attempts to cause insubordination, disloyalty, mutiny, or refusal of duty within the military or the obstruction of military recruitment or enlistment. In practice, this law was used as the springboard for massive prosecutions of antiwar speeches and publications of all kinds across the United States, based on the theory that many such viewpoints were false and, in any case, aimed at undermining recruitment or other aspects of the war effort.

Despite the sweeping language and even more sweeping prosecutions associated with the 1917 law, a far more draconian amendment to the Espionage Act, sometimes known as the Sedition Act, was enacted in 1918 in response to complaints that the original law was not stringent enough to suppress antiwar sentiment. The 1918 amendments outlawed virtually all conceivable criticism of the war, including any expressions of support for "any country with which the United State is at war" or that opposed "the cause of the United States therein." Also banned was the oral or printed dissemination of all "disloyal, profane, scurrilous, or abusive language" about the "form of government" of the country, the Constitution, the flag, the military, and military uniforms, as well as any language intended to bring any of the above into "contempt, scorn, contumely, or disrepute."

Under these laws, more than two thousand people were indicted for written or verbal criticism of the war and more than one thousand were convicted, resulting in more than one hundred jail terms of ten years or more. No one was convicted under the espionage acts during World War I for spying activities. The 1918 amendments to the Espionage Act were repealed in 1920. Although the original 1917 law remains in effect, it was virtually never used after World War I to prosecute expressions of opinion (partly because the 1940 Smith Act included more updated sedition provisions); it has, however, been used in cases involving alleged theft of information, including in the prosecutions of Julius Rosenberg and Ethel Rosenberg during the Cold War and the Vietnam War-era prosecution of Daniel Ellsberg for dissemination of the Pentagon Papers.

COURT RULINGS

The Supreme Court handed down six rulings concerning the constitutionality of Espionage Act prosecutions in 1919-1920, during a severe "red scare." In every case, it upheld lower court convictions. Although the Court's rulings no doubt reflected the anticommunist climate, they had long-term significance because they were the first cases in which the Court sought to interpret the free speech clauses of the First Amendment and thus helped shape decades of subsequent debate and interpretation of this subject. In *Schenck v. United States* (1919), the Court upheld the conviction (under the original 1917 law) of a group accused of seeking to obstruct enlistment in the armed forces by mailing antidraft leaflets. Despite the lack of evidence that Schenck's mailings had any effect whatsoever, the Court, in a famous ruling penned by Justice Oliver Wendell Holmes, rejected Schenck's First Amendment claims. Holmes wrote that although the defendants would have been within their constitutional rights in saying what they did in ordinary times, the character of "every act depends upon the circumstances in which it is done." Just as "the most stringent protection of free speech would not protect a man in falsely shouting fire in a theater and causing a panic," the question was always whether the expression was used in such circumstances and was of such a nature as to create a "clear and present danger " that it would cause the "substantive evils" that Congress has the right to prevent.

In *Abrams v. United States* (1919), a second landmark case (based on the 1918 amendment), the Court upheld the conviction of a group of defendants who had thrown from a New York City rooftop leaflets critical of U.S. military intervention against the new Bolshevik government in Russia. This case became known especially because of a dissent by Holmes, who essentially maintained that no clear and present danger had been demonstrated and that Congress could not constitutionally forbid "all effort to change the mind of the country." In words that became famous both for their eloquence and because, after 1937, most Court rulings in First Amendment cases reflected their sentiment more than the those of the majorities in either *Abrams* or *Schenck*, Holmes declared that U.S. constitutional democracy was based on giving all thought an opportunity to compete in the free trade in ideas, and as long as that experiment remained part of the Constitution, Americans should be "eternally vigilant against attempts to check the expression of opinions that we loathe and believe to be fraught with death, unless they so imminently threaten interference with the lawful and pressing purposes of the law that an immediate check is required to save the country."

In the only significant Espionage Act case involving First Amendment claims to be decided by the Court after 1920, a Court majority reflected Holmes's *Abrams* dissent. In *Hartzel v. United States* (1944), involving a man who had mailed articles attacking U.S. policies during World War II to Army officers and draft registrants (circumstances almost identical to *Schenck*), the Court reversed Hartzel's conviction on the grounds that there was no proof he had willfully sought to obstruct the activities of the armed forces.

Robert Justin Goldstein

Sources for Further Study

Chafee, Zechariah. *Free Speech in the United States.* New York: Atheneum, 1969.

Goldstein, Robert Justin. *Political Repression in Modern America: 1870 to the Present.* Boston: G. K. Hall, 1978.

Polenberg, Richard. *Fighting Faiths: The Abrams Case, the Supreme Court, and Free Speech.* New York: Viking Penguin, 1987.

Preston, William. *Aliens and Dissenters: Federal Suppression of Radicals, 1903-1933.* New York: Harper & Row, 1966.

See also: First Amendment (1789); Alien and Sedition Acts (1798); Sedition Act of 1798 (1798).

Migratory Bird Treaty Act

Date: July 3, 1918
U.S. Statutes at Large: 40 Stat. 755
U.S. Code: 16 § 703
Categories: Agriculture; Animals; Environment and Conservation; Treaties and Agreements

The act established federal ownership of economically important migratory birds, thus shifting the power to regulate wildlife away from the states.

Until 1920, wildlife management was a state-level activity. In 1913, however, the federal Migratory Bird Act was passed to protect migratory game and insectivorous birds from excessive hunting pressure. Lower federal courts found the act unconstitutional. In 1916, Congress concluded a treaty with Great Britain for the protection of migratory birds, and in 1918, Congress passed the Migratory Bird Treaty Act to implement the provisions of the treaty. In 1920, this act withstood a constitutional challenge brought to the Supreme Court in *Missouri v. Holland*. The Court decided that the treaty power of the federal government, unlike its legislative power, is not constrained by the constitutional rights of the states. The decision destroyed the doctrine of state ownership of wildlife and set the stage for further assertions of federal supremacy.

The Migratory Bird Treaty Act was the first successful challenge to the established legal doctrine that ownership and control of wildlife were vested in state governments and held in trust for state citizens. Based on English common law, the state-ownership doctrine evolved as states sought to protect their dwindling fish-and-game resources from heavy commercial demand. The height of the state-ownership doctrine was reached in *Geer v. Connecticut* (1896). A Connecticut law that prohibited interstate transportation of game that had been lawfully killed in Connecticut was successfully defended against the charge that this was unconstitutional interference with interstate commerce. The Supreme Court decided that the state, as owner of the wildlife, could impose any reasonable restriction on its use, alive or dead.

LACEY ACT

While *Geer* established the states' rights to prohibit the export of wildlife, states still had no mechanism to prohibit the importation of wildlife. Many states had laws restricting hunting and the sale of illegally harvested game, but they were hampered in enforcing such laws by market hunters who brought in game killed in other states. Dealers charged with violating state laws could claim that their product was taken in another state, and it was virtually impossible to disprove such assertions. Solving such problems was clearly a federal concern, since the matter involved interstate commerce. In 1900, Representative John Lacey of Iowa introduced a bill in Congress to remedy this problem. Passed in 1900, the Lacey Act provided federal sanction to state laws that prohibited interstate transportation of unlawfully killed animals. The act also allowed states to assume that any dead wildlife found within a state had been killed in the state and thus was subject to state game laws.

The Lacey Act helped the states in their efforts to enforce existing laws, but it did nothing to regularize or to enhance protection for migratory birds. Across the nation, a patchwork of hunting regulations and irregular enforcement left many species at the mercy of the casual hunter. Lobbyists such as T. Gilbert Pearson began to work toward federal regulation, and in a political climate that increasingly supported centralization of governmental power, they soon found supporters in Congress.

WEEKS-MCLEAN MIGRATORY BIRD ACT

The first congressional attempt to establish federal control over migratory birds came in 1904, when Pennsylvania congressman George Shiras III introduced a bill to put the birds under the protection of the national government. His first bill died in the Agriculture Committee; a second attempt in 1906 failed as well. Two years later, after Shiras had retired, Massachusetts congressman John Weeks introduced a similar but also unsuccessful bill. By 1912, when Weeks, joined by Connecticut senator George McLean, tried again, other interest groups had begun to rally around the cause. The firearms manufacturers and dealers were interested in protecting their markets. Game associations wished to preserve their sport. Some advocates were moved by the plight of the disappearing species and the wanton slaughter, especially for feathers in women's hats. The bill was expanded to include insectivorous birds, bringing agricultural interests into the fold.

The legislation was hidden as a rider to an agricultural appropriations bill and was signed by President William Howard Taft on March 4, 1913, as his administration was rushing to a close. Taft later said that he thought the migratory bird provisions of the bill were unconstitutional and that he would have vetoed the bill had he been aware of its contents.

Relying on the interstate commerce clause of the Constitution, the Weeks-McLean Migratory Bird Act gave jurisdiction over migratory birds to the federal Department of Agriculture. Challenges to the Migratory Bird Act reached the federal courts in *United States v. Shauver* in 1914 and *United States v. McCullagh* in 1915; in both cases, the courts relied on *Geer,* finding the Migratory Bird Act to be an unconstitutional exercise of federal power.

CONVENTION FOR THE PROTECTION OF MIGRATORY BIRDS
President Taft had not been alone in his misgivings over the act. Only a month after the act became law, the rapid state response challenging the bill led Senator McLean to introduce a resolution asking the president to negotiate a North American treaty to protect migratory birds. The resolution passed, aided considerably by the public furor over the death in 1914 of the last known passenger pigeon. Treaty negotiations with Great Britain (on behalf of Canada) began almost at once. The Convention for the Protection of Migratory Birds was signed on August 16, 1916, and swiftly ratified by the Senate; the convention entered into force on August 22, 1916.

MIGRATORY BIRD TREATY ACT
Opposition in Congress to the enabling act for the Migratory Bird Treaty was stiff. Members of Congress were dismayed that the treaty power was being used to give the federal government an authority that would otherwise be unconstitutional. Issues of states' rights were hotly debated. Even members who recognized the need to protect diminishing bird populations feared that this use of the treaty power to limit state authority might undermine the federal system of government. They warned that the national government might use the same vehicle to invade other areas constitutionally reserved to the states. Nevertheless, Congress passed enabling legislation in 1917, and on July 3, 1918, the Migratory Bird Treaty Act was signed by President Woodrow Wilson.

The states moved promptly to challenge the enabling legislation in court, but use of the federal treaty power complicated their arguments considerably. The landmark case that decided the supremacy of the treaty power over the reserved rights of the states was *Missouri v. Holland* (1920). This case arose in federal district court against federal game warden Ray P. Holland, whose enforcement of the Migratory Bird Treaty Act in Missouri was interfering with the amount of state revenues generated by hunting. The district judge found that the treaty-making power of the United States was supreme over state authority; therefore, he ruled, the Migratory Bird Treaty Act was constitutional. Missouri appealed to the Supreme Court, but the Court upheld the lower-court decision. The Migratory Bird Treaty Act was indeed constitutional; the erosion of the state ownership doctrine confirmed in *Geer* had begun.

IMPACT OF THE ACT

Federal assumption of control over wildlife was part of a larger effort to centralize national power. Virtually all congressional debates over the Migratory Bird Act and the Migratory Bird Treaty Act focused on the constitutional issues of the proper relationship between the state and federal governments. It is clear from the congressional debates and judicial opinions that all parties were agreed that game in general, and migratory birds in particular, needed protection. They also agreed that the federal acts would provide protection, yet they argued bitterly over the legislation. For the most part, the arguments were not on scientific or administrative grounds but rather on constitutional ones. Even men who favored the policy ends were driven to object to the policy means.

Using a popular policy agenda to achieve a hidden agenda is an ancient political ploy. Environmental policy is often used to camouflage less respectable goals, partly because environmental issues have such high social appeal. For example, Arthur McEvoy notes in *The Fisherman's Problem: Ecology and Law in California Fisheries, 1850-1980* (1986) that regulation of California shrimp fisheries was as much an attempt to force Chinese immigrants out of business as it was scientific regulation of a natural resource.

Having flexed its muscles over migratory birds, the federal government allowed the states to retain some control over wildlife. Throughout much of the twentieth century, the states were given considerable autonomy in choosing how and to what extent they complied with federal guidelines, subject of course to the silken chains of federal money through such programs as the Pittman-Robertson Act (1937), which redistributes a federal tax on ammunition and firearms sales to the states for wildlife restoration. Yet some protective legislation, such as the Marine Mammal Protection Act (1972), the Endangered Species Act (1973), and implementation legislation for the Convention on International Trade in Endangered Species (1975), places responsibility for compliance with the national government. The courts have continued to support federal authority over wildlife: For example, federally owned lands within state borders are not subject to state regulation (*Hunt v. United States,* 1928), the federal government may kill animals on national land without state permits (*New Mexico State Game Commission v. Udall,* 1969), and the interstate commerce clause gives Congress the power to protect wildlife in navigable waters when such wildlife is affected by dredge and fill operations conducted on privately owned riparian land (*Zabel v. Tabb,* 1970).

None of this would have been possible had the state ownership doctrine enunciated in *Geer* been allowed to stand. The Migratory Bird Treaty Act, which withstood a legal challenge to the constitutional right of the federal government to regulate wildlife, was thus the beginning of a unified national policy for wildlife regulation.

Susan J. Buck

SOURCES FOR FURTHER STUDY

Bean, Michael. *The Evolution of National Wildlife Law.* New York: Praeger, 1983.

Belanger, Dian Olson. *Managing American Wildlife: A History of the International Association of Fish and Wildlife Agencies.* Amherst: University of Massachusetts Press, 1988.

Chandler, William. "The U.S. Fish and Wildlife Service." In *Audubon Wildlife Report 1985,* edited by Roger Di Silvestro. New York: National Audubon Society, 1985.

Fox, Stephen. *The American Conservation Movement: John Muir and His Legacy.* Madison: University of Wisconsin Press, 1981.

Hays, Samuel. *Conservation and the Gospel of Efficiency: The Progressive Conservation Movement, 1890-1920.* Cambridge, Mass.: Harvard University Press, 1959.

Orr, Oliver H., Jr. *Saving American Birds: T. Gilbert Pearson and the Founding of the Audubon Movement.* Gainesville: University Press of Florida, 1992.

Tober, James A. *Who Owns the Wildlife? The Political Economy of Conservation in Nineteenth Century America.* Westport, Conn.: Greenwood Press, 1981.

SEE ALSO: Migratory Bird Act (1913); Migratory Bird Hunting and Conservation Stamp Act (1934); Endangered Species Preservation Act (1966); Endangered Species Act (1973); Convention on the Conservation of Migratory Species of Wild Animals (1979).

EIGHTEENTH AMENDMENT

ALSO KNOWN AS: Prohibition

DATE: Ratified January 16, 1919; certified January 29, 1919; repealed December 5, 1933

U.S. STATUTES AT LARGE: 40 Stat. 1059

CATEGORIES: Constitutional Law; Crimes and Criminal Procedure; Food and Drugs

Called a "noble experiment" by President Herbert Hoover, the amendment imposed a national ban on the production, sale, and distribution of alcoholic beverages; its failure brought an end to a major reform effort.

The prohibitionist movement existed as early as the colonial period, but most historians date the modern form to the 1850's. The movement met with local and state successes in the late nineteenth century. By 1900 a quarter of the U.S. population was living in "dry" areas (areas where the sale of alcohol was illegal); by 1917, twenty-nine states were dry.

PASSAGE OF THE ACT

Congress first enacted a temporary prohibition of the sale of alcohol in 1917 as a war measure. Then, in December, 1917, a proposed amendment to the U.S. Constitution stating that the "manufacture, sale, or transportation of intoxicating liquors within, the importation thereof into, or the exportation thereof from the United States and all territory subject to the jurisdiction thereof for beverage purposes is hereby prohibited" was introduced into Congress. It speeded its way through the Senate and the House of Representatives and was sent to the states for ratification. Mississippi was the first state to ratify (on January 8, 1918), and a little more than a year later, Nebraska became the thirty-sixth, the last required. Passage of the Volstead Act, a measure designed both to continue the wartime prohibition and to provide enforcement of Prohibition as mandated by the Eighteenth Amendment, followed on October 28, 1919. The Volstead Act defined alcoholic beverages as those containing at least 0.5 percent alcohol.

THE PROHIBITION ERA

Almost from the first, Prohibition appeared to be largely unenforceable. Those who wanted to drink had little trouble locating bootleggers, and speakeasies (clubs that served alcohol illegally) abounded. The Prohibition Bureau's budget was small, and all the presidents of the period—Warren G. Harding, Calvin Coolidge, and Herbert Hoover—expressed doubts about its viability.

One of the side effects of Prohibition was the rise of organized crime. Until the 1920's gangs had been local, but that soon changed. Although there were bootleggers and illicit distillers and brewers in all parts of the country, "Scarface Al" Capone, who operated out of Chicago, became the symbol of them all. By 1927 the Capone gang was grossing an estimated $60 million a year on beer alone, and by 1929 the figure approximated $100 million. Capone's beer earnings were said to be larger than the profits of Standard Oil of Indiana, Ford, or General Electric. Without Prohibition, this situation would have been impossible. That Prohibition was considered the most divisive American political question of the 1920's is generally conceded by historians who study the period. The matter was addressed directly in the 1928 presidential election, when the country was presented with a choice between Republican Herbert Hoover, who supported Prohibition, and Democrat Al Smith, who opposed it. The election resulted in a Hoover landslide, although it was attributable more to the fact that the nation was basking in prosperity than to other issues. Despite his support of Prohibition, Hoover indicated his conviction that the Volstead Act was unenforceable. On May 29, 1929, he appointed a group to study Prohibition and make recommendations. The National Commission on Law Observation and Enforcement, headed by former attorney general George Wickersham, released its findings in 1931. The Wickersham Report concluded that a more serious attempt at enforcement would be required if Washington expected the public to take the Volstead Act seriously.

Prohibition was a major issue in the 1932 presidential race. The Republicans renominated Hoover and at his insistence adopted a conciliatory position on Prohibition, calling for the Eighteenth Amendment to be resubmitted to the states for ratification. The Democrats, led by Franklin D. Roosevelt, supported outright repeal.

REPEAL OF PROHIBITION
Roosevelt's election spelled the end of Prohibition. On December 7, 1932, the House Ways and Means Committee held hearings on the matter of modifying the Volstead Act. Shortly thereafter, Representative James Collier introduced a measure to legalize beer with a 2.75 percent alcohol content. It won approval in the House and was sent on to the Senate. There it became the Collier-Blaine Bill, which in its new form upped the alcoholic content to 3.05 percent—another sign that Prohibition was a fading crusade.

On February 20, 1933, Congress passed what would become the Twenty-first Amendment, repealing the Eighteenth. It was sent to the states for ratification. Roosevelt did not have to wait until ratification to ask for changes in the Volstead Act, however; legislation based on the Collier-Blaine Bill, now known as the Cullen-Harrison Bill, which legalized 3.2 percent beer, was passed by Congress. On March 22, in the midst of his famous "hundred days," in which a rush of legislation was passed to fight the Great Depression, Roosevelt signed into law the Beer and Wine Revenue Act—the title was significant—which legalized beer and wine with an alcohol content of 3.2 percent, effective April 7, 1933, in those states and areas without local laws to the contrary. At the same time, the proposed amendment made its way through the states. Utah ratified it on December 5, whereupon it became part of the Constitution. Prohibition at the federal level died.

Most historians agree that Prohibition marked a major step in the development of a federal presence in law enforcement. The modern Federal Bureau of Investigation had its origins in the enforcement of Prohibition statutes. Prohibition also made possible the growth of organized crime. Defenders of the "war against drugs" observe that liquor consumption fell in the 1920's; opponents point to the experience of Prohibition as an indication that criminalization of such behavior does not work. Both sides agree, however, that the way in which the laws were enforced (or not enforced) prompted a disrespect for law in general.

Robert Sobel

SUPREME COURT DECISIONS
The Supreme Court's decisions in such cases as *Crane v. Campbell* (1917), *Hawke v. Smith* (1920), and the *National Prohibition Cases*

(1920) strengthened the basis for and strongly endorsed the amendment.

In *Crane,* the Court supported national prohibition by ruling that possessing alcohol for personal use was not a constitutional right. In *Hawke,* the Court upheld the ratification of the Eighteenth Amendment by the Ohio General Assembly over the referendum by Ohio voters who rejected the amendment. According to the Court, when Congress requested that a constitutional amendment be ratified by state legislatures, it neither authorized nor permitted a referendum. In the *National Prohibition Cases,* the Court completed the process of making national prohibition part of the law of the United States. In these cases, the justices upheld the constitutionality of the Eighteenth Amendment and approved the method by which the state legislatures had ratified it.

On December 5, 1933, the Twenty-first Amendment to the Constitution was ratified. This amendment repealed the Eighteenth Amendment and ended constitutional prohibition of alcoholic beverages.

Louis Gesualdi

SOURCES FOR FURTHER STUDY

Asbury, Herbert. *The Great Illusion: An Informal History of Prohibition.* New York: Alfred A. Knopf, 1950.

Cashman, Sean D. *Prohibition: The Lie of the Land.* New York: Free Press, 1981.

Chidsey, Donald Barr. *On and Off the Wagon: A Sober Analysis of the Temperance Movement from the Pilgrims Through Prohibition.* New York: Cowles, 1969.

Dobyns, Fletcher. *The Amazing Story of Repeal.* Chicago: Willett, Clark, 1940.

Engelmann, Larry. *Intemperance: The Lost War Against Liquor.* New York: Free Press, 1979.

Furnas, J. C. *The Life and Times of the Late Demon Rum.* London: W. H. Allen, 1965.

Kerr, K. Austin. *Organized for Prohibition: A New History of the Anti-Saloon League.* New Haven, Conn.: Yale University Press, 1985.

Krout, John. *The Origins of Prohibition.* New York: Alfred A. Knopf, 1925.

Kyvig, David E., ed. *Law, Alcohol, and Order: Perspectives on National Prohibition.* Westport, Conn.: Greenwood Press, 1985.

Merz, Charles. *The Dry Decade.* Garden City, N.Y.: Doubleday, Doran, 1931.

Root, Grace C. *Women and Repeal: The Story of the Women's Organization for National Prohibition Reform.* New York: Harper & Brothers, 1934.

Rumbarger, John J. *Profits, Power, and Prohibition: Alcohol Reform and the Industrializing of America, 1800-1930.* Albany: State University of New York Press, 1989.

Schlesinger, Arthur M. *The Age of Roosevelt: The Crisis of the Old Order, 1919-1933.* Boston: Houghton Mifflin, 1957.

Sinclair, Andrew. *Era of Excess: A Social History of the Prohibition Movement.* New York: Harper & Row, 1964.

Spinelli, Lawrence. *Dry Diplomacy: The United States, Great Britain, and Prohibition.* Wilmington, Del.: Scholarly Resources, 1989.

Vile, John R. *Encyclopedia of Constitutional Amendments, Proposed Amendments, and Amending Issues, 1789-1995.* Santa Barbara, Calif: ABC-CLIO, 1996.

SEE ALSO: Hundred Days legislation (1933); Twenty-first Amendment (1933).

TREATY OF VERSAILLES

DATE: Signed June 28, 1919
CATEGORIES: Foreign Relations; Treaties and Agreements

The treaty brought World War I to a close, establishing a fragile basis for European peace. The agreement created the League of Nations, the first global collective security organization, but dealt harshly with Germany.

While World War I had been raging in Europe, President Woodrow Wilson had begun to articulate the hopes of many people in the United States for a liberal peace. He believed that the victors could not indulge themselves in the luxury of vengeance: Only a just and merciful settlement could ensure a lasting peace. In early 1917, three months before the United States entered the conflict, Wilson called for a "peace without victory," with no indemnities and annexations to sow the seeds of future wars.

WILSON'S FOURTEEN POINTS

Wilson sought more than a just settlement; he wanted to create a new, rational, international order. On January 8, 1918, addressing a joint session of Congress, he outlined his famous Fourteen Points. The first five applied to all nations: open diplomacy, freedom of the seas, removal of barriers to free trade, arms reductions, and impartial adjustments of colonial claims. The next eight revolved around the principle of national self-determination, listing the French, Belgian, and Russian territory that Germany must evacuate and promising autonomy to the subject nationalities of Eastern Europe. The capstone was Wilson's fourteenth point: the creation of an international League of Nations. Wilson envisioned, above all, the United States playing a permanent role in world affairs through membership in a collective security organization. Great Britain and France had already made secret treaties that violated several of Wilson's points, but on November 11, 1918, representatives of Germany, the United States, and the Allies, meeting in a railroad car in the Compiègne Forest, signed an armistice based substantially on Wilson's program. The Great War was over.

THE PEACE CONFERENCE

Two months later, on January 18, 1919, the peace conference convened at Paris amid an atmosphere of crisis. The war had left Europe in confusion. Half a dozen small wars still raged. As the Bolsheviks tightened their hold on Russia, communist hysteria swept through Eastern Europe. The conference, although sensing the need for haste, had to consider calmly the fate of much of the world. Thirty-two nations sent delegations, but the actual decision making devolved on the Big Four: Great Britain's David Lloyd George, France's Georges Clemenceau, Italy's Vittorio Orlando, and the United States' Woodrow Wilson.

Clemenceau, the cynical French "Tiger," was suspicious of Wilsonian idealism. "God gave us the Ten Commandments, and we broke them," he said. "Wilson gives us the Fourteen Points. We shall see." The Big Four approved the demilitarization of Germany, Allied occupation of the Rhineland, the return of Alsace-Lorraine to France, and an Anglo-French-U.S. mutual defense pact. These provisions, if maintained, would guarantee French security. Italy received Southern Tyrol, a region populated by some two hundred thousand Austrians. The conference also redrew the map of Eastern Europe. A series of new, independent nations sprang to life: Poland, Czechoslovakia, Yugoslavia, Austria, Hungary, Estonia, Lithuania, and Finland. The boundary areas of Poland and Czechoslovakia included large populations of German-speaking people. In the Far East, Japan took over German economic rights in the Chinese province of Shantun, while Great Britain and France divided up the other German colonies in the Pacific and Africa. The conference forced Germany not only to take full responsibility for causing the war but also to provide a "blank check" for reparations, including damages to civilian properties and future pensions. The Germans signed the treaty on June 28. They would later learn that they owed thirty-three billion dollars.

The Treaty of Versailles hardly lived up to Wilson's ideas of self-determination, although it left a smaller proportion than ever of European people living under foreign governments. Nor was it a peace without victory. Wilson did win acceptance for the League of Nations, however, with the League Covenant being incorporated into the treaty itself. The League, he hoped, would later correct any imperfections in the work of the conference.

AMERICAN RESPONSE TO THE LEAGUE OF NATIONS

When Wilson returned to the United States from Paris, public opinion favored ratification of the treaty and membership in the League of Nations, but the Senate would have the final decision. In March, 1919, Senator Henry Cabot Lodge had ominously secured a "round robin" resolution with the signatures of thirty-seven senators—more than enough to kill the treaty—announcing their opposition to the League Covenant in its current form. Wilson could count on the support of most of the Senate Democrats, but he could not meet the two-thirds majority necessary for ratification without a large block of Republican votes. A dozen or so Republican senators had mild reservations about the League; another group had strong reservations. These latter opposed Article 10 of the League Covenant, a provision binding nations to preserve the territorial integrity and independence of all League members against aggression. Senator William E. Borah was the leader of the "irreconcilables," who unconditionally opposed the treaty with or without reservations.

As chairman of the Senate Foreign Affairs Committee, Lodge played a crucial role in the fight over the League of Nations. Unlike the irreconcilables, he was no isolationist. He claimed to favor the League but with strong reservations. Yet Lodge possessed an intense personal dislike for Wilson and a distrust of his leadership. For two weeks, Lodge stalled for time by reading aloud the text of the treaty, all 268 pages of it. Then he held six weeks of hearings, calling witnesses who opposed ratification. At last, he drew up a list of fourteen reservations, as if to ridicule Wilson's Fourteen Points. Gradually, the mood of the country shifted against the treaty.

Wilson, overworked and ill, decided to go to the people in a whirlwind speaking tour. In three weeks, he traveled eight thousand miles and delivered thirty-six major speeches, typing them out himself on his portable typewriter. On the night of September 25, he fell ill in Pueblo, Colorado. The presidential train rushed him back to Washington. On October 20, in the White House, he collapsed: He had suffered a stroke that paralyzed his left side. For the next six weeks, the country was virtually without a president, and Wilson never fully recovered. When the treaty came to a vote, he passed word for Democrats to vote against the treaty with the Lodge reservations. On November 19, 1919, and in a second vote on March 19, 1920, a coalition of Democrats and irreconcilables sent the treaty to defeat.

The failure of Wilson's efforts to win support for unqualified U.S. participation in the League of Nations ultimately reduced the League's effective operation. As for the peace itself, the U.S. Congress passed a joint resolution formally bringing hostilities to an end on July 2, 1921. Despite the isolationist mood of the country, the United States eventually participated in a number of League activities, although never as a formal member. The absence of the United States from the League Council hampered its peacemaking capacity. More deadly to the League's future, however, were the growing nationalism throughout Europe, the deep resentment among the Germans with regard to what they viewed as unfair Versailles Treaty provisions, and the lack of consensus about how to deal with violations of League Covenant provisions.

Like many of Wilson's idealized Fourteen Points, the League of Nations was a noble experiment that foundered on political realities. The world was not ready for a global collective security organization, but the League's work in a number of economic and humanitarian areas did substantially advance international cooperation. These efforts, coupled with greater realism about power politics and keeping international peace, led to more realistic structures in the League's successor, the United Nations. U.S. policymakers played the lead role in fashioning the new organization, as Wilson had with the League, but they were more careful to build bipartisan domestic support for the United Nations as they seized, rather than spurned, global leadership.

Donald Holley, updated by
Robert F. Gorman

SOURCES FOR FURTHER STUDY

Bennet, A. LeRoy. *International Organizations: Principles and Issues.* 6th ed. Englewood Cliffs, N.J.: Prentice-Hall, 1995.

Boemeke, Manfred F., Gerald D. Feldman, and Elisabeth Glaser-Schmidt, eds. *The Treaty of Versailles: A Reassessment After Seventy-five Years.* New York: Cambridge University Press, 1998.

Dockrill, Michael L., and John Fisher, eds. *The Paris Peace Conference 1919: Peace without Victory?* Palgrave, 2001.

Hay, Jeff, ed. *Treaty of Versailles.* Detroit: Gale Group, 2001.

Heckscher, August. *Woodrow Wilson.* New York: Charles Scribner's Sons, 1991.

Levin, N. Gordon. *Woodrow Wilson and World Politics: America's Response to War and Revolution.* New York: Oxford University Press, 1968.

Mayer, Arno J. *The Politics and Diplomacy of Peacemaking: Containment and Counterrevolution at Versailles, 1918-1919.* New York: Alfred A. Knopf, 1967.

Northedge, F. S. *The League of Nations: Its Life and Times, 1920-1946.* New York: Holmes and Meier, 1986.

Stone, Ralph A. *The Irreconcilables: The Fight Against the League of Nations.* Lexington: University Press of Kentucky, 1970.

SEE ALSO: National Defense Act (1916).

MOTOR VEHICLE THEFT ACT

ALSO KNOWN AS: Dyer Act; National Motor Vehicle Theft Act
DATE: October 29, 1919
U.S. STATUTES AT LARGE: 41 Stat. 324
CATEGORIES: Crimes and Criminal Procedure

Establishing penalties for motor vehicle theft involving interstate commerce, this act was one of a series of bills utilizing the Constitution's commerce clause to expand federal involvement in the enforcement of criminal law.

In 1919, approximately 6.5 million motor vehicles were registered in the United States. Criminals and criminal rings, particularly in larger cities, were taking advantage of this rapidly expanding opportunity, so that automobile theft was a burgeoning problem and insurance rates were rising significantly. Although all states already had established laws against automobile theft, the Motor Vehicle Theft Act (the Dyer Act) made the theft of motor vehicles and the receipt of stolen vehicles a federal offense when state boundaries were crossed. It specified penalties of five thousand dollars, up to five years in prison, or both.

The commerce clause of the Constitution thus was used to justify federal involvement in what had been the jurisdiction of state and local authorities. Some opposed the legislation out of concern for states' rights, and President Woodrow Wilson did not support the bill, which became law without his signature. In following years, federal regulation of business and labor would be expanded significantly on the basis of the commerce clause.

Steve D. Boilard

SOURCES FOR FURTHER STUDY
Cooke, Frederick H. *Commerce Clause of the Federal Constitution.* Reprint. Buffalo, N.Y.: William S. Hein, 1987.
Kallenbach, Joseph Ernest. *Federal Cooperation with the States Under the Commerce Clause.* Reprint. New York: Greenwood Press, 1970.

SEE ALSO: Motor Vehicle Theft Law Enforcement Act (1984).

MINERAL LEASING ACT

DATE: February 25, 1920
U.S. STATUTES AT LARGE: 41 Stat. 437
U.S. CODE: 30 § 181
CATEGORIES: Land Management; Natural Resources

> *The act gave statutory effect to the policy of leasing government lands containing mineral deposits such as coal, gas, oil, oil shale, phosphates, potassium, and sodium to private parties for development.*

On February 25, 1920, President Woodrow Wilson signed the Mineral Leasing Act, giving statutory effect to the policy of leasing government lands containing mineral deposits such as coal, gas, oil, oil shale, phosphates, potassium, and sodium to private parties for development. The law did not satisfy everyone. Many Westerners, businesspeople, and conservatives preferred a policy of permanent alienation or sale of government lands to private parties without conditions. Some conservationists and Progressives desired that the government not only own the public lands but also conserve and develop the resources contained within them. After more than a century of uncontrolled development and exploitation, however, the act represented a victory for conservation.

RISE OF THE CONSERVATION MOVEMENT

Prior to the twentieth century, federal lands were generally sold for nominal fees or given away outright. The General Mining Act of 1872 turned public-land mineral deposits of gold, silver, and copper over to developers at a minimal cost with few restrictions by the federal government. Lands containing coal deposits were treated in much the same way. In the early twentieth century, however, as the exhaustion of the nation's vast lands and resources became a possibility, a conservation movement emerged during the administration of President Theodore Roosevelt. Yet not everyone was a conservationist. Many people in the West, for example, claimed that conservationists tended to be Easterners whose lands were already developed and who were thus enforcing a double standard on the West, denying opportunities to the citizens of those states. Others argued that government conservation policies were a violation of the rights of property and individualism as set forth in the Declaration of Independence; some complained that government conservation was paternalistic and autocratic.

In 1906, Roosevelt proposed a coal-leasing bill to Congress. In order to protect the public interest and increase government revenues, the government would retain ownership of the land but would lease it to private interests for a royalty. Some critics argued that the proposal was a socialistic violation of states' rights. Others, such as Wisconsin senator Robert M. La Follette, wanted tighter legislative controls, fearing that a loose leasing law might result in increased private monopoly of the nation's resources. No leasing law resulted, but Roosevelt and his successors William Howard Taft and Woodrow Wilson began withdrawing certain government lands containing mineral deposits from the public domain. By 1916, more than 140 million acres had been set aside, including fifty oil reserves totaling 5,587,000 acres. To many private interests, leasing became a viable approach in developing the mineral resources on federal lands, both to generate income and to preserve and develop the nation's resources.

OIL AND THE LEASING DEBATE

It was oil rather than coal, however, that became the focus of the debate. Oil was destined to be the energy source of the future, and part of the oil debate revolved around naval power and U.S. defense policy. In 1912, Taft created two naval oil reserves in California's San Joaquin Valley: reserve number 1, Elk Hills, and reserve number 2, Buena Vista Hills. Taft's successor, Woodrow Wilson, established a third reserve in 1915 in Wyoming, at Teapot Dome. Wilson's secretary of the interior, Franklin K. Lane, a Progressive from California, supported leasing for oil and other minerals. Lane's major opponent in the administration, Josephus Daniels, the secretary of the navy and also a Progressive, was a strong advocate of oil reserves for exclusive naval use and was critical of leasing.

Most conservationists, notably Gifford Pinchot, Roosevelt's chief forester, advocated the concept of leasing. Several leasing bills were introduced during the Wilson years. The leasing debate was a regional, rather than a political, issue at that time. Scott Ferris, an Oklahoma Democrat, and Irvine Lenroot, a Wisconsin Republican, led the leasing campaign in the House. Daniels was opposed to any leasing bill that would alienate public oil lands, particularly those set aside for the navy. Progressives such as Idaho's Senator William Borah argued that natural resources should be maintained and operated by the government for the people. Others, such as William King of Utah, wanted no government conservation program of any kind. Secretary Lane was caught in the middle. He admired the private businesspeople who had built America, and he was sympathetic to those who claimed that they had established a stake in the withdrawn oil reserves. He also wished to open Alaska to development, and his water-power sites policy came under attack for lacking sufficient government controls. In 1916, Pinchot called Lane an anticonservationist. Pinchot did not believe that administrators should be narrowly bound by restrictive regulations, but he believed that Lane had acted unwisely.

Wilson's Democrats suffered defeat in the 1918 congressional elections. Losses were particularly severe in the West, and in February, 1919, Wilson, risking the wrath of conservationists, gave his support to a mineral-leasing bill, which included both leasing and sale provisions. Many conservationists were dismayed. The naval reserves were not protected, and the national forests, Grand Canyon National Park, and Mount Olympus National Monument were opened to prospectors. The bill easily passed the House by a vote of 233 to 109, La Follette kept the bill from coming to a vote in the Senate, and it died when the congressional session ended in March, 1919.

With Republican control of Congress, the long campaign for a leasing bill came to fruition. The Republican leadership needed to appear constructive, particularly after the party's opposition to the Treaty of Versailles and Wilson's League of Nations. Westerners and conservatives, both Democrats and Republicans, worried that without a leasing bill government operation might result. Utah's Reed Smoot, the chairman of the Senate Public Lands Committee, preferred no government involvement but recognized the political need to compromise if any development was to occur. With the prodding of the Pinchot bloc from the outside and Lenroot's actions within the committee, the Smoot bill evolved during the summer of 1919 in a manner pleasing to conservationists. Unlike the previous bill, it was entirely a leasing bill, with no sales or alienation alternatives. The Grand Canyon and Mt. Olympus were removed from coal and other mineral exploration. LaFollette led the fight on the Senate floor and supported the bill as an improvement over previous bills, although he wished for additional controls over possible monopolies and unfair prices.

PROVISIONS OF THE LEASING ACT

The bill was passed by the Senate in September, 1919, was passed by the House at the end of October, and was signed into law by Wilson on February 25, 1920. The Mineral Leasing Act applied to oil and gas as well as to coal, sodium, and phosphates. Prospecting was allowed on unproven lands, some preference was given to those with earlier claims, and each state was allocated 37.5 percent of resource royalties from lands within its borders. The secretary of the interior was given considerable responsibility for administering the new law.

The Mineral Leasing Act of 1920 established the principle that the government would retain ownership of the public lands containing mineral deposits and would lease those lands and their resources to private developers. In so doing, the federal government became permanently involved in managing the mineral resources of the nation. By the 1980's, more than 100 million acres of public lands were under oil and gas lease, and approximately 70 million tons of coal were mined on federal lands. The people's interests were to be protected, and preservation and planning would be possible—or, at least, so it seemed in 1920.

EFFECTS OF LEASING

In operation, the mineral-leasing law proved to be controversial, and within a few years it led to one of the most famous scandals in U.S. history. The early twentieth century Progressives trusted the advice of supposedly apolitical experts. Objective in their assessments, such experts, according to Progressives, would provide the necessary scientific knowledge to elected or appointed administrators, who were given broad leeway to implement the laws. In practice, however, experts' opinions often differed on specific points, such as whether the naval reserves could intentionally or inadvertently be drained by outside drilling. During debate on the Smoot bill, La Follette proposed an amendment to the bill to exclude the naval reserves from the leasing bill, and, citing expert opinion, denied that separate naval reserves would be damaged by nearby drilling. Montana's Democratic senator Thomas J. Walsh, who fa-

473

vored Western development, claimed that his expert, E. L. Doheny, predicted that the naval reserves would be drained and thus should be developed and the oil stored or sold. La Follette's amendment failed, but in June, 1920, in an amendment to another bill, the naval reserves were made the responsibility of the secretary of the navy.

Administrators, who were given the broad discretion that the Progressives deemed necessary, did not always administer the laws as some had anticipated. New Mexico's Republican senator Albert Fall, the archetypal Westerner distrustful of federal conservation policies, opposed leasing and any other governmental restrictions on development. Gifford Pinchot hoped to be chosen as the new secretary of the interior after the Republican victory in the 1920 presidential election, but President Warren G. Harding selected Fall for the position. Republican conservationists were concerned, but they hoped for the best. They received the worst.

THE TEAPOT DOME AFFAIR

In May, 1921, Fall persuaded Harding's secretary of the Navy, Edwin Denby, to turn the naval reserves over to Fall's interior department. This was legal but was antithetical to the spirit of the mineral-leasing legislation. Fall then surreptitiously but legally leased Elk Hills to the Doheny oil interests and Teapot Dome to Harry Sinclair. When Fall went to jail years later, it was not because he had violated provisions of the Mineral Leasing Act but because he had received financial and other compensation from Doheny and Sinclair.

There were several paradoxes in the Teapot Dome affair. First, the scandal was misnamed, as the Teapot Dome reserves were less important than those at California's Elk Hills. Second, the original justification for establishing the reserves was to offset a perceived shortage of oil, a scenario that did not materialize. Third, although LaFollette was one of the chief figures in exposing the Teapot Dome scandal, the primary investigator was Senator Thomas J. Walsh, who had been sympathetic to Western developers during Wilson's administration. Senator Lenroot, one of the conservationist architects of the Smoot bill, defended the Harding administration's conservation decisions. When the Leasing Act of 1920 was passed, it was viewed as a conservation measure; however, the scandal demonstrated that, in the hands of a willful administrator opposed to the spirit of conservation, the act's outcome could be radically different.

LONG-RANGE IMPACT

The intent of the law, at least as far as conservationists were concerned, was better served by the administration of Franklin D. Roosevelt. New Deal liberals were not the direct political heirs of the earlier Progressives, but conservation was a common concern, and Roosevelt's secretary of the interior, Harold Ickes, was a former Progressive Republican. Ickes was a committed conservationist, and during his tenure he conscientiously supervised the mineral-leasing program through the General Land Office, as well as through the Bureau of Mines, the U.S. Fuel Administration, the Bituminous Coal Commission, the U.S. Coal Commission, and the Federal Oil Conservation Board.

The battle between conservationists and developers continued. The Wilderness Act of 1964 established 9.1 million acres as wilderness areas largely exempt from mining and drilling. At the same time, the nation needed additional amounts of oil and other resources, needs that were increasingly met by imports. In the 1970's, a movement developed in the West to give greater say to states and local areas in the use of federal public lands and resources. Many conservationists reacted by demanding revisions in the Mineral Leasing Act that would place a higher priority on environmental considerations. Conservationists warned about the threat of monopoly and price fixing, noting that 70 percent of the coal leases were held by only fifteen corporations. The oil embargoes instituted by the Organization of Petroleum Exporting Countries (OPEC), however, added another justification for additional development: The nation's survival seemed to require it.

By the end of the 1970's, Western demands, known popularly as the Sagebrush Rebellion, were paralleling those of the years prior to 1920. "Sagebrush Rebels" claimed that federal government policies were infringing upon needed development. Most disputants agreed that the government would retain ownership of the public lands and lease them to private parties for development, but there remained the contentious questions of how much, how fast, by whom, and at what environmental cost should such development be undertaken. These issues would necessarily be fought out in the political arena by each generation. The Mineral Leasing Act of

1920 established the principle of continued government owner-ship of mineral lands, but enactment of the law did not end the de-bate about the actual use of those lands.

Eugene Larson

SOURCES FOR FURTHER STUDY
Bates, J. Leonard. *The Origins of Teapot Dome.* Urbana: University of Illinois Press, 1963.
Cawley, R. McGreggor. *Federal Land, Western Anger.* Lawrence: University Press of Kansas, 1993.
Hays, Samuel P. *Conservation and the Gospel of Efficiency.* Cambridge, Mass.: Harvard University Press, 1959.
Noggle, Burl. *Teapot Dome.* New York: W. W. Norton, 1965.
Robbins, Roy M. *Our Landed Heritage.* 2d ed. Lincoln: University of Nebraska Press, 1976.
Wyant, William K. *Westward in Eden.* Berkeley: University of California Press, 1982.

SEE ALSO: General Mining Act (1872); Wilderness Act (1964); Mining and Minerals Policy Act (1970); Surface Mining Control and Reclamation Act (1977).

FEDERAL POWER ACT

ALSO KNOWN AS: Water Power Act
DATE: June 10, 1920
U.S. STATUTES AT LARGE: 41 Stat. 1063
CATEGORIES: Agriculture; Energy; Natural Resources

The Federal Power Act created the Federal Power Commission to regu-late hydroelectric development on rivers in the United States.

The Federal Power Act provided for the secretaries of the Depart-ments of Interior, Agriculture, and War to regulate water power de-velopment jointly. Prior to passage of the Water Power Act, each of these cabinet departments had individually overseen hydroelectric plants on streams falling under their respective jurisdictions: Agriculture oversaw development in national forests, for example, and the War Department bore responsibility for navigable rivers. The new agency would review permit applications and approve engineering designs for dams and powerhouses.

The act was approved in 1920 after many years of lobbying, negotiation, and compromise in Congress. The first hydropower development in the United States occurred in 1882, but despite its advantages hydropower development lagged behind steam plants. A 1914 report found sixteen different sources of potential problems in obtaining water rights for hydro-projects. Lobbyists representing interest groups ranging from conservationists to industrialists pushed for a coherent federal water power policy.

BACKGROUND

By 1915 Congress had two bills to consider, the Adamson Bill, which was an amendment to the Federal Dam Act of 1906 and dealt with navigable waters, and the Ferris Bill, which dealt with power development on public lands. The major differences between the Ferris and the Adamson Bills lay in two areas—what specific waters were covered and who would have the administrative responsibilities—not with actual provisions regarding water power development. Both bills allowed for a fifty-year permit system with the permit being nonrevocable. Under the old system, permits could be revoked at any time. Both bills also provided for payment of fees by permit holders to the federal government. Licensing fees meant the public could benefit from development of public resources by private firms. Water power continued to be debated for several more years, despite claims by lobbyists that emergency situations caused by World War I required quick action.

It was not until 1918 that a compromise bill was introduced. This bill proposed a commission consisting of the three departments already involved in waterpower regulation (War, Interior, and Agriculture) and covering water power on navigable streams, public lands, and national forests. Oscar C. Merrill, chief forester with the U.S. Forest Service, was the primary author of the proposed legislation. Still, legislative inertia following World War I slowed the act's passage.

PROVISIONS

It was not until June 10, 1920, that the Federal Water Power Act became law. By then, numerous compromises necessary to ensure its approval had weakened conservationists' intentions. The act as passed reads as though its goal had always been regulation of technology rather than wise use of natural resources. It provided for fees to be collected and engineering design work to be submitted for approval. The FPC's executive secretary, Merrill, supported conservation, but he was only one man. Congress failed to allocate funding for even one clerk-typist for the FPC; all staff had to be "borrowed" from component departments. It was not until the FPC's reorganization in 1930 that it began to function as a truly regulatory agency.

Nancy Farm Männikkö

SOURCE FOR FURTHER STUDY

Baum, Robert David. *The Federal Power Commission and State Utility Regulation.* Washington, D.C.: American Council on Public Affairs, 1942.

SEE ALSO: Natural Gas Act (1938); Price-Anderson Act (1957); Niagara Power Act (1957); Department of Energy Organization Act (1977).

NINETEENTH AMENDMENT

DATE: Ratified August 18, 1920; certified August 26, 1920
U.S. STATUTES AT LARGE: 41 Stat. 362
CATEGORIES: Civil Rights and Liberties; Constitutional Law; Voting and Elections; Women's Issues

After more than a century of struggle, the Nineteenth Amendment gave women the right to vote.

"We hold these truths to be self-evident, that all men and women are created equal. . . ." Written in 1848 at the first Women's Rights Convention, held at Seneca Falls, New York, these words announced the opening of a new movement in which the goal was to establish political, social, and economic equality for men and women.

THE FIRST WOMEN'S MOVEMENT

Although the campaign for the vote created the greatest public outcry, suffrage was merely one facet of the larger struggle of women to enter the professions, to own property, and to enjoy the same legal rights as men. By attaining these goals, nineteenth century reformers hoped to see women emerge from second-class citizenship to a status equal to that of their male counterparts.

The 1848 meeting was not an isolated phenomenon; it was part of the general reform spirit of the period. Prosperous middle and upper classes had developed in large urban centers along the Atlantic seaboard. This prosperity had created a new, leisured class of women who could devote at least part of their time to worthy causes. Many chose to support the cause of women's rights in some way. Both men and women worked for social reforms. As each effort was successful, it inevitably led to others, thus creating a climate in which reform prospered. This process could be seen most clearly in the 1830's and 1840's, again in the Reconstruction period following the Civil War, and in the first two decades of the twentieth century. These three periods saw changes in the legal, social, and economic positions of African Americans,women, and labor. As their problems were interrelated, advancement for one group normally brought some gains for the others.

The moving force behind the 1848 meeting and the establishment of an Equal Rights Association was Elizabeth Cady Stanton. Like many other activists for women, Stanton came to the issue from the abolitionist movement. Many of the mid-nineteenth century reformers saw parallels between the position of slaves and the position of all women. Both groups were regarded by society as inherently inferior. Many abolitionists also believed that only when women enjoyed full rights to participate in the political process would they achieve their goal of a more egalitarian society. Thus, from the outset, the idea of women's political rights was regarded by their supporters as both a means and an end in itself. In the early years, Stanton's most important coworkers were Susan B. Anthony and Lucy Stone. Anthony later emerged as the organizing genius of the suffrage drive. Her administrative talents provided a perfect complement to Stanton's gifts as a writer and theoretician.

Although the Equal Rights Association was chronically short of funds, it managed to establish a short-lived newspaper, sponsor hundreds of speeches, and organize women's groups to petition and lobby for the vote in their home states. During the Civil War era, pressure for equal rights was submerged, first by the demand for the abolition of slavery and later by the drive to pass the Fifteenth Amendment. Male abolitionists promised that if women would work to secure suffrage for black men, their turn would come next. Thus the Equal Rights Association was placed in the position of working for a suffrage amendment that did not include women among its beneficiaries.

Anthony and Stanton found such a position intolerable and founded the National Woman Suffrage Association (NWSA) in 1869. Stone, who accepted that women must step aside during "the Negro's hour" of Reconstruction, formed the rival American Woman Suffrage Association (AWSA) that same year. The split in suffrage organizations reflected differences of personality and strategy. The AWSA concentrated on suffrage as its sole issue and followed a plan to educate citizens to try to achieve votes for women on a state-by-state basis. The NWSA at first allied itself with anyone who supported women's rights, including the self-proclaimed free-love advocate and presidential candidate Victoria Woodhull. After enduring great criticism and financial loss for its endorsement of Woodhull, the NWSA also decided to focus most of its efforts on suffrage. In 1889, the rival woman suffrage organizations decided to present a united front, and they merged to form the National American Woman Suffrage Association.

THE SECOND WOMEN'S MOVEMENT: PUSH FOR SUFFRAGE

The 1890's saw the death or retirement of most of the original suffrage leaders, but fortunately for the movement, the new century brought new leaders, such as Harriot Stanton Blatch, Carrie Chapman Catt, and Alice Paul; new organizations, such as the Boston Equal Suffrage Association for Good Government, the College Equal Suffrage League (1901), and the Congressional Union (1912), later called the Woman's Party; and the adoption of new techniques and ideas. Leaders and participants were better educated and better funded than before, and in the early twentieth century, the woman suffrage movement joined with other efforts to make the U.S. system more democratic and more just. The crusade for votes for women was an integral part of the Progressive movement and took strength from the widespread support for reform.

Suffragists had learned from the more militant English movement the value of publicity to call attention to themselves. To speeches and petitions, they added mass picketing, demonstrations, and rallies, including a huge suffrage parade in Washington, D.C., in 1913. On that day, when president-elect Woodrow Wilson arrived for his inauguration, he wondered why no crowd met him at the station. People were watching the suffrage parade instead, seeing marchers attacked by boisterous bystanders and rescued by federal troops. The parade drew national attention to the suffrage movement and led to congressional hearings.

Not only did the method of focusing attention on the issue of suffrage change, but also the means for attaining the end. The NAWSA realized that the only way to achieve national woman suffrage was through an amendment to the federal constitution. In 1915, Carrie Chapman Catt became the organization's president. Having helped to orchestrate adoption of woman suffrage in the states of Idaho, Colorado, Washington, California, and Illinois, Catt brought superb organizing skills to the NAWSA. In 1916, she developed her Winning Plan, by which suffragists would move on all fronts. In the states where women could vote, they would pressure their legislatures to urge Congress to pass a federal amendment. The NAWSA set up a Washington, D.C., office with a million-dollar budget to lobby President Wilson and the legislators. Alice Paul and the Woman's Party picketed the White House with banners asking, "Mr. President! How Long Must Women Wait for Liberty?"

Inside and outside Washington, opponents of suffragists also prepared for a struggle. In the conservative South, white supremacists believed that raising the question of votes for women would reopen the question of the black vote. In other states, the traditional friendship between prohibitionists and advocates of women's rights led to liquor interests' financing successful campaigns against woman suffrage. Anti-suffragist groups also drew support from business groups that feared that voting women would eliminate child labor and lead to pressure to improve other working conditions.

Although both political parties included statements endorsing woman suffrage in their 1916 platforms, they failed to translate the words into action after the election, when national attention was focused on European events. The United States' entry into World War I in 1917 led to arguments about the priority of winning the vote versus winning the war. While the more conservative women worked harder for the second goal, others redoubled their efforts for suffrage. How, Paul demanded, could President Wilson talk of fighting for democracy abroad and deny American women the right to vote? The Woman's Party continued picketing the White House, carrying placards addressed to "Kaiser Wilson." Suffragists were denounced as traitors, and many were arrested and sentenced to jail for disturbing the peace. There, the women protested conditions and demanded to be treated as political prisoners. They finally went on a hunger strike. When the public read of the women's miserable imprisonment, including the painful force-feeding of the hunger strikers, popular opinion forced the administration to release the prisoners and drop the charges.

PUBLIC BACKING

President Wilson endorsed woman suffrage but considered other problems to be more pressing. With his recommendation, the amendment passed the House in 1918 in a dramatic vote, with one member leaving the deathbed of his suffragist wife to cast an affirmative ballot. Although the Senate rejected the amendment in 1918, public opinion was firmly on the side of woman suffrage, and by the following year, passage was inevitable. On June 4, 1919, the proposed amendment passed the Senate and was submitted to the states. On his mother's advice, the youngest member of the Tennessee legislature cast the deciding vote in the decisive state. On August 16, 1920, U.S. women were enfranchised, after seventy-two years and countless hours of work and determination, beginning with the Seneca Falls meeting. Passage of the Nineteenth Amendment opened the door to full citizenship for women in the United States, a necessary step on the road to full equality.

Anne Trotter, updated by
Mary Welek Atwell

SOURCES FOR FURTHER STUDY
Cott, Nancy F. *The Grounding of Modern Feminism.* New Haven, Conn.: Yale University Press, 1987.
Evans, Sara M. *Born for Liberty: A History of Women in America.* New York: Free Press, 1989.
Flexner, Eleanor. *Century of Struggle: The Woman's Rights Movement in the United States.* Rev. ed. Cambridge, Mass.: Harvard University Press, 1975.
Scott, Anne Firor, and Andrew M. Scott. *One Half the People: The Fight for Woman Suffrage.* Philadelphia: J. B. Lippincott, 1975.
Woloch, Nancy. *Women and the American Experience.* 2d ed. New York: McGraw-Hill, 1994.

SEE ALSO: Fifteenth Amendment (1870); Equal Rights Amendment (1923).

IMMIGRATION ACT OF 1921

ALSO KNOWN AS: Emergency Quota Act of 1921
DATE: May 19, 1921
U.S. STATUTES AT LARGE: 42 Stat. 5
PUBLIC LAW: 67-5
CATEGORIES: Asia or Asian Americans; Immigration

Immigration legislation in 1921 created a quota system that favored the nations of northern and western Europe and put an end to the ideal of the United States as a melting pot.

Throughout most of the nineteenth century, immigration to the United States was open to anyone who wanted to enter. By the 1880's, however, this unlimited freedom was beginning to disappear. The first law restricting immigration came in 1882, when Chinese were excluded from entering American territory. Hostility to Chinese workers in California sparked Congress to pass a bill amid warnings that Chinese worked for lower wages than whites and came from such a culturally inferior civilization that they would never make good Americans. The law became permanent in 1902. Five years later, under a gentlemen's agreement with the Japanese government, citizens of that country were added to the excluded list. The only other people barred from entering the United States were prostitutes, insane persons, paupers, polygamists, and anyone suffering from a "loathsome or contagious disease." Under these categories, compared to more than a million immigrants per year from 1890 to 1914, less than thirteen thousand were kept out annually.

NATIVIST XENOPHOBIA

The small number of those excluded troubled anti-immigrant groups, such as the American Protective Association, founded in 1887, and the Immigration Restriction League, created in Boston in 1894. Both organizations warned of the "immigrant invasion" which threatened the American way of life. These opponents of open immigration argued that since 1880, most new arrivals had come from different areas of Europe from that of the pre-1880 immigrants, who came largely from Germany, England, Ireland, and Scandinavia. The "new" immigrants—mainly Slavs, Poles, Italians, and Jews—came from poorer and more culturally "backward" areas of Europe. Many of these immigrants advocated radicalism, anarchism, socialism, or communism, and were unfamiliar with ideas of democracy and progress. Furthermore, they preferred to live in ghettoes in cities, where they strengthened the power of political machines and corrupt bosses. Those who considered themselves guardians of traditional American values found support for their position among trade unionists in the American Federation of Labor (AFL), whose president, Samuel Gompers, argued that the new immigrants provided employers with an endless supply of cheap labor, leading to lower wages for everyone.

Advocates of restriction found their chief congressional spokesperson in Senator Henry Cabot Lodge, a member of the Immigration Restriction League, who sponsored a bill calling for a literacy test. Such a law, which called upon immigrants to be able to read and write in their native language, was seen as an effective barrier to most "new" immigrants. Congress passed the bill in 1897, but President Grover Cleveland vetoed it, arguing that it was unnecessary and discriminatory. Cleveland believed that American borders should remain open to anyone who wanted to enter and that there were enough jobs and opportunities to allow anyone to fulfill a dream of economic success. Advocates of this vision of the American dream, however, were lessening in number over time.

DILLINGHAM COMMISSION

The assassination of President William McKinley in 1901 led to the exclusion of anarchists and those who advocated the violent overthrow of the government of the United States. A more important step to a quota system, however, came in 1907, when the House and Senate established the United States Immigration Commission, under the leadership of Senator William P. Dillingham. In 1910 and 1911, the commission issued a forty-two-volume report advocating a reduction in immigration because of the "racial inferiority" of new immigrant groups. Studies of immigrant populations, the commission concluded, showed that people from southern and eastern Europe had a higher potential for criminal activity, were more likely to end up poor and sick, and were less intelligent than other Americans. It called for passage of a literacy test to preserve American values. Congress passed legislation in 1912 calling for such a test, but President William Howard Taft vetoed it, saying that illiteracy resulted from lack of educational opportunity and had little to do with native intelligence. Open entrance to the United States was part of American history, and many of America's wealthiest and hardest working citizens had come without knowing how to read and write. If the United States barred such people, Taft argued, America would become weaker and less wealthy.

WAR, IMMIGRATION POLICY, AND RACISM

In 1915, Woodrow Wilson became the third president to veto a literacy bill, denouncing its violation of the American ideal of an open door. Two years later, in the wake of American entrance into World War I and growing hostility against foreigners, Congress overrode Wilson's second veto and the literacy test became law in the Immigration Act of 1917. Along with establishing a reading test for anyone over age sixteen, the law also created a "barred zone" which excluded immigrants from most of Asia, including China, India, and Japan, regardless of whether they could read. As it turned out, the test that asked adults to read a few words in any recognized language did little to reduce immigration. Between 1918 and 1920, less than 1 percent of those who took it failed. Representative Albert Johnson, chair of the House Committee on Immigration, had been a longtime advocate of closing the borders of the United States. In 1919, he called for the suspension of all immigration. Johnson's proposal was defeated in the House of Representatives.

In 1920, however, immigration increased dramatically, as did fears that millions of refugees from war-torn Europe were waiting to flood into the United States. Much of the argument for restriction was based on ideas associated with scientific racism. The Republican candidate for the presidency, Warren G. Harding, advocated restriction in several speeches, warning of the dangers inherent in allowing open admission. He called for legislation that would permit entrance to the United States only to people whose background and racial characteristics showed that they could adopt American values and principles. The next year, Vice President Calvin Coolidge authored a magazine article claiming that laws of biology proved that "Nordics," the preferred type, deteriorated intellectually and physically when allowed to intermarry with other races.

These views reflected the growing influence of eugenics, the science of improving the human race by discouraging the birth of the "unfit." Madison Grant, a lawyer and secretary of the New York Zoological Society, and later an adviser to Albert Johnson's Immigration Committee, wrote the most influential book advocating this racist way of thinking, *The Passing of the Great Race in America* (1916). In it, he described human society as a huge snake. Nordic races made up the head, while the inferior races formed the tail. It would be this type of scientific argument, more than any other, that would provide the major rationale for creation of the 1921 quota system. The tail could not be allowed to rule the head.

LABOR, RADICALISM, QUOTAS

Early in 1921, the House debated and passed Johnson's bill calling for a two-year suspension of all immigration. The Senate Committee on Immigration, chaired by Senator LeBaron Colt, held hearings on a similar proposal but refused to support a total ban after hearing arguments from business groups fearful that complete exclusion would stop all access to European laborers. Representatives from the National Association of Manufacturers testified on the need to have access to inexpensive labor, even though some business leaders were beginning to fear that too many in the immigration pool were influenced by communism and socialism, especially after the communist victory in Russia in 1918. The possibility of thousands of radical workers with a greater tendency to strike coming into the country seemed too high a price to pay in return for lower wages. Unions, especially the AFL, continued to lobby for strict regulation of immigration. To keep wages high, Samuel Gompers told Congress, foreign workers had to be kept out. By 1921, the only widespread support for free and open immigration came from immigrant groups themselves. Although a few members of Congress supported their position, it was a distinctly minority view.

Senator William Dillingham, whose report had renewed efforts to restrict immigration, offered a quota plan which he hoped would satisfy business and labor. He called for a policy in which each nation would receive a quota of immigrants equal to 5 percent of that country's total population in the United States according to the 1910 census. Dillingham's suggestion passed the Senate with little opposition and gained favor in the House. Before its final approval, however, Johnson and his supporters of total suspension reduced the quota to 3 percent and set 350,000 as the maximum number of legal immigrants in any one year. Woodrow Wilson vetoed the bill shortly before leaving office, but it was passed with only one dissenting vote in the Senate during a special session called by President Harding on May 19, 1921. The House approved the Emergency Quota Act the same day without a recorded vote. The only opposition came from representatives with large numbers of immigrants in their districts. Adolph Sabath, a Democratic congressperson from Chicago, led the dissenters, arguing that the act was based on a "pseudoscientific proposition" that falsely glorified the Nordic nations. His comments had little effect on the result. One of the most important changes in American immigration history went into effect in June of 1921.

THE QUOTA ACT: PROVISIONS

The Emergency Quota Act of 1921 severely reduced immigration into the United States. In 1922, its first full year of operation, only 309,556 people legally entered the country, compared with 805,228 the previous year. Quotas for Europe, the Middle East, Africa, Australia, and New Zealand were generally filled quickly, although economic depressions in England, Ireland, and Germany kept many potential immigrants at home. Less than half the legal number of immigrants came to America the first year; the southern and eastern Europeans filled almost 99 percent of their limit. No limits existed for Canada, Mexico, and other nations of the Western Hemisphere. To keep an adequate supply of cheap agricultural labor available to farmers in Texas and California, Congress refused to place a quota on immigration from these areas of the world. Japan and China were the only countries with a quota of zero, as Congress continued its policy of exclusion for most areas of Asia.

The 1921 act provided for "special preferences" for relatives of America citizens, including wives, children under eighteen, parents, brothers, and sisters. The commissioner of immigration was to make it a priority to maintain family unity; however, this was to be the only exception to the strict quota policy.

Congress extended the "emergency" law in May, 1922, for two more years. This move, however, did not satisfy Representative Johnson and others supporting complete restriction. Johnson's Immigration Committee continued to hold hearings and gather evidence supporting an end to all immigration. Johnson became increasingly interested in eugenics and remained in close contact with Madison Grant. In 1923, Johnson was elected president of the Eugenics Research Association of America, a group devoted to gathering statistics on the hereditary traits of Americans. He seemed especially interested in studies showing a large concentration of "new" immigrants in mental hospitals, prisons, and poorhouses. Such information led him to call for a change in the law. A reduction in the quota for "new" immigrants was necessary, he claimed, to save the United States from even larger numbers of paupers, mental patients, and criminals. The Immigration Committee voted to change the census base from 1910 to 1890, when there were far fewer southern and eastern Europeans in the country, and to reduce the quota from 3 percent to 2 percent. Congress would adopt those ideas in 1924.

Under the 1921 law, boats filled with prospective immigrants were returned to their homelands. These actions, however, were only the beginning, and the guardians of racial purity in Congress were already moving toward even tighter controls. Restrictionists had gotten most of what they wanted.

Leslie V. Tischauser

SOURCES FOR FURTHER STUDY
Bennett, Marion T. *American Immigration Policies.* Washington, D.C.: Public Affairs Press, 1963.
Divine, Robert. *American Immigration Policy, 1924-1952.* New Haven, Conn.: Yale University Press, 1957.
Gains, Roy. *Immigration Restriction.* New York: Macmillan, 1928.
Higham, John. *Strangers in the Land: Patterns of American Nativism, 1860-1925.* New York: Atheneum, 1975.
Lipset, Seymour M., and Earl Raab. *The Politics of Unreason: Right-Wing Extremism in America, 1790-1970.* New York: Harper & Row, 1970.
Solomon, Barbara. *Ancestors and Immigrants.* Cambridge, Mass.: Harvard University Press, 1956.

SEE ALSO: Chinese Exclusion Act (1882); Gentlemen's Agreement (1907); Alien land laws (1913); Immigration Act of 1917 (1917); Immigration Act of 1924 (1924); Immigration Act of 1943 (1943).

SHEPPARD-TOWNER ACT

ALSO KNOWN AS: Public Protection of Maternity and Infancy Act; Maternity Act
DATE: November 23, 1921
U.S. STATUTES AT LARGE: 42 Stat. 224
CATEGORIES: Children's Issues; Health and Welfare; Women's Issues

The first federal social welfare legislation authorized matching funds to the states for programs in maternal and child hygiene.

The Public Protection of Maternity and Infancy Act of 1921, commonly known as the Sheppard-Towner Act, linked a chain of ideas and actions about the proper role of government in the economy and society from the presidency of Theodore Roosevelt to that of Franklin Delano Roosevelt. The link began with the White House Conference on Child Welfare Standards in 1909 and ended with the Social Security Act of 1935. Aside from veterans' pension appro-

priations, the Sheppard-Towner Act was in many ways the first federal welfare legislation. It authorized matching funds to the states
for programs in maternal and child hygiene. The act also broke
with the legacy of mothers' aid by providing non-means-tested assistance, although it retained social-control aspects whereby visiting nurses offered advice and help according to the Children's Bureau's norms of good child care (for example, against feeding or
cuddling babies on demand), even if these norms went against a
client's customs. The Sheppard-Towner Act also represented the
first major dividend of women's national enfranchisement.

MATERNAL AND INFANT MORTALITY
The U.S. Children's Bureau developed from the White House Conference of 1909, and the Bureau first investigated the causes of infant and maternal mortality. Studies revealed that the United
States had high rates, showing, for example, that the nation ranked
seventeenth in maternal and eleventh in infant mortality among
world nations in 1918. Studies also linked poverty and mortality
rates, revealing that 80 percent of America's expectant mothers received no advice or trained care. To remedy this situation, Jean-
nette Rankin, the first woman to serve in Congress, introduced in
1918 a measure to provide public protection of maternity and infancy. Julia Lathrop, chief of the Children's Bureau, sponsored the
measure, and Senator Morris Sheppard of Texas and Representative Horace Towner of Iowa reintroduced the bill in the Sixty-sixth
Congress. The bill made little progress until the full enfranchisement of women in 1920.

PASSAGE AND PROVISIONS
The League of Women Voters urged the national parties to endorse the maternity bill in their 1920 platforms. The Democratic,
Socialist, Prohibition, and Farmer-Labor parties did, while the Republican platform ignored it. President Warren G. Harding, however, supported the bill in his Social Justice Day speech on October 1, 1920. Sheppard and Towner resubmitted the bill in April,
1921, and it passed the Senate on July 22 by a vote of 63 to 7. Samuel Winslow, chair of the House Committee on Interstate and Foreign Commerce, which oversaw the bill, refused to hold hearings
for months. President Harding prodded Winslow only after influential women such as Republican National Committee vice chair

Harriet Upton warned him that delay alienated many women. The House finally passed the measure by a vote of 279 to 39, while the only woman in Congress, the anti-suffragist Alice Robertson, voted against it. Harding signed the bill on November 23, 1921.

At the time of debate and passage, the inclinations of women voters were an unknown quantity. Suffragists had promised to clean house when they got the vote, and many politicians feared that women voters would vote en bloc or remain aloof from the main parties. Passage of the maternity bill was a goal of newly enfranchised women and took precedence over all other efforts. In 1920, the League of Women Voters helped to create the Women's Joint Congressional Committee (WJCC), which coordinated the lobbying efforts in Washington, D.C., for nearly two dozen women's organizations. Florence Kelley, executive secretary of the National Consumers' League, chaired the WJCC subcommittee responsible for enactment of the measure.

Kelley's successful lobbying efforts overcame powerful opponents who assailed the measure as a threat to the moral foundation of the nation. Such organizations as the National Association Opposed to Woman Suffrage and the Woman Patriots equated feminism and woman suffrage with socialism and communism. Mary Kilbreth, a leading anti-suffragist, wrote Harding that many believed the bill was inspired by communism and backed by American radicals, thereby striking at the heart of American civilization. Organizations such as the Woman's Municipal League of Boston, the American Constitutional League, the Constitutional Liberty League of Massachusetts, and the Massachusetts Public Interest League concurred.

Fearing state-run medicine, the American Medical Association (AMA) also targeted the Sheppard-Towner Act. State medical societies in Massachusetts, New York, Illinois, Ohio, and Indiana spearheaded the opposition. The *Illinois Medical Journal*, official organ of the Illinois State Medical Society, for example, attacked the act as a product of Bolshevist forces that sought to set up bureaucratic autocracy in the nation's capital. The *Journal of the American Medical Association* campaigned against the Sheppard-Towner Act from February 5, 1921, until its repeal in June of 1929. In 1922, the AMA's house of delegates condemned the legislation as a socialistic machination. Many women physicians, such as Josephine Baker, a constant ally of the National Consumers' League and the League of Women Voters and president of the Medical Woman's National Association in the early 1930's, supported the Sheppard-Towner Act.

The act authorized an appropriation of $1.48 million for fiscal 1921-1922 and $1.24 million for the next five years ending June 30, 1927. Of this sum, $5,000 would go to each state outright; $5,000 more would go to each state if matching funds were provided; and the remainder would be allocated on a population percentage and matching basis. The Children's Bureau would channel the money through state child welfare or health divisions. States retained the right to reject aid. The act provided for instruction in hygiene of maternity and infancy through public health nurses, visiting nurses, consultation centers, child care conferences, and literature distribution. Forty-one states joined the program in 1922, whereas until the act's repeal in 1929, only Connecticut, Illinois, and Massachusetts rejected Sheppard-Towner money.

RESPONSE AND DEMISE

The attorney general of Massachusetts issued an opinion that the act would misuse the state's tax money and that it was unconstitutional because it violated the rights of the states. Massachusetts filed a suit with the U.S. Supreme Court on behalf of its taxpayers to enjoin the law. Harriet Frothingham, president of the Woman Patriots, filed another suit in the Supreme Court of the District of Columbia in the event that states were deemed ineligible to file a taxpayer's suit. The District of Columbia court dismissed Frothingham's case and the U.S. Court of Appeals concurred. She then appealed to the U.S. Supreme Court. In the interim, U.S. Solicitor General James Beck, who considered the Sheppard-Towner Act to be unconstitutional, encouraged Massachusetts to pursue its case. These suits threatened the range of federal programs which provided either direct aid or matching grants to states. On June 5, 1923, the U.S. Supreme Court dismissed both suits for want of jurisdiction and without ruling on the constitutionality of the act.

Although the Sheppard-Towner Act was considered a permanent law, federal appropriations under the act's provisions were scheduled to cease automatically on June 30, 1927. In 1926, proponents moved to have the authorization extended. The House of Representatives quickly approved a two-year extension by a vote of 218 to 44. The AMA, Woman Patriots, Daughters of the American

Revolution, and other opponents, however, mobilized to stop the bill in the Senate. Opponents iterated many of the same themes that had been less persuasive in 1921: primarily that the Sheppard-Towner Act was part of a feminist-socialist-communist plot to sovietize the United States. In the end, proponents accepted a compromise which extended the appropriations for two more years but repealed the law itself automatically on June 30, 1929.

Although progressive women still lobbied for the bill, President Herbert Hoover refused to press the matter and allowed the first federal social security law to lapse. The Great Depression precluded any revival of national provisions in the early 1930's, and the loss of federal funds severely restricted many of the forty-five state programs that had continued to provide maternity and infancy aid on their own. Restoration, however, came with the Social Security Act of 1935. Title V of the 1935 act authorized appropriations for the Children's Bureau of $5.82 million for maternity and infancy protection, in addition to $3.87 million for crippled children and $34.75 million for aid to dependent children.

Richard K. Caputo

SOURCES FOR FURTHER STUDY
Bremner, Robert H., ed. *1866-1932.* Vol. 2 in *Children and Youth in America: A Documentary History.* Cambridge, Mass.: Harvard University Press, 1971.
Caputo, Richard K., ed. *Federal Responses to People in Need.* Vol. 1, *Welfare and Freedom American Style I: The Role of the Federal Government, 1900-1940.* Lanham, Md.: University Press of America, 1991.
Gordon, Linda. *Pitied but Not Entitled: Single Mothers and the History of Welfare 1890-1935.* New York: Free Press, 1994.
Lemons, J. Stanley. "The Sheppard-Towner Act: Progressivism in the 1920's." *Journal of American History* 55 (March, 1969): 776-786.

SEE ALSO: Social Security Act (1935); Aid to Families with Dependent Children (1935).

CABLE ACT

DATE: September 22, 1922
U.S. STATUTES AT LARGE: 42 Stat. 1021
PUBLIC LAW: 346
CATEGORIES: Asia or Asian Americans; Immigration; Women's Issues

*The Cable Act reformed the rules by which women lost or obtained
U.S. citizenship through marriage to foreigners.*

Representative John L. Cable of Ohio noted when introducing his
bill that "the laws of our country should grant independent citizenship to women." By this act, the United States took the lead among
nations in the world in acknowledging the right of a woman to
choose her citizenship rather than to lose or gain it upon marriage.
In the early twentieth century, under the laws of virtually all nations, a woman automatically lost her citizenship and took that of
her husband upon marriage to a foreigner. The Cable Act, supported by all major women's groups at the time, was viewed as
an important piece of reform legislation aimed at protecting a
woman's right to choose her citizenship. As Representative Cable
noted upon the bill's passage into law: "Justice and common sense
dictate that the woman should have the same right as the man to
choose the country of her allegiance."

The effects of the Cable Act were varied. Although aimed primarily at rectifying cases in which American women, under the
1907 Expropriation Act, automatically lost their U.S. citizenship
upon marriage to an alien, it also revoked provisions of an 1885 act
that automatically conferred U.S. citizenship on alien women who
married Americans. Therefore, a foreign woman could not automatically become an American citizen upon marriage to an American, even if that were her desire. Instead, like any other alien, she
would have to undergo an independent process of naturalization.

One effect of this aspect of the law was to discourage Chinese
American men from marrying immigrant women. For these reasons, the Cable Act has been considered anti-immigrant and anti-women by some latter-day observers. However, although an alien
woman who married a U.S. citizen or whose husband became natu-

ralized would no longer automatically be granted citizenship, she was not excluded from seeking U.S. citizenship. The act made the process of becoming an American citizen a matter of deliberate choice rather than an automatic effect of marriage. The Cable Act did not revoke the citizenship of any woman who before its passage had received American citizenship automatically by marriage.

The ultimate effect of the Cable Act was to treat women of all ethnic and racial backgrounds with complete equality insofar as the acquisition of U.S. citizenship was concerned. Modern human rights treaties generally follow this U.S. practice, recognizing that acquisition of citizenship should be a matter of free and independent consent.

Robert F. Gorman

SOURCES FOR FURTHER STUDY
Kansas, Sidney. *Citizenship of the United States of America.* New York: Washington Publishing, 1936.
Von Glahn, Gerhard. *Law Among Nations: An Introduction to Public International Law.* New York: Macmillan, 1992.

SEE ALSO: War Brides Act (1945).

EQUAL RIGHTS AMENDMENT

DATE: Proposed 1923; defeated 1983
CATEGORIES: Civil Rights and Liberties; Women's Issues

A proposed amendment to the United States Constitution which would have guaranteed equality of rights regardless of sex. Though it did not secure enough states for its ratification, the Equal Rights Amendment focused debate on issues of gender equity.

After the ratification in 1920 of the Nineteenth Amendment, which awarded women the vote, demand grew for legislation providing other rights for women. The first equal rights amendment, introduced in 1923, failed mainly because of the strong opposition of organized labor. Labor opposed it because it would have invalidated protective legislation for women workers such as mandatory rest periods or limits on hours to be worked or weight to be lifted.

TEXT AND CONGRESSIONAL PASSAGE

The text of the Equal Rights Amendment was extremely simple:

Section 1. Equality of rights under the law shall not be denied or abridged by the United States or by any State on account of sex.

Section 2. The Congress shall have the power to enforce, by appropriate legislation, the provisions of this article.

Section 3. The Amendment shall take effect two years after the date of ratification.

Through the efforts of two Democratic congresswomen, Martha Griffiths of Michigan and Edith Green of Oregon, the ERA passed the House of Representatives in 1970. Previous obstructions were bypassed through a discharge petition which received bipartisan support, especially from President Richard Nixon. When the ERA was reintroduced in 1971, it easily passed with overwhelmingly favorable votes in the House and in the Senate the following year.

Some members of Congress proposed amendments that would have retained protective legislation or exempted women from the draft. Supporters of the ERA viewed these amendments as permitting inequalities in pay, hiring, and advancement. Although these amendments had been defeated, their arguments surfaced in later debates over ratification.

SUPPORTERS OF THE ERA

To become law, the amendment now need to be ratified by two-thirds of the states. The principal rationale for the ERA was that it was a statement of principle that women were entitled to equal status with men. It would set a national standard to prevent discrimination on local or state levels. The Fifth and Fourteenth Amendments, ERA supporters argued, were not designed to deal with sex-related discrimination; moreover, stereotypes regarding gender roles were perpetuated in common law, and women were under-represented in legislative bodies and courts.

Groups of middle-class women such as the Business and Professional Women's Clubs and League of Women Voters were among the earliest supporters of the ERA, and they were joined by the National Education Association and reform groups such as Common Cause. The National Organization for Women (NOW), founded in 1966, was a more militant group that sought to apply the tactics of civil rights groups to women's causes and aggressively supported the ERA. Between 1970 and 1973 organized labor changed its position from opposition to support.

OPPONENTS OF THE ERA

Several religious denominations opposed the ERA: Mormons because it could interfere with the traditional family, Catholics because it might require ordaining women despite the church's insistence on a male priesthood, and fundamentalist Protestants because of biblical prohibitions against women clergy. Among other objections was the idea that the ERA was unnecessary because of the equal protection clause of the Fourteenth Amendment and such legislation as Title VII of the Civil Rights Act of 1964 (extending the same protection to sex as to race) and the Equal Pay Act of 1963. Under the ERA, its opponents feared, even women with small children could not only be drafted but also assigned to combat duty. Homosexuals would gain the right to marry and to adopt children. Abortion would be protected through the amendment, and state regulations thereof would be preempted. Unisex dormitories, prisons, and restrooms could not be prohibited.

Philosophically, the ERA would shift state policy powers from the legislature to the judiciary, and from the states to the federal government. Some worried that the vague wording of the ERA could lead to unpredictable court decisions, and previous decisions on school integration, criminal rights, and abortion had led to a profound distrust of the federal courts, especially in the South.

FAILURE OF RATIFICATION

Twenty-two states ratified the Equal Rights Amendment in 1972, and eight more did so in 1973. Yet only five more states ratified: The last, Indiana, did so in 1977. The holdout states were mainly in the South and West; Illinois was the only northern industrial state among them.

The ERA failed for several reasons. Nixon was the only president to give it his personal support, whereas Ronald Reagan actively opposed it. The Republican Party platforms had included the ERA for several decades, but it did not in 1980 or thereafter. Conservative activist Phyllis Schlafly became a highly articulate and effective opponent of the ERA, raising arguments that it would force women to support idle husbands and would deprive them of preference in divorce and child custody cases. Some members of minority groups perceived the ERA as providing gains for middle-class white women at the expense of men and women of color. Male government workers feared that the ERA would undermine laws that gave war veterans preference in employment. The Soviet invasion of Afghanistan in 1979 brought about draft registration for men in 1980 and raised concerns about women in combat.

The ERA's supporters were unprepared for the intensity of the debate which arose in the late 1970's. Their last victory was getting Congress to vote a three-year extension of the ratification deadline in 1978, which proved fruitless: No additional states ratified despite boycotts, demonstrations, and even hunger strikes by the more radical ERA supporters. In 1983 the ERA was reintroduced in Congress, but it did not receive enough votes in the House to pass.

R. M. Longyear

SOURCES FOR FURTHER STUDY

Berry, Mary Frances. *Why ERA Failed: Politics, Women's Rights, and the Amending Process of the Constitution.* Bloomington: Indiana University Press, 1986.

Boles, Janet K. *The Politics of the Equal Rights Amendment: Conflict and the Decision Process.* New York: Longman, 1979.

Gillmore, Inez Haynes. *The Story of Alice Paul and the National Woman's Party.* Fairfax, Va.: Denlinger's, 1977. First published in 1921 as *The Story of the Woman's Party.*

Hammer, Roger A. *American Woman: Hidden in History, Forging the Future.* 2d ed. Vol. 3 in *Hidden America.* Golden Valley, Minn.: The Place in the Woods, 1993.

Hoff-Wilson, Joan, ed. *Rights of Passage: The Past and Future of the ERA.* Bloomington: Indiana University Press, 1986.

Lee, Rex E. *A Lawyer Looks at the Equal Rights Amendment.* Provo, Utah: Brigham Young University Press, 1980.

Lunardini, Christine A. *From Equal Suffrage to Equal Rights: Alice Paul and the National Woman's Party, 1910-1928.* New York: New York University Press, 1986.

Mansbridge, Jane J. *Why We Lost the ERA.* Chicago: University of Chicago Press, 1986.

Mathews, Donald G., and Jane Sherron De Hart. *Sex, Gender, and the Politics of ERA: A State and the Nation.* New York: Oxford University Press, 1990.

Pole, J. R. *The Pursuit of Equality in American History.* Berkeley: University of California Press, 1978.

Steiner, Gilbert Yale. *Constitutional Inequality: The Political Fortunes of the Equal Rights Amendment.* Washington, D.C.: Brookings Institution Press, 1985.

Woodward, Carolyn. "The Growth of the Modern Women's Movement." In *Changing Our Power: An Introduction to Women's Studies,* edited by Jo Whitehorse Cochran, Donna Lengston, and Carolyn Woodward. 2d ed. Dubuque, Iowa: Kendall/Hunt, 1991.

SEE ALSO: Fifth Amendment (1789); Fourteenth Amendment (1868); Fifteenth Amendment (1870); Nineteenth Amendment (1920); Sheppard-Towner Act (1921); Equal Pay Act (1963); Civil Rights Act of 1964 (1964); Title VII of the Civil Rights Act of 1964 (1964).

WORLD WAR ADJUSTED COMPENSATION ACT

ALSO KNOWN AS: Bonus Act
DATE: May 19, 1924
U.S. STATUTES AT LARGE: 43 Stat. 121
PUBLIC LAW: 68-120
U.S. CODE: not available
CATEGORIES: Health and Welfare

In the wake of the Great Depression, the failure to pay veterans their full compensation under this act virtually assured the defeat of Herber Hoover in his second bid for the presidency.

Answering their nation's call to enter the armed forces, millions of Americans left their jobs to fight in World War I, which led to an economic disparity between those who fought and those who did not. While the military paid soldiers only a small salary per month, civilian wages grew tremendously and those who did not sacrifice for their country benefited while the soldiers who fought gained nothing. To rectify the situation, Congress in 1924 proposed a compensation act to reward World War I veterans with a monetary sum when the veteran neared retirement age. Veterans were to be compensated at a set fee for each day in military service ($1.25 for overseas duty, $1.00 for stateside duty) with the full sum to be paid in 1945. Concerned that the financial commitment would harm the economy, President Calvin Coolidge vetoed the legislation, but Congress overrode the veto and the Bonus Act became law on May 19, 1924.

When the Great Depression began in 1929, however, most veterans could not wait until 1945. Unemployed, hungry, and desperate, approximately fifteen thousand veterans, the so-called Bonus Army, converged on Washington, D.C., in the summer of 1932 to demand early payment of their bonuses. Establishing squatter camps around Washington, the veterans waited to see what Congress would do. When Congress refused to pass the necessary legislation, most veteran camps dispersed and went home, leaving about five thousand diehards. Claiming that communists had influenced the remaining veterans, President Herbert Hoover ordered the U.S. Army to remove the veterans by force if necessary. Led by Army Chief of Staff Douglas MacArthur, soldiers backed by tanks and machine guns burned the Bonus Army camps and forced the veterans from the city. Two soldiers and two policemen were killed in the clash. The dispersal of the Bonus Army, conducted in full view of the national media, virtually assured the defeat of Herbert Hoover in the 1932 presidential elections, leading to the victory of Franklin D. Roosevelt.

In 1935, to alleviate the suffering of unemployed veterans, Congress voted to issue the soldiers their bonuses immediately, but Roosevelt vetoed the bill (introduced by a Republican rival) because it was not part of his established New Deal plan for Depression relief. A year later, Congress again voted for immediate compensation, but this time it successfully overrode Roosevelt's veto, and cash payments were issued in 1936.

Steven J. Ramold

SOURCES FOR FURTHER STUDY
Keene, Jennifer D. *Doughboys, the Great War, and the Remaking of America*. Baltimore: The Johns Hopkins University Press, 2001.
Lisio, Donald J. *The President and Protest: Hoover, Conspiracy, and the Bonus Riot*. Columbia: University of Missouri Press, 1974.

SEE ALSO: Dependent Pension Act (1890); Social Security Act (1935); G.I. Bill (1944); Employee Retirement Income Security Act (1974).

IMMIGRATION ACT OF 1924

ALSO KNOWN AS: Johnson-Reid Act; National Origins Act
DATE: May 26, 1924
U.S. STATUTES AT LARGE: 43 Stat. 153
PUBLIC LAW: 68-139
CATEGORIES: Asia or Asian Americans; Immigration

Also known as the National Origins Act, this law restricted immigration by nationality using a quota system.

There was no clearly defined official U.S. policy toward immigration until the late nineteenth century. The United States was still a relatively young country, and there was a need for settlers in the West and for workers to build industry. Chinese immigrants flowed into California in 1849 and the early 1850's, searching for fortune and staying as laborers who worked the mines and helped to build the transcontinental railroad.

ANTI-ASIAN PREJUDICE

The earliest immigration restriction focused on Asians. In 1875, the federal government restricted the number of Chinese and Japanese coming into the country. The push for restriction of Asian immigrants was led by U.S. workers. After the depression of 1877, Denis Kearney, an Irish-born labor organizer, helped found the Workingman's Trade and Labor Union of San Francisco, an anti-Chinese and anticapitalist group. Kearney and others believed that lower-paid Chinese workers took jobs away from white workers, and they agitated for expulsion of the Chinese and legal restrictions on future immigrants. Their efforts were successful in 1882, when the Chinese Exclusion Act was passed. The act exempted teachers, students, merchants, and pleasure travelers, and remained in effect until 1943. With the act of 1882, the federal government had, for the first time, placed restrictions on the immigration of persons from a specific country. More specific policy toward European immigration began in the 1880's. In 1882, the federal government excluded convicts, paupers, and mentally impaired persons. Organized labor's efforts also were successful in 1882, with the prohibition of employers' recruiting workers in Europe and paying their passage to the United States.

RESTRICTIVE CHANGES

Federal law became more aggressive by the early twentieth century, with the passage of the Act of 1903, which excluded epileptics, beggars, and anarchists. In 1907, the United States Immigration Commission was formed. This group, also known as the Dillingham Commission, published a forty-two-volume survey of the impact of immigration on American life and called for a literacy test and further immigration restriction. Although several presidential vetoes had prevented a literacy requirement, in 1917, the U.S. Congress overrode President Woodrow Wilson's veto and passed a law requiring a literacy test for newcomers. The test was designed to reduce the number of immigrants, particularly those from southeastern Europe, where the literacy rate was low.

The marked change in official policy and in the view of a majority of people in the United States was caused by several factors. A strong nativist movement had begun after World War I with such groups as the American Protective Association, an organization that began in the Midwest in the 1880's and was fueled by prejudice against aliens and Catholics. Senator Henry Cabot Lodge organized the Immigration Restriction League in Boston, indicating the addition of U.S. leaders and intellectuals to the restriction movement. Political and economic problems in Europe, including the war and a postwar economic depression, had led to rising immigration from Europe. Changes in the U.S. economy reduced the need for manual labor.

IMMIGRATION IN THE PROGRESSIVE ERA

The push for restriction coincided with the most intensive era of immigration in United States history. From the late 1880's until the 1920's, the nation experienced wave after wave of immigration, with millions of persons coming into the country each decade. The growth of new physical and social sciences that emphasized heredity as a factor in intelligence led many people to believe that persons such as Slavs or Italians were less intelligent than western Europeans such as the Norwegians or the English. The belief in genetic inferiority gave credence to the immigration restriction movement and helped sway the government.

At the same time that millions of newcomers were entering the United States, a spirit of reform, the Progressive Era, had grown throughout the country. Americans who saw themselves as progressive and forward-looking pushed for change in politics, society, and education, particularly in the crowded urban areas of the Northeast. Europeans had emigrated in large numbers to the cities, and newer groups, such as Italians and Poles, were seen by many progressive-minded reformers as the root of urban problems. Thus it was with the help of progressive leaders that a push was made at the federal level to restrict the number of immigrants.

In 1921, Congress passed a temporary measure that was the first U.S. law specifically restricting European immigration. The act established a quota system that held the number of immigrants to 3 percent of each admissible nationality living in the United States in 1910. Quotas were established for persons from Europe, Asia, Africa, Australia, and New Zealand. Although only a temporary measure, the Immigration Act of 1921 marked the beginning of a permanent policy of restricting European immigration. It began a bitter three-year controversy that led to the Immigration Act of 1924.

THE 1924 ACT
Congress amended the 1921 act with a more restrictive permanent
measure in May of 1924, the Johnson-Reid Act. This act, which became known as the National Origins Act, took effect on July 1,
1924. It limited the annual immigration to the United States to 2
percent of a country's U.S. population as of the census of 1890.
With the large numbers of northern and western Europeans who
had immigrated to the country throughout the nation's history,
the act effectively restricted southern and eastern European immigrants to approximately 12 percent of the total immigrant population. Asian immigration was completely prohibited, but there was
no restriction on immigration from independent nations of the
Western Hemisphere.

The new law also changed the processing system for aliens by
moving the immigration inspection process to U.S. consulates in
foreign countries and requiring immigrants to obtain visas in the
native country before emigrating to the United States. The number of visas was held to 10 percent in each country per month and
thus reduced the number of people arriving at Ellis Island, leading
to the eventual closing of the facility.

The Immigration Act of 1924 reflects a change in the controversy that occurred in the three-year period after the act of 1921.
By 1924, the major factor in immigration restriction was ethnic
prejudice. By using the U.S. Census of 1890 as the basis for quotas,
the government in effect sharply reduced the number of southern
and eastern Europeans, who had not begun to arrive in large numbers until after that census year. The passage of the act codified an
official policy of preventing further changes in the ethnic composi-
tion of U.S. society, and it was to remain in effect until passage of
the Immigration and Nationality Act of 1965.

Judith Boyce DeMark

SOURCES FOR FURTHER STUDY
Bolino, August C. *The Ellis Island Source Book.* Washington, D.C.:
    Kensington Historical Press, 1985.
Curran, Thomas J. *Xenophobia and Immigration, 1820-1930.* Boston:
    Twayne, 1975.
Divine, Robert A. *American Immigration Policy, 1924-1952.* New Ha-

ven, Conn.: Yale University Press, 1957. Reprint. New York: Da Capo Press, 1972.

Reeves, Pamela. *Ellis Island: Gateway to the American Dream.* New York: Crescent Books, 1991.

Seller, Maxine S. "Historical Perspectives on American Immigration Policy: Case Studies and Current Implications." In *U.S. Immigration Policy,* edited by Richard R. Hofstetter. Durham, N.C.: Duke University Press, 1984.

SEE ALSO: Page Law (1875); Chinese Exclusion Act (1882); Gentlemen's Agreement (1907); Alien land laws (1913); Immigration Act of 1917 (1917); Immigration Act of 1921 (1921); Immigration Act of 1943 (1943).

INDIAN CITIZENSHIP ACT

ALSO KNOWN AS: American Indian Citizenship Act
DATE: June 2, 1924
U.S. STATUTES AT LARGE: 43 Stat. 253
U.S. CODE: 8 § 1401
CATEGORIES: Native Americans

The act conferred citizenship on all American Indians born within territorial limits of the United States, thus encouraging the dissolution of tribal nations.

American Indians hold a unique position in U.S. society and law, so the question of their citizenship was complicated. By the time of the Revolutionary War (1775-1783), it was established practice for European colonial powers to negotiate treaties with American Indian tribes, as they were considered to be independent nations, and this policy was continued by the United States. The Constitution regards tribes as distinct political units separate and apart from the United States, although not foreign nations. As long as American Indians were members of tribes or nations that negotiated treaties with the United States government as independent

505

political units, they could not be considered U.S. citizens. Two significant rulings made it clear that an act of Congress would be required in order to grant citizenship to American Indians.

THE QUESTION OF CITIZENSHIP

The issue of whether American Indians were citizens came into question when the Fourteenth Amendment to the Constitution was adopted in 1868. The amendment stated that "All persons born or naturalized within the United States and subject to the jurisdiction thereof, are citizens of the State wherein they reside." This amendment was intended to grant citizenship to newly emancipated slaves; however, there was a question as to whether it covered American Indians as well. In 1868, Senator James Doolittle of Wisconsin led the opposition to the extension of citizenship to American Indians under the Fourteenth Amendment. Many tribes were not yet settled on reservations, there were ongoing tribal wars in the Great Plains, and Doolittle felt strongly that the natives were not yet prepared for citizenship. There was considerable confusion in the Senate as to whether Indians living with tribal connections were subject to the jurisdiction of the United States. It was decided that Fourteenth Amendment rights did not extend to American Indians, when the Senate Committee on the Judiciary ruled, in 1870, that tribal Indians were not granted citizenship under the Fourteenth Amendment because they were not subject to the jurisdiction of the United States in the sense meant by the amendment.

Once this matter was settled, issues arose over the status of American Indians who voluntarily severed relationships with their tribe. John Elk, an American Indian who terminated relations with his tribe and lived and worked in Omaha, Nebraska, sought to register to vote in a local election. Elk met all the requirements to vote in the state of Nebraska, but he was refused the right to vote because election officials, and later the courts, ruled that as an American Indian, he was not a United States citizen. In 1884, the U.S. Supreme Court upheld the lower court decisions; it ruled, in *Elk v. Wilkins*, that an Indian born as a member of a tribe, although he disassociated himself from that tribe and lived among whites, was not a citizen and therefore was ineligible to vote. This ruling indicated it would take a specific act of Congress to naturalize American Indians.

ENDING TRIBAL SOVEREIGNTY

By the 1880's, many persons in the United States sought to end tribal sovereignty, individualize Indians (end their status as tribal members), and grant citizenship to them so they eventually would be amalgamated into the general population. As a means toward this end, Senator Henry L. Dawes of Massachusetts, a leader in reform legislation for American Indian issues, sponsored the General Allotment Act, which became law in 1887. This act carried provisions for citizenship as a reward for leaving the tribe and adopting "the habits of civilized life." In part, this meant that American Indians had to accept small plots of land, successfully farm their lands, and learn the English language. Provisions in the General Allotment Act meant that eventually every American Indian could become a citizen, except members of tribes specifically excluded in legislation. Indians in Oklahoma were originally excluded from these provisions, but in 1901, a congressional act granted Indians in Oklahoma Territory citizenship. By 1917, through a variety of federal statutes, as many as two-thirds of all Native Americans were United States citizens. However, it was World War I that reopened the debate about citizenship for American Indians as a whole.

American Indians actively supported the war effort through increased food production, purchase of war bonds, contributions to the Red Cross, and most dramatically, enlistment: Between six and ten thousand Indians, many of whom were not citizens, enlisted for military service. In return for their service to the country, Representative Homer P. Snyder of New York authored the Veterans Citizenship bill, which became law on November 6, 1919. This law granted any American Indian who had received an honorable discharge from military service during World War I the right to apply for citizenship with no restriction on the right to tribal property. Still, by 1920, some 125,000 American Indians were not citizens. Many people in the United States believed that all Indians should be rewarded for their patriotism in World War I. Therefore, Snyder introduced a bill in Congress proposing to declare all remaining noncitizen Indians born in the United States as citizens. Political maneuverings began at once.

CITIZENSHIP WITH SOVEREIGNTY

Many people favored citizenship as a way to sever the legal relationship between the tribes and the federal government, and many

American Indians were aware that citizenship could alter their tribal governments and possibly dissolve the reservation land base. In particular, full-bloods in many tribes were fearful that citizenship would end tribal sovereignty, bring them under state jurisdiction, and ultimately destroy tribal life and values. Compromise was required to resolve these conflicting views. In January, 1924, Congressman Snyder introduced House Resolution 6355, authorizing the secretary of the interior to grant citizenship to all American Indians, but ensuring that "the granting of such citizenship shall not in any manner impair or otherwise affect the right of any Indian to tribal or other property." The bill was approved by Congress, and the American Indian Citizenship Act, signed into law on June 2, 1924, by President Calvin Coolidge, made Native Americans both citizens of the United States and persons with tribal relations.

Ultimately, citizenship had little impact on American Indian life. The Bureau of Indian Affairs continued its policy of treating tribal members as wards of the government and administering affairs for American Indian citizens. The right to vote was denied to many American Indians until the 1960's, because the states had the power to determine voter eligibility and did not consider tribal members living on reservations to reside in the state. With federal protections in place, American Indians have been granted the right to vote in federal, state, and local elections, and as members of tribes, they also can vote in tribal elections.

Carole A. Barrett

SOURCES FOR FURTHER STUDY

Cohen, Felix. *Handbook of Federal Indian Law.* Washington, D.C.: Government Printing Office, 1942.
Debo, Angie. *A History of the Indians in the United States.* Norman: University of Oklahoma Press, 1989.
Olson, James S., and Raymond Wilson. *Native Americans in the Twentieth Century.* Chicago: University of Illinois Press, 1984.
Prucha, Francis Paul. *The Great Father: The United States Government and the American Indians.* Lincoln: University of Nebraska Press, 1984.
Smith, Michael T. "The History of Indian Citizenship." In *The American Indian Past and Present.* 2d ed. New York: John Wiley & Sons, 1981.

Washburn, Wilcomb, ed. *Indian-White Relations.* Vol. 4 in *Handbook of North American Indians.* Washington, D.C.: Smithsonian Institution Press, 1988.

Sᴇᴇ ᴀʟsᴏ: Indian Appropriation Act (1871); General Allotment Act (1887); Burke Act (1906); Indian Reorganization Act (1934).

Oɪʟ Pᴏʟʟᴜᴛɪᴏɴ Aᴄᴛ ᴏғ 1924

Dᴀᴛᴇ: June 7, 1924
U.S. Sᴛᴀᴛᴜᴛᴇs ᴀᴛ Lᴀʀɢᴇ: 43 Stat. 604-606
U.S. Cᴏᴅᴇ: 33 § 431
Cᴀᴛᴇɢᴏʀɪᴇs: Environment and Conservation

The act established civil and criminal penalties for the grossly negligent or intentional discharge of oil from a vessel into U.S. waters.

President Calvin Coolidge signed the Oil Pollution Act into law on June 7, 1924, as the first law to deal specifically with oil pollution of the navigable waters of the United States and its shorelines. The law imposed civil and criminal penalties for grossly negligent or willful discharge of oil into the sea from U.S. and foreign ships. The act made exceptions for unavoidable accidents and for cases in which oil was discharged to avoid danger to life or property. In the context of the law, "oil" is defined as petroleum hydrocarbons that are obtained from underground deposits and that may exist in the form of crude oil, fuel oil, heavy diesel oil, and lubricating oil. The law was limited to offshore pollution within fifty nautical miles of land.

Dᴜᴍᴘɪɴɢ Oɪʟʏ Bᴀʟʟᴀsᴛ
In 1924, preventing the deliberate discharge of oil by transport tankers was impeded by the technical inability of ships to separate residue oil, called "clingage," from water in their ballast tanks (ballast is the water used in a ship to balance it on heavy and stormy

seas, especially when the ship is empty of cargo and is returning to its home port). The oily ballast water had to be discharged before the ship reached port in order to avoid polluting the harbor. To clean the tank, the entire contents were pumped overboard, and the tank was then refilled with seawater. If the journey was long enough and the seas were not too heavy, the oil would float to the top. This small amount of oil from each ship—0.3 percent of a tank—could have been saved, but a practical method to do so was not generally available. (Some British ports had barges in their harbors for pumping this clingage oil off the top layer of ballast.) Upon nearing a home port, most ships simply dumped the oily ballast water over the side and refilled the tank with more water. The oil that had been pumped out before arrival in port, however, eventually washed to shore along all the tanker routes of the world. In addition, harbors became intolerably polluted, because some oil was dumped from engines and pipelines in harbors and at docks. One of the worst examples of such pollution was in New York Harbor, where it was reported that, in 1921, the wharves and pilings on the harbor front were oil-saturated and the water was coated with a layer of oil. This oil saturation devastated marine life and posed a fire hazard.

DESTRUCTION OF FISH AND FOWL
Various organizations, such as the Audubon Society and the National Coast Anti-Pollution League, as well as newspaper editors speaking for local groups, began to urge congressional action. The Audubon Society reported that thousands of waterfowl were dying annually as a result of their plumage being covered with oil. The fishing industry was being affected to a serious extent. In 1880, the coastal waters of the United States produced 600,000 barrels of salt mackerel in one year; by 1921, the catch had dropped to 43,000 barrels. The destruction of spawning fish from the effects of oil pollution was a major factor. It was also estimated that oil pollution between 1918 and 1923 caused an 80 percent decrease in oyster production off the coast of Connecticut. In 1923, Los Angeles had become the world's largest oil market. There, the editor of *The Express* reported that the damage to ships, port, fishermen's income, and residents had become a paramount issue.

The problem of oil dumping was reaching dramatic levels: The number of oil-burning and oil-carrying ships rose from 364 in 1911 to 2,536 in 1921. In 1924, the U.S. exported 4,428,110,720 gallons of petroleum products. If 0.3 percent of this amount was clingage, then nearly 13 million gallons of oil products were dumped from that source alone.

PREVIOUS REGULATIONS

Prior to the Oil Pollution Act of 1924, the only law that could be applied to tanker dumping was the Refuse Act of 1899. This law made it illegal to discard any detrimental substance into the sea in territorial waters to a three-mile limit. The law also applied to dumping from land locations. The law required violators to pay fines and removal costs, and it rewarded informants. In 1868, the Canadian government prohibited the discharge of ballast, coal, chemicals, and other polluting substances into waters where fishing was practiced, although the law did not mention oil specifically. In 1918, the United States and Canada signed the Migratory Bird Treaty Act to protect migratory birds, but the act did not recognize damage to birds by oil pollution until 1948, when an addendum was written. Although it is one of the few treaties in North America that acknowledges that valuable resources cross political boundaries, this and other laws have not been consistently applied.

CONGRESSIONAL DEBATE AND PASSAGE

The debate in Congress that produced two bills leading to the Oil Pollution Act elicited strong opinions from the oil industry. The Willis Bill, written by Senator Frank Willis of Delaware on January 8, 1924, proposed to make it unlawful to dump any kind of oil product, crude or refined, from either ships or land-based refineries. The law would have continued to be administered by the War Department, because the problem was an issue of navigable waters. The Willis Bill also imposed fines and imprisonment at the option of the courts. The oil industry objected to the provisions of this bill and wanted to exempt controls on land operations. The Lineberger Bill, proposed by Walter F. Lineberger, a House representative from Long Beach, California, was different from the Willis Bill in several respects: It included regulation of oil from ships only, the law would be administered by the Department of Commerce, no prison penalties were imposed, and fines could be waived in some cases. The bill also provided for investigations of land industry. The oil industry, the secretary of the interior, and the deputy commissioner of fisheries supported this bill.

The two houses of Congress reached a compromise on the two bills in order to protect the interests of the public and industry as quickly as possible. The law limited liability to vessels in coastal navigable waters. Violation of the act could result in fines and prison terms. The Coast Guard was given authority to revoke licenses of ship captains. Administration of the law was left with the War Department until 1966, when it was transferred to the secretary of the interior.

A BEGINNING

The Oil Pollution Act of 1924 was a starting point for the regulation of an industry that was growing so quickly that technology could not keep up with safety and pollution standards. Ship builders constructed tankers of such enormous size that, at first, the ships' engines were not powerful enough to stop the giant ships in time to avert accidents. At the request of Congress, President Coolidge called an International Conference on Oil Pollution, which was held from June 8 to 17, 1926. The conference included the representatives of thirteen maritime nations that recognized that coastal oil pollution was a problem. The conference recommendations included extending the prohibition on dumping from 50 to 150 nautical miles in order to protect marine life and encouraging ships to install oil separators to conserve oil and protect natural resources.

Traditionally, international laws concerning liability for accidents on the open sea have focused on damage to the beneficial uses of the sea, and prosecution has been vested in the government of the ship's origin. Enforcement, if it conflicted with economic concerns, was therefore often lax. To the extent that oil pollution resulted in public protest and damage of domestic resources, the laws that were passed in each country called attention to the need for international action. This was the case with the Oil Pollution Act of 1924. In practice, the law proved difficult to enforce, because the high seas of international territory constitute a vast region. Adherence to a law that depended upon international commitment to an honor code was difficult to verify. The law of 1924 primarily relied on the Coast Guard to discipline domestic vessels polluting territorial waters and to control foreign ships that acted with negligence. Unless a ship was caught in the act of committing a violation, however, there was no way to prove responsibility for an infraction.

LATER LEGISLATION AND IMPROVED TECHNOLOGIES

The deficiencies in the 1924 law eventually set in motion legislation that culminated in the 1970 Water Quality Improvement Act, which amended the 1924 act. The 1970 law prohibits discharges of oil from offshore and onshore facilities. The president is allowed to order measures to prevent damage to the environment and to remove spilled oil. The 1970 law removed the need for criminal prosecution if the violation is reported by the ship owner. Any other domestic or foreign ship owned by the person operating the violating ship can be denied permission to gain access to a domestic port. Responsibility was thus placed on ship owners to keep all of their ships in good operating condition. In this way, Congress attempted to focus attention on prevention of oil spills rather than on after-the-fact punishment.

The establishment of oil-pollution laws motivated the oil industry to develop the technology to prevent excess discharge of oil in the cleaning of tanks and in the handling of dirty ballast water. The new methods included load-on-top systems, by which oil and water are separated and the water is drawn out. The new load of oil is added on top of the remaining oil, and all of it is discharged at the port of destination. Another method, called crude-oil washing, uses the oil itself to disperse and clean the tank residues. Ballast water is taken onboard after the cleaning. These methods are cleaner than the methods of tank washing used in the 1920's. The load-on-top method discharges only 25 percent of the oil of older methods, and the crude-oil washing method discharges only 10 percent of the oil of the load-on-top method.

The Oil Pollution Act of 1924 set a precedent for action on a federal level to control oil pollution from domestic and foreign vessels. The deficiencies of the law encouraged stronger laws and public action, which eventually required industry to develop technology to prevent spills.

Laura R. Broyles

Sources for Further Study

Abbott, Lawrence F. "Oil on Troubled Waters." *The Outlook* 136 (April 16, 1924): 638.

_____. "To Clean the Ocean of Oil." *The Outlook* 143 (May 5, 1926): 16.

Edwards, Max N. "Oil Pollution and the Law." In *Oil Pollution: Problems and Policies*, edited by Stanley E. Degler. Washington, D.C.: Bureau of National Affairs, 1969.

Ross, William M. *Oil Pollution as an International Problem*. Seattle: University of Washington Press, 1973.

Wagnalls, Adam W. "The Oil Trouble on the Waters." *Literary Digest* 79 (November 10, 1923): 14.

Wardley-Smith, J. "Source of Oil Discharged into Water." In *The Control of Oil Pollution*, edited by J. Wardley-Smith. London: Graham and Trotman, 1983.

See also: Migratory Bird Treaty Act (1918); Water Pollution Control Act (1948); Water Pollution Control Act Amendments of 1956 (1956); Coastal Zone Management Act (1972); Marine Mammal Protection Act (1972); Water Pollution Control Act Amendments of 1972 (1972); Port and Tanker Safety Act (1978); Marine Plastic Pollution Research and Control Act (1987); Oil Pollution Act of 1990 (1990).

Halibut Treaty

Date: October 21, 1924

Categories: Animals; Environment and Conservation; Foreign Relations; Natural Resources; Treaties and Agreements

After five years of negotiation, an agreement was reached to save the fisheries of the North Pacific, displaying U.S.-Canadian cooperation.

On March 21, 1919, a Canadian-American Fisheries Conference called for a closed season on halibut fishing in the North Pacific every year for the next ten years. The commission, made up of scientists and fisheries experts, reported that halibut would totally disappear from the seas unless fishing were prohibited for at least this period. In October of the same year, the Canadian government sent a draft treaty to the United States secretary of state calling for an end to halibut fishing from November 15, 1920, to February 15, 1921, and similar dates until 1930. Boats violating this season would be seized by either country's navy and their owners suitably punished. The treaty also contained provisions concerning regulations on lobster fishing, tariffs on fish traded between the two nations, rules for port privileges for fishing boats, and a call for a scientific investigation into the life history of the Pacific halibut.

The United States took no immediate action on the proposal. In February, 1921, however, another commission of fisheries experts issued another report predicting disaster unless halibut received protection. This conference report likened the troubles of the halibut industry to the terrible conditions faced by salmon fishermen on the Pacific coast. The value of salmon shipped from U.S. and Canadian canneries had dropped by more than 90 percent since 1913 (from $30 million to $3 million) and was heading quickly toward zero. The halibut industry faced similarly depressed conditions unless something was done quickly to save the fish.

SENATE REFUSES RATIFICATION

Secretary of State Charles Evans Hughes and Secretary of Commerce Herbert Hoover recognized the need for action on the treaty. President Warren G. Harding sent it to the Senate for ratification, a procedure requiring a two-thirds vote of approval. Senators began debating the various sections of the proposal but refused to ratify it after objections from the governor, members of Congress, and fisheries authorities in Washington State. They claimed the halibut question properly belonged in the hands of state officials, not the federal authorities in Washington, D.C.; thus, the province of British Columbia should be discussing limits with the state of Washington. Canadian authorities argued that the provinces had no jurisdiction over such international questions as fisheries. Therefore, direct negotiations with the state of Washington were not permitted. Another problem had to do with punishing violators of the closed season. Canada suggested that ships caught with halibut during the closed season could be tried in both countries if authorities desired. Several senators argued that this constituted double jeopardy, a violation of the U.S. Constitution.

Violators should be tried only once and in only one court for the same crime. Because of these objections, the treaty was withdrawn from Senate consideration in late August. It seemed to have no chance of ratification.

Canadian fisheries experts expressed outrage at the Senate's failure to ratify the treaty and asked whether any modifications would change the results. Secretary Hughes replied that he knew of no modifications that would change the minds of those senators who were opposed. He did suggest a meeting between Washington State officials and Canadian experts in the Pacific Northwest, and both sides agreed to that proposal. In February, 1922, representatives from the Canadian Marine and Fisheries Department met with the Fisheries Board of the state of Washington. They reached no agreement on protecting halibut, although they did decide to stop sockeye salmon fishing totally for five years, so desperately low was the population of that species. Washington State officials refused to give assurance that they would help control halibut fishing.

REVISING THE TREATY

In August, 1922, the Canadian government, tired of waiting for action by the United States, sent the United States a new draft proposal asking for immediate action. On December 14, the United States agreed in principle to the new treaty, although it still needed Senate approval. The new treaty provided for a closed season on halibut. Violators would be turned over either to the U.S. Department of Commerce or to the Canadian Ministry of Marine and Fisheries of the Dominion of Canada, but not to both agencies. The United States representatives suggested that halibut taken accidentally during the closed season be used only to feed the crew of the detained vessel but not be sold. This provision was added to the final draft.

A new complication arose when the revised treaty was sent back to Canada. In February, 1923, the British Colonial Office in London demanded that the treaty's title be changed before it could be given final approval by the English government. Canada, at this time, was still officially part of the British Empire. The title was to be changed from "A Convention for the Regulation of Halibut Fisheries on the Pacific Coast of Canada and the United States" to "A Convention for the Regulation of Halibut Fisheries on the Pacific Coast of His Majesty the King of the United Kingdom, of Great Britain and Ireland and the British Dominions Beyond the Seas, Emperor of India and the United States." The first version would signify that Canada had the right to negotiate its own treaties, something that had never happened before and that the British wished to ensure never would.

Governor General Julian Byng of Canada suggested that, because the treaty concerned only the United States and Canada, the signature of a Canadian minister should be enough to make it official. The British refused to back down, however, and when the final document was signed in Washington, on March 2, 1923, it included the signature of the British colonial secretary. The closed season was established from November 16 to February 15; halibut taken during this season could be used only for food for the crew. Violators would have their boats seized and would be tried in the courts of the nation from which they came. The treaty also established an International Fisheries Commission of four members to study the life and environment of halibut and present recommendations for future regulations needed to save the fish. The treaty and ban would be in effect for five years and then renewed if both parties agreed.

The Senate began debate on the treaty in March and voted to ratify it with only one change. It added a provision stating that none of the nationals and inhabitants of any other part of Great Britain should engage in halibut fishing. This prohibition included people from all parts of the British Empire. When Canada received this change, it raised an objection. This amendment put the Canadians in an embarrassing position. It seemed to champion the British cause, at the expense of Canada, by insisting that Canada had to secure the consent of the entire British Empire before the treaty could be agreed upon. Canada could not accept this demand; the document would not be presented to the parliament in Ottawa because it would face certain defeat. The government of William Lyon Mackenzie King wanted to make the point that it could sign treaties without British consent, and they would block passage of the Halibut Treaty if necessary.

FINAL RATIFICATION

In October, the Harding administration agreed to resubmit the treaty without the offensive reservation. The Senate, however, was not scheduled to meet again until December, too late to approve a closed season for 1923-1924. Canada asked if the president could impose a ban on halibut fishing but was told that such action was beyond the powers of the chief executive of the United States. Halibut fishing had suffered greatly reduced supplies of fish since the first draft treaty had been proposed, more than four years earlier. Still, both sides reluctantly had to announce there would be no closed season that winter either.

By January, 1924, Canadian authorities declared that since the waters off Washington State and southern British Columbia had almost been depleted of halibut, fishing vessels would have to move north to the coast of Alaska. Supplies in that region were more abundant. Still, the halibut industry faced serious trouble and possible bankruptcy if fishing was not halted quickly. Both sides eventually backed down from their positions. The British king, George V, signed the Halibut Treaty on July 31, and Canadian and U.S. officials added their signatures on October 21, 1924. A closed season began in November and continued into the 1990's.

Leslie V. Tischauser

Sources for Further Study
Clark, Lovell C., ed. *1919-1925*. Vol. 3 in *Documents on Canadian External Relations*. Ottawa: Department of External Affairs, 1970.
McInnis, Edgar. *Canada: A Political and Social History*. 4th ed. Toronto: Holt, Rinehart and Winston of Canada, 1982.

See also: Reciprocal Trade Act (1936).

Federal Corrupt Practices Act

Also known as: Corrupt Practices Act
Date: February 28, 1925
U.S. Statutes at Large: 43 Stat. 1070
Categories: Voting and Elections

*This law, inadequate except symbolically, remained the basic legisla-
tion regulating political financing until 1971.*

Political parties are generally credited with making America's striv-
ings toward its evolving democracy work. Democracy entails parties' competition for an ever-increasing number of offices by selecting candidates and then aiding their campaigns. At no time in the
American past, however, has the general electorate been prepared
to pay for the privilege of nominally belonging to or voting for a
political party. The competition for political offices, however, almost year by year has become more expensive for parties and their
candidates. Consequently, combinations of ingenuity and loosely
defined corruption persistently marked attempts by parties and
politicians to pay for the very party mechanisms that made democracy a viable form of governance.

POLITICAL CORRUPTION AND EARLIER LEGISLATION
One price paid for this has been widespread public cynicism and
periodic public condemnations of party and campaign financing.
Until after the Civil War ended in 1865, political candidates usually
were men of sufficient means to contribute in one fashion or another to their own and to their party's struggles at the polls. By the
1930's, as the "spoils system" increasingly characterized office seeking, officeholders, whether elected or appointed, were expected to
have their salaries "taxed" by party leaders to finance party operations.

America's spectacular leap to world preeminence in industry in
the half century after 1865 was marked by the rise of the corporation. Corporate influence quickly penetrated the realm of politics, where it served its interests by funding candidates and parties. On the local level, men such as New York City politician
William Marcy "Boss" Tweed not only looted the treasuries with
an entrepreneurial panache entirely their own but also allied
themselves with business interests. The phenomenon was national.
Pennsylvania's Boies Penrose, the state's political boss for years,
was famous for encouraging business and corporate leaders to
pay the toll for his party's candidates and elections. Businessmen who did not cooperate faced "sandbag" legislation that would
cost them heavily. Inevitably, the crude couplings of politics and
business emerged as a factor in congressional and presidential

elections. Ohio's Marcus Alonzo Hanna, a wealthy industrialist in his own right, converted much of the corporate world into a money machine for an always money-hungry Republican Party. His fund-raising in William McKinley's presidential campaign against William Jennings Bryan was a landmark in American political financing.

A few years later President Theodore Roosevelt was accurately accused of receiving secret corporate funds to aid his election, although it ran contrary to his principles. By way of mitigation, Roosevelt called for the public funding of elections. In 1907, Congress passed the Tillman Act (which had been under consideration since 1902). The act made it unlawful for corporations or national banks to make political contributions to candidates for any federal office.

With Progressive reformism in full flood, Congress enacted the Federal Corrupt Practices Act of 1910, requiring every political committee that in two or more states attempted to influence or influenced the results of elections to the House of Representatives to file names of contributors and recipients with the clerk of the House. In 1911, similar legislation was extended to Senate elections, and candidates for all congressional seats were obliged to file financial reports. In addition, limitations were placed on candidates' spending for House and Senate seats.

PASSAGE AND PROVISIONS
The scandals tainting the administration of President Warren G. Harding, Teapot Dome prominent among them, encouraged Congress to enact the Federal Corrupt Practices Act of 1925 (FCPA). Until passage of the Federal Election Campaign Act (FECA) of 1971, the FCPA operated as the country's basic statute on political financing.

Seeking to regulate campaign spending and calling for disclosures of receipts and expenditures by congressional candidates, the FCPA also revised existing ceilings on expenditures. Bans on political contributions by national banks and by corporations, a major feature of the 1907 Tillman Act, were also embodied in the new legislation. So, too, were prohibitions against candidates or parties soliciting campaign funds from federal employees. Barring states prescribing lower ceilings, Senate candidates were allowed to spend $10,000 and House candidates $5,000 on their campaigns. Reports on campaign financing were required in addition, and giving or taking money for anyone's vote was made illegal. Such restrictions were limited to general election campaigns, since congressional power to regulate the fairly new practice of primary elections had not yet been tested in the courts. Few historians, even of the 1920's, mentioned the 1925 act, for good reason. As campaign costs were rising rapidly at all levels and just as the new medium of radio presented candidates with novel opportunities for campaigning, the costs of running parties and political campaigns had begun to soar. Law and political reality were thus starkly juxtaposed.

Experts commenting on the FCPA have consistently drawn attention to its numerous deficiencies. On its face, the FCPA was a sop to public opinion rather than a serious attempt at the reform of party and campaign election expenditures. It was a Swiss cheese of loopholes. The act contained no enforcement provisions. It likewise left reportage of spending by candidates and by parties incomplete and indicative only. Finance reports did not have to be presented publicly, and there were no mandates for reviewing them for accuracy. Contributions or expenditures in the critical instances of presidential or congressional primary campaigns, as well as spending intended to fuel presidential nominations, did not fall within the act.

Excluded by the act as well was money contributed to or spent by political committees, the activities of which were confined solely to one state and which were not literal affiliates of parties. Thus political committees were free to solicit and spend campaign contributions at will. These committees were relatively innocuous during the 1920's and 1930's, but after the 1940's, in the form of political action committees or PACs, they became extremely important, even integral, parts of election financing. The activities of PACs allowed candidates to disavow "knowledge and consent" of committees' fund-raising machinations in their behalf. Candidates evaded spending limitations imposed by the FCPA by having PACs spend for them.

THE FORD-NEWBERRY SENATORIAL RACE

Because of the importance of primary elections, particularly after passage of the Seventeenth Amendment (1913) calling for popular election of U.S. senators, the exclusion of primaries from the FCPA proved to be a major deficiency. In this regard, the defect was attributable not to Congress but to the U.S. Supreme Court. The matter had come to issue in 1921 as the result of an election contest between one of America's folk heroes and leading industrialists, Henry Ford, and Truman Handy Newberry. Ford lost to Republican Newberry in the general election for U.S. senator in 1918. Newberry proceeded to take his Senate seat. Ford, however, charged Newberry with having exceeded the $10,000 spending limit set by 1911 amendments to the Tillman Act. Initially, Newberry was convicted, but in 1921, on appeal, a divided Supreme Court ruled the primaries were not "elections" as construed by the Tillman Act. The decision obscured Congress's right to regulate primary nominations and in fact was one of the factors that motivated Congress to enact the FCPA in 1925.

Nevertheless, with the Court ruling in mind, Congress shied away from the regulation of primary financing by not requiring accounts either of receipts or of expenditures. In many states, however, a candidate's victory in the primary was tantamount to election. Not surprisingly, no House or Senate candidate was ever prosecuted for violations of the FCPA, despite, as experts have noted, general knowledge that campaign contributions and expenditures wildly exceeded legal limits.

THE VARE AND SMITH CASES

After review of their campaign finances by a special Senate Committee on Privileges and Elections, however, two senators-elect in 1927 were refused their Senate seats. In one instance, the Senate Committee discovered that proponents of Philadelphia's political boss, William Vare, in seeking to win a Republican factional fight for nomination to a Senate seat, had spent $785,000, or $760,000 over the legal limit. In the other case, Republican William McKinley had expended $500,000 in a primary renomination effort, while his ultimately successful challenger, Republican Frank L. Smith, had spent $450,000 to win. Smith's Democratic opponent, on the other hand, had not exceeded the $25,000 limit. Smith was not prosecuted, but his Democratic opponent was not declared a victor.

The Vare and Smith cases were distinguished only by revealing the commonplace. Politicians faced rising campaign costs in all quadrants, and their hunger for funds was unslakable. Veteran political reporters such as the *Baltimore Sun*'s Frank R. Kent recorded that no law effectively regulating campaign fund-raising or expenditures "has been enacted through which politicians cannot drive a four-horse team." Implicit was the belief that such a law never would be enacted. Wealthy contributors along with Prohibition-enriched gangsters such as Al Capone ignored the FCPA. So, too, did special interests such as the Anti-Saloon League and the Methodist-backed Southern Anti-Smith Democrats, in company with hundreds of other cause-oriented groups.

THE HATCH ACT AND LATER LEGISLATION

Several changes, some observers believed for the better, occurred during the 1930's and 1940's. The Supreme Court ruled in January, 1934, in *Burroughs and Cannon v. United States* that the FCPA did apply to elections of presidential electors, thereby implicitly acknowledging that federal regulation of the financing of congressional elections was also permissible. To that degree, the Court had overruled its 1927 decision in *Newberry v. United States.* Furthermore, in 1939, the Clean Politics Act, sponsored by New Mexico's Senator Carl A. Hatch (frequently known as the Hatch Act) amended campaign finance laws with several new restrictions. The Hatch Act barred federal employees from participation in national politics and further prohibited the collection of political contributions from anyone receiving federal relief funds.

Amendments to the Hatch Act in 1940 further barred federal contractors, whether individuals or companies, from contributing to any political committees, including PACs, or to any candidates. In addition, the amended act asserted Congress's authority over regulation of primary elections of candidates for federal office, limiting financial contributions to federal candidates or political committees to $5,000 per year. A ceiling of $3 million, moreover, was placed on the annual expenditures of political committees operating in two or more states.

Well-intentioned law, however, effected little positive change. In 1967, President Lyndon B. Johnson, his own political career revealing countless examples of dubious and unlawful campaign financing, described the FCPA, the Hatch Act, and similar legislation as inadequate in scope, obsolete from the outset, and more loophole than law. Only in 1971, with congressional passage of the Federal

Election Campaign Act, were serious attempts renewed to rectify the endemic and epidemic illegalities associated with political financing. As experts noted, although money did not invariably win elections, the costs of democracy were high and the morality involved was low.

Clifton K. Yearley

SOURCES FOR FURTHER STUDY

Alexander, Herbert E. *Money in Politics.* Washington, D.C.: Public Affairs Press, 1972.

Drew, Elizabeth. *Policies and Money.* New York: Macmillan, 1983.

Heard, Alexander. *The Costs of Democracy.* Chapel Hill: University of North Carolina Press, 1960.

Malbin, Michael J., ed. *Parties, Interest Groups, and Campaign Finance Laws.* Washington, D.C.: American Enterprise Institute for Public Policy Research, 1980.

Mutch, Robert E. *Campaigns, Congress, and Courts.* New York: Praeger, 1988.

Sorauf, Frank J. *Money in American Elections.* Glenview, Ill.: Scott, Foresman/Little, Brown College Division, 1988.

Thayer, George. *Who Shakes the Money Tree?.* New York: Simon and Schuster, 1973.

SEE ALSO: Hatch Act (1939); Federal Election Campaign Act (1972); Bipartisan Campaign Reform Act (2002).

GENEVA PROTOCOL

DATE: June 17, 1925
CATEGORIES: Foreign Relations; Treaties and Agreements

Representatives from several nations, including most of the great powers, signed a protocol banning the use of poison gas and bacteriological weapons in war.

On June 17, 1925, representatives from several nations met in Geneva, Switzerland, and signed a protocol to prohibit "the use in war of asphyxiating, poisonous or other gases, and of all analogous liquids, materials or devices," and further consented to extend this prohibition to bacteriological methods of warfare as well. This relatively brief document acknowledged that gas warfare had been condemned by civilized opinion and expressed the hope that the accord would one day become an accepted part of international law. The swiftness with which the agreement was reached was a tribute to the negotiating skills of the U.S. representative, Theodore E. Burton, and also to the strong support that President Calvin Coolidge gave to the project.

BAN ON CHEMICAL WEAPONS
The protocol was a response to the widespread use of poison gas in World War I. Poison gas was first used at the Battle of Ypres in April, 1915, when the Germans released clouds of chlorine gas against French positions. Other nations, including Great Britain, France, and eventually the United States, either conducted extensive research or actually used poison gas in battle. Each year of the war witnessed an increase in use of this nefarious weapon. There is no consensus on the actual number of people affected, but after the war, the figures of one million casualties and 100,000 deaths were frequently cited. Although these numbers were undoubtedly an exaggeration, they were readily accepted by the general public. When these statistics were combined with graphic accounts of gas attacks in antiwar poems and novels and with photographs depicting pathetic columns of soldiers with bandages covering their eyes or hideous blisters marring their bodies, the effect on public opinion was dramatic. A significant body of opinion soon began to call for an end to gas warfare.

By the time that delegates gathered in Geneva in 1925, there were already three international agreements on the subject. Even before World War I, several nations had signed the 1899 Hague Declaration, promising to abstain from using "projectiles" to deliver poison gas. Advances in technology, however, later made it possible to disperse gas from cylinders or from aerial bombs. After the war, the victorious Allied governments inserted Clause 171 into the Treaty of Versailles, which prohibited Germany from possessing, manufacturing, or importing chemical weapons. A more extensive agreement was reached at the Washington Arms Limita-tion Conference in 1921 and 1922, when the Five Powers (the United States, Great Britain, Japan, Italy, and France) adopted Article 5, which banned the use of poison gas in war. All five coun-tries signed the agreement, but it never came into force because France subsequently refused to ratify it over a dispute concerning submarines.

ASSESSMENT

The Geneva Protocol was in many respects an unexpected and un-planned success. Originally, the delegates had a rather narrow mandate: to regulate the international arms trade. Although the is-sue was not on the agenda, Theodore E. Burton suggested that chemical weapons be included in the discussions. Smaller nations did not like the idea of a ban on the export of chemical weapons, since such a ban would help to perpetuate the substantial gap that already existed between the arsenals of the great powers and those of the lesser ones. Moreover, enforcement of such a law would have been complicated by the difficulty of distinguishing between chemi-cals destined for legitimate use and those intended to be converted into poison gas; such uses often overlapped. Finally, some dele-gates feared that regulating the trade in poison gas would in effect legitimize gas as a weapon by placing it on the same level with con-ventional weapons.

Responding to these concerns, Burton therefore proposed a to-tal ban on the use of chemical weapons in war, not simply a ban on trade. About the same time, President Coolidge stated that if the delegates in Geneva failed to agree to a ban on use, he would invite them to Washington for a conference in order to achieve that ob-jective. Burton's proposal was warmly received, however, and the U.S. delegation readily accepted a friendly amendment from the Polish delegate that the prohibition be extended to bacteriological warfare. Initially, some two dozen nations signed the protocol, but several nations, including the United States, had to have their na-tional legislatures ratify it to give it the force of law.

INITIAL U.S. FAILURE TO RATIFY

Ironically, the United States, the nation given credit for negotiat-ing the agreement, failed to ratify it. Since the protocol was a treaty, it needed to be approved by two-thirds majority in the U.S. Senate.

The protocol had the support of Coolidge, the Navy, and the War Department and the personal backing of General John Pershing, who had been commander-in-chief of the U.S. forces in World War I. Nevertheless, the military establishments in many countries, including the United States, did not wish to give up the new weapon. Moreover, there were powerful voices that asserted that chemical weapons designed to incapacitate or immobilize were less horrible than other weaponry designed to kill or maim. A particularly telling statistic often quoted by opponents of the protocol was that 25 percent of the soldiers hit by artillery shells died, as compared to only 3 percent of gas casualties. In addition, influential organizations such as the American Legion, the Veterans of Foreign Wars, the Association of Military Surgeons, and the prestigious American Chemical Society were opposed to ratification. The protocol was deliberated for only one day on the Senate floor before being withdrawn by its supporters, who feared certain defeat. Despite this failure, the protocol came into force in 1928. By the outbreak of World War II, more than thirty countries had ratified it, including all of the great powers save the United States and Japan.

LIMITATIONS OF THE PROTOCOL

Over the decades, there has been a tendency for the public to expect too much of the protocol, mainly as a result of several misunderstandings. The agreement did not ban further research, manufacture, or importation of chemical weapons, only their use in war. Significantly, there were neither provisions for verification nor penalties for noncompliance. The wording of the protocol obligated the signees only with respect to those nations that also signed the pact; in other words, it was permissible for a signee to use poison gas against an enemy that was not a signatory. Furthermore, many nations that ratified the protocol did so with the reservation that they would be at liberty to retaliate if an enemy first employed chemical methods of warfare. Many observers have pointed out that this meant the protocol was tantamount to an agreement renouncing first use of chemical weapons, nothing more.

Moreover, diplomats, scholars, and jurists skilled in international law have found some disturbing ambiguities in the agreement. It was unclear whether the protocol banned all chemical agents or only those that were clearly intended to kill, wound, or seriously maim. It was also unclear whether the agreement applied only to international wars or to all wars, including civil wars and undeclared wars such as the U.S. conflict in Vietnam. Some scientists wondered whether references to bacteria should be interpreted narrowly or broadly, since there are some highly toxic substances, such as viruses or fungi, that technically are not bacteria.

LATER CONCERNS: CHEMICAL AND BIOLOGICAL WEAPONS
The Geneva Protocol did not stop the practice of chemical warfare. The first nation to breach the agreement was Italy, which unleashed poison gas against Ethiopia in 1935 and 1936. Japan used gas against China beginning in the late 1930's. Chemical weapons were not employed in World War II. Most scholars believe that a universal fear of retaliation prevented such use, and most of the belligerents in the war were not adequately prepared, offensively or defensively, for chemical warfare. After World War II, fears of chemical warfare partially receded. The atomic bomb replaced poison gas as the "doomsday" weapon.

However, during the later twentieth century, chemical weapons again became a concern: The United Arab Republic employed chemical weapons in Yemen's civil war in 1967; the United States used nonlethal chemicals, such as riot-control agents, herbicides, and defoliants, in the Vietnam conflict during the late 1960's; Iraq employed both mustard and nerve gas in the Gulf War with Iran in 1983 and later against the Kurds; the Soviet Union was suspected of using chemical weapons in Afghanistan during the 1980's, and Vietnam was alleged to have used chemical agents in Laos and Kampuchea.

In addition, the major powers shrouded much of their research into new biological and toxic agents in secrecy, thus temporarily allaying the public's apprehension. The protocol, however, was not forgotten. In 1966, the United Nation's General Assembly voted unanimously to observe the principles and objectives of the Geneva Protocol. By 1970, the number of signatories to the treaty had reached eighty-four; the United States remained a significant exception.

On November 25, 1969, however, President Richard Nixon reaffirmed U.S. support for the Geneva Protocol and renounced first use of lethal chemical weapons. Nixon also renounced the use of all biological weapons, even in retaliation, and stated that the Department of Defense had been ordered to dispose of existing stocks of such weapons. The following year, Nixon submitted the Geneva Protocol to the Senate for ratification, where it ran into opposition from liberal senators. The Republican Nixon administration made it clear that it believed the protocol did not prohibit the use of nonlethal chemical agents. Democrats, however, were upset that the United States was using nonlethal herbicides, defoliants, and riot-control agents in Vietnam; many liberal senators argued that the protocol banned all chemical weapons, not only lethal chemicals.

The stalemate was finally resolved during the presidency of Gerald R. Ford. Senate opposition was stilled when Fred Icke, the director of the United States Arms Control and Disarmament Agency, promised that nonlethal chemicals would be used in the future only under stringent limitations. The Senate ratified the protocol by a vote of 90 to 0, and on January 22, 1975, President Ford signed the agreement, fifty years after it had been negotiated. On the day the Senate ratified the protocol, it also unanimously ratified the Convention on the Prohibition of Bacteriological and Toxin Weapons (1972), or Biological Weapons Convention. This agreement banned development and production of biological toxins, and as of 2000 it had been signed by 143 nations. A similar agreement was reached for chemcial weapons in the Chemical Weapons Convention of 1993, to which 135 nations are parties. The importance of these agreements became clear when, not long after the fall of the Soviet Union in 1989 and a subsequent rise in world terrorism, such weapons were threatening nations worldwide.

In 1998, President Bill Clinton addressed these issues in his state of the Union speech before Congress:

On this seventy-fifth anniversary of the Geneva Protocol, I call on the countries of the world who have not yet done so to join the Geneva Protocol, CWC and BWC. I call on all parties to strictly adhere to these agreements and to work to strengthen them. It is more urgent than ever that, true to the words of the Geneva Protocol, their prohibitions shall be universally accepted . . . binding alike the conscience and the practice of nations.

After the September 11, 2001, terrorist attacks on the World Trade Center towers and the Pentagon, the seriousness and unscrupulousness of the parties who promulgated the attacks made the future use of chemical and biological weapons appear likely.

David C. Lukowitz, updated by
Christina J. Moose

SOURCES FOR FURTHER STUDY
Adams, Valerie. *Chemical Warfare, Chemical Disarmament.* Bloomington: Indiana University Press, 1990.
Friedman, Leon, ed. *The Law of War: A Documentary History.* Vol. 1. New York: Random House, 1972.
Haber, L. F. *The Poisonous Cloud: Chemical Warfare in the First World War.* Oxford, England: Clarendon Press, 1986.
Spiers, Edward. *Chemical Warfare.* Urbana: University of Illinois Press, 1986.
Thomas, Ann Van Wynen, and A. J. Thomas, Jr. *Legal Limits on the Use of Chemical and Biological Weapons.* Dallas: Southern Methodist University Press, 1970.

SEE ALSO: Genocide Treaty (1948); USA Patriot Act (2001).

AIR COMMERCE ACT

DATE: May 20, 1926
U.S. STATUTES AT LARGE: 44 Stat. 568
CATEGORIES: Business, Commerce, and Trade; Transportation

The federal government moved to develop air commerce, the airways system, and air navigation.

The U.S. Post Office Department, through its development of an airmail distribution system, was directly responsible for the development of commercial air transportation and, subsequently, the airline industry. Many credit the Post Office as the progenitor of the United States commercial air transportation system. Benjamin Franklin, by establishing the postal service at the birth of the nation, recognized the importance of such postal service and communication systems at large. His policy for the Post Office focused on its role in assisting and developing all new forms of transportation, which would in turn provide better mail delivery. Early subsidies were paid to stagecoach lines, and the Pony Express was established solely because of the lucrative mail payments given to the contractors involved. Likewise, federal policy provided government assistance to early railroads, including loans for equipment and land grants. Such a policy thrust also involved the Post Office in airmail service development.

THE POST OFFICE'S AIRMAIL SERVICE

By 1925, the Post Office had conducted airmail service long enough to prove the practicality of this commercial nonmilitary use of the airplane. Throughout the initial period of Post Office support for airmail operations, it was firmly understood that government investment and control would be temporary, with a move by the mid-1920's to involve private industry in airmail operations. Through the involvement of private firms in airmail, attention was given to the growth of the commercial airline industry.

The last direct flight of the Post Office operation took place on September 9, 1927. Beginning in June of that year, Post Office pilots were released as newly formed airlines took over various airmail routes. There had been more than forty pilots involved in the postal airmail service and more than six hundred employees in ground jobs. These employees had contributed to the more than twelve million airmail miles flown.

From the beginning of government's airmail service in 1918 until the last flight in 1927, the entire cost totaled $17.5 million, with more than $5 million in airmail postage sold. The balance cannot be counted as a loss, since it led to the establishment of commercial air transportation and the entirety of the U.S. airline industry. It should instead be counted as an investment.

CIVILIAN AIR MAIL: THE KELLY ACT

Civilian air transportation largely began in the United States with the passage of the Kelly Air Mail Act on February 2, 1925. The act made possible the awarding of contracts to private contractors for the transport of airmail and, hence, led to the development of private airmail contractors. The act held that the amount of compensation paid to an air carrier would not be more than 80 percent of the revenue derived from the sale of airmail postage for such mail.

In the middle of 1925, the postmaster general advertised for bids on eight airmail routes. Only five routes were immediately awarded, but by the beginning of 1926 twelve contract airmail routes had been awarded. The awards went to entrepreneurs of various backgrounds, many of them pioneers in commercial operations in the United States. The routes all focused on feeder lines branching off into the main transcontinental routes. Bids were accepted on main routes beginning in 1927, and contracts were written for major as well as feeder routes throughout that year.

Subsequent amendments to the Kelly Act abandoned difficult methods of apportioning payments for letters carried and, over time, reduced airmail postage, leading to a substantial increase in airmail traffic. The young airlines, entrepreneurs, and inventors involved in airline service benefited through the adjustments and the growth in the market, which led to substantial progress in the establishment of commercial aviation.

THE AIR COMMERCE ACT

Although the Kelly Act and Post Office policy provided that airlines could carry airmail, it became clear that airlines were not financially stable or large enough to provide for the maintenance and operation of the airways system organized for Post Office operation. Therefore, Congress passed another major piece of legislation known as the Air Commerce Act of 1926, the purpose of which was to promote air commerce. The law charged the federal government with the development, operation, and maintenance of the airways system and all aids to air navigation. It also charged the federal government with providing safety in air commerce generally through a system of regulation. Air transportation presented new and serious safety issues for the federal government to consider. Unlike many forms of surface transportation, it involved such speed and distance from the surface of the earth that it pointed to potentially hazardous safety situations. Any failures in maintenance, construction, or operation could lead to serious problems of efficiency and safety. The initiative of the 1925 act gave rise also to a complex, continuing structure of safety regulation.

The act of 1926 was unlike other acts dealing with airmail, leaving no hesitancy or reluctance in the belief that the federal government was strongly in the picture of growth and development of aviation by way of its aid and encouragement. Safety regulation was to be carried out by the Department of Commerce, and that agency established a department of air commerce. Among the earliest safety regulations provided were requirements of registration and licensing of aircraft and the certification and medical examination of pilots. Civil penalties were allowed in the enforcement of these regulations. This structure was the foundation of what later became the Civil Aeronautics Administration and the Federal Aviation Administration. The Air Commerce Act of 1926, along with the Kelly Act, provided a firm foundation for the development of civilian air transportation in the United States.

IMPACT OF THE 1926 ACT

The Air Commerce Act of 1926 has had several impacts. First, it reinforced the movement of aviation into the civilian or private sector, beginning with the handling of airmail operations. Secondly, it brought the firm recognition of a new and different role for the government by virtue of government provision of support for infrastructure development and operating assistance in that industry. From the act grew considerable investment in the development of a usable and progressive air traffic control system (largely federally funded and developed), considerable investment in airport expansion and maintenance, and subsidies for airlines. Finally, it established the precursors of regulation in the industry by focusing federal attention on safety mandates for craft and pilots.

Theodore O. Wallin

SOURCES FOR FURTHER STUDY

Davis, Grant M. *Transportation Regulation: A Pragmatic Assessment.* Danville, Ill.: Interstate Printers & Publishers, 1976.
Fair, Marvin L., and John Guandolo. *Transportation Regulation.* 8th ed. Dubuque, Iowa: William C. Brown, 1979.

Harper, Donald V. *Transportation in America Users, Carriers, Government.* 2d ed. Englewood Cliffs, N.J.: Prentice-Hall, 1982.
Hazard, John L. *Transportation Management, Economics, Policy.* Cambridge Maryland: Cornell Maritime Press, 1977.
Kane, Robert M., and Allan D. Vose. *Air Transportation.* 8th ed. Dubuque Iowa: Kendall/Hunt, 1982.
Locklin, D. Philip. *Economics of Transportation.* 7th ed. Homewood, Ill.: Richard D. Irwin, 1972.

SEE ALSO: Comstock Act (1873); Interstate Commerce Act (1887); Airline Deregulation Act (1978); Aviation and Transportation Security Act (2001).

RAILWAY LABOR ACT

DATE: May 20, 1926
U.S. STATUTES AT LARGE: 44 Stat. 577
U.S. CODE: 45 § 151-188
CATEGORIES: Labor and Employment

> *This law established a mechanism for mediating labor disputes between organized labor and the railroad companies, in the process guaranteeing the right to collective bargaining for workers.*

The 1926 Railway Labor Act brought peace to an industry plagued by strikes and violence. It created machinery acceptable to the railroad carriers and labor to mediate their disputes while guaranteeing labor's long-sought goal of collective bargaining. The carriers submitted to these terms in exchange for excluding specific bargaining agents (unions) for labor from the act. This enabled the railroads to maintain their company unions, despite the intent of the act.

THE RAILROAD STRIKE OF 1922
The origins of the Railway Labor Act lie in a fiercely contested strike in 1922. That action stemmed from wage cuts ordered by the

Railroad Labor Board (RLB), an agency charged by the 1920 Transportation Act with monitoring and regulating wages and rates in the railroad industry. Staffed by appointees of President Warren G. Harding, who held strong antilabor views, the RLB rescinded wage increases granted in 1920. This action hit hardest the shopcraft and other workers not directly included in operating the railroads. At the same time, the RLB tolerated the Pennsylvania Railroad's defiance of the RLB's orders that carriers restore union contracts that they had unilaterally abrogated and that the carriers also dismantle recently established company unions. Fearing for their long-term survival, the shopcraft and nonoperating unions struck the railroad carriers on July 1, 1922, primarily over the issues of wages and hours. Hurt least by the reductions and conciliated by the RLB's promise of no further wage cuts, the operating employees remained on the job.

Soon the strike look a new turn, as the carriers demanded an end to seniority rights, the very heart of union strength. In order to sustain operations, the companies recruited scores of strikebreakers to fill the positions held by striking workers. By eliminating seniority, the carriers eased their task of rehiring strikers and, as the unions asserted, created a massive surplus of railroad workers. By this measure, the railroad companies had raised the stakes from mere wages to union survival. The unions complained bitterly about the RLB's decision to urge the carriers to try to break the strike and to allow the companies to broach the seniority issue.

Working behind the scenes, Secretary of Commerce Herbert Hoover proved unable to persuade the carriers to negotiate. The refusal angered Harding. By the fall of 1922, Harding had reversed his early stand. Frustrated by the unions' continued rejection of the RLB demands for wage cuts, the president placed the blame for the prolonged strike squarely on the shoulders of organized labor. By the late summer, he had embraced Attorney General Harry Daugherty's position of the strike's illegality and agreed that only drastic action could prevent the country's transportation system from grinding to a halt. With presidential backing, Daugherty used a sweeping injunction to end the strike action, forcing compliance with the RLB wage cuts. The injunction, issued by Judge James Wilkerson of the District Court of Chicago on September 1, 1922, exceeded past judicial orders by prohibiting picketing and even minimal communications among the strikers and their supporters.

The measure outraged many moderate Republicans such as Hoover, who had advocated a cooperative rather than confrontational solution to the strike.

Faced with a hostile government and determined carriers, the unions had no choice but to return to work. Most unions followed the Baltimore & Ohio plan suggested by Hoover ally Daniel Willard, president of that railroad. The plan entailed negotiating with the companies on a separate basis in exchange for salvaging their seniority rights.

THE NEED FOR A GRIEVANCE MECHANISM

In the wake of this massive confrontation, union members and moderate Republicans agreed that the industry needed a new mechanism to cope with grievances and disputes. The Special Committee Representing Railroad Labor Organizations prepared an initial report that outlined labor's objectives in its relationships with the carriers. Union representatives turned this document over to Donald Richberg, who had earned a reputation as the leading labor attorney for his work in the 1922 strike. Charged with resolving the problems inherent in the carrier-union relationship, Richberg integrated these recommendations into his proposed legislation aimed at establishing new negotiating procedures.

Richberg's early drafts inevitably sparked controversy. The original proposal, known as the Howell-Barkley Bill, contained a provision that the carriers found particularly objectionable. It designated sixteen railroad labor organizations as specific bargaining agents for the rail employees. Acceptance of this condition would acknowledge carrier recognition of the unions, a position the railroad companies fiercely resisted. The two parties worked out a compromise, which President Calvin Coolidge signed on May 20, 1926.

PROVISIONS OF THE ACT

The final version of the act disbanded the RLB and substituted new procedures for settling disputes. As a first step, these included conferences between the two parties to iron out differences on wages, hours, and other items in the contract. If the parties remained deadlocked, an adjustment board, which would handle disputes over interpretation of the terms of a contract, assumed jurisdiction. The act was vague as to whether a national board (favoring the unions) or a systemwide board (implicitly allowing for company unions) would hear the grievances. The carriers seized upon the ambiguity of the act to maintain their employee representation schemes and bring grievances to systemwide boards. As late as 1933, 147 of the 233 largest carriers still maintained company unions that predated the 1926 law. The law included neither the means to enforce decisions nor the power to inflict penalties on guilty parties, therefore emboldening the railroad carriers. The weaker shopcraft and nonoperating workers proved most vulnerable to the company union strategy.

A National Mediation Board was to intervene in disputes involving changes in a contract. The act required either party to provide a thirty-day prior notice before such changes went into effect. Once that period elapsed, the board would step in to negotiate a settlement. Arbitration stood as the absolute last choice of the board and occurred only if both parties agreed. If the mediation board perceived that the dispute endangered the transportation system, it could so inform the president, who could appoint an emergency board to deal with the crisis. The emergency board lacked enforcement power. The National Mediation Board's course of moderation and accommodation contrasted sharply with the aggressive and hostile character of the RLB.

A MODEL FOR MANAGEMENT-LABOR RECONCILIATION
The Railway Labor Act of 1926 established peace throughout the railroad industry and acted as a model for other industries seeking accommodation between company owners and union advocates. Its recognition of collective bargaining as an employee right opened alternatives for workers throughout the economy who had no access to any form of bargaining procedure.

The 1926 Railway Labor Act marked an important turning point in organized labor's drive for recognition and the right to collecting bargaining. It drew on earlier legislation such as the Erdman and Newlands Acts and would play a critical role in the formulation of the 1933 Bankruptcy Act, the 1934 amendments to the Railway Labor Act, and the 1935 Wagner Act.

The Erdman Act of 1898 attempted to restore equality to the bargaining process between the railroad carriers and organized labor. The act applied only to operating employees—specifically engineers, firemen, conductors, and trainmen—yet it moved toward establishing mediation procedures that dealt fairly with unions. It banned the "yellow dog" contract, which threatened workers engaged in union activity with dismissal. The act also outlawed blacklisting, which permanently barred union supporters from employment through a system of files that carriers maintained on dissidents. A court test struck down these last two provisions. The 1913 Newlands Act sought to keep alive the negotiation process by setting up the U.S Board of Mediation and Conciliation, which again dealt only with the operating workers.

World War I created an atmosphere more favorable to union demands. The urgency of continued production, the need for industrial peace, and the government's desire to placate unions sparked administrative and legislative decisions that favored organized labor. Even before the declaration of war, the railroad unions had won the eight-hour day with the passage of the Adamson Act in 1916. During the conflict, the federal government assumed control of the nation's rail system. The government promoted standard wages and hours, long favored by the rail unions, and ensured that union members remained free of discriminatory practices by the carriers.

The union found federal control far more in tune with their interests than was private ownership. The end of the war and the specter of company interests reclaiming their control worried the unions. Quickly, their representatives brought forth the Plumb plan, which outlined a scenario in which the unions, the bondholders, and the shippers exercised administrative control of the industry. Organized labor clearly wished to hold on to the gains made during the war and sustain what it perceived as favorable conditions.

The war's end proved disappointing to organized labor. Collective bargaining faced a sustained assault by carriers. Railroads pushed for open shops, in which workers did not have to belong to unions, and workers saw a resurgence of yellow dog contracts. The passage of the Railway Labor Act transformed the hostile environment that menaced the very existence of unions. The act salvaged the union goals first articulated in the Erdman Act and pursued through World War I. It revived collective bargaining and ended yellow dog contracts in the rail industry while guaranteeing the long-term survival of unions. Its success provided a model that greatly influenced subsequent legislation regarding labor relations through the mid-1930's and acted as a beacon for pro-union forces in the economy.

The revision of the 1890 Bankruptcy Law in June of 1933 demonstrated the continued influence of the Railway Labor Act. The Great Depression forced many railroads to the brink of ruin. Bankruptcy offered one alternative for troubled companies. It also opened the possibility of companies suspending all union contracts. To prevent such an action, the unions insisted on amendments that enabled the terms of the Railway Labor Act to prevail despite economic contingencies and secured the right to organization free from carrier intrusion. The Emergency Transportation Act of 1933, with a one-year life, reiterated these provisions. Designed to promote efficiencies and reduce waste in the industry, that act ensured that no workers would lose their jobs as a result of measures enacted under this law.

In 1934, the unions sought permanent legislation to create a more stable workplace. Specifically, they intended to change the conditions that allowed company unions to persist in more than half the carriers. The 1934 amendments to the Railway Labor Act guaranteed employees the right to organize independent of carrier influence. The act also established a National Board of Adjustment, which acknowledged the unions as bargaining agents for the workers and created a new board of national mediation. The act gave the president the power to appoint members to this board, subject to congressional confirmation. The mediation board also exercised the authority to certify representatives from either side, a measure that preserved the autonomy of the unions. As important, workers had the right to select their representatives through secret ballots, which isolated them from company pressures.

The success of the rail workers was illustrated most prominently in the formulation of the Wagner Act of 1935, which culminated a drive for collective bargaining throughout the economy. Already the National Industrial Recovery Act (NIRA) had incorporated boards of mediation and arbitration that had assumed a central role in the rail industry. Donald Richberg, who oversaw the writing of the Railway Labor Act, participated in the preparation of the NIRA, leading to similarities between the 1926 measure and the NIRA.

The Wagner Act, or National Labor Relations Act, replaced the NIRA, which was found to be unconstitutional. It repeated many of the staples of the Railway Labor Act and its 1934 revisions. Company unions and yellow dog contracts fell by the wayside, and the law recognized the right of workers to organize free of company interference throughout all industries. Collective bargaining assumed a central role in labor-company relations. The Wagner Act, unlike the Railway Labor Act, acknowledged closed shops, in which workers had to belong to the union before beginning work. By the mid-1930's, the unions had achieved their long-sought autonomy.

Edward J. Davies II

SOURCES FOR FURTHER STUDY

Bernstein, Irving. *The Lean Years: A History of the American Worker, 1920-1933*. Baltimore: Penguin Books, 1960.

_____. *Turbulent Years: A History of the American Worker, 1933-1941*. Boston: Houghton Mifflin, 1970.

Campbell, Michael H., and Edward C. Brewer, eds. *Railway Labor Act of 1926: A Legislative History*. Buffalo, N.Y.: William S. Hein, 1988.

Fleming, R. W., and Edwin Young. "The Significance of the Wagner Act." In *Labor and the New Deal*, edited by Milton Derber. New York: Da Capo Press, 1972.

Foner, Philip S. *History of the Labor Movement in the United States on the Eve of America's Entrance into World War I, 1915-1916*. Vol. 6. New York: International Publishers, 1982.

Keller, Morton. *Regulating a New Economy Public and Economic Change in America, 1900-1930*. Cambridge, Mass.: Harvard University Press, 1990.

Locklin, Philip D. *Economics of Transportation*. 3d ed. Chicago: Richard D. Irwin, 1947.

Montgomery, David. *The Fall of the House of Labor: The Workplace, the State, and American Labor Activism, 1865-1925*. New York: Cambridge University Press, 1987.

Tomlins, Christopher L. *The State and the Unions Labor Relations, Law, and the Organized Labor Movement in America, 1889-1930*. New York: Cambridge University Press, 1985.

Vadney, Thomas E. *The Wayward Liberal: A Political Biography of Donald Richberg.* Lexington: University of Kentucky Press, 1970.
Zieger, Robert H. *Republicans and Labor, 1919-1929.* Lexington: University of Kentucky Press, 1969.

SEE ALSO: Norris-La Guardia Act (1932); National Labor Relations Act (1935); Fair Labor Standards Act (1938); Labor-Management Relations Act (1947).

MCFADDEN ACT

DATE: February 25, 1927
U.S. STATUTES AT LARGE: 44 Stat. 1224
PUBLIC LAW: 69-639
CATEGORIES: Banking, Money, and Finance

The McFadden Act granted national banks the right to open branches in their head-office cities in order to reduce the comparative disadvantages they had suffered and to retain government control over banking and monetary policies.

The McFadden Act was passed on February 25, 1927. Its main provisions permitted branch banking by federally chartered banks (national banks) that were located in the states in which laws granted such authority to state-chartered banks (state banks). The act was intended to remove some of the handicaps under which national banks had been competing with state banks.

STATE VS. BRANCH BANKS
The Federal Reserve Act of 1913 prohibited national banks from branching; they could operate from only one full-service office. State banks, however, were often allowed to branch within their head-office cities or counties, or even statewide. The purpose of this differential regulation was to protect small (state) banks from competition from branches of large (national) banks. This disad-

vantage to national banks in competing with state banks caused many banks to convert to state charters. During the 1920's, 127 large national banks (with total assets of $5 million or more at that time) converted to state charters.

Unlike national banks, state banks were not required to be members of the Federal Reserve System and were not subject to the reserve requirements set by the Federal Reserve, under which banks had to keep certain percentages of deposits available as reserves to meet demands for withdrawals. Therefore, the Federal Reserve's ability to maintain direct control over banking policies and the money supply was weakened as national banks converted to state charters.

To alleviate this problem, Daniel Richard Crissinger, chairman of the Office of the Comptroller of the Currency (OCC), in 1921 authorized national banks (in states that permitted state banks to branch) to open teller windows that would only accept deposits and cash checks. These acted as limited-service branches. The problem of conversion to state charters nevertheless continued. Between 1924 and 1927, the issue of branch banking was extensively debated in the banking industry, in state governments, and in Congress.

PRESERVING THE NATIONAL BANKING SYSTEM

The McFadden Act allowed national banks to open full-service branches. Under the McFadden Act, national banks were allowed to branch within the cities or towns in which they were located, provided that state banks had the same privilege. State banks were permitted to retain all branches established prior to the McFadden Act but were forbidden to establish new branches outside their head-office cities.

The purpose of the McFadden Act was to reduce the comparative disadvantage suffered by national banks, thereby reducing the incentive to abandon federal charters in favor of state charters. The bill was designed to slow defections from the national banking system. The disadvantage to national banks remained, however, in states in which state banks had already established branches outside their head-office cities, since the branching of national banks was limited to the cities in which they were located.

According to Louis Thomas McFadden, it was not the purpose

of his act to encourage branch banking in the broadest sense. The act was in fact an "anti-branch banking bill" that cut the number of bank branches per capita by about half between 1920 and 1930. The reduction came about because of the restrictions on branching by state banks.

GLASS-STEAGALL ACT

On June 16, 1933, Congress passed the Glass-Steagall Act, amending the McFadden Act by extending the branching privilege of national banks to outside their head-office cities if state law permitted state banks this freedom. Under this bill, national banks and state banks had the same branching rights. Branching authority for both national and state banks was subject to state branching laws.

TYPES OF BRANCHING

Bank branching can be classified into three categories. First, unit-banking states permitted only single-office banks. Second, limited-branching states allowed state banks to branch within a city, county, or portion of the state. Third, statewide-branching states allowed banks to open branches anywhere within the state.

Branch banking began on a large scale after passage of the Glass-Steagall Act. National banks took advantage of the right to branch outside their head-office cities. For example, the number of branches of Bank of America increased to five hundred by 1946 and to more than a thousand by 1976, with at least one branch in every county in California. During the period from 1933 to 1951, three-fourths of new branches created were outside head-office cities.

GUARDING AGAINST MONOPOLIES

Although banks were granted more freedom to branch intrastate, neither national nor state banks were allowed to branch across state lines. The purpose of this interstate branching restriction was to prevent monopolistic tendencies in the banking system. That is, the restriction was intended to prevent development of a bank that would have control over loan and deposit markets in the entire nation. In addition, the interstate branching restriction was intended to prevent banks from draining funds from one state to lend in another state. Local banks were believed to be more likely to commit to serving local businesses and investments within the state. In supporting this argument, president Herbert Hoover stated in 1929 that the American credit system should be subject to the restraint of local interest.

Some banks were interested in branching beyond their intrastate branching rights. These banks evaded the interstate branching restriction by setting up holding company organizations to acquire banks in other states. Until the 1950's, the multibank holding company was frequently used as a mechanism to expand across state lines. Forty-seven bank holding companies existed in 1960.

THE BANK HOLDING COMPANY ACT OF 1956

This loophole in the McFadden Act was closed on May 9, 1956, by the Douglas Amendment to the Bank Holding Company Act, which prohibited bank holding companies from acquiring banks in other states. Those bank holding companies that had already acquired bank subsidiaries in other states were allowed to keep them and operate them. The Douglas Amendment effectively prohibited banks from branching across state lines unless specifically authorized to do so by state authorities.

The Bank Holding Company Act of 1956 was amended in 1970 to define a bank as an institution that accepts deposits that can be withdrawn on demand and also makes commercial loans. A branch office that did not provide one of these services would not satisfy the definition of a full-service bank. These branch offices were called "nonbank banks" and were not regulated by the Federal Reserve System. Some banks evaded the interstate branching restriction by opening nonbank banks in other states as a way to expand across state lines.

COMPETITIVE BANKING EQUALITY ACT OF 1987

The Competitive Banking Equality Act of 1987 closed this loophole by defining a bank as any institution insured by the Federal Deposit Insurance Corporation (FDIC), but it exempted nonbank banks established before March 5, 1986. Branch liberalization within states (intrastate branching) continued as more and more states converted from unit banking to statewide banking. For example, New Jersey and New York converted to statewide branching in 1973 and 1975, respectively. Florida converted from unit banking to countywide branching in 1977, and then to statewide branching in 1980. By the end of 1990, forty-two states had statewide branching, and Colorado was the only unit-banking state in the nation.

THE GARN-ST. GERMAN ACT OF 1982

More important than allowing national banks to branch within their head-office cities, the McFadden Act had imposed interstate branching restrictions for both national and state banks, one of the most important restrictions on the nation's banking industry. All banks were prohibited from branching across state lines in order to prevent monopolistic tendencies in the banking system. This interstate branching law had an unintended effect. Besides tampering with the degree of competition in the banking industry, the law also imposed restrictions on banks' ability to diversify geographically, since banks were not able to open branches in other states to diversify their loan and investment portfolios.

The limitation on geographic diversification increased bank risks. An economic downturn in a state could have a disastrous effect on banks with business concentrated in the state and cause a chain of bank failures in that state. For example, First Republic Bank of Texas, the fourteenth largest bank in the nation at the time, went bankrupt in the late 1980's, as did several other Texas banks. Problems in the oil industry and real estate in Texas caused the failures, which used up a large part of the FDIC insurance fund.

As the number of bank failures increased dramatically in the 1980's the FDIC attempted to minimize depositor losses and resulting communitywide or nationwide disruption by arranging for troubled banks to be merged with healthy ones, with FDIC financial assistance. This policy was applied particularly to large banks, which were considered by regulators to be too big to be allowed to fail because of the disruptions that would result from failure. The FDIC sometimes had a difficult time finding a healthy bank within the same state to acquire a troubled bank, since problems in a state tended to affect all the state's banks.

The Garn-St. Germain Depository Institutions Act was passed on October 15, 1982, to affirm the power of the FDIC to arrange interstate mergers if an acquirer from the same state was not found.

For example, First Republic Bank of Texas was acquired by the North Carolina National Bank (NCNB) in July, 1988, under an FDIC emergency rescue program. The FDIC emergency rescue program helped to promote nationwide banking and improve geographic diversification in the U.S. banking system.

In addition, starting in the early 1980's, states began to pass laws that would allow out-of-state banks to enter under specified circumstances. Some states required a reciprocal arrangement that allowed banks and bank holding companies from other states to enter by acquiring existing banks within their borders only if the home state of an entering bank granted similar privileges to banks headquartered in the state being entered. A trend toward nationwide banking, which would help to reduce bank's vulnerability to regional economic downturns, had begun.

Julapa Jagtiani

SOURCES FOR FURTHER STUDY

Burns, Helen M. *The American Banking Community and New Deal Banking Reforms, 1933-1935.* Westport, Conn.: Greenwood Press, 1974.

Chapman, John M., and Ray Westerfield. *Branch Banking.* New York: Harper & Brothers, 1942.

Frieder, Larry A. *Commercial Banking and Interstate Expansion Issues, Prospects, and Strategies.* Ann Arbor, Mich.: UMI Research Press, 1985.

Johnson, Richard B., ed. *The Bank Holding Company, 1973.* Dallas, Tex.: Southern Methodist University Press, 1973.

Klebaner, Benjamin J. *American Commercial Banking: A History.* Boston: Twayne, 1990.

Ostrolenk, Bernhard. *The Economics of Branch Banking.* New York: Harper & Brothers, 1930.

SEE ALSO: Federal Reserve Act (1913); Banking Act of 1933 (1933); Banking Act of 1935 (1935).

KELLOGG-BRIAND PACT

ALSO KNOWN AS: Pact of Paris
DATE: Signed August 27, 1928
CATEGORIES: Foreign Relations; Treaties and Agreements

This multilateral treaty pledged to renounce war as an instrument of national policy and to maintain peace by common action.

The Kellogg-Briand Multilateral Pact, also known as the Pact of Paris, held out the promise of a new era of international harmony. It was signed on August 27, 1928. The chief architects of the treaty, Aristide Briand and Frank Kellogg, and the other member signatories took a formal pledge "not to have recourse to war as an instrument of national policy, and to settle all disputes arising between them by peaceful means." The treaty was signed originally by fifteen countries and embraced the participation of sixty-four nations by 1934, the exceptions being Argentina, Brazil, and the tiny countries of Andorra, Liechtenstein, Monaco, and San Marino.

A TREATY TO RENOUNCE WAR
The movement to outlaw war was initiated by Salmon Levinson in the United States in the aftermath of World War I and became a global movement in a few years. This movement was of great importance in bringing about the negotiation and general ratification of the Kellogg-Briand Pact. The idea of a definitive treaty was proposed by Briand on April 6, 1927, when he suggested the conclusion of a bilateral Pact of Perpetual Friendship between France and the United States for the renunciation of war. Briand's aim was to bind the United States—which still remained outside existing international accords, such as the League of Nations' Covenant and the Locarno Pact—to France through a separate bilateral pact, in an effort to reinforce the international movement toward world peace.

REVISING THE FRENCH PROPOSAL
At the beginning, the French proposal was ignored completely by Kellogg and the Department of State. It was Nicholas Murray Butler, the president of Columbia University, and Professors J. T.

Shotwell and Joseph P. Chamberlain who developed the implications of Briand's offer by drawing up a draft treaty celebrated as the "American Locarno." The idea had an overwhelming impact on Americans, creating widespread support for the antiwar idea. Encouraged by these developments, Briand formally presented a "Draft Pact of Perpetual Friendship between France and the U.S." to the Department of State on June 20, 1927.

Levinson's untiring campaign to make the United States the champion of the movement to outlaw war bore fruit. He persuaded William Borah to introduce a resolution in the Senate on December 27, 1927, calling for the outlawing of war. Kellogg, now responding to public enthusiasm, made a new proposition to the French minister: that "the two governments would make a more signal contribution to world peace by joining in an effort to obtain the adherence of all of the principal powers of the world to a declaration renouncing war as an instrument of national policy." There ensued a long period of complex negotiations between France, the United States, the other great powers except Russia, and some lesser powers.

The French did not immediately endorse the suggested alterations to their original proposal. They feared that a new multilateral agreement would conflict with the obligations and machinery of sanctions embodied in the League Covenant and the Locarno Pact. Because the United States was not a signatory to those international accords, France desired only a bilateral pact with the United States. In his reply of February 27, 1928, Kellogg allayed French fears by assuring that the multilateral pact would neither conflict with nor violate the specific obligations of the Covenant and the Locarno Pact. Rather, it would act as an effective instrument for strengthening the foundations of world peace. On March 30, 1928, the French accepted the revised United States proposal to universalize the treaty. It is historically accurate to say that the Briand offer formed the basis of the multilateral Kellogg-Briand Pact, and its wording, with slight modifications, became the wording of the final treaty.

INVITING OTHER NATIONS

On April 7, 1928, Kellogg secured an understanding with the French ambassador that both France and the United States would separately address the other four great powers—Great Britain,

Germany, Italy, and Japan—inviting their opinions and participation. According to *The New York Times* of April 14, 1928, a copy of the U.S. draft treaty and a note were sent to those powers and to France. The U.S. note stated that the United States government "desires to see the institution of war abolished and stands ready to conclude with the French, British, German, Italian, and Japanese governments a single multilateral treaty open to subsequent adherence by any and all other governments binding the parties thereto not to resort to war with one another." The draft treaty contained two articles calling for the renunciation of war as an instrument of national policy and peaceful settlement of all international disputes. The French sent their draft on April 20. The French draft contained six articles, adding other clauses concerning matters such as self-defense, violation and release of obligation by others, and ratification by all before the treaty would be enforced.

The responses of the four great powers to both drafts were more than favorable. The only concern, expressed by the British minister, Sir Austen Chamberlain, was the restrictions that the treaty would place on British freedom of action over its far-flung empire. This fear was lessened by the sovereign right of self-defense implicit in the pact. Every sovereign state, Kellogg emphasized, possessed the inherent right to defend its territory, and wars fought to repulse aggression would be entirely legal and not a violation of the pact. On the suggestion of the British, other signatories of the Locarno Pact—Belgium, Poland, and Czechoslovakia—were included among the principal signatories, along with India and the five British Dominions of Australia, Canada, the Irish Free State, New Zealand, and South Africa. The U.S. interpretation of the treaty was sent to fourteen governments. The vital element in the fourteen replies received in July was that all the governments had agreed to sign the treaty as proposed by Kellogg.

The diplomatic exchanges thus came to a successful conclusion. This represented a personal triumph for Kellogg, who was awarded the Nobel Peace Prize in 1929. Since December 28, 1927, he had unremittingly pursued the aim of a global multilateral treaty for the renunciation of war as an instrument of national policy, and he had achieved his goal. The other great hero and the original inspiration, Briand, also was awarded the Nobel Peace Prize. He had accomplished everything that he deemed essential for France.

GOALS AND FLAWS

The most important aim of the pact had been to prevent war. The treaty linked the United States to the League of Nations as the guardian of world peace and in turn strengthened the sanctions of the Covenant. It simultaneously enhanced the feeling of security in Europe and in the rest of the world, and abetted the motive for general disarmament. The practical influence of the pact lay in the mobilization of the moral and legal conscience of humankind against aggressive militarism.

The treaty remained permanently flawed, however. Although it outlawed war, it did not codify this into a principle or rule of international law. Hence, a breach of the resolution—many of which happened in subsequent years—was not tantamount to a crime or a violation of international law. Italy's attack on Ethiopia in 1935 and Japanese imperialism in China in the 1930's could not be prevented, as the pact had neither moral sanctions nor any tribunals to enforce its provisions. Moreover, the blanket interpretation of self-defense allowed many a nation to justify its war of aggression. Nevertheless, the pact, although violated many times, was never officially repealed. It acted as the legal basis for the Nuremberg and Tokyo war crimes' trials after World War II.

Sudipta Das

SOURCES FOR FURTHER STUDY

Ferrell, Robert H. *Peace in Their Time: The Origins of the Kellogg-Briand Pact.* New York: W. W. Norton, 1969.

Marks, Sally. *The Illusion of Peace: International Relations in Europe, 1918-1933.* London: Macmillan, 1976.

Miller, D. H. *The Peace Pact of Paris: A Study of the Briand-Kellogg Treaty.* New York: G. P. Putnam's Sons, 1928.

Shotwell, J. T. *War as an Instrument of National Policy and Its Renunciation in the Pact of Paris.* New York: Harcourt, Brace, 1928.

Vinson, John C. *William E. Borah and the Outlawry of War.* Athens: University of Georgia Press, 1957.

SEE ALSO: Treaty of Versailles (1919); Geneva Protocol (1925); Yalta Conference agreements (1945).